P9-EEB-785

Urban Economics

NINTH EDITION

Arthur O'Sullivan

Department of Economics
Lewis & Clark College

URBAN ECONOMICS, NINTH EDITION

Published by McGraw-Hill Education, 2 Penn Plaza, New York, NY 10121.

Some ancillaries, including electronic and print components, may not be available to customers outside the United States.

This book is printed on acid-free paper.

1 2 3 4 5 6 7 8 9 LCR 21 20 19 18

ISBN 978-0-078-02178-7
MHID 0-078-02178-2

Portfolio Manager: *Katie Hoenicke*
Product Developer: *Kevin White*
Marketing Manager: *Virgil Lloyd*
Content Project Manager: *Maria McGreal*
Buyer: *Sue Culbertson*
Design: *MPS Limited*
Content Licensing Specialist: *Shannon Manderscheid*
Cover Image: *Shutterstock/Taras Vyshnya*
Compositor: *MPS Limited*

Library of Congress Cataloging-in-Publication Data

O'Sullivan, Arthur, author.
Urban economics / Arthur O'Sullivan, Department of Economics, Lewis & Clark College.
Ninth edition. | New York, NY : McGraw-Hill Education, [2018]
LCCN 2017038923 | ISBN 9780078021787 (alk. paper)
LCSH: Urban economics.
LCC HT321 .O88 2018 | DDC 330.9173/2–dc23 LC record available at https://lccn.loc.gov/2017038923

mheducation.com/highered

To Professor Ed Whitelaw, the most talented teacher I've ever known.
It has been almost 30 years since I've been in Ed's class, but whenever
I start thinking about how to teach some new material,
my first thought is "How would Ed present this material?"

About the Author

ARTHUR O'SULLIVAN is a professor of Economics at Lewis and Clark College in Portland, Oregon. After receiving his B.S. degree in economics from the University of Oregon, he spent two years in the Peace Corps, working with city planners in the Philippines. He received his Ph.D. degree in economics from Princeton University in 1981 and taught at the University of California, Davis, and Oregon State University, winning teaching awards at both schools. He is the Robert B. Pamplin Junior Professor of Economics at Lewis and Clark College in Portland, Oregon, where he teaches microeconomics and urban economics. He is the coauthor of the introductory textbook, *Economics: Principles and Tools*, currently in its eighth edition.

Professor O'Sullivan's research explores economic issues concerning urban land use, environmental protection, and public policy. His articles appear in many economics journals, including *Journal of Urban Economics, Regional Science and Urban Economics, Journal of Environmental Economics and Management, National Tax Journal, Journal of Public Economics*, and *Journal of Law and Economics*.

Preface

This book is designed for a course in urban economics, the discipline that lies at the intersection of geography and economics. Economics is the study of choice, exploring the decisions of optimizing households, firms, governments, and other organizations. Urban economics places these choices in a geographical context.

- A household chooses the utility-maximizing residential location.
- A firm chooses the profit-maximizing production site.

As we'll see throughout the book, the incorporation of locational concerns into models of optimization behavior provides important insights into the nature of cities and the causes of urban problems such as poverty, congestion, segregation, and crime. The geographical perspective also helps us evaluate the merits of alternative policies to address these urban problems.

The book is organized into five parts. Part I introduces the field of urban economics and reviews six key concepts of microeconomics that are used repeatedly throughout the book. Part II explores a variety of market forces that cause firms and people to cluster in cities of various size and scope. Part III looks at the spatial organization of cities, exploring the economic and public-policy forces that determine the spatial distribution of activity within cities. Part IV explores the two components of the urban transportation system–cars and roads, and public transit. Part V looks at local government, exploring the rationale for local government in a federal system of government, and taking a closer look at two particular public goods–education and public safety.

The text is designed for use in undergraduate courses in urban economics and urban affairs. It could also be used for graduate courses in urban planning, public policy, and public administration. All of the economic concepts used in the book are covered in the typical intermediate microeconomics course. For readers whose exposure to microeconomics is limited to an introductory course–or readers could benefit from a review of microeconomics concepts–Chapter 24 ("Models of Microeconomics") provides a review of the key concepts developed in an intermediate course.

CHANGES FOR THE 9TH EDITION

The text has been thoroughly revised to provide a clear and concise presentation of the field of urban economics. While the overall sequence of topics in the book has not changed, the changes in individual chapters are substantial and too numerous to list. The best way to get a sense of the changes is to consult the Table of Contents.

WEB SITE

The web site for the book www.mhhe.com/osullivan9e has color versions of the maps in the book, PowerPoint presentations, and lecture notes.

Acknowledgments

I am indebted to many people who read the book and suggested ways to improve the coverage and the exposition. In particular I would like to thank those instructors who participated in surveys and reviews that were indispensable in the development of the Ninth Edition of *Urban Economics*. The appearance of their names does not necessarily constitute their endorsement of the text or its methodology.

Oliver D. Cooke
Richard Stockton College of New Jersey

Jonathan Diskin
Earlham College

Kristie A. Feder
Bard College

Gary Frimann
Gavilan College

Anthony Joseph Greco
University of Louisiana-Lafayette

Peter E. Howe
Cazenovia College

Haydar Kurban
Howard University

Thomas J. Muench
State University of New York Stony Brook

Steven R. Nivin
St. Mary's University

Joseph Michael Pogodzinski
San Jose State University

Jeffrey Pompe
Francis Marion University

Margaret A Ray
University of Mary Washington

Jesse J. Richardson, Jr
Virginia Tech

Paul Rivera
Wheaton College

Frederica Shockley
California State University, Chico

John D. Wong
Wichita State University

In addition, dozens of instructors provided feedback and suggestions for earlier editions of the book.

Richard Arnott
Boston College

Randall Bartlett
Smith College

Charles Becker
Department of Economics, Duke University

Charles Berry
University of Cincinnati

Bradley Braun
University of Central Florida

Jerry Carlino
University of Pennsylvania

Paul Carrillo
George Washington University

Suparna Chakraborty
Dept. of Economics and Finance, Zicklin School of Business, Baruch College, CUNY

Brian J. Cushing
West Virginia University

Maria N. DaCosta
University of Wisconsin-Eau Claire

Joseph Daniel
University of Delaware

Minh Quang Dao
Eastern Illinois University

Gilles Duranton
University of Toronto

Steven Durlauf
University of Wisconsin

Ingrid Gould Ellen
Wagner School, New York University

Erwin F. Erhardt, III
University of Cincinnati

David Figlio
University of Oregon

Edward J. Ford
University of South Florida

Tom Fullerton
University of Texas at El Paso

Andrew Gold
Trinity College

Alan Day Haight
SUNY-Cortland

Bríd Gleeson Hanna
Rochester Institute of Technology

Julia L. Hansen
Western Washington University

Daryl Hellman
Northeastern University

Barry Hersh
Steven L. Newman Real Estate Institute, Baruch College, City University of New York

Diane Hite
Auburn University

Bruce K. Johnson
Centre College

Christopher K. Johnson
University of North Florida

Stanley Keil
Ball State University

Sukoo Kim
Washington University

MaryJane Lenon, Ph.D.
Providence College, Providence, RI

James P. LeSage
Texas State University-San Marcos

Kenneth Lipner
Florida International University

Roxanne Ezzet-Lofstrom
University of Texas at Dallas

Vijay Mathur
Cleveland State University

Dr. Warren McHone
University of Central Florida

Kevin J. Murphy
Oakland University

James K. O'Toole
California State University, Chico

Bruce Pietrykowski
University of Michigan-Dearborn

Florenz Plassmann
Binghamton University, State University of New York

Michael J. Potepan
San Francisco State University

David A. Quart
NYU-Wagner Graduate School of Public Service

Steven Raphael
University of California, San Diego

Donald Renner
Minnesota State University

Jesse J. Richardson, Jr.
Virginia Tech

Craig Rogers
Canisius College

Jonathan Rork
Vassar College

Stuart S. Rosenthal
Syracuse University

Jeffrey Rous
University of North Texas

William A. Schaffer
Georgia Institute of Technology

Steve Soderlind
Saint Olaf College

Dean Stansel
Florida Gulf Coast University

Mary Stevenson
University of Massachusetts, Boston

Will Strange
University of Toronto

Edward F. Stuart
Northeastern Illinois University

Timothy Sullivan
Towson University

Jacques-Francois Thisse
Universite Catholique de Louvain-la-Neuve

Wendine Thompson-Dawson
University of Utah

Mark R. Wolfe
University of California, Berkeley

Anthony Yezer
George Washington University

King Yik
Idaho State University

John Yinger
Syracuse University

Arthur O'Sullivan

The McGraw-Hill Series Economics

ESSENTIALS OF ECONOMICS

Brue, McConnell, and Flynn
Essentials of Economics
Fourth Edition

Mandel
Economics: The Basics
Third Edition

Schiller
Essentials of Economics
Tenth Edition

PRINCIPLES OF ECONOMICS

Asarta and Butters
Principles of Economics

Colander
Economics, Microeconomics, and Macroeconomics
Tenth Edition

Frank, Bernanke, Antonovics, and Heffetz
Principles of Economics, Principles of Microeconomics, Principles of Macroeconomics
Seventh Edition

Frank, Bernanke, Antonovics, and Heffetz
Streamlined Editions: Principles of Economics, Principles of Microeconomics, Principles of Macroeconomics
Third Edition

Karlan and Morduch
Economics, Microeconomics, and Macroeconomics
Second Edition

McConnell, Brue, and Flynn
Economics, Microeconomics, Macroeconomics
Twenty-First Edition

McConnell, Brue, and Flynn
Brief Editions: Microeconomics and Macroeconomics
Second Edition

Samuelson and Nordhaus
Economics, Microeconomics, and Macroeconomics
Nineteenth Edition

Schiller
The Economy Today, The Micro Economy Today, and The Macro Economy Today
Fifteenth Edition

Slavin
Economics, Microeconomics, and Macroeconomics
Eleventh Edition

ECONOMICS OF SOCIAL ISSUES

Guell
Issues in Economics Today
Eighth Edition

Register and Grimes
Economics of Social Issues
Twenty-First Edition

ECONOMETRICS AND DATA ANALYTICS

Gujarati and Porter
Basic Econometrics
Fifth Edition

Gujarati and Porter
Essentials of Econometrics
Fourth Edition

Hilmer and Hilmer
Practical Econometrics
First Edition

Prince
Predictive Analytics for Business Strategy
First Edition

Managerial Economics

Baye and Prince
Managerial Economics and Business Strategy
Ninth Edition

Brickley, Smith, and Zimmerman
Managerial Economics and Organizational Architecture
Sixth Edition

Thomas and Maurice
Managerial Economics
Twelfth Edition

Intermediate Economics

Bernheim and Whinston
Microeconomics
Second Edition

Dornbusch, Fischer, and Startz
Macroeconomics
Twelfth Edition

Frank
Microeconomics and Behavior
Ninth Edition

Advanced Economics

Romer
Advanced Macroeconomics
Fifth Edition

Money and Banking

Cecchetti and Schoenholtz
Money, Banking, and Financial Markets
Fifth Edition

Urban Economics

O'Sullivan
Urban Economics
Ninth Edition

Labor Economics

Borjas
Labor Economics
Seventh Edition

McConnell, Brue, and Macpherson
Contemporary Labor Economics
Eleventh Edition

Public Finance

Rosen and Gayer
Public Finance
Tenth Edition

Environmental Economics

Field and Field
Environmental Economics: An Introduction
Seventh Edition

International Economics

Appleyard and Field
International Economics
Ninth Edition

Pugel
International Economics
Sixteenth Edition

Brief Contents

Contents

Part IV
URBAN TRANSPORTATION 285

Part V
LOCAL GOVERNMENT, EDUCATION, AND CRIME 323

PART ONE

Introduction and Key Concepts

The first two chapters set the stage for later chapters. Chapter 1 provides an overview of the field of urban economics and explains the organization of the book. The chapter also discusses various geographical definitions developed by the U.S. Census Bureau, including urban area, metropolitan area, and principal city. Chapter 2 reviews six key concepts of urban economics, five of which will be familiar to students who have completed a course in intermediate microeconomics. These concepts will reappear throughout the book.

CHAPTER 1

Introduction

Cities have always been the fireplaces of civilization, whence light and heat radiated out into the dark.

—THEODORE PARKER

I'd rather wake up in the middle of nowhere than in any city on earth.

—STEVE MCQUEEN

This book explores the economics of cities and urban problems. The quotes above from Parker and McQueen reflect our mixed feelings about cities. On the positive side, cities facilitate innovation, production, and trade, so they increase our standard of living. On the negative side, cities can be crowded, noisy, and dirty. As we'll see in the first part of this book, firms and people locate in cities because the obvious costs are more than offset by the subtle benefits of producing and consuming in close proximity to other firms and people. As we'll see later in this book, policies that address urban problems such as congestion, pollution, and crime are likely to increase the vitality of cities, causing them to grow.

Urban economics is defined as the intersection of geography and economics. Economics explores the choices people make when resources are limited, while geography studies how various activities are arranged across space. Urban economics puts economics and geography together, exploring the location choices of utility-maximizing households and profit-maximizing firms. Urban economics also explores the causes and consequences of urban problems such as congestion, pollution, and crime and evaluates alternative policy responses to these problems. In addition, urban economics explores the efficiency and distributional effects of the policies of local governments, including municipalities and school districts.

1. URBAN ECONOMICS AND CITIES

Urban economics can be divided into four related areas, providing an organizational framework for this book.

1. *Market forces in the development of cities.* The interurban location decisions of firms and households generate cities of different sizes and economic structures. We explore the issues of why cities exist, where they develop, and why cities vary in size and scope.

2. *Land use within cities.* The intraurban location decisions of firms and households generate urban land-use patterns. In modern cities, employment is spread throughout the metropolitan area, in sharp contrast to the highly centralized cities of just 100 years ago. We explore the economic forces behind the change from centralized to decentralized cities. We also use a model of neighborhood choice to explore the issue of segregation with respect to race, income, and educational level. Housing choices are linked to location choices because housing is immobile. We will discuss why housing is different from other products and how housing policies work.
3. *Urban transportation.* We explore some possible solutions to the urban congestion problem and look at the role of mass transit in the urban transportation system. One issue is whether a bus system is more efficient than a light-rail system or a heavy-rail system such as BART (San Francisco) or Metro (Washington).
4. *Local government, education, and crime.* Most large U.S. metropolitan areas have dozens of local governments, including municipalities, school districts, and special districts. This fragmented system of local government generates interesting locational choices for households and firms as well as complex policy interactions. The provision of public K–12 education (kindergarten through high school) is the responsibility of local governments. Local governments are also responsible for controlling crime.

An urban economist defines an urban area as a geographical area that contains a large number of people in a relatively small area. In other words, an urban area has a population density that is high relative to the density of the surrounding area. This definition accommodates urban areas of vastly different sizes, from a small town to a large metropolitan area. The definition is based on population density because an essential feature of an urban economy is frequent contact between different economic activities, which is feasible only if firms and households are concentrated in a relatively small area.

The U.S. Census Bureau has developed a variety of geographical definitions relevant to urban economics. Since much of the empirical work in urban economics is based on census data, a clear understanding of these definitions is important. Part 2 of this chapter provides the details of the census definitions. There are four key census definitions.

1. *Urban area.* A densely settled geographical area with a minimum population of 2,500 people and a minimum density of 500 people per square mile.
2. *Metropolitan area.* A core area with a substantial population nucleus, together with adjacent communities that are integrated, in an economic sense, with the core area. To qualify as a metropolitan area, the minimum population is 50,000 people. In 2010, there were 366 metropolitan statistical areas in the United States.
3. *Micropolitan area.* A smaller version of a metropolitan area with a concentration of 10,000 to 50,000 people. In 2010, there were 576 micropolitan statistical areas in the United States.

4. *Principal city.* The largest municipality in a particular metropolitan area or micropolitan area. A municipality is defined as an area over which a municipal corporation exercises political authority and provides local government services such as sewage service, crime protection, and fire protection.

This book uses three terms to refer to spatial concentrations of economic activity: *urban area, metropolitan area,* and *city*. These three terms, which will be used interchangeably, refer to the economic city (an area with a relatively high population density that contains a set of closely related activities), not the political city. When referring to a political city, we use the term *municipality*.

Figure 1-1 shows the shares of U.S. population in cities of various size. Overall, about 94 percent of the population lives in urban areas, with 84 percent in 366 metropolitan areas and 10 percent in 576 micropolitan areas. Roughly one quarter of the population lives in the largest metropolitan areas, defined as metropolitan areas with at least 5 million residents, leaving 30 percent in medium metropolitan areas and 30 percent in small metropolitan areas. Together the two largest metropolitan areas, New York and Los Angeles, have over 10 percent of the U.S. population.

Figure 1-2 shows the share of people living in urban areas in the United States from 1790 to 2010. Over this period, the share of the population living in urban areas increased from 5 percent to 81 percent, a remarkable transformation that also

FIGURE 1-1 Proportions of U.S. Population by CBSA Status and Size Category

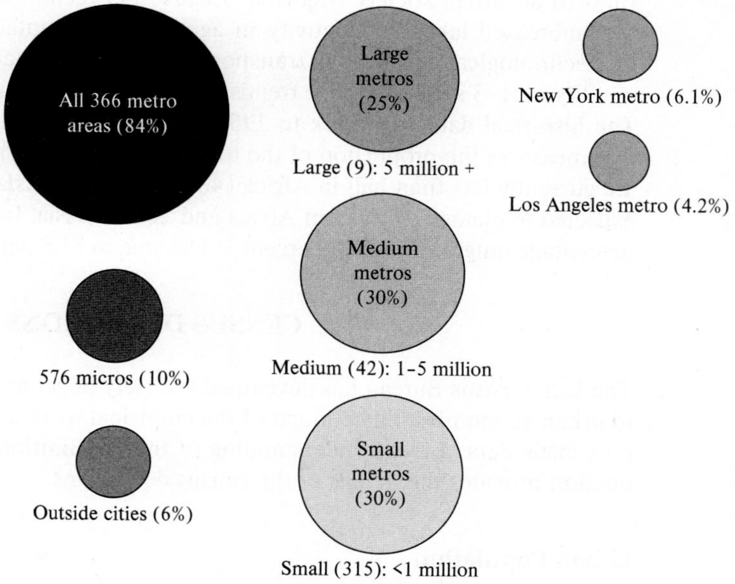

Source: Wilson, Steven et al., "U.S. Patterns of Metropolitan and Micropolitan Population Change: 2000-2010," U.S. Census Bureau, 2012.

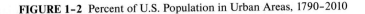

FIGURE 1-2 Percent of U.S. Population in Urban Areas, 1790–2010

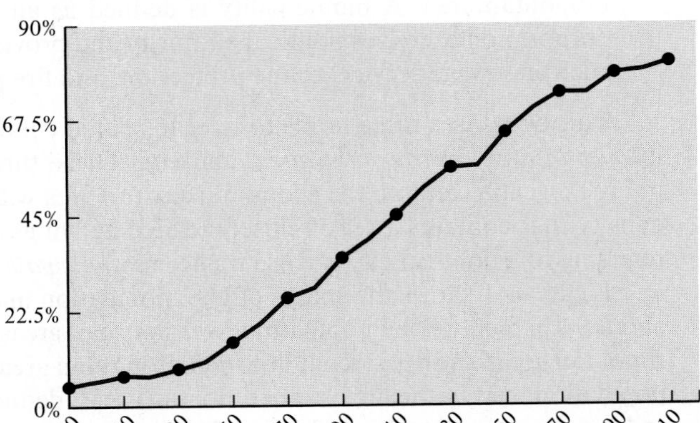

Source: U.S. Census, *United States Summary: 2010 Population and Housing Unit Counts, 2010 Census of Population and Housing,* 2012.

occurred in other parts of the world. Urbanization was nearly stagnant during the 1930s, the decade associated with the Great Depression. Urbanization was also stagnant a few decades later in the 1970s, a decade that included a deep recession in 1973–1975. As we will see in the first part of the book, the transformation from a rural to an urban society occurred because (1) technological advances in production increased labor productivity in agriculture, manufacturing, and services; and (2) technological advances in transportation increased accessibility.

Figure 1-3 shows the time trends in urbanization for six major areas in the world. The historical data goes back to 1950 and the projections go to 2050. The vertical axis measures the proportion of the total population in urban areas. The proportions are currently less than half in Africa (40 percent) and Asia (47.5 percent), but that is expected to change by 2035 in Africa and 2018 in Asia. In the other areas, the urban percentage ranges from 70.8 percent in Oceania to 81.5 percent in Northern America.

2. CENSUS DEFINITIONS

The U.S. Census Bureau has developed a variety of geographical definitions relevant to urban economics. Since much of the empirical work in urban economics is based on census data, a clear understanding of these definitions is important. This introduction provides the details of the census definitions.

Urban Population

The geographical definitions developed by the Census Bureau are based on the census block, the smallest geographical unit in census data. A census block is defined

FIGURE 1–3 Urban Population as Percentage of Population, 1950–2050

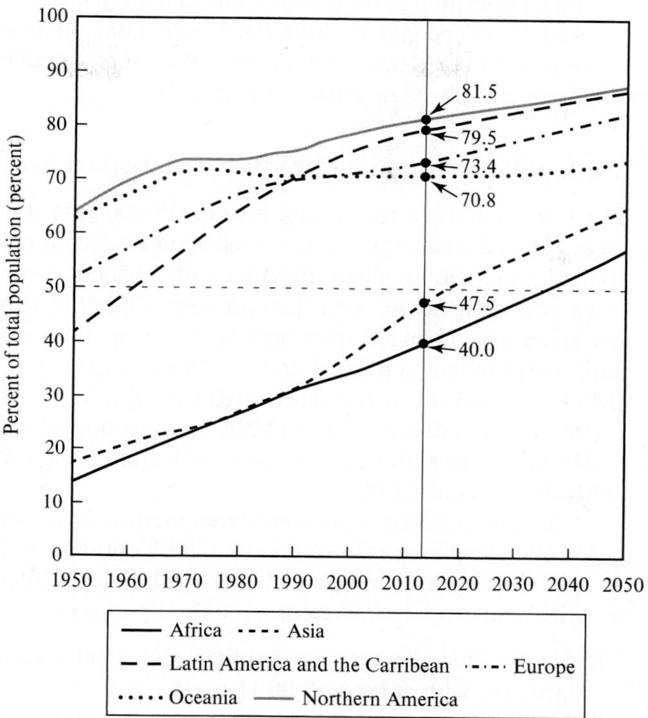

Source: United Nations, *World Urbanization Prospects, 2014,* New York: United Nations, 2016.

as an area bounded on all sides by visible features (streets, streams, or tracks) or invisible features (property lines or political boundaries). The typical census block has between a few dozen and a few hundred residents. A block group is a group of contiguous census blocks. A census tract is a contiguous set of census blocks. The target population range for a census tract is 4,000 residents. In 2010, there were more than 72,531 census tracts, with an average population of 4,256. Roughly 90 percent of the tracts had between 1,500 and 7,500 residents.

The Census Bureau uses tracts to define two types of urban areas. The urban population is defined as all people living in urbanized areas and urban clusters.

1. *Urbanized area.* An urbanized area is a densely settled core of census tracts and surrounding tracts that meet minimum population density requirements. In most cases, the density requirement is 1,000 people per square mile for the core block groups and 500 people per square mile for the surrounding blocks. Together, the densely settled tracts must encompass a population of at least 50,000 people. In 2010, there were 486 urbanized areas in the United States.

2. *Urban clusters.* An urban cluster is a scaled-down version of an urbanized area. The total population of the census tracts that make up an urban cluster is between 2,500 and 50,000 people. In 2010, there were 3,087 urban clusters in the United States. Based on the Census definition of the urban population, 81 percent of the U.S. population lived in urban areas in 2010.

Metropolitan Area aka Core-Based Statistical Area

The Census Bureau has a long history of changing its definitions of metropolitan areas. The general idea is that a metropolitan area includes a core area with a substantial population nucleus, together with adjacent communities that are integrated, in an economic sense, with the core area. Over the years, the labels for metropolitan areas have changed from standard metropolitan area (SMA) in 1949, to standard metropolitan statistical area (SMSA) in 1959, to metropolitan statistical area (MSA) in 1983, to metropolitan area (MA) in 1990, which referred collectively to metropolitan statistical areas (MSAs), consolidated metropolitan statistical areas (CMSAs–the largest metropolitan areas), and primary metropolitan statistical areas (PMSAs–parts of CMSAs).

The new label for areas considered metropolitan, implemented in 2000, is core-based statistical area (CBSA). Each CBSA contains at least one urban area (either an urbanized area or an urban cluster) with at least 10,000 people and is designated as either a metropolitan area or a micropolitan area.

1. *Metropolitan area.* A metropolitan statistical area includes at least one urbanized area with at least 50,000 people.
2. *Micropolitan area.* A micropolitan statistical area includes at least one urban cluster of between 10,000 and 50,000 people. In 2010, there were 366 metropolitan statistical areas and 576 micropolitan statistical areas in the United States.

The building blocks for metropolitan and micropolitan areas are counties. For a particular CBSA, central counties are ones in which at least 5,000 people or 50 percent of the population resides within urban areas with at least 10,000 people. Additional outlying counties are included in the CBSA if they meet minimum thresholds of commuting rates to or from the central counties. Specifically, at least 25 percent of workers in an outlying county must work in one of the central counties, or at least 25 percent of the jobs in an outlying county must be filled by residents of one of the central counties.

Together CBSAs contain 94 percent of the nation's population, with 84 percent in metropolitan areas and 10 percent in the smaller micropolitan areas. The percentage of the population in CBSAs (94 percent) exceeds the percentage in urban areas (81 percent) because CBSAs encompass entire counties, including areas outside urban areas (defined by the smallest geographical unit, the census block).

Principal City

The largest municipality in each metropolitan or micropolitan statistical area is designated a principal city. Additional cities qualify as "principal" if they meet minimum requirements for population size (at least 250,000 people) and employment (at least 100,000 workers). The title of each metropolitan or micropolitan statistical area consists of the names of up to three of its principal cities and the name of each state into which the metropolitan or micropolitan statistical area extends. For example, the name for the Minneapolis metropolitan area is Minneapolis-St. Paul-Bloomington, MN-WI, indicating that it includes parts of two states with two other municipalities large enough to merit listing. For most metropolitan areas, the label includes only one principal city. About a dozen large metropolitan areas are divided into smaller groupings of counties called metropolitan divisions.

REFERENCES AND READING

1. U.S. Government. "Standards for Defining Metropolitan and Micropolitan Statistical Areas." *Federal Register* 65, no. 249 (December 17, 2000).

CHAPTER 2

Key Concepts of Urban Economics

Two campers awake in their tent to the sound of a rustling bear. Camper A calmly puts on his running shoes and starts stretching.

Camper B: What are you doing? You can't outrun a hungry bear.

Camper A: I don't have to outrun the bear. I just have to outrun you.

This chapter discusses six key concepts from microeconomics that provide a foundation for urban economics.

1. Opportunity cost
2. Marginal principle
3. Nash equilibrium
4. Comparative statics
5. Pareto efficiency
6. Self-reinforcing changes

The first five concepts are employed in many other fields in economics, while the sixth concept is special to urban economics and a few other fields in economics.

1. OPPORTUNITY COST

Economic cost is opportunity cost. The opportunity cost of something is what you sacrifice to get it. More precisely, the opportunity cost of using a resource is the value of that resource in its next-best use. For example, the opportunity cost of reading this chapter is the value of your time in its next-best use, such as earning money, playing sports, or studying another subject. On a larger scale, the opportunity cost of waging war is the value of resources such as soldiers and tanks in their next-best use. If soldiers could be science teachers, the opportunity cost of each soldier is the value of a science teacher. If the resources used to build a tank could instead be used to build 12,000 bicycles ($6 million tank vs. $500 bicycles), the opportunity cost of each tank is the value of 1,000 bicycles. One role of economic analysis is to highlight the opportunity cost and thus improve the decision-making process.

To illustrate the notion of opportunity cost, consider a firm that will take one year to build a tall office building—a skyscraper—in a city. A firm's economic cost is the cost of all the inputs used in the production process, computed as the opportunity cost of the inputs. The economic cost can be divided into types. An explicit cost involves an explicit monetary payment for an input. For example, suppose the firm hires a workforce of 500 construction workers and pays each worker $60,000, for a total of $30 million in labor cost. Similarly, suppose the firm pays $100 million for building materials such as concrete, steel, and glass. These are opportunity costs because the $130 million spent on labor and materials cannot be spent on something else.

A firm's implicit cost is the opportunity cost of inputs that are not subject to an explicit monetary payment. There are two common implicit costs.

1. *Opportunity cost of an entrepreneur's time.* The opportunity cost of running a business such as a construction firm is the income foregone in the next-best use of the entrepreneur's time. Suppose the firm uses a team of five partners to manage the skyscraper project, and each partner could earn $200,000 as an employee of another firm. In this case, the opportunity cost of running the skyscraper project is $1 million.
2. *Opportunity cost of an entrepreneur's funds.* If an entrepreneur uses his or her own money to set up and run a business, the opportunity cost is the interest that could be earned in a bank account. For example, suppose the construction firm has machinery and equipment that could be sold today for $200 million. If the annual interest rate is 10 percent, the opportunity cost of the $200 million is the $20 million in foregone interest that could be earned during the one-year project.

In the skyscraper example, the implicit cost is $21 million, the sum of $1 million for entrepreneur time and $20 million for the entrepreneur funds.

In an urban environment, travel time—for commuting to work, shopping, and recreation—plays an important role in the location decisions of households and firms. The opportunity cost of travel time is the value of time in its next-best use, for example, work, education, or recreation. Firms compensate workers for commuting costs in the form of higher wages, so the cost of production is lower in locations that are relatively accessible to a firm's workforce. On the consumer side of the urban economy, households are willing to pay more for housing where commuting cost is relatively low. The opportunity cost of travel time affects wages, production cost, and housing prices, so it influences the spatial distribution of activity within cities.

Economic cost is opportunity cost, and opportunity cost appears in other contexts in urban economics. The opportunity cost of housing is the value of capital in its next-best use, for example, in factories or educational facilities. The opportunity cost of open space is the value of land used in production or housing. The opportunity cost of an urban light-rail transit system could be a larger fleet of buses. In the crime environment, the opportunity cost of a person's time in prison is the foregone production in a lawful job, and the opportunity cost of a prison facility is the value of capital (buildings and machines) in alternative uses.

2. MARGINAL PRINCIPLE

Economic reasoning often focuses on marginal or incremental changes. The marginal benefit of an activity is the additional benefit resulting from a one-unit increase in the activity. The marginal cost of an activity is the additional cost resulting from a one-unit increase in the activity. The marginal principle provides a simple decision-making rule for choosing the appropriate level of an activity.

Marginal Principle: Choose the level of an activity at which the marginal benefit equals the marginal cost.

If the marginal benefit of some activity exceeds the marginal cost, the marginal rule says to do more: a decision-maker should increase the level of the activity until the marginal benefit equals the marginal cost.

We can apply the marginal principle to a firm's decision on the height of a new structure. The profit-maximizing number of floors is determined by the marginal benefit and marginal cost of building up.

1. *Marginal benefit.* The marginal benefit of height equals the rent collected on the additional floor. In Figure 2–1, the marginal-benefit curve is negatively sloped, because a taller building devotes more space to vertical transportation (stairs and elevators), leaving less rentable space. As the number of floors increases, total rental revenue increases, but at a decreasing rate. Therefore, the marginal-benefit curve is negatively sloped.
2. *Marginal cost.* The marginal cost of height equals the additional construction cost from building one more floor. In Figure 2–1, the marginal-cost curve is positively sloped because a taller building requires more reinforcement to support its more concentrated weight. As the number of floors increases, construction cost increases at an increasing rate. Therefore, the marginal-cost curve is positively sloped.

FIGURE 2–1 The Marginal Principle

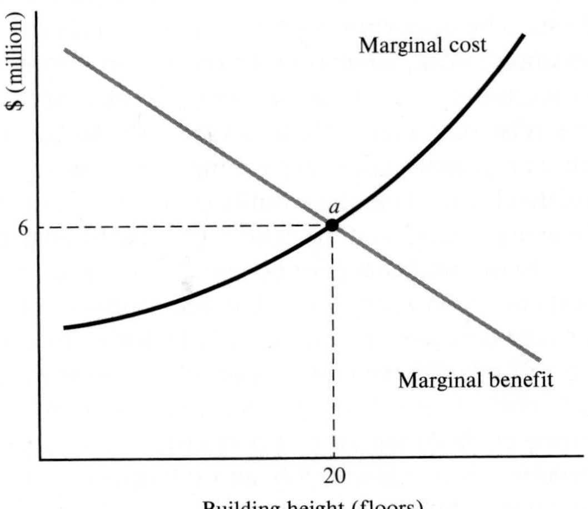

The firm maximizes profit at point *a*, with 20 floors at a marginal cost of $6 million. The firm stops at 20 floors because the cost of adding the 21st floor exceeds the rental revenue from the additional floor.

We will use the marginal principle throughout the book to explore decisions by households, firms, and other organizations. Households use the marginal principle in choosing a residential location and how to vote in local elections. Firms use the marginal principle to decide how much output to produce, how many workers to hire, and where to locate a production facility. Local governments use the marginal principle to decide how many teachers to hire and how many resources to devote to public safety. In the urban transportation system, drivers use the marginal principle to decide how fast to drive, and transit authorities use the principle to decide how many buses to run and what fare to charge.

3. NASH EQUILIBRIUM

An economic environment has reached an equilibrium if there is no pressure to change things. In microeconomics, a key equilibrium concept is Nash equilibrium, named after John Nash, the recipient of the 1994 Nobel Prize in economics and the subject of the movie *A Beautiful Mind.*

Nash Equilibrium: There is no incentive for unilateral deviation.

We have a Nash equilibrium if no single decision-maker has an incentive to change his or her behavior, given the choices made by other participants. In more casual terms, we have a Nash equilibrium if there are no regrets: no single decision-maker wishes that he or she had made a different choice, given the choices made by other participants.

Nash Equilibrium in a Model of Supply and Demand

Figure 2–2 shows the market equilibrium in the market for new housing. At the equilibrium price of $300,000, the quantity supplied by firms equals the quantity demanded by consumers at 200 new houses per year. A key assumption of the model of supply and demand is that both consumers and producers are price takers: each decision-maker in the market takes the price as given. In other words, we assume that no single participant can move the market price in a favorable direction: a firm cannot increase the price by producing less; a consumer cannot decrease the price by consuming less. The market equilibrium is a Nash equilibrium because each participant is doing the best he or she can, given the market price.

1. *Individual firm.* The market supply curve shows the profit-maximizing responses of individual firms to different prices. At the market equilibrium, each firm is doing the best it can, given the market price. Therefore, no single firm has an incentive to unilaterally change the quantity it produces.
2. *Individual consumer.* The market demand curve shows the utility-maximizing responses of individual consumers to different prices. At the market equilibrium,

FIGURE 2–2 Market Equilibrium

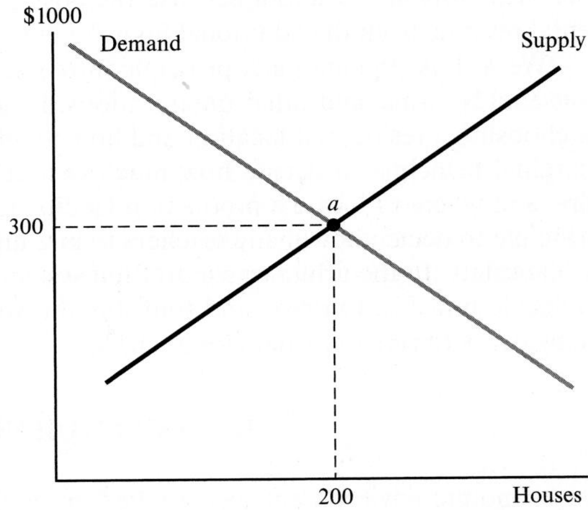

each consumer is doing the best he or she can, given the market price. Therefore, no single consumer has an incentive to unilaterally change the quantity he or she purchases.

Figure 2–3 shows two cases of market disequilibrium. In both cases, there is an incentive for unilateral deviation, so the market has not reached a Nash equilibrium.

1. *Excess supply.* At any price above the equilibrium price, there will be excess supply of the product. At a price of $420,000, the excess supply is shown by the gap between point *b* on the demand curve and point *c* on the supply curve. In this

FIGURE 2–3 Disequilibrium

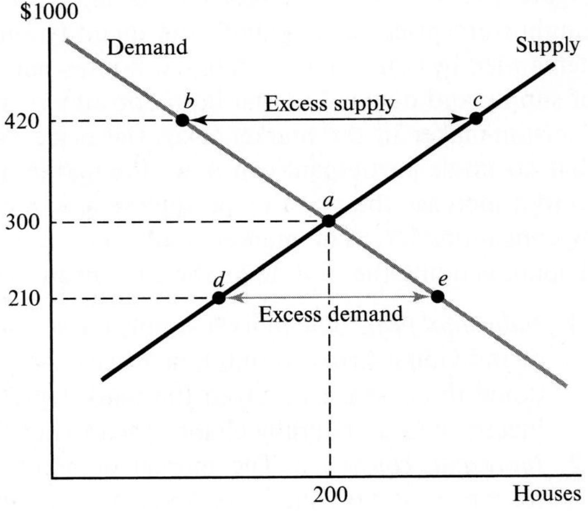

case, there are firms that are willing to sell new houses at a price of $420,000 but cannot find consumers who are willing to pay the relatively high price. These firms have an incentive to unilaterally cut the price to attract consumers.

2. *Excess demand.* At any price below the equilibrium price, there will be excess demand for the product. At a price of $210,000, the excess demand is shown by the gap between point *d* on the demand curve and point *e* on the supply curve. In this case, there are consumers who are willing to buy new houses at the relatively low price but cannot find a firm to build a new house at a price of $210,000. These consumers have an incentive to unilaterally offer a higher price and thus outbid other consumers for new houses.

Nash Equilibrium in Location

The concept of Nash equilibrium applies to all sorts of decision-making environments. Consider the location decisions of two competing firms that sell a homogeneous product. For example, suppose two vendors sell vanilla ice cream along a beach that is 11 blocks long. Consumers are uniformly distributed along the beach, with one customer each block. Each consumer patronizes the closest ice-cream vendor. In the initial location pattern shown in the upper panel of Figure 2–4, vendors Lefty and Righty divide the beach into two equal market areas, and each locates at the center of its market. Lefty's consumers are in blocks 1 through 5, while Righty's

FIGURE 2–4 Nash Equilibrium on the Beach

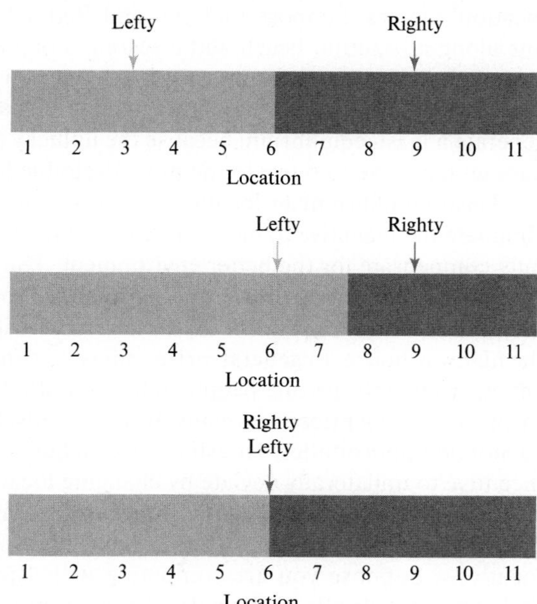

customers are in blocks 7 through 11. The consumer in block 6 is indifferent and choose a vendor randomly. Each vendor has 5 customers for sure and a 50-50 chance at a sixth customer.

Although the initial location pattern seems sensible, it is not a Nash equilibrium because each vendor has an incentive to unilaterally deviate. The second and third panels in Figure 2–4 show the transition from the initial positions (in the upper panel) to the Nash equilibrium.

- *Middle panel.* Lefty moves to the median location. Suppose Lefty moves to block 6. This is the median location, defined as the location that splits consumers into two equal groups: 5 consumers are to the left, and 5 customers are to the right. Lefty's unilateral deviation increases her number of customers to 7. In contrast, Righty now has only 4 consumers.
- *Lower panel.* Righty moves to the median location. Righty's unilateral deviation from the pattern in the middle panel allows him to restore an equal splitting of the market.

When both vendors reach the median location, there is no incentive for unilateral deviation. A vender who moved away from the median would move away from a majority of consumers and toward a minority of consumers, resulting in fewer customers. In the Nash equilibrium, both vendors are located at the median location, and each gets half the customers.

Nash Equilibrium and Spatial Variation in Prices

In an urban environment, prices play an important role in Nash equilibria involving location choices. Suppose that you and Bud are competing for two rental houses, one along a beautiful beach and a second along a noisy highway. If the two houses have the same price (the same monthly rent), you would prefer the beach house, and so would Bud. Flipping a coin and giving the beach house to the winner would not generate a Nash equilibrium because the unlucky person in the highway house would have an incentive to move to the more desirable house.

Nash equilibrium in location requires a higher price for the beach house. To eliminate the incentive to move, the price of the beach house must be high enough to fully compensate for the better environment. The question is, How much money are you willing to sacrifice to live on the beach? If your answer is \$300 and Bud agrees, then the equilibrium price of the beach house will be \$300 higher than the price of the highway house. In general, prices adjust to generate the same utility level in different environments, getting people to live in both desirable and undesirable locations. In cities, housing prices are relatively high to offset the better access to jobs and other economic opportunities. Housing prices adjust to ensure that no household has an incentive to unilaterally deviate by changing location.

The same sort of economic forces operate in the labor market. Workers compete for jobs in desirable locations, causing lower wages in those more desirable locations. Suppose you are competing with Ricki for two jobs, one in Dullsville and one in Coolsville, a city with a more stimulating social environment. If a \$500 gap in the monthly wage fully compensates for the difference in the social environment, the equilibrium wage will be $500 lower in Coolsville. The two workers will be indifferent between the two cities because a move to Coolsville means a $500 wage cut. In the labor market, wages adjust to get people to work in both desirable and undesirable environments. For workplaces within a city, workers demand a premium to work at locations with relatively high commuting costs. Wages adjust to ensure that no worker has an incentive to unilaterally deviate by changing workplaces.

The same logic applies to urban land markets. The price of land adjusts to ensure Nash equilibrium in location among firms. For manufacturers, quick access to ports and highways economizes on freight cost, and the price of manufacturing land is highest near highways and ports. Office firms are in the business of information exchange and are willing to pay more for central locations because they provide quick access to information from other firms and institutions. Land prices adjust to ensure that no office firm has an incentive to unilaterally deviate by changing location.

4. COMPARATIVE STATICS

We can use comparative statics to predict the responses of decision-makers and markets to changes in economic circumstances. We can distinguish between two types of comparative-statics exercises.

1. *For a choice variable.* Comparative statics explores the effect of a change in the value of a parameter on the value of a choice variable. In a choice environment, a parameter is defined as a variable whose value is taken as given by a decision-maker. For example, an increase in the price of steel (a parameter to the builder) decreases the profit-maximizing building height (the choice variable).
2. *For an equilibrium variable.* Comparative statics explores the effect of a change in the value of a parameter on the value of an equilibrium variable. In a market setting, a parameter is defined as a variable whose value is determined outside the market being studied. For example, an increase in the price of fertilizer (a parameter to the market) increases the equilibrium price of apples (the equilibrium variable).

Comparative Statics for Choice Variables

We will start with comparative statics for choice variables. Figure 2–5 illustrates the effects of a change in the price of steel on building height.

1. *Initial steel price.* As we saw in Figure 2–1, the marginal principle is satisfied at point *a*, where the marginal-cost curve intersects the marginal-benefit curve. The profit-maximizing height is 20 floors.
2. *Lower steel price.* A decrease in the price of steel decreases the marginal cost of building, shifting the marginal-cost curve downward. The marginal principle

FIGURE 2–5 Comparative Statics: Choice Variable

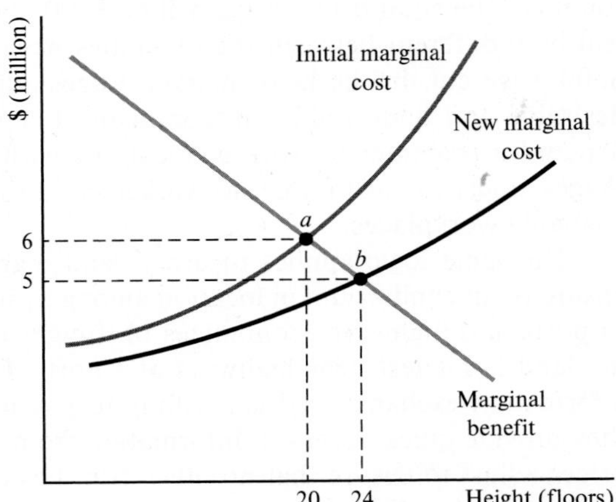

is satisfied at point *b*, so the profit-maximizing height increases to 24 floors. The decrease in marginal cost means that for floors 21 through 24, the marginal benefit is now greater than or equal to the marginal cost.

This comparative-statics exercise shows a negative relationship between the price of steel (a parameter) and building height (a choice variable).

The urban economy provides many opportunities to do comparative statics for choice variables. For firm location choices, we can explore the effects of changes in transport costs on the profit-maximizing location. For commuters' modal choice, we can explore the effects of more frequent mass-transit service on transit ridership. For household location choices, we can explore the effect of a change in the number of low-income households on the neighborhood choices of high-income households. In general, whenever people or organizations make rational choices, we can use comparative statics to see how a change in the value of a parameter affects choice.

Comparative Statics for Market Equilibrium

Economics also explores the economic forces that generate a market equilibrium. We can distinguish between two types of variables in a market.

1. *Equilibrium variable.* The value is determined within the market under consideration, for example, the equilibrium price of housing.
2. *Parameter.* The value is determined beyond the market under consideration. For the housing market, the parameters include the price of wood and other building materials, and the wages of carpenters and other construction workers. The values of these variables are determined outside the local housing market.

FIGURE 2–6 Comparative Statics of a Change in Supply

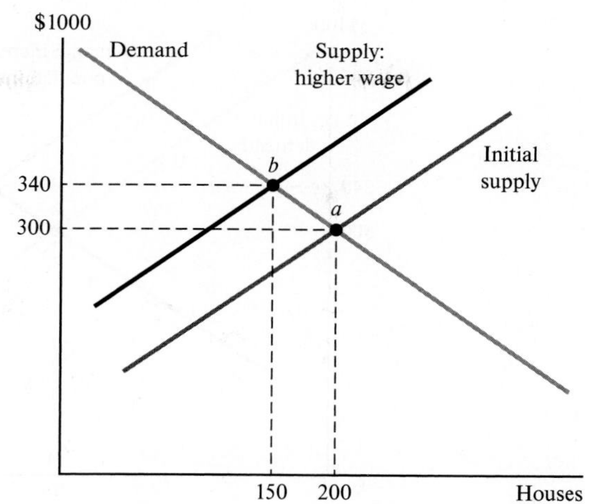

We can use comparative statics to predict the effect of a change in the value of a parameter on the value of an equilibrium variable. For example, we could predict the effect of an increase in the carpenter wage (a parameter) on the equilibrium price of new houses (an equilibrium variable). The word *static* is a synonym for equilibrium, and comparative statics compares an equilibrium generated by one set of parameter values to an equilibrium generated by a second set of parameter values.

Figure 2–6 shows that an increase in the carpenter wage increases the equilibrium price of houses and decreases the equilibrium quantity of houses.

1. *Initial equilibrium: point a.* The wage is relatively low, generating an equilibrium house price of $300,000.
2. *New equilibrium: point b.* An increase in the carpenter wage increases the cost of producing houses, shifting the supply curve upward. The equilibrium price of houses increases to $340,000 and the equilibrium quantity decreases from 200 to 150.

This comparative-statics exercise shows that there is a positive relationship between the carpenter wage (a parameter) and the price of houses (an equilibrium variable).

Consider next the effect of a change in the value of a demand-side parameter on the market equilibrium. Figure 2–7 shows the effects of an increase in a city's population.

1. *Initial equilibrium: point a.* The equilibrium price of $300,000 and the equilibrium quantity is 200 houses.
2. *New equilibrium: point b.* An increase in the city's population increases the demand for new housing, shifting the demand curve to the right. The equilibrium price increases to $340,000 and the equilibrium quantity increases to 250 houses.

FIGURE 2-7 Comparative Statics of a Change in Demand

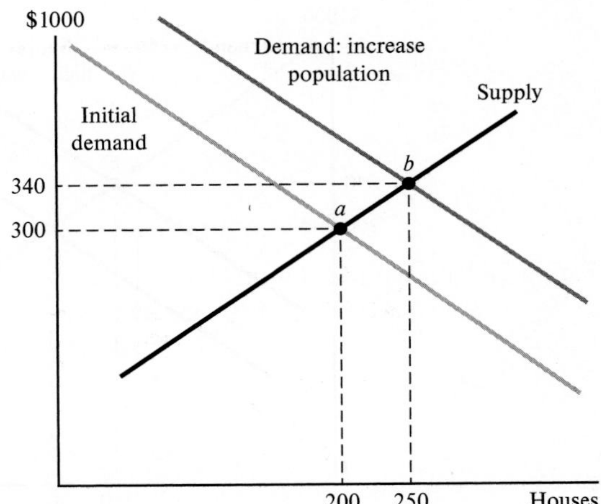

This comparative-statics exercise shows that there is a positive relationship between city population (a parameter) and the price of housing (an equilibrium variable).

The urban economy provides many opportunities to do comparative statics for market equilibria. In the urban labor market, we can predict the effects of a change in labor demand on the equilibrium wage and equilibrium employment. In the urban land market, we can predict the effects of changes in public policy on land prices and land-use patterns. In the urban transportation sector, we can predict the effects of a congestion tax on the equilibrium number of drivers and transit riders. For any market equilibrium, we can use comparative statics to predict the effect of a change in the value of a parameter on the market equilibrium.

5. PARETO EFFICIENCY

The notion of economic efficiency is embodied in the concept of Pareto efficiency, named after Italian economist Vilfredo Pareto. The concept of Pareto efficiency is based on a simple thought experiment. Starting from some initial allocation of resources, could we do better? We could do better if there is a Pareto improvement.

Pareto improvement: a reallocation of resources that makes at least one person better off without making anyone worse off.

To determine whether an allocation is Pareto efficient, we check for Pareto improvements.

An allocation is Pareto inefficient if there is a Pareto improvement.
An allocation is Pareto efficient if there are no Pareto improvements.

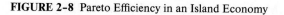

FIGURE 2–8 Pareto Efficiency in an Island Economy

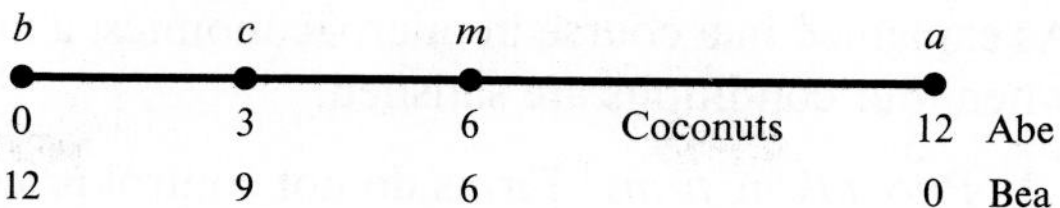

Pareto Efficiency in an Exchange Economy

In Figure 2–8, an island economy has 12 coconuts to divide between two people, Abe and Bea. Every allocation of the coconuts between the two people is Pareto efficient because any reallocation of coconuts makes one person better off at the expense of the other. Starting at point *b*, we can make Abe better off by giving him his first coconut, but only by taking a coconut from Bea and making her worse off. Similarly, starting at point *c*, Abe could go from 3 to 4 coconuts, but only if Bea goes from 9 to 8 coconuts. Each allocation is Pareto efficient because any change harms someone.

This simple example highlights the distinction between economic efficiency and equity or fairness. A 50-50 split of the coconuts may be appealing for reasons of equity or fairness, but an equal division is one of many efficient allocations. In a real economy, there are many efficient allocations of resources and goods across consumers, and reasonable people can disagree about which efficient allocation is the most equitable.

If we add a second good (bananas) to the island economy, there are likely to be Pareto improvements. Suppose Abe starts with all 12 bananas, while Bea starts with all 12 coconuts. If Abe and Bea, like most consumers, prefer variety in consumption, there is a Pareto improvement: if they exchange a few coconuts and bananas, both can be better off because each gets a more balanced bundle of goods. For example, suppose Abe is willing to pay 3 bananas to get a coconut, and Bea is willing to accept 1 banana to give up a coconut. If they split the difference between the willingness to pay (3 bananas) and the willingness to accept, they will exchange 2 bananas and 1 coconut.

1. Abe is better off because he pays 2 bananas for a coconut, compared to his willingness to pay 3 bananas.
2. Bea is better off because she gets 2 bananas for a coconut, compared to her willingness to accept 1 banana.

We would expect Abe and Bea to exchange coconuts and bananas until all the mutually beneficial trades have occurred. At that point, they have reached a Pareto efficient allocation.

This example illustrates the connection between markets and efficiency. Voluntary trade in markets generates Pareto improvements, and trade is likely to continue until all the mutually beneficial trades have been executed. At that point, the new allocation is Pareto efficient. In short, markets generally promote Pareto efficiency. A recurring theme of microeconomics is that a fully functioning market promotes efficiency, while the absence of a market–or a market that operates imperfectly–generates inefficient outcomes.

Market Equilibrium and Pareto Efficiency

As explained in a course in microeconomics, a market equilibrium is Pareto efficient when four conditions are satisfied.

1. *Price-taking firms.* Firms do not control prices but instead take the market price as given. This rules out monopolies, oligopolies, and other markets in which an individual firm is large enough to affect the market price.
2. *No external costs.* All the costs of production are incurred by firms. This rules out production that generates external costs such as air pollution or water pollution. It also rules out travel on congested highways because an additional vehicle slows down traffic and imposes costs on others.
3. *No external benefits in consumption and production.* All the benefits of consumption go to the consumer who buys a particular product. This rules out public goods such as fireworks displays, parks, and childhood education. In addition, all the benefits from producing a product go to the individual producer. This rules out agglomeration economies, defined later in the book as economic benefits (increases in productivity or decreases in cost) experienced by nearby producers.
4. *Perfect information for consumers and producers.* Consumers are fully informed about product characteristics. This rules out used cars and other goods for which a consumer has imperfect information about the characteristics of the good. Producers are fully informed about the cost of providing goods and services to consumers. This rules out insurance and other services for which a producer has imperfect information about the cost of serving customers.

Pareto Inefficiency in the Urban Economy

In an urban economy, the second efficiency condition–no external cost–is sometimes violated, generating Pareto inefficient allocations. To make the case for the inefficiency of a particular outcome, we simply identify a Pareto improvement.

1. *Air pollution.* Suppose one ton of sulfur dioxide increases the cost of health care by \$500, and a firm can cut pollution at a cost of only \$100 per ton. For a Pareto improvement, suppose pollution victims pay the polluter \$300 to cut pollution by one ton. In this case, each party will be better off by \$200: victims pay \$300 to get a \$500 reduction in the cost of health care, and the polluter incurs a \$100 cost and gets \$300. We've found a Pareto improvement, so the initial allocation is inefficient.
2. *Congestion.* Suppose the marginal driver slows traffic on a highway, and each of the 100 drivers incurs an additional opportunity cost of \$0.07. Suppose the value of the trip to the marginal driver is \$2. As a Pareto improvement, suppose each of the 100 victims pays \$0.03 to a driver to keep him or her off the road. The diverted driver has a net gain of $\$1 = \$3 - \$2$, and each continuing driver has a net gain of $\$0.04 = \$0.07 - \$0.03$. We've found a Pareto improvement, so the initial allocation is inefficient.

Of course, these transactions are simple thought experiments. As a practical matter, a number of policies could be deployed to reduce pollution and congestion to their efficient levels.

The violation of the third efficiency condition–no external benefits–provides an incentive for consumers and firms to cluster in cities. External benefits in the consumption of local public goods such as fireworks and childhood education cause consumers to cluster to share public goods. As we'll see later in the book, there are external benefits in production: firms benefit from being close to one another. These external benefits in production cause firms to cluster in cities. For external benefits in consumption and production, clustering is a Pareto improvement in response to external benefits.

6. SELF-REINFORCING CHANGES

The typical market analysis in microeconomics involves markets subject to self-limiting changes in market conditions. For example, an increase in the demand for a product initially causes excess demand for the product. The resulting increase in price eliminates excess demand by increasing the quantity supplied and decreasing the quantity demanded. This is a self-limiting change because a change in one direction (excess demand) triggers changes in the opposite direction: the price continues to increase until excess demand is eliminated. Similarly, an increase in supply causes excess supply, and the price continues to decrease until excess supply is eliminated.

In an urban economy, some markets are subject to self-reinforcing changes. A self-reinforcing change leads to additional changes in the same direction rather than the opposite direction. This process can lead to extreme outcomes, for example, large concentrations of economic activity in cities. To illustrate the effects of self-reinforcing changes in location choice, we start with an initial uniform distribution of activity. Then we explore the effects of a small change in the location pattern. If the change is self-reinforcing, the uniform distribution is replaced by clusters of economic activity.

To illustrate the effects of self-reinforcing changes, consider the location of automobile sellers. Suppose four sellers are initially distributed uniformly throughout a city and earn the same profit. In Figure 2–9, we start in panel A, with small profit rectangles. If one seller moves to a location next to another seller, what happens next?

- *Panel B.* Auto consumers compare brands before buying. The two-firm cluster will facilitate comparison shopping, so the number of car shoppers at location 1 will more than double. The profit per firm increases, as indicated by the larger profit rectangles for firms in the cluster.
- *Panel C.* The higher profit in the cluster attracts a third firm, causing a disproportionate increase in the number of shoppers, a result of enhanced comparison shopping. The cluster profit increases, increasing the profit gap between a firm in the cluster and the isolated firm at location 10.
- *Panel D.* The fourth firm joins other firms in the cluster, causing a disproportionate increase in the number of shoppers and an increase in profit per firm.

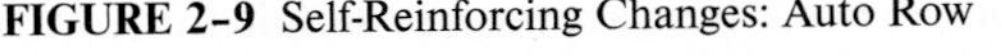

FIGURE 2-9 Self-Reinforcing Changes: Auto Row

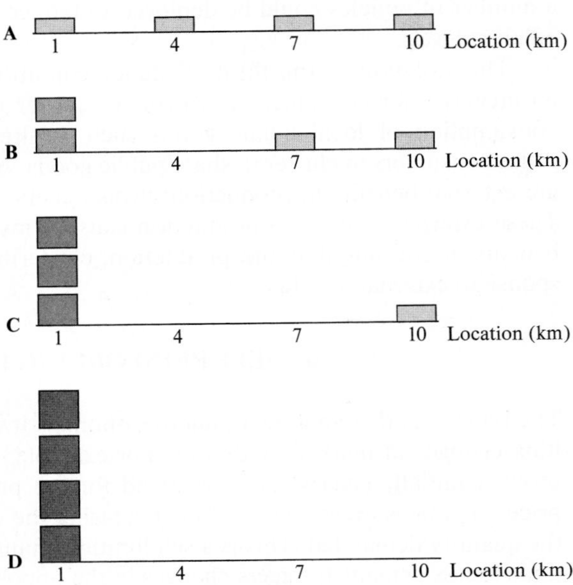

In this "auto row," firms that compete against one another locate close to one another. Self-reinforcing changes (relocations) lead to the extreme outcome–a cluster of competing firms.

Self-reinforcing changes also occur in the location decisions of people. Suppose artists and creative workers are initially spread out evenly across a dozen cities in a region. If by chance one city experiences an influx of artists, its creative environment could improve as artists are exposed to more ideas and fabrication techniques, and can share studios, print shops, tool suppliers, and other facilities. The cluster of artists may attract other artists from the region, causing a concentration of artistic production in one city.

As we will see later in the book, self-reinforcing effects are at the heart of many urban phenomena. In the first part of the book, self-reinforcing effects in production generate large clusters of employment in cities. In addition, self-reinforcing effects in consumption generate large clusters of consumer activities in large cities. In the residential environment, self-reinforcing effects generate substantial segregation with respect to income, education, and race.

REVIEW THE CONCEPTS

1. To compute the monthly cost of an entrepreneur's time, we need a number for the monthly [______]. To compute the annual cost of $100,000 that an entrepreneur invests in a business, we need a number for the [______].

2. The fundamental rule for economic decision making is to choose the level of an activity at which [______] = [______].
3. A decision-maker should do more of an activity if [______] > [______].
4. An airline has two flights per day and its average cost is $5,000 per flight. Adding a third flight would decrease the average cost to $4,000 per flight. Adding the third flight is rational if the marginal benefit (additional revenue) is at least $[________].
5. In a Nash equilibrium, there is no incentive for [______] deviation.
6. In a model of demand and supply, excess demand occurs when the price is [______] than the equilibrium price, and [______] have an incentive to unilaterally deviate by offering a [______] price.
7. In a model of demand and supply, excess supply occurs when the price is [______] than the equilibrium price, and [______] have an incentive to unilaterally deviate by offering a [______] price.
8. In a Nash equilibrium in residential location choice, a difference in an environmental feature such as noise causes differences in [______].
9. Economists use comparative statics to predict the effect of a change in the value of a [______] on the value of an [______] variable or a [______] variable.
10. In a model of market equilibrium, a change in the value of a supply-side parameter changes the equilibrium price and the equilibrium quantity in [______] direction(s).
11. In a model of market equilibrium, a change in the value of a demand-side parameter changes the equilibrium price and the equilibrium quantity in [______] direction(s).
12. Consider an economy with 24 apples and 2 people. An allocation in which each person gets 12 apples is Pareto [______]. An allocation in which one person gets all 24 apples is Pareto [______].
13. Suppose one ton of water pollution decreases a fishing firm's harvest by $200, and a paper mill can cut pollution at a cost of $100 per ton. For a Pareto improvement with an equal sharing of the efficiency gains, the [______] firm pays the [______] $[______] to reduce pollution.
14. In an urban economy, self-reinforcing changes cause changes in [______] direction(s), sometimes leading to [______] outcomes.

APPLY THE CONCEPTS

1. *The Cost of an Expedition*

   The 6 members of the BukoUlo tribe differ in their productivity in harvesting coconuts: 1 coconut harvested per day for worker one, 2 coconuts per day for worker two, and so on up to 6 coconuts per day for worker six. The tribe will choose 2 people to serve as scouts in a one-day expedition to explore the island.

   a. If the tribe randomly picks two members to serve as scouts, the economic cost of an expedition could be as high as [______] coconuts.
   b. If the tribe switches to a labor market, the market-clearing scout wage is [______] and the economic cost of an expedition is [______] coconuts.

2. *Orchard to Park*
   A citizen of Freeburg recently donated a 10-hectare orchard to the city. The city has decided to convert the orchard to a public park, using 1,000 hours of volunteer time and machinery that has a current market value of $36,000. The project will be completed in one month. Your task is to estimate the cost of the new park.
   a. List the additional information needed to compute the cost of the park.
   b. Provide plausible values for the economic variables and compute the cost of the park.
3. *Building Height*
   The total revenue from a building is $R(h) = 5400 \cdot ln(h)$, where ln is the natural logarithm and h is building height in floors. The total construction cost is $C(h) = 1000 + 3h^2$. Using a bit of calculus, the marginal benefit is $mb(h) = 5400/h$ and marginal cost is $mc(h) = 6h$. To satisfy the marginal principle, $h^* =$ [______] floors. Illustrate.
4. *Driving Speed*
   For Otto, the marginal benefit of driving speed is constant at MB = 2 utils per mph. As speed increases, the expected cost associated with an accident increases at an increasing rate. The marginal cost of speed is $MC(s) = 0.05 \cdot s$, where s is miles per hour. The marginal principle is satisfied with a speed of $s^* =$ [______] mph. Illustrate.
5. *Median Voter*
   Consider a school-board election in which each citizen votes for the candidate whose expressed budget position is closest to the citizen's preferred budget. The distribution of voter preferences is uniform, with 10 voters in each $1 interval from $1 to $11. True to their names, Penny initially proposes a small budget ($3) and Buck proposes a large budget ($9).
   a. Is the initial set of proposals ($3 and $9) a Nash equilibrium? Illustrate with a unilateral deviation by Penny of +$3.
   b. Describe the Nash equilibrium in terms of proposed budgets by Penny and Buck.
6. *Outrun a Hungry Bear?*
   Two campers awake in their tent to the sound of a rustling, pawing bear. Camper A calmly puts on his running shoes and starts stretching.
   Camper B: What are you doing? You can't outrun a hungry bear.
   Camper A: I don't have to outrun the bear. I just have to outrun you.
   Suppose that a person who wears shoes outruns a person without shoes. Describe the Nash equilibrium in terms of the number of campers who wear shoes.
7. *Quiet House vs. Noisy House*
   Consider two houses that are identical except that one is located along a quiet street (noise level = 40 decibels) and a second is located along a noisy highway (noise level = 60 decibels).
   a. Suppose the daily rent on the quiet house equals the daily rent on the noisy house. Is this a Nash equilibrium? Illustrate with a unilateral deviation.
   b. Suppose the willingness to pay for housing is $R = 600/d$, where d is the noise level in decibels. Compute the Nash equilibrium prices. Illustrate.

8. *Airbags and Speed*
Recall the earlier exercise on driving speed. Suppose Otto gets a new car, with mandated airbags that protect the driver in the event of an accident. As a result, the marginal cost of speed decreases by one fifth, to $MC(s) = 0.04 \cdot s$. As before, the marginal benefit of speed is constant at MB $= 2$. Illustrate the effects of air bags on Otto's driving speed, including values for the driving speeds before and after airbags.
9. *Changes in the Marijuana Market*
Over the past year in your state, the price of marijuana decreased, while the quantity of marijuana increased. These facts are consistent with a change on what side of the market? Illustrate.
10. *Pollution Permits*
Consider a state where each power plant initially generates one ton of pollution. Plant H can reduce its pollution at a cost of \$50 per ton, while plant L can reduce its pollution at a cost of \$20 per ton. Under a uniform-reduction policy, the state requires each plant to reduce its pollution by one ton. Describe a Pareto improvement that generates the same 2-ton reduction of pollution and makes each firm better off by the same amount. Which firm pays *how much* to the other firm to *do what*?
11. *Twins Outrun a Bear?*
Recall the exercise, "Outrun a Hungry Bear." Suppose the two campers, Dash and Slog, are identical twins, so they have the same shoe size. Dash is a faster runner if (i) both twins wear shoes, and (ii) neither twin wears shoes. A person wearing shoes outruns a person without shoes. The bear will eat one camper, along with any shoes worn by the victim.
    a. Describe the Nash equilibrium in terms of the number of campers who wear shoes.
    b. Describe the Pareto-efficient outcome in terms of the number of campers who wear shoes.
    c. The efficiency gain from switching from the Nash equilibrium to the Pareto-efficient outcome is . . .
12. *Cluster for Advertising*
Each corporation in a region purchases one advertising campaign per year from an advertising company in the same city as the corporation. The total cost for an advertising firm is $C(q) = 120 + 20q$, where q is the number of advertising campaigns per year. Initially, there is one corporation in each of the region's four cities (A, B, C, D).
    a. Suppose the corporation in city C relocates to city A. Is this a self-reinforcing or self-limiting change? Use the notion of Nash equilibrium to explain.
    b. Describe the Nash equilibrium in terms of the locations of the firms.
13. *Pizzerias vs. Food Carts*
Consider the location patterns of pizzerias and food carts. Which type of establishments tend to cluster, and which type tend to disperse? Explain the difference.

PART TWO

Market Forces in the Development of Cites

Part two of the book explores a variety of market forces that cause firms and people to cluster in cities of various size and scope. As explained in Chapter 3, cities exist because the benefits of concentrated production dominate the costs associated with living at high densities. Specifically, trading cities emerge because comparative advantage generates trade, and scale economies in exchange cause trading firms to cluster. Factory cities emerge because of economies of scale in production. Chapter 4 explores the economic forces that generate large cities: the presence of one firm reduces production costs for other firms, and this external economy causes firms to cluster in large cities. As explained in Chapter 5, the *where* of urban development is the result of a multifaceted tug-of-war, with many forces pulling firms and people in different directions. Chapter 6 shifts the focus from production to consumption, and explains the role of consumer choice in the development of cities of various size and scope. Chapter 7 takes a regional perspective, and explores the interactions between cities in a regional economy. Chapter 8 develops a model of the urban labor market and explores the effects of various public policies on equilibrium wages and total employment. Chapter 9 digs into the archeological evidence to discuss what we know about the first cities, including Jericho, Catalhouyuk, and Uruk.

CHAPTER 3

Trading and Factory Towns

Nobody ever saw a dog make a fair and deliberate exchange of one bone for another with another dog.

—ADAM SMITH

This is the first of several chapters on the economic rationale for cities. In an economy that experiences comparative advantage in production and scale economies in exchange, a trading town will develop around a trading firm. In an economy with scale economies in production, a factory town will develop around a factory.

We start with the model of backyard production, which predicts that all production happens in backyards rather than in shops and factories. Each household produces the goods it consumes in its backyard, so there is no reason to concentrate workers in cities. When we relax the assumptions of the backyard production model, the more realistic models predict the development of cities.

1. A MODEL OF BACKYARD PRODUCTION

Consider a region that produces and consumes two products, milk and shoes. People use the raw materials from cattle (milk and hides) to produce the two consumer products. The following assumptions eliminate the possibility of cities.

1. *Equal productivity.* All land is equally productive in producing the two products, and all workers are equally productive.
2. *Constant returns to scale in exchange.* The unit cost of exchange (the cost of executing one transaction, including transportation cost) is constant, regardless of how much is exchanged.
3. *Constant returns to scale in production.* The quantity of shoes produced per hour is constant, regardless of how many shoes a worker produces. The same is true for milk production.

Together these assumptions eliminate the possibility of exchange and guarantee that each household will be self-sufficient. If a person were to specialize in milk and then trade some milk for shoes, the transaction cost is the opportunity cost of the time spent in exchange rather than production. If all workers are equally productive (assumption 1), there is no benefit from specialization and exchange, so no trade will occur. If production is subject to constant returns to scale (assumption 3), there is no benefit from producing shoes in factories because an individual is just as efficient as a factory worker. In sum, because there are no productivity benefits from specialization and exchange, every household will be self-sufficient, producing everything it consumes.

The absence of exchange guarantees a uniform distribution of population. If population were concentrated at some location, competition for land would bid up its price. People in the city would pay a higher price for land without any compensating benefit, giving them an incentive to leave the city. In the Nash equilibrium, the price of land is the same at all locations, and population density is uniform.

2. COMPARATIVE ADVANTAGE AND A TRADING TOWN

The model of backyard production provides a short list of assumptions under which cities do not develop. We will proceed by dropping the assumptions, one by one, and observe the logical implications of changing the model. We will start by dropping the assumption of equal productivity for all workers.

Comparative Advantage and Trade

Consider a region with two islands, Stitch and Squeeze. Suppose that Stitch workers are more productive in producing both milk and shoes, a result of differences in soil conditions, climate, or worker skills. The first two rows of Table 3-1 show output per hour: Stitch workers are twice as productive in milk and 12 times as productive in shoes. For shoe production, the opportunity cost is 1 gallon of milk per shoe in Squeeze, compared to 1/6 of a gallon in Stitch. In the time required for a Stitch worker to produce one shoe, he or she could have instead produced 1/6 gallon of milk. Stitch has a lower opportunity cost for shoes, so Stitch has

TABLE 3-1 Production and Opportunity Cost

	Stitch	Squeeze
Shoes per hour	12	1
Milk per hour (gallons)	2	1
Opportunity cost: shoe	1/6 gallon	1 gallon
Opportunity cost: milk	6 shoes	1 shoe

a comparative advantage in shoes. For milk, the opportunity cost is 1 shoe in Squeeze, compared to 6 shoes in Stitch. Therefore, Squeeze has a comparative advantage in producing milk.

Figure 3-1 shows the gains from specialization and trade. Suppose the two islands are initially self-sufficient, with each household producing all the milk and shoes it consumes.

- *Production.* A Stitch household switches one hour from milk to shoe production, while a Squeeze household switches two hours from shoes to milk. The changes in production for Stitch are +12 shoes and −2 gallons of milk and −2 shoes and +2 gallons of milk for Squeeze. The switch to exploit comparative advantages increases the total quantity of shoes by 10 (+12 in Stitch −2 in Squeeze) while the total quantity of milk is unchanged.
- *Exchange.* Suppose the exchange rate is 3 shoes per gallon of milk. The Stitch household trades 6 shoes for 2 gallons, generating a gain of +6 shoes. The Squeeze household trades 2 gallons of milk for 6 shoes, for a gain of 4 shoes.
- *Net gains.* Each household has just as much milk and more shoes.

So far we have ignored transaction cost, defined as the opportunity cost of the time required to exchange products. For Stitch, the opportunity cost per hour is 12 shoes, so the transaction is beneficial as long as it requires less than 1/2 hour (6 shoes). For Squeeze, the opportunity cost is 1 shoe per hour, so the transaction is beneficial as long as it takes fewer than 4 hours. For example, if the exchange time is 1/4 hour, the net gain is 3 shoes for Stitch (6 − 3) and 3.75 shoes for Squeeze

FIGURE 3-1 Gains from Specialization

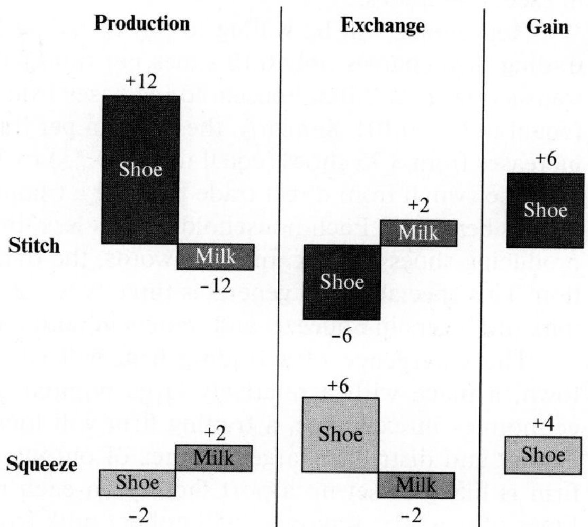

(4 − 0.25). In general, trade will occur if the differences in productivity that generate comparative advantage are large relative to transaction cost.

Scale Economies in Exchange, Trading Firms, and Trading Towns

The presence of specialization and trade will not necessarily cause the development of a trading firm. Recall the second assumption of the backyard-production model: constant returns to scale in production and exchange. Under this assumption, an individual household can exchange shoes and milk just as efficiently as a trading firm, so there is no reason to pay a firm to execute a transaction. Therefore, each Stitch household can link up with a Squeeze household to exchange shoes and milk directly. In a world of direct exchange, people in our little island economy paddle their boats to the midpoint between the two islands and exchange shoes and milk.

A trading firm will emerge if there are economies of scale associated with exchange. Scale economies could result from two economic phenomena.

1. *Indivisible inputs.* A trading firm uses indivisible inputs such as a large wagon to collect and distribute output, and a ship to transport output between the two islands.
2. *Labor specialization.* A trading firm that employs many workers can assign each worker a specialized task. Specialization increases productivity through continuity (each worker spends less time switching from one task to another) and repetition (each worker learns the most efficient way to accomplish a specific task). For example, some workers could specialize in driving wagons, while others could specialize in sailing ships.

The economies of scale from indivisible inputs and labor specialization decrease transaction cost, meaning that a trading firm will be more efficient than an individual in executing trades.

Households will be willing to pay a trading firm to execute trades. Suppose a trading firm charges only 0.10 shoes per transaction. In this case, the net gain per transaction for a Stitch household increases from 3 shoes (equal to 6 − 3) to 5.90 (equal to 6 − 0.10). Similarly, the net gain per transaction for a Squeeze household increases from 3.75 shoes (equal to 4 − 0.25) to 3.90 (equal to 4 − 0.10).

The switch from direct trade to using a trading firm makes households on both islands better off. Each household spends less time executing trades and more time producing shoes or milk. In other words, the trading firm allows further specialization. This specialization generates three types of workers: shoe producers in Stitch, milk producers in Squeeze, and traders in both locations.

The emergence of a trading firm will cause the development of a trading town, a place with a relatively large population density. To fully exploit scale economies in exchange, a trading firm will locate at a place that can efficiently collect and distribute large volumes of output. In our island model, the trading firm is likely to set up a port facility on each island. The firm will employ four types of workers: wagoners will collect milk from farmers on Squeeze and shoes from shoemakers on Stitch; dock workers will transfer the products between carts and ships; sailors will transport the products across the channel between the two islands; and accountants will collect and disperse money.

Recall that a city is defined as a place with a relatively high population density. In our island model, workers employed by the trading firm will compete for land near the ports to economize on commuting time, and the competition for land will bid up its price. The increase in price will cause workers to economize on land by choosing relatively small residential lots. In other words, workers living close to trading firms will occupy less land and thus live at a higher density. The result is a place of relatively high population density–a trading town or a small city.

Trading Cities in Urban History

Our simple model suggests that trading cities develop when comparative advantage is combined with scale economies in transport and exchange. This observation provides some important insights into the history of cities before the Industrial Revolution of the 1800s. Most of the workers in these trading cities didn't produce goods, but instead collected and distributed goods produced elsewhere, such as agricultural products from the hinterlands and handcrafted goods from various locations.

Trading cities have a long history. In the third millennium B.C., Phoenicians used fast sailing ships to serve as traders for the entire Mediterranean basin, exploiting comparative advantage to trade dye, raw materials, foodstuffs, textiles, and jewelry. They established trading cities along the Mediterranean coast in present-day Lebanon. By around 500 B.C. Athens was a thriving site for regional trade, exchanging household crafts and olive products for food and raw materials from the countryside. During the 11th and 12th centuries, Italian city-states forged agreements with the Byzantine and Islamic rulers for trade with North Africa and the East. The city-states traded wood, iron, grain, wine, and wool cloth for medicines, dyes, linen, cotton, leather, and precious metals. This trade was the major force behind the growth of Venice, Genoa, and Pisa.

Comparative advantage also played a role in U.S. urban history. Eli Whitney's cotton gin (1794) provided a means of removing the sticky seeds of green-seed cotton, which could be grown throughout the south. Within 15 years, the total output of cotton increased by a factor of 50, with most of the output coming from inland areas far from the east coast ports. American cotton was transported along rivers to New Orleans for shipment to textile firms in New England and Europe. The increase in cotton trade caused the rapid growth of New Orleans at the mouth of the Mississippi and the development of upriver commercial cities.

The history of urban America illustrates the role of transport costs in the development of trading cities. In the 1700s, most cities served largely as trading cities for ocean trade. On the eastern seaboard, cities collected agricultural products from their hinterlands to the west and shipped them overseas. The volume of trade was limited by the dirt roads serving the interior: Travel was always slow and, in times of rain and melting snow, slippery. A number of innovations decreased transport costs and increased trade.

1. *Turnpikes.* The Pennsylvania Turnpike, built with stone and gravel in 1792, increased travel speeds to a steady two miles per hour, increasing the market area and trading volume of the city of Philadelphia.
2. *Canals.* New York State completed the 360-mile Erie Canal in 1825. The canal linked New York City's natural harbor to vast agricultural areas to the north and west, and it cut freight costs from about 20 cents per ton mile to 1.5 cents. An additional canal connecting Lake Champlain to the Hudson River extended the market area of New York City to northern New England. The vast transportation network increased the volume of trade through New York City, increasing its size. By 1850, the city had a population of half a million, about 20 times its size at the end of the American Revolution. Other cities, including competitors to the south (Baltimore and Philadelphia), responded by building canals to connect hinterlands and ports, and by 1845 there were more than 3,300 miles of artificial waterways in the United States.
3. *Steamboats.* Before the introduction of the steamboat in 1807, traffic was strictly downstream: After cargo was unloaded at the terminal point, wooden boats were broken up for lumber. The steamboat allowed two-way traffic and cut river freight costs, increasing the volume of trade and the size of river cities.
4. *Railroads.* The steam engine was eventually used to power locomotives, and railroad freight replaced river shipping as the principal means of transporting goods. Between 1850 and 1890, the ratio of railroad freight to river freight went from 0.10 to 2.0, and the volume of railroad freight increased by a factor of 240. The shift from rivers to railroad caused the decline of commercial cities along rivers and the rise of cities along the vast railroad network.

3. SCALE ECONOMIES AND A FACTORY TOWN

The third assumption of the backyard-production model is that production is subject to constant returns to scale. We will maintain this assumption for milk production, but assume that shoes are produced with increasing returns to scale. Shoe producers use indivisible inputs and specialized labor, and as a result, a factory worker produces more shoes than a home worker. To continue our example, suppose that a factory worker produces 10 shoes per hour, meaning that each shoe requires just 6 minutes of labor and capital. In contrast, home workers produce one shoe or one gallon of milk per hour.

The Price of Factory Shoes

What is the market price of factory shoes? We assume that the market for shoes is competitive, so the price must be just high enough to cover the average cost of producing shoes. The average cost of production is the sum of the average capital cost and the average labor cost.

The average labor cost is defined as the cost of labor per shoe. The average labor cost is the wage w divided by the quantity of shoes produced per unit of labor q:

$$\text{Average labor cost} = \frac{w}{q}$$

The market wage ensures that workers are indifferent between working in the shoe factory and working as dairy farmers. A dairy farmer earns one gallon of milk per hour, and if the cost of living near the factory were the same as the cost of living on a dairy farm, the factory wage would be one gallon of milk per hour. But competition among factory workers for land near the factory will bid up the price of land. For Nash equilibrium in location, factory workers must receive a higher wage to offset the higher cost of city living. In addition, they must be compensated for commuting cost within the city. Continuing our numerical example, suppose the higher cost of living and commuting requires compensation of 0.80 gallons of milk per hour. In that case, the Nash equilibrium for workers requires a factory wage of 1.80 gallons of milk per hour of work. Each worker produces 10 shoes per hour, so the average labor cost is 0.18 gallons of milk:

$$\text{Average labor cost} = \frac{w}{q} = \frac{1.80}{10} = 0.18 \text{ gallons}$$

Consider next the cost of capital. Suppose the shoe firm rents the machinery and equipment from capital owners outside the region. Suppose the rental rate for the capital used in the factory is 1.2 gallons of milk per hour. Since the firm produces 10 shoes per hour, the capital cost per shoe is 0.12 gallons of milk:

$$\text{Average capital cost} = \frac{1.2}{10} = 0.12 \text{ gallons}$$

Figure 3-2 summarizes the computation of the average cost of production. The average cost is the sum of the average labor cost and the average capital cost:

$$\text{Average cost} = 0.18 + 0.12 = 0.30 \text{ gallons}$$

In a competitive market, a firm will charge a price equal to the average production cost.

$$\text{Factory price} = \text{Average cost} = 0.18 + 0.12 = 0.30 \text{ gallons}$$

With a factory price of 0.30 gallons of milk per shoe, the factory gets just enough to pay the cost of the labor and capital required to produce shoes.

FIGURE 3–2 Average Production Cost

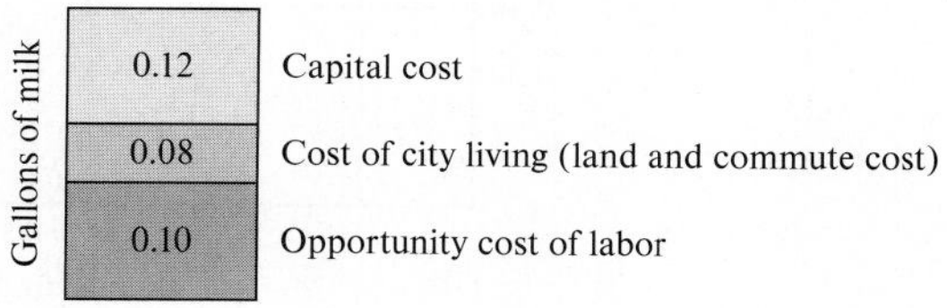

The Market Area of a Factory

Suppose there is a single shoe factory in the region. The factory competes with homemade shoes and will sell shoes to any household for which the net price of factory shoes is less than the cost of homemade shoes. The cost of a homemade shoe is the opportunity cost of the time required to make the shoe at home, that is, the one gallon of milk that could be produced instead. In Figure 3–3, the horizontal line shows the cost of homemade shoes.

The net price of factory shoes is the sum of the factory price and the household's opportunity cost of travel to the factory to buy the shoes. The net price is

$$p(x) = p' + t \cdot x$$

where $p(x)$ is the net price, p' is the factory price (equal to the average production cost), t is the opportunity cost per round-trip mile of travel, and x is the distance from the household to the factory. A round-trip mile involves one mile of travel to a location and one mile back, for a total distance of two miles. Suppose the typical person takes 1/10 of an hour per round-trip mile. In Figure 3–3, the factory price, shown by point a, is 0.30 gallons of milk. The net price curve has a slope of 0.10 per mile. For example, as shown by point b, the net price is 0.40 for a distance $x = 1$ mile:

$$p(1) = 0.30 + 0.10 = 0.40$$

The net price increases to 1.00 at a distance of 7 miles:

$$p(7) = 0.30 + 0.10 \cdot 7 = 1.0$$

The market area of the factory is the area over which it underprices the home production of shoes. In Figure 3–3, the net price of factory shoes is less than the cost

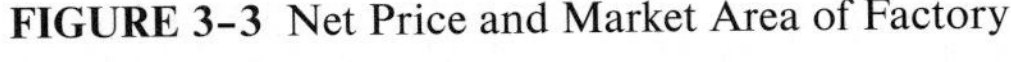

FIGURE 3–3 Net Price and Market Area of Factory

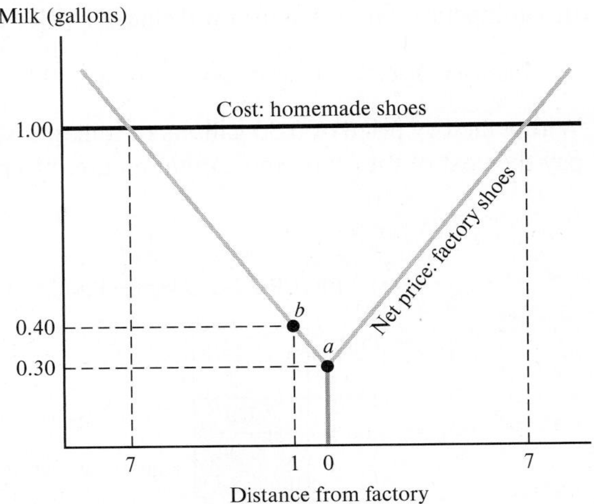

of homemade shoes for up to 7 miles from the factory. In other words, the radius of the factory's market area is 7 miles. Within this area, workers who do not work in the factory will specialize in milk production and use some of the milk they produce to purchase factory shoes. In contrast, factory workers will produce shoes in exchange for milk. Households who live farther than 7 miles from the factory will be self-sufficient, producing their own milk and shoes.

Factory Towns

A factory town will develop around the shoe factory. Workers will economize on travel costs by living close to the factory, and competition for land will bid up its price. The higher price of land will cause workers to economize on land, leading to a higher population density. The result is a place of relatively high population density, a factory town or city. Note that we have already incorporated the higher land price into the factory wage and the factory price: Workers receive an hourly wage of 1.8 gallons of milk to cover the opportunity cost of their time (1 gallon) and the higher cost of living in a city (0.80 gallons).

Our simple model of the factory city suggests that a factory city develops because scale economies make factory shoes cheaper than homemade shoes. The Industrial Revolution of the 19th century produced innovations in manufacturing and transportation that shifted production from the home and the small shop to large factories in industrial cities. In contrast to the earlier trading cities, workers in factory cities produced products rather than simply distributing products produced elsewhere.

A key innovation of the Industrial Revolution was Eli Whitney's system of interchangeable parts for manufacturing, developed around 1800. Under the traditional craft approach, the component parts of a particular product were made individually—and imprecisely. Skilled craftsmen and craftswomen were necessary to produce the parts and then fit them all together. Under Whitney's system, the producer made a large batch of each part, using precise machine tools to generate identical parts. The identical parts were interchangeable, so unskilled workers could be quickly trained to assemble the parts. The replacement of handcraft production with standardized production generated large-scale economies, causing the development of factories and factory cities.

As an illustration of the role of scale economies in the development of cities, consider the sewing machine, which was developed in the middle of the 19th century. At the beginning of the century, about four-fifths of the clothing worn in the United States was hand-sewn in the home for members of the household, and the rest was hand-sewn by tailors. The sewing machine (patented in 1846) allowed factories to underprice home producers, and by 1890 nine-tenths of U.S. clothing was being made in factories. New cities developed around the clothing factories. Innovations in the sewing machine for shoemaking (in 1858) mechanized the process of sewing soles to uppers, generating large-scale economies in shoe production that generated large shoe factories and cities developed around the shoe factories.

Innovations in intercity transportation contributed to industrialization and urbanization. As we saw earlier in the chapter, the dirt roads of the 1700s were replaced

FIGURE 3–4 Industrial Revolution and Market Area

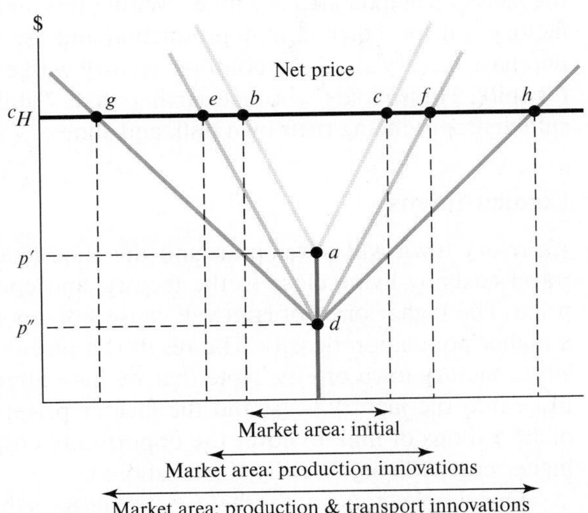

by turnpikes, and the construction of canals allowed a more dense network of inland water transport. The development of the steamship allowed two-way travel on major rivers, and the railroad system increased the speed and reach of the transportation system. All of these innovations decreased the relative price of factory goods, contributing to the growth of factory cities.

Figure 3–4 illustrates the effects of the transportation and production innovations of the Industrial Revolution on the market area of a factory.

- *Initial conditions.* The factory price p' is relatively high because of relatively small economies of scale, and the net-price curve is relatively steep because of relatively high transport cost. The market area (defined by points b and c) is relatively small.
- Innovations in production decrease the factory price from p' to p'' and increase the market area, as indicated by points e and f.
- Innovations in transportation flatten the net price curve. The market area increases in size, as indicated by points g and h.

REVIEW THE CONCEPTS

1. Region A has a comparative advantage over region B in producing a product if region A has a lower [______] for the product.
2. Trade occurs when differences in [______] are large relative to [______].
3. A region will specialize in a product for which the region has a [______].
4. In an economy that experiences comparative advantage and trade, trading cities will not exist if the economy experiences [______] in exchange.

5. Economies of scale result from [______] inputs and labor [______].
6. A city is defined as a place with relatively high [______] and occurs if workers bid up the price of [______].
7. Eli Whitney's cotton gin promoted the development of trading cities because it boosted [______].
8. Turnpikes promoted the development of cities because they increased [______] by decreasing [______].
9. In a factory town, the wage equals [______] of factory time plus the extra cost of [______].
10. The average labor cost in production equals [______] divided by [______].
11. The average capital cost in production equals [______] divided by [______].
12. Suppose the factory wage is 2 gallons of milk per hour and the capital cost is 1 gallon of milk per hour. If labor productivity is 15 shoes per hour, the average cost of production is [______] gallons. If the consumer travel cost is 1/10 hour per round-trip mile, at a distance of 6 miles, the net price of a factory shoe is [______] gallons.
13. In the model of backyard production, the absence of factory cities is explained by the assumption of [______] in production.
14. The sewing machine promoted the development of factory cities because it increased [______] in production.
15. Innovations in intercity transportation promoted the development of factory cities because the innovations decreased the price of [______] relative to the cost of [______].
16. For each pair of variables, indicate whether the relationship is positive, negative, neutral, or ambiguous.

Parameter	Choice Variable	Relationship
unit travel cost	volume of trade	[______]
economies of scale in exchange	volume of trade	[______]
unit travel cost (consumers)	net price at given location	[______]
unit travel cost (workers)	market area of factory	[______]
factory labor productivity	market area of factory	[______]
factory price	market area of factory	[______]
factory capital cost	market area of factory	[______]

APPLY THE CONCEPTS

1. *Innovation and Trading City*

   In the Stitch and Squeeze example, suppose the shoe output per hour in Stitch increases to 16 and the exchange rate increases to 4 shoes per gallon of milk. A Stitch household switches 1 hour of production time, and a Squeeze household switches 2 hours of production time.

   a. Ignoring any transaction cost, what are the gains from trade for each type of household?
   b. If the exchange time is 1/4 hour, what are the gains from trade for each type of household?

2. *Dragons and Trading Cities*
Consider a nation with two islands separated by water infested with fire-breathing dragons. Initially both islands are self-sufficient, and there are no cities. Suppose a dragon-whisperer tames the dragons and harnesses them to serve as air cargo carriers.
    a. The dragon re-purposing will cause trade if . . .
    b. If the dragon re-purposing causes trade, a trading city will develop if . . .
3. *Wagoneers and Bankers in a Trading City*
Consider an island economy with two products that are transported by horse-drawn wagon. In the single trading city, there are 60 wagoneers and 60 bankers. For each product, transport cost is 40 percent of the average cost (and delivered price), and the price elasticity of demand for the product is −2.50. Suppose a mud road is replaced by a turnpike, doubling travel speed and thus cutting in half the number of wagoneers required to handle any given volume of trade. The number of bankers is proportional to the volume of trade.
    a. The volume of trade increases by [______] percent.
    b. Compute the effects of the turnpike on (i) the number of bankers, (ii) the number of wagoneers, and (iii) total employment.
4. *Drones and a Trading City*
Consider an island economy with two goods and a single trading city that is initially occupied by wagoneers and bankers. Suppose wagons are replaced by solar-powered drones with on-board GPS (imported from another region), and banks are replaced by electronic financial systems accessible through the Internet.
    a. How will the introduction of drones and electronic banking affect the volume of trade? Explain.
    b. The introduction of drones and electronic banking cause the trading city to disappear if . . .
5. *Innovation and Average Cost of Shoes*
Using Figure 3–2 as a starting point, suppose a new production technology has five times the capital cost and five times the labor productivity. Compute the new value for the average cost of production.
6. *Hoverboards and the Factory Market Area*
Using Figure 3–3 as a starting point, consider the effect of introducing hoverboards.
    a. Suppose hoverboards decrease travel time for consumers from 1/10 per round-trip mile to 1/20 per round-trip mile. Illustrate the implications for the radius of the market area of the factory, including a value for the new radius.
    b. Suppose hoverboards also decrease the commuting cost of factory workers, decreasing the cost of urban living from 0.80 gallons to 0.30 gallons. Illustrate the effect on radius of the market area of the factory, including a value for the new radius.
7. *Matter Transmitter in Factory Town*
Consider the effects of a new matter transmitter on a factory town. The matter transmitter can instantly transport goods (but not people) from the factory to

any consumer up to 12 miles away, with a zero marginal cost of transport. The hourly rental cost of a transmitter is 1 gallon of milk.

a. Using Figure 3–3 as a starting point, show the effects of the matter transmitter on the market area of the factory.
b. An apt descriptor of the new figure is . . . (martini glass, goal post, pitched roof, shed roof, peace sign).

8. *Drama City*
Consider a region where households produce and consume drama, either live performances or broadcast television. After accounting for prices, the utility from a live performance is 24 utils, compared to 6 utils for a televised performance. There are scale economies in the production of live drama, which is provided at a performance venue at the center of the region. The travel cost is 2 utils per round-trip mile. Illustrate the equilibrium market area of the performance venue, including a value for the radius of the market area.

REFERENCES AND READING

1. Combes, P., and H. Overman. "The Spatial Distribution of Economic Activities in the European Union." Chapter 64 in *Handbook of Regional and Urban Economics 4: Cities and Geography,* eds. V. Henderson and J. F. Thisse. Amsterdam: Elsevier, 2004.
2. Davis, Kingsley. "Urbanization." In *The Urban Economy,* ed. Harold Hochman. New York: W. W. Norton, 1976.
3. Ellison, Glen, and Edward Glaeser. "The Geographic Concentration of Industry: Does Natural Advantage Explain Agglomeration?" *American Economic Review* 89 (1999), pp. 311–316.
4. Hohenberg, Paul M., and Lynn H. Lees. *The Making of Urban Europe 1000–1950.* Cambridge, MA: Harvard University Press, 1985.
5. Holmes, T., and J. Stevens., "Spatial Distribution of Economic Activities in North America." Chapter 63 in *Handbook of Regional and Urban Economics 4: Cities and Geography,* ed. V. Henderson and J. F. Thisse. Amsterdam: Elsevier, 2004.
6. Kim, Sukkoo. "Regions Resources, and Economic Geography: Sources of U.S. Regional Comparative Advantage, 1880–1987." *Regional Science and Urban Economics* 29 (1999), pp. 1–32.
7. Mills, Edwin and Bruce Hamilton. *Urban Economics.* Scott Foresman, 1997.
8. Mumford, Lewis. *The City in History.* New York: Harcourt Brace Jovanovich, 1961.

CHAPTER 4

Agglomeration Economies

The modern metropolis is jam-packed. People are living atop one another; their ideas are as well.

—PETER DIAMANDIS

People don't go there anymore. It's too crowded.

—YOGI BERRA

Firms cluster in cities to exploit external economies of scale in production, which occur when the activity of one firm decreases the production costs of nearby firms. Economists distinguish between two sorts of agglomeration economies.

1. *Localization economies.* The external effects are confined to firms in a specific industry. A more accurate label would be "intra-industry external economies."
2. *Urbanization economies.* The external effects cross industry boundaries. A more accurate label would be "inter-industry external economies." We discuss agglomeration economies in general terms that are applicable to externalities within industries (localization economies) and across industries (urbanization economies).

1. AGGLOMERATION ECONOMIES

Agglomeration economies generate relatively low production costs for firms that cluster. The cost advantages of clustering generate large concentrations of employment. This part of the chapter will explore four types of agglomeration economies.

1. Sharing intermediate input producers
2. Tapping a common labor pool
3. Improving skills matching
4. Sharing knowledge

In each case, the cost of production is lower for a firm in a cluster compared to an isolated firm.

Sharing an Intermediate Input

Some firms locate close to one another to share a supplier of intermediate inputs. An intermediate input is something produced by one firm and used by a second firm as an input to the production process. For example, a buttonmaker produces buttons that are used as intermediate inputs by dressmaking firms.

Firms will cluster to share the producer of an intermediate input if two conditions are satisfied.

1. *Economies of scale.* The production of the intermediate input is subject to economies of scale that are large relative to the demand of a single firm. By sharing a single supplier, final-good producers are able to exploit economies of scale and get the intermediate input at a lower average cost.
2. *Face time.* The design and fabrication of the intermediate input requires face-to-face interaction between the producer of the intermediate input and the producer of the final good. The intermediate input is not a standardized input that can be ordered online, but instead requires face time to ensure that the input is suited to the final product.

The first condition means that final-good producers share an intermediate input supplier, and the second condition means that final-good producers locate close to the intermediate input supplier.

In Figure 4–1, when there are economies of scale in the production of an intermediate good, the long-run average cost curve is negatively sloped. If each final-good producer demands z' units of the intermediate input and uses its own intermediate-input supplier, the average cost of the intermediate input is c' (point a). In contrast, if several final-good producers together demand z'' units of the intermediate good from a single supplier, the average cost is $c'' < c'$ (point b).

The classic example of clustering around an intermediate input supplier is the clustering of dressmakers around a buttonmaker (Vernon, 1972). The demand for high-fashion dresses is subject to the whims of fashion, so dressmaking firms must

FIGURE 4–1 Average Cost of an Intermediate Input

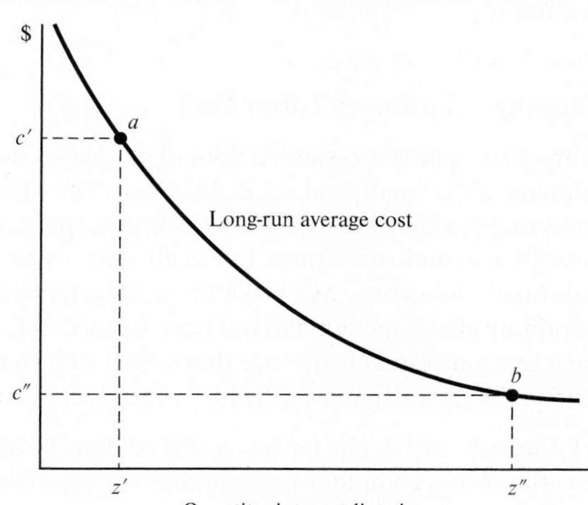

be small and nimble, ready to respond quickly to changes in fashion. Given the large economies of scale in producing buttons, the average cost will be lower if several small dressmakers share a single buttonmaker. A button for a high-fashion dress is not a standardized input that can be ordered online, but instead requires interaction between a dressmaker and a buttonmaker to design and produce the ideal button for each dress model. For example, two firms may collaborate to produce several button prototypes that vary in size, shape, and color, and then choose the most suitable prototype.

A more recent example of clustering to share intermediate inputs comes from the movie industry. Movie production is concentrated in the area in and around Hollywood, home to seven major studios and hundreds of independent movie producers. One of the many intermediate inputs shared by movie producers is props. The objects used in film scenes include mundane items such as table lamps and chairs, special items such as castoff medical instruments and vintage cars, and signature props such as elf ear tips and Gryffindor scarves. To exploit economies of scale in supplying props, movie producers share firms known as "prop houses."

Trading firms also gain from sharing the suppliers of intermediate inputs. A trading firm uses intermediate inputs such as repair services to fix leaky ships and revive balky truck engines. If the economies of scale in repair services are large relative to the demand for repair services per trading firm, repair costs will be lower if several trading firms share a single repair firm. In this case, clustering is necessary to exploit scale economies in repair services because repairs cannot be performed remotely, at least not until repair drones are developed.

In some cases, firms in different industries share the supplier of an intermediate input. The economies of scale in banking services are large relative to the demand from a single firm, so the average cost of banking service is lower in a cluster of trading firms and manufacturers of different products. The same logic applies to other business services such as insurance, accounting, and legal services: firms in different industries cluster to get these services at a lower price. Recall that when agglomeration economies cross industry boundaries, they are sometimes labeled "urbanization economies."

Tapping a Common Labor Pool

Some firms cluster to share a pool of workers. Consider an industry in which market demand for a final product is constant over time, but the demand per firm varies from one period to the next. For example, the number of television program slots is roughly constant over time, but each year, some firms will produce "hits" that will continue, and others will produce "duds" that will be cancelled. In an environment of rapidly changing demand per firm, unsuccessful firms will fire workers at the same time that successful firms hire them. Firms cluster to reduce the costs of transferring workers from unsuccessful firms to successful firms.

1. *Search cost.* A cluster has a higher density of information about job opportunities. For a computer programmer who has friends and colleagues in the software

industry, everyday interactions generate information about job openings. In addition, a job applicant in a cluster spends less time traveling from one prospective employer to the next.

2. *Relocation cost.* A worker who switches to a nearby firm can avoid the cost of a change in residence.

Workers are mobile between cities, and for a Nash equilibrium in location choice, workers must achieve the same utility level at different workplaces. In an uncertain world where a worker might be fired from a job, the expected utility from a particular job location is

$$\text{expected utility} = r \cdot u(w) + (1 - r) \cdot u(w - s)$$

where w is the wage, r is the probability of keeping the job, $(1 - r)$ is the probability of being fired and switching jobs, and s is the cost of switching jobs. The expected utility is the weighted average of the two outcomes (keep the job and earn w, or lose the job and earn $w - s$), with the weights equal to the probabilities of the two outcomes. An isolated site has a relatively high cost of switching jobs (large s), so it has a relatively high wage. For example, a software worker will demand a higher wage from an isolated firm because if the worker is fired, switching costs will be higher.

Figure 4–2 uses the concept of expected utility (reviewed in Chapter 24, Models of Microeconomics) to show the logic of a lower wage in a cluster. The worker's utility curve is concave, indicating diminishing marginal utility of income. In this example, the utility function is

$$u(\text{income}) = w^{1/2}$$

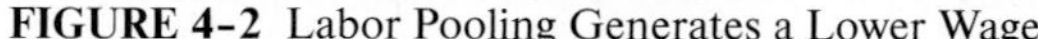

FIGURE 4–2 Labor Pooling Generates a Lower Wage

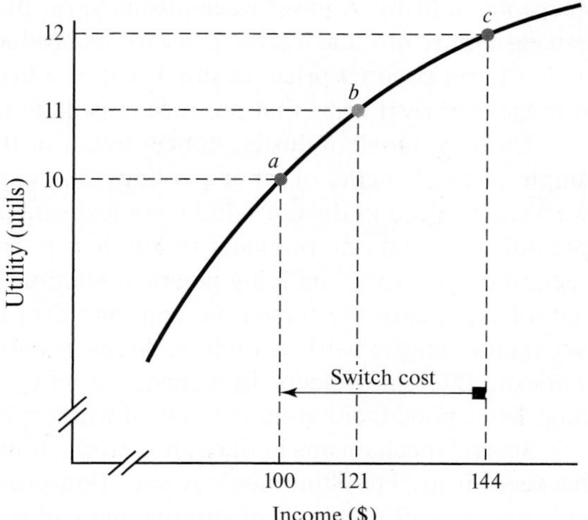

There is a 50 percent chance of being fired from either firm. Suppose for the isolated firm, the wage is $w = \$144$ and switching cost is \$44. The favorable outcome (keep the job) is shown by point c, with net income $w - s = \$144$ and utility = 12 utils. The unfavorable outcome (get fired and incur a \$44 switch cost) is shown by point a, with net income $w - s = \$100$ and utility = 10 utils. The expected utility is the average of 12 utils and 10 utils, or 11 utils.

We can use the concept of certainty equivalent to translate the expected utility of the risky isolated job into dollars. As explained in Chapter 24 (Models of Microeconomics), the certainty equivalent is the certain payment in dollars that makes a decision-maker indifferent between taking a risk (50-50 chance of either \$100 or \$144) and taking the certain payment. In this case, the certainty equivalent is \$121. The worker is indifferent between a certain payment of \$121 (a certain utility of 11 utils) and taking the risk of either earning \$144 by keeping the job or earning only \$100 by losing the job and relocating.

As noted earlier, switching costs are lower for a worker in a cluster of firms because of superior employment information and a smaller chance of being forced to change residence. To simplify the calculations, suppose the switching cost for a worker in a cluster of firms is zero. For Nash equilibrium in the labor market, the wage in the cluster is simply the \$121 certainty equivalent of the risky job in an isolated firm. A worker in a cluster who loses a job finds another at the same wage without any switching cost, so the \$121 is a sure thing. The certain \$121 makes the worker indifferent between working in the cluster and taking the risk of equal chances of either \$144 or \$100 in the isolated firm.

The same logic applies if the switching cost of the cluster are positive, but smaller than the switching cost of an isolated site. In this case, working in the cluster carries some risk because losing a job means incurring some switching cost. But because the switching cost is lower in the cluster, there is a smaller income loss in the event of losing a job, so Nash equilibrium requires a lower wage in the cluster.

The relatively low wage in a cluster has important implications for the location decisions of firms. A lower wage means lower production cost, so a firm in a cluster can earn more profit at a given price for its product, or can earn zero economic profit with a lower product price. In other words, a firm in a cluster has a competitive advantage over rival firms that produce in isolation.

The U.S. movie industry, concentrated in the Hollywood area, provides an example of the benefits of labor pooling. One segment of the labor market includes workers involved in the craft and technical side of the industry. These workers move periodically from one producer to another as projects come and go and rely on an "economy of favors," building personal relationships to keep informed about potential jobs and ease the transition from one firm to another. The same phenomenon occurs for creative workers (actors, directors, writers) as they move between firms to work on different projects. In a cluster of movie producers, firms draw from a common labor pool, facilitating the flow of workers between firms.

Several mechanisms in the movie-production cluster improve the flow of workers between firms. The Stuntmen's Association provides free online access to a searchable database of hundreds of stuntpeople and stunt coordinators. A movie producer can enter the keyword "yanked through air" and instantly get a list of dozens of stunt performers who make their living being yanked off the ground by pressurized air ratchets. Other intermediaries such as agents, casting directors, and talent managers match labor demanders and suppliers. Colleges and universities in the area have professional programs that train students in the production of film and television. These coordinating mechanisms improve the efficiency of the labor market and help maintain the competitive advantages of the movie-production cluster.

Skills Matching

The third type of agglomeration economies is related to the matching of workers and jobs. In a traditional economic model of a labor market, we assume that workers and firms are matched perfectly: each firm hires workers who have precisely the skills the firm requires. In the real world, things are not so tidy. Workers and firms are not always perfectly matched, and skill mismatches require costly worker training to better match workers and jobs. As we'll see, a large city can improve the matching of workers and firms, decreasing training costs and labor costs.

To illustrate skills matching, consider computer programmers hired by a software firm. Programmers have different skill sets, depending on their facility with different programming languages (e.g., Java, Javascipt, Python, HTML) and their experience with different programming tasks (e.g., graphics, artificial intelligence, e-commerce). Although some programmers are more productive than others, what matters for the matching model is that they have different skill sets. A firm enters the market with a particular skill requirement and hires workers who provide the best skill matches.

The classic model of labor matching has four key assumptions.

1. *Variation in worker skills.* Each worker has a skill described by a position or "address" on a line of unit length, and the workers are equally spaced. In the first panel of Figure 4–3, the four workers (triangles) are positioned at addresses 0, 1/3, 2/3, and 1.
2. *Economies of scale in production.* Production is subject to economies of scale, and each firm hires more than one worker. In our example, each firm hires two workers.

FIGURE 4–3 Agglomeration Economies: Labor Skills Matching

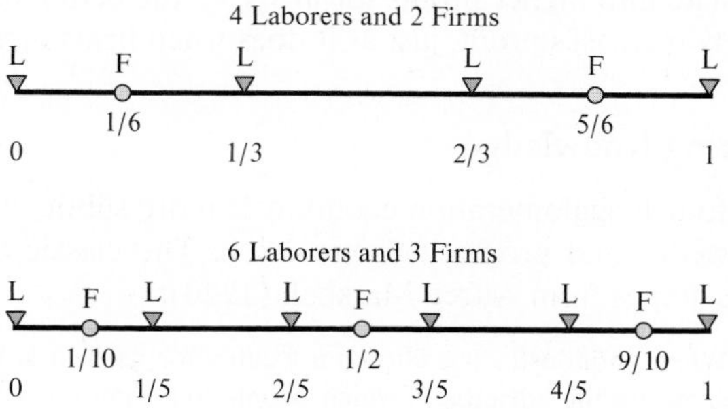

4 Laborers and 2 Firms

L F L L F L

1/6 5/6

0 1/3 2/3 1

6 Laborers and 3 Firms

L F L L F L L F L

1/10 1/2 9/10

0 1/5 2/5 3/5 4/5 1

3. *Firm skill requirements.* Each firm enters the market by picking a product and the associated skill requirement. In Figure 4–3 firms are shown as circles. One firm enters with skill address 1/6 and a second enters with skill address 5/6.
4. *Training cost.* A firm bears the cost of closing the gap between worker skills and the firm's skill requirement.

Figure 4–3 illustrates two equilibria in a labor matching model, one for a small city and a second for a large city.

- *Upper panel: Small city.* In a city with four skill types and two firms, the skills mismatch is 1/6. For example, workers at skill addresses 0 and 1/3 are hired by a firm with skill requirement 1/6, so each worker has a skills gap of 1/6. If the training cost of closing a unit gap (from 0 to 1) is \$30, the training cost per worker is 1/6 of \$30, or \$5.
- *Lower panel: Large city.* In a city with six skill types and three firms, the skills mismatch is 1/10. For example, the workers at skill addresses 0 and 1/5 are hired by a firm with skill requirement 1/10, so each worker has a skills gap of 1/10. If the training cost of closing a unit gap is \$30, the training cost per worker is 1/10 of \$30, or \$3.

A firm that moves from the small city to the large city will cut its training cost per worker from \$5 to \$3. The general lesson is that an increase in the number of workers improves skills matching and decreases training cost.

This simple model illustrates the agglomeration economies associated with improved matching of workers and firms as a city's workforce grows. In general, if the number of workers in the city is n, the average skills mismatch is

$$m = \frac{1}{2(n-1)}$$

As n increases, the skills mismatch decreases ($m = 1/6$ for $n = 4$ and $m = 1/10$ for $n = 6$), decreasing training costs.

We have assumed that firms bear the training costs required to close skills gaps. If instead workers bear training costs, agglomeration economies persist. In that case, workers experience lower training costs in larger cities, generating downward pressure on wages. For locational equilibrium, workers reach the same utility level in each city, and lower training costs cause lower wages, ceteris paribus. Lower wages translate into higher profits for firms, so the better skill matching in large cities ultimately increases profit, just as it does when firms incur training costs.

Sharing Knowledge

The fourth agglomeration economy is more subtle, involving the benefits of sharing knowledge and promoting innovation. The classic description of knowledge spillovers comes from Alfred Marshall (1920):

> When an industry has chosen a locality for itself, it is likely to stay there for long; so great are the advantages which people following the same skilled trade get from near

> neighborhood to one another. The mysteries of the trade become no mysteries; but are as it were in the air, and children learn many of them unconsciously. Good work is appreciated; inventions and improvements in machinery, in processes and the general organization of the business have their merits promptly discussed; if one man starts a new idea, it is taken up by others and combined with suggestions of their own; and thus it becomes the source of new ideas.

The sharing of knowledge provides an incentive for firms to cluster because innovation leads to lower costs and higher profit. Some knowledge spillovers occur within an industry (localization economies), but the spillovers often cross industry boundaries (urbanization economies).

Other Benefits of City Size

So far we have explored four types of agglomeration economies that increase productivity and decrease production cost. Three other advantages of city size generate lower wages production cost.

1. *Joint labor supply.* A household with two workers confronts the problem of joint labor supply: the household chooses a single residence and two workplaces. If the skills of the two workers are suited to different industries, the household will be attracted to locations with a mix of industries, and workers are willing to accept lower wages in cities with a more favorable mix of industries. The role of cities in resolving the issue of joint labor supply has a long history. In the 1800s, mining and metal-processing firms (employing men) located close to textile firms (employing women), and each industry benefited from the presence of the other. More recently, power couples (defined as a pair of college graduates) are concentrated in large cities, where they are more likely to find good job matches for both workers.
2. *Learning.* Human capital is defined as the knowledge and skills acquired by workers in formal education, work experience, and social interaction. Human capital can be increased through learning by imitation—observing other workers and imitating the most productive workers. A larger city provides a wider variety of role models for workers, so it attracts workers pursuing learning opportunities. Empirical studies show that a worker who moves from a rural area to a city experiences wage increases over time as learning increases productivity. If the worker moves back to the rural area, his or her rural wage will be higher than before, a result of the higher productivity from urban learning.
3. *Social interactions.* So far we have ignored the social aspects of life. People enjoy interacting with one another, and a larger city provides more opportunities for social interactions. Imagine a model of hobby matching, an analog of the model of labor skill matching. A larger city provides better matching of hobbies and other social interests. For example, you are more likely to find a book club that focuses on your favorite author and more likely to find a dance club that dances your favorite dances. Some people live in cities to take advantage of better opportunities for social matching.

2. EQUILIBRIUM SIZE OF A CLUSTER

How large will the typical cluster of firms be? We can use a simple model to explore the factors that determine the equilibrium size of a cluster. Each firm chooses the location that maximizes profit, and in the Nash equilibrium, no firm has an incentive to change its location.

Agglomeration Diseconomies

So far we've seen that agglomeration economies generate external benefits that provide an incentive for firms to cluster. On the other hand, the clustering of firms increases total employment, generating agglomeration diseconomies that at least partly offset agglomeration economies. Consider the effects of an increase in the number of workers in a cluster. The additional workers can be accommodated by (a) an increase in density (building up) or (b) an increase in land area (building out). In both cases, an increase in the size of the workforce increases wages and production cost, at least partly offsetting the lower production cost generated by agglomeration economies.

Consider first the effects of an increase in population density. In this case, an increase in building height increases the production cost per square foot of housing for two reasons.

1. *Extra reinforcement.* A taller building requires sturdier walls to support its greater weight. For example, a doubling of building height from 3 levels to 6 levels more than doubles construction cost because of the extra reinforcement of walls.
2. *Less housing space per floor.* The taller the building, the larger the fraction of floor space devoted to intra-building transportation systems (stairways and elevators) and thus the smaller the amount of housing space per floor. For example, a doubling of building height from 3 levels to 6 levels less than doubles housing space. The smaller the amount of housing space per floor, the higher the construction cost per square foot of housing.

Higher housing costs lead to higher wages. Firms must offer wages high enough to attract workers to the cluster, and the higher the cost of urban housing, the higher the wage demanded by workers. So when an increase in the workforce is accommodated by building taller buildings, firms pay higher wages to offset the higher cost of housing. The higher wages mean higher production costs for all firms in the cluster.

Consider next the possibility of an increase in the land area of the cluster. In the case of building out to accommodate a larger workforce, the average commuting distance increases, increasing the monetary and time cost of travel to work. So when an increase in the workforce is accommodated by increasing commuting distances, firms pay higher wages to offset the higher commuting cost. The higher wages mean higher production costs for all firms in the cluster.

Equilibrium vs. Efficient Cluster Size

Figure 4–4 shows the tradeoffs associated with different cluster sizes. The horizontal axis shows the number of firms in a cluster, and the vertical axis shows profit per firm. Over the positively sloped portion of the profit curve, as the number of firms increases, agglomeration economies dominate agglomeration diseconomies, so profit per firm increases. Over the negatively sloped portion, as the number of firms increases, agglomeration diseconomies dominate agglomeration economies, so profit per firm decreases.

To illustrate the economic forces behind clustering, consider a growing region. In Figure 4–4, we start with a single firm at point *a*, and the region grows by one firm per time period. The first firm is isolated (a single firm in the cluster) and earns profit π_1. The second firm will either join the first firm to form a two-firm cluster or choose an isolated site. As shown by point *b*, profit in a two-firm cluster is higher ($\pi_2 > \pi_1$), so clustering happens. As additional firms enter the region, they will continue to join the cluster, causing movement upward and then downward along the profit curve until we reach point *c*. Firms will continue to enter the cluster as long as the profit in the cluster exceeds the profit of an isolated firm (π_1). Starting from point *c*, an additional firm in the cluster would earn less profit than an isolated firm, so the next entering firm will start a new cluster.

As firms continue to enter the regional economy, they form new clusters. For each additional cluster, we move from point *a* to point *c*. Once we reach point *c*, an additional cluster will develop, and the up-and-over movement along the profit curve will repeat for as many clusters as it takes to accommodate all the entering firms.

The equilibrium cluster size exceeds the efficient size. To illustrate, suppose that growth in the region stops once the region reaches 30 firms. In Figure 4–5, the equilibrium is shown by point *c*, with a single cluster with $z^* = 30$ firms and a total profit of 30 times π_1. In contrast, the efficient allocation is two clusters, each

FIGURE 4–4 Profit and Cluster Size

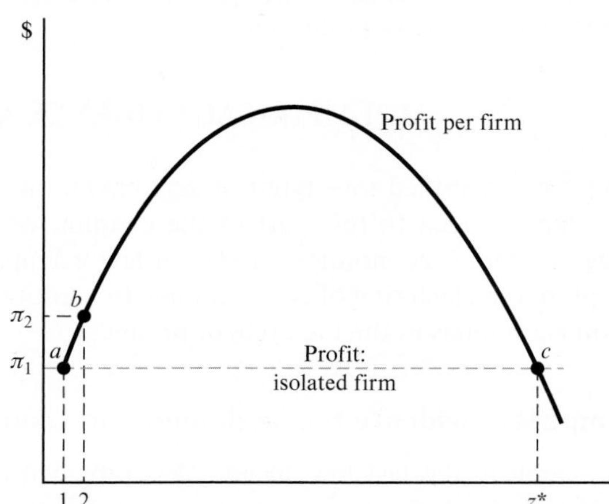

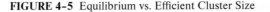

FIGURE 4–5 Equilibrium vs. Efficient Cluster Size

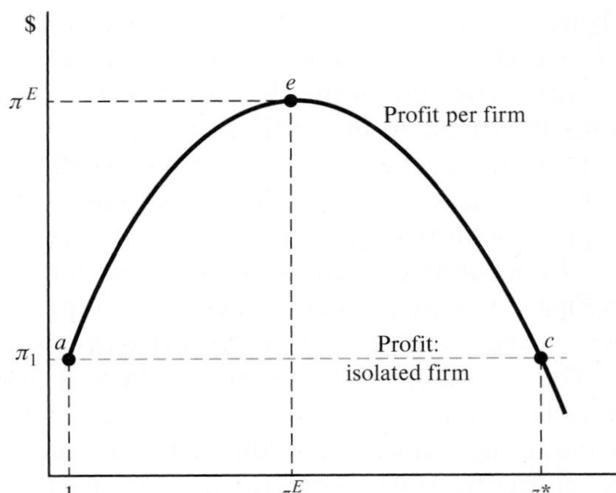

with $z^E = 15$ firms (point *e*). In this case, the total profit is 30 times the profit of the typical firm, π^E. For example, if $\pi_1 = \$5$ and $\pi^E = \$12$, the equilibrium total profit is $150, compared to $360 for the efficient outcome.

Why do the individual location decisions lead to an inefficient outcome? In making a location decision, each individual firm ignores the external benefit of agglomeration economies as well as the external cost from agglomeration *diseconomies.* Once the region reaches the efficient number of firms per cluster at point *e* (the peak of the profit curve), an additional firm in the cluster decreases the profit per firm. At this point, the external cost from agglomeration diseconomies dominates the external benefit from agglomeration economies. An individual firm ignores both the external benefit and the external cost, but because the external cost is relatively large, the firm's choice generates "too much" of the activity–too large a cluster. This is similar to the case of pollution: a firm ignores the external cost of pollution, resulting in an excessive volume of pollution.

3. EMPIRICAL EVIDENCE AND EXAMPLES

We have identified four types of agglomeration economies that encourage firms to cluster in cities. In this part of the chapter, we summarize empirical evidence of agglomeration economies, provide a few examples of single-industry clusters, and explore the clustering of corporations. In addition, we discuss the role of agglomeration economies in the life cycle of products.

Empirical Evidence for Agglomeration Economies

Research in the last few decades has provided ample evidence that the clustering of firms in cities increases worker productivity, promotes the development of new production facilities, and increases employment. This research is summarized by Combes and Gobillon (2015).

1. *Productivity.* The conventional measure is the elasticity of labor productivity with respect to industry output, equal to the percentage change in output per worker divided by the percentage change in industry output.
2. *New plants.* The conventional measure is the elasticity of firm births (new production facilities) with respect to industry output. In the classic study by Carlton of three industries (plastics products, electronic transmitting equipment, and electronic components), the estimated elasticity is 0.43: A 10 percent increase in industry output increases the number of births by 4.3 percent (Carlton).
3. *Employment growth.* In the classic study by Rosenthal and Strange of the software industry, a zip-code area that starts out with 1,000 more software jobs than another zip-code area experiences a larger increase in software employment—about 12 more jobs. On average, the boost in employment from agglomeration economies peters out at a rate of about 50 percent per mile.

Economic Effects of Million-Dollar Plants

A recent study (Greenstone, Hornbeck, & Moretti, 2010) explores the effects of a large manufacturing plant on a metropolitan economy. The study focuses on competition between local governments (U.S. counties) for large manufacturing plants. A regular feature in the corporate real-estate journal *Site Selection,* "Million Dollar Plants," documents corporate decisions about where to locate a new plant, including the role of incentives from county governments. For each site-selection contest between counties, the journal lists the winning county as well as one or two finalist counties. The study compares the economic experience of a winning county to the experience of a losing county.

The study focuses on the effects of a million-dollar plant (MDP) on productivity, output, and wages in the local economy. The study highlights agglomeration economies and diseconomies associated with large production facilities.

1. *Agglomeration economies.* On average, worker productivity in existing manufacturing plants increases by 12 percent. The productivity gains are larger for firms that are economically proximate to the MDP in terms of production technology and the flow of workers. This is evidence of agglomeration economies between firms that share workers and knowledge. The increase in productivity generates an additional $430 million in annual county manufacturing output (five years after the opening of the MDP).
2. *Agglomeration diseconomies.* The location of an MDP increases the average wage by roughly 2.7 percent. For firms that benefit from agglomeration economies, the higher wage offsets roughly 13 percent of the productivity gains from agglomeration.

For firms that do not benefit from agglomeration economies, higher wage increases production cost and decreases profit. This explains the clustering tendency of firms subject to agglomeration economies: firms with the most to gain from a cluster crowd out firms that bear a cost (higher wages) without an offsetting productivity boost.

Evidence of Knowledge Spillovers

There is evidence that knowledge spillovers cause firms to cluster. This research is summarized by Carlton and Kerr (2015). Knowledge spillovers increase the size of the clustered industry by increasing the number of firms (more firm births) and increasing total employment. The studies draw several other conclusions.

1. The largest knowledge spillovers occur in the most innovative industries.
2. Knowledge spillovers are highly localized, petering out over a distance of a few miles.
3. Knowledge spillovers are more prevalent in industry clusters with small, competitive firms (e.g., the electronics cluster in Silicon Valley) and less prevalent in industry clusters dominated by a few firms (e.g., the electronics cluster along Route 128 in Boston).

One measure of knowledge generation is the incidence of patents for new products and processes. The classic study by Carlino and Hunt (2009) explores the factors that determine the incidence of patents across metropolitan areas. After adjusting the raw number of patents to incorporate their relative importance (as measured by the number of times a patent is cited in other patents), they estimated the elasticities of patent intensity with respect to several variables.

1. *Employment density (jobs per square mile).* The overall elasticity is 0.22: a 10 percent increase in employment density increases patent intensity by about 2.20 percent. There are diminishing returns to density: the positive relationship levels off at an employment density of roughly 2,200 jobs per square mile.
2. *Total employment.* The overall elasticity is 0.52: a 10 percent increase in total employment increases patent intensity by about 5.2 percent. There are diminishing returns to total employment: the positive relationship levels off at a metropolitan population of about 1.8 million.
3. *Human capital (share of workforce with a college degree).* The elasticity is 1.05: A 10 percent increase in the share of the population with a college degree increases patent intensity by 10.5 percent.
4. *Establishment size.* The elasticity is −1.4: a 10 percent increase in the average establishment size decreases patent intensity by 14 percent. This provides evidence that workers in cities with relatively competitive environments are more innovative.

There is substantial variation in patent intensity across metropolitan areas. The average patent intensity is 2.0, and the values ranging from 0.07 (in McAllen, Texas) to 17 (in San Jose, California). Following San Jose in the rankings are Rochester, New York; Trenton, New Jersey; Ann Arbor, Michigan; Austin, Texas; Wilmington, Delaware; Raleigh-Durham, North Carolina; Boston, Massachusetts; and San Francisco, California.

Single-Industry Clusters

When external economies in production are confined to firms in a specific industry, these "localization economies" can generate large clusters of firms producing the same product. In the United States, the most famous industry clusters are carpets in Dalton, Georgia (41 percent of national employment in carpets); costume jewelry in Providence, Rhode Island (55 percent); and elevators in Indianapolis, Indiana (20 percent); and video production in Los Angeles, California (44 percent).

The cluster of carpet makers in Dalton had its origin in 1895. Catherine Evans of Dalton used an outdated technique–known as tufting or candle wicking–to make a bedspread as a wedding gift. The gift was a big hit, and in the next few years, Evans made tufted items for her friends and even sold a few. After she discovered a few production tricks such as a technique for locking the tufts onto the backing, she and her neighbors launched a local handicraft industry, producing handmade tufted items for sale. When a new machine for producing tufted carpets made tufted carpets cheaper than woven carpets, firms entered the carpet market and located in Dalton to hire workers with knowledge and experience in tufting, and to share the suppliers of intermediate inputs such as dyes and backing. Some carpet makers moved from the Northeast to the Dalton area and switched to the new techniques. Dalton became the carpet capital of the country, with most of the top manufacturers locating in and near the city.

The rapid urbanization of China has generated large clusters of firms that exploit agglomeration economies. Sock producers in the city of Datang produce 12 billion pairs of socks per year, about 35 percent of the world production. The city has 10,000 sock-making enterprises that employ a total of 200,000 workers, so the average enterprise has only 20 workers. The small- and medium-sized enterprises cluster to share the suppliers of intermediate inputs, tap common labor pools, and share knowledge.

Table 4–1 lists some of the features of eight industry clusters. For each cluster, the table shows the most prominent clusters as measured by industry employment, and the location quotient for the industry in the city. The location quotient is computed as the share of the city's total employment in the industry divided by the share of national employment in the industry. A large location quotient indicates a relatively large concentration of the industry in the city. For example, Seattle's location quotient for software publishers is 12.3, indicating that Seattle's software job count of 53,800 is 12.3 times the job count that would occur if the city's software employment share matched the national software employment share. Other software clusters occur in San Francisco (20,700 jobs and a location quotient of 3.9), San Jose, Atlanta, and Madison, Wisconsin. Los Angeles hosts clusters in motion pictures, insurance claims, aerospace, and ophthamalic goods. New York hosts clusters in sound recording, motion pictures, and investment banking and securities. Although the cluster of sound producers in Nashville is smaller than the clusters in Los Angeles and New York, the Nashville cluster is a much larger fraction of the city's economy.

TABLE 4-1 Industry Clusters

Industry	Metropolitan Area	2015 Employment	Location Quotient	Industry	Metropolitan Area	2015 Employment	Location Quotient
Software publishers	Seattle, WA	53,800	12.3	Investment banking & securities	New York, NY	53,888	5.71
	San Francisco, CA	20,700	3.9		Chicago, IL	8,381	1.52
	San Jose, CA	16,900	6.91		Bridgeport, CT	3,782	8.42
	Atlanta, GA	12,300	2.16	Ship building & repairing	Virginia Beach, VA	26,232	59.61
	Madison, WI	8,900	10.17		Mobile, AL	5,645	49.15
Motion pictures & video	Los Angeles, CA	106,800	11.74	Ophthamalic goods	Los Angeles, CA	2,953	2.82
	New York, NY	35,500	2.48		Rochester, NY	1,924	29.63
	New Orleans, LA	2,900	3.33		Dallas, TX	1,837	2.28
	Bridgeport, CT	2,300	3.3		Tampa, FL	1,355	6.73
Sound recording	New York, NY	3,076	2.94	Aerospace products	Seattle, WA	91,424	12.67
	Los Angeles, CA	2,718	4.09		Los Angeles, CA	49,934	2.48
	Nashville, TN	1,936	19.23		Dallas, TX	32,121	2.79
Insurance claims	Los Angeles, CA	3,257	1.86		Wichita, KS	28,062	27.52
	Atlanta, GA	2,382	2.43		St. Louis, MO	16,228	3.57
	Las Vegas, NV	1,030	3.04				

Corporate Headquarters and Functional Specialization

Corporations locate their headquarters in cities to exploit agglomeration economies that cross industry boundaries (urbanization economies). Corporate executives and managers perform a variety of tasks. For example, they develop strategic plans for production and marketing, pick locations for new plants, and handle legal disputes. Corporations cluster to share firms that specialize in providing information that is vital to corporate decisions, for example, accounting and legal firms. In other words, clustering allows corporations to outsource accounting and legal services and to exploit scale economies in providing intermediate inputs.

Corporations in a cluster can also share firms that provide other business services. For example, given the large economies of scale in producing advertising campaigns, corporations cluster to share advertising firms, and they get specialized marketing campaigns at a lower cost. Similarly, corporations are attracted by the large concentrations of firms that provide financial and business services in midtown Manhattan, the Loop in Chicago, and the financial district of San Francisco.

In the last several decades, there has been a fundamental shift in the specialization of cities. Large cities have become increasingly specialized in managerial functions, while smaller cities have become more specialized in production. One measure of managerial specialization for a city is the ratio of management workers to production workers. The classic study by Duranton and Puga (2005) shows that in the last few decades, the ratio has increased in relative terms in large cities. Since 1950, the ratio in the largest cities (population greater than 5 million) increased from just 10 percent above the national average to well above average. In contrast, the ratio in the smallest cities (population between 75,000 and 250,000) went from just 2 percent below average to well below average.

These changes in functional specialization were caused by decreases in the cost of managing production facilities from afar. Firms are better equipped to operate multi-plant firms from headquarters in large cities, where agglomeration economies generate lower production costs. The most important cost reductions have come from innovations in telecommunications, in particular the development of duplicators (photocopiers, fax machines, and e-mail) that have facilitated the rapid transmission of information and reduced the cost of coordination.

Agglomeration and the Product Cycle: The Radio Industry in New York

Agglomeration economies contribute to the development of new products. The classic study by Vernon (1972) identifies the radio industry in New York as an example of an industry that benefited from agglomeration economies in its early design and development stage.

> In the 1920s that industry had all the earmarks of an activity whose establishments were heavily dependent on external [agglomeration] economies, speed, and personal contact. Its technology was unsettled and changing rapidly; its production methods were untried; its market was uncertain. Accordingly, at that stage, producers were typically small in size, numerous, agile, nervous, heavily reliant upon subcontractors and suppliers. Mortality in the industry was high. In those circumstances, the attraction of an urban area like the New York Metropolitan Region was especially strong.

New York was attractive because it provided a wide variety of intermediate inputs and a large and diverse workforce. The area also provided production knowledge–embodied in a wide variety of production processes–that proved useful in developing a production process for the radio.

Vernon explains why the radio industry eventually left the New York metropolitan area.

> A decade or two later, however, the technology of the industry had settled down. Production methods were standardized and sets were being turned out in long runs. Now, the critical competitive questions had become transport and labor costs, rather than product design. The small firm faded from the picture and large assembly plants appeared at lower-range locations more centrally placed for national markets.

When a product reaches its mature stage, with a settled design and established production process, producers have less to gain from diversified cities, and they can relocate to places with lower production costs because of lower wages or lower land rent.

Nursery Cities

Recent work has explored the notion of "nursery cities," defined as large diverse cities that provide a nurturing environment for early product design and development. Diverse cities foster new ideas and experimentation, so they serve as nurseries for innovative firms. Once a firm settles on a product design and production process, production is likely to be more efficient in a specialized city that fully exploits external economies in production that are specific to an industry (also known as localization economies). In other words, diverse cities foster innovation, while specialized cities facilitate efficient production.

The classic study by Duranton and Puga (2001) provides evidence that diverse cities serve as nurseries for firms in innovative industries. Among French firms that change locations, more than 7 in 10 relocated from a diverse city to a specialized city. The frequency of moves from a diverse to a specialized city is highest for the most innovative industries: the frequency is 93 percent for research and development, 88 percent for pharmaceuticals and cosmetics, and 82 percent for information technology. Other industries have relatively high frequencies of moves from diverse to specialized cities, including business services, printing and publishing, aerospace equipment, and electronic equipment. In contrast, the frequency of moves from diverse to specialized cities is relatively low for less innovative sectors such as furniture, food, beverages, clothing, and leather.

REVIEW THE CONCEPTS

1. Dressmakers will share a buttonmaker if [_____] in button production are large relative to [_____] in dress production, and will cluster if [_____] is required to produce buttons.
2. Labor pooling can occur for an industry in which [_____] demand for a final product is constant over time, but the [_____] varies from one period to the next.
3. Suppose the wage offered by an isolated firm is \$64 and there is a 50 percent chance of being fired. The switching cost is \$28 and the utility function is $u(w) = w^{1/2}$. The expected utility for a job with the isolated firm is [_____] and the certainty equivalent of a job in the isolated site is \$[_____]. If the moving cost in a cluster is zero, the wage in the cluster is \$[_____].
4. In the model of labor matching, the assumption that each firm hires more than one worker is consistent with [_____] in production.
5. As the number of firms in a city increases, the skills mismatch [_____] and training cost [_____].
6. An increase in building height [_____] the production cost per square foot of housing because of [_____] and more space for [_____].
7. A city that accommodates a larger workforce by building out experiences increases in [_____] and [_____].
8. For the [_____] number of firms in a cluster, the profit curve is at its [_____] value. For the equilibrium number of firms, the profit of a(n) [_____] firm equals the profit of a(n) [_____] firm.

9. The empirical evidence for agglomeration economies comes from data showing that an increase in industry output increases [_____] and increases the number of [_____].
10. As a cluster of firms grows, clustering firms crowd out firms that [_____] without an offsetting [_____].
11. Knowledge spillovers are more prevalent in industry clusters with [_____] firms.
12. Patent intensity [_____] as population density increases and [_____] as firm size increases.
13. In the last several decades, large cities have become increasingly specialized in [_____], while smaller cities have become more specialized in [_____].
14. The radio industry in 1920 is a classic example of agglomeration economies because the technology was [_____] and the firms were [_____] in size, [_____] in number, [_____] in their response to changing circumstances, and [_____] in temperament.
15. The notion of nursery cities suggest that firms start in [_____] cities and then move to [_____] cities.
16. The notion of nursery cities suggests that diverse cities foster [_____], while specialized cities facilitate [_____].
17. For each pair of variables, indicate whether the relationship is positive, negative, neutral, or ambiguous.

Parameter	Choice Variable	Relationship
economies of scale in intermediate input	number of firms in cluster	[_____]
economies of scale in final good	number of firms in cluster	[_____]
job switching cost for isolated job	expected utility for isolated job	[_____]
number of workers in cluster	average skills mismatch	[_____]
number of workers in cluster	average training cost	[_____]
commuting cost per km in cluster	number of firms in cluster	[_____]

APPLY THE CONCEPTS

1. *Product Testing*
The total cost for a product-testing firm is $C(q) = 60 + 10q$, where q is the number of products tested. The price of a product test equals the average cost per test, and each corporation in a region purchases one product test per year from a product-testing firm in the same city. All other inputs are ubiquitous (available at the same price at all locations). Suppose five corporations are initially distributed uniformly, with one corporation in each city (A, B, C, D, E).
    a. Is the initial distribution a Nash equilibrium? Demonstrate with a suitable unilateral deviation.
    b. Describe the Nash equilibrium in terms of (i) the distribution of firms and (ii) the price of a product test.
2. *Switching Cost and Labor Pooling*
Consider the model of labor pooling shown in Figure 4–2. As before the utility function is $u(w) = w^{1/2}$. The isolated wage is \$144 and the switching cost for the

cluster is zero. Suppose the switching cost for the isolated site increases to \$80. Illustrate the implications for the expected utility and certainty equivalent of the isolated job, including values for both variables.

3. *Risk Neutrality and Labor Pooling*
Consider the model of labor pooling shown in Figure 4–2. Suppose the next generation of workers is risk neutral rather than risk averse, with a utility function $u(income) = w - s$. For the isolated site, the wage is \$144 and the switching cost is \$44. The switching cost is zero for jobs in the cluster. How does the change to risk neutrality affect the advantage of larger cities related to labor pooling? Explain.
4. *Model Management and Extreme Makeover*
In the model-management industry, firms supply human models for advertisements. Models vary in skin color, which is measured on a line of unit length. Skin color can be modified with makeup, and the makeup costs are incurred by the firm. Each firm enters the market at an address on the color line, and each firm manages two models. Suppose the cost of an extreme makeover (the cost of going from one end of the color line to the other) is \$90. Illustrate the determination of makeup cost in (i) a city with 4 models (2 firms) and (ii) a city with 6 models (3 firms), including values for the makeup cost per model.
5. *Matching in a Spatial Context*
Consider the matching model in a spatial context. Workers are uniformly distributed along a roadway. Each firm chooses an address along the roadway of unit length and hires two workers. The cost of commuting is incorporated into the market wage: $wage = 50 + 60 \cdot d$, where d is the distance from the worker to the nearest firm.
   a. Illustrate the determination of the wage in (i) a city with 4 workers (2 firms) and (ii) a city with 6 workers (3 firms), including values for the wages.
   b. Suppose the industry experiences an increase in economies of scale, increasing the number of workers per firm to 3 workers per firm. Illustrate the determination of wages in a city with 2 firms and 6 workers. For the worker with the longest commute, the wage is \$[_____].
6. *Cluster Size and Efficiency*
Consider an industry subject to agglomeration economies. The profit per firm is \$120 for an isolated firm and increases to the maximum of \$180 per firm in a 7-firm cluster. The profit curve is linear, with a slope of +\$10 per firm along the positively sloped portion and −\$15 per firm along the negatively sloped portion. Illustrate the determination of the Nash equilibrium, including values for the number of firms and profit per firm.
7. *Equilibrium vs. Efficient Corporate Clustering*
Consider corporations that use advertising firms to develop marketing campaigns. The marketing cost per firm is $M = 120/n$ and the labor cost per firm is $L = 30 \cdot n$, where n is the number of corporations. Total revenue is $R = \$300$ and profit is $\pi = R - M - L$.
   a. Illustrate the determination of the Nash equilibrium, including values for the number of firms and profit per firm.
   b. Illustrate the determination of the Pareto-efficient outcome, including values for the number of firms and profit per firm.

REFERENCES AND READING

1. Berens, Kristian, and Frederic Robert-Nicoud, "Agglomeration Theory," Chapter 4 in *Handbook of Urban and Regional Economics Volume 5,* edited by Gilles Duranton, J. Vernon Henderson, and William C. Strange. Amsterdam: Elsevier, 2015.
2. Carlino, Gerald, and William Robert Kerr, "Agglomeration and Innovation," Chapter 6 in *Handbook of Urban and Regional Economics Volume 5,* edited by Gilles Duranton, J. Vernon Henderson, and William C. Strange. Amsterdam: Elsevier, 2015.
3. Carlino, Gerald, and Robert Hunt, "What Explains the Quantity and Quality of Local Inventive Activity?" *Brookings-Wharton Papers on Urban Affairs* (January 2009), pp. 65–109.
4. Carlton, D.W., "The Location and Employment Choices of New Firms." *Review of Economics and Statistics* 65 (1983), pp. 440–49.
5. Combes, Pierre-Philippe, and Laurent Gobillon, "The Empirics of Agglomeration," Chapter 5 in *Handbook of Urban and Regional Economics Volume 5,* edited by Gilles Duranton, J. Vernon Henderson, and William C. Strange. Amsterdam: Elsevier, 2015.
6. Duranton, G., and D. Puga, "Nursery Cities: Urban Diversity, Process Innovation, and the Life Cycle of Products." *American Economic Review* 91.5 (2001), pp. 1454–77.
7. Duranton, Gilles, and Diego Puga, "From Sectoral to Functional Specialization." *Journal of Urban Economics* 57 (2005), pp. 343–70.
8. Duranton, Gilles, "Human Capital Externalities in Cities: Identification and Policy Issues," Chapter 2 in *A Companion to Urban Economics,* edited by Richard J. Arnott and Daniel P. McMillen. New York: Wiley-Blackwell, 2006.
9. Ellison, Glenn, Edward Glaeser, and William Kerr, "What Causes Industry Agglomeration? Evidence from Coagglomeration Patterns," *American Economic Review,* 100.3 (2010), pp. 1195–1213.
10. Fujita, Mashisa, and Jacques-Francois Thisse, *Economics of Agglomeration.* Cambridge: Cambridge University Press, 2002.
11. Glaeser, Edward, and D. C. Mare, "Cities and Skills," *Journal of Labor Economics* 19.2 (2001), pp. 316–42.
12. Glaeser, Edward, "Learning in Cities." *Journal of Urban Economics* 46 (1999), pp. 254–277.
13. Greenstone, Michael, Richard Hornbeck, Enrico Moretti. "Identifying Agglomeration Spillovers: Evidence from Winners and Losers of Large Plant Openings." *Journal of Political Economy* 118 (2010), pp. 536–98.
14. Harvard Business School, Cluster Mapping Project. http://data.isc.hbs.edu/isc/.
15. Head, K., J. Ries, and D. Swenson, "Agglomeration Benefits and Location Choice." *Journal of International Economics* 38 (1995), pp. 223–48.
16. Helsley, R., and W. Strange, "Matching and Agglomeration Economies in a System of Cities." *Regional Science and Urban Economics* 20 (1990), pp. 189–212.
17. Jacobs, Jane. *The Economy of Cities.* New York: Random House, 1969.
18. Marshall, Alfred. *Principles of Economics.* London: Macmillan, 1920, p. 352.

19. McCann Philip, "The Role of Industrial Clustering and Increasing Returns to Scale in Economic Development and Urban Growth," Chapter 8 in *The Oxford Handbook of Urban Economics and Planning,* edited by Nancy Brooks, Kieran Donaghy, and Gerrit-Jan Knaap. New York: Oxford University Press, 2011.
20. Moretti, Enrico, "Workers' Education, Spillovers and Productivity," *American Economic Review* (2004).
21. Rosenthal, S. S., and W. C. Strange, "Geography, Industrial Organization, and Agglomeration," *Review of Economics and Statistics* 85 (May 2003), pp. 377–93.
22. Saxenian, Annalee, *Regional Advantage: Culture and Competition in Silicon Valley and Route 128*. Cambridge, MA: Harvard University Press, 1994.
23. Scott, Allen J., *On Hollywood: The Place, the Industry*. Princeton, NJ: Princeton University Press, 2005.
24. Vernon, Raymond, "External Economies." In *Readings in Urban Economics,* eds. M. Edel and J. Rothenberg. New York: Macmillan, 1972.

CHAPTER 5

Where Do Cities Develop?

We're not lost. We're locationally challenged.

—Mitch Hedberg

The location decisions of profit-maximizing firms cause the development of cities in different locations. A firm's location decision is the outcome of a multidimensional tug-of-war. This chapter explores the economic forces pulling a firm in different directions, including low transport costs, productive workers, other firms that generate external economies in production, and low energy costs. The analysis provides important insights into the *where* of urban development.

1. TRANSPORT-INTENSIVE FIRMS

The solution to a firm's location task is the outcome of a multidimensional tug-of-war. Among the forces pulling a firm in one or more direction is low transport costs. Consider the location decision of a transport-intensive firm, defined as a firm for which transport costs are responsible for a relatively large fraction of total cost. For a transport-intensive firm, the dominant location factor is the cost of transporting inputs and outputs. The firm's objective is to choose the location that minimizes total transport costs, defined as the sum of input transport cost (for transporting materials from their source to the production site) and output transport cost (for transporting output from the production site to the output market).

The classic model of a transport-intensive firm has four assumptions that make transportation cost the dominant location factor.

1. *Single transportable output.* The firm produces a fixed quantity of a single product, which is transported from the production facility to an output market.
2. *Single transportable input.* The firm may use several inputs, but only one input is transported from an input source to the firm's production facility. All other inputs are ubiquitous, meaning that they are available at all locations at the same price.
3. *Fixed-factor proportions.* The firm produces its fixed quantity with fixed amounts of each input. In other words, the firm uses a single recipe to produce its good, regardless of the prices of its inputs. There is no factor substitution.
4. *Fixed prices.* The firm is so small that it does not affect the prices of its inputs or its product.

Under these assumptions, the firm maximizes its profit by minimizing its transportation costs. The firm's profit equals total revenue (price times the quantity of output) minus input costs and transport costs. Total revenue is the same at all locations because the firm sells a fixed quantity of output at a fixed price. Input costs are the same at all locations because the firm buys a fixed amount of each input at a fixed price. The only costs that vary across space are input transport costs and output transport costs, so the firm will choose the location that minimizes its total transport cost. In the locational tug-of-war, the firm is pulled toward its input source and its output market, and the outcome of the tug-of-war is determined by the relative strengths of the two conflicting forces.

Resource-Oriented Firms

A resource-oriented firm is defined as a firm that has a relatively high cost of transporting its input. Table 5-1 shows the key transport features of a firm that produces baseball bats. The firm uses five tons of wood to produce one ton of bats, so the firm is involved in a weight-losing activity. Its output is lighter than its materials because the firm shaves logs to make bats.

The outcome of the locational tug-of-war is determined by the monetary weights of the firm's inputs and outputs. The monetary weight of the input equals the physical weight of the input (5 tons) times the transport cost rate ($1 per ton per mile), or $5 per mile. Similarly, the monetary weight of the output is one ton times $2, or $2 per mile. This firm is resource-oriented because the monetary weight of its transportable input exceeds the monetary weight of its output. Although the unit cost of transporting output is higher (because finished bats must be packed carefully, but logs can be tossed onto a truck), the weight loss in the production process dominates the difference in the transport rate, so the monetary weight for the output is lower.

Figure 5-1 shows the firm's transport costs. The variable x measures the distance from the factory to the output market in a city. If the forest is 10 kilometers from the output market, the distance from the factory to the forest is $10 - x$. The input transport cost equals the monetary weight of the input (the physical weight w_i times the transport cost rate t_i) times the distance between forest and factory:

$$\text{Input transport cost} = w_i \cdot t_i \cdot (10 - x)$$

In Figure 5-1, the input transport cost is $50 in the city and decreases at a rate of $5 per km (the monetary weight of the input) to zero at the forest.

TABLE 5-1 Monetary Weights for a Resource-Oriented Firm

	Material (wood)	Output (bats)
Physical weight (tons)	5	1
Transport cost rate ($ per ton per mile)	$1	$2
Monetary weight = weight times rate	$5	$2

FIGURE 5-1 A Resource-Oriented Firm at the Input Source

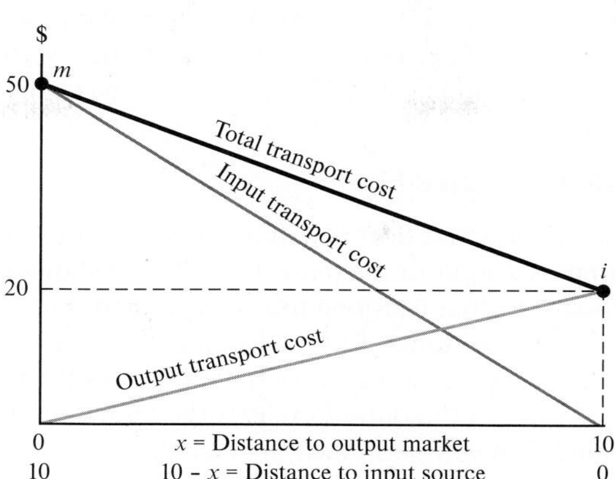

The firm's output transport costs are computed in an analogous way. The output transport cost equals the monetary weight of the output (weight w_Q times unit transport cost rate t_Q) times the distance from the factory to the market:

$$\text{Output transport cost} = w_Q \cdot t_Q \cdot x$$

In Figure 5-1, output transport cost is zero at the market and increases at a rate of \$2 per km (the monetary weight of the output). At the forest, the output transport cost is \$20.

Total transport cost is the sum of input and output transport costs. In Figure 5-1, total transport cost is minimized at the forest site at \$20. Starting at any location except the forest, a one-kilometer move toward the forest would decrease input transport cost by \$5 (the monetary weight of the input) and increase output transport cost by \$2 (the monetary weight of the output), for a net reduction of \$3. The firm's total transport cost is minimized at the input source because the monetary weight of the input exceeds the monetary weight of the output. Some other examples of weight-losing firms that locate close to their input sources are beet-sugar factories, onion dehydrators, and ore processors.

Some firms are resource oriented not because inputs are heavier, but because they are more costly to transport. For example, a cannery produces one ton of canned fruit with roughly a ton of raw fruit. The firm's input is perishable and must be transported in refrigerated trucks, while its output can be transported less expensively on regular trucks. Because the cost of shipping a ton of raw fruit exceeds the cost of shipping a ton of canned fruit, the monetary weight of the input exceeds the monetary weight of the output, and the firm locates near its input source, a farm. In general, a firm's input will be more expensive to ship if the input is more bulky, perishable, fragile, or hazardous than the output.

There are many examples of industries that locate close to their transportable inputs. The producers of soybean and vegetable oil are concentrated in Nebraska,

North Dakota, and South Dakota, close to the farms that supply soybeans and corn. Milk and cheese producers are concentrated in South Dakota, Nebraska, and Montana, close to dairy farms. Sawmills and other wood processors are concentrated in Arkansas, Montana, and Idaho, close to vast timberlands.

Market-Oriented Firms

A market-oriented firm is defined as a firm that has relatively high costs for transporting its output to the market. Table 5-2 shows the transport characteristics for a bottling firm that uses one ton of sugar and four tons of water (a ubiquitous input) to produce five tons of bottled beverages. The firm is involved in a weight-gaining activity in the sense that its output is heavier than its transportable input. The monetary weight of the output exceeds the monetary weight of the input, so the market-oriented firm will locate near its market.

As shown in Figure 5-2, a market-oriented firm's transport cost is minimized at the market. Because the monetary weight of the output exceeds the monetary weight of the input, a one-mile move away from the market increases output transport cost by more than it decreases input transport cost. Specifically, such a move increases output transport cost by $10 but decreases input transport cost by only $2, for a net increase in cost of $8. For this weight-gaining activity, the tug-of-war between input source and market is won by the market because there is more physical weight on the market side.

TABLE 5-2 Monetary Weights for a Market-Oriented Firm

	Material (sugar)	Output (beverages)
Physical weight (tons)	1	5
Transport cost rate ($ per ton per mile)	$2	$2
Monetary weight = weight times rate	$2	$10

FIGURE 5-2 A Market-Oriented Firm at the Market

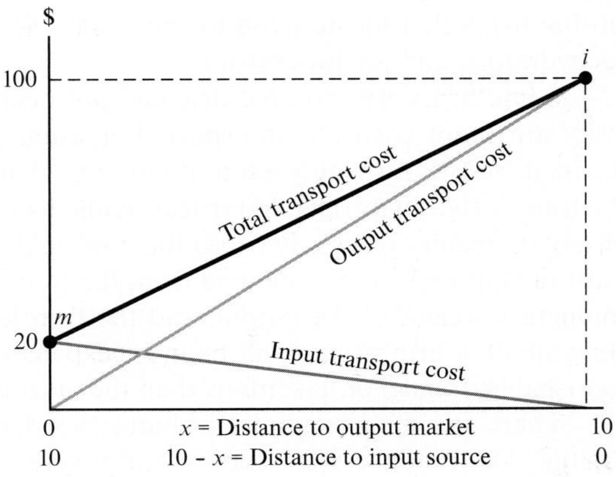

Some firms are market oriented because their output is relatively expensive to transport. Output will be relatively costly to transport if it is bulky, perishable, fragile, or hazardous.

1. *Bulky.* The output of an automobile assembly firm (assembled cars) is more bulky than the inputs (e.g., rolls of wire, sheets of metal). The cost of shipping a ton of automobiles exceeds the cost of shipping a ton of component parts, so the monetary weight of the output exceeds the monetary weight of the inputs, pulling the firm toward the market.
2. *Perishable.* The output of a bakery is more perishable than its inputs, pulling bakeries toward consumers.
3. *Hazardous.* A weapons producer combines harmless inputs into a lethal output, and the firm locates near its output market to avoid transporting the hazardous (or fragile) output long distances.

In general, when a firm's output is relatively bulky, perishable, fragile, or hazardous, the tug-of-war will be won by the market, not because the output is heavier, but because it is more expensive to transport.

2. THE PRINCIPLE OF MEDIAN LOCATION

The classic model of the transport-intensive firm assumes that the firm has a single input source and a single market. For more complex cases involving multiple inputs or markets, we can use the principle of median location to predict where a firm will locate.

Principle of Median Location: The median location minimizes total travel distance

The median location splits destinations into two equal halves, with half the destinations in one direction and half in the other direction.

Illustration: Intercity Location Choice

We can illustrate this principle with the location decision of Fixit, who repairs machinery in factories that are located in five cities strung along a highway. Under the following assumptions, Fixit's objective is to minimize the total travel distance.

1. All inputs (tools and parts) are ubiquitous (available at all locations for the same price), so the cost of transporting inputs cost is zero.
2. The price of repair service is fixed, and Fixit visits each factory once per week.
3. Each repair trip to a factory requires a separate trip.

Figure 5-3 shows the distribution of factories along the highway. There are two factories in city A, eight factories in city B, one factory in city M, one factory in city C, and nine factories in city D. Cities A, B, M, and C are 20 miles apart, and city D is 100 miles from city C.

FIGURE 5–3 Principle of Median Location

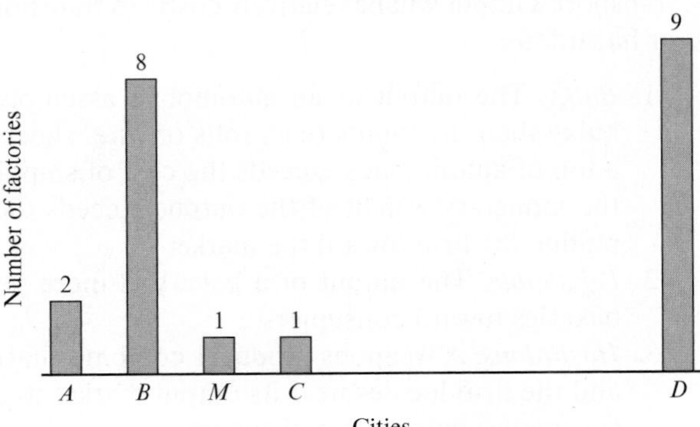

Fixit will minimize the total travel distance by locating in city M, the median location. City M is the median because there are 10 customers to the west (in cities A and B) and 10 customers to the east (in cities C and D). To show the superiority of the median location, suppose Fixit starts in city M, and then moves 20 miles east to city C. The move reduces the travel distance to factories to the east (in cities C and D) by 200 miles (10 factories times 20 miles) but increases the travel distance to factories to the west (in cities A, B, and M) by 220 miles (11 factories times 20 miles). The total travel distance increases because Fixit moves closer to 10 factories but farther from 11 factories. In general, any move away from the median location will increase travel distances for the majority of factories, so the total travel distance increases.

It is important to note that the distance between the consumers is irrelevant to the firm's location choice. For example, if city D were located 300 miles from city A instead of 100 miles, the median location would still be city M. Fixit's total travel distance would still be minimized (at a higher level) in city M.

The Median Location and Large Cities

The principle of median location provides another explanation of why large cities become larger. In Figure 5–4, suppose the number of factories in city D increases to 13. Now city D is the median location, and Fixit will minimize total travel cost by locating there. If Fixit starts in M and then moves eastward toward D, travel cost increases for a minority of customers (11 factories in A, B, and M) and decreases for a majority (14 factories in C and D), so the total travel cost decreases. Moving eastward beyond C, the travel cost to western cities increases for 12 factories and decrease for 13 factories. Total travel cost is minimized in city D, the median location. The lesson from this example is that the concentration of demand in large cities causes large cities to grow.

FIGURE 5-4 Why Do Big Cities Get Bigger?

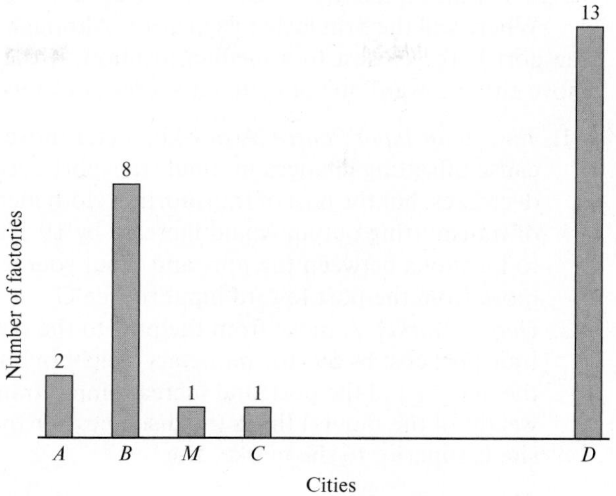

Number of factories

A: 2, B: 8, M: 1, C: 1, D: 13

Cities

Transshipment Points and Port Cities

The principle of median location also explains why some industrial firms locate at transshipment points such as ports. A transshipment point is defined as a place where a good is transferred from one transport mode to another. For example, at a port, goods are transferred from trucks or trains to ships. The location of industrial firms in port cities means that port cities host both shipping firms and manufacturing firms.

Figure 5-5 illustrates the attraction of a transshipment point. A furniture factory gets wood from a forest at site F and cloth from another firm at site G. To simplify, assume that the monetary weights of the two inputs are equal. The firm processes the wood and cloth into furniture in its factory and sells its furniture in an overseas market at site M. Highways connect input sites F and G to the port, and ships travel from the

FIGURE 5-5 Port Location: Trans-Shipment Point

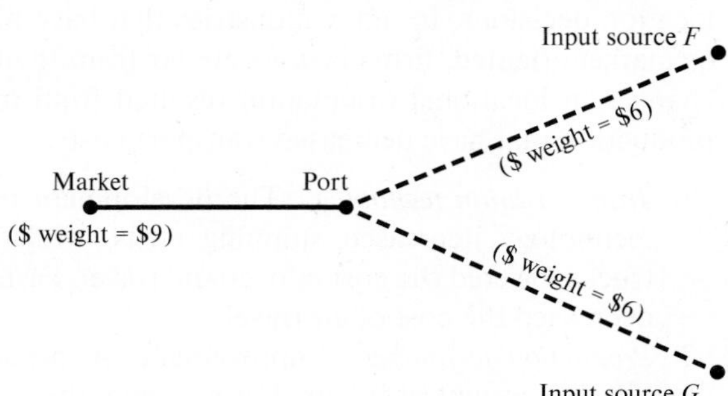

port to the market at M. The furniture maker is a weight-losing activity: The monetary weights of the inputs ($12 = $6 + $6) exceeds the $9 monetary weight of the output.

Where will the firm locate its factory? Although there is no true median location, the port is the closest to a median location. If the firm starts at the port, it could move either toward one of its input sources or to its market.

1. *Toward an Input Source.* A one-kilometer move from the port toward site F will cause offsetting changes in input transport costs: the cost of transporting wood decreases, but the cost of transporting cloth increases. At the same time, the cost of transporting output would increase by $9. Therefore, the port site is superior to locations between the port and input source G. The same logic applies for a move from the port toward input source G.
2. *Output Market.* A move from the port to the output market will decrease output transport cost by $9 (the monetary weight of output) times the distance between the market and the port, and increase input transport cost by $12 (the monetary weight of the inputs) times the distance. For this weight-losing activity, the port site is superior to the market site.

There are many examples of port cities that developed as a result of the location decisions of industrial firms. On the west coast, Seattle started in 1880 as a sawmill town: Firms harvested trees in western Washington, processed the logs in Seattle sawmills, and then shipped the wood products to other states and countries. On east coast, Baltimore was the nation's first boomtown: Flour mills processed wheat from the surrounding agricultural areas for export to the West Indies. Later in the midwest, Buffalo, New York, was the center for flour mills, providing consumers in eastern cities with flour produced from midwestern wheat. Wheat was shipped from midwestern states across the Great Lakes to Buffalo, where it was processed into flour for shipment by rail to cities in the eastern United States. Although both Baltimore and Buffalo were flour mill towns, they differed in their use of ships: Baltimore exported its output (flour) by ship, while Buffalo imported its input (wheat) by ship.

3. LABOR, ENERGY, AND AGGLOMERATION ECONOMIES

In the last several decades, transport costs have become less important in firms' location decisions. In many industries that have historically been resource-oriented or market-oriented, firms now locate far from their input sources and markets. The changes in locational orientation resulted from innovations in transportation and production that have decreased transport costs.

1. *Transportation technology.* The development of fast ocean ships and container technology decreased shipping costs, while improvements in railroads and trucks lowered the cost of overland travel. Faster and more efficient aircraft have decreased the cost of air travel.
2. *Production technology.* Improvements in production techniques decreased the physical weight of inputs. For example, the amount of coal and ore required to

produce one ton of steel has decreased steadily, a result of improved production methods and the use of scrap metal (a local input) instead of iron ore (a transportable input).

In this part of the chapter we explore the role of labor costs, energy, and agglomeration economies.

Labor Cost

What is the role of labor in location choices? On average, labor is responsible for about three-fourths of the cost of production, so firms' location decisions are sensitive to the cost of labor and labor productivity. Labor is a local input in the sense that it is impractical for workers to commute outside metropolitan areas. The long-term trend of declining transportation costs has contributed to the shift in location patterns to areas with relatively low labor costs. The most obvious cases are at the international level, where production has shifted to low-wage countries. At the national level, manufacturing shifted to the south, where labor costs are relatively low.

How do wages affect location decisions at the metropolitan level? Bartik (1991) summarizes the results of dozens of studies and concludes that the long-run elasticity of business activity with respect to the metropolitan wage is between -1.0 and -2.0. This means that a 10 percent decrease in the metropolitan wage will increase business activity between 10 percent and 20 percent. An earlier study of the relationship between metropolitan wages and the number of new firms estimated that the elasticity of the number of plant births with respect to the metropolitan wage is roughly -1.0. In other words, a 10 percent increase in the wage decreases firm births by 10 percent.

Weather affects location patterns through its influence on wages. Consider a nation that has two regions–with warm weather in the south and cold weather in the north–and workers prefer warm weather. To achieve Nash equilibrium for workers, wages in the south must be lower than wages in the north; otherwise, there would be an incentive for workers to move to the south, getting the same wage and better weather as well. In the Nash equilibrium, the wage for a given skill level will be lower in the south, and northern workers will be compensated for bad weather by a higher wage.

The lower wage caused by favorable weather provides an incentive for firms to locate their production facilities in the south. In this case, the firm's location depends on the location choice of its workforce: instead of workers following firms, firms follow workers. Rappaport (2007) shows that starting around 1920, U.S. residents have migrated to places with nicer weather, and that a key factor in this migration is an increase in the value of nice weather as a consumption amenity.

Energy Technology

What is the role of energy in the location decisions of firms? In the first half of the 19th century, energy was a local input, defined as an input that cannot be transported. The waterwheel was the first device use to generate non-animal mechanical energy. The first factories used waterwheels turned by waterfalls and fast-moving streams to translate moving water into mechanical motion. The power was transmitted by systems of belts and gears. Textile manufacturers built factories along backcountry streams in New England and used waterwheels to run their machines. Some examples of waterwheel cities are Lowell, Lawrence, Holyoke, and Lewiston.

The refinement of the steam engine in the second half of the 19th century made energy a transportable input. The steam engine could be operated anywhere, with the only constraint being the availability of coal to fuel the engine. Some energy-intensive manufacturers located near the coal mines in Pennsylvania. Others located along navigable waterways and shipped coal from the mines to their factories. In New England, textile firms shifted from backcountry waterfall sites to locations along navigable waterways. The later development of the railroad gave coal users another transport option, causing the development of factories along the vast network of rail lines. In general, the steam engine widened the location options for factories.

The development of electricity changed the location patterns of factories. Electricity generators were refined in the 1860s, and the electric motor was developed in 1888. Factories replaced belt-and-gear systems driven by a central steam engine with small electric motors for individual machines. The first factory to use electric power was adjacent to a hydroelectric generating facility at Niagara Falls. Rapid improvements in the long-distance transmission of electricity allowed factories to be hundreds of miles from hydroelectric and coal-powered generating plants. In general, the development of electricity decreased the importance of energy considerations in location decisions, causing firms in many industries to base their location choices on the accessibility to other inputs and to consumers.

For some production facilities, the availability of cheap energy is still an important location factor. In the production of primary aluminum, energy costs are responsible for about 30 percent of total cost, and producers are attracted to locations that provide cheap electricity. In the production of clay tiles and fertilizer, natural gas is responsible for a relatively large fraction of total cost, and producers are attracted to areas with relatively low prices for natural gas.

Agglomeration Economies

As discussed in previous chapters, firms cluster to exploit agglomeration economies. A cluster may facilitate sharing–of infrastructure, the suppliers of intermediate inputs, labor pools, and knowledge–and may improve the matching of workers' skills and firms' skill requirements. Although locating in a cluster may generate higher wages and other costs, the benefits from agglomeration more than offsets the higher costs. As we saw in an earlier chapter, there is evidence that agglomeration economies increase firm births and total employment, indicating the effect of agglomeration economies on firm location choices.

U.S. Manufacturing Belt–Growth and Decline

Our discussion of the location decisions of firms some insights into the growth and decline of the manufacturing belt in the Northeast and Great Lakes regions of the United States. The manufacturing belt developed in the second half of the

19th century. Innovations in production allowed firms to exploit scale economies, and many of the production processes required large volumes of relatively immobile resources (e.g., coal and iron ore). The manufacturing belt had a natural advantage in its access to these resources, so manufacturing was concentrated there. As late as 1947, the manufacturing belt contained 70 percent of the nation's manufacturing employment. By the 2000, the manufacturing belt contained only about 40 percent of the nation's manufacturing employment, just above its share of total employment. An important factor in the dispersion of manufacturing was a general reduction in transport costs that reduced the natural advantage of the historical manufacturing belt.

Glaeser (1991) explores the decline of the manufacturing belt and its implications for cities. The dispersion of manufacturing decreased the demand for manufacturing workers throughout the historical manufacturing belt. Some cities experienced decreases in equilibrium total employment and population. Among the cities that lost population over the period 1970–2000 were Detroit (7% loss), Cleveland (28% loss), and Pittsburgh (5% loss). In contrast, many cities grew despite the loss of manufacturing employment. Among the cities that gained population over the 30-year period were Boston (11% gain) and Minneapolis (50% gain).

A key factor in the different experiences of manufacturing cities is the stock of human capital. In declining cities (Detroit, Cleveland, and Pittsburgh), the share of the workforce with college degrees was relatively low. In contrast, in growing cities such as Boston and Minneapolis, the college share was relatively high. In the last four decades, the demand for low-skilled manual labor (in manufacturing and other industries) decreased, while the demand for high-skilled thinking labor (in services such as finance, legal services, and medical care) increased. The cities with relatively educated workforces were better equipped to make the transition to an economy with a greater share of high-skilled thinking jobs. In contrast, the cities with poorly educated workforces were ill-equipped to cope with changing economic circumstances, so their economies suffered. Glaeser (1991) estimates that the elasticity of population growth with respect to the share of the adult population with a college degree is 1.2: a 10 percent increase in the college share increases the population growth rate by 12 percent.

REVIEW THE CONCEPTS

1. The monetary weight of an input equals its [_____] times its [_____].
2. For a resource-oriented firm, the monetary weight of [_____] exceeds the monetary weight of [_____], and transport cost is minimized at the [_____].
3. A firm will be resource-oriented if its [_____] is relatively heavy, bulky, perishable, fragile, or hazardous.
4. For a market-oriented firm, the monetary weight of [_____] exceeds the monetary weight of [_____], and transport cost is minimized at the [_____].
5. In general, a firm will be market-oriented if its [_____] is relatively bulky, perishable, fragile, or hazardous.

FIGURE 5–6

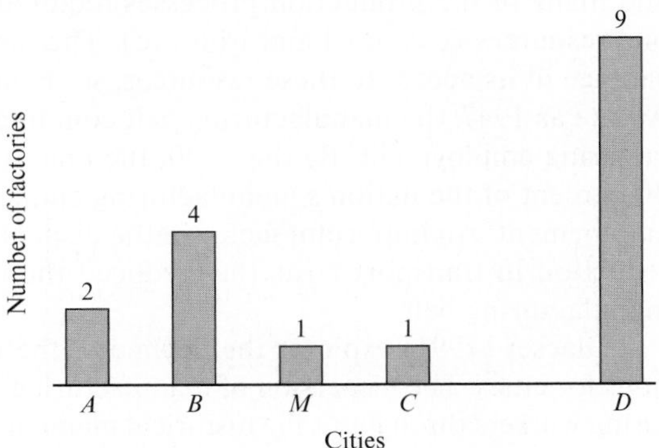

6. Suppose the physical weight of a firm's input is three tons and the physical weight of output is two tons. The transport rates are $5 for input and $6 for output. The monetary weight of input is $[_____] and the monetary weight of output is $[_____]. The firm is [_____] oriented. The firm will switch orientation if the transport rate for input drops below $[_____].
7. The forces pulling assembly plants toward a [_____] are relatively strong because output is [_____] than inputs.
8. The median location, defined as the location that [_____] destinations into [_____], minimizes [_____].
9. The principle of median location explains why [_____] cities tend to grow [_____] and why many firms locate at [_____] points such as [_____].
10. Use Figure 5–6. The median location is in city [_____]. As the distance between cities C and D increases, the median location [_____].
11. The time path of location choices of manufacturers reflects changes in energy technology: the waterwheel caused factories to locate along [_____]; the steam engine caused factories to locate near [_____] and along [_____].
12. The most powerful variable in explaining the differences in employment growth across U.S. cities in the historical manufacturing belt is differences in [_____].
13. The estimated elasticity of population growth with respect to the share of the adult population with a college degree is [_____] (choose 0, 0.23, 0.50, 1.20).

APPLY THE CONCEPTS

1. *Skunk Deodorizing*

   Edgar Hoover captures wild skunks in a forest at milepost 12, performs a brief operation in a deodorizing facility to remove odor-distribution organs, and then sells deodorized skunks as pets in the city at milepost 0. Edgar's objective is to minimize transport cost. Illustrate Edgar's location choice and explain his choice in terms of the monetary weights of inputs and outputs.

2. *Beer and Wine*
Consider the location choices of beer brewers and wineries. Most breweries are located close to their customers and far from some inputs (barley, wheat, and hops), while most wineries are located far from customers and close to the key input (grapes). Illustrate the two cases and explain the differences in terms of the monetary weights of inputs and outputs.

3. *Location of Shipyards*
The production of wooden ships is a weight-losing activity (as shown by the large piles of sawdust and wood scraps), and yet most shipyards are located far from a forest. Shipyards locate far from the forest because . . . Illustrate.

4. *Manufacturing Location within City*
Consider the intracity location choice of a factory. The workforce commutes from a suburb 8 miles from the city center to the factory, and a one-mile increase in the distance between the factory and the suburban workforce increases the firm's labor cost by t_L. The other inputs to the production process are ubiquitous. The firm transports its output from the factory to a central port for export at $x = 0$. A one-mile increase in the distance between the factory and the port increases the firm's freight cost by t_Q. The firm will choose the suburban location ($x = 8$) if . . . Illustrate.

5. *Ice-Cream Vendors on the Beach*
Two ice-cream vendors compete for customers who are uniformly distributed (at 20 customers per km) along a 12 km beach. Each consumer buys one unit of ice cream per day, and each customer generates a profit of $3 for a vendor. The initial location are vendor L at location $x = 3$ and vendor R at location $x = 9$.

a. Is the initial set of locations ($x = 3$ and $x = 9$) a Nash equilibrium? Demonstrate with a unilateral deviation by vendor R of 2 km.
b. Illustrate the Nash equilibrium.

6. *Location Incentives*
Consider the spatial distribution of factories shown in Figure 5–4. The distance between city M and city C is 1 km, and the distance between city C and city D is 7 km. Mr. Fixit is currently in city M and is considering relocating. The urban development agency in city M will develop a subsidy plan to keep Mr. Fixit in the city. Suppose that Mr. Fixit's cost per mile of travel is $2.

a. To prevent a move from city M to city C, the minimum weekly subsidy is $. . . .
b. To prevent a move from city M to city D, the minimum weekly subsidy is $ . . .

REFERENCES AND READING

1. Bartik, Timothy J., *Who Benefits from State and Local Economic Development Policies?* Kalamazoo, MI: Upjohn Institute, 1991.
2. Combes, Pierre-Philippe, and Henry Overman, "The Spatial Distribution of Economic Activities in the European Union," Chapter 64 in *Handbook of Regional and Urban Economics 4: Cities and Geography*, edited by Vernon Henderson and Jacques-Francois Thisse. Amsterdam: Elsevier, 2004.

3. Desmet, Klaus, and J. Vernon Henderson, "The Geography of Development within Countries," Chapter 22 in *Handbook of Urban and Regional Economics Volume 5,* edited by Gilles Duranton, J. Vernon Henderson, and William C. Strange. Amsterdam: Elsevier, 2015.
4. Fujita, Masahisa, and Jacques-Francois Thisse, *Economics of Agglomeration.* Cambridge: Cambridge University Press, 2002.
5. Fujita, Masahisa, Tomoya Mori, Vernon Henderson, and Yoshitsuga Kanemoto. "The Spatial Distribution of Economic Activities in Japan and China," Chapter 65 in *Handbook of Regional and Urban Economics 4: Cities and Geography*, edited by Vernon Henderson and Jacques-Francois Thisse. Amsterdam: Elsevier, 2004.
6. Glaeser, Edward, "Growth: The Death and Life of Cities," Chapter 2 in *Making Cities Work,* edited by Robert P. Inman. Princeton, NJ: Princeton University Press, 2009.
7. Hohenberg, Paul M., and Lyann H. Lees, *The Making of Urban Europe 1000–1950.* Cambridge, MA: Harvard University Press, 1986.
8. Holmes, Thomas, and John Stevens, "The Spatial Distribution of Economic Activities in North America," Chapter 63 in *Handbook of Regional and Urban Economics 4: Cities and Geography*, edited by Vernon Henderson and Jacques-Francois Thisse. Amsterdam: Elsevier, 2004.
9. Hoover, Edgar, and Frank Giarrantani, *Introduction to Regional Economics.* McGraw-Hill, 1984.
10. Kim, Sukkoo, and Robert Margo, "Historical Perspectives on U.S. Economic Geography," Chapter 66 in *Handbook of Regional and Urban Economics 4: Cities and Geography*, edited by Vernon Henderson and Jacques-Francois Thisse. Amsterdam: Elsevier, 2004.
11. Rappaport, Jordan, "Moving to Nice Weather." *Regional Science and Urban Economics* 37 (2007), pp. 375–98.
12. Wolman, Harold, Edward Hill, Pamela Blumenthal, and Kimberly Furdell, "Understanding Economically Distressed Cities," in *Retooling for Growth: Building a 21st Century Economy in America's Older Industrial Areas*, edited by Richard McGahey and Jennifer Vey. Washington, DC: Brookings, 2008.

CHAPTER 6

Consumer Cities and Central Places

Barber: And how old are you, little man?

Bill: Eight.

Barber: And do you want a haircut?

Bill: Well, I certainly didn't come in for a shave!

Up to this point we have taken the perspective of firms, exploring the role of cities in producing goods and facilitating trade. In this chapter, we switch to the perspective of consumers and explore the role of cities as markets for consumer goods and services. We'll see how consumer decisions generate cities of varying size and product variety, with larger cities offering a wider variety of consumer goods and services.

1. MONOPOLISTIC COMPETITION IN LOCATION

Our analysis of consumer cities starts with the model of monopolistic competition, a model developed in microeconomics courses. The model is based on two key assumptions.

1. *No artificial barriers to entry.* There are no patents or regulations that prevent a firm from entering the market. Entry into the market does have a cost, which we will model as a fixed setup cost. For example, if you want to enter the restaurant business, there are costs associated with buying or renting space and equipment.
2. *Product differentiation.* Firms in the market make products that are close but not perfect substitutes. In other words, each firm differentiates its product in some way. In a spatial context, firms differentiate their products with respect to location and accessibility to consumers. For example, a centrally located restaurant is more accessible than a restaurant located on the fringe.

These assumptions explain the label "monopolistic competition." Although the label appears to be an oxymoron like "tight slacks," "act naturally," and "Dodge

Ram," the label reveals the essential features of the market. Each firm has a local monopoly for its narrowly differentiated product. For example, a restaurant may be the only Italian restaurant in its neighborhood. But each firm also faces competition from other restaurants that are differentiated with respect to location (similar restaurants at different locations) or products (different cuisines at nearby restaurants).

Structure of Monopolistic Competition

In a model of a market subject to firm entry and exit, it is natural to use long-run cost curves, which show production cost when firms are perfectly flexible in choosing their inputs. The expressions for total and average cost are

$$C(q) = k + cq \qquad ac(q) = \frac{k}{q} + c$$

where q is the quantity produced by a firm. The setup cost of a firm is k, and the marginal cost of production is c. In Figure 6-1, the long-run average-cost curve is negatively sloped and is asymptotic to the horizontal-marginal cost curve.

Imagine that we start with a single firm in the market, so we have a monopoly. In Figure 6-1, the demand curve for the firm is the market demand curve. Applying the marginal principle (marginal benefit = marginal cost), the firm chooses the quantity at which marginal revenue equals marginal cost. The profit-maximizing choice is shown by point a, with a quantity q' and average cost ac'. At this quantity, the firm charges the price p', as shown by the demand curve at point b. The firm's economic profit is shown by the shaded rectangle: the height is the gap between the price and average cost, and the width is the quantity produced.

FIGURE 6-1 Monopoly Outcome

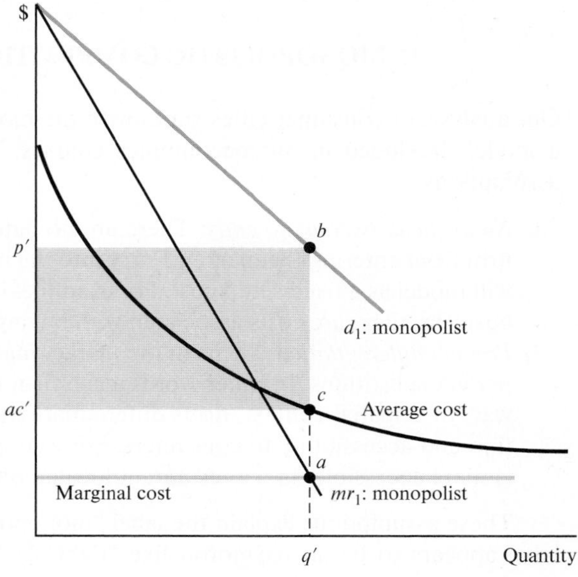

If there are no barriers to entry into this market, the situation in Figure 6-1 is not a long-run equilibrium. The monopolist is earning a positive economic profit, and other firms will enter the lucrative market. In the model of monopolistic competition, each firm will enter the market with a slightly differentiated product.

Effects of Market Entry

Figure 6-2 shows the transition from monopoly to monopolistic competition. Starting from the monopoly outcome shown in Figure 6-1, the entry of a second firm shifts the demand curve of the typical firm (also known as the residual demand curve) to the left.

1. *Upper panel: Duopoly.* A second firm enters the lucrative market, shifting the residual demand curve to the left: at each price, the typical duopolist will sell a smaller quantity than a monopolist. The shift of the residual demand curve shifts

FIGURE 6-2 Entry and Monopolistic Competition

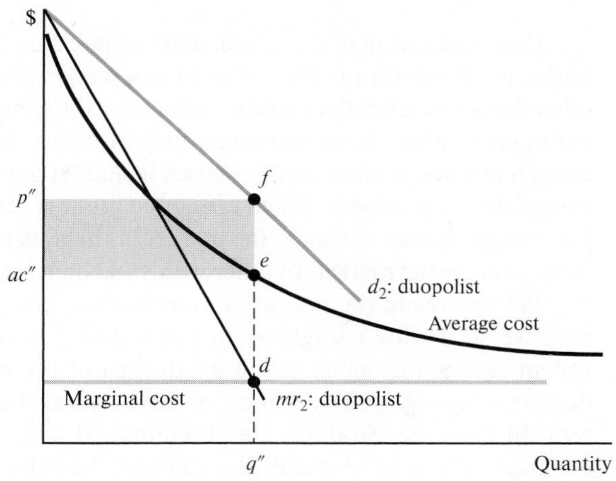

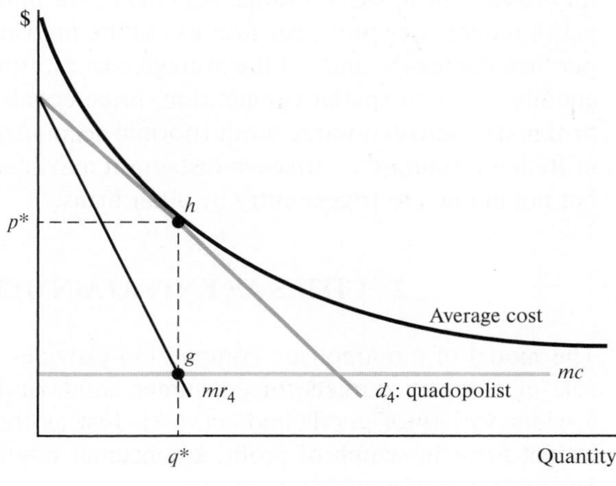

the marginal-revenue curve in the same direction. Each duopolist produces q'' units of output at price p'' and average cost ac''. Entry squeezes profit from above (lower price), the right (smaller quantity per firm), and below (higher average cost).

2. *Lower panel: Long-Run Equilibrium.* Entry continues until economic profit is zero. Entry shifts the residual demand curve to the left, along with the marginal-revenue curve. In this case, the market is a quadopoly, with four firms. This is a Nash equilibrium because there is no incentive for unilateral deviation. For each firm, marginal revenue equals marginal cost, meaning that each firm is maximizing its profit. The market price equals average cost, meaning that each firm earns zero economic profit. Therefore, firms in the market do not have an incentive to exit, and other firms do not have an incentive to enter the market.

The equilibrium number of firms equals the market quantity Q^* divided by the quantity per firm q^*:

$$n^* = \frac{Q^*}{q^*}$$

One implication of the model of monopolistic competition is that the long-run economic profit per firm is zero. If firms in a market are earning positive economic profit, other firms will enter the market, each with a differentiated product. Entry will continue until competition drives economic profit to zero: each firm in the market earns just enough revenue to cover all of its costs, including the cost of capital and the opportunity cost of the entrepreneur. When economic profit is zero, every firm in the market is making enough money to stay in the market in the long run, but not enough to cause other firms to enter the market. In other words, each firm earns a "normal" accounting profit.

We can relate the notion of monopolistic competition to a spatial context. Suppose we start with a single profitable Italian restaurant in a city center. If a second Italian restaurant opens in the north area of the city, some people who live in the northern part of the city will economize on travel cost and switch to the new restaurant. In this case, products are differentiated with respect to location and access. In a market subject to spatial differentiation, the entry of a new firm decreases the territory of each firm, so its residual demand curve shifts to the left. The increase in competition decreases profit per firm as (a) the market price decreases, (b) the quantity per firm decreases, and (c) the average cost of production increases. In the long-run equilibrium with spatial competition, price equals average cost, meaning that each firm makes zero economic profit (normal accounting profit). A city may have dozens of Italian restaurants, with each restaurant making enough money to stay in business, but not enough to trigger entry by other firms.

2. CITIES AS ENTERTAINMENT MACHINES

The model of monopolistic competition provides some important insights into the role of cities as markets for consumer goods and services. A larger city supports a wider variety of goods and services. Just as trading cities and production cities attract firms in search of profit, a consumer city attracts consumers in search of a favorable mix of goods and services.

Minimum Market Size

When there is a fixed setup cost associated with producing a particular product, there is a minimum market size required to support a firm. Recall the expression for the average cost of production:

$$ac(q) = \frac{k}{q} + c$$

where k is the fixed setup cost per firm. In the retail and service sectors of the economy, the setup cost is determined by the cost associated with setting up a facility such as a restaurant, store, movie house, or theater. Space must be leased and perhaps remodeled, and equipment such as shelves and tables must be installed. When the setup cost is relatively large, the long-run average-cost curve will have a relatively large negative slope over a relatively large quantity of output. In other words, a large setup cost indicates relatively large economies of scale.

When the setup cost is relatively large, a producer will be profitable only if its quantity sold is relatively large. The citywide demand for a product equals per-capita demand $d(p)$ times city population N:

$$\text{citywide demand} = d(p) \cdot N$$

For a large total quantity demanded in a city, we need either high per-capita demand or a large population.

Figure 6–3 illustrates the notion of minimum market size. When scale economies are relatively large, it takes a relatively large market demand to support at least one firm.

1. *Large Economies of Scale.* In the case of high setup cost and large economies of scale, the average-cost curve will be relatively high, and it takes a relatively large

FIGURE 6–3 Economies of Scale and Minimum Market Size

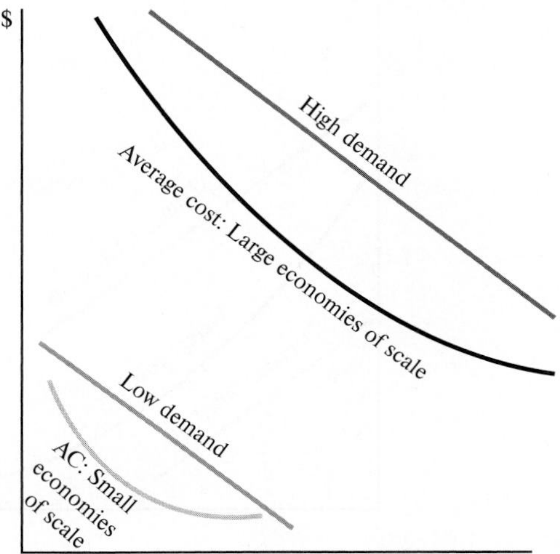

market demand to support at least one firm. In other words, the market demand curve must be high enough to lie at least partly above the relatively high average-cost curve. Demand could be relatively high because of high per-capita demand, a large population, or both.

2. *Small Economies of Scale.* In the case of low setup cost and small economies of scale, a market can support at least one firm even if the market demand is relatively low.

The general lesson from Figure 6–3 is that a market will support at least one firm if market demand is large relative to the economies of scale in production.

City Size and Product Variety

For a good with a relatively low per-capita demand, it takes a relatively large population to support a firm. In Figure 6–4, a large city has sufficient demand to make production profitable for at least one firm: the demand curve lies above the average-cost curve. In contrast, the demand curve for a small city lies below the average-cost curve, so the city does not have sufficient demand to support a firm. For example, the per-capita demand for Peruvian food is relatively low, and Peruvian restaurants can survive in large cities, but not small cities.

Our restaurant example illustrates an essential feature of a relatively large city. Some products will be provided in the large city but not the small city. In our restaurant example, the large city has a Peruvian restaurant because its large population generates sufficient demand to support a restaurant that produces a good with relatively low per-capita demand.

FIGURE 6–4 A Product Sold in a Large City, But Not a Small City

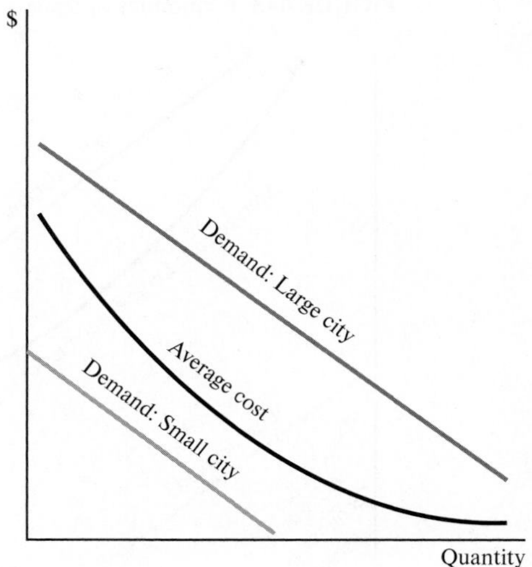

As another example of the difference between small and large cities, consider barbers and brain surgeons. Although both types of workers operate in roughly the same area of the body, they face different per-capita demands relative to economies of scale in production.

1. *Barbers in All Cities.* The typical person gets a haircut every two months, so per-capita demand is relatively high. In addition, the setup cost for a barber is relatively low: all a barber needs is a pair of scissors, about 12 cubic meters of space ($2 \times 2 \times 3$), and a chair. As a result, a barber can survive in a city with just a few thousand people.
2. *Brain Surgeons in Large Cities.* Because only a small fraction of the population ever needs brain surgery, the per-capita demand for brain surgery is relatively low. In addition, the facilities and equipment required for brain surgery are costly, so the economies of scale in brain surgery are relatively large. The per-capita demand for brain surgery is low relative to the economies of scale, so brain surgeons locate in cities with millions of potential customers.

There are many examples of goods and services that are provided in large cities but not in small cities. In the art sector, large cities host museum exhibits and live performances of music and theater. In the retail sector, large cities host specialized retailers such as clothing stores that sell products at both ends of the price spectrum, from high-fashion clothing to used clothing. In the consumer service sector, large cities host firms that provide specialized services such as medical procedures and self-help services. In each case, per-capita demand is small relative to economies of scale in production, so it takes a large city to generate sufficient demand to exploit scale economies.

Cities as Entertainment Machines

So what? In earlier chapters, we saw that agglomeration economies in production cause firms to cluster and thus make large cities larger. In this chapter, we have seen that firms providing some types of consumer goods and services can survive only in large cities. As a result, consumer interests tend to make large cities larger: the presence of a large workforce and consumer base attracts museums, theaters, sports teams, and specialized medical facilities.

Over the last few decades, the cities with the greatest product variety have grown relative to other cities. Using data from the United States and France, Glaeser, Kolko, and Saiz (2001) show that the cities with relatively large numbers of live-performance venues (per capita) grew faster on average. They found the same positive correlation between population growth and the number of restaurants per capita. In contrast, they found a negative correlation between population growth and the numbers of movie theaters and bowling alleys. They argue that cities are "entertainment machines" and that in the last few decades the most productive entertainment machines–including New York, Chicago, and San Francisco–have experienced the most rapid growth.

3. CENTRAL PLACE THEORY

The model of monopolistic competition provides a framework to explore the development of consumer cities in a regional economy. Central place theory is based on a regional perspective and addresses two questions.

1. How many cities will develop?
2. How do cities vary in size and in the variety of consumer goods?

The theory predicts a hierarchical system of cities in the regional economy. At the top of the hierarchy are large cities that have a complete set of goods and services. As we move down through the hierarchy, cities become progressively smaller and provide progressively fewer goods and services. The simple punchline is that you can get anything you want in a large city, but not in a small city.

Simplifying Assumptions

Central place theory is based on a number of simplifying assumptions. The model focuses attention on the location choices of market-oriented firms, defined as firms that base their location decisions on access to consumers.

1. *Fixed population.* The population of the region is fixed.
2. *Ubiquitous inputs.* All inputs are available at all locations in a region at the same price.
3. *Uniform demand.* For each product, the per-capita demand is the same at all locations within the region.
4. *Perfect substitutes.* For a given good, the products made by different firms are perfect substitutes. There are no advantages from comparison shopping and thus no advantages from the clustering of firms selling the same product.
5. *No complementarity between goods.* The different goods are not complementary, so there are no advantages from the clustering of firms selling different goods.

The first two assumptions are essential to the model. As we will see later in the chapter, we can relax the other assumptions to explore urban development in a more realistic economic environment.

We can use a simple example to illustrate the theory of central places. Consider a region with a population of 48,000. Three goods differ in their per-capita demand relative to economies of scale.

1. *Clothing.* The per-capita demand is small relative to economies of scale, so a clothing store needs a population of 48,000 to survive. There will be a single clothing store in the region.
2. *Groceries.* The per-capita demand is moderate relative to economies of scale, so a grocery store can survive with a population of 12,000 people. There will be four grocery stores in the region.
3. *Barbers.* Per-capita demand is high relative to economies of scale, so a barber can survive with a population of 3,000 people. There will be 16 barbers in the region.

The Central Place Hierarchy

Imagine that we start with a uniform population density in the region. In addition, imagine that consumers are located along a line, so we have a one-dimensional region. In Figure 6–5, the region is 48 miles long, and initially there are 1,000 consumers per mile. This linear approach simplifies the explanation without affecting the basic results.

The firms will choose locations that minimize the distances to their customers. As we saw in a previous chapter, travel distances are minimized at the median location. In Figure 6–5, the single clothing store chooses the median location, which is at the center because population density is uniform. The clothing store employs workers who live nearby, so the location of the clothing store increases population density in the area around the clothing store. In Figure 6–5, a city—a place with a relatively high population density—develops at the center of the region, shown by the tallest bar.

Consider next the location decisions of the four grocery stores. If the region's population density were uniform, the grocery stores would divide the region into four equal market areas, and each store would have a 12-mile territory. But because population density is higher in the city centered on the location of the clothing store, there will be sufficient demand to support more than one grocery store. Suppose the city and the surrounding area has enough demand to support two grocery stores. In that case, there will be two remaining grocery stores for the rest of the region. In Figure 6–5, the two grocery stores split the rest of the region into two equal market areas, and each locates at the median location of its market area. Grocery workers will live near the stores, causing the development of two additional cities, shown as mid-sized bars to the west and east of the regional center.

FIGURE 6–5 Central Place Theory

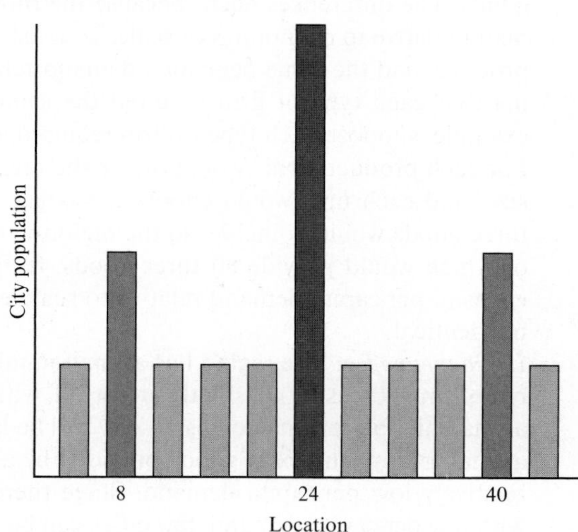

Consider finally the location of the 16 barbers. Some barbers will locate in the cities, where population density is relatively high, and the rest will divide the remainder of the region into small market areas with populations of 3,000. Suppose that the big city is large enough to support four barbers and each of the two medium-sized cities is large enough to support two barbers. That leaves eight barbers for the rest of the region, causing the development of eight additional cities, shown as short bars in Figure 6–5.

The region has a total of 11 cities that differ in size and the variety of consumer goods. The large city has one clothing store, two grocery stores, and four barbers. It has a wide variety of goods because it is large: its large population can support all three types of firms. And the city is large because it has a wide variety of goods, and is home to people who work in clothing stores, grocery stores, and barber shops. At the other extreme, the small city has only barbershops. In the middle, the mid-sized city has barbershops and grocery stores, but no clothing stores.

The simple central-place model generates a hierarchy of cities. At the top of the hierarchy, the largest city provides a full set of goods. At the bottom of the hierarchy, the smallest cities provide a single good. Each city exports goods to lower ranked cities: the large city exports clothing to medium and small cities and exports groceries to nearby small cities. In the middle of the hierarchy, the medium cities export groceries to small cities. At the low end, the small cities import goods: their consumers travel to larger cities for groceries and clothing.

Insights from Central Place Theory

The simple central place model provides some important insights into the features of a regional system of cities.

1. *Differences in size and variety.* The cities differ in size and variety of consumer goods. The differences occur because the three products differ in per-capita demand relative to economies of scale. To illustrate, suppose instead that the three products had the same per-capita demand relative to economies of scale, meaning that each type of firm required the same population base to survive. For example, suppose each type of firm required a consumer base of 12,000 people. For each product, firms would divide the region into four market areas of equal size, and each firm would choose a median location. The market areas of the three goods would coincide, so the region would have four identical cities, each of which would provide all three goods. In other words, if there are no differences in per-capita demand relative to scale economies, cities in the region will be identical.
2. *Large means few.* The region has a small number of large cities and a large number of small cities. Why isn't this reversed, with a large number of large cities and a small number of small cities? A city will be large if it provides more goods than a smaller city. The extra goods provided by a large city are the goods that have relatively low per-capita demand. Since there are few stores selling the goods with low per-capita demand, few cities can be large. In our example, there is only

one clothing store, and its host city becomes the largest city. There are more medium-sized cities because there are more grocery stores to distribute across the region. There are many small cities because there are many barbers to distribute across the region.

3. *Shopping paths.* Consumers travel to bigger cities, not to smaller cities or to cities of the same size. For example, consumers who live in a medium city travel to the large city to buy clothing, but they do not travel to the other medium city to buy groceries and do not travel to a small city for a haircut. Similarly, consumers in small cities travel to larger cities for clothing and groceries but do not travel to other small cities.

Figure 6-6 shows cities of varying sizes in the state of Indiana in 2014. The map shows census tracts as jigsaw pieces, which are extruded (pushed up) to a height equal to employment density, the number of workers per hectare. The largest concentration of employment is the Indianapolis metropolitan area, which is close to the geographic center of the state. Indianapolis has a relatively large mass of jobs, as indicated by the relatively large footprint (areas over which census tracts are extruded) and relatively tall bars (high employment density). The other concentrations of employment are in cities of varying size, as indicated by their footprints and job

FIGURE 6-6 Central Places in Indiana, 2014

densities. The map illustrates the notion of central place theory, with an urban hierarchy of cities of different sizes distributed across the state.

Relaxing the Assumptions

Several of the assumptions of the simple central place theory are unrealistic. In this section we relax some of the assumptions, exploring the implications for the equilibrium number and size of cities in the urban hierarchy.

Consider first the assumption that the products from different firms are perfect substitutes. Under this assumption, there is no need for consumers to do comparison shopping, and thus no tendency for grocery stores or barbers to cluster to facilitate comparison shopping. Suppose that grocery stores are replaced by car sellers, and imagine that cars from different sellers are imperfect substitutes. People shopping for cars benefit from comparing the products of different firms, and comparison shopping will encourage car sellers to cluster rather than disperse. For example, if the equilibrium cluster is four car sellers, a single cluster will develop at the center of the region. In this case, the region will have only two types of cities: large cities will have clothing stores, car sellers, and barbers, while small cities will have barbers. The introduction of imperfect substitutes reduces the equilibrium number of cities and increases the size of the largest city.

Another assumption of the simple model is that the three products are not complementary goods. Suppose that grocery stores are replaced by shoe stores, and that clothing and shoes are complementary goods: the typical consumer purchases clothing and shoes on the same shopping trip. In this case, shoe stores will locate in the large city, close to the clothing store, to facilitate one-stop shopping. The region will have two types of cities, large (clothing, shoes, barbers) and small (barbers). Again, the clustering of firms to exploit agglomeration economies in shopping decreases the number of cities and increases the size of the largest city.

A key assumption of the simple central place model is that per-capita demand does not vary with city size. Systematic variation in per capita demand may disrupt the urban hierarchy. We can add various types of goods to see what happens to the size and scope of cities of various sizes.

1. *Country music.* Suppose the per-capita demand for country music is high in small cities and low in large cities. If the large city does not have sufficient demand to support a country-music venue, the urban hierarchy will be disrupted: some goods that are available in the small city will not be available in the large city. On the other hand, a large city may overcome the problem of low per-capita demand with its large population, generating at least one country-music venue.
2. *Opera.* Suppose the per-capita demand for opera is high in large cities and zero in small cities. In this case, large cities will naturally become larger, reinforcing the urban hierarchy as the gap between large and small cities grows.

Although the introduction of systematic variation in per-capita demand may generate an urban hierarchy that is less tidy than implied by the simple central place model, the essential features of the hierarchy persist. Larger cities provide a wider variety of goods and services.

REVIEW THE CONCEPTS

1. The model of monopolistic competition is based on two assumptions: (i) [_____]; (ii) [_____].
2. Suppose the long-run cost of production is $C(q) = 120 + 2 \cdot q$. For $q = 30$, total cost = $[_____], average cost = $[_____], and marginal cost = $[_____].
3. Consider an equilibrium in monopolistic competition. For profit maximization, [_____] = [_____]. For zero economic profit, [_____] = [_____].
4. The entry of a second firm into a market [_____] profit per firm for three reasons: (i) [_____] decreases, (ii) [_____] decreases, and (iii) [_____] increases.
5. The entry of a firm into a market causes movement along a firm's [_____] curve and [_____] curve, along with a shift of the firm's [_____] curve and the firm's [_____] curve.
6. Consider the example shown in Figure 6-2. An outcome with six firms [_____] be an equilibrium because d_6 would be [_____] the [_____] curve. [_____].
7. A market will support at least one firm producing a product if [_____] is large relative to [_____] in production. Market demand in a city will be relatively large if the product has relatively high [_____] or the city has a [_____].
8. For pizzerias and sushi bars, the average-cost curve reaches its minimum at 200,000 meals per year. The per-capita demand for pizza is 20 meals per year and the per-capita demand for sushi is 2 meals per year. The smallest city with a pizzeria has a population of [_____], and the smallest city with a sushi bar has a population of [_____].
9. Barbers locate in [_____] (choose large, small, or large and small) cities because the [_____] for haircuts is [_____] relative to [_____].
10. Brain surgeons locate in [_____] (choose large, small, or large and small) cities because the [_____] for brain surgery is [_____] relative to [_____].
11. Over the last few decades, the cities with relatively large numbers of [_____] venues grew faster than cities with relatively large numbers of [_____] alleys.
12. The theory of central places generates a [_____] of cities. Cities in the economy differ in [_____] and [_____]. Consumers travel to [_____] cities, but not to [_____] cities.
13. The introduction of imperfect substitutes into the central-place framework [_____] the equilibrium number of cities and [_____] the size of the largest city.
14. The introduction of complementary products into the central-place framework [_____] the equilibrium number of cities and [_____] the size of the largest city.

APPLY THE CONCEPTS

1. *Entry and Profit*

   Paige initially has the only license to operate a bookstore in Bookville. She charges a price of $9 per book, has an average cost of $4 per book, and sells 1,001 books per year. Suppose Paige's license expires, and the city decides to auction two bookstore licenses to the highest bidders. Suppose the relevant variables (price, average cost, and quantity per firm) take on only integer values (no fraction or decimals). The maximum possible bid for each license is $[_____] Illustrate.

2. *How Many Pizzerias?*
Your city initially restricts the number of pizzerias to one. The existing monopolist sells 2,000 pizzas per day. The number of firms is $n = Q/q$, where Q is the market quantity and q is the quantity per firm. In the case of monopoly,

$$n = \frac{Q}{q} = \frac{2000}{2000} = 1$$

A pizzeria reaches the horizontal portion of its long-run average cost curve at an output of $q = 1000$. Suppose the city eliminates the entry restrictions, and other firms enter the market. According to the economic consultant Difford Qq, "The equilibrium number of pizzerias is not two." Explain Difford's economic logic. Illustrate.

3. *Pizza vs. Sushi*
Suppose pizzerias and sushi bars experience roughly the same economies of scale, with a common minimum market size of 200,000 meals per year. The per-capita demand for pizza is 20 meals per year and the per-capita demand for sushi is 4 meals per year. Suppose you move from a city with a population of 20,000 to a city with a population of 60,000.
   a. The number of pizzerias will change from [_____] to [_____]
   b. The number of sushi restaurants will change from [_____] to [_____]

4. *Barbers and Brain Surgeons for an Aging Population*
Consider Greyland, a regional economy where the smallest city with a barber has a population of 10,000 ($N_B = 10{,}000$) and the smallest city with a brain surgeon has a population of 200,000 ($N_S = 200{,}000$). Over the next 10 years, the average age of Greyland will increase. The aging process affects heads in two ways: hair volume decreases and the frequency of brain problems increases.
   a. Predict the qualitative effect of the aging of the population on the ratio N_S/N_B. Explain.
   b. Suppose the average age doubles. The elasticity of haircuts with respect to the average age is -1.0 and the elasticity of brain surgery with respect to average age is $+1.0$. Predict the quantitative effect (numbers) of the aging of the population on the ratio N_S/N_B.

5. *One City Size*
Consider a consumer region with only two consumer goods, tattoos (per-capita demand = 3) and manicures (per-capita demand = 6). According to Mr. Wizard, "If my assumption is correct, all consumer cities in the region will be identical." Mr. Wizard's assumption is . . .

6. *Boring Capital Cities*
Some people claim that state capitals (Sacramento, CA; Salem, OR; Olympia, WA) are relatively boring for consumers in the sense that they have less variety in consumer goods than other cities of equal size (population). Check a map of the western states. The three capitals are relatively boring because . . .

REFERENCES AND READING

1. Glaeser, Edward L., Jed Kolko, and Albert Saiz, "Consumer City." *Journal of Economic Geography* 1 (2001), pp. 27–50.
2. Rappaport, Jordan, "Consumption Amenities and City Population Density." *Regional Science and Urban Economics* 38 (2008), pp. 533–52.
3. Christaller, Walter, *Central Places in Southern Germany,* trans. C. W. Baskin. Englewood, NJ: Prentice Hall, 1966.
4. Losch, August, *The Economics of Location*. New Haven, CT: Yale University Press, 1954.

CHAPTER 7

Cities in a Regional Economy

There is no need to worry about mere size. Sir Isaac Newton was very much smaller than a hippopotamus, but we do not on that account value him less.

—Bertrand Russell

The typical regional economy has many inter-connected cities that vary in size and economic scope. This chapter explores the economic forces that shape a regional system of cities. A key assumption underlying the long-run analysis of a regional economy is that workers and firms are perfectly mobile between cities.

1. URBAN UTILITY AND CITY SIZE

Cities in a regional economy are linked through the labor market. In the long run, workers are perfectly mobile between cities, and in the Nash equilibrium in city choice, workers are indifferent between cities in the regional economy. As we'll see, intercity labor mobility means that changes in one city spill over to other cities in the regional economy.

The Urban Utility Curve

How does an increase in total employment in a city affect the utility level of the typical worker? As usual, there are trade-offs. Consider first the positive effects of an increase in a city's workforce. An increase in total employment generates two sorts of agglomeration economies that provide upward pressure on worker utility.

1. *Agglomeration economies in production.* As we saw in Chapter 3, an increase in the workforce generates agglomeration economies as firms share suppliers of intermediate inputs, tap common labor pools, improve skills matching, and benefit from knowledge spillovers. These agglomeration economies increase labor productivity and wages, increasing worker utility.
2. *Agglomeration economies in consumption.* As we saw in Chapter 5, an increase in population increases the variety of consumer goods, which increases consumer utility.

Consider next three sorts of agglomeration diseconomies that provide downward pressure on worker utility.

1. *Commuting and housing cost.* As we saw in Chapter 3, an increase in the workforce increases the unit cost of housing (building up) and/or increases the average commuting distance (building out), so worker utility decreases.
2. *Disease.* As late as the early 1900s, living in a large city in the United States reduced life expectancy by roughly five years. Before the development of modern water and sanitation systems, high-density living facilitated the spread of germs and bacteria, with deadly results. Since then, improvements in water and sanitation systems have reversed the life-expectancy gap: in many of the nation's largest cities (New York, Boston, and San Francisco), life expectancy exceeds the national average. In contrast, in many less developed countries, inferior sanitation systems generate lower life expectancies in cities.
3. *Pollution.* If an increase in a city's workforce increases air or water pollution, worker utility decreases.

Figure 7-1 represents the tradeoffs associated with city size. The urban utility curve shows worker utility as a function of the number of workers. Over the positively sloped portion up to point *i*, as the number of workers increases, the benefits of a larger city (agglomeration economies in production and greater product variety) dominate the costs (agglomeration diseconomies from higher housing cost, longer commuting distance, disease, pollution) and utility increases. Over the negatively sloped portion beyond point *i*, the agglomeration diseconomies dominate the agglomeration economies, so utility decreases.

FIGURE 7-1 Urban Utility Curve

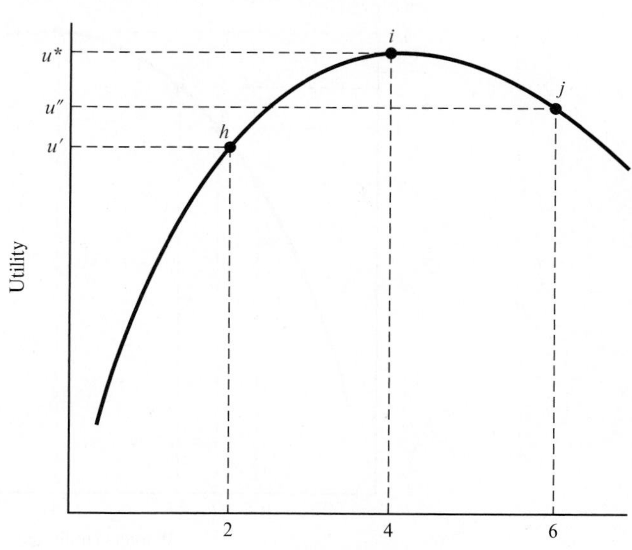

Regional Equilibrium: Cities Are Not Too Small

Suppose for the moment that all cities in a regional economy are identical. The question is whether the region will have a large number of small cities, a small number of large cities, or something between the extremes. To simplify matters, consider three possible configurations of a workforce of 12 million workers.

1. Six cities (A, B, C, D, E, F), each with 2 million workers.
2. Three cities (A, B, C), each with 4 million workers.
3. Two cities (A, B), each with 6 million workers.

Let's start with the six-city configuration. In Figure 7–2, the common utility level with 2 million workers is u' (shown by point h). This is an equilibrium: every worker in the region achieves the same utility level, so no one has an incentive to move. But this equilibrium is unstable because a small deviation will cause the economy to move to a different configuration. Imagine that some workers move from city D to city A. The growing city (A) moves upward along the utility curve from point h to point g, and utility increases to u''. In contrast, the shrinking city (D) moves downward along the utility curve from point h to point s, and utility decreases to u'''. Utility is now higher in the growing city, and the utility gap encourages other workers to move from city D to city A. As migration proceeds, the utility gap grows, and city D will eventually disappear. The population of city A will double and its utility level will reach u^*.

We can apply the same logic to the other four cities in the regional economy. An initial random move of workers from city E to city B will trigger self-reinforcing

FIGURE 7–2 Cities Are Not Too Small

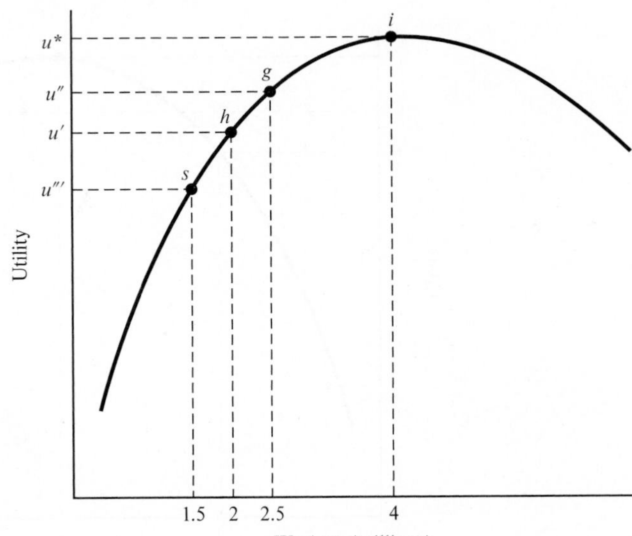

moves that will double the population of city B at the expense of city E. Similarly, if workers move from city F to city C, city F will eventually disappear because other workers will relocate from the shrinking city to the growing city. Under this tidy example, the six-city configuration is replaced by a three-city configuration.

The configuration with six small cities is unstable because migration is self-reinforcing. Migration is self-reinforcing because the small cities are operating along the positively sloped portion of the utility curve. As workers migrate from one city to another, the utility gap between the two cities grows, increasing the incentive to relocate to the growing city. This self-reinforcing migration ultimately eliminates the small cities that experience random out-migration.

The punchline of this analysis is that cities will never be too small. In Figure 7–2, a city would be too small if its workforce is less than the utility-maximizing workforce (4 million workers at point *i*). In other words, being too small means the city is on the positively sloped portion of the utility curve. As we've seen, a configuration that includes at least one city on the positively sloped portion of the utility curve is unstable, so cities can never be too small.

Regional Equilibrium: Cities May Be Too Large

The two-city configuration is shown by point *j* in Figure 7–3. This is an equilibrium: All workers achieve the same utility level u'', so there is no incentive to move. To test for stability, imagine that some workers move from B to A. The city that has grown (A) moves downward along the utility curve from point *j* to point *g*, and utility

FIGURE 7–3 Cities May Be Too Large

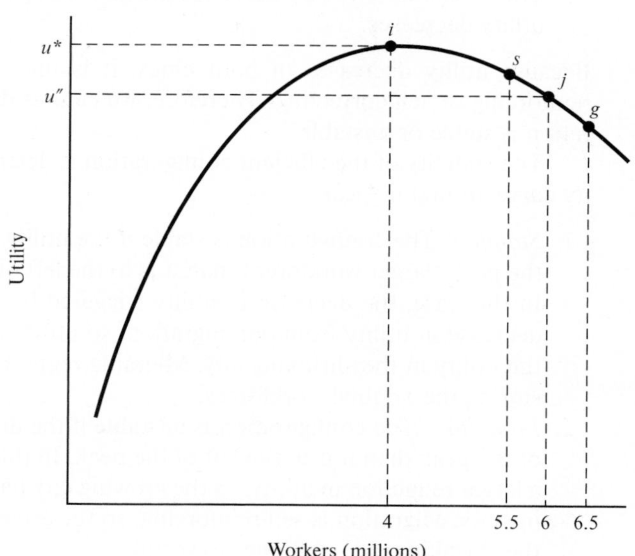

decreases to a utility level below u''. The city that has shrunk (B) moves upward along the utility curve from point j to point s, and utility increases to a level above u''. In this case, utility is higher in the smaller city, so workers will reverse the earlier moves: A will grow and B will shrink, and the migration will continue until each city returns to the original workforce of 6 million and original utility u''.

The two-city configuration is stable because migration is self-correcting. Migration is self-correcting because both cities are on the negatively sloped portion of the utility curve. Movement from city B to city A opens a utility gap, with higher utility in the city that migrants left behind. In a sense, migrants regret their moves to the now-larger city, and the reversal of the migration restores the original utility level u''.

The punchline of this analysis is that equilibrium cities may be too large. In Figure 7–3, a city will be too large if its workforce exceeds the utility-maximizing workforce (4 million workers at point i). In other words, being too large means the city is on the negatively sloped portion of the utility curve. As we've seen, a configuration with cities on the negatively sloped portion of the utility curve is stable, so cities can be too large.

Regional Equilibrium: Efficient Cities?

Consider finally the three-city configuration, with all three cities at the peak of the utility curve at point i. This is an equilibrium because all workers achieve the same utility level u^*, which happens to be the maximum utility. To test for stability, imagine that some workers move from city B to city A.

1. The growing city (A) moves downward along the utility curve to the right, so utility decreases.
2. The shrinking city (B) moves downward along the utility curve to the left, so utility decreases.

Because utility decreases in both cities, it is unclear whether migration is self-reinforcing or self-correcting. Therefore, we cannot determine whether the configuration is stable or unstable.

The stability of the efficient configuration is determined by the slope of the utility curve around its peak.

1. *Stability.* The configuration is stable if the utility curve is steeper to the right of the peak (larger workforce) than it is to the left of the peak (smaller workforce). In this case, the decrease in utility triggered by in-migration is larger than the decrease in utility from out-migration, so utility in the growing city is less than the utility in the shrinking city. Migrants regret their moves and move back, restoring the original workforces.
2. *Instability.* The configuration is unstable if the utility curve is flatter to the right of the peak than it is to the left of the peak. In this case, out-migration generates a larger reduction in utility, so the growing city has higher utility than the shrinking city. Migration is self-reinforcing, so the growing city continues to grow and the shrinking city continues to shrink.

In the case of instability, it is difficult to predict the ultimate outcome in terms of the size and number of cities. The outcome is unpredictable unless we know more about the slope and position of the utility curve.

2. DIFFERENCES IN CITY SIZE

Up to this point we have assumed that a regional economy generates identical cities. In fact, cities in a regional economy differ in size and economic scope. New York, the largest urban area in the United States, has a population of more than 18 million, while the smallest urban area (Andrews, Texas) has a population of about 13,000. Figure 7-4 shows the size distribution of U.S. metropolitan areas, split into two graphs, one for the top 50 metropolitan areas and a second for all 365 metropolitan areas.

Equilibrium City Sizes in a Regional Economy

We can use utility curves to explain the development of cities of different size. In Figure 7-5, the utility curve that includes point *s* is for a city that experiences relatively small agglomeration economies in production and consumption. As the workforce increases, agglomeration diseconomies quickly overwhelm agglomeration economies, so the peak of the utility curve occurs with a relatively small workforce. For the city represented by the utility curve that includes point *m*, agglomeration economies are moderate, and the peak utility occurs with a medium workforce. For the city represented by the utility curve that includes point *b*, agglomeration economies are relatively large, and the peak utility occurs with a large workforce.

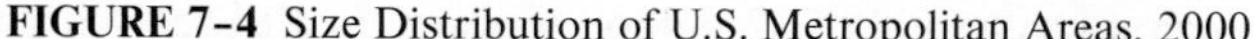

FIGURE 7-4 Size Distribution of U.S. Metropolitan Areas, 2000

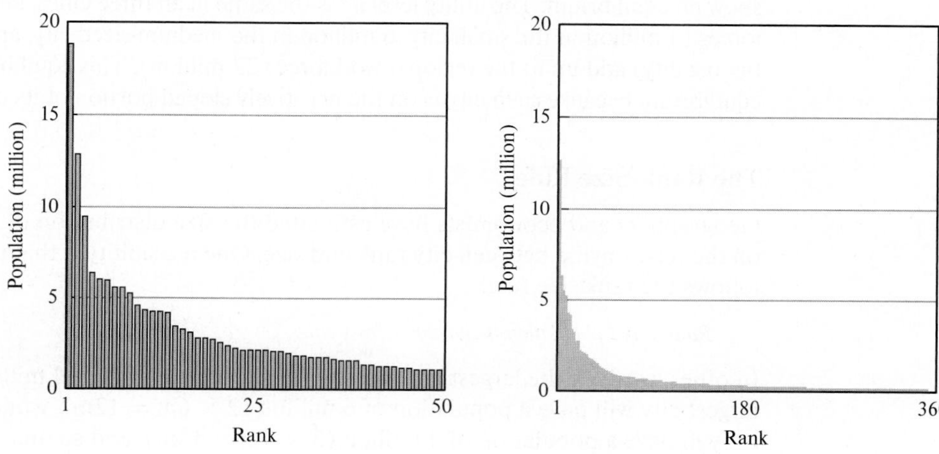

FIGURE 7–5 Differences in City Size

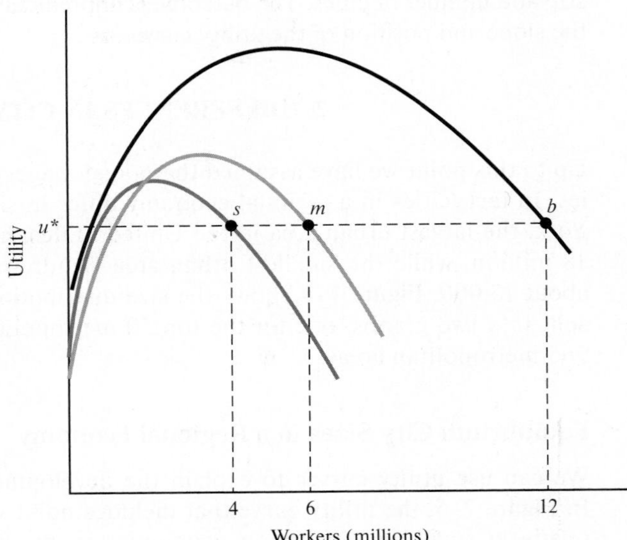

In the equilibrium allocation of workers across cities in the regional economy, workers are indifferent between the three cities and every worker has a workplace. There are two conditions for locational equilibrium.

1. *Nash equilibrium: Equal utility across cities.* Workers in the three cities achieve the same utility level, so there is no incentive for unilateral deviation.
2. *Adding up.* The sum of the workers in the three cities adds up to the fixed regional workforce.

Suppose the region has a total of 22 million workers. In Figure 7–5, points s, m, and b show an equilibrium. The utility level u^* is the same in all three cities, and the city workforces (4 million in the small city, 6 million in the medium-sized city, and 12 million in the big city) add up to the regional workforce (22 million). This equilibrium is a stable equilibrium because each city is on the negatively sloped portion of its utility curve.

The Rank-Size Rule

Geographers and economists have estimated the size distribution of cities, focusing on the relationship between city rank and size. One possibility is that the relationship follows the rank-size rule:

Rank times population is constant across cities.

In other words, if the largest city (rank 1) has a population of 12 million, the second largest city will have a population of 6 million ($2 \times 6\text{m} = 12\text{m}$), while the third largest will have a population of 4 million ($3 \times 4\text{m} = 12\text{m}$), and so on.

Nitsche (2005) summarizes the results of 29 studies of the rank-size relationship, with data from countries around the world. The hypothesized relationship is

$$R = \frac{c}{N^b}$$

where c is a constant, N is population, and the exponent b is to be estimated from the data on rank and population. If $b = 1.0$, the rank-size rule holds. The example shown in Figure 7–5 is consistent with the rank-size rule, with $c = 12$ million and $b = 1$. The largest city has a population of 12 million workers, followed by a city with 6 million workers and then a city with a population of 3 million workers:

$$R_1 = \frac{c}{N^b} = \frac{12m}{12m} = 1 \qquad R_2 = \frac{c}{N^b} = \frac{12m}{6m} = 2 \qquad R_3 = \frac{c}{N^b} = \frac{12m}{4m} = 3$$

In other words, rank times size is constant at 12 million. In the studies considered by Nitsche, two-thirds of the estimates of b are between 0.80 to 1.20, and the median estimate is 1.09. This is consistent with earlier cross-country studies that generate estimates of b in the range 1.11 to 1.13. In other words, the urban population is more evenly distributed across cities than would be predicted by the rank-size rule.

It is important to note that many of the studies of the rank-size rule use political definitions of cities rather than the economic definition. A political city is defined by boundaries that separate political jurisdictions. In contrast, the economic definition of a city ignores political boundaries and includes all the people who are economically involved in the urban economy. In practical terms, the economic city is typically defined as a metropolitan area (e.g., the San Francisco Bay Area) that includes the central (political) city along with all the surrounding communities. For the studies of the rank-size rule that use economic cities rather than political cities, the median estimate for b is 1.02, which is much closer to the value consistent with the rank-size rule.

3. URBAN ECONOMIC GROWTH

In economics, economic growth is defined as an increase in per-capita income. In an urban context, economic growth is defined as an increase in the utility level of the typical resident. In other words, the urban definition accounts for factors other than market income (the wage), including the other benefits (product variety) and costs of urban living (housing cost, commuting cost, pollution).

What causes economic growth in an urban context? There are four sources of economic growth, including three traditional (non-geographic) factors and one geographical factor.

1. *Capital deepening.* Physical capital includes the objects made by humans to produce goods and services, such as machines, equipment, and buildings. Capital deepening is defined as an increase in the amount of capital per worker. Capital deepening provides workers more capital, so it increases productivity and income.

2. *Increases in human capital.* A person's human capital includes the knowledge and skills acquired through education and experience. An increase in human capital increases productivity and income.
3. *Technological progress.* Any idea that increases productivity–from a worker's commonsense idea about how to better organize production, to a scientist's invention of a faster microprocessor–is a form of technological progress. The resulting increase in productivity increases income per worker.
4. *Agglomeration economies.* Physical proximity increases productivity as firms share suppliers of intermediate inputs, tap common labor pools, improve skills matching, and benefit from knowledge spillovers. Cities increase productivity and income because they bring together the inputs to the production process and facilitate face-to-face communication. In the words of Lucas (2001), cities are the "engines of economic growth."

Innovation and Regionwide Utility

We can use the urban utility curve to show the connection between technological progress and utility. Consider a region of 12 million workers and two identical cities, each with 6 million workers. In Figure 7–6, the initial utility curve has the familiar hill shape, reflecting the tension between agglomeration economies and diseconomies. The two cities have the same initial utility curve, and the initial equilibrium is shown by point *a*. The region's workforce is split equally between two cities of 6 million workers, and the common utility level is u^*.

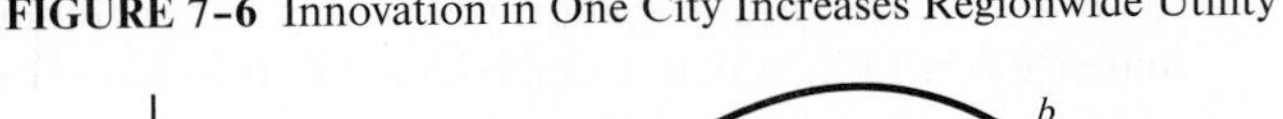

FIGURE 7–6 Innovation in One City Increases Regionwide Utility

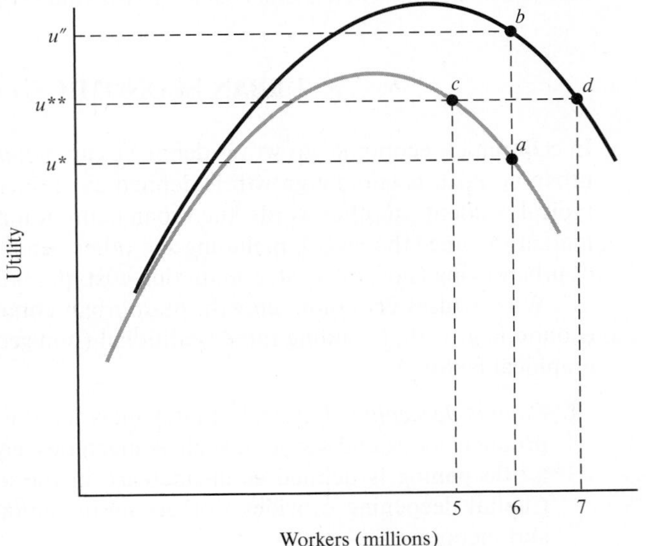

Suppose one of the two cities experiences technological progress that increases worker productivity. The city's utility curve shifts upward, with a higher productivity (and utility) for each workforce. For example, for a workforce of 6 million in the innovative city, the utility level increases from u^* (point *a*) to u'' (point *b*). So in the absence of migration, utility in the innovative city would exceed utility in the other city by $u'' - u^*$. In response to the utility gap, workers will migrate to the innovative city, and migration will continue until utility is equalized across the two cities.

The new equilibrium is shown by points *c* and *d*. This is a locational equilibrium because both cities have the same utility level u^{**}, and the workforces in the two cities add up to the fixed regional workforce. The innovative city (shown by point *d*) gains 1 million workers, while the other city (shown by point *c*) loses 1 million workers. Utility increases from u^* to u^{**} in both cities, meaning that workers in both cities benefit from innovation in one city. Workers in the other city benefit because the decrease in population causes the city to move upward along its negatively sloped utility curve, from point *a* to point *c*, where $u^{**} > u^*$.

We've seen that the benefits of technological progress in a one city spread to other cities in the region. Any initial gap in utility will be eliminated by labor migration to the city with the higher utility level, and migration will continue until the utility gap is eliminated. In our two-city region, the initial utility gap (shown by points *a* and *b*) is $(u'' - u^*)$ and in equilibrium, workers in each city experience an increase in utility equal to roughly half this initial gap: $(u^{**} - u^*)$ is roughly half of $(u'' - u^*)$.

In a larger region, the increase in per-capita utility would be smaller. If the region had 10 cities instead of two, there would be five times as many workers to share the benefits of the innovation. As a rough approximation, the increase in utility would be about one-tenth (rather than one-half) the initial utility gap. Similarly, if the region had 50 cities, the increase in utility would be roughly 1/50 of the initial gap. In general, the larger the number of workers over which to spread the benefits of innovation, the smaller the benefit per worker.

Consider next the effect of simultaneous technological progress in both cities. Suppose the two cities experience the same increase in productivity, and thus experience the same upward shift of the utility curve. In this case, both cities would move from point *a* to point *b*, and point *b* would be the new equilibrium. There would be no utility gap to overcome with migration because both cities would experience the same change in productivity and utility. As a result, each city would maintain its workforce of 6 million workers.

We've seen that technological progress–represented by an upward shift of the utility curve–increases the equilibrium utility of workers throughout the region. The same logic applies to other sources of higher productivity: capital deepening, increases in human capital, and agglomeration economies.

Human Capital and Economic Growth

Consider next the role of human capital in economic growth. Urban economists have explored the effects of human capital on urban productivity and income. An increase in the education or job skills of a specific worker has three effects.

1. *Higher wage.* The worker's productivity increases, and competition among employers increases the wage to match the worker's higher productivity.
2. *Spillover benefits.* Workers learn from one another by sharing knowledge–in both formal and informal settings–and a worker with more human capital has more knowledge to share and is better equipped to share the skills.
3. *Technological progress.* An increase in human capital increases the rate of technological innovation, which increases productivity and income.

There is evidence that the largest beneficiaries of human-capital spillovers are less-skilled workers. One study estimated that a 1 percent increase in a city's share of college-educated workers increases the wage of high-school dropouts by 1.9 percent, while it increases the wage of high-school graduates by 1.6 percent and increases the wage of college graduates by 0.4 percent (Moretti, 2004). This is consistent with the general observation that urban economic growth tends to reduce income inequality (Wheeler, 2004).

A recent study of the biotechnology industry shows that physical proximity to top-notch "star" researchers is an important factor in the birth of biotechnology firms (Zucker, Darby, and Brewer, 1998). The new biotechnology firms located close to scientists with specific human capital (those involved in the discovery of genetic sequences). Although many of the scientists were connected to universities and research centers, the key location factor was the human capital of the scientists, not the presence of a university or research center.

In less developed countries, secondary (high-school) education is an important factor in income growth. According to a recent study of Chinese cities (Mody and Wang, 1997), when enrollment in secondary education increases from 30 percent to 35 percent of the eligible population in a city, the growth rate of total output increases by 5 percentage points. This effect diminishes as the enrollment rate increases: an increase in the enrollment rate from 55 percent to 60 percent increases the growth rate by only 3 percentage points. The largest productivity boost from secondary education occurs in cities with relatively high levels of foreign investment, suggesting that foreign investment and human-capital investments are complementary inputs.

REVIEW THE CONCEPTS

1. An increase in a city's total employment generates agglomeration economies in [_____] as firms share [_____], tap [_____], improve [_____], and experience [_____] spillovers.
2. An increase in a city's total employment generates agglomeration economies in [_____] because an increase in population increases [_____].
3. An increase in a city's total employment generates agglomeration diseconomies as the costs of [_____] and [_____] increase.
4. The urban utility curve is shaped like a [_____] (young volcano, rounded hill, plateau, crevasse), a result of the interplay of agglomeration [_____] and [_____].
5. In the equilibrium in a regional system of cities, cities may be too [_____] but will not be too [_____].

FIGURE 7–7

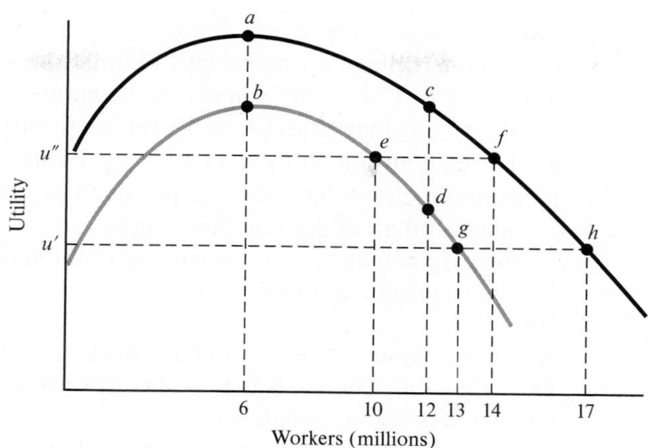

6. Suppose each city in a regional economy is on the positively sloped portion of an urban utility curve. A random deviation leads to [_____] changes: a city that has grown will [_____] in size, and a city that has shrunk will [_____] in size.
7. Suppose each city in a regional economy is on the negatively sloped portion of an urban utility curve. A random deviation leads to [_____] changes: a city that has grown will [_____] in size, and a city that has shrunk will [_____] in size.
8. The conditions for locational equilibrium for cities in a regional are (i) [_____]; (ii) [_____].
9. According to the rank-size rule, if the largest city in an economy has a population of 12 million, the fourth largest city has a population of [_____].
10. Use Figure 7–7. Consider a two-city region with 24 million workers.
    a. The regional equilibrium is shown by points [_____] and [_____] and the equilibrium utility is [_____].
    b. Points [_____] and [_____] satisfy the equal-utility condition but not the adding-up condition.
    c. Points [_____] and [_____] satisfy the adding-up condition but not the equal-utility condition.
11. Economic growth is defined as an increase in [_____].
12. There are four sources of urban economic growth: (i) [_____], (ii) [_____], (iii) [_____], and (iv) [_____].
13. Suppose one of two cities in a regional economy experiences an increase in labor productivity. In the new regional equilibrium, the other city experiences a(n) [_____] in utility because the city moves [_____] along its utility curve as its workforce [_____].
14. An increase in one worker's human capital [_____] the worker's wage and generates [_____] for other workers. The largest beneficiaries of educational spillovers are [_____].

APPLY THE CONCEPTS

1. *Carplanes and City Size*
   Consider a regional economy with 12 million workers and an urban utility curve $u(n) = 15 + 12n - 2n^2$, where n is the number of workers in millions. Initially the region has four cities (A, B, C, D), each with a population of 3 million.
   a. The equilibrium utility level is [______] utils.
   b. Suppose city A introduce carplanes to replace regular cars for commuting, and its urban utility function is $u(n) = 15 + 12n - n^2$. Predict the effect of the carplane on (i) equilibrium distribution of population between the cities and (ii) regional utility. Illustrate.
2. *New Cities*
   A regional economy has 11 million workers and an urban utility curve $u(n) = 15 + 12n - n^2$, where n is the number of workers in millions. Initially, all 11 million workers are in a single city.
   a. Suppose the regional government establishes a new city with 1 million workers, leaving 10 million workers in the old city. Predict the new equilibrium distribution of population between the two cities. Illustrate.
   b. Suppose the regional government provides a subsidy to the residents of the new city. The subsidy (in utils) is $s = 12 - 2n$, that is, 10 utils in a city with 1 million workers, 8 utils for 2 million workers, and so on. Predict the new equilibrium distribution of population between the two cities. Illustrate.
3. *Equilibrium in a Two-City Region*
   Consider a region with two cities and a total workforce $24 = A + B$, where A is the workforce in city 1 and B is the workforce in city 2. For the negatively sloped portion of the utility curves,

   $$u(A) = \frac{480}{A} \qquad u(B) = \frac{240}{B}$$

   Illustrate the regional equilibrium, including values for the workforces of the two cities and the regional utility.
4. *Innovation in a Two-City Region*
   Consider a region with two cities and a total workforce $24 = A + B$, where A is the workforce in city 1 and B is the workforce in city 2. For the negatively sloped portion of the utility curves,

   $$u(A) = \frac{480}{A} \qquad u(B) = \frac{240}{B}$$

   a. Illustrate the regional equilibrium, including values for the workforces of the two cities and the regional utility.
   b. Suppose technological innovation in the first city shifts the utility curve upward, so along the negatively sloped portion $u(A) = 720/A$. Illustrate the regional equilibrium, including values for the workforces of the two cities and the regional utility.

5. *Air Pollution and Economic Decline*
Consider a two-city (A and B) regional economy where each city operates on the negatively sloped portion of its utility curve. In the initial equilibrium, the two cities are identical. Then air pollution (lead emissions) in city B decreases the brain power and productivity of workers in the city by 20 percent. Illustrate the effects of lead emissions on the regional equilibrium, indicating the direction of changes in city size (the number of workers) and regional utility.
6. *Rural vs. Urban Development*
In the initial equilibrium, a region's workforce of 24 million is divided equally between a city and a rural area. The initial common utility level is 50 utils. The urban utility curve peaks at 8 million people, and in the population range of 8–12 million, the slope of the utility curve is −2 utils per million. The rural utility curve reflects mildly increasing returns to scale. In the population range of 12–16 million, the slope is 1 util per million. Suppose the nation invests in rural infrastructure, which increases rural productivity and shifts the rural utility curve upward by 3 utils. Illustrate the implications on the regional economy, including values for (i) the city population, (ii) the rural population, and (iii) regional utility.
7. *Capital City Circus*
Consider a nation with a fixed population of 12 million that is initially divided equally between two cities, Circusville and Dullsville. The urban utility curve is $u(w) = 15 + 12w - w^2$. Suppose a dictator in Circusville initiates free circuses, financed by coercive transfer payments from people outside the region. The circus program initially increases the utility of living in Circusville by 3 utils. Illustrate the effects of the circuses on the regional economy, including values for (i) city sizes and (ii) regional utility.

REFERENCES AND READING

1. Abdel-Rahman, H., and A. Anas, "Theories of Systems of Cities," Chapter 52 in *Handbook of Regional and Urban Economics 4: Cities and Geography,* edited by V. Henderson and J. F. Thisse. Amsterdam: Elsevier, 2004.
2. Ades, Alberto F., and Edward L. Glaeser, "Trade and Circuses: Explaining Urban Giants." *Quarterly Journal of Economics* (1995), pp. 195–227.
3. Au, Chun Chung, and J. Vernon Henderson, "Are Chinese Cities Too Small?" *Review of Economic Studies* (2006).
4. Brueckner, Jan, and Somik Lall, "Cities in Developing Countries: Fueled by Rural-Urban Migration, Lacking in Tenure Security, and Short of Affordable Housing," Chapter 21 in *Handbook of Urban and Regional Economics Volume 5,* edited by Gilles Duranton, J. Vernon Henderson, and William C. Strange. Amsterdam: Elsevier, 2015.
5. Davis, Donald, and David Weinstein, "Bones, Bombs, and Break Points: The Geography of Economic Activity." *American Economic Review* (2002).
6. Duranton, Gilles, "Urban Evolutions: The Fast, the Slow, and the Still." *American Economic Review,* 97.1 (2007), pp. 197–221.

7. Findeisen, Sebastian, and Jens Sudekum, "Industry Churning and the Evolution of Cities: Evidence for Germany." *Journal of Urban Economics,* 64.2 (2008), pp. 326–339.
8. Gabaix, X., and Y. Ioannides, "Evolution of City Size Distributions," Chapter 53 in *Handbook of Regional and Urban Economics 4: Cities and Geography,* edited by V. Henderson and J. F. Thisse. Amsterdam: Elsevier, 2004.
9. Henderson,V., *Urban Development: Theory, Fact, and Illusion*. Oxford: Oxford University Press, 1988.
10. Henderson, J. V., "Efficiency of Resource Usage and City Size." *Journal of Urban Economics* 19 (1986), pp. 47–90.
11. Lucas, Robert, "Externalities and Cities." *Review of Economic Dynamics* 4 (2001), pp. 245–74.
12. Malpezzi, Stephen, "Cross-Country Patterns of Urban Development," Chapter 4 in *A Companion to Urban Economics,* edited by Richard J. Arnott and Daniel P. McMillen. New York: Wiley-Blackwell, 2006.
13. Mody, Ashoka, and Fang-Yi Wang, "Explaining Industrial Growth in Coastal China: Economic Reforms . . . and What Else?" *World Bank Economic Review* 11 (1997), pp. 293–325.
14. Moomaw, R., and A. Shatter, "Urbanization and Economic Development: A Bias Toward Large Cities." *Journal of Urban Economics,* July 1996.
15. Moretti, Enrico. "Human Capital Externalities and Cities," Chapter 51 in *Handbook of Regional and Urban Economics 4: Cities and Geography,* edited by Vernon Henderson and J. F. Thisse. Amsterdam: Elsevier, 2004.
16. Nitsche, V., "Zipf Zipped." *Journal of Urban Economics* 57 (2005), pp. 86–100.
17. Wheeler, Christopher H., "On the Distributional Aspects of Urban Growth." *Journal of Urban Economics* 55 (2004), pp. 1371–97.
18. Zucker, L.G., M.R. Darby, and M.B. Brewer, "Intellectual Human Capital and the Birth of U.S. Biotechnology Enterprises." *American Economic Review* 88 (1998), pp. 290–306.

CHAPTER 8

The Urban Labor Market

An economic forecaster is like a cross-eyed javelin thrower: He doesn't win many accuracy contests, but he keeps the crowd's attention.

—ANONYMOUS

This chapter explores the workings of the urban labor market. We discuss the economic forces that determine equilibrium wages and total employment in an urban area and explore the effects of various public policies on wages and employment. We address three key questions.

1. Who benefits from an increase in total employment?
2. How does tax policy affect total employment?
3. What are the economic effects of professional sports teams and mega-events such as the World Cup?

1. URBAN LABOR SUPPLY AND DEMAND

We can use a model of the urban labor market to explore the market forces that determine equilibrium wages and total employment in a city. We take a long-run perspective. We assume that the metropolitan area is part of a larger regional economy in which households and firms are perfectly mobile between cities in the region. The demand for labor comes from firms in the city, while supply comes from households living in the city.

The Labor Supply Curve

Figure 8-1 shows the supply curve for an urban labor market. The labor supply curve is positively sloped, indicating that an increase in the wage increases the quantity of labor supplied. In drawing the supply curve, we make two simplifying assumptions.

1. *Fixed work hours per worker.* Empirical estimates suggest that an increase in the wage causes some workers to work more and others to work less; on average, the change in work hours is relatively small.
2. *Fixed labor-force participation rate.* We assume that a change in the wage does not change the fraction of the city's population in the workforce.

FIGURE 8–1 Urban Labor Supply

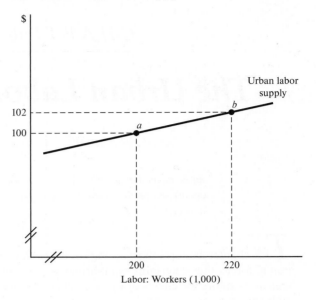

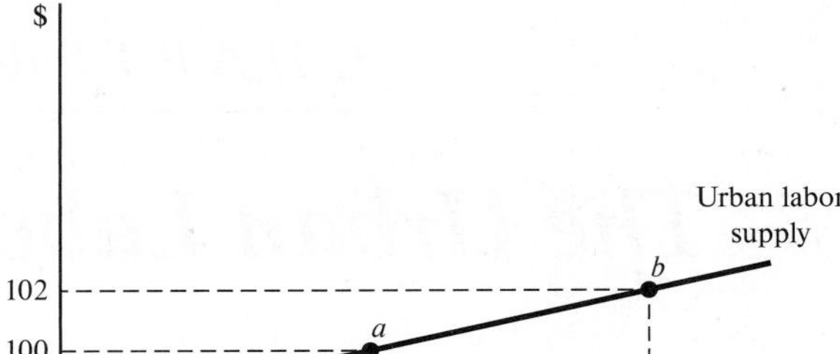

An increase in a city's wage increases the quantity of labor supplied because the higher wage attracts more workers to the city.

Why is the supply curve positively sloped? An increase in total employment in a city increases the total demand for housing and land, increasing their prices. To ensure locational equilibrium in the labor market, a larger city must offer a higher wage to compensate workers for the higher cost of living. The estimated elasticity of the cost of living with respect to the size of the workforce is 0.20 (Bartik, 1991):

$$e(\text{Cost of living, Workforces}) = \frac{\%\Delta\text{Cost of living}}{\%\Delta\text{Workforce}} = 0.20$$

For example, a 10 percent increase in the workforce increases the cost of living by about 2 percent. This means that to keep real wages constant as total employment increases, the elasticity of the wage with respect to the size of the workforce is 0.20:

$$e(\text{wage, Workforce}) = \frac{\%\Delta\text{Wage}}{\%\Delta\text{Workforce}} = 0.20$$

We can use these numbers to compute the wage elasticity of the supply of labor, which is the inverse of the elasticity of the wage with respect to the size of the workforce.

$$e(\text{Workforce, wage}) = \frac{\%\Delta\text{ Workforce}}{\%\Delta\text{ Wage}} = 5.0$$

For example, if the labor-supply elasticity is 5.0, a 2 percent increase in the wage increases the workforce by 10 percent (equal to 5 times 2 percent). This elasticity applies to the labor market of an individual city in a regional economy. The city labor-supply elasticity is larger than the national labor-supply elasticity (close to zero) because migration between cities is less costly than migration between nations.

What causes the supply curve to shift to the right or left? The position of the supply curve is determined by the following factors:

1. *Amenities.* Any change that increases the relative attractiveness of the city (other than a change in the wage) shifts the supply curve to the right. For example, an improvement in air or water quality causes migration that increases the supply of labor.
2. *Disamenities.* Any change that decreases the relative attractiveness of a city (other than a change in the wage) decreases labor supply and shifts the supply curve to the left. For example, an increase in crime causes people to flee the city, decreasing labor supply.
3. *Residential taxes.* An increase in residential taxes (without a corresponding change in public services) decreases the relative attractiveness of the city, causing out-migration that shifts the supply curve to the left.
4. *Residential public services.* An increase in the quality of residential public services (without a corresponding increase in taxes) increases the relative attractiveness of the city, causing in-migration that shifts the supply curve to the right.

The Labor Demand Curve

A labor demand curve shows the relationship between the quantity of labor demanded and the market wage. Figure 8–2 shows the market demand curve for an

FIGURE 8–2 Urban Labor Demand

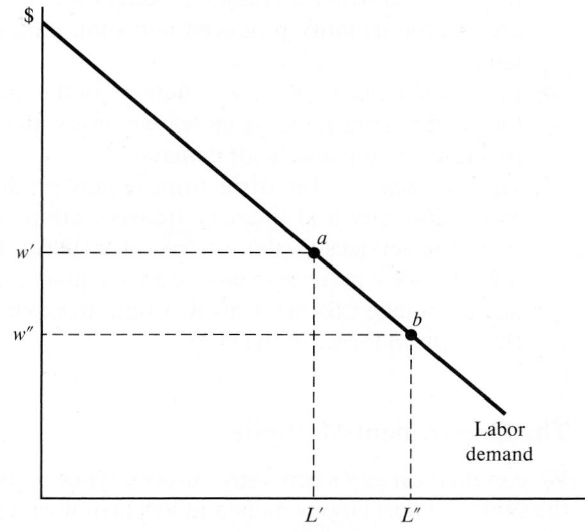

urban economy. As explained in a course in microeconomics, labor demand curves are negatively sloped. A decrease in the market wage increases the quantity of labor demand for two reasons.

1. *Input substitution effect.* A decrease in the wage causes firms to substitute labor for other inputs, including capital, land, and materials.
2. *Output effect.* A decrease in the wage decreases production costs, and firms respond by cutting their prices. Consumers respond to lower prices by purchasing more output, so firms produce more output and hire more workers.
3. *Agglomeration effect.* In the urban labor market, the presence of agglomeration economies adds a third effect of a decrease in the wage. A decrease in the wage and the resulting increase in the quantity of labor demanded allows firms to exploit agglomeration economies that increase labor productivity. The increase in labor productivity decreases production costs and prices, and firms produce more output and hire more workers.

What causes the demand curve to shift to the right or the left? As in the case of other demand curves, a change in something other than the price (the wage) shifts the entire curve. The following factors determine the position of the curve:

1. *Demand for exports.* An increase in the demand for the city's exports increases export production and shifts the demand curve to the right: at every wage, more workers will be demanded.
2. *Labor productivity.* An increase in labor productivity decreases production costs, allowing firms to cut prices, increase output, and hire more workers. As we saw in an earlier chapter, labor productivity increases with capital deepening, technological progress, increases in human capital, and agglomeration economies.
3. *Business taxes.* An increase in business taxes (without a corresponding change in public services) increases production costs, which increases prices and decreases the quantity produced and sold, ultimately decreasing the demand for labor.
4. *Industrial public services.* An increase in the quality of industrial public services (without a corresponding increase in taxes) decreases production costs and thus increases output and labor demand.
5. *Land-use policies.* Industrial firms require production sites that (i) are accessible to the intracity and intercity transportation networks and (ii) have a full set of public services (water, sewers, electricity). By coordinating its land-use and infrastructure policies to ensure an adequate supply of industrial land, a city can accommodate existing firms that want to expand their operations and new firms that want to locate in the city.

The Employment Multiplier

We can divide a city's economy into two types of jobs. Total employment in a city is the sum of export employment and local employment. People who work in export industries produce goods that are sold to people who live outside the city. To illustrate, consider Providence, Rhode Island, the center of the costume-jewelry industry and a regional center for medical care.

1. *Costume-jewelry workers.* Almost all the costume jewelry produced in Providence is sold to people who live in other cities, so jewelry workers are counted as export workers.
2. *Medical workers.* If two-thirds of the patients served by Rhode Island Hospital live in other cities, two-thirds of the hospital workers are counted as export workers.

To count a city's export workers, we add up all the workers who produce goods that are sold to people who live elsewhere. Another label for export goods is "tradeable goods."

People who produce goods and services that are sold to local residents are considered local workers. In some cases, it is obvious that a worker produces a local good. For example, almost all barbers in Providence cut local hair, so all barbers would be counted as local workers. In other cases, the distinction between export and local workers is more subtle. In our example, the one-third of hospital workers who serve local residents would count as local workers. Another label for local goods is "nontradeable goods."

The relationship between export employment and local employment is determined by the multiplier process. Suppose a jewelry firm in Providence hires 100 additional workers to produce jewelry for export. These workers spend part of their wage income on local goods such as haircuts and groceries, increasing the number of barbers and grocery clerks. These newly hired local workers in turn spend part of their wage income on local goods, supporting additional local jobs. Because the spending and respending of income supports local jobs, a 100-job increase in export employment increases total employment by more than 100 jobs. The employment multiplier is defined as the change in total employment per unit change in export employment.

$$\text{Employment multiplier} = \frac{\Delta\text{Total employment}}{\Delta\text{Export employment}}$$

For example, suppose an increase of 100 export jobs increases local employment by 160 jobs, for a total employment effect of 260 jobs. In this case the employment multiplier is 2.60:

$$\text{Employment multiplier} = \frac{\Delta\text{Total employment}}{\Delta\text{Export employment}} = \frac{260}{100} = 2.60$$

Economists use two techniques to estimate employment multipliers. The traditional approach, input-output analysis, requires a full accounting of the transactions between all firms and households. This accounting exercise reveals the interactions (spending and re-spending) between different sectors of the economy. For example, a study of Portland, Oregon, estimated an average employment multiplier of 2.13. The estimated multipliers vary across industries, from a low of 1.46 for optical instruments to a high of 2.77 for independent artists. The input-output approach is problematic because based on two assumptions about the consequences of changes in total employment.

1. *Constant wage.* We've seen that an increase in a city's workforce increases the cost of living, increasing wages. An increase in the wage decreases the quantity of labor demanded, so the input-output approach overestimates the stimulative effect of an increase in export demand.
2. *Constant labor productivity.* As a city's total employment increases, the city may realize agglomeration economies that increase labor productivity. The realization of agglomeration economies increases labor productivity and thus increases labor demand, so the input-output approach underestimates the stimulative effect of an increase in export demand.

An alternative approach is to estimate multipliers from the data on the actual employment experiences of cities. The key question is how past changes in export employment affected local employment and total employment. Because this approach is based on actual employment data, it incorporates both the wage and productivity effects of changes in total employment. For example, a recent study estimates a multiplier of 2.60 for manufacturing employment (Moretti, 2010). The estimated multipliers vary across industries, with the largest multipliers for high-technology industries (machinery and computing equipment, electrical machinery and professional equipment).

We can use a simple numerical example to illustrate the implications of the employment multiplier. Moretti estimates the elasticity of local employment with respect to export employment (also known as employment in the tradeable sector) as +0.33, or roughly one-third. Therefore, a 12 percent increase in export employment increases local employment by about 4 percent. In the typical city, local employment is roughly five times export employment. In Table 8-1, suppose a city starts with total employment of 600,000, with 100,000 export jobs and 500,000 local jobs. If export employment increases by 12 percent to 112,000, local employment will increase by 4 percent to 520,000, and total employment will increase by just over 5 percent. The change in total employment (+32,000) is about 2.6 times the change in export employment (12,000).

Figure 8-3 illustrates the multiplier process. In the initial equilibrium (point *a*), the equilibrium wage is w^* and equilibrium quantity of labor is 100,000 units. An increase in the demand for a city's export good increases labor demand in a two-step process.

1. *Increase in demand.* An increase in export production increases the demand for export workers, shifting the demand curve to the right, from D′ to D″. At the

TABLE 8-1 The Multiplier Process

Employment	Initial (1000)	New (1000)
Export	100	112
Local	500	520
Total	600	632

FIGURE 8–3 Multiplier Effects of an Increase in Exports

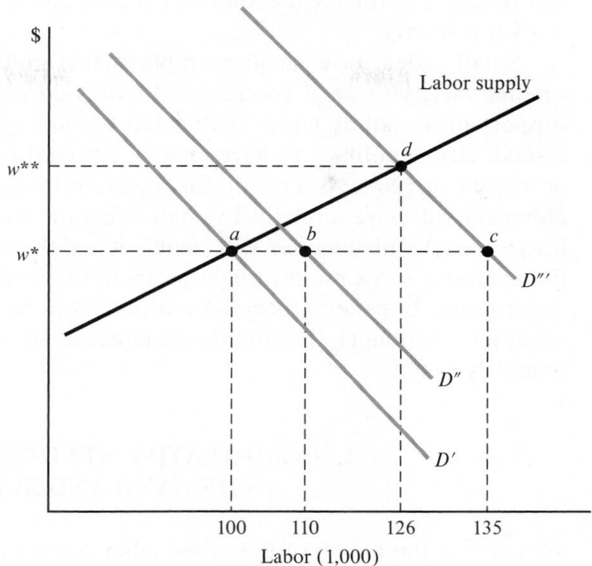

initial wage, the quantity of labor demanded increases from 100,000 (point *a*) to 110,000 (point *b*).

2. *Multiplier effect.* The increase in local production and local labor demand shifts the demand curve to right, from D″ to D‴. At the initial wage, the quantity of labor demanded increases from 110,000 (point *b*) to 135,000 (point *c*).

The two-step increase in labor demand causes excess demand for labor in the city. The excess demand increases the city's wage, and equilibrium is restored at point *d*. The increase in the demand for the city's export good increases the equilibrium wage ($w^{**} > w^*$) and increases the equilibrium quantity of labor from 100,000 to 126,0000. In this example, the employment multiplier is $2.60 = 26{,}000/10{,}000$.

Multipliers in Small and Large Cities

The multiplier process occurs in cities of all sizes, but the multiplication through spending and re-spending is larger in large cities. As we saw in a previous chapter, larger cities have a wider variety of consumer goods because they have more consumers. In particular, large cities have enough total demand to support firms selling products with relatively low per-capita demand. For example, a large city can support a specialized restaurant such as a Peruvian restaurant because it can draw from a large population to fill the restaurant. Similarly, a large city can support an opera company, brain surgeons, and professional sports. As a result, when an export industry in a large city expands by hiring more workers and injects more income into the urban economy, a relatively large fraction of the additional income will be spent in the local economy because consumers buy most consumer goods in their own city.

Small cities have smaller employment multipliers because they provide a smaller variety of local goods. Small cities do not have enough total demand to support firms selling goods with relatively low per-capita demand. For example, a small city is unlikely to have enough demand to support a Peruvian restaurant or a brain surgeon. As a result, the injection of money from additional export employment will have a relatively small effect on the local economy because a large fraction of the new money will "leak" out of the small city to be spent elsewhere. For example, some money might be spent on Peruvian meals and brain surgery in larger cities. In general, because consumers in small cities choose from a smaller set of local products, the stimulative effect of an increase in export employment is relatively small.

2. COMPARATIVE STATICS: CHANGES IN DEMAND AND SUPPLY

We can use the model of the urban labor market to explore the effects of changes on either side of the market on the city's equilibrium wages and total employment. Of particular interest are the effects of an increase in export sales on a city's total employment and wages. A related issue concerns what fraction of any new jobs are filled by existing city residents as opposed to new residents.

Market Effects of an Increase in Demand

Figure 8–4 shows the effects of an increase in export sales on the urban labor market. Suppose the demand for export workers increases by 10,000 workers and because of the multiplier process, the demand for local workers increases by 20,000. In this case, the demand curve shifts to the right by 30,000 workers, or 30 percent. As the population of the city increases, the prices of housing and land increase, requiring an increase in the wage to compensate workers for the higher cost of living. In other words, the city moves upward along its supply curve. The equilibrium wage rises from \$100 per day to \$105, and the equilibrium number of laborers increases from 100,000 to 125,000.

We can use two simple formulas to predict the effect of an increase in demand on a city's equilibrium wage and employment. The formula for the change in the equilibrium wage is

$$\%\Delta w^* = \frac{\%\Delta Demand}{e_S - e_D}$$

where the numerator is the percentage horizontal shift of the demand curve, e_S is the wage elasticity of labor supply, and e_D is the wage elasticity of labor demand (a negative number). In the example depicted in Figure 8–4, the demand curve shifts

FIGURE 8-4 Market Effects of Increase in Labor Demand

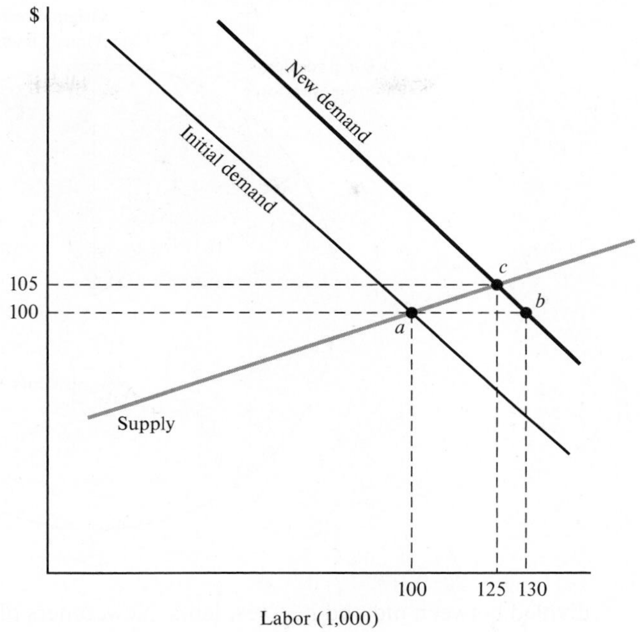

horizontally by 30 percent (30,000/100,000). If the demand elasticity is −1.0, and the supply elasticity is 5.0, the predicted change in the equilibrium wage is

$$\%\Delta w^* = \frac{\%\Delta Demand}{e_S - e_D} = \frac{30}{5+1} = 5\%$$

The market moves upward along the supply curve, so we can use the supply elasticity to predict the change in the equilibrium quantity:

$$\%\Delta N^* = e_s \cdot \%\Delta w^* = 5 \cdot 5\% = 25\%$$

In this case, a 30 percent increase in demand leads to a 5 percent increase in the equilibrium wage and a 25 percent increase in equilibrium employment. In other words, the market-based employment multiplier is 2.50: an initial increase in export employment of 10,000 jobs triggers multiplier effects that increase total employment by 25,000 jobs.

Who Gets the New Jobs?

Bartik (1991) studied the effects of increases in employment on migration and employment in 89 metropolitan areas. He measures the effects of an additional 1,000 jobs in a city that starts with 100,000 jobs. Figure 8-5 shows how the new jobs are

FIGURE 8–5 Distribution of New Jobs: New versus Original Residents

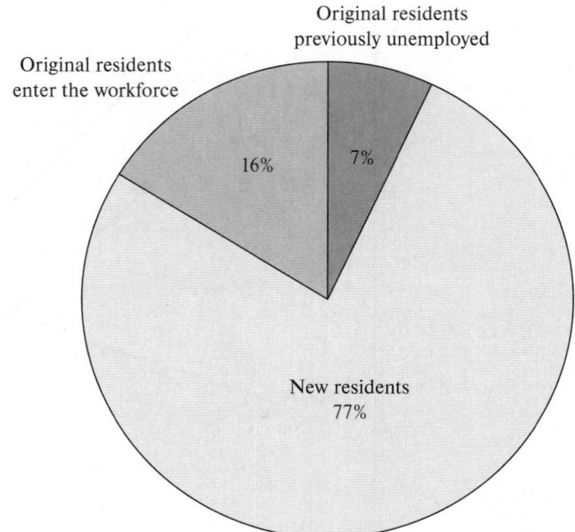

divided between old and new residents. Newcomers fill 770 of the 1,000 jobs, leaving 230 jobs for the original residents. The 230 jobs filled by original residents are split between people who were previously unemployed (70 jobs) and people who were previously not in the labor force (160 jobs). The simple lesson from Figure 8–5 is that increases in employment cause in-migration and population growth, so a small fraction of the new jobs are filled by original residents.

Market Effects of an Increase in Labor Supply

As we saw earlier in the chapter, the position of the urban labor supply curve is determined by a number of factors that affect the relative attractiveness of a city. For example, an increase in amenities (environmental quality) shifts the supply curve to the right, while an increase in disamenities (crime) shifts the supply curve to the left. In the public sector, an increase in taxes shifts the supply curve to the left, while an increase in the quality of public services shifts the supply curve to the right.

Figure 8–6 shows the effects of an increase in the supply of labor. Suppose the city increases the efficiency of its public education system: the city hires better teachers, and the benefits associated with better teachers exceed the cost to taxpayers. The labor-supply curve shifts to the right: at each wage, more people are willing to work and live in the city. The shift of the supply curve increases equilibrium employment and decreases the equilibrium wage. The implication of this analysis is that workers accept lower wages in cities that provide more efficient local public goods.

We can also use Figure 8–6 to illustrate the effects of other favorable changes on the supply side of the market. For example, a decrease in a city's crime rate increases

FIGURE 8–6 Market Effects of an Increase in Labor Supply

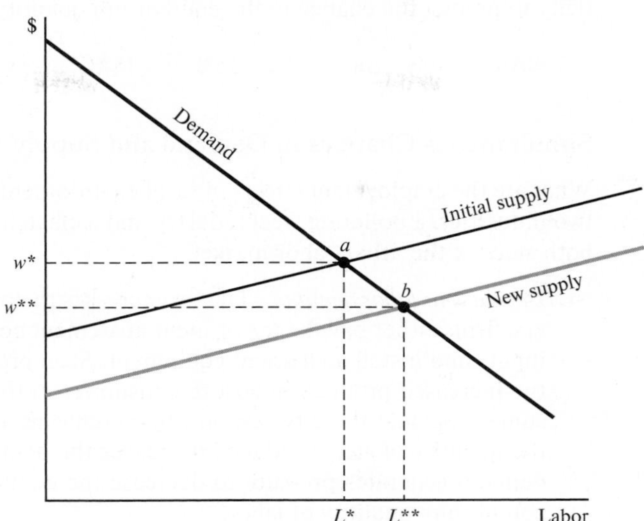

the relative attractiveness of the city, and the labor-supply curve shifts to the right. As a result, the equilibrium employment increases while the equilibrium wage decreases. Workers accept lower wages in cities with relatively low crime rates.

We can use a simple formula to predict the effect of a change in labor supply on a city's equilibrium wage and employment. The formula for the change in the equilibrium wage is

$$\%\Delta w^* = \frac{\%\Delta Supply}{e_S - e_D}$$

where $\%\Delta Supply$ is the percentage horizontal shift of the supply curve, e_S is the wage elasticity of labor supply, and e_D is the wage elasticity of labor demand (a negative number).

It is often convenient to measure a change in labor supply as the vertical shift of the labor-supply curve. In this case, the formula for the change in the equilibrium wage is

$$\%\Delta w^* = \frac{e_S}{e_S - e_D} \cdot \%\Delta WTA$$

where w^* is the equilibrium wage and $\%\Delta WTA$ is the percentage change in workers' willingness to accept (the percentage vertical shift of the supply curve). For example, suppose the willingness to accept increases by 18 percent, indicating an 18 percent upward shift of the supply curve. If $e_S = 5.0$ and $e_D = -1$, the equilibrium wage will increase by 3 percent:

$$\%\Delta p^* = \frac{5}{5 - (-1)} \cdot 18\% = \frac{5}{6} \cdot 18\% = 15\%$$

The market moves upward along the demand curve, so we can use the demand elasticity to predict the change in the equilibrium quantity of labor:

$$\%\Delta N^* = e_d \cdot \%\Delta w^* = -1 \cdot 15\% = -15\%$$

Simultaneous Changes in Demand and Supply

What are the employment effects of local environmental policy? Consider a city with two industries, a polluting steel industry and a clean industry. A pollution tax affects both sides of the urban labor market.

1. *Decrease in labor demand.* The tax increases the production cost of steel producers: firms either pay the tax or incur abatement cost as they switch to alternative inputs and install abatement equipment. Steel producers respond by passing on the increased production cost to consumers in the form of a higher price. Consumers outside the city respond by purchasing less steel, and the decrease in the quantity of steel produced decreases the demand for labor. The decrease in demand generates pressure to decrease the equilibrium wage and decrease the equilibrium quantity of labor.
2. *Increase in labor supply.* The tax will decrease the volume of pollution as (i) the quantity of steel produced decreases and (ii) steel producers adopt pollution-control methods that decreases the volume of pollution per ton of steel. The improvement of the city's air quality increases the relative attractiveness of the city, causing workers to migrate to the cleaner city. The increase in supply generates pressure to decrease the equilibrium wage and increase the equilibrium quantity of labor.

Because a pollution tax affects both sides of the labor market, it shifts both the supply curve and the demand curve. As shown in Figure 8–7, a pollution tax could either increase or decrease the equilibrium employment.

1. *Upper panel: Increase equilibrium employment.* The increase in supply is larger than the decrease in demand. This case applies when (i) the increase in production cost triggered by the tax is relatively small, (ii) the demand for the export good is relatively inelastic, (iii) the improvement in environmental quality is relatively large, and (iv) workers are relatively sensitive to changes in environmental quality.
2. *Lower panel: Decrease equilibrium employment.* The decrease in demand is larger than the increase in supply, which happens when (i) the increase in production cost triggered by the tax is relatively large, (ii) the demand for the export good is relatively elastic, (iii) the improvement in environmental quality is relatively small, and (iv) workers are relatively insensitive to changes in environmental quality.

The pollution tax has conflicting effects on production cost. The direct effect (higher taxes and abatement cost) is at least partly offset by a decrease in labor cost from the decrease in the city's wage. For some firms, the decrease in labor cost dominates, so production cost decreases. This is the case for relatively "clean" firms, so employment in "clean" industries increases at the expense of employment in polluting industries.

FIGURE 8–7 Environmental Policy and Employment

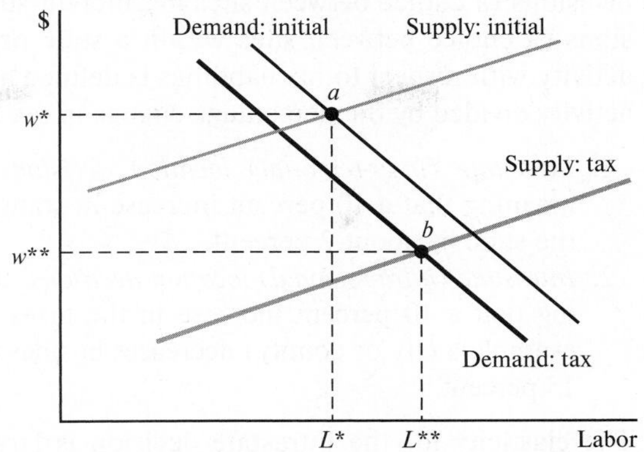

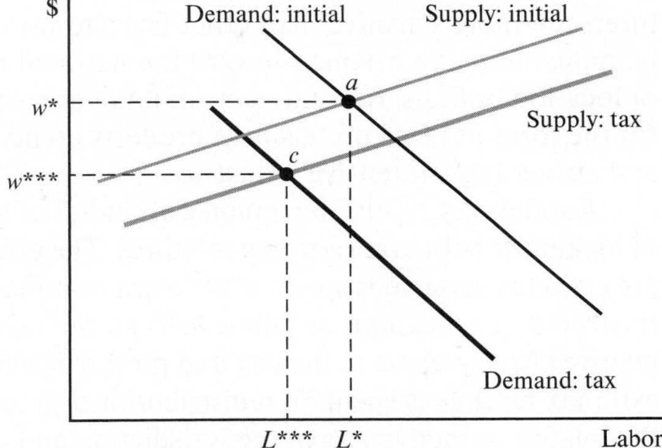

3. PUBLIC POLICY: TAXES AND SPORTS

As we saw earlier in the chapter, local governments can shift the demand curve for labor in a number of ways. In this part of the chapter we explore the effects of taxes on firm location decisions and urban employment. We also explore the employment effects of professional sports and mega-events such as the Super Bowl and the World Cup.

Taxes and Firm Location Choices

There is convincing evidence that local taxes have a strong negative effect on employment growth. A high-tax city will grow at a slower rate than a low-tax city, everything else being equal. One of the items included in everything else is public services. If two cities have the same level of public services but different tax liabilities, the high-tax city will grow at a slower rate.

We can distinguish between two types of business location decisions, interstate decisions (a choice between sites in different states or regions) and intra-state decisions (a choice between sites within a state or region). The elasticity of business activity with respect to tax liabilities is defined as the percentage change in business activity divided by the percentage change in tax liabilities.

1. *Interstate (inter-regional) location decisions.* The elasticity is around −0.20, meaning that a 10 percent increase in state taxes decreases business activity in the state by about 2 percent.
2. *Intrastate (intra-regional) location decisions.* The elasticity is around −1.5, meaning that a 10 percent increase in the taxes in a jurisdiction within a state (for example a city or county) decreases business activity in the jurisdiction by about 15 percent.

The elasticity for the intrastate decision is larger because firms are more mobile within states than between them. Alternative locations within a state are better substitutes than alternative locations in different states.

Two other results from recent empirical studies are worth noting. First, manufacturers are more sensitive than other firms to tax differences. This is sensible because manufacturers are oriented toward the national market and thus have a wider range of location options. Second, metropolitan areas with relatively high taxes on capital (in the form of taxes on business property) tend to repel capital-intensive industries and attract labor-intensive industries.

Another key result from empirical studies of local taxes highlights the importance of looking at both taxes and expenditures. The effect of a tax increase depends on how the extra tax revenue is spent. If the extra revenue is spent on local public services (infrastructure, education, or public safety), the tax/expenditure program increases the relative attractiveness of the city and promotes employment growth. In contrast, if the extra tax revenue is spent on redistributional programs for the poor, the tax decreases the relative attractiveness of the jurisdiction and decreases the growth rate.

Tax Incentive Programs

Many cities try to attract new firms by offering tax incentives such as relatively low tax rates over some period, sometimes known as tax holidays. Bartik (2010) estimates that state and local governments provide over $20 billion per year (roughly $60 per capita) in tax incentives to encourage employment growth. The typical tax-incentive package provides tax credits and deductions worth about $1,200 per job per year for a 10-year period. Of course, many of the subsidized jobs would have been created even without the subsidy. The typical incentive package is decisive for only about 4 percent of jobs: 96 percent of the new jobs would have been created without the incentives.

Bartik (2010) estimates the effects of Michigan's MEGA (Michigan Economic Growth Authority) tax-incentive program. The program offers refundable tax credits to firms that bring new jobs to the state or retain old jobs. In contrast to the typical local tax-incentive program, MEGA is strongly targeted to export industries and focuses on the traditional manufacturing strengths of Michigan. As a result, MEGA promotes projects that create jobs with relatively high wages and large multiplier effects. On average, the tax incentive per job covered under the program is $2,188. Based on the estimated elasticity of business activity with respect to state taxes (−0.20), Bartik estimates that the program generated 18,000 new jobs, including both export jobs and local jobs resulting from multiplier effects. The additional tax revenue from these new jobs partly offsets the direct fiscal cost of the tax-incentive program. The net fiscal cost per new job is roughly $4,000 per job year (one year of employment).

Geographically Targeted Subsidies: Empowerment and Enterprise Zones

Cities and states use a number of other programs to promote economic development. Some governments establish enterprise zones within cities, defined as areas where firms pay low taxes, receive subsidies for worker training, and are exempt from some local regulations. Studies of enterprise zones suggest that these policies do not attract many firms and do not generate many new jobs. When a program succeeds in increasing employment in the target area, it is often because a firm chooses a site in the enterprise zone rather than another site within the city. In other words, job growth in the special zone often comes at the expense of other areas in the city.

Under the Empowerment Zone (EZ) program funded by the federal government, firms that locate in economically distressed areas receive tax credits on wages paid to workers who live within the zone boundaries. The program also provides incentives for capital investment. Hanson and Rohlin (2011) conclude that the EZ program generates relatively small employment gains in the target areas, with most of the new jobs in retail and service employment. The estimated fiscal cost per new business is $19 million and the cost per new job in new businesses is roughly $2.9 million. The job gains in EZs are at least partly offset by job losses in nearby areas, and in some cases the net employment effect of the program is zero or negative.

Sport Stadiums and Mega-Events

Many cities subsidize the construction of facilities for professional sports, building stadiums that cost $200 million or more. The logic behind the job-creation effects of a sports stadium is straightforward. A new stadium may help attract a professional sports team or retain an existing team. Like other organizations, a professional team sells a product and hires workers, including athletes, groundskeepers, ticket takers, accountants, and media personnel. In addition, some of the money the team's employees earn is spent in the local economy, generating multiplier effects that increase employment in restaurants, dental offices, and hardware stores.

The employment effects of stadiums are modest. The stadium for the Arizona Diamondbacks cost $240 million but increased total employment in the area by only 340 jobs. This figure includes both the direct effect (people hired by the team) and the multiplier effect (local jobs). In other words, the cost per new job was $705,882. Employment gains were modest for other host cities, with between 128 and 356 additional jobs in Denver, Kansas City, and San Diego. A comprehensive study of cities that host professional teams showed small positive effects in only one quarter of cases (Baade and Sanderson, 1997). In about a fifth of the cases, the presence of a sports team actually decreased total employment.

The employment effects of stadiums are relatively small because professional sports is for the most part a local good, not an export good. A large fraction of sports fans live in the metropolitan area. For example, only about 5–20 percent of fans at a typical MLB game are visitors from outside the metropolitan area. As a result, most of the money spent on professional sports events comes at the expense of local goods such as movies and restaurant meals. When a sports team comes to town, a large fraction of the money spent by consumers on the team is diverted from local consumer products. For example, there may be more popcorn sold in the stadium but less popcorn sold in movie theaters. Similarly, a sports event provides a different place to drink beer. To the extent that consumers switch from movies and other local goods to sport events, the employment effects of sports teams will be relatively small.

Sport mega-events such as the Super Bowl and the World Cup are often cited as opportunities to increase metropolitan employment. The National Football League (NFL) announced that Super Bowl XXXIII increased taxable sales in South Florida by $670 million, but a study by Baade, Baumann, and Matheson (2008) estimated an economic impact of only $100 million. The economic effects of the Super Bowl and other mega-events are relatively small for three reasons.

1. *Local substitution.* Some people spend money on mega-events that they would have otherwise spent elsewhere in the local economy. Even visitors to the host metropolitan area may choose a mega-event instead of some other local spending opportunity.
2. *Crowding out.* A mega-event causes crowding out in the local economy. For example, hotels may be filled with football fans rather than tourists.
3. *Leakage.* A large fraction of the money spent on mega-events goes to people who live outside the metropolitan area, and this leakage decreases the multiplier effects. For example, few of the athletes and coaches in the Super Bowl live in the host city, so most of the money paid to athletes and coaches generates multiplier effects elsewhere.

The same logic applies to other sports mega events such as the World Cup, the Olympics, and All-Star games. The widely publicized estimates of economic impacts do not account for the three factors listed above, so they typically overstate the economic impacts by a large margin.

REVIEW THE CONCEPTS

1. An increase in a city's wage [_____] the quantity of labor supplied because of [_____]. For a city economy, the wage elasticity of the supply of labor is roughly [_____] (choose 0, 1, 2, 5, 10).

2. The city labor-supply elasticity is larger than the national labor-supply elasticity because migration [_____] is less costly than migration [_____].
3. A decrease in a city's crime rate will shift the labor [_____] curve to the [_____].
4. In an urban labor market, a decrease in the wage [_____] the quantity of labor demanded because of (i) the [_____] effect, (ii) the [_____] effect, and (iii) the [_____] effect.
5. Consumers play a role in the output effect of a decrease in the urban wage: the resulting decrease in [_____] decreases the [_____], increasing the quantity of the product [_____].
6. The employment multiplier is defined as the change in [_____] employment per unit change in [_____].
7. If an additional 100 export jobs increases total employment by 240 jobs, the employment multiplier is [_____].
8. In computing a city's employment multiplier, input-output analysis assumes a constant [_____] and constant [_____].
9. An alternative to input-output analysis is to use market data to estimate the effect of a change in [_____] employment on [_____] employment. A plausible elasticity for the relationship is one [_____].
10. The employment multiplier of a large city [_____] (>, <, =) the employment multiplier of a small city because the large city has a [_____].
11. Suppose the wage elasticity of labor supply is 5.0 and the wage elasticity of labor demand is −2.0. A 21 percent increase in labor demand will [_____] the equilibrium wage by [_____] percent.
12. If total employment in a metropolitan economy increases by 100 jobs, roughly [_____] of the jobs will be filled by new residents and roughly [_____] of the jobs will be filled by city residents who were previously unemployed.
13. A decrease in a city's crime rate [_____] the supply of labor. As a result, the equilibrium wage [_____] and the equilibrium employment [_____].
14. The imposition of a pollution tax will increase equilibrium employment if the increase in [_____] is large relative to the decrease in [_____].
15. A pollution tax will cause a net decrease in production cost if the decrease in [_____] is large relative to the increase in [_____] cost.
16. For each pair of variables, indicate whether the relationship is positive, negative, neutral, or ambiguous.

Parameter	Choice Variable	Relationship
demand for export good	wage	[_____]
demand for export good	total employment	[_____]
efficiency of public schools	wage	[_____]
efficiency of public schools	total employment	[_____]
crime rate	wage	[_____]
pollution tax	wage	[_____]
pollution tax	total employment	[_____]

APPLY THE CONCEPTS

1. *Labor Supply Elasticity*
Island City is located on a small island, while Plains City is located at the center of a large, flat, featureless plain. Draw two labor supply curves, one for each city, and explain why one curve is steeper than the other.
2. *Elasticity of Demand for Labor*
Consider the computer software industry. Assume (i) labor is responsible for 80 percent of production costs, (ii) software is produced with fixed factor proportions (no capital-labor substitution), (iii) the software market is perfectly competitive, and (iv) the price elasticity of demand for software is −1.50. Suppose the wage of software workers increases by 20 percent.
   a. Compute the effects of the increase in the wage on the equilibrium price of software and the quantity of software labor demanded.
   b. Suppose we relax assumption (ii). The decrease in the quantity of software labor demanded would be [______] (larger, smaller, the same) because . . .
3. *Predict Wages and Employment*
In the city of Growville, the equilibrium employment is 100,000 workers and the equilibrium wage is $100 per day. The wage elasticity of demand for labor is −1.0 and the wage elasticity of supply of labor is 5.0. Suppose the demand for labor increases by 18 percent. Illustrate the effects of the increase in labor demand on the urban labor market, including values for the equilibrium wage and equilibrium total employment.
4. *Growth Control and Employment*
Consider two cities, ControlCity and Freeburg, that are initially identical, with an equilibrium wage $100, equilibrium employment 100,000 jobs, and 50 million square feet of housing (500 square feet per worker). The government in ControlCity fixes the maximum total square footage in the city at its current level: new housing can be built, but every square foot of new housing requires that one square foot of old housing be retired from the market. Each city experiences an increase in labor demand that shifts the market demand curve to the right by 24 percent. In both cities, the wage elasticity of demand for labor is −1.0.
   a. In Freeburg, the wage elasticity of labor supply is 5.0. Illustrate the market effect of the increase in labor demand, including a value for the new equilibrium wage.
   b. In ControlCity, a plausible value for the wage elasticity of labor supply is [______] (choose 0, 2, 5, 7). Illustrate the market effect of the increase in labor demand, including a value for the new equilibrium wage.
5. *Economic Impact of a Football Team*
Consider the results of a consultant report on the economic effects of moving the Raiders (a professional football team) to Sacramento. The consultant estimated that the team would increase total spending in the Sacramento economy by $61.6 million per year, computed as

$$\Delta Spending = s \cdot N \cdot m = \$40 \cdot 700{,}000 \cdot 2.20 = \$61.6 \text{ million}$$

where s is spending per fan, N is the number of fans attending the games, and m is the average spending multiplier for the Sacramento economy. Define an outsider as a person who lives outside Sacramento and an insider as a person who lives in Sacramento. The consultant's calculation [_____] (choose overstates or understates) the change in total spending because . . .

6. *Negative Impact of Shearing Championship?*
ClipCity will host the one-day World Sheep Shearing Championship. A total of 1,000 people will pay the $12 admission price, and all admission revenue will be paid to the champion. The spending multiplier for ClipCity is 2.0. According to Ms. Wizard, "If my two assumptions are correct, hosting the competition will decrease total spending in the ClipCity economy." Define an outsider as a person who lives outside ClipCity and an insider as a person who lives in ClipCity.
a. Ms. Wizard's assumptions are (i) [_____] and (ii) [_____]
b. The largest possible negative effect is a change in spending of −$ [_____]

7. *Environmental Policy and Employment*
Consider two cities, each of which initially experiences 100 tons of pollution per day (50 tons from each polluting firm). City T imposes a pollution tax, resulting in an overall pollution reduction of 20 percent and a decrease in equilibrium employment. City U implements a uniform-reduction policy under which each firm cuts its pollution by 20 percent. Which city will experience a larger reduction in equilibrium employment? Illustrate.

REFERENCES AND READING

1. Baade, Robert A., and Allen R. Sanderson, "The Employment Effects of Teams and Sports Facilities." *Sports, Jobs and Taxes*, eds. Roger Noll and Andrew Zimbalist. Washington, D.C.: Brookings, 1997.
2. Baade, Robert A., Robert Baumann, and Victor A. Matheson, "Selling the Game: Estimating the Economic Impact of Professional Sports through Taxable Sales." *Southern Economic Journal* 74 (2008), pp. 794–810.
3. Bartik, Timothy J., and Randall Eberts, "The Roles of Tax Incentives and Other Business Incentives in Local Economic Development," Chapter 28 in *The Oxford Handbook of Urban Economics and Planning,* edited by Nancy Brooks, Kieran Donaghy, and Gerrit-Jan Knaap. Oxford: Oxford University Press, 2011.
4. Bartik, Timothy J., and Randall W. Eberts, "Urban Labor Markets," Chapter 23 in *A Companion to Urban Economics,* edited by Richard J. Arnott and Daniel P. McMillen. New York: Wiley-Blackwell, 2006.
5. Bartik, Timothy J., *Who Benefits from State and Local Economic Development Policies?* Kalamazoo, MI: Upjohn Institute, 1991.
6. Bartik, Timothy J., and George Erickcek, "The Employment and Fiscal Effects of Michigan's MEGA Tax Credit Program." Upjohn Institute Working Paper No. 10-164 (2010).
7. Black, Dan, Natalia Kolesnikova, and Lowell Taylor, "Why Do So Few Women Work in New York (and So Many in Minneapolis)? Labor Supply of

Married Women Across U.S. Cities." *Journal of Urban Economics* 79(2014), pp. 59–71.

8. Chen, Yong, and Stuart Rosenthal, "Local Amenities and Life Cycle Migration: Do People Move for Jobs or Fun?" *Journal of Urban Economics* 65.3 (2008), pp. 519–537.
9. Courant, Paul, "How Would You Know a Good Economic Development Policy if You Tripped over one? Hint: Don't Just Count Jobs." *National Tax Journal* 47.4 (1994), pp. 863–881.
10. Hanson, Andrew, and Shawn Rohlin, "Do Location-Base Tax Incentives Attract New Business Establishments?" *Journal of Regional Science* 51 (2011), pp. 427–449.
11. Lewis, Ethan, and Giovanni Peri, "Immigration and the Economy of Cities and Regions," Chapter 10 in *Handbook of Urban and Regional Economics Volume 5,* edited by Gilles Duranton, J. Vernon Henderson, and William C. Strange. Amsterdam: Elsevier, 2015.
12. Moretti, Enrico. "Local Multipliers." *American Economic Review: Papers & Proceedings* 100 (2010), pp. 1–7.
13. Neumark, David, and Helen Simpson, "Place Based Policies," Chapter 18 in *Handbook of Urban and Regional Economics Volume 5*, edited by Gilles Duranton, J. Vernon Henderson, and William C. Strange. Amsterdam: Elsevier, 2015.
14. Noll, Roger G., and Andrew Zimbalist, "Build the Stadium–Create the Jobs!" *Sports, Jobs and Taxes,* edited by Roger Noll and Andrew Zimbalist. Washington, D.C.: Brookings, 1997.
15. Wheeler, Christopher H., "On the Distributional Aspects of Urban Growth." *Journal of Urban Economics* 55 (2004), pp. 1371–97.
16. Zenou, Yves, "Urban Labor Economic Theory," Chapter 25 in *A Companion to Urban Economics,* edited by Richard J. Arnott and Daniel P. McMillen. New York: Wiley-Blackwell, 2006.

CHAPTER 9

The First Cities

The author, an Assyriologist of renown in his day, was not always able to control his imagination and his weakness for paradoxes.
— Jean Bottero

This chapter has a brief overview of the first cities, which developed in the Jordan Valley (now in a Palestinian territory), the Konya Plain (in present-day Turkey), and southern Mesopotamia (in present-day Iraq). For a detailed discussion of the origins of these first cities, see O'Sullivan (2006).

Archaeologists have excavated piles of rubble from the first cities, uncovering city walls, buildings, household implements, tools used in fabrication, and religious objects. The first cities exploited the public-good aspects of religion and defense against coercive transfer payments. Religion is a public good if worship is assumed to be more effective in a concentration of worshipers. Defense is a public good because there is greater safety in numbers. Given our limited knowledge about these early cities, many puzzles remain.

1. JERICHO

Archaeological evidence suggests that the first city in the world was Jericho (Tell es Sultan), situated at a junction of travel routes in the fertile Jordan Valley. The site was occupied in the period 8400 to 7300 B.C., with a population of about 2,000. The Jordan Valley was a fertile area with a good supply of water, and the residents of Jericho domesticated crops (barley and wheat) and animals (goats and sheep). In addition, the spring near the city attracted wild game, making it relatively easy to hunt gazelle and other wild animals. There may have been some trade in raw materials from the nearby Dead Sea, but what appears to be a small volume of trade could not have supported a city of 2,000 people.

The most startling feature of Jericho is a formidable system of defense, consisting of a wall, a surrounding ditch, and a tower. The wall was about 7 meters tall and 3 meters thick at the base, and was built with undressed stone to surround an area of about 10 acres. The ditch surrounding the wall was 9 meters wide and 3 meters deep and presumably served as a moat to discourage assaults on the city's protective wall. The tower was located just inside the wall and was at least 8 meters tall and 9 meters in diameter. The tower presumably served as an observation post to monitor the movement of hostile forces.

The building of the fortifications involved enormous amounts of resources, both labor and material. The undressed stone for the walls was transported long distances to the city site. To dig the moat, the workers scooped out solid rock at the base of the wall, a task apparently performed with the simplest of tools, the stone maul. There is no evidence of even simple stone digging tools, and metal tools weren't available for another 5,000 years.

The presence of these massive fortifications suggests that agricultural productivity in the area was relatively high. A high level of productivity was required to free a large fraction of the population from agricultural tasks to allow them to work on building and maintaining the city's fortifications. In addition, a high productivity is required for a society to accumulate enough wealth to attract thieves. In sifting through the rubble of several thousand years of occupation, archaeologists have not yet found any stores of wealth that would have attracted raiders, so the nature of Jerico's presumed booty (goods stolen in war) remains a mystery.

The fortifications also suggest the presence of persistent raiders. The city was located at the junction of several travel routes, making it a convenient target. The city was surrounded by hunter-gatherer groups, and archaeologists speculate that these groups occasionally supplemented their hunting and gathering with stealing. At the time, the technology of war involved attacking at a distance with bows and arrows (range of 100 meters) and slings (range of 200 meters). For close combat, the weapon of choice was the mace. Artwork dating from the time of Jericho suggests that attacks were well organized, with warriors arranged in columns.

Given the technology of war at the time, the fortifications would have been the appropriate response to frequent raids (Ferrill, 1997). Archers could position themselves atop the walls to keep attackers at a distance and prevent them from scaling the walls. Methods for assaulting city walls—the battering ram and undermining—hadn't been invented yet, so the wall was an effective defense. Fending off attacks wasn't costless: archaeologists estimate that about a quarter of the population served as defenders.

Based on archaeological evidence, it appears that Jericho developed to provide defense as a public good. Given the frequency of raids, the wealth of households needed protection, and the collective provision of defense is more efficient than the provision by individual households. A small group of raiders, armed with spears, maces, and bows, could overwhelm an individual household and steal its accumulated wealth. A group of households could match the personnel and weaponry of a raiding band, but would fare better by combining resources to build fortifications that discouraged attacks. Given the substantial labor cost associated with its fortifications, the residents of Jericho apparently had something to protect.

2. CATALHOYUK

Catalhoyuk was a city of around 5,000 people in the sixth and seventh millennium B.C. The city was on a 32-acre site in the Konya plain, an area that is now part of Turkey. The city fed its residents with domesticated crops and animals and produced a wide variety of craft products, some of which were exported to other regions.

The food economy of the city was based on simple agriculture and domesticated cattle. The domestication of cattle, which provided the bulk of meat as well as transport, contrasts with the domestication of sheep and goats by other cultures. The city grew wheat and barley on irrigated land and also harvested legumes, nuts, fruits, and berries. The city's residents hunted boar, deer, bear, and leopard for supplementary meat and skins. In addition, the residents of the city consumed dairy products and beer.

The religious activities of Catalhoyuk were not concentrated in a single large temple, but distributed throughout the city in shrine rooms in individual houses. The wall paintings and plaster reliefs in the shrine rooms show a mother goddess exhibiting unusual feats of fertility. The shrine rooms also have bucrania, sculptures of wild ox heads, complete with long horns. One object that appears in many shrines is a bench with up to seven pairs of sharp ox horns pointing upward, making for uncomfortable sitting but presumably a better relationship with the gods.

The people of Catalhoyuk were involved in highly sophisticated and specialized production of products made of wood, stone, and obsidian. The black obsidian from a nearby volcano was flaked and polished to produce points (for spearheads and arrowheads), wedges (for scraping and butchering), blades, and mirrors. Imported flint was fashioned into daggers. The city's polished stone industry produced a wide variety of products, including statuettes, perforated mace heads, stone bowls, greenstone axes, and chisels. Workers in the city processed shell and bone into ornaments and tools. Woodworkers squared oak and juniper for construction purposes and also produced bowls, dishes, and boxes with lids.

The production of obsidian products had several stages. Itinerant workers chipped obsidian collected from a volcanic site about 150 km from the city and processed the raw obsidian into "cores," reducing the bulk and weight of the material. The itinerants then transported the cores to Catalhoyuk for further processing. In the city, skilled workers used pressure and punching techniques to fashion obsidian products from the cores. The itinerant workers then served as transporters and traders, exchanging obsidian products for products from other regions.

In recent experiments, workers tried to duplicate the production process for obsidian tools in Catalhoyuk. The experiments revealed the high level of skill required for tool production:

> Recent studies indicate that pressure flaking (of blades) is a difficult and demanding practice, which requires extensive knowledge of rock flaking properties as well as good neuromuscular coordination. The latter takes several years to acquire, but allows

> thereafter a very high productivity. Consequently, pressure flaking conforms to the typical criteria one associates with the highly skilled and productive practice of a specialist. (Connolly, 1999)

Connolly (1999) concludes that specialization occurred within a kin group, with some members of the extended family engaging in part-time obsidian tool production for the kin group.

The production of obsidian tools required a high skill level, meaning that two phenomena were present in the industry.

1. *Innovation.* Someone must develop the innovations that lead to a sophisticated production process.
2. *Learning.* The skills must be passed on to new workers.

The concentration of production in a city–with workers located close to one another–would hasten both innovation and learning. In general, cities facilitate innovation because they bring together people of different backgrounds and skills to exchange ideas. Cities facilitate learning because workers learn by observation, and there are more people to observe in cities. In general, there are benefits from physical proximity of production facilities–even if they are in tightly packed houses rather than in factories–and Catalhoyuk may have been the center for innovation and learning in the production of obsidian tools.

There is evidence that Catalhoyuk was involved in interregional trade. The city exchanged its craft products–obsidian and stone tools, ornaments, and wood products–for resources that were not available locally. Archaeologists have discovered flint from Syria, shells from the Mediterranean, and bitumen from the Dead Sea. The city also imported wood and copper from nearby sources. Two recent archeological discoveries–smaller settlements close to Catalhoyuk and evidence of the spreading of Catalhoyuk culture to the entire Konya plain–has generated to speculation that Catalhoyuk was a sort of regional trading center, the largest city in a system of cities that traded with each other and with people outside the region.

Could the provision of defense as a public good be partly responsible for the development of Catalhoyuk? The architecture of Catalhoyuk appears somewhat defensive: the houses were stuck together, with roof entryways and high windows. But given the massive fortifications of Jericho, the idea that Catalhoyuk's defensive features would deter raiders seems far-fetched. But perhaps the booty-seekers in the time of Catalhoyuk were different from the raiders who tormented Jericho. If the simple defensive features of Catalhoyuk were combined with a system of organizing people for defense, the city could have provided protection from potential raiders. If so, defense could have been a public good that encouraged people to cluster in the city.

3. BABYLONIA

Starting in the middle part of the fourth millennium B.C., several cities developed in southern Mesopotamia (also known as Babylonia), near the Tigris and Euphrates Rivers in present-day Iraq. The population of Uruk, the largest city in Babylonia, reached 50,000 at the end of the fourth millennium B.C. Other cities developed nearby, including Ur, Erudi, and Kish, each with tens of thousands of people. In this part of the chapter, we focus on the economic features of these cities from the middle of the late fourth millennium B.C. to the early part of the third millennium B.C.

The Ecological Setting

Babylonia had a number of rich and varied ecosystems, including alluvial plains, rivers, and grasslands. These ecosystems were suitable for a wide variety of food-producing activities, including farming (barley, emmer, fruit), fishing, hunting (wild pig, gazelle, wild asses), and grazing (sheep and goats for wool, hair, and milk). In contrast to its rich agricultural resources, Babylonia lacked many basic raw materials, including hardwood, basic metals (copper, tin, silver, lead), and precious stones. The dry climate did not support rain-fed agriculture, but the water from the Tigris and the Euphrates Rivers was easily diverted into canals, allowing the cultivation of lands beyond the banks of the rivers. The first rudimentary irrigation canals date back to 5500 B.C.

Given its ecological setting, Babylonia was a perfect candidate for specialization and trade. The varied ecosystems generated comparative advantages in different parts of the region, opening the possibility of specialization and gains from trade. Similarly, the combination of rich agricultural resources and limited raw materials generated a comparative advantage in agricultural goods, opening the possibility of interregional trade, with agricultural goods being traded for raw materials.

Given its many comparative advantages, it seem likely that Babylonia would eventually develop a system of specialization and trade, causing the development of trading cities. In the middle of the fourth millennium B.C., however, there were two major impediments to widespread specialization and trade. First, there was no money, and exchange was based on barter, an awkward system with high transaction costs. Second, writing had not been invented, so there was no system of recording transactions. People involved in trade were dependent on human memory and honesty to keep track of transactions, and it appears that most people were reluctant to trade with strangers. As a result, specialization and trade typically occurred at the kin-group or village level.

The appearance of cities in Babylonia in the middle of the fourth millennium, before the invention of writing and money, remains a puzzle. The question is, How did the Babylonians overcome the obstacles of barter and illiteracy to develop widespread specialization and trade? One possibility is that the Sumerians, who migrated to the region some time between 4000 B.C. and 3500 B.C., brought a social system that made cities possible. The Sumerians provided the region with the dominant spoken language and a system of religion. Over the second half of the fourth millennium, Sumerian priests developed a system of recording transactions, culminating in the invention of writing in 3100 B.C.

Religious Beliefs

The Sumerian religion adopted in Babylonia was based on the belief that the gods determined the fertility of flora and fauna. The gods were responsible for all natural phenomena, with each of the 2,400 gods responsible for a piece of the natural order. For example, the crop gods included Innana, originally responsible for ripening dates, and Ashnan, responsible for producing grain. The gods for domesticated herd animals included Dumazi, who determined the timing of livestock births, and Lahar, who was responsible for the productivity of sheep. There were also gods for hunting, including Suagan, who was responsible for generating large and accessible herds of gazelles and wild asses. Together the gods were responsible for ecological continuity, keeping nature working as it had in the past. The Babylonians did not ask the gods to perform miracles but simply asked them to continue the "miracle" of nature. The role of the gods was to keep the crops growing, the dates ripening, and the wild asses running on time.

The role of humans was to provide goods to the materialistic gods, freeing them to manage the natural world. According to the Sumerian legend of the origin of humans, second-rate gods originally tilled the soil to provide for the needs of greater gods, who were busy with the tasks of nature management. When the second-rate gods tired of tilling, they persuaded the other gods to create humans to feed, clothe, and shelter all the gods. In the words of Bottero (2001),

> The faithful were convinced that humans were created and put on earth for the sole purpose of ensuring, through human industry and solicitude, that the gods led an opulent and worry-free life, free to concentrate on the government of the world and its inhabitants.

In other words, the gods were not mystical beings with mysterious motives, but simply hungry managers.

People offered huge volumes of goods to the gods, and most of the goods were ultimately consumed by members of the temple staff. The gods were accommodated in large, luxurious temples and were fed four elaborate meals per day. After the fully prepared food sat in front of the statues of the gods for a while, the food was distributed to the religious elite and members of the temple staff, which numbered in the hundreds. An old Sumerian saying is "the priests eat off the altar." Some members of the staff lived in the temple area, sharing the luxurious accommodations with the icons.

Religious Offerings and Temple Enterprises

The religion of Babylon is an example of a public good, at least a perceived one. An increase in aggregate contributions to the gods freed the gods to better manage the ecosystem (e.g., by bringing favorable weather) so the fertility of flora and fauna increased. A more fertile ecosystem made everyone more productive, so a single contribution to the gods benefited everyone. The challenge for society was to persuade people to contribute to the support of the public good, preventing free riding.

The Babylonian response to the free rider problem was a centrally planned economy administered by the religious authorities. The temple collected the aggregate output of the economy, reserved the appropriate share for the gods, and distributed the leftover output to workers and other citizens. In the fourth millennium,

Babylonia had a mixed economy, with a wide variety of temple enterprises as well as some private enterprise. According to Potts,

> Herding, weaving, pottery manufacture, metalworking, woodworking, stone working, agriculture, gardening, forestry, fishing, beer production, and baking, just to name the most obvious activities, all came within the purview of the temple administration, as did the distribution of rations in naturalia (e.g., barley, oil, wool, etc.) . . . (Potts, 1997, p. 237) Although the archaeological evidence is insufficient to determine the fraction of the economy directly administered by the temple, it is clear that the temple was the dominant force in the economy.

The temple's output–the sum of output from a wide variety of temple enterprises and contributions from private enterprises–was distributed in several ways.

1. *Gods and temple personnel.* Offered to the gods and then consumed by temple personnel, including priests involved in rituals and others who managed the temple enterprises.
2. *Worker rations.* Compensation for workers who built and maintained the irrigation canals, worked on temple farms and workshops, and worked in interregional trade.
3. *Welfare.* Distributed to people incapable of working, including children and the aged.
4. *Interregional Trade.* Exchanged for imported goods.

Why was the temple involved in so many economic activities? In the fourth millennium, one advantage of temple enterprise was related to the barter system. In an economy without money or writing, people tended to trade with people they knew and trusted, that is, members of their kin group in the local village. To get people to trade beyond the kin group, there must be a system that engenders trust, and the temple provided such a system. The temple specified the terms of trade, in particular the temple ration for each occupation, and also produced the goods (barley, oil, and wool) that could either be consumed by the recipient or bartered for other goods. The temple served as a trusted broker, encouraging specialization and trade beyond the kin group.

Another advantage of temple enterprise system that it solved the free-rider problem in religious contributions. Rather than asking citizens to contribute some fraction of the output of private enterprise, the temple managers simply took a share for the gods and redistributed the rest. For the remainder of the economy engaged in private enterprise, the temple managers used sharecropping arrangements to collect contributions to the gods.

Transactions and Writing

An important part of the economic history of Babylonian cities was the invention and refinement of writing. This development freed people engaged in trade from their reliance on human memory and honesty. Writing was developed by priests, and the immediate effect was to strengthen the dependence of the economy on the temple organization. In the long run, writing allowed traders to put their trust in permanent and verifiable records, which may have contributed to the increase in private enterprise at the expense of temple enterprises.

The earliest attempts to record transactions, developed in Babylonia in the fourth millennium, employed bullae, closed clay containers with counters inside. For example, when a person contributed 10 goats to the temple, the priest would record the transaction with a container holding 10 icons representing the goats, with the container marked with the contributor's unique seal. The bullae were used by temple authorities to record the inputs and outputs of temple enterprises, and to track the contributions of private enterprises. One problem with the bullae system was that to verify the transaction (to tally the goat counters), the container had to be broken. A second problem was that it required each person to have a unique seal for identification purposes, and these personal seals were costly.

Writing developed in Uruk in about 3100 B.C. The first writing involved etching symbols (pictograms) into clay tablets, with a unique symbol for each object. For example, the symbol for an ear of corn looks like a cornstalk, while the symbol for an ox is an inverted pyramid with two lines coming out the top. Similarly, each person was assigned a unique personal symbol. Clay tablets recovered from Uruk use pictograms to record the number of oxen received by the temple from different individuals. The symbols were etched into wet clay, which was then baked or left to dry to serve as a permanent record. This simple system allowed information to be retained and conveyed to other people.

The pictogram system was awkward because it required a unique symbol for each object. Archaeologists estimate that the Babylonian pictogram system had about 1,500 symbols. About 100 years after the first object-oriented pictograms, the Babylonians shifted to using symbols to represent sounds (syllables) rather than objects. This allowed objects to be represented by different combinations of a smaller set of symbols. For example, the Sumerian word for "arrow" was pronounced ti, and so was the word for "life." Under the phonetic system, the word for life was represented by the symbol for its homophone, arrow. In general, each word was depicted with a series of symbols, one for each syllable. The phonetic innovation reduced the number of symbols used to about 400. Eventually, most of the pictograms were replaced by symbols that combined straight lines and wedges, known as cuneiform script (cuneus is Latin for "wedge").

Writing was invented by temple priests and first used to keep track of temple business. Writing emerged after several hundred years of collecting offerings for the gods and managing temple enterprises. In the Sumerian language, the words for "priest" and "accountant" refer to the same people, suggesting that the priests used their invention to serve as the city's accountants. Writing was used exclusively for commerce between 3100 and 2600 B.C. Starting about 2600 B.C., writing was used for hymns, prayers, myths, and the relaying of wisdom. This first step toward literature occurred before cuneiform text, so much of the meaning of the texts is obscure.

The timing of the invention and refinement of writing reveals an important feature of innovation. It appears that writing didn't just happen, but instead was a response to the practical problem of how to keep track of transactions in a barter economy. The priests in Uruk had been tracking the transactions of the temple for a long time before they came up with the idea of recording transactions on clay tablets. Over the next several centuries, they perfected the practice of writing, motivated by the challenges of record keeping.

The development of writing contributed to urban development because it facilitated specialization and trade. Writing decreased transaction costs, so it increased the net gains from trade, allowing a fuller exploitation of underlying comparative advantages. As writing spread beyond Mesopotamia, the opportunities for specialization widened and trade increased, causing the development of trading cities. In the case of Babylonian cities, writing came after the development of cities, so it merely reinforced the growth of cities.

REFERENCES AND READING

1. Adams, Robert McCormick, *The Evolution of Urban Society: Early Mesopotamia and Prehispanic Mexico*. Chicago: Aldine, 1966.
2. Aharoni, Yohanan, *The Archaeology of the Land of Israel: From the Prehistoric Beginnings to the End of the First Temple Period.* Edited by Miriam Aharoni; translated by Anson F. Rainey. Philadelphia: Westminster Press, 1982.
3. Bottéro, Jean, *Mesopotamia: Writing, Reasoning, and the Gods.* Translated by Zainab Bahrani and Marc Van De Mieroop. Chicago: University of Chicago Press, 1995.
4. Bottéro, Jean, *Religion in Ancient Mesopotamia.* Translated by Teresa Lavender Fagan. Chicago: University of Chicago Press, 2001.
5. Conolly, James, *The Çatalhöyük Flint and Obsidian Industry: Technology and Typology in Context.* Oxford: Archaeopress, 1999.
6. Ferrill, Arther, *The Origins of War: From the Stone Age to Alexander the Great.* Boulder, Colo.: Westview Press, 1997.
7. Kenyon, Kathleen Mary, Dame, *Archaeology in the Holy Land.* New York: W. W. Norton, 1979.
8. Kenyon, Kathleen Mary, Dame, *Digging up Jericho.* London: E. Benn, 1957.
9. Mellaart, James, *Çatal Hüyük; a Neolithic Town in Anatolia*. New York: McGraw-Hill, 1967.
10. Mellaart, James, *The Neolithic of the Near East.* New York: Scribner, 1975.
11. Oppenheim, A. Leo, *Ancient Mesopotamia: Portrait of a Dead Civilization.* Chicago: University of Chicago Press, 1964.
12. O'Sullivan, Arthur, "The First Cities," Chapter 4 in *A Companion to Urban Economics,* edited by R. Arnott and Daniel P. McMillen. Malden, MA; Oxford: Blackwell, 2006.
13. Potts, Daniel T., *Mesopotamian Civilization: The Material Foundations.* Ithaca, NY: Cornell University Press, 1997.
14. Todd, Ian, *Çatal Hüyük in Perspective.* Menlo Park, Calif.: Cummings, 1976.
15. Van de Mieroop, Marc, *The Ancient Mesopotamian City.* Oxford: Clarendon Press, 1997.

PART THREE

Urban Land Use and Housing

Part Three of the book looks at the spatial organization of cities. Chapter 10 introduces the market for land and explores the intraurban location decisions of manufacturing firms. Chapter 11 considers the economic activity in office buildings and explores the economic forces that generate tall buildings in city centers and subcenters. Chapter 12 looks at the spatial aspects of urban housing, focusing on the factors that determine the price of housing at different locations within a city. Chapter 13 describes the distribution of jobs and people within modern metropolitan areas. Chapter 14 discusses the market forces that generated large monocentric cities, the dominant urban form until early in the 20th century. The chapter also develops a model that captures the interactions between the urban labor market and the urban land market. Chapter 15 considers residential location choice when people value different types of neighbors. The key question is, who gets the neighbors who are most highly valued? Chapter 16 discusses a variety of public policies that affect the land market, including zoning, building-permit limits, growth boundaries, and development taxes. Chapter 17 takes a close look at the urban housing market and evaluates the merits of various public policies that respond to the problem of affordability.

CHAPTER 10

Land Rent and Manufacturing Land

The trouble with land is that they're not making it anymore.
—Will Rogers

This chapter starts our exploration of the factors that determine the price of land. Competition for the fixed supply of land means that land is the residual claimant: land rent (the price of land) equals a firm's total revenue minus the non-land cost of production. In more casual terms, the landowner gets what's left over after a firm pays for all of its other inputs. The price of agricultural land reflects is fertility, and the price of manufacturing land reflects its accessibility to customers and workers.

1. FERTILITY AND THE LEFTOVER PRINCIPLE

David Ricardo (1821) is credited with the idea that the price of agricultural land is determined by its fertility. An increase in the fertility of land decreases production cost, so a farmer is willing to pay more to grow crops on the land. Competitive bidding among farmers for fertile land drives its price up to the level at which the winning bidder makes zero economic profit. This is known as the leftover principle: the rent paid by the winning bidder equals total revenue minus non-land cost. In other words, the landowner gets the money left over after the farmer pays for other inputs.

Land Rent, Market Value, and the Price of Land

It will be useful to define two terms, *land rent* and *market value*. Land rent is an annual payment for the right to use a plot of land. For example, a farmer could pay a landowner $300 per year to use a hectare of land to grow corn. The market value of land is the purchase price for land ownership, the amount of money paid to take ownership of the land. For example, the market value of land suitable for growing corn could be $6,000 per hectare.

The market value of a plot of land is determined by the land rent it generates. Land is an asset that yields a stream of income (land rent), and the maximum amount an investor is willing to pay for the asset equals the present value of the stream of income. Suppose the market interest rate is $i = 5$ percent, meaning that \$6,000 invested in a bank account generates interest income of \$300 per year. If an annual stream of rental income $R = \$300$ lasts forever, the present value of the income stream is

$$PV = \frac{R}{i} = \frac{\$300}{0.05} = \$6000$$

The present value of an asset is the maximum amount an investor is willing to pay for the rights to the income stream of the asset. In this case, the maximum amount you would be willing to pay for a hectare of land that generates \$300 of rental income per year is \$6,000, an amount that makes you indifferent between owning the land and earning \$300 per year in rental income, or putting the \$6,000 in the bank and earning \$300 in interest income. In other words, the present value incorporates the opportunity cost of investing in land rather than in a bank account.

In this book, we define the price of land as the annual payment in exchange for the right to use the land. In other words, the price of land is synonymous with land rent. Most other relevant economic variables are defined as streams of revenue or costs. For example, a worker earns an hourly wage or monthly income, and a firm computes its annual profits as annual revenue minus annual cost. Given the simple relationship between rent and market value, it's easy to make the translation from land rent to market value: just divide the annual rent by the market interest rate. Going the other way, if we know the market value of land, the implied price (annual rent) is the market value times the interest rate.

Willingness to Pay for Agricultural Land

The price of land is determined by the profit that can be earned on the land. To illustrate, we start with agricultural land, where profitability is determined by the fertility of land. Consider a region where tenant farmers grow corn on land of varying fertility. The model of agricultural rent has five key assumptions.

1. *Perfect competition in the output market.* Farmers are price takers, and economic profit is zero in the long run.
2. *Common input prices.* The prices of non-land inputs (materials, labor, capital) are the same throughout the region.
3. *Land to highest bidder.* Landowners rent land to the highest bidder.
4. *Zero transport costs.* Transport costs are zero.
5. *National prices.* All prices are determined in the national market and are unaffected by events in the region.

Figure 10–1 shows how to determine a farmer's profit on land that is highly fertile and thus has relatively low production cost. The marginal-cost curve is positively sloped and passes through the average total-cost curve at its minimum point. The cost curves include all the non-land costs of production, including the costs of material, capital, hired labor, and the opportunity cost of being a farmer. The national price of corn is p^*, as shown by the horizontal green dashed line. Applying the marginal principle, a farmer maximizes profit at quantity q^*, where price (marginal revenue)

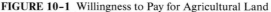

FIGURE 10–1 Willingness to Pay for Agricultural Land

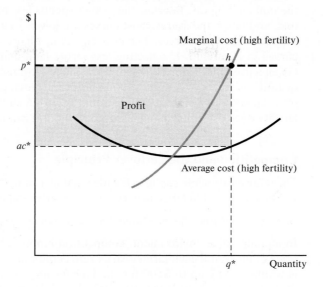

equals marginal cost. The shaded area is the profit rectangle, with height ($p^* - ac^*$) and width q^*. For example, if $p^* = 11$, $ac^* = 6$, and $q^* = 100$, profit = \$500. The economic profit is a farmer's willingness to pay for high-fertility land.

Figure 10–2 shows that the willingness to pay for land is determined by its fertility. The fertility of land determines the positions of the cost curves. A farmer on

FIGURE 10–2 Fertility and the Willingness to Pay for Land

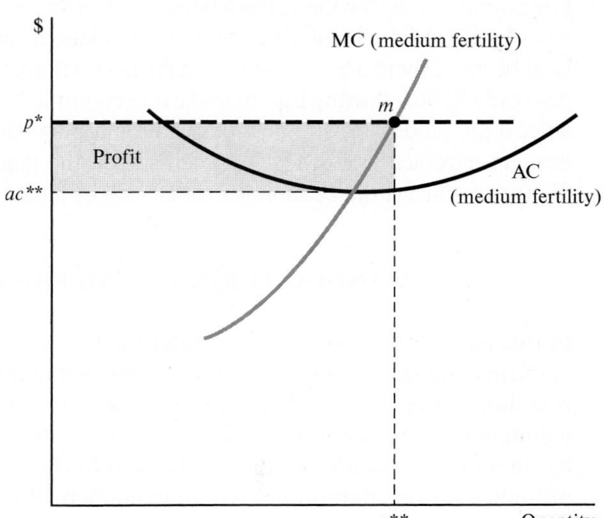

relatively fertile land can produce the same amount of corn with smaller quantities of the non-land inputs. Because the farmer spends less money on seeds, fertilizer, tractors, and labor, the average-cost curves are lower. In general, the higher the fertility, the lower the cost curves. The cost curves in Figure 10–2 are higher than the cost curves in Figure 10–1, reflecting less fertile land and thus higher production cost. Given a fixed market price for corn, the higher cost means that the profit-maximizing quantity is lower ($q^{**} < q^{*}$) and the profit rectangle is smaller. For example, if $p^{*} = 11$, $ac^{**} = 8$, and $q^{**} = 90$, profit = \$270. A shift from high fertility to medium fertility decreases the willingness to pay for land from \$500 to \$270.

Competition and the Leftover Principle

The leftover principle captures the idea that in a competitive land market, a landowner will be paid the difference between a land user's total revenue and non-land cost.

Leftover principle: The equilibrium land rent equals total revenue minus non-land cost.

In a competitive environment, competition among prospective farmers bids up the price of land until each farmer earns zero economic profit. For example, each farmer is willing to pay up to \$500 for the high-fertility land and is forced by competition to do so. At any rent less than \$500, the landowner would be able to find another farmer willing to pay slightly more to use the land. Similarly, the equilibrium rent on the medium-fertility land is \$270. Because the equilibrium land rents make economic profits equal to zero, farmers are indifferent between different plots of land. Although the high-fertility land has lower production costs, the savings in production costs are exactly offset by higher land costs. The leftover principle assumes that although individual plots of land differ in their fertility, farmers are identical in the sense that they have access to the same production technology and input prices.

The leftover principle is inapplicable there are restrictions on market entry. For example, suppose Gene has a patent on a farming technique that reduces production costs by \$200. The landlord cannot expect Gene to pay a rent of \$700 for high-fertility land because there are no competing farmers willing to pay this amount. Instead, Gene pays only \$500, allowing him to make an economic profit of \$200. This surplus attributable to the patent is also known as economic rent. But once the patent expires and all farmers have access to the same technology, the landowner can increase land rent to \$700 and convert the economic rent earned by a patent holder into higher land rent.

2. MANUFACTURING: LAND PRICE AND LOCATION

In this part of the chapter we consider the intracity location patterns of manufacturing firms. We start by exploring the factors that determine how much a manufacturer is willing to pay for land at different locations in a city. In an urban environment, the willingness to pay for a plot of land depends on its accessibility rather than its fertility. In a market economy, land is allocated to the highest bidder, and so the land bid of manufacturers determines where manufacturing firms locate. As we'll see, urban manufacturing employment is decentralized and dispersed, with most firms locating close to highways connected to the intercity highway system.

Freight Cost versus Labor Cost

We can use a simple model of a manufacturing sector to develop the basic concepts of the land bids of manufacturers. Suppose manufacturing firms produce bicycles, using land, labor, and intermediate inputs such as spokes, frames, and tires. The simple model has a number of assumptions about inputs and outputs.

1. *Fixed input and output quantities.* Each firm produces a fixed quantity of bicycles with a fixed quantity of each input, including one hectare of land.
2. *Fixed input and output prices.* The price of bicycles is fixed, and so are the prices of intermediate inputs.
3. *Central freight terminal.* Firms import intermediate inputs from other cities and export bicycles to other cities, and both imports and exports go through a central freight terminal (a train terminal or port).
4. *Intracity freight.* Firms use horse carts to transport intermediate inputs and bicycles between a factory site and the central freight terminal. For the typical firm, freight cost per kilometer is $f = \$10$; if a firm moves 1 kilometer farther from the center, its freight cost increases by \$10.
5. *Labor cost.* The wage paid to bicycle workers compensates workers for commuting costs. The wage is highest at the city center and decreases as a firm moves toward its suburban workforce. For the typical firm, a 1 kilometer move away from the center decreases the labor cost by $c = \$2$.

Figure 10–3 shows that spatial variation in labor and freight cost generates spatial variation in the manufacturing bid for land.

- *Spatial variation in cost.* The horizontal measures distance to the central freight terminal. The lower horizontal line is the cost of intermediate inputs. Freight cost increases linearly at a rate $f = \$10$ per km. Labor cost is \$40 at the center, and decreases at a rate $c = \$4$ per km. Total cost increases linearly from \$50 at the center to \$80 at a distance of 5 km. The slope of the total-cost curve is \$6: a one-unit increase in distance increases freight cost by \$10 and decreases labor cost by \$4, for a net increase of \$6.
- *Bid for land.* By assumption, total revenue (price times quantity) is the same at all locations. The vertical arrows show the bids for land, equal to the excess of total revenue over total cost. At the central freight terminal, the bid is \$42 = \$92 − \$50. As the distance to the terminal increases, total cost increases at a rate of \$6 per km, so the bid decreases by \$6 per km. For example, the bid is \$36 at a distance of 1 km and \$12 at a distance of 5 km.

We can use some simple algebra to gain insights into the position and slope of the bid curve. Applying the leftover principle, a firm's willingness to pay for land at location x equals total revenue minus non-land cost:

$$r(x) \cdot T = \text{Total revenue} - \text{Freight cost}(x) - \text{Labor cost}(x) - \text{Intermediate input cost}$$

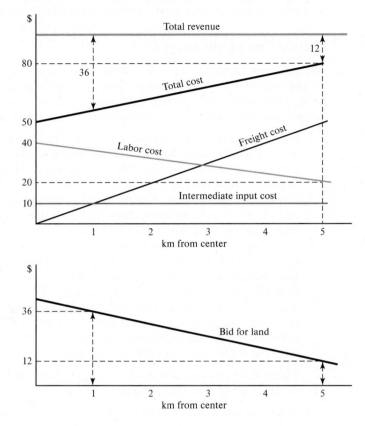

FIGURE 10–3 Manufacturing Rent in a Horse Cart City

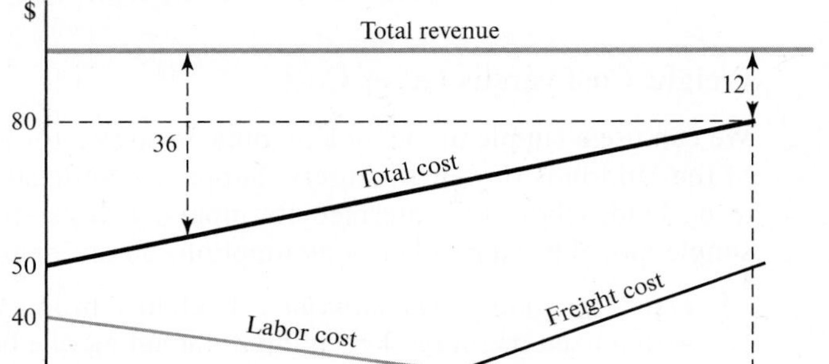

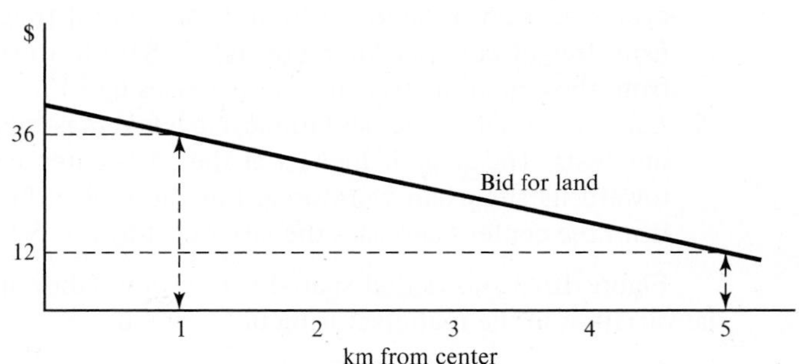

where $r(x)$ is the bid per unit land and T is the quantity of land occupied by the firm (lot size). The bid per unit of land is simply the willingness to pay divided by the lot size:

$$r(x) = \frac{\text{Total revenue} - \text{Freight cost}(x) - \text{Labor cost}(x) - \text{Intermediate input cost}}{T}$$

Freight cost and labor cost vary with distance x (at a rate f for freight and c for labor), so the slope of the bid curve is

$$\frac{\Delta r}{\Delta x} = \frac{-f + c}{T}$$

If $f = \$10$ and $c = \$4$ the slope of the bid curve is

$$\frac{\Delta r}{\Delta x} = \frac{-f + c}{T} = \frac{-10 + 4}{1} = -\$6$$

The simple model incorporates the transportation technology of the early 20th century. The truck had not yet been invented, so intracity freight was by horse cart, a relatively slow and costly freight system. In addition, intercity freight was by ship or train, so manufacturers were tied to a central port or railroad terminal. In contrast, workers commuted on relatively fast streetcars from suburban residential areas to central core areas. In other words, the cost of transporting inputs and outputs (represented by f) was high relative to the cost of transporting workers (represented by c). Because $f > c$, the manufacturing bid curve is negatively sloped, and manufacturers outbid other land users for sites close to the central freight terminal.

The Intracity Truck

The intracity truck, developed in 1910, was twice as fast as a horse cart and less costly to operate. The use of the truck increased rapidly: between 1910 and 1920, the number of trucks in Chicago increased from 800 to 23,000. Figure 10–4 shows manufacturing rent in a city with intracity trucks. The change from Figure 10–3 is that the freight-cost curve is flatter, reflecting the lower freight cost per km.

FIGURE 10–4 Manufacturing Rent in a Truck City

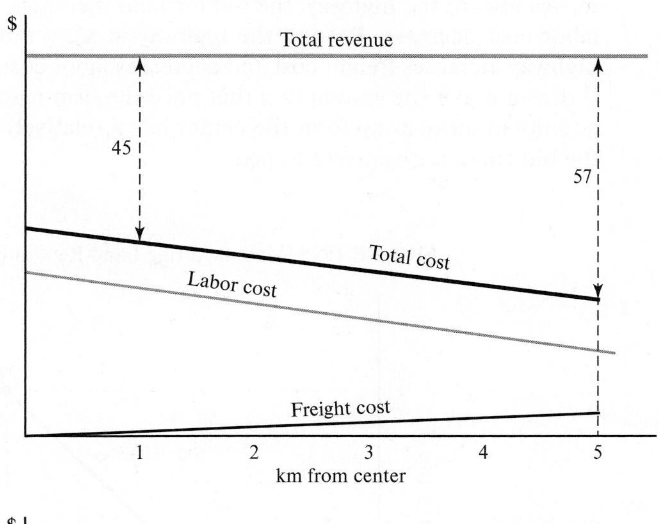

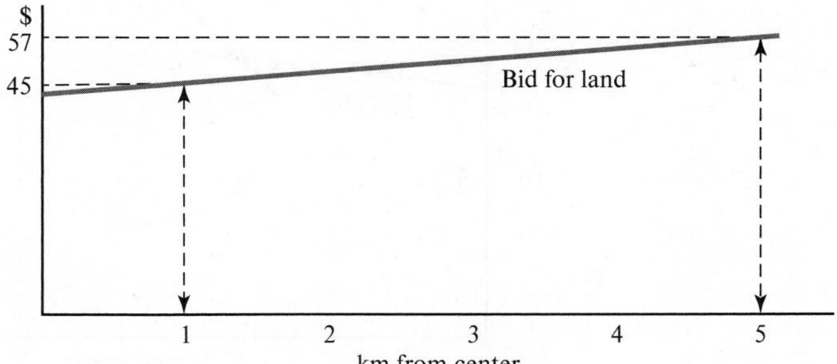

The total-cost curve is now negatively sloped because as a firm moves away from the center, the savings in labor cost dominates the increase in freight cost. As a result, the rent curve is positively sloped. To illustrate the positive slope, suppose the unit freight cost f decreases from \$10 to \$1. In this case, the slope of the bid curve is +\$3:

$$\frac{\Delta r}{\Delta x} = \frac{-f + c}{T} = \frac{-1 + 4}{1} = \$3$$

When the cost of transporting inputs and outputs is low relative to the cost of transporting workers, a firm bids more for land farther from the freight terminal, and thus closer to its suburban workforce.

Intercity Truck and Highways in a Beltway City

Consider next the implications of introducing an intercity highway network. The combination of the intercity truck and the highway system freed manufacturers from their dependence on the central port or rail terminal. Figure 10–5 shows the effects of a circumferential highway at x''. The bid curve peaks at the highway: as a firm moves toward the highway, the bid for land increases because both freight cost and labor cost decrease. Beyond the highway at x'', a move away from the center and highway increases freight cost and decreases labor cost. The bid curve in Figure 10–5 is drawn under the assumption that once the firm reaches the suburban highway, an additional move away from the center has a relatively small effect on labor cost, so the bid curve is negatively sloped.

FIGURE 10–5 Manufacturing Land Rent in Beltway City

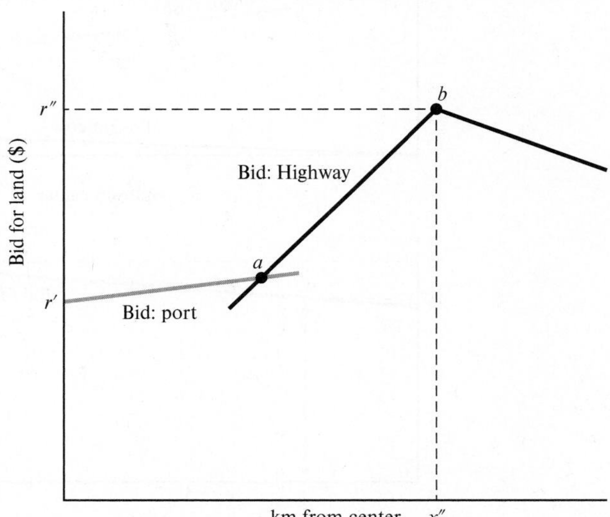

FIGURE 10–6 Land Rent Surface in Beltway City

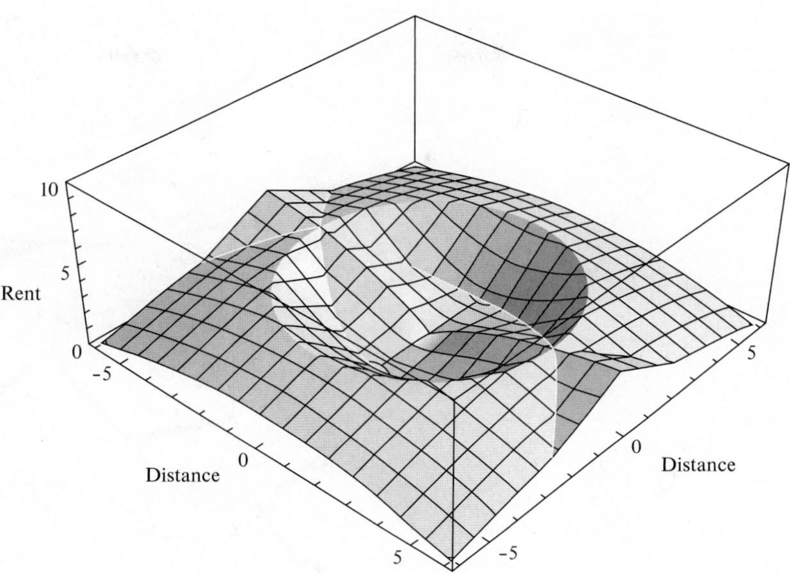

It will be useful to compare the land bid for the central location ($x = 0$) to the bid for the highway location ($x = x''$). At both locations, freight cost is zero because the firm is located next to either the central terminal or the highway. The difference between the two locations is that workers demand a higher wage at the center to compensate for longer commuting distances. The central location has a higher labor cost, so manufacturers' bid for land is lower: $r' < r''$. This is consistent with the leftover principle: a higher wage generates a lower bid for land.

Figure 10–6 shows the land bid surface in a highway-based city. There is no port or central rail terminal, so manufacturers rely on highways to import intermediate inputs and export output. An intercity highway runs through the city center and a circumferential highway is connected to the intercity highway. Wages incorporate commuting costs, so labor cost per firm decreases as the distance to the center increases. Starting from the center, a move along the intercity highway increases the bid for land because labor cost decreases. The bid for land reaches its maximum at the beltway, where the freight cost is zero and the labor cost is lower than at highway locations closer to the center. Beyond the beltway, labor cost decreases at a relatively low rate, so the bid for land decreases as freight cost increases.

Manufacturing Rent and the Spatial Distribution of Manufacturing

Figure 10–7 shows the spatial distribution of manufacturing in Denver in 2015. The maps show census tracts as jigsaw pieces, which are extruded (pushed up) to a height equal to its manufacturing employment density. The manufacturing density equals

FIGURE 10–7 Spatial Distribution of Manufacturing Employment in Denver, 2014

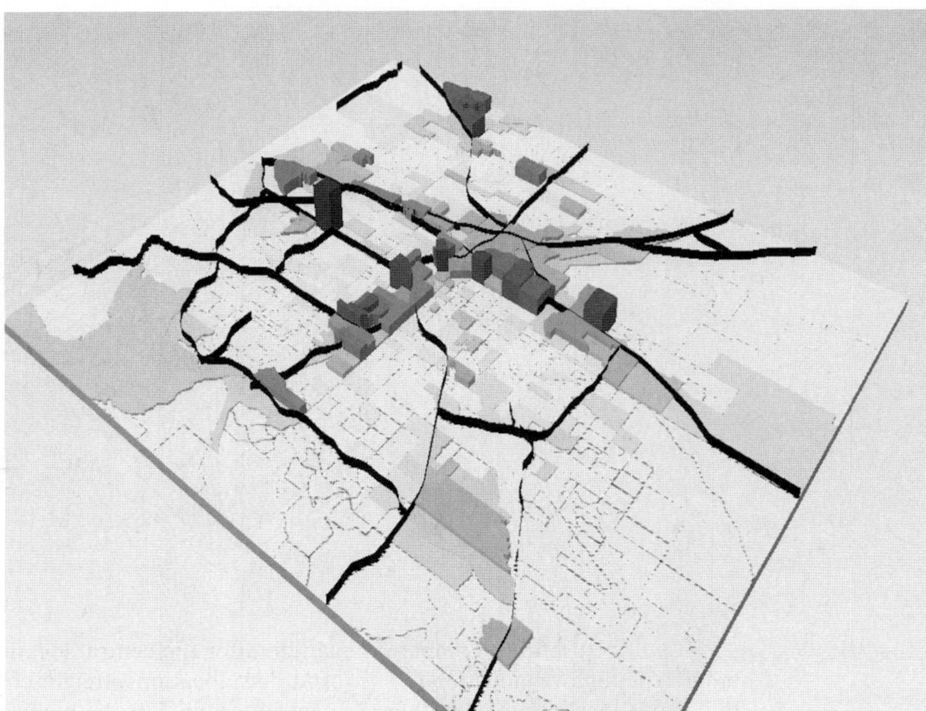

the number of manufacturing workers per hectare in the census tract. Recall that a hectare is a 100-meter square, roughly twice the area of a football field. The ribbons in the maps show the freeways that run through the metropolitan area. As in many large metropolitan areas, the bulk of manufacturing employment is in areas accessible to highways.

REVIEW THE CONCEPTS

1. If a hectare of land generates $100 of rental income per year and the market interest rate is 5 percent, the market value of the land is $[______].
2. The price of agricultural land increases with its [______], and the price of urban land increases with its [______].
3. According to the [______] principle, a firm's bid for land equals [______] minus [______]. The key assumption underlying this principle is [______] in the market for land.
4. Suppose a new fertilizer decreases the production cost per hectare by $120. Suppose a farmer offers to split the benefits of the new fertilizer equally with

the landowner. The landowner will [_____] (accept, reject) the offer, and the equilibrium price of land will increase by $[_____].

5. In a city with a central export node, the expression for the slope of the bid curve for manufacturing land is [_____] /lot size. The curve will be negatively sloped if [_____] is large relative to [_____], that is, if the cost of moving [_____] is large relative to the cost of moving [_____].
6. Consider the bid curve for manufacturing land in a city with a central export node and horse carts. An increase in the unit freight cost makes the curve [_____] (choose steeper or flatter). An increase in the unit commuting cost makes the curve [_____] (choose steeper or flatter). An increase in the price of manufacturing goods shifts the curve [_____] {↑, ↓, −}.
7. The replacement of horse carts with the intracity truck decreased the cost of moving [_____] relative to the cost of moving [_____], making it possible that the bid curve for manufacturing land is [_____] sloped.
8. Consider a city with a central export node (a port), trucks, and a suburban beltway. The bid for land adjacent to the beltway will be [_____] than the bid for land adjacent to the central export node because [_____] is lower at the [_____].
9. Comparative Statics–What's Your Sign?
For each pair of variables, indicate whether the relationship is positive, negative, neutral, or ambiguous.

Parameter	Choice Variable	Relationship
land fertility	willingness to pay for farm land	[______]
price of cotton	willingness to pay for cotton land	[______]
price of irrigation water	willingness to pay for watermelon land	[______]
wage	willingness to pay for manufacturing land	[______]

APPLY THE CONCEPTS

1. *Innovative Farmer and Land Rent*
Greengenes grows corn on the land he rents at a price of $500. Suppose Greengenes develops a new genetically modified organism (GMO) that decreases production cost for corn by $300. Greengenes will pay land rent of $800 if . . . Illustrate.
2. *Gandhi and the Leftover Principle*
In 1917, Mahatma Gandhi settled a dispute between Indian farmers and British landowners. Under a sharecropping arrangement, each indigo farmer paid 15 percent of the harvest to the landowner. When landowners heard about the development of synthetic indigo, they quickly sold the land to the farmers, before the farmers heard about synthetic indigo. When the price of indigo dropped, the farmers who had purchased land demanded their money back. As Gandhi's research assistant, your task is to compute the appropriate refund for the typical

new landowner. You can assume that (i) the annual output is 100 units of indigo per hectare; (ii) the initial price of indigo is $10; (iii) farmers have bank accounts that earn 10 percent per year; and (iv) the non-land production cost per hectare is $850.

a. The sharecropping arrangement is consistent with the leftover principle because . . . The market value of land is [_____].
b. Suppose the development of synthetic indigo decreases the price of indigo to $8.51. The new market value for indigo land is $[_____].
c. Suppose the land can produce rice, with a price of $7 per unit, a quantity of 110 units per hectare per year, and a non-land cost of $660 per hectare per year. The appropriate compensation for a farmer who purchased a hectare before knowing about synthetic indigo is $[_____].

3. *Fair Trade Cocoa*

You are the economist for an NGO that is organizing a certification program for "fair-trade" cocoa producers. Assume (i) the annual output of land is 100 units of cocoa per hectare; (ii) the initial price of cocoa is $12.40; (iii) farmers have bank accounts that earn 10 percent per year; (iv) the labor cost (wages) for cocoa workers is $400 per hectare; and (v) the other non-land cost for cocoa is $200 per hectare. Under a fair-trade agreement, farmers will increase wages to $500 per hectare.

a. Predict the quantitative effect (a number) of the wage boost on the market value of cocoa land. Illustrate.
b. Describe an amendment to the fair-trade agreement that would make it neutral with respect to the market value of cocoa land.

4. *Matter Transmitter for Manufacturing*

Consider a manufacturing industry that exports its output by ship. Each firm has total revenue per month of $1,400 and a monthly non-land production cost of $400. Each firm initially transports its output from its factory at location x to the port ($x = 0$) on trucks. A firm's freight cost is $100 per block from the port. Suppose a second transport option is developed: For a monthly rental cost of $300, a firm can use a matter transmitter to transport its output from its factory to a matter receiver at the port, up to a distance of seven blocks. For a firm using the matter transmitter, the marginal cost of transportation is zero. A product can be transported using a matter transmitter only once (chaining transmitters is impossible) and a firm must use either the truck or the transmitter, not both. All the relevant markets are competitive.

a. Illustrate the effects of the matter transmitter on the bid-rent curve for manufacturers from $x = 0$ to $x = 10$.
b. Firm's will use the transmitter for locations . . .
c. Among economic agents within the city, the transmitter generates benefits for [_____] Illustrate.

5. *Manufacturers and Airports*

Consider a manufacturing firm that occupies one hectare of land. The firm transports over half of its output on trucks via an interstate highway four miles east of the city center ($x = 4$) and transports less than half its output on airplanes that leave from an airport seven miles east of the city center ($x = 7$). Draw the firm's bid-rent curve for $x = 0$ to $x = 10$.

6. *Space Z Location*
You are the economist for Space Z, a producer of space satellites with total revenue = \$246 million per year. The material inputs are imported though a port at the center of a semicircular coastal city, and the output (satellites) are launched into earth orbit from the production site. For technical reasons, the firm must locate its production site along the coast. The firm's annual costs (in \$ million) are as follows. The cost of materials is \$30 at the port, and a one-mile increase in distance to the port (x) increases material transport cost by \$16. Labor cost is $w(x) = 100 + (144/x)$.
a. The cost-minimizing location is $x^* = $ [______].
b. At the cost-minimizing site (x^*), the firm is willing to pay \$[______] per year for land.

REFERENCES AND READING

1. Anas, Alex, Richard Arnott, and Kenneth A. Small. "Urban Spatial Structure." *Journal of Economic Literature* 34 (1998), pp. 1426–64.
2. Baum-Snow, Nathaniel, "Did Highways Cause Suburbanization?" *Quarterly Journal of Economics* 122.2 (2007), pp. 775–805.
3. Duranton, Gilles, and Diego Puga, "Urban Land Use," Chapter 8 in *Handbook of Urban and Regional Economics Volume 5,* edited by Gilles Duranton, J. Vernon Henderson and William C. Strange. Amsterdam: Elsevier, 2015.
4. George, Henry. *Progress and Poverty.* New York: Schalkenbach Foundation, 1954.
5. Glaeser, Edward, and Matthew Kahn, "Decentralized Employment and the Transformation of the American City." NBER Working Paper, March 2001.
6. Glaeser, Edward, Matthew Kahn, and Chenghuan Chu, "Job Sprawl: Employment Location in U.S. Metropolitan Areas." Brookings Institution Survey Series, May 2001, pp. 1–8.
7. Irwin, Elena G., and Nancy E. Bockstael, "The Spatial Pattern of Land Use in the United States," Chapter 6 in *A Companion to Urban Economics,* edited by Richard J. Arnott and Daniel P. McMillen. New York: Wiley-Blackwell, 2006.
8. Lang, Robert E., "Office Sprawl: The Evolving Geography of Business." The Brookings Institution Survey Series, October 2000.
9. Lang, Robert E., *Edgeless Cities.* Washington, DC: Brookings, 2003.
10. McMillen, Daniel P., "One Hundred Fifty Years of Land Values in Chicago: A Nonparametric Approach." *Journal of Urban Economics* 40 (1996), pp. 100–24.
11. Mills, Edwin S., *Studies in the Structure of the Urban Economy.* Baltimore: Johns Hopkins, 1972.

12. Moses, Leon, and Harold Williamson, "The Location of Economic Activity in Cities," in *Readings in Urban Economics,* edited by Matthew Edel and Jerome Rothenberg. New York: Macmillan, 1972.
13. Redding, Stephen J., and Matthew Turner, "Transportation Costs and the Spatial Organization of Economic Activity," Chapter 20 in *Handbook of Urban and Regional Economics Volume 5,* edited by Gilles Duranton, J. Vernon Henderson, and William C. Strange. Amsterdam: Elsevier, 2015.
14. Sivitanidou, R., and P. Sivitanides, "Industrial Rent Differentials: The Case of Greater Los Angeles." *Environment and Planning A* 27 (1995), pp. 1133–46.

CHAPTER 11

Office Space and Tall Buildings

This chapter explores the links between the price of office space, the height of buildings, and the price of land. The price of office space is relatively high in office clusters, where office workers from different firms can interact at a relatively low cost. Office buildings are relatively tall where the price of space is relatively high. The price of commercial land is relatively high where the price of office space is relatively high and buildings are relatively tall. In some cases, tall buildings result from inefficient competition to be the tallest building in the city.

1. THE PRICE OF OFFICE SPACE

In this part of the chapter we explore the pricing of office space. Firms that use offices as production facilities gather, process, and distribute tacit information, defined as information that cannot be codified for distribution on a piece of paper or a web page. The transmission of tacit information requires face-to-face contact between high-skilled workers who have a high opportunity cost of travel. Some examples of workers who transmit input and output in this way are bankers, accountants, financial consultants, marketing strategists, product designers, and lawyers. The transmission of tacit information involves interactions between workers from different firms, and firms can reduce travel time for interaction by locating close to related firms.

A key factor in the price of office space is accessibility. Office firms are willing to pay more for more office space that is accessible to other office firms. The price of office space varies in three dimensions: latitude, longitude, and altitude. We will start by exploring how the price of office space varies across surface locations: latitude and longitude. Then we consider how the price of office space varies with altitude (building height).

Interaction Travel Cost for Office Firms

To focus first on the price of office in terms of surface location, consider office space on the ground floor of a one-floor office building. Suppose that office firms are

FIGURE 11-1 Interaction Travel Distances

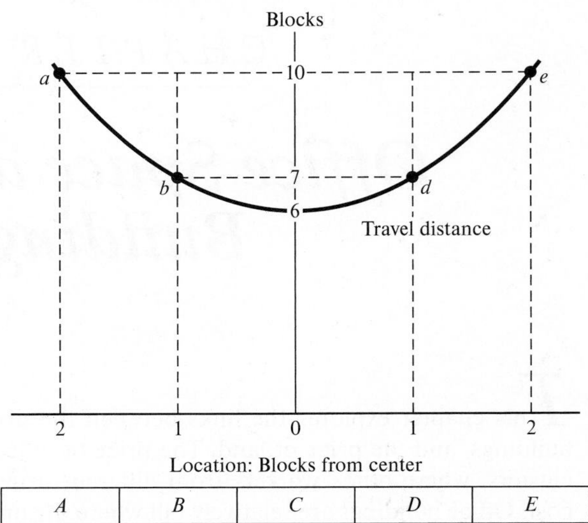

identical: each firm produces the same quantity of output and uses the same bundle of inputs, including one unit of office space. Each firm sells its output at the same market price.

The willingness to pay for office space at a particular location depends in part on the site's accessibility to office firms at other locations. In Figure 11-1, five firms in a central business district (CBD) are spaced one block apart in a straight line. Workers from each firm travel to each of the other firms to exchange information. A firm's total travel distance for interaction depends on the firm's location relative to other firms.

1. *Median firm (C).* The firm travels 1 block to *B* and *D*, and 2 blocks to *A* and *E*, for a total of 6 blocks of travel.
2. *Intermediate firms (B) and (D).* Firm *B* travels one block to *A* and *C*, 2 blocks to *D*, and 3 blocks to *E*, for a total of 8 blocks. Similarly, firm *D* travels a total of 7 blocks.
3. *Endpoint firms (A) and (E).* Firm *A* travels 1 block to *B*, 2 blocks to *C*, 3 blocks to *D*, and 4 blocks to *E*, for a total of 10 blocks. Similarly, firm *E* travels a total of 10 blocks in the opposite direction.

The principle of median location states that the total travel distance is minimized at the median location. In Figure 11-1, firm *C* is at the median location, defined as the location that separates the other firms into two equal halves, with two firms on each side. As we move away from the median location, total travel distance increases because the new location is farther from at least half of the other firms and closer to fewer than half of the other firms. As shown in Figure 11-1, a move from the median location (*C*) to an intermediate location (*B* or *D*) increases travel distance from 6 blocks to 7 blocks.

As we move away from the median location, travel distance increases at an increasing rate. A one-block move away from the median location increases travel distance from 6 to 7, but an additional one-block move increases travel distance from 7 blocks to 10 blocks. As we move in one-block steps away from the median location, we move farther from progressively more firms and closer to progressively fewer firms. As a result, total travel distance increases by progressively larger amounts.

Willingness to Pay for Office Space

Figure 11–2 shows how to determine a firm's willingness to pay for office space at different sites. The total cost is the sum of interaction travel costs and other costs. To simplify, we assume for now that other costs do not vary across space. The interaction cost is determined by the total interaction travel distance, travel speed, and the opportunity cost of travel time. As the distance from the center increases, the travel distance increases at increasing rate, so the interaction cost increases at an

FIGURE 11–2 Location and the Willingness to Pay for Office Space

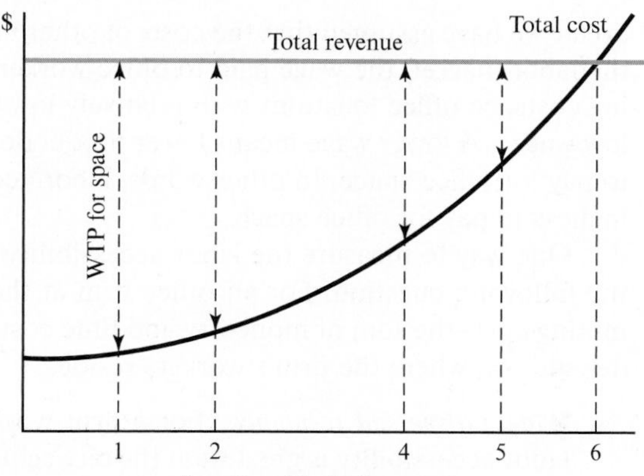

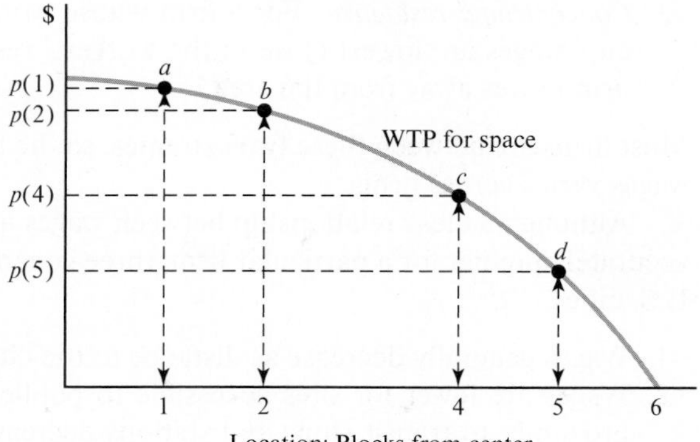

increasing rate as well. As a result, total cost increases at an increasing rate. In the upper panel of Figure 11-2, the total-cost curve is convex.

The firm's willingness to pay for space equals total revenue minus total cost. In Figure 11-2, total revenue does not vary with location. The willingness to pay is shown as the gap between the horizontal total-revenue curve and the convex total-cost curve. This is shown by the dashed arrows and the negatively sloped WTP curve in the lower panel.

The WTP curve is negatively sloped and concave. The curve is negatively sloped because interaction cost increases with the distance to the center: more distant locations are more costly and less profitable, so firms are willing to pay less for office space. The WTP curve is concave because as we move away from the center, interaction cost increases at an increasing rate, meaning that the willingness to pay decreases at an increasing rate. For example, a move from one block from the center to two blocks increases travel cost by a relatively small amount and decreases the WTP by a small amount, $p(1) - p(2)$. A move from four blocks to five blocks increases travel cost by a larger amount and decreases the WTP per hectare by a larger amount, equal to $p(4) - p(5)$.

Labor Accessibility, Wages, and the Willingness to Pay for Office Space

So far we have assumed that the costs of other inputs are the same at all locations. In the labor market, the wage paid to office workers compensates workers for commuting costs, so office locations with relatively low commuting costs will have relatively low wages. A lower wage means lower production cost, and thus a higher willingness to pay for office space. In other words, labor accessibility translates into higher willingness to pay for office space.

One way to measure the labor accessibility of a particular location is to answer the following question. For an office firm at the location, what is the average commuting cost–the sum of monetary and time cost–for the firm's workers? The answer depends on where the firm's workers reside.

1. *Widely dispersed residence.* For a firm whose workers live throughout the city, labor accessibility is greatest at the city center, the median location for the firm's workforce. As a result, central locations have relatively low wages and labor cost.
2. *Concentrated residence.* For a firm whose workers live in a specific area of the city, wages are lowest close to the workers' residential area and increase as the firm moves away from the area.

Most firms are between these two extremes, so the relationship between location and wages varies across firms.

Although a clear relationship between wages and location may be impossible to accurately predict for a particular firm, three general patterns have been observed in U.S. cities.

1. Wages generally decrease as distance to the city center increases.
2. Wages are lower for sites accessible to public transit. This is sensible because proximity to transit stops and stations decreases commuting time and thus decreases wages.

FIGURE 11–3 Willingness to Pay and Commuting Mode

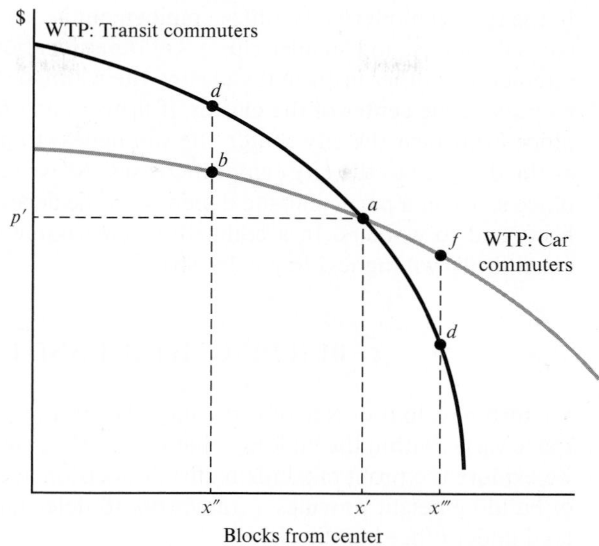

3. Wages are lower for sites close to suburban highways. This is sensible because proximity to highways decreases commuting time between a highway and the workplace, decreasing wages.

Figure 11–3 shows the implications of variation in labor accessibility and wages on the willingness to pay for office space.

1. *Public transit commuters.* If there is a transit node such as a subway station at the city center and a firm's workers commute by public transit, wages are lower closer to the city center. Starting from block x', a move to block $x'' < x'$ increases the willingness to pay for office space for two reasons: (i) lower interaction cost and (ii) lower wages. Therefore, the willingness to pay increases by a relatively large amount. In contrast, a move away from the center decreases the willingness to pay as both wages and interaction cost increase. In general, accessibility to central transit increases the slope of the willingness to pay curve as the advantage of a central location increases.
2. *Car commuters.* If a firm's workers live in a suburban area and commute by car, wages are higher closer to the city center. Starting from block x', a move to block $x'' < x'$ has conflicting effects on the WTP: interaction cost decreases but wages increase. Therefore, the willingness to pay increases by a relatively small amount. A move in the opposite direction reverses the tradeoff: interaction cost increases while wages decrease. In general, the employment of a suburban workforce decreases the slope of the willingness to pay curve because there are tradeoffs associated with a central location: interaction costs are lower, but wages are higher.

Office Subcenters

In the typical modern city, office employment is divided between a city center, suburban subcenters, and smaller clusters at other locations. For each cluster where firms interact with other firms in the cluster, the willingness to pay for office space reaches its peak at the center of the cluster. If firms in an office subcenter also interact with office firms near the city center, the willingness to pay for office space will decrease as the distance to the city center increases. As we've seen, the willingness to pay for office space at a particular site depends on the accessibility of the site to other office firms and to workers. In a competitive environment, the price of office space will equal firms' willingness to pay for space.

2. BUILDING HEIGHT AND LAND PRICES

We turn next to the issue of verticality. We start by looking at how the price of office space varies within the building, that is, how the price varies from floor to floor. Then we explore the profit-maximizing firm's decision about building height. The analysis of building height provides a framework to determine the willingness to pay for the land under office buildings.

The Price of Office Space and Building Height

Consider an office firm that has chosen a particular location x'. The base price of office space (for ground-level office space in a one-floor building) is $p(x')$. The base price reflects the accessibility of the site to other office firms and the office workforce. The question is, How much more (or less) is the firm willing to pay for office space on higher floors–the second, third, fourth, and so on? There are two effects to consider.

1. *Intra-building travel cost.* As the floor level increases, the firm's workers will spend more time traveling within the building on their way to interact with other firms in the cluster. In other words, the firm's vertical travel cost increases, so the firm's willingness to pay for office space decreases.
2. *Altitude amenity.* Suppose workers get a thrill from working at a greater altitude, because of a better view or a sense of higher status. In a competitive labor market, better working conditions generate lower wages and thus lower production costs for a firm. If wages decrease as altitude increases, the willingness to pay for office space increases with the floor level.

Figure 11–4 shows the combined effects of intra-building travel cost and altitude amenities on the price of office space. We consider two types of vertical transportation technology.

- *Stairways.* Intra-building travel cost increases rapidly with height, pulling down the willingness to pay for office space. Although the amenity effect dampens the negative effect of travel cost on willingness to pay, the amenity effect is never

FIGURE 11-4 Price of Office Space and Building Height

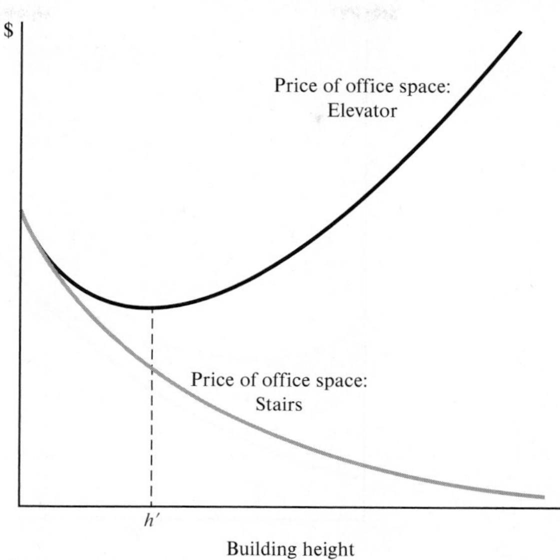

strong enough to offset the relatively high intra-building travel cost. The willingness to pay curve is negatively sloped.

- *Elevator.* Intra-building travel cost increases rapidly for the first few floors: workers either use the stairs or incur the fixed time cost of waiting for an elevator. Beyond the first few floors, as altitude increases, travel cost increases slowly because an elevator moves quickly from one floor to the next. For the first h' floors, the altitude amenity partly offsets the travel-cost effect. For higher floors, the altitude amenity dominates the travel-cost effect. The willingness to pay curve is positively sloped for building height of at least h' floors.

Profit-Maximizing Building Height

Consider next the role of a building firm. The firm builds an office structure and rents space to office firms. The key decision concerns building height, and the firm's task is to choose the building height (number of floors of office space) that maximizes the firm's economic profit.

The firm can use the marginal principle to choose the profit-maximizing height. The marginal benefit of an additional floor is the additional revenue that can be collected from office firms on the floor. Suppose that each floor has one unit of office space, so the additional revenue is simply the price of office space. Figure 11-5 shows the marginal-benefit curve for a building with elevators. On the cost side, the marginal cost of a floor equals the additional construction cost from building one more floor. The marginal-cost curve is positively sloped because a taller building

FIGURE 11-5 Profit-Maximizing Building Height

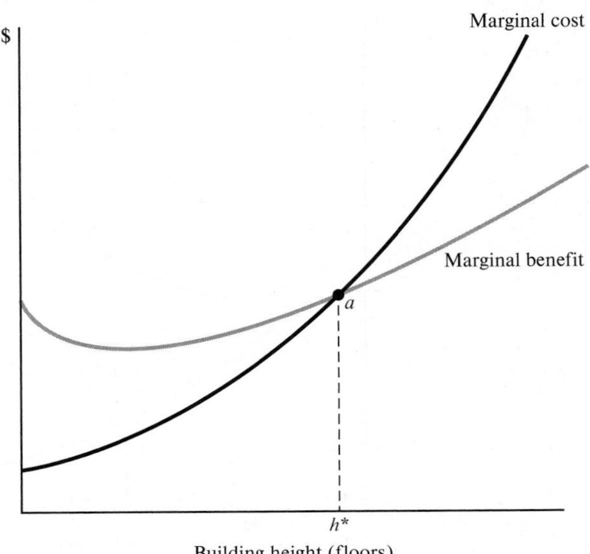

requires more reinforcement to support its more concentrated weight. As the number of floors increases, construction cost increases at an increasing rate, so the marginal-cost curve is positively sloped.

In Figure 11-5, the profit-maximizing height is h^* floors, where the marginal benefit equals the marginal cost. For a shorter building, the marginal benefit of building up (revenue from an additional floor) exceeds the marginal cost, so it would be sensible to build a taller building. For a building taller than h^* floors, the marginal cost of building up exceeds the marginal benefit, so a shorter building would be more profitable.

The Willingness to Pay for Land

We can use the building-height framework to show how much a building firm is willing to pay for the land under the building. The willingness to pay for land equals the economic profit to be earned by the building firm. In other words, the building firm is willing to pay up to its economic profit for the rights to build a profitable building.

In graphical terms, we compute the economic profit as the gap between the marginal-benefit curve and the marginal-cost curve up to the profit-maximizing building height h^*. In Figure 11-6, the economic profit from floor h' is shown by the gap between the marginal-benefit curve (rental revenue on the first floor, shown by point b) and the marginal-cost curve (construction cost for the floor h', shown by point c). In other words, the economic profit for floor h' equals $mb' - mc'$. For each floor of the building, we can compute the economic profit by measuring the gap between the

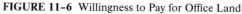

FIGURE 11–6 Willingness to Pay for Office Land

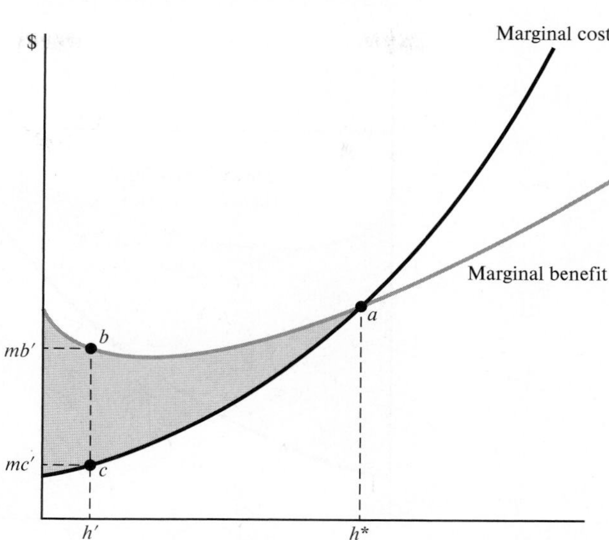

marginal-benefit curve and marginal-cost curve. Adding up these floor profits across the h^* floors in the building, we get the shaded area between the two curves.

Competition among building firms ensures that the price of land equals the willingness to pay for land. If one builder offered to pay less than the willingness to pay (economic profit), the landowner could find another builder who is willing to pay more. Bidding among competing builders will bid up the price of land until it reaches the economic profit from using the land. This is the leftover principle: Competition among potential land users ensures that economic profit (total revenue − total nonland cost) goes to landowners.

The next step in our analysis of office land use is to explore the effects of spatial variation in the base price of office space. Recall that the base price of office space (for ground-level space) varies with the accessibility of the location to other office firms. Figure 11–7 shows the effects of moving closer to the center, where greater accessibility to other office firms generates a higher base price of office space. The higher base price of office space generates a higher marginal-benefit curve for building height. The marginal principle is satisfied with a taller building: $h^{**} > h^*$. An increase in the base price of office space—a result of increased accessibility to other office firms—increases the profit-maximizing building height.

A second result is that the price of land is higher close to the city center. In Figure 11–7, the economic profit of the more accessible building is higher, as indicated by the larger shaded area between the marginal-benefit curve and marginal-cost curve. The greater accessibility of a more central location translates into a higher price of land. In other words, taller buildings and higher land prices go together.

FIGURE 11-7 Greater Accessibility Generates a Taller Building and a Higher Land Price

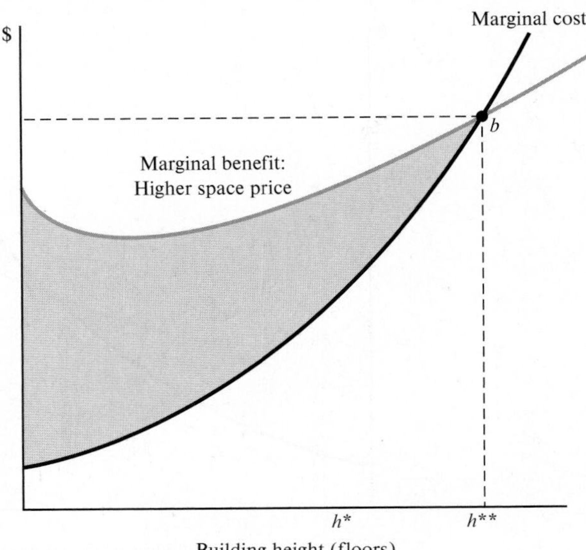

Input Substitution

For a different perspective on the link between the price of land and building height, consider a firm that is evaluating alternative sites for an office building. At each location, the firm takes the price of land as given, and the firm's objective is to minimize the cost of producing a building with a fixed amount of office space. The solution to the cost-minimization task involves a choice of two inputs to the production process, capital and land.

The isoquant in Figure 11-8 shows the different combinations of land and capital that generate the same quantity of office space. Point s is the input bundle required for a short building (k' is small) on a large quantity of land (L' is large). Moving upward along the isoquant, point m represents a medium-height building, and point t represents a tall building. A taller building requires more capital because it requires (i) extra reinforcement to support its more concentrated weight and (ii) transport systems for vertical travel within the building.

We can illustrate the rationale for a negatively sloped isoquant with a simple thought experiment. Suppose you use a crane to build a 25-story office building by stacking 25 standard mobile homes on top of one another. There are two problems with this construction plan.

1. *Accordion problem: upper floors will crush lower floors.* This problem can be prevented by extra reinforcement (more capital).
2. *Rappelling problem: workers must rappel from one floor to another.* This problem can be avoided by adding elevators and stairs (more capital).

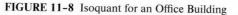

FIGURE 11-8 Isoquant for an Office Building

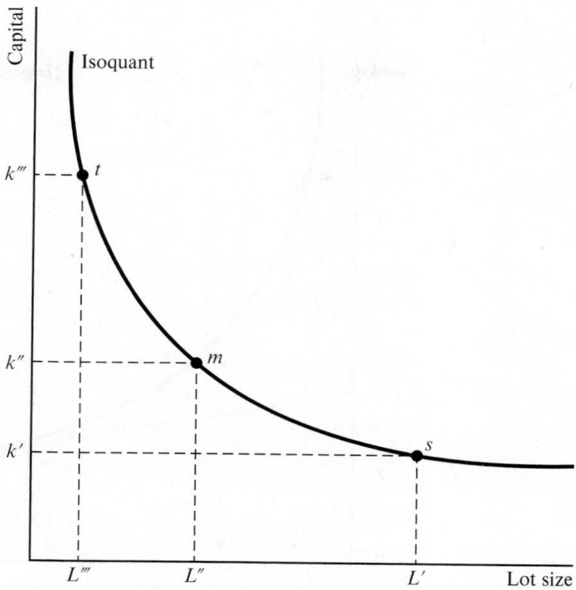

Figure 11-8 illustrates the solution to these two problems. A tall building (point t) requires roughly three times as much capital as the short building (point s): k''' is roughly three times k'.

Recall the input-choice model of microeconomics (reviewed in Chapter 24, Models of Microeconomics). At the cost-minimizing input bundle, the marginal rate of technical substitution between two inputs (MRTS) equals the input price ratio. In the case of land (price R) and capital (price p_k) as inputs to the construction process,

$$\text{MRTS} = \frac{R}{p_k}$$

In other words, the production tradeoff between the two inputs (MRTS) equals the market tradeoff (the price ratio). In graphical terms, the slope of the isoquant (MRTS) equals the slope of the isocost (price ratio).

Figure 11-9 shows that spatial variation in the price of land causes spatial variation in building heights. There is a single isoquant and three isocosts, each of which is relevant for a location in the city.

1. *Point s: Low land price at remote location.* The isocost is relatively flat at remote locations, so MRTS = input price ratio at a relatively low capital:land ratio (a short building).
2. *Point t: High land price at highly accessible location.* The isocost is relatively steep, so MRTS = input price ratio at a high capital:land ratio (a tall building). When the price of land is relatively high, the benefit of building up (less land

FIGURE 11-9 Input Substitution in Response to Higher Price of Land

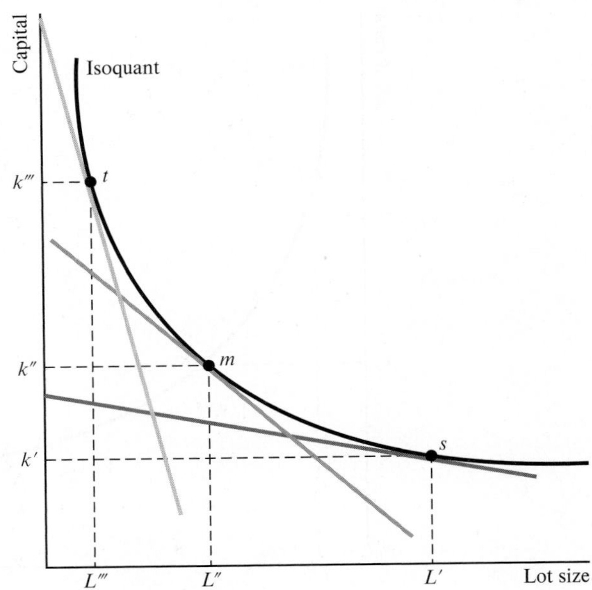

used) exceeds the cost of building up (more capital for reinforcement and vertical transportation).

3. *Point m: Medium land price.* The isocost has a midrange slope, so MRTS = input price ratio at a medium capital:land ratio (a medium-height building).

3. SKYSCRAPER GAMES

We've seen that a high price of land generates tall buildings as firms substitute capital for relatively expensive land. Does the high price of land fully explain the massive skyscrapers in modern cities? A recent study suggests that skyscrapers result from competition between firms for the tallest building in a city (Helsley and Strange, 2008). The competition to be the tallest building increases building heights beyond the efficient height.

A Model of Competition to Be the Tallest

Consider a firm that will construct an office building on a given plot of land. The firm chooses a building height, measured in the number of floors. The firm uses the marginal principle to decide how high to go, choosing the height that makes the marginal benefit equal to the marginal cost. In Figure 11-10, profit is maximized at point *a*, with $h^* = 50$ floors, where the marginal benefit of height equals

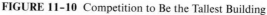

FIGURE 11–10 Competition to Be the Tallest Building

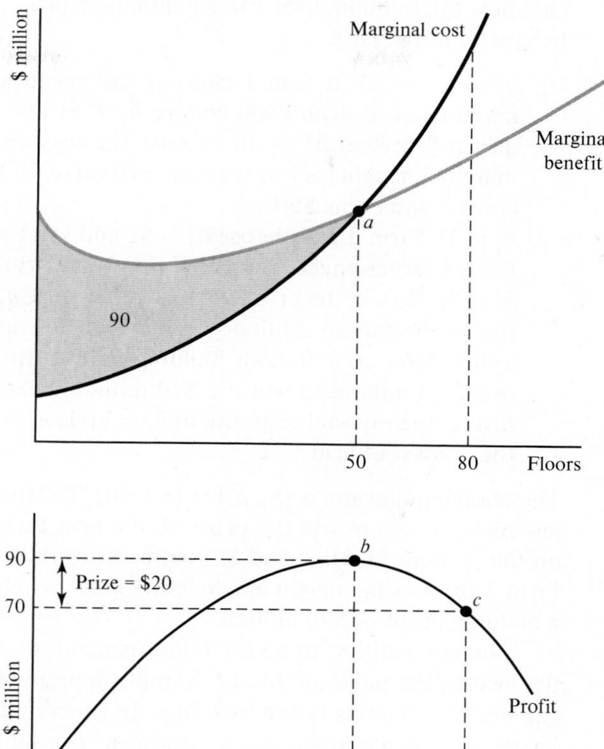

the marginal cost. In the upper panel, economic profit is shown by the shaded area between the marginal-benefit curve and the marginal-cost curve. In the lower panel, the profit is shown by the peak of the profit function, at $90 million. Beyond $h^* = 50$ floors, the marginal cost of an additional floor exceeds the marginal benefit, so profit decreases.

Consider the implications of competition for being the tallest building in the city. Suppose a second construction firm has access to the same construction technology and input markets. Suppose each firm places a value of $V =$ $20 million on having the tallest building. This could be the value of free corporate advertising from being labeled the tallest building. Alternatively, V could be the value of signaling to potential investors that the firm is sufficiently profitable that it can spend money on a tall building. Only one firm can have the tallest building, so the firms are in a noncooperative game for the $20 million prize.

To simplify matters, suppose the two firms play a sequential game. Firm 1 builds first, and then firm 2 follows after observing firm 1's building. To predict the outcome of the skyscraper game, we take the perspective of firm 1, the first mover. To decide how tall to build, firm 1 must anticipate firm 2's responses to different building heights of firm 1 (h_1).

1. $h_1 = h^* = 50$. If firm 1 chooses the height at which marginal benefit equals marginal cost, firm 2 will choose $h_2 = 51$ and win the prize. Firm 2 chooses a quantity beyond $h^* = 50$ because the loss on the 51st floor (marginal cost > marginal benefit) is less than the $20 prize for being the tallest. Firm 1 loses the contest and earns $90.
2. $h_1 = 51$. Firm 2 will choose $h_2 = 52$ and win the prize because the prize exceeds the loss experienced on floors 51 and 52. Firm 1 loses the contest.
3. $h_1 = 80$. To win the prize, firm 2 must choose $h_2 = 81$. As shown in Figure 11–10, the profit for an 81-floor building is just under $70 million, compared to $90 million on a 50-floor building. To win the prize, firm 2 must sacrifice just over $20 million to win the $20 million prize. This would be irrational, so for firm 2, the rational response to $h_1 = 80$ is $h_2 = 50$. In this case, firm 2 concedes the contest to firm 1.

The Nash equilibrium is $\{h_1, h_2\} = \{80, 50\}$. The first mover (firm 1) chooses a height just high enough to win the prize, so the firm earns a building profit of $70 million on the 80-floor building and $20 million in prize money, for a total of $90 million. Firm 2 chooses the height at which marginal benefit equals marginal cost, and earns a building profit of $90 million.

The competition to be the tallest generates a large gap between the tallest and the next tallest building. In our example, a prize of $20 million generates a 30-floor gap between the two tallest buildings. In general, the larger the prize, the largest the height gap. To win the prize, a firm must "overbuild" to make the building profit of the tallest building *plus* the prize equal to the building profit of the next tallest building. In other words, the building profit of the tallest building will be $V (the prize) less than the building profit of the second tallest building. Overbuilding decreases building profit, and the larger the prize, the greater the amount of overbuilding and thus the larger the height gap between the tallest and second tallest building.

The model predicts a large gap between the heights of the two tallest buildings in a city. This prediction is consistent with observation in real cities. In the largest 20 U.S. cities, the average gap between the tallest building and the second tallest building is about 27 percent.

Nash Equilibrium versus Pareto Efficiency

The Nash equilibrium in the skyscraper game is Pareto inefficient. As usual, we can demonstrate inefficiency by identifying a Pareto improvement, defined as a reallocation that makes someone better off without harming anyone. In the Nash equilibrium (80 floors for firm 1 and 50 floors for firm 2), each firm earns a profit of $90 million.

1. Firm 1: Profit = $90 million = $70 million building profit + $20 million prize.
2. Firm 2: Profit = $90 million building profit.

For a Pareto improvement, suppose firm 1 switches from an 80-floor building to a 51-floor building, while firm 2 again chooses a 50-floor building. As in the Nash equilibrium, firm 1 wins the prize.

1. Firm 1: Profit = \$109 million = \$89 building profit (just below \$90 million) + \$20 million prize.
2. Firm 2: Profit = \$90 building profit.

The move from (80, 50) to (51, 50) is a Pareto improvement because firm 1 is better off by \$19 million and firm 2 is no worse off.

The competition to be the tallest building generates an inefficient outcome because it increases the equilibrium building height beyond the efficient height. The pursuit of the prize decreases the surplus from the market. The efficient outcome is a pair of 50-floor buildings and building profit of \$180 million. If one building were just one millimeter taller than the other, one builder could collect the \$20 million prize with a trivial increase in cost, and the total value of the market would be \$200 million. In contrast, in the Nash equilibrium, the total value of the market is only \$180 million, including \$90 million in building profit for firm 2, \$70 million in building profit for firm 1, and the \$20 million prize. The reduction in the total value of the market is roughly equal to the prize.

4. THE SPATIAL DISTRIBUTION OF OFFICE ACTIVITY

Figure 11–11 shows the spatial distribution of jobs in finance and insurance in Boston. The map shows census tracts as jigsaw pieces, which are extruded (pushed up) to a height equal to the employment density. The employment density equals the number of finance and insurance workers per hectare in the census tract. As in other other large cities, the density of finance and insurance employment is highest in the central business district, and as we move away from the center, employment density decreases rapidly.

Table 11–1 shows the distribution of office space across three types of locations in 13 metropolitan areas.

1. High density (at least 7.5 million square feet [sf] per square mile): primary downtowns.
2. Medium density (2 million to 3.5 million sf per square mile): secondary downtowns (office clusters geographically distinct from primary downtowns), edge cities (clusters distinct from both types of downtowns), urban envelopes (clusters contiguous to primary downtowns), and corridors (linear clusters that commonly follow major highway routes).
3. Low density (less than 2 million sf per square mile): dispersed. The average density is 20,000 sf per square mile.

There is substantial variation across the 13 metropolitan areas in the distribution of office space. For the metropolitan areas as a whole, roughly one-third of office space is in high-density downtowns and two-fifths is in low-density areas, leaving 28 percent

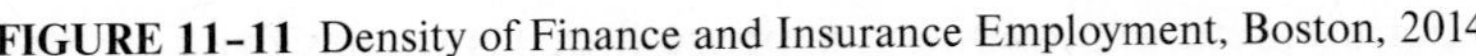

FIGURE 11-11 Density of Finance and Insurance Employment, Boston, 2014

TABLE 11-1 Distribution of Office Space

	High Density (center)	Medium Density (subcenter)	Low Density (dispersed)
13 Metros	0.33	0.28	0.40
Atlanta	0.07	0.55	0.38
Boston	0.39	0.11	0.50
Chicago	0.49	0.11	0.39
Dallas-Ft. Worth	0.21	0.39	0.34
Denver	0.27	0.22	0.51
Detroit	0.17	0.29	0.54
Houston	0.23	0.43	0.35
Los Angeles	0.16	0.38	0.46
Miami	0.09	0.19	0.72
New York	0.55	0.13	0.32
San Francisco	0.39	0.21	0.39
Washington, DC	0.23	0.53	0.24

Source: Lang, Robert E. "Office Sprawl: The Evolving Geography of Business." The Brookings Institution Survey Series, October 2000.

for medium-density areas. The largest downtown shares are in New York, Chicago, and Boston. The smallest downtown shares are in Atlanta, Miami, and Los Angeles. At the other end, the largest low-density shares are in Miami, Detroit, and Philadelphia.

REVIEW THE CONCEPTS

1. As distance to the city center increases, the travel cost for information exchange [______] {↑, ↓, −} at a(n) [______] {↑, ↓, −} rate.
2. As distance to the city center increases, an office firm's willingness to pay for space [______] {↑, ↓, −} at a(n) [______] {↑, ↓, −} rate.
3. Workers in firm T commute by public transit, while workers in firm C commute by car. Firm [______] has a steeper willingness-to-pay curve for office space. Firm [______] will outbid firm [______] for land close to the city center.
4. In an office building, as height increases, the [______] effect tends to decrease the price of office space, while the [______] effect tends to increase the price of space. The [______] effect is relatively strong in buildings with [______].
5. The rule for the profit-maximizing building height is [______] = [______].
6. In graphical terms, the willingness to pay for office land is shown by the area between the [______] and [______] curves up to [______].
7. An increase in the accessibility of an office site [______] {↑, ↓, −} the base price of office space, [______] {↑, ↓, −} building height, and [______] {↑, ↓, −} the willingness to pay for office land.
8. As building height increases, the amount of capital required to produce a fixed quantity of output (interior space) [______] {↑, ↓, −} to prevent two problems: [______] and [______].
9. In the input-choice model of microeconomics, the rule for cost minimization with respect to building height is [______] = [______].
10. A building at a central location is [______] than a building at a remote site because the price of [______] is higher at the [______] site.
11. As we move from a remote location to a central location, the MRTS between land and capital [______]. {↑, ↓, −}
12. Competition to be the tallest building generates a relatively [______] gap between the height of the tallest building and the second tallest building. As the prize increases, the size of the gap [______].
13. Competition to be the tallest building [______] {↑, ↓, −} the efficiency of the building market.
14. Comparative Statics. For each pair of variables, indicate whether the relationship is positive, negative, neutral, or ambiguous.

Parameter	Choice Variable	Relationship
price of office space	building height	[______]
price of office space	willingness to pay for office land	[______]
price of office land	office lot size	[______]
wage	bid for office land	[______]
prize for tallest building	surplus of building market	[______]

APPLY THE CONCEPTS

1. *Hoverboards for Information Workers*
Consider a CBD where workers from office firms interact to exchange tacit information. Suppose hoverboards are introduced, doubling travel speed on sidewalks.
   a. Illustrate the effects of hoverboards on the willingness to pay for office space at different locations in the CBD.
   b. In the long run, the bulk of the benefits of hoverboards go to [______] (choose landowners, workers, capital owners).
2. *Stairs vs. Elevator*
Each firm in an office building occupies one floor of space, earns total revenue R = \$380, and incurs a labor cost L = \$300. Define h as the height (floor level) of the building. The intrabuilding travel cost is $c_S(h) = 10 \cdot h$ per floor for travel by stairs, compared to $c_E(h) = 27 + h$ for travel by elevator.
   a. Illustrate the WTP for office space for the two travel modes for $h = 1$ to $h = 53$. What sort of firms use the stairs?
   b. Suppose that as h increases beyond the third floor, the view improves, and workers are willing to accept lower wages. The saving in labor cost is \$3 per floor. Draw the WTP curve for the building with elevators, including a value for $h = 53$.
3. *Price of Office Space*
Consider the price of office space within a building with favorable views of the surrounding area. The horizontal axis measures the vertical distance from the street in floors (h), and the vertical axis measures the price per square foot of office space, $p(h)$.
   a. Draw the price curve $p(h)$ for a building with stairs and no windows.
   b. Draw the price curve $p(h)$ for a building with elevators and no windows.
   c. Draw the price curve $p(h)$ for a building with elevators and windows.
4. *Space Price and WTP for Office Land*
The marginal benefit of building height (h) is $mb(h) = 2 \cdot p + h$, where p is the price of office space. The marginal cost of building height is $mc(h) = 4 \cdot h$.
   a. Illustrate the effects of an increase in the price of office space on the profit-maximizing height. Specifically, show the effects of an increase in price from $p = 30$ (height h^*), to $p = 60$ (height h^{**}).
   b. For $p = 60$, the willingness to pay for office land is \$[______]. Illustrate.
5. *Steel Frame and Building Height*
Consider the implications of the switch from office buildings made of stone to buildings made with steel framing. Suppose the switch in technology does not affect the capital required for a one-floor building. For a standard office building (5,000 square meters of space), a one-floor building requires 5,000 square meters of land and \$100 in capital, regardless of the construction technology. The common input bundle (5000, \$100) anchors the isoquants for stone and steel.

a. Draw two office-building isoquants, one for stone and one for steel.
b. Suppose that before steel framing, the cost-minimizing height of a stone building is 2 floors (2,500 square meters of land). Illustrate the effect of a switch to steel buildings on the cost-minimizing quantity of land.

6. *LegoSpiderCity*
ConCity is a conventional city, with diminishing returns to building height and vertical transportation in elevators within buildings. When an innovation in construction allows stackable buildings (no additional reinforcement is required for taller buildings), the city changes its name to LegoCity. When workers acquire new climbing skills and are able to rappel up and down the outside of the buildings, the city changes its name to LegoSpiderCity.
a. Draw a trio of isoquants for ConCity, LegoCity, and LegoSpider city.
b. Rank the three cities with respect to the willingness to pay for land close to the city center.

7. *Prize for the Tallest Building*
For an office building in a large city, the profit increases with the number of floors for the first 40 floors at a rate of $3 per floor, and then decreases as the number of floors increases at a rate of $2 per floor. In addition, the prize or bonus profit from the tallest building is $30. Two firms, A and B, will each build one office building, and A builds first. In the event of a tie (two buildings of the same height) there is no prize.
a. The Nash equilibrium is . . .
b. The competition to be the tallest changes total building profit by $[______]
c. Design a Pareto improvement under which the two firms share the gain equally. Assume that the number of floors is an integer. Firm A gives *how much* to firm B to *do what*?

REFERENCES AND READING

1. Anas, Alex, Richard Arnott, and Kenneth A. Small, "Urban Spatial Structure." *Journal of Economic Literature* 34 (1998), pp. 1426–64.
2. Baum-Snow, Nathaniel, "Did Highways Cause Suburbanization?" *Quarterly Journal of Economics* 122.2 (2007), pp. 775–805.
3. Bollinger, Christopher, Keith Ihlanfeldt, and David Rowes, "Spatial Variation in Office Rents within the Atlanta Region." *Urban Studies* 35 (1998), pp. 1097–1118.
4. Duranton, Gilles, and Diego Puga, "Urban Land Use," Chapter 8 in *Handbook of Urban and Regional Economics Volume 5,* edited by Gilles Duranton, J. Vernon Henderson, and William C. Strange. Amsterdam: Elsevier, 2015.
5. Garreau, Joel. *Edge City: Life on the New Frontier.* New York: Doubleday, 1991.
6. George, Henry. *Progress and Poverty.* New York: Schalkenbach Foundation, 1954.
7. Giuliano, Genevieve, and Kenneth Small, "Subcenters in the Los Angeles Region." *Regional Science and Urban Economics* 21 (1991).

8. Glaeser, Edward, and Matthew Kahn, "Decentralized Employment and the Transformation of the American City." NBER Working Paper, March 2001.
9. Glaeser, Edward, Matthew Kahn, and Chenghuan Chu, "Job Sprawl: Employment Location in U.S. Metropolitan Areas." Brookings Institution Survey Series, May 2001, pp. 1–8.
10. Helsley, Robert, and William Strange, "A Game-Theoretic Analysis of Skyscrapers." *Journal of Urban Economics* 64 (2008), pp. 49–64.
11. Irwin, Elena G., and Nancy E. Bockstael, "The Spatial Pattern of Land Use in the United States," Chapter 6 in *A Companion to Urban Economics,* edited by Richard J. Arnott and Daniel P. McMillen. New York: Wiley-Blackwell, 2006.
12. Lang, Robert E. "Office Sprawl: The Evolving Geography of Business." The Brookings Institution Survey Series, October 2000.
13. Lang, Robert E., *Edgeless Cities.* Washington, DC: Brookings, 2003.
14. McMillen, Daniel P. "One Hundred Fifty Years of Land Values in Chicago: A Nonparametric Approach." *Journal of Urban Economics* 40 (1996), pp. 100–24.
15. Liu, Crocker, Stuart Rosenthal, and William Strange, "The Vertical City: Rent Gradients and Spatial Structure," working paper.
16. McMillen, Daniel P., and John F. McDonald, "Suburban Subcenters and Employment Density in Metropolitan Chicago." *Journal of Urban Economics* 43 (1998), pp. 157–80.
17. Mills, Edwin S. *Studies in the Structure of the Urban Economy.* Baltimore: Johns Hopkins, 1972.
18. Moses, Leon, and Harold Williamson, "The Location of Economic Activity in Cities," in *Readings in Urban Economics,* edited by Matthew Edel and Jerome Rothenberg. New York: Macmillan, 1972.
19. Nivola, Pietro. "Fat City: Understanding American Urban Form from a Transatlantic Perspective." *Brookings Review,* Fall 1998, pp. 17–20.
20. O'Hara, D. J., "Location of Firms within a Square Central Business District." *Journal of Political Economy* 85 (1977), pp. 1189–1207.
21. Redding, Stephen J., and Matthew Turner, "Transportation Costs and the Spatial Organization of Economic Activity," Chapter 20 in *Handbook of Urban and Regional Economics Volume 5,* edited by Gilles Duranton, J. Vernon Henderson, and William C. Strange. Amsterdam: Elsevier, 2015.
22. Sivitanidou, R., and P. Sivitanides, "Industrial Rent Differentials: The Case of Greater Los Angeles." *Environment and Planning A* 27 (1995), pp. 1133–46.
23. Sivitanidou, Rena, "Do Office-Commercial Firms Value Access to Service Employment Centers? A Hedonic Value Analysis within Polycentric Los Angeles." *Journal of Urban Economics* 40 (1996), pp. 125–49.
24. Sivitanidou, Rena, "Urban Spatial Variations in Office-Commercial Rents: The Role of Spatial Amenities and Commercial Zoning." *Journal of Urban Economics* 38 (1995), pp. 23–49.

CHAPTER 12

Housing Prices and Residential Land Use

What is a cynic? A man who knows the price of everything and the value of nothing.

—OSCAR WILDE

This chapter explores the spatial variation in the prices of housing and residential land. The hedonic approach to the housing market is based on the notion that dwellings differ in physical characteristics and accessibility to jobs and other features of the urban economy. Under the hedonic approach, a dwelling is a bundle of attributes. Each attribute has an implicit price, and the market value of a dwelling is the sum of the values of the attributes. The following hedonic equation incorporates five attributes: dwelling size, job access, school quality, air quality, and crime.

$$V = p_B \cdot B + p_J \cdot J + p_S \cdot S + p_A \cdot A + p_C \cdot C$$

where p_i is the price of component i, B is the number of bedrooms, J is the distance to a concentration of jobs, S is the average test score of local schools, A is a measure of air quality, and C is the neighborhood crime rate. The prices are positive for desirable attributes (bedrooms, test score, air quality) and negative for undesirable attributes (distance to jobs, crime rate).

1. JOB ACCESSIBILITY

In this first part of the chapter, we consider the job-access component of the bundle of dwelling attributes. We explore how the price of housing varies with the distance to jobs.

Utility Maximization with Commuting Cost and Housing

As a starting point, consider a simple city where all employment is in a central business district. Workers commute from their residential locations to central jobs, and

FIGURE 12–1 Commuting Cost and Utility-Maximizing Housing Consumption

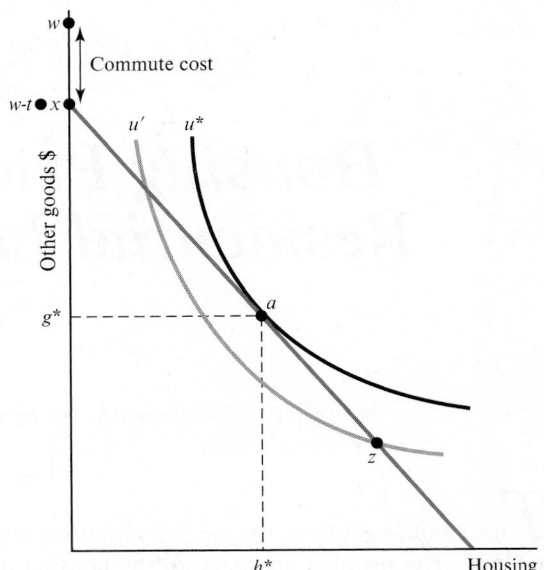

the distance to the center is x (in kilometers). Each household has a fixed income w to spend each month on housing, commuting, and other goods. The monetary cost of commuting is $t =$ \$50 per km per month: when a household moves 1 kilometer further away from the center, its monthly commuting cost increases by \$50. The price of housing $p(x)$ is defined as the monthly price per square meter of living space, and depends on x (distance to the center).

Figure 12–1 shows a variation on the standard consumer-choice model from microeconomics (reviewed in Chapter 24, Models of Microeconomics). The horizontal axis shows housing consumption (in square meters), and the vertical axis shows the consumption of all other goods. The price of other goods is fixed at \$1. The linear curve is the budget line and shows all the affordable bundles, given household income w, commuting cost t, and the price of housing p. The position of the budget line depends on the distance to the center. The vertical intercept is computed as

$$\text{vertical intercept} = w - t \cdot x$$

For example, if $w =$ \$2,000, $t =$ \$50 per km, and $x =$ 10 km, the vertical intercept is \$1,500.

Each indifference curve (labeled u' and u^*) shows alternative bundles of housing and other goods that generate the same level of utility (satisfaction). Utility is maximized at point a, where the marginal rate of substitution (the slope of the indifference curve and the consumer's subjective tradeoff between housing and other goods) equals the price ratio (the market tradeoff between housing and other goods). Although the other point shown (point z) is on the budget line and therefore is affordable, point a is on a higher indifference curve, indicating higher utility: $u^* > u'$. At point z, MRS is less than the price ratio, so the consumer's rational response is to consume less housing and more other goods. The household moves upward along the budget line up to point a, where MRS equals the price ratio and utility is maximized.

Commuting Distance and the Price of Housing

We can use a simple thought experiment to illustrate the negative relationship between commuting distance x and the price of housing $p(x)$. Consider a household that initially locates at $x = 10$ km from the center, where its housing consumption is $h^* = 100$ and its commuting cost is \$500 (\$50 times 10 km). In Figure 12–2, the initial budget line (labeled p^*) is tangent to the indifference curve at point a. Suppose the household moves 4 kilometers closer to the center, to $x = 6$. The 4-kilometer decrease in commuting distance decreases commuting cost by \$200:

$$\Delta\text{commute cost} = \Delta x \cdot t = 4 \cdot \$50 = \$200$$

For the Nash equilibrium in residential location, the \$200 decrease in commuting cost must be offset by some other change such that the utility at $x = 6$ equals the

FIGURE 12–2 A Decrease in Commuting Cost Increases the Housing Price for Affordability

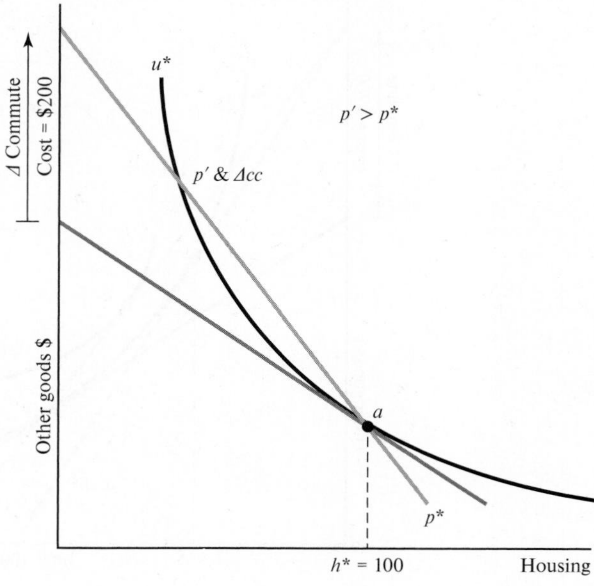

utility at $x = 10$. The other change is an increase in the price of housing. A higher price at the more accessible location ($x = 6$) offsets the lower commuting cost, with a price gap just large enough that no resident has an incentive to change its location.

Figure 12–2 shows the effect of a \$2 increase in the price of housing. The \$2 increase in price is just large enough to offset the \$200 decrease in commuting cost in a budgetary sense. The combination of a \$200 decrease in commuting cost and a \$2 increase in the price of housing means that the original bundle of consumer goods (shown by point *a*) is just affordable. In other words, the budget line labeled (p' & Δcc) goes through the original bundle. When a \$200 decrease in commuting cost is combined with a \$2 increase in the price of housing, one option for the household is to choose point *a* and consume 100 units of housing.

As shown in Figure 12–3, the rational response to the new (steeper) budget line is to consume less housing. At point *a*, the budget line (p' & \$$\Delta cc$) is steeper than the indifference curve, indicating that the marginal rate of substitution exceeds the new price ratio. With the new budget line, utility is now maximized at point *b*, where MRS = the price ratio. At point *b*, utility is higher at $x = 6$ than it was at $x = 10$, so point *b* (with p') is not a Nash equilibrium. With a price of p' at $x = 6$, each resident at $x = 10$ would have an incentive to move to $x = 6$. In other words, there is an incentive for unilateral deviation.

To reach a Nash equilibrium, the price of housing at $x = 6$ must be higher than p'. An increase in price to $p^{**} > p'$ tilts the budget line inward (marked p^{**} & Δcc), and the resident maximizes utility at point *c*, with $h^{**} < h^{*}$ units of housing.

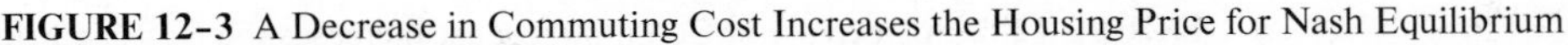

FIGURE 12–3 A Decrease in Commuting Cost Increases the Housing Price for Nash Equilibrium

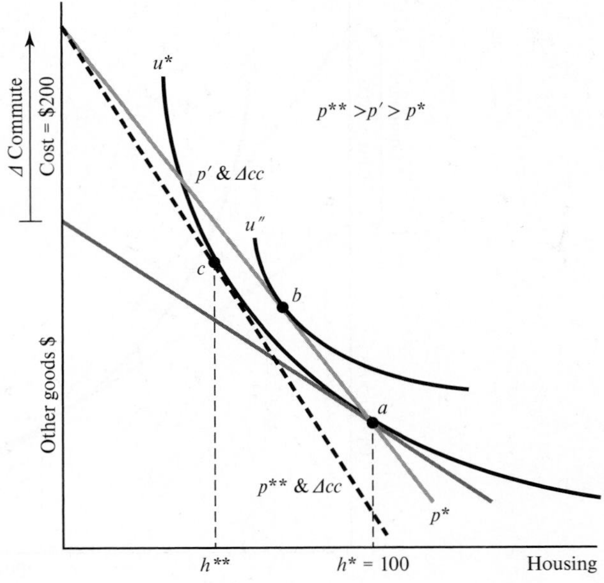

With the higher price, the original utility is restored at u^*, meaning that the utility at $x = 6$ (point c) equals the utility at $x = 10$ (point a). The increase in price eliminates the incentive for unilateral deviation.

Figure 12–3 provides an example of the substitution effect of an increase in the price of a consumer good. As explained in a course in microeconomic theory, the substitution effect is the change in consumption when the price of a good increases, but the consumer's utility level is held fixed. In Figure 12–3, the price of housing increases, and the budget line tilts inward from the original line labeled p^* to the line labeled (p^{**} & Δcc). Utility is held constant (a requirement for Nash equilibrium), so the consumer moves along the original indifference curve. Given the fixed utility and a higher price, housing consumption decreases from h^* to h^{**}.

The Convex Housing-Price Curve

The lesson from Figure 12–3 is that the premium for accessibility exceeds the difference in price that offsets the change in commuting cost in a budgetary sense. A \$2 price difference (from p^* to p') makes the original bundle just affordable, but a larger price increase (from p' to p^{**}) is required for Nash equilibrium. The larger premium occurs because consumers respond to a higher price by engaging in consumer substitution away from the product (housing) whose price has increased. The substitution increases utility, so a larger price increase is required to restore the original utility level.

Figure 12–4 shows that consumer substitution generates a convex housing-price curve. The price of housing is anchored at point a: at a distance of 10 kilometers

FIGURE 12–4 Convex Housing-Price Curve: Inward

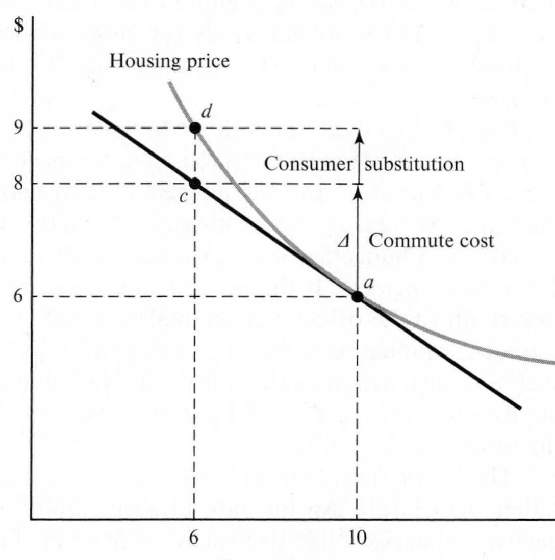

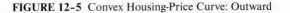

FIGURE 12–5 Convex Housing-Price Curve: Outward

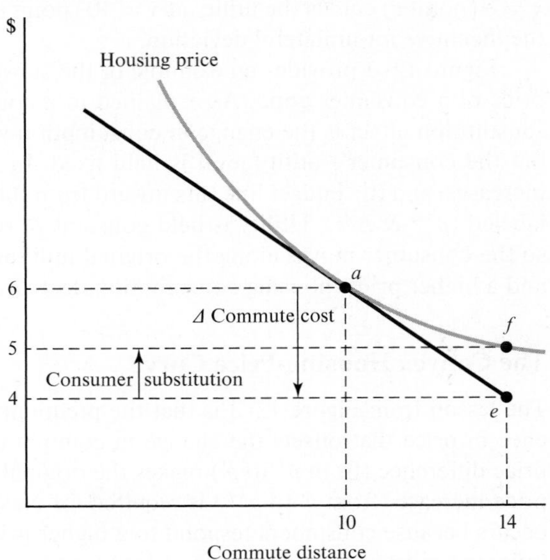

from the center, the price is $p^* = \$6$. Consider the implications of moving inward. We've seen that a 4-kilometer move closer to the center increases the price from $p^* = \$6$ to $p' = \$8$ because of lower commuting cost (a \$2 premium), and then from $p' = \$8$ to p^{**} because of consumer substitution. For example, if $p^{**} = \$9$, there is an additional \$1 premium caused by consumer substitution. To summarize, an inward move increases the price of housing for two reasons: (i) lower commuting cost, and (ii) consumer substitution in response to a higher price of housing.

Figure 12–5 uses similar logic to illustrate the price effects of an outward move to a less accessible residential location. Suppose a household starts at $x = 10$, with $h^* = 100$ and $p^* = \$6$. The household then makes a 4-kilometer move away from the center, increasing commuting cost by \$200. To offset the increases in commuting cost in a budgetary sense, we need a \$2 reduction in price (\$200 = \$2 times 100 square meters). If the price decreases to $p'' = \$4$, the consumer will be able to just afford the original consumption bundle with $h^* = 100$. But given the lower price, the rational response to a lower price is to increase housing consumption, and such a change will increase utility. For Nash equilibrium in location, the price must increase to a price $p^{***} > \$4$ to restore the original utility level u^*. In Figure 12–5, the price at $x = 14$ is \$5.

The lesson from Figures 12–4 and 12–5 is that the housing-price curve is convex rather than linear. An increase in accessibility increases the price by \$3, while a decrease in accessibility decreases the price by only \$1. This happens because housing consumers engage in consumer substitution in response to changes in the price of housing.

The Algebra of the Convex Housing-Price Curve

We can use some simple algebra to show the convexity of the housing-price curve. To simplify matters, suppose the household has a fixed sum of money to spend on housing and commuting cost. The equilibrium housing-price curve makes residents indifferent among all locations. Consider a move toward or away from the employment center. Such a move changes commuting cost by the change in distance Δx times the commuting cost per km (t) and changes housing cost by the change in price of housing Δp times housing consumption $h(x)$. For locational indifference, the two changes must sum to zero:

$$\Delta p \cdot h(x) + \Delta x \cdot t = 0$$

We can rewrite this expression to show that the change in housing cost equals the negative of the change in commuting cost:

$$\Delta p \cdot h(x) = -\Delta x \cdot t$$

We can use this trade-off to derive an expression for the slope of the housing-price curve. Dividing each side of the expression by Δx and h,

$$\frac{\Delta p}{\Delta x} = -\frac{t}{h(x)}$$

We have seen that an increase in accessibility (a decrease in x) increases the price of housing, and the rational response is to consume less housing: $h^{**} < h^{*}$ in Figure 12–3. Therefore, the denominator of the slope equation decreases, meaning that the slope of housing-price curve increases in absolute value. In other words, the housing-price curve is steeper closer to the city center. Moving in the opposite direction, a decrease in accessibility (increase in x) decreases the price of housing, increases housing consumption, and increases the denominator of the slope expression. In other words, the housing-price curve becomes flatter. Putting it all together, the housing-price curve is convex: as we move away from the city center to locations with less accessibility, the curve becomes flatter.

So far we have focused on the monetary cost of commuting while ignoring the time cost. The opportunity cost of commuting time is the value of the time in its next-best use. Define T as the time cost per kilometer of distance per month: a 1-kilometer increase in distance increases the time cost of commuting per month by $\$T$. The value of T is determined by the opportunity cost of travel time, the frequency of travel to the center (more trips means a larger value), and travel speed (slower travel means a larger value). The expression for the slope of the housing-price curve is

$$\frac{\Delta p}{\Delta x} = -\frac{t + T}{h(x)}$$

The time cost of commuting affects the slope of the housing-price curve: an increase in T increases the absolute value of the slope, generating a steeper housing-price curve.

Job Accessibility within a Metropolitan Area

In our discussion of housing prices and job accessibility, so far we have assumed that all workers commute to jobs in a central business district. In this case, the metric for

FIGURE 12–6 Employment Density, Boston in 2014

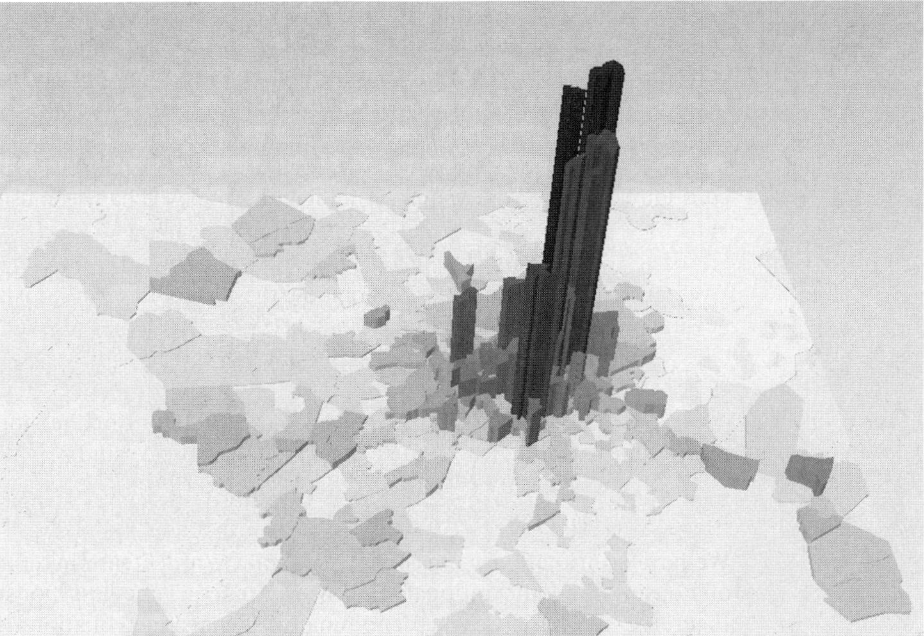

job accessibility is the distance to the city center. In modern metropolitan areas, jobs are widely distributed across the metropolitan area. Figure 12–6 shows employment density for the Boston metropolitan area. Each jigsaw puzzle piece represents a census tract, and is extruded (pushed up) to the employment density (jobs per hectare) of the tract. The highest density occurs near the city center. The central area hosts a large fraction of the jobs, and there are jobs in subcenters at varying distances from the center. In addition, a large fraction of jobs are dispersed in low-density areas outside the center and subcenters.

We can use an accessibility index to measure the number of jobs accessible to each residential location. The index is based on the following thought experiment. Suppose commuting speed is 20 kilometers per hour and commuting time comes at the expense of work time. Consider the job accessibility of residential area *i*. Suppose census tract *j* has *J* actual jobs. The number of jobs in workplace area *j* that are accessible to residential location (the effective number of jobs after accounting for commuting time) *i* is

$$J^* = J \cdot \left[\frac{8 - \text{commute hours } i \text{ to } j}{8}\right]$$

For example, if there are $J = 800$ jobs and commuting from a residential area *i* to census tract *j* requires a 1-hour commute, the number of accessible jobs is 7/8 of *J*, or $J^* = 700$. Similarly, if another workplace area has the same number of jobs but requires 2 hours of commuting time, the number of accessible jobs is $J^* = 600$. For

FIGURE 12–7 Metropolitan Accessibility in Boston, 2014

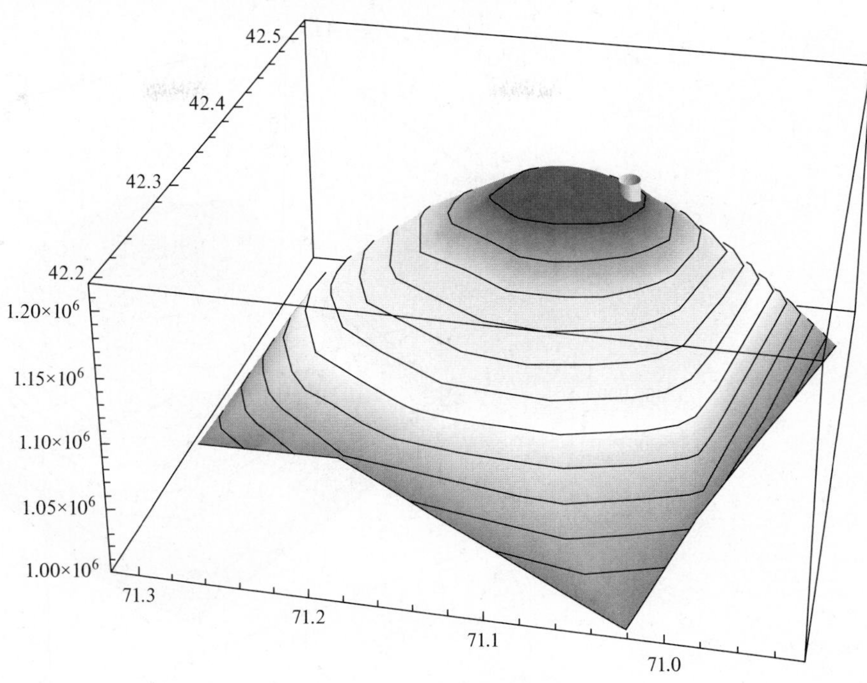

each residential area, we can add the numbers of accessible jobs across workplace areas in the metropolitan area. In our example, if there were just two workplace areas, the total accessibility for residential area *i* would be $1300 = 700 + 600$. If for another residential area the commuting times to the workplace areas were 3 hours and 4 hours, the total accessibility of the less accessible residential area would be $900 = 500 + 400$.

Figure 12–7 uses LEHD (longitudinal employer-household dynamics) data on the location of jobs and workers to compute the values of the job accessibility index for residential locations in Boston. The floor of the box shows longitude (range 70.9 to 71.3) and latitude (range 40.2 to 42.6). The height of the surface shows the number of accessible jobs at a particular (longitude, latitude). The gray column that pierces the surface shows the city center, defined as the census tract with the highest employment density. The value of the accessibility index is highest close to the city center, and then generally decreases as we move away from the center.

Figure 12–8 shows another way compute job accessibility, using a metric based on access to local jobs. For each residential location, we define a catchment area of 10 kilometers and measure the accessibility index for jobs within the 10-kilometer catchment area. This contrasts with the metropolitan accessibility index shown in Figure 12–8, which measures access to jobs throughout the metropolitan area. As in the case of the metropolitan accessibility index, the value of the local accessibility index is highest near the city center and generally decreases as distance to the center increases.

FIGURE 12–8 Local Job Accessibility in Boston, 2014

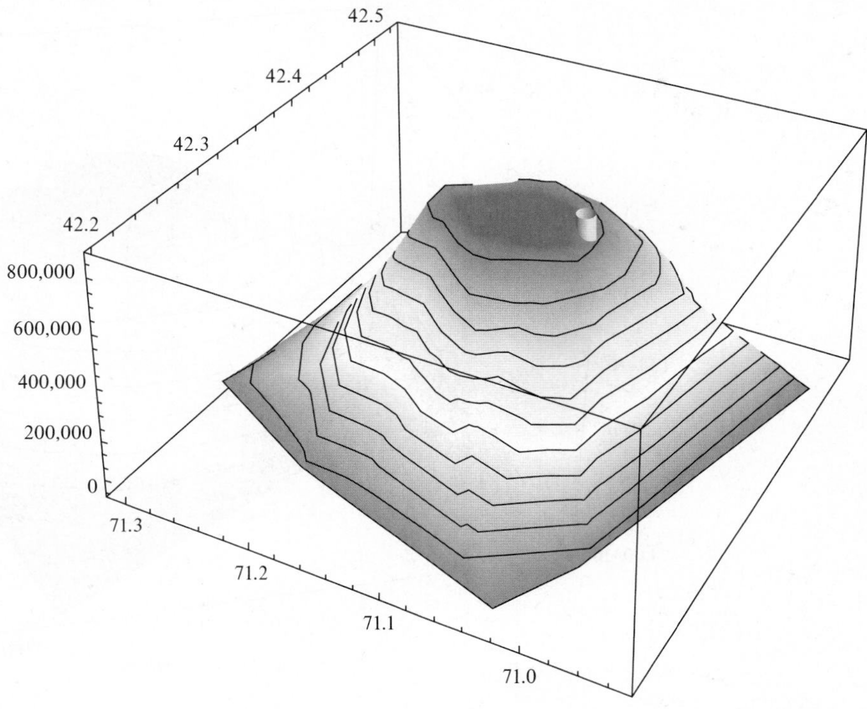

The lesson from Figures 12–7 and 12–8 is that job accessibility decreases as distance to the city center increases. Although jobs in a metropolitan area are not confined to a central business district, the distance to the city center is a useful measure of job accessibility. Hedonic studies of urban housing show that the price of housing generally decreases as the distance to the city center increases, and job accessibility plays a role in this negative relationship.

2. CRIME, ENVIRONMENTAL QUALITY, SCHOOLS

We've seen that the price of housing increases with accessibility to jobs. We turn next to other features of the urban economy that affect housing prices. We start with neighborhood crime rates, then explore the influence of air quality and schools.

Crime and Housing Prices

In the typical city, there is substantial geographical variation in crime. To illustrate the negative relationship between crime and housing prices, consider the case of

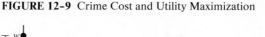

FIGURE 12-9 Crime Cost and Utility Maximization

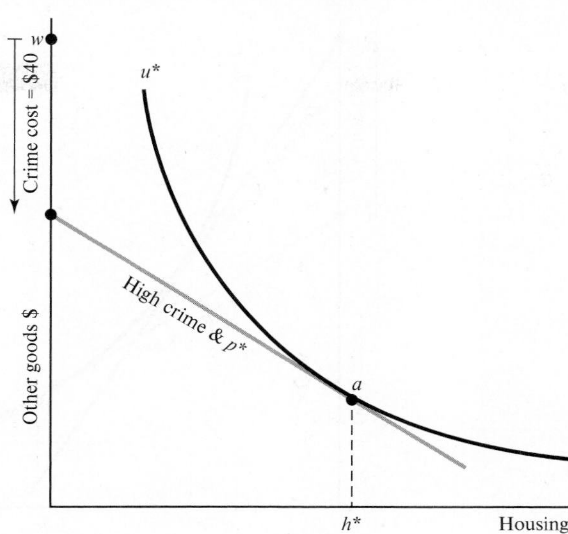

burglary. Suppose the property loss from each burglary is L and the probability of being victimized is r. The expected cost from burglary is the probability times the property loss:

$$\text{Expected cost} = r \cdot L$$

For example, if $r = 0.005$ and $L = \$8{,}000$, the expected cost is \$40:

$$\text{Expected cost} = r \cdot L = 0.005 \cdot \$8{,}000 = \$40$$

For a household with market income w, disposable income is

$$\text{Disposable income} = w - r \cdot L = w - \$40$$

We can use the consumer choice model to show the relationship between crime and housing prices. Figure 12-9 shows a variation on the familiar consumer choice model. Market income is w, and disposable income (the vertical intercept of the budget line) equals market income w minus the expected cost of crime. For an expected cost of \$40, the vertical intercept of the budget line is \$40 less than market income w. Given a housing price p^*, utility is maximized at point a, with housing consumption h^*. This analysis is analogous to the earlier model employed for accessibility to jobs: we simply replace commuting cost with expected crime cost.

Figure 12-10 shows the logic of the negative relationship between crime and the price of housing. Using the outcome shown in Figure 12-9 as a starting point,

FIGURE 12–10 Lower Crime and Higher Housing Price for Nash Equilibrium

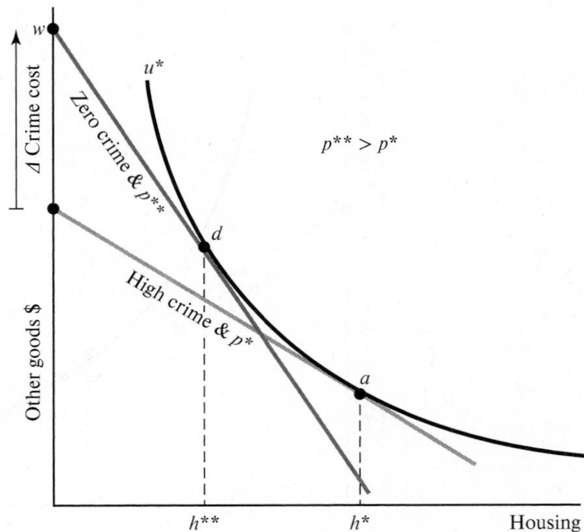

suppose the household moves from a high-crime area to a location with zero crime: at the new location, the probability of being burglarized is zero. In this case, the vertical intercept of the budget line is market income w. As we saw before in the case of job access, Nash equilibrium requires an increase in the price of housing to restore the original utility level. The budget line shifts upward to reflect lower crime cost and then tilts downward to reflect a higher price. The price increases until we achieve a tangency between the new budget line and the original indifference curve. Utility is maximized at point d, with the original utility level u^*, a higher price of housing, and a lower housing consumption $h^{**} < h^*$.

The lesson from Figure 12–10 is that a decrease in crime increases housing prices. In a Nash equilibrium in residential location, no one has an incentive for unilateral deviation, meaning that a household in a low-crime area pays more for housing. Along with a higher housing price, residents of low-crime neighborhoods have lower housing consumption ($h^{**} < h^*$), a result of the substitution effect of a higher price.

Air Quality and Housing Prices

So far we have seen that job accessibility and public safety result in higher housing prices. We can use similar logic to show a positive relationship between environmental quality and housing prices. The components of environmental quality include air quality, water quality, and exposure to hazardous waste facilities. Housing prices will

FIGURE 12-11 Better Air Quality and Higher Housing Prices for Nash Equilibrium

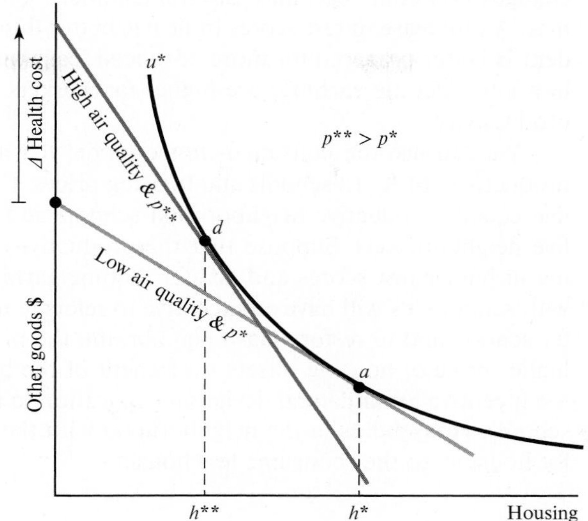

be higher in neighborhoods with better environmental quality–better air and water quality, or greater distance from hazardous waste facilities.

Figure 12-11 shows the effects of a relocation from a heavily polluted area to less polluted area. The position of the budget line is determined by disposable income, defined in this case as the market income minus health care costs. A move to a less polluted area decreases health care cost and shifts the budget line upward. To restore the original utility level u^*, the price of housing increases, tilting the budget line downward. The Nash equilibrium is shown by points a and d: an area with less pollution has a higher housing price ($p^{**} > p^*$) and lower housing consumption ($h^{**} < h^*$).

School Productivity and Housing Prices

As we see later in the book, we can measure the production or "output" of K-12 schools (kindergarten through grade 12) as the value-added of students over the course of a school year. One measure is the gain, from the beginning to the end of the school year, in student scores on standardized tests. As we'll see later in the book, there is spatial variation in the productivity of schools across the typical metropolitan area. For a Nash equilibrium in residential location, areas with highly productive schools (large gains in test scores) will have higher housing prices.

A more refined measure of school productivity is the change in a student's lifetime earnings attributable to attending a particular school for a year. Economists have developed a number of procedures to translate changes in test scores to changes in lifetime earnings. Several channels connect test scores to lifetime earnings. An increase in test scores indicates better thinking skills, meaning that the student is better prepared for more advanced learning in college and more productive in a job. Lifetime earnings are higher for workers with college degrees and higher productivity.

We can use the consumer-choice model to show the connection between the productivity of K–12 schools and housing prices. Consider a metropolitan area with five equally productive neighborhood schools and equal housing prices across the five neighborhoods. Suppose that the productivity of one school increases, resulting in higher test scores and greater lifetime earnings for its students. Households with school kids will have an incentive to relocate to the neighborhood with the better school, and to restore Nash equilibrium, the price of housing will increase. The higher price of housing offsets the benefit of the better school and thus eliminates the incentive for unilateral deviation (relocation to the neighborhood with the better school). Households in the neighborhood with the better school pay a higher price for housing, so they consume less housing.

3. HOUSING PRODUCTION AND THE PRICE OF RESIDENTIAL LAND

In this part of the chapter we explore the factors that determine housing density (living space per unit of land) and the market price of residential land. We take the perspective of a firm that produces housing, with land as one input to the production process. We assume that the housing industry is perfectly competitive, so economic profit is zero and land is the residual claimant. In other words, the leftover principle holds.

Profit-Maximizing Quantity of Housing

Consider a firm that will build housing on a one-hectare site at location x'. The price of housing is $p(x')$ per unit of housing, for example, per square meter of living space. As we saw in the previous section of the chapter, the housing price reflects the site's attributes, including job accessibility, environmental quality, crime rate, and school productivity. For the housing firm, the marginal benefit of housing at x' is the price $p(x')$.

The firm's task is to decide how much housing to produce on its one-hectare site, and the firm can use the marginal principle to choose the profit-maximizing quantity of housing. At one extreme, the firm could build a small house on the site, for example, $H = 100$ square meters. At the other extreme, the firm could build a 30-floor residential tower that covers the entire hectare, for $H = 300{,}000$ square meters. Given the fixed amount of land, housing production is subject to diminishing returns and rising marginal cost. In Figure 12–12, the horizontal marginal-benefit curve intersects the positively sloped marginal-cost curve at point a, satisfying the marginal principle with H^* units of housing.

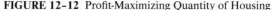

FIGURE 12–12 Profit-Maximizing Quantity of Housing

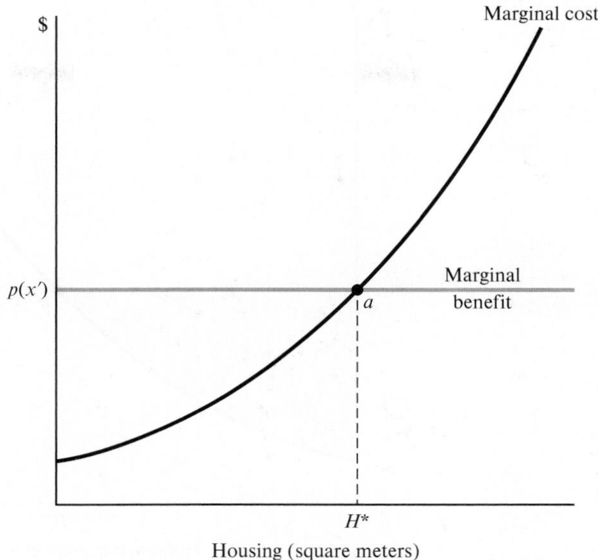

The Price of Residential Land

For a housing production firm, the willingness to pay for land equals the economic profit that can be earned from housing. As we saw earlier in the market for land in the office sector, we can use the marginal-benefit curve and the marginal-cost curve to compute a builder's economic profit. The economic profit is shown as the area between the marginal-benefit curve and the marginal-cost curve up to the profit-maximizing quantity of housing H^*. In Figure 12–13, the economic profit is shown by the shaded area between the two curves.

Competition among building firms ensures that the price of land equals the willingness to pay for land. If one housing producer offered to pay less than the potential economic profit, the landowner could find another producer who is willing to pay more. Bidding among competing producers will bid up the price of residential land until it reaches the potential economic profit from using the land. This is the leftover principle: Competition among potential land users ensures that economic profit (total revenue − total nonland cost) goes to landowners.

The next step in our analysis of residential land use is to explore the effects of spatial variation in the price of housing. Suppose the housing producer chooses a different location, where the price of housing is higher. The price could be higher because the new site (i) is more accessible to jobs, (ii) has a lower crime rate, (iii) has higher environmental quality, or (iv) has better schools.

Figure 12–14 shows the implications of a higher price of housing on the profit-maximizing quantity of housing. The higher price generates a higher marginal-benefit

FIGURE 12–13 Housing Production and the Price of Residential Land

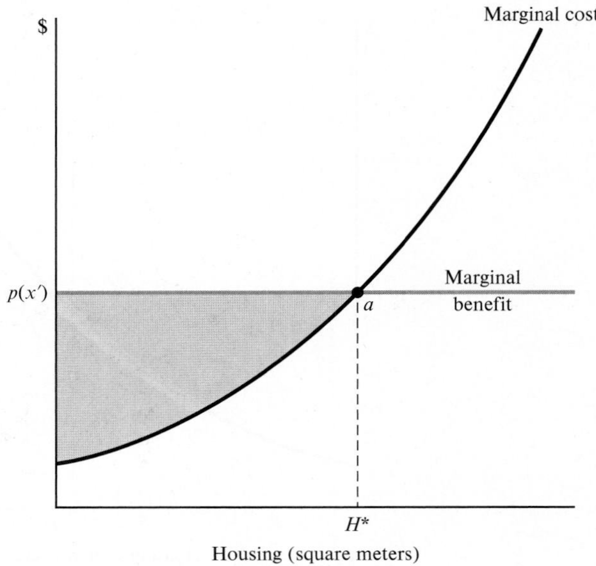

FIGURE 12–14 Effects of a Higher Housing Price

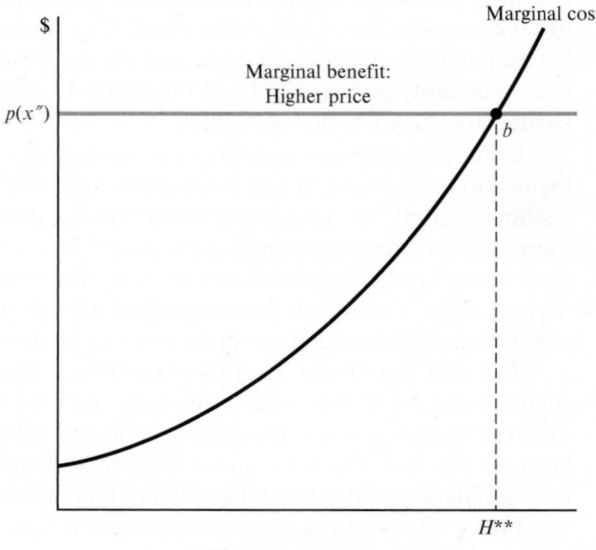

FIGURE 12-15 An Increase in the Price of Housing Increases the Price of Residential Land

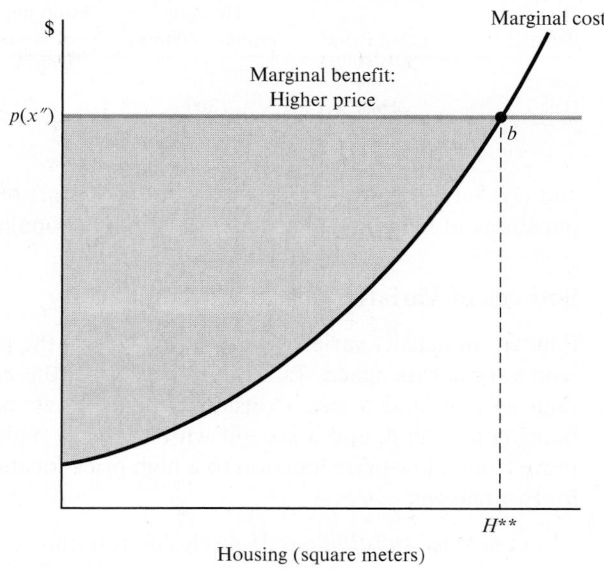

curve for housing, and the marginal principle is satisfied with a larger quantity of housing: $H^{**} > H^{*}$. In other words, an increase in the price of housing increases the profit-maximizing quantity of housing on the one-hectare site. Wherever housing prices are relatively high—because of job access, better environmental quality, lower crime, better schools—we expect more housing per unit of land, that is, a higher housing density. A higher housing density means (i) a larger share of land will be covered by structures, and (ii) buildings will be taller.

Figure 12-15 shows the implications of a higher price of housing on the price of residential land. The upward shift of the marginal-benefit curve increases the potential economic profit, measured as the area between the marginal-benefit curve and the marginal-cost curve. Competition among housing producers transforms this potential economic profit into land rent: landowners benefit from higher housing prices. The lesson from Figures 12-3 and 12-15 is that wherever housing prices are relatively high—because of job access, better environmental quality, lower crime, better schools—the price of residential land will be relatively high.

4. POPULATION DENSITY

We have seen that the prices of housing and residential land vary within a metropolitan economy. Both prices are relatively high in areas with (i) relatively high job accessibility, (ii) relatively low crime rates, (iii) relatively high environmental quality,

TABLE 12–1 Population Density

Housing Price	Land Price	Housing (square meters)	Land per Unit of Housing	Land per Dwelling	Households per Hectare
Low	Low	250	2	500	20
High	High	200	0.25	50	200

and (iv) relatively productive schools. In this part of the chapter we explore the implications of high housing and land prices on population density.

Sources of Variation in Population Density

Population density varies within a city because the prices of housing and residential land vary across space. Table 12–1 illustrates the combined effects of variation in housing and land prices. Consider two locations, one with relatively low prices of housing and land, and a second with relatively high prices of housing and land. A move from a low-price location to a high-price location increases population density for two reasons.

1. *Consumer substitution.* Households respond to a higher housing price by consuming fewer square meters of space. Housing consumption is 250 square meters at the low-price location, compared to 200 at the high-price location.
2. *Input substitution.* Housing producers economize on land when its price is relatively high. With a low land price, there are 2 square meters of land per square meter of housing: the footprint of a one-story house is half the lot. With a high land price, there are only 0.25 square meters of land per square meter of housing: people live in four-story residential structures.

As shown in the fifth column, the land per dwelling is 500 square meters at a low-price location, compared to 25 at the high-price location. The sixth column shows population density, measured as households per hectare. The density at a low-price location is 20 per hectare (10,000 square meters divided by 500), compared to 200 per hectare (10,000/50) at the high-price location.

Population Density within Cities

Figure 12–16 shows population density in Boston. Each jigsaw piece represents a census tract and is extruded (pushed up) to a height equal to the tract's population density (residents per hectare). The ribbons in the map represent freeways, extruded to a value of 25 to provide a measuring rod for population density. Density reaches its highest level in the central area, where relatively high prices of housing and land cause residents and housing producers to economize on housing and land. In general, population density decreases as the distance to the city center increases, reflecting decreasing housing and land prices.

The phenomenon of relatively high central density is widespread. In Paris, the population density in the central area is roughly six times the density at a distance of

FIGURE 12–16 Residential (Population) Density, Boston, 2005

20 kilometers. In New York, population density near the center is roughly four times the density at a distance of 20 kilometers. One exception to the general pattern of higher central density is Moscow, a planned city (as opposed to a market-based city) where density decreases as we approach the city center. Specifically, population density is 300 people per hectare at a distance of 20 kilometers from the center, and decreases to roughly 150 people per hectare at a distance of 3 kilometers from the center.

Population Density across Cities

Population density varies considerably across U.S. metropolitan areas (Fulton, Pendall, Nguyen, and Harrison, 2001). Among the 20 most densely populated areas, the range is 40 people per hectare in New York to 14 per hectare in Santa Barbara. In contrast with popular perceptions, 12 of the 14 most densely populated metropolitan areas (and 13 of the top 20) are in the West, including eight cities in California. The high density in western cities reflects relatively high land prices. In fact, the two poster-cities for sprawl, Los Angeles (number 2, with 21 people per hectare) and Phoenix (number 11, with 18 per hectare), are more dense than Chicago (number 15, with 15 per hectare) and Boston (number 19, with 14 per hectare).

FIGURE 12–17 Built-Up Density in World Cities

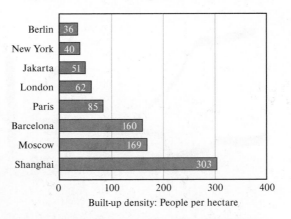

	Built-up density: People per hectare
Berlin	36
New York	40
Jakarta	51
London	62
Paris	85
Barcelona	160
Moscow	169
Shanghai	303

Source: Bertraud, Alain, "Metropolis: A Measure of the Spatial Organization of 7 Large Cities," *Disponible sur*, 2001; Bertraud, Alain, and Malpezzi, Stephen, "The Spatial Distribution of Population in 48 World Cities: Implications for Cities in Transition," Working Paper, The Center for Urban Land Research, University of Wisconsin, 2003.

Figure 12–17 shows the built-up density in selected cities around the world. Built-up density equals the total population of a metropolitan area divided by the amount of land in urban use, including residential areas, industrial districts, commercial areas, roads, schools, and city parks. Asian cities are at the top of the density list, and U.S. cities are at the bottom. New York is the densest U.S. metropolitan area, yet its density is about half the density of Paris, one-fourth the density of Barcelona, and roughly one-eighth the density of Shanghai. Los Angeles, the second densest U.S. metropolitan area, is roughly half as dense as New York, while Chicago is roughly one-third as dense, and Atlanta is roughly one-fifth as dense.

REVIEW THE CONCEPTS

1. In a city where all employment is in a central business district, the housing price curve is [____] sloped because of [____] and is convex because of [____].
2. Suppose at location $x = 10$, households consume 120 units of housing and the monthly commuting cost per kilometer is \$60. The slope of the housing-price curve is $-$\$[____].
3. Use Figure 12–18. A move from 12 kilometers to 6 kilometers increases the price of housing by \$[____] from the savings in [____] and by \$[____] from the benefits of [____].
4. For each additional 1 kilometer of distance between work and home, commute expense increases by \$10 and commute time increases by 3 hours. The opportunity cost of commuting time is \$20 per hour. If at $x = 10$, housing consumption is $h(10) = 200$, the slope of the housing price curve is $-$\$[____].

FIGURE 12-18

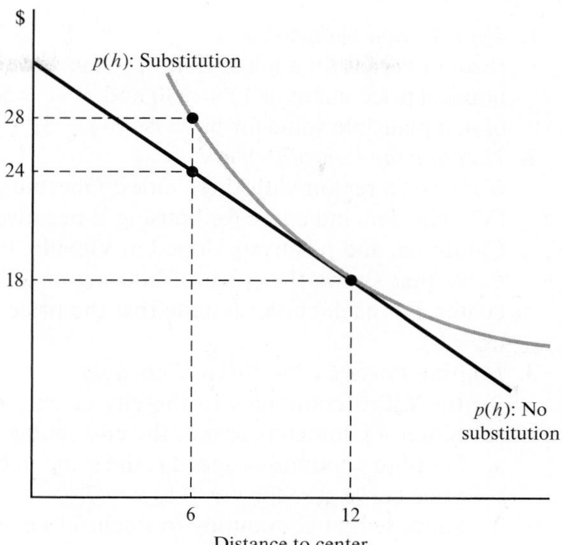

5. A household that relocates to a neighborhood with a higher crime rate will pay a [______] housing price.
6. A household that relocates to a neighborhood with a lower level of air pollution will pay a [______] housing price.
7. The bid for residential land is shown by the area between a housing producer's [____] curve and its [____] curve.
8. As we move from a location with relatively low housing prices to a location with relatively high housing prices, population density [____] because (i) [____] decreases in response to [____] and (ii) [____] decreases in response to [____].
9. In Paris, the population density of the central area is roughly [____] (choose 2, 6, or 10) times the density at a distance of 20 kilometers.
10. For each pair of variables, indicate whether the relationship is positive, negative, neutral, or ambiguous.

Parameter	Choice or Equilibrium Variable	Relationship
price of housing	housing consumption per household	[______]
h: housing consumption	slope of housing-price curve (absolute value)	[______]
T: time cost of commuting per km	slope of housing-price curve (absolute value)	[______]
number of trips to city center	slope of housing-price curve (absolute value)	[______]
neighborhood crime rate	price of housing	[______]
price of residential land	land per unit of housing	[______]

APPLY THE CONCEPTS

1. *Job Interview with Zillow*
In an interview for a job at Zillow, you are given the following exercise. Along the housing-price curve, $p(1) = \$30$ and $p(7) = \$12$. For the intermediate distance of 4, a plausible value for price is $p(4) = \$[\_\_\_\_]$ (choose 15, 21, 27). Illustrate.
2. *Violating the Law of Demand*
Consider a region with three cities: Obeyburg (B), Catatonia (C), and Vioville (V). The demand curve for housing is negatively sloped in Obeyburg, vertical in Catatonia, and positively sloped in Vioville. For each city, draw a housing-price curve that shows the price of housing as a function of x, the distance to city center. For each curve, assume that the price of housing is \$1 at the city center ($x = 0$).
3. *Housing Prices for the YoPro Household*
Sentra YoPro commutes to the city center, while Suba YoPro commutes to a subcenter 4 kilometers east of the city center.
   a. Suppose commuting speed is the same in both directions. Draw the housing-price curve $p(x)$ for $x = 0$ to $x = 7$.
   b. Suppose that commuting to a central job is slower than commuting to a sub-center job. Draw the housing-price curve $p(x)$ for $x = 0$ to $x = 7$.
   c. Suppose commuting speed is the same for both types of commuting, but Suba earns a higher wage. Draw the housing-price curve $p(x)$ for $x = 0$ to $x = 7$.
4. *Housing Prices: Detroit vs. Paris*
People in Detroit travel in air-conditioned land yachts on uncongested freeways, while people in Paris travel on slow, crowded buses subject to strong armpit effects. The central area of Detroit is deserted after work hours, while central Paris bustles with activity in restaurants, museums, concert halls, and theaters. For Detroit, t_D is the travel cost per trip per km of distance to the city center and n_D is the number of trips to the center. For Paris, t_P is the travel cost per trip per km of distance to the city center and n_P is the number of trips to the center. Assume that in each city, the housing-price curve is negatively sloped.
   a. Illustrate the housing-price curves for the two cities, and explain why one is steeper than the other.
   b. Suppose $\{t_D, t_P, n_D, n_P\} = \{20, 50, 1, 6\}$ and housing consumption is $h =$ 200 square meters. The slope of the housing-price function is $-\$[\_\_\_\_]$ in Detroit, compared to $-\$[\_\_\_\_]$ in Paris.
5. *Pollution and Housing Prices*
Consider a household in which a single worker commutes to the city center. For each additional 1 kilometer of distance between work and home, the monthly cost of commuting increases by \$20. Housing consumption is the same at all locations: $h = 100$ square meters. A polluting factory is located at $x = 6$. At $x =$ 0, the price of housing is \$10 per square meter. For each additional 1 kilometer of distance between the factory and a home, the monthly health care cost of a

household decreases by \$30. Draw the housing-price curve, and indicate the slope at $x = 2$, the slope at $x = 7$, and the price at $x = 10$.

6. *Crime and Housing Prices*
Consider a city where no one has theft insurance and everyone commutes to the city center. Each household occupies a 100-square-meter dwelling with \$7,000 worth of possessions. The probability that any particular household will be burglarized and lose all its possessions is 0.10 at the city center and decreases by 0.01 per mile. The price of housing is \$10 per square meter at the city center. Commuting cost is \$40 per mile per month. Draw the housing-price curve, and indicate the slope at $x = 5$, the slope at $x = 12$, the price at $x = 10$, and the price at $x = 12$.

7. *Housing Prices and Land Prices*
A household located $x = 10$ km from the city center occupies a pays an annual rent of \$9,000 for a standard dwelling. The annual non-land cost per dwelling is \$5,000, and there are 8 dwellings per hectare. The annual interest rate is 5 percent.

a. At $x = 10$, the willingness to pay for land is \$[____] per hectare per year and the market value (purchase price) of land is \$[____] per hectare.

b. Suppose we shift attention to $x = 11$. How would the calculations change? For what variables would we use (i) a larger value, (ii) a smaller value, or (iii) the same value?

8. *Who Pays a Development Tax?*
Consider the effects of a development tax of \$10 per square meter of living space, paid in legal terms by developers. Suppose each developer produces 9,000 square meters of housing on one hectare of land. Predict the effect of the tax on (i) the profit of the typical developer and (ii) land rent per hectare. Illustrate.

REFERENCES AND READING

1. Bertaud, Alain, and Stephen Malpezzi, "The Spatial Distribution of Population in 48 World Cities: Implications for Cities in Transition." Working Paper, The Center for Urban Land Research, University of Wisconsin, 2003.
2. Bertaud, Alain, "Clearing the Air in Atlanta: Transit and Smart Growth or Conventional Economics?" *Journal of Urban Economics* 54 (2003), pp. 379–400.
3. Brueckner, J., "Urban Sprawl: Lessons from Urban Economics," in W. Gale and J. Pack, eds. Brookings-Wharton Papers on Urban Affairs, 2001.
4. Brueckner, Jan K., Jacques-Francois Thisse, and Yves Zenou, "Why Is Central Paris Rich and Downtown Detroit Poor? An Amenity-Based Theory." *European Economic Review* 43 (1999), pp. 91–107.
5. Burchfield, M., H. G. Overman, D. Puga, and M. A. Turner, "Causes of Sprawl: A Portrait from Space." *Quarterly Journal of Economics,* May 2006.
6. Cullen, J. B., and S. D. Levitt, "Crime, Urban Flight, and the Consequences for Cities." *Review of Economics and Statistics* 81 (1999), pp. 159–69.

7. Davis and Heathcote, "The Price and Quantity of Residential Land in the US." *Journal of Monetary Economics* (2007).
8. Fulton, William, Rolf Pendall, Mai Nguyen, and Alicia Harrison, "Who Sprawls Most? How Growth Patterns Differ across the U.S." The Brookings Institution Survey Series. July 2001, pp. 1–23.
9. Glaeser, Edward, and Matthew Kahn, "Sprawl and Urban Growth," Chapter 56 in *Handbook of Regional and Urban Economics 4: Cities and Geography,* edited by Vernon Henderson and Jacques-Francois Thisse. Amsterdam: Elsevier, 2004.
10. Glaeser, Edward, Joshua Gottlieb, and Kristina Tobio, "Housing Booms and City Centers." *American Economic Review* 102.3 (2012), pp. 127–133.
11. Glaeser, E. and M. Kahn, "Sprawl and Urban Growth," in J.V. Henderson and J.-F. Thisse, eds., *Handbook of Regional and Urban Economics Volume 4* (2006).
12. Guerrieri, Veronica, Daniel Hartley, and Erik Hurst, "Within-City Variation in Urban Decline: The Case of Detroit." *American Economic Review* 102.3 (2012), pp. 120–126.
13. Kahn, Matthew, "The Environmental Impact of Suburbanization." *Journal of Policy Analysis and Management* 19 (2000).
14. Kahn, Matthew, and Randall Walsh, "The Role of the Amenities (Environmental and Otherwise) in Shaping Cities," Chapter 7 in *Handbook of Urban and Regional Economics Volume 5,* edited by Gilles Duranton, J. Vernon Henderson, and William C. Strange. Amsterdam: Elsevier, 2015.
15. O'Sullivan, Arthur, "The Distribution of Jobs within Cities: Integration, Density, and Accessibility *or* There's a Lot of πr^2 Out There." Working Paper, 2016.
16. Patacchini, Eleonora, and Yves Zenou, 2009, "Urban Sprawl in Europe," Brookings-Wharton Papers on Urban Affairs, pp. 125–149.
17. Persky, Joseph, and Wim Wiewel, "Urban Decentralization, Suburbanization and Sprawl: An Equity Perspective," Chapter 7 in *The Oxford Handbook of Urban Economics and Planning,* edited by Nancy Brooks, Kieran Donaghy, and Gerrit-Jan Knaap. New York: Oxford University Press, 2011.
18. Wilson, Beth, and James Frew, "Apartment Rents and Locations in Portland, Oregon: 1992–2002." *Journal of Real Estate Research* 29 (2007), pp. 201–217.

CHAPTER 13

Spatial Distribution of Employment and Residence

Forget the damned motor car and build the cities for lovers and friends.

—LEWIS MUMFORD

1. THE SPATIAL DISTRIBUTION OF EMPLOYMENT AND RESIDENCE

There are several ways to represent the spatial distribution of employment and residence within a metropolitan area. One approach is to distinguish between the central city and the rest of the metropolitan area. Recall that a central city is defined as the principal municipality of a metropolitan area, for example, the political city of Chicago or San Francisco. The rest of the metropolitan area includes other municipalities, which together constitute the "suburban" area of the metropolitan area.

Commuting Patterns

Figure 13-1 uses commuting patterns to show the changes in the spatial distributions of residence and jobs between 1960 and 2000. The data include the 152 metropolitan areas that had at least 100,000 residents in 1960. The areas (central city and suburbs) are defined in terms of 1960 geography, using the 1960 boundaries of central cities to distinguish between the two areas. Over the period 1960–2000, the fraction of workers commuting within central cities decreased from 0.45 to 0.15, while the fraction of workers commuting within suburban areas increased from 0.34 to 0.62. The fraction of workers commuting between central cities and suburbs didn't change in total (0.22) but tilted slightly in favor of "reverse" commuting from central cities to suburban jobs.

We can use the commuting data to compute the shares of employment in central cities and suburbs. Over the 40-year period, the fraction of jobs in central cities

FIGURE 13–1 Distribution of Residence and Jobs: Central City versus Suburbs

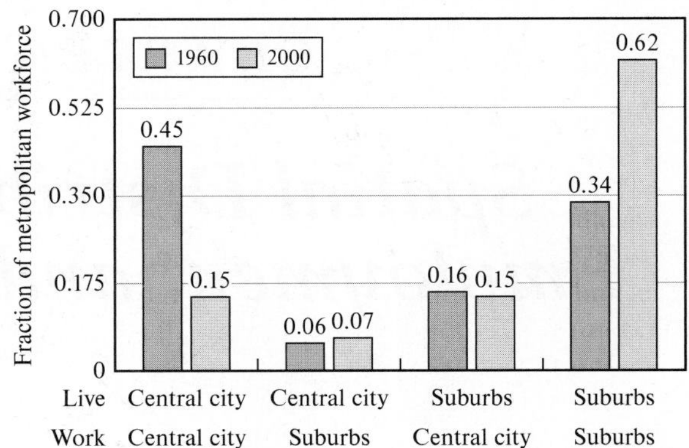

Source: Baum-Snow, Nathaniel, "Changes in Transportation Infrastructure and Commuting Patterns in US Metropolitan Areas, 1960–2000," *American Economic Review,* 100, 2010, 378–382.

decreased from 0.61 (equal to 0.45 + 0.16) to 0.30 (equal to 0.15 + 0.15). In contrast, the fraction of jobs in suburban areas increased from 0.40 (equal to 0.06 + 0.34) to 0.69 (equal to 0.07 + 0.62).

Five-Kilometer Shares and Median Locations

We can also distinguish between activity in a fixed central area and in the rest of the metropolitan area. For the largest 25 metropolitan areas, roughly 14 percent of jobs are within 5 kilometers of the center. The median workplace is defined as the distance that splits jobs into two equal quantities, with half the jobs closer to the center and the other half farther from the center. For the largest 25 metropolitan areas, the median workplace is 22 kilometers from the center. For workers in these large metropolitan areas, the median homeplace (the distance that separates workers' residences into two equal halves, with half living closer and half living farther) is 27 kilometers from the center.

Table 13–1 uses data from LEHD (longitudinal employer-household dynamics) to show the spatial distribution of workplaces and homeplaces in the 25 largest U.S. metropolitan areas. The first column shows total employment in the metropolitan area. The median workplace ranges from 12 kilometers in Portland to 30 kilometers in Chicago and Miami. The 5-kilometer workplace share ranges from 4 percent in Baltimore to 27 percent in San Francisco. The median homeplace ranges from 15 in Portland to 36 in Chicago. The 5-kilometer homeplace share ranges from 1 percent in Orlando and Detroit to 13 percent in San Francisco.

Table 13–2 shows data on the spatial distribution of workplaces and homeplaces in a selection of mid-size and small U.S. cities. The first column shows

TABLE 13–1 Distribution of Workplaces and Homeplaces, Largest U.S. Metro Areas, 2014

City	Jobs (1000)	Median Workplace	Median Homeplace	Percent Jobs within 5 km of Center	Percent Workers Living within 5 km of Center
New York	8736	20	25	17	5
Los Angeles	5777	24	27	9	3
Chicago	4348	30	36	18	4
Dallas	3167	25	33	10	2
Washington, DC	2896	17	24	6	4
Houston	2779	21	29	9	3
Philadelphia	2682	23	25	15	7
Atlanta	2340	25	34	10	3
Miami	2302	30	31	9	4
Boston	2285	18	23	26	8
San Francisco	2136	19	25	27	13
Detroit	1803	27	30	8	1
Phoenix	1801	16	24	13	2
Minneapolis	1783	15	22	18	5
Seattle	1720	19	24	7	3
Denver	1300	21	23	5	2
St. Louis	1289	21	26	12	4
San Diego	1276	14	19	9	3
Baltimore	1265	21	23	4	3
Tampa	1162	22	27	12	4
Pittsburgh	1135	16	21	22	8
Orlando	1086	25	29	10	1
Charlotte	1054	16	25	18	5
Portland	1039	12	15	24	8
Indianapolis	970	16	19	20	4

total employment in the metropolitan area. The median workplace ranges from 8 kilometers in Spokane to 14 kilometers in San Antonio. The 5-kilometer workplace share ranges from 7 percent in Harrisburg to 38 percent in Spokane. The median homeplace ranges from 10 in Toledo to 20 in Birmingham. The 5-kilometer homeplace share ranges from 6 percent in Birmingham to 19 percent in Spokane.

Employment Density

As shown earlier in the chapter, employment density varies within cities, with relatively high density near city centers and close to highways. Table 13–3 uses LEHD data to show employment density classes in select metropolitan areas. The first column of numbers shows the share of jobs in areas with an employment density of at least 10 jobs per hectare. Moving to the right in the table, the threshold density increases, to 25 jobs per hectare and 75 jobs per hectare. The last column shows the maximum job density, which ranges from 345 per hectare in Atlanta to 2622 per hectare in Chicago.

There is substantial variation in the fraction of jobs in high-density areas. Economists define an employment center as an area where (a) employment density is

TABLE 13-2 Distribution of Workplaces and Homeplaces, Mid-Size U.S. Metro Areas, 2014

City	Jobs (1000)	Median Workplace	Median Homeplace	Percent Jobs within 5 km of Center	Percent Workers Living within 5 km of Center
Columbus	960	13	16	15	7
San Antonio	883	14	17	14	7
Austin	871	10	19	29	8
Salt Lake City	618	11	12	15	13
Louisville	612	9	14	13	8
Memphis	593	12	17	13	9
Oklahoma City	590	11	17	12	9
Birmingham	498	13	20	26	6
Rochester	498	9	15	29	9
Grand Rapids	493	12	15	19	13
Des Moines	335	10	11	31	16
Harrisburg	324	12	15	7	7
Wichita	292	11	14	9	7
Syracuse	290	9	15	28	13
Toledo	278	10	10	20	18
Boise	276	10	15	27	14
Jackson	269	9	16	30	10
Portland ME	247	10	24	31	16
Chattanooga	228	9	15	33	9
Spokane	218	8	11	38	19

TABLE 13-3 Employment Density in Select U.S. Cities, 2014

Metro Area	>10 Jobs per Hectare	>25 Jobs per Hectare	>75 Jobs per Hectare	Maximum Density (jobs per hectare)
Atlanta	0.438	0.239	0.102	345
Boston	0.852	0.614	0.41	1073
Chicago	0.608	0.344	0.201	2622
Los Angeles	0.811	0.551	0.199	1572
Portland	0.638	0.339	0.138	501

at least 25 workers per hectare and (b) contiguous census tracts contain at least 10,000 jobs. In Atlanta, roughly 24 percent of jobs are in areas with density high enough to be considered an employment center, meaning that roughly three-fourths of jobs are considered dispersed. At the other extreme, roughly 62 percent of jobs in Boston are in employment centers, leaving only 38 percent as dispersed. For the highest density class (density > 75 jobs per hectare) the share is 0.41 in Boston, compared to roughly 0.20 in Chicago and Los Angeles, and only 0.102 in Atlanta.

Employment Subcenters

As we saw in Chapter 4, agglomeration economies encourage firms to locate close to one another, and one manifestation of clustering is an *employment center,* a term that includes the principal employment center for the metropolitan area and smaller subcenters. Recall that firms cluster to improve skills matching and share intermediate inputs, labor pools, and information. For example, manufacturing firms in a cluster can purchase intermediate goods (components) and services (testing and repair services) from a common supplier. A cluster of office firms facilitates face time between workers in different firms and allows office firms to share banks, law firms, and advertising firms. Firms in office clusters also share restaurants and hotels. One rule of thumb is that a cluster of 2.5 million square feet of office space can support a 250-room hotel.

The typical large urban area includes at least a few employment centers, including a principal employment center and some subcenters. Any census tract with employment density above 25 workers per hectare can be part of an employment center, and it doesn't take many high-density census tracts to generate 10,000 workers, the conventional threshold for an employment center.

1. A study of Los Angeles revealed 36 employment centers in 1980, compared to 48 centers in 2000 (Guliano, Agarwal, and Redfearn, 2007). For Los Angeles County, the share of employment in centers was 0.46 in 2000, compared to 0.43 for Orange County (Giuliano and Small, 1991).
2. A study of Chicago revealed 20 subcenters (McMillen and McDonald, 1998), including specialized industrial areas and diverse subcenters that mix industry, services, and retailing.

A study of employment subcenters in 62 metropolitan areas shows that the number of subcenters varies considerably across metropolitan areas (McMillen and Smith, 2003). At the upper end, the study counted 46 subcenters in Los Angeles, compared to 38 in New York, 14 in Seattle, and 12 in Chicago, Dallas, and San Francisco. At the lower end, among the metropolitan areas with a single subcenter were Charlotte, North Carolina; Colorado Springs, Colorado; Honolulu, Hawaii; Miami, Florida; Pittsburgh, Pennsylvania; and Spokane, Washington. Among the 62 urban areas in the sample, several areas with populations of at least 700,000 had no subcenters: Austin, Texas; Buffalo, New York; Nashville, Tennessee; and Salt Lake City, Utah.

The study concludes that the number of subcenters in an urban area is determined in large part by two factors. First, the number of subcenters increases with the population of the metropolitan area. A second factor is the level of traffic congestion: an urban area with relatively high congestion has a relatively large number of subcenters. Stated another way, an urban area with relatively high congestion develops its first subcenter at a relatively low population.

We can draw several conclusions about the role of subcenters in the metropolitan economy.

1. Subcenters are numerous in both new and old large metropolitan areas.
2. In most metropolitan areas, most jobs are dispersed rather than concentrated in CBDs and subcenters.
3. Many subcenters are highly specialized, indicating the presence of large agglomeration economies.

4. The central area of the city remains the largest and densest concentration of employment.
5. Employment density (jobs per hectare) decreases as distance from the center increases.
6. Firms in subcenters interact with firms in the center, and the value of access to firms in the center is reflected in higher land prices near the center.
7. Firms in different subcenters interact, indicating that subcenters have different functions and are complementary.

What is the economic relationship between a central business district and the surrounding subcenters and dispersed firms? The central business district provides superior opportunities for the face time required for the production of services such as advertising, accounting, legal counsel, and investment banking. Although advances in telecommunications have reduced the need for some types of interaction, face time is still required to exchange complex and tacit information as well as to establish trust among economic agents involved in financial and production relationships.

2. SUBURBANIZATION AND SPRAWL

Over the last several decades, urban jobs and residents have decentralized, moving outward from central areas to suburban areas. As shown in Figure 13–1, between 1960 and 2000, the fraction of urban workers living in central cities decreased from roughly one half to roughly one quarter. In U.S. cities today, the most frequent commuting trip is suburban: over three-fifths of workers (62%) commute within suburban areas.

Decentralization of Population

The decentralization of metropolitan population is a longstanding and worldwide phenomenon. Mills (1972) documents suburbanization dating back to 1880. In a study of four cities (Baltimore, Milwaukee, Philadelphia, and Rochester), the fraction of people living within three miles of the center decreased from 0.88 in 1880 to 0.24 in 1963. Between 1801 and 1961, the share of London's population living within three miles of the city center dropped from 0.88 to 0.24, and similar changes occurred in Paris. In cities throughout the world, population has been shifting outward away from the city center.

What factors contributed to the decentralization of population over the last several decades? One factor is rising income. The demand for housing increases with income, and because housing prices are generally lower in suburban areas, rising income increases the relative attractiveness of suburban locations. An increase in income also increases the opportunity cost of commuting, increasing the relative attractiveness of locations close to workplaces. So it is not clear, in theory, whether higher income leads to more distant residential locations. There is evidence that income growth encourages suburbanization (Anas, Arnott, and Small, 1998).

Another factor in suburbanization of population is lower commuting costs. Transportation innovations over the last 180 years, from the horse-drawn omnibus of 1827 to the fast and comfortable automobiles of today, have decreased the monetary and time costs of commuting. A decrease in commuting costs decreases the relative cost of living far from employment areas, contributing to suburbanization. In addition, the suburbanization of jobs and people reinforce one another: some jobs follow workers to the suburbs, and some workers follow jobs to the suburbs.

Several other factors contribute to the suburbanization of population.

1. *Old housing.* The deterioration of central-city housing encourages households to move to the suburbs, where most new housing is built.
2. *Central-city fiscal problems.* Many central cities have relatively high taxes, encouraging households to move to low-tax suburbs. The causality goes both ways: Fiscal problems cause suburbanization, and suburbanization contributes to central-city fiscal problems.
3. *Crime.* Many central cities have higher crime rates than suburban areas, encouraging households to move to the suburbs. Cullen and Levitt (1999) estimated that during the 1970s and 1980s, that for each additional central-city crime, one additional person relocates from the central city to a suburb. In the largest metropolitan areas (population exceeding 1 million), central cities now have lower crime rates than suburban areas. This is a dramatic reversal of historical patterns, and has increased the relative attractiveness of living in central-cities.
4. *Education.* Suburban schools are often considered superior to central-city schools, encouraging households to relocate to the suburbs. Later in the book, we'll explore the reasons for differences between central-city and suburban schools.

Sprawl and Density Facts

There is a spirited debate among policy makers about "urban sprawl." As a city's population increases, the city can grow up by building taller buildings, or it can grow out by occupying more land. The people concerned about urban sprawl suggest that there is too little "up" and too much "out." For several decades, the amount of urbanized land in the United States has increased more rapidly than urban population, resulting in sprawling urban landscapes.

What causes urban sprawl and low-density cities? Living at a low density means consuming a large quantity of land. Land is a normal good, so the higher the income, the larger the consumption of land and the lower the population density. A second factor is a low cost of travel, which allows workers and shoppers to live relatively long distances from jobs, shops, and destinations for social interaction. Distant land is cheaper, so lot sizes are larger and population density is lower. Putting these two factors together, high income makes people demand large lots, and a low travel cost allows them to move to the suburbs where land is relatively cheap. So we get low density development at distant locations, also known as urban sprawl.

Is there a cultural dimension to urban density and sprawl? Bertaud and Malpezzi (2003) suggest that cultural differences explain some of the dramatic differences in urban density across world cities. Asia has much higher urban density than other continents, much higher than could be explained by other factors such as income. Similarly, the variation in density across other continents could reflect differences in preferences for living space. In U.S. metropolitan areas, the presence of immigrants tends to increase density, suggesting that culture is relevant (Fulton, Pendall, Nguyen, and Harrison, 2001).

A number of government policies in the United States encourage low densities in large metropolitan areas.

1. *Congestion externalities.* As we discuss later in the book, people who use streets and highways during peak travel periods slow other drivers, imposing external costs on other travelers. This underpricing of urban transportation encourages people to commute relatively long distances from locations far from the city center, where the low price of land encourages large lots.
2. *Mortgage subsidy.* Interest on housing mortgages is a deductible expense for federal and state income taxes, providing a subsidy for housing that increases housing consumption. Land and housing are complementary goods, so the mortgage subsidy increases lot sizes, decreasing density.
3. *Underpricing of fringe infrastructure.* In some metropolitan areas, the infrastructure cost of new development at the urban fringe is not fully borne by developers and their customers. In response, many states use development fees (impact fees) to impose the cost of fringe development on developers and their customers.
4. *Zoning.* Many suburban municipalities use zoning to establish minimum lot sizes. One motivation is to exclude low-income households, whose tax contribution may fall short of the costs they impose on municipal government.

Glaeser and Kahn (2004) argue that sprawl is caused mainly by the automobile and the truck. These two travel modes eliminated the orientation of firms and workers toward the indivisible transportation infrastructure near the city center (hub-spoke transit systems, ports, and rail terminals). The authors show that sprawl is ubiquitous across metropolitan areas with all levels of income, poverty, and government fragmentation, suggesting that something else–the internal combustion engine–is the driving force behind sprawl. The authors suggest that the subsidies for highways and housing are too small to have much of an effect.

The Consequences of Low Density

A recent study measures some of the consequences of low-density living in U.S. cities (Kahn, 2000). Compared to the typical central-city household, a suburban household requires 58 percent more land (1,167 square meters versus 739). A suburban household actually consumes about the same amount of energy in housing: Although suburban dwellings are larger, they are newer and more energy-efficient. A suburban household drives about 30 percent more than a central-city household. In general, low density means more travel: The elasticity of vehicle miles traveled with respect to urban density is −0.36, meaning that a 10 percent decrease in density increases vehicle miles by 3.6 percent. As a result, sprawl increases automobile-generated air pollution and the volume of greenhouse gases.

What about the loss of farmland to urban uses? For the United States as a whole, the elasticity of farmland acreage with respect to urban population is relatively small at 0.02: a 10 percent increase in population causes a 0.2 percent decrease in farmland. The loss of farmland at the city fringe indicates that the land is more valuable in urban use. As we saw earlier in the chapter, various public policies increase the residential value of fringe land, and the solution is to correct the distortionary policies. There is no evidence that urban sprawl has created a shortage of either agricultural land or agricultural products. If it had, the prices of agricultural products would increase, allowing farmers to bid more for land and thus outbid developers for land on the urban fringe.

Bertaud (2003) discusses the challenges associated with providing mass transit in low-density areas. Mass transit is feasible only if density around bus stops or transit stations is high enough to attract a sufficient number of riders. For the typical commuter, the maximum walking time to a transit stop is about 10 minutes, so a transit stop can serve households within an 800-meter radius. To support a bus system with an intermediate service level (two buses per hour and a half mile between stops), the population density in the service area must be at least 31 people per hectare. There are two U.S. metropolitan areas with at least 31 people per hectare: New York (40) and Honolulu (31). Of course, density is higher closer to centers and subcenters, and may be high enough to support mass transit. For example, the density of New York City is 80 people per hectare (compared to 40 for the metropolitan area). Later in the book, we'll explore various issues concerning the provision and pricing of mass transit.

A comparison of Barcelona to Atlanta reveals the transit challenge for U.S. cities (Bertaud, 2003). As shown in Figure 13–2, Barcelona is 28 times as dense

FIGURE 13–2 Population Density and Transit Accessibility, Atlanta vs. Barcelona

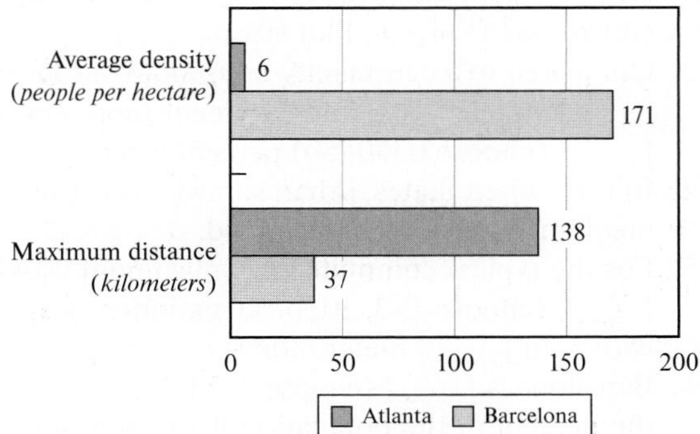

Source: Bertaud, Alain. "Clearing the Air in Atlanta: Transit and Smart Growth or Conventional Economics?" *Journal of Urban Economics* 54, 2003, 379–400.

as Atlanta. In Barcelona, 60 percent of the population lives within 600 meters of a transit station, compared to only 4 percent living within 800 meters of a transit station in Atlanta. To duplicate the accessibility and ridership of the Barcelona system, Atlanta would have to build an additional 3,400 kilometers of metro tracks and 2,800 more stations. In contrast, the Barcelona system has just 99 kilometers of tracks and 136 stations.

Policy Responses to Sprawl?

There are many factors behind urban sprawl. It partly reflects consumer choice–a rational choice of a large lot at the expense of other consumer products. A number of public policies contribute to urban sprawl, and the appropriate response is to eliminate these distortions. Would land-use patterns change by a little or a lot? If the relatively low density in U.S. cities results in large part from high income, low transport costs, and strong preferences for space, eliminating the policy distortions won't change density very much. But if the distortions–from congestion externalities, mortgage subsidies, underpricing of fringe infrastructure, and large-lot zoning–are significant, we would expect larger changes in density.

An alternative approach is to adopt anti-sprawl policies such as urban growth boundaries and development taxes. We'll discuss the trade-offs associated with these policies later in the book. An anti-sprawl policy may succeed in increasing density, but the question is whether the benefit of the policy exceeds its cost.

REVIEW AND APPLY THE CONCEPTS

1. Several factors contributed to the decentralization of population in cities: (i) [____] income; (ii) [____] commuting cost; (iii) [____] housing; (iv) fiscal problems in [____]; (v) [____] suburban schools.
2. Several government policies encourage low densities in large metropolitan areas: (i) [____] externalities; (ii) [____] subsidy; (iii) underpricing of fringe [____]; (iv) zoning for [____] lot size.
3. Compared to a central-city household, a suburban household consumes roughly [____] (choose 0, 30, 50) percent more energy in housing and drives roughly [____] (choose 0, 30, 50) percent more.
4. In the United States, urban sprawl has caused a relatively [____] (choose small, medium, large) loss in farmland.
5. For the typical commuter, the maximum walking time to a transit stop is about [____] (choose 1, 3, 10, or 40) minutes, so a transit stop can serve households within an [____] meter radius.
6. Barcelona is [____] (choose 2, 10, or 28) times as dense as Atlanta. In Barcelona, the percent of the population living within walking distance of a transit station is [____] (choose 10, 30, 60, or 90), compared to [____] (choose 4, 14, 24, or 34) percent in Atlanta.

REFERENCES AND READING

1. Bertaud, Alain, "Clearing the Air in Atlanta: Transit and Smart Growth or Conventional Economics?" *Journal of Urban Economics* 54 (2003), pp. 379–400.
2. Craig, Steven G., Janet E. Kohlhase, and Adam W. Perdue, "Empirical Polycentricity: The Complex Relationship Between Employment Centers," Working Paper, Department of Economics, University of Houston (2014).
3. Giuliano, Genevieve, Ajay Agarwal, and Christian Redfearn, "Metropolitan Trends in Employment and Housing: Literature Review." Prepared for the Transportation Research Board, 2008.
4. Giuliano, Genevieve, Ajay Agarwal, and Christian Redfearn, "Strangers in Our Midst: The Usefulness of Exploring Polycentricity." *Annals of Regional Science* 48 (2012), pp. 433–450.
5. McMillen, Daniel P., and Stefani C. Smith, "The Number of Subcenters in Large Urban Areas." *Journal of Urban Economics* 53 (2003), pp. 321–338.
6. O'Sullivan, Arthur, "The Distribution of Jobs within Cities: Integration, Density, and Accessibility *or* There's a Lot of πr^2 Out There." Working Paper, 2016.
7. Redfearn, Christian L., "The Topography of Metropolitan Employment: Identifying Centers of Employment in a Polycentric Urban Area." *Journal of Urban Economics* 61 (2007) 519–541.

CHAPTER 14

The Monocentric City and Urban General Equilibrium

One man's wage rise is another man's price increase.

—Harold Wilson

In the heyday of the monocentric city 100 years ago, most jobs in the typical city were near the city center. Manufacturers located close to ports and railroad terminals to economize on transport costs, and office firms clustered in the central business district to facilitate the exchange of information. Some workers lived near the city center, while others lived in suburbs and commuted by streetcars.

This chapter develops a model of the urban economy that is based on the traditional monocentric city. The model incorporates the interactions between the urban land market and the urban labor market. We use the model to explore the effects of changes in technology, climate, and public policy on land use, wages, and total employment. Although modern cities are not monocentric, the simple monocentric model provides insights into the workings of the urban economy.

1. THE MONOCENTRIC MODEL

The classic model of the monocentric city is based on the transportation and communication technology around the beginning of the 20th century. There are four key assumptions in the monocentric model.

1. *Central export node.* Manufacturing firms export their output from the city through a central export node: a port or railroad terminal.
2. *Horse carts.* Manufacturing firms use horse carts to transport output from factories to the central node.
3. *Hub-and-spoke streetcar.* Workers travel by streetcar from residential areas to their jobs in the central business district (CBD).
4. *Central information exchange.* Office workers travel between office firms to exchange information, the output of the office sector.

These assumptions make the city center the focal point of the metropolitan area. Manufacturers are oriented toward the export node, while office firms are oriented toward each other. Households are oriented toward jobs in factories and offices.

The Industrial Revolution and the Monocentric City

During the 19th century, the innovations of the Industrial Revolution caused the development of large monocentric cities. Technological innovations in production and energy increased economies of scale in production, leading to large-scale production in factories. The agglomeration economies in production–from sharing intermediate inputs, tapping common labor pools, knowledge spillovers, and improved labor matching–caused factories to cluster in large industrial cities. In addition, the Industrial Revolution generated innovations in intercity transportation that allowed the wider exploitation of comparative advantage, leading to increased trade and larger trading cities. An important question is, Why were the large cities monocentric, with highly centralized employment?

Consider first the transportation of people within cities. Before the 1820s, most urban travel was by foot, although a few wealthy people traveled by private horse carriage. In the hub-spoke system developed during the Industrial Revolution, the hub was the city center, and spokes radiated out from the center to residential areas. Over the course of the Industrial Revolution the efficiency of the hub-spoke system increased: the system became more efficient in transporting large numbers of workers and shoppers between residential areas and the central core area.

1. *Omnibus (1827).* The horse-drawn cart on rails had a top speed of six miles per hour. The word "omnibus" is Latin for "for all" and was later shortened to "bus."
2. *Cable cars (1873).* Steam-powered cable cars were introduced in San Francisco in 1873 and spread to other cities.
3. *Electric trolley (1873).* The trolley was powered by an on-board electric motor connected to overhead power lines with dangling wires that apparently reminded harried city dwellers of fishing (trolling).
4. *Subway (1890).* The world's first practical subway operated in London in 1890 with electric traction replacing smoky steam power. Boston built the first U.S. subway, a 1.5-mile line that used streetcars. It was followed by systems in New York (1904) and Philadelphia (1907).

These innovations decreased commuting costs and increased the feasible radius of cities. One rule of thumb is that the radius of a city is the distance that can be traveled in an hour. In the "walking city" of the early 19th century, the maximum radius was about two miles. The series of innovations in intracity transport increased travel speeds and increased the feasible radius of cities.

Consider next the course of construction technology over the 19th century. In the early 1800s, wood buildings were made of posts and beams with 16-inch timbers, and the practical height limit was three floors. The construction of a three-story building required highly skilled labor to fasten the posts and beams, so labor cost was relatively high. Although masonry buildings could be a bit taller, the height was limited by the thick walls required to support upper floors. In addition, masonry buildings were inflexible because every wall was load-bearing. A series of innovations decreased the cost of building taller buildings.

1. *Balloon frame building (1832).* A balloon frame uses small pieces of lumber, fastened by nails using relatively low-skill labor. A critical element in the spread of the balloon-frame building was the introduction of inexpensive manufactured nails. Before they were introduced in the 1830s, handcrafted nails were expensive enough to be listed as valued possessions in wills. The switch from high-skilled labor for beam-post buildings to low-skilled labor for balloon framed buildings decreased the labor cost of taller buildings. The first balloon-frame building was a warehouse in Chicago.
2. *Cast iron columns (1848).* Office buildings were transformed by the switch from masonry to metal frames. In 1848, a five-story building in New York used cast-iron columns instead of masonry walls.
3. *Steel frame (1885).* Steel is stronger and more elastic and workable than cast iron. The world's first skyscraper, an 11-story building housing the Home Insurance Company, was built in 1885 with a steel skeleton frame.

Building heights are constrained by the cost of vertical transportation. The burden of walking up stairs imposed a practical height limit on buildings. In 1854, Elisha Otis demonstrated the safe use of a steam-powered elevator. The key innovation was a safety latch that prevented the elevator car from plummeting down when the rope connecting the car to the pulley system broke. By 1857, the Otis elevator was deployed in a five-story building. When the power source for elevators switched from steam engines to electric motors, the cost of running elevators decreased and their range increased. In the world's first skyscraper, a bank of elevators carried people at a speed of 500 feet per minute.

Consider finally the transportation technology for the raw materials, intermediate inputs, and output of producers. As we saw earlier in the book, most intercity freight in the 1800s and early 1900s traveled by railroad or ship. For the transport of inputs and outputs within the city–between production sites and the port or rail terminal–firms relied on horse-drawn carts. A horse cart is slow and costly, and firms had an incentive to locate their production facilities close to ports, railroad terminals, and other central firms that produced intermediate inputs.

Land Use in the Monocentric City

Figure 14–1 shows the bid curves for four land users. Consider first the bid curves of business–office firms and manufacturers. The steepest curve is for the office sector. Recall that the output of office firms is transported in the minds and briefcases of office workers. In the simple monocentric model, the slope of a bid curve is determined by transport cost. The office bid curve is relatively steep because the opportunity cost

FIGURE 14–1 Land Rent and Land Use in a Monocentric City

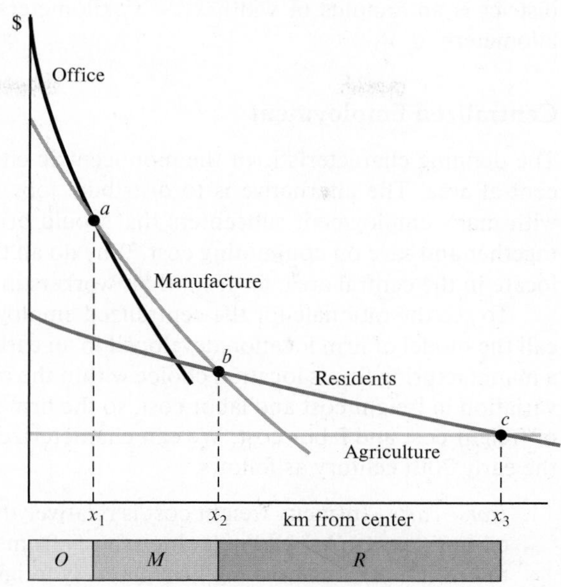

of travel for office workers is relatively high. The manufacturing bid curve is relatively flat because the opportunity cost of horses and wagoneers is lower than the opportunity cost of office workers.

Land within the central business district (CBD) is allocated to the highest bidder, either office firms or manufacturers. The office district is the area over which the office bid exceeds the manufacturing bid. In Figure 14–1, the office district is a circular area with a radius of x_1 kilometers. The manufacturing district is the area over which manufacturers outbid office firms and residents, shown in Figure 14–1 as an annulus of width $x_2 - x_1$ kilometers.

Why is the central area of the city occupied by office firms rather than manufacturing firms? Although both types of land users benefit from being close to the center, office firms have relatively high transport cost, generating a steeper bid curve and the ability to outbid manufacturing firms for the most accessible locations. This allocation is efficient because the office industry has more to gain from proximity to the city center. If an office firm were to swap places with a manufacturing firm, the travel cost of the office firm would increase while the freight cost of the manufacturing firm would decrease. Given the higher unit transport cost for office firms, total transport costs would increase. The market allocation, which gives central land to the office industry, economizes on transport costs.

The residential district is the area over which residents outbid other land users, urban and agricultural. In Figure 14–1, the resident bid curve is flatter than the manufacturing bid curve but steeper than the agricultural bid curve. The residential district is an annulus of width $x_3 - x_2$ kilometers, and the radius of the city is x_3 kilometers.

Centralized Employment

The defining characteristic of the monocentric city is that all employment is in the central area. The alternative is to distribute jobs more evenly throughout the city, with many employment subcenters that would bring workers and employers closer together and save on commuting cost. Why do all the manufacturers and office firms locate in the central area, far from their workers in the residential district?

To see the rationale for the centralized employment in the monocentric city, recall the model of firm location developed in an earlier chapter. To apply the model to a manufacturing firm's location choice within the city, we assume that there is spatial variation in freight cost and labor cost, so the firm's objective is to minimize the sum of freight cost and labor cost. We can characterize the transportation technology of the early 20th century as follows.

1. *Horse carts.* Intracity freight cost is relatively high because output is transported on horse carts. A 1-kilometer move away from the central export node (a port or rail terminal) increases the firm's weekly freight cost by \$6.
2. *Streetcars.* The market wage compensates workers for commuting cost, so the wage decreases as a firm moves away from the city center toward its suburban workforce. As a firm moves away from the city center, the savings in labor cost is relatively small because commuters use a fast and efficient streetcar. A 1-kilometer move away from the city center decreases the firm's weekly labor cost by \$1.

Under this transportation technology, the cost of transporting output (on horse carts) is high relative to the cost of transporting workers (in streetcars).

Figure 14–2 shows the freight cost and labor cost for different locations within the city. The firm's workforce lives 10 kilometers from the center. For the typical firm, freight cost increases from zero at the city center to \$60 at $x = 10$. In contrast, labor cost is \$25 at the center, and decreases to \$15 at the location of the firm's workforce at $x = 10$. Total cost $TC(x)$ is minimized at the city center (at \$25) because the cost of transporting output is large relative to the cost of transporting workers: a move away from the center increases freight cost by \$6 per kilometer but decreases labor costs by only \$1 per kilometer. The firm's rational choice is to locate far from its workforce but close to the export node.

The same logic applies to the location decision of office firms. The production of the office sector involves information exchange, which requires travel by office workers from one firm to another. An office firm that moved from the city center toward its suburban workforce would save on commuting cost and thus pay a lower wage. But the firm's workers would spend much more time traveling to the other office firms near the city center, so the firm would require more worker hours to produce a given quantity of output. For an office firm with relatively frequent interactions with other office firms, total cost will be lower near the city center.

FIGURE 14–2 Rationale for Centralized Manufacturing

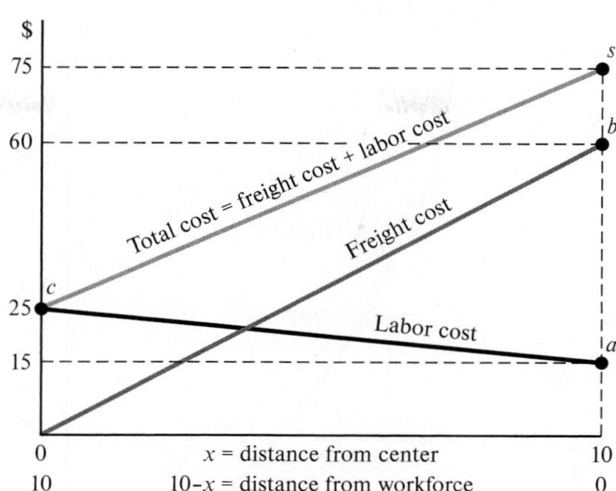

2. GENERAL-EQUILIBRIUM MODEL

We can use the model of the monocentric city to explore the interactions between the urban labor market and the urban land market. The model considers a city that is small (one of many in a nation) and open (people move costlessly between cities). The utility level of residents is determined at the national level and is unaffected by changes in the city. In other words, the utility level of city residents is fixed, but the population of the city varies.

Interactions between the Land and Labor Markets

To simplify matters, we adopt two assumptions. First, we assume for the moment that there is no consumer substitution or input substitution. Therefore, population density is the same at all residential locations, and employment density is the same at all business locations. Later in the chapter we'll see how variation in density affects the analysis. Second, we assume that the city is not circular, but rectangular with a fixed width of 10 kilometers and a length to be determined by the bids of business and residents.

The left panel of Figure 14–3 shows the urban land market. The business bid curve intersects the residential curve at point *a*, generating a 2-kilometer CBD. The total demand for labor equals the land area of the CBD (20 square km) times the employment density (6,000 workers per square km), or 120,000 workers. The residential bid curve intersects the agricultural curve at point *b*, generating a 4-km residential area (from km 2 to km 6). The total supply of labor in the city equals the land area of the residential area (40 square km) times residential density (3,000 workers per square km), or 120,000 workers.

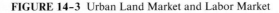

FIGURE 14-3 Urban Land Market and Labor Market

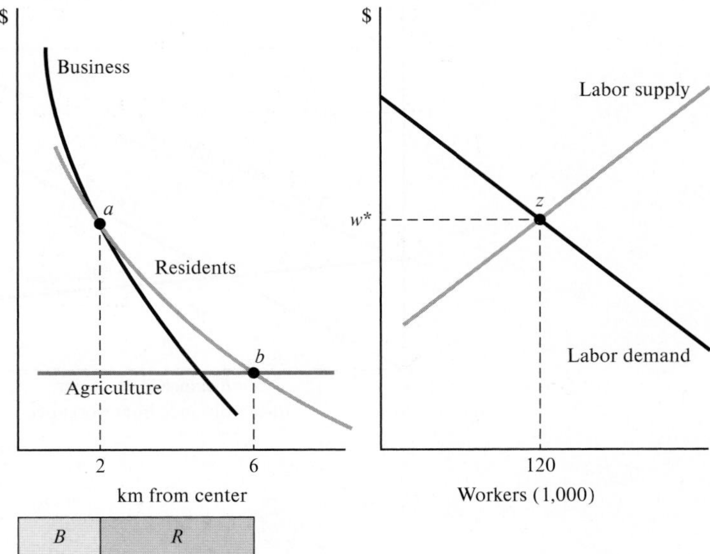

The right panel of Figure 14-3 shows the urban labor market, with a negatively sloped demand curve and a positively sloped supply curve.

1. *Negatively sloped demand curve.* An increase in the wage increases production costs. Applying the leftover principle, the bid for business land decreases, so the business territory shrinks. A decrease in the business territory decreases the quantity of labor demanded.
2. *Positively sloped supply curve.* An increase in the wage increases households' willingness to pay for housing and housing prices. Applying the leftover principle, an increase in housing prices increases the bid for residential land, increasing the territory of the labor-supply sector and thus increasing the quantity of labor supplied.
3. In the initial equilibrium shown by point z, the wage is w^* and the quantity of labor demanded (from the business district) equals the quantity supplied (from the residential district), with 120,000 workers.

The General Equilibrium Effects of the Streetcar

Consider the effects of introducing a streetcar into the monocentric city. The streetcar replaces walking as a commuting mode, so it decreases the unit commuting cost. Figure 14-4 shows the effects of the streetcar on land use within a city. The initial equilibrium, a continuation of Figure 14-3, is shown by points a and b. The streetcar decreases the unit commuting cost, so it decreases the slope of the housing-price curve and residential bid curve. The intersection of the residential bid curve and the

FIGURE 14–4 Short-Run Effects of Streetcar

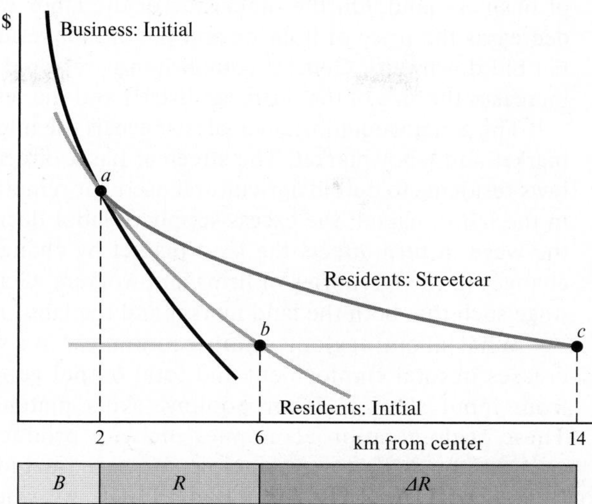

agricultural bid curve shifts from point b to point c, and the residential area grows by the shaded area (ΔR). The expansion of the residential area increases labor supply, causing excess supply of labor.

The excess supply of labor decreases the city wage, causing changes in the business land market. In Figure 14–5, the decrease in the wage shifts the business bid curve upward in accordance with the leftover principle: a decrease in the wage

FIGURE 14–5 Equilibrium Effects of the Streetcar

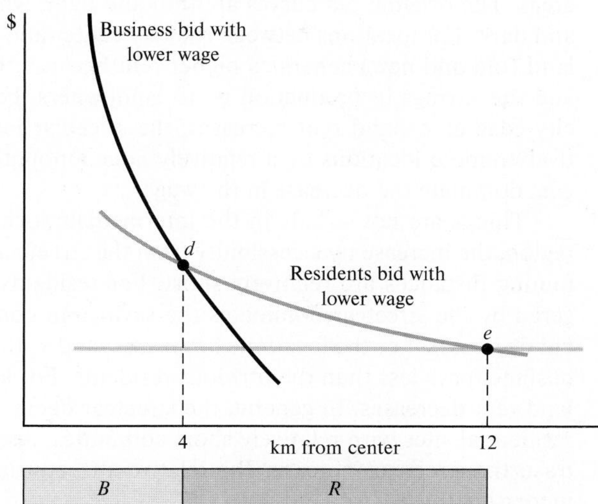

decreases production cost, and competition among firm for land bids up the price of business land. On the other side of the labor market, the decrease in the wage decreases the price of housing and the bid for residential land, shifting the residential bid downward. General equilibrium is restored at points *d* and *e*. The streetcar increases the size of the business district and the residential district.

The general-equilibrium analysis reveals the interactions between the urban land market and labor market. The streetcar has a direct effect on the land market: it allows residents to outbid agricultural users for remote land. The indirect effect occurs in the labor market: the excess supply of labor decreases the wage. The decrease in the wage in turn affects the land market by changing the bids for land, triggering changes in the territories of firms and workers. General equilibrium is restored at a wage such that both the land market and the labor market are in equilibrium.

What about agglomeration economies? As we saw earlier in the book, increases in total employment and total output generate agglomeration economies from input sharing, labor pooling, skills matching, and knowledge spillovers. These agglomeration economies increase productivity and decrease production cost, and by the leftover principle, increase the bid for business land. To represent agglomeration economies in Figure 14–5, we would shift the business bid curve upward. In the labor market, the resulting increase in labor demand would shift the labor demand curve to the right, generating a higher wage. In the residential land market, the higher wage would increase housing prices and the residential bid. Equilibrium would be restored with a larger business district and a larger residential district.

The Streetcar and Land Rent

How does the streetcar affect land rent in the city? In general, land rent is higher in the larger city. But as shown in Figure 14–6, the streetcar decreases land rent in some areas. The original bid curves are thin and light, while the new bid curves are thick and dark. For locations between the city center and x_1, land rent increases: business land (old and new) generates higher rent because the streetcar decreases the wage, and the savings in production go to landowners. For locations between x_2 and the city edge at x_3, land rent increases: the streetcar increases the accessibility of relatively remote locations by a relatively large amount, and the savings in commuting cost dominate the decrease in the wage.

Things are not so tidy in the intermediate locations between x_2 and x_3. In this region, the increase in accessibility from the streetcar is relatively small because commuting distances are relatively short. For residents, the decrease in the wage triggered by the streetcar dominates the savings in commuting cost, so the residential bid decreases. For the locations between x_1 and x_2 that are converted to business use, business pays less than the previous residents. For locations that remain residential, land rent decreases. In general, the streetcar decreases the relative attractiveness of residential sites with relatively short commutes, decreasing the bid for land. In contrast, the streetcar increases the relative attractiveness of relative distant locations, increasing the bid for land.

FIGURE 14-6 Effects of the Streetcar on Land Rent

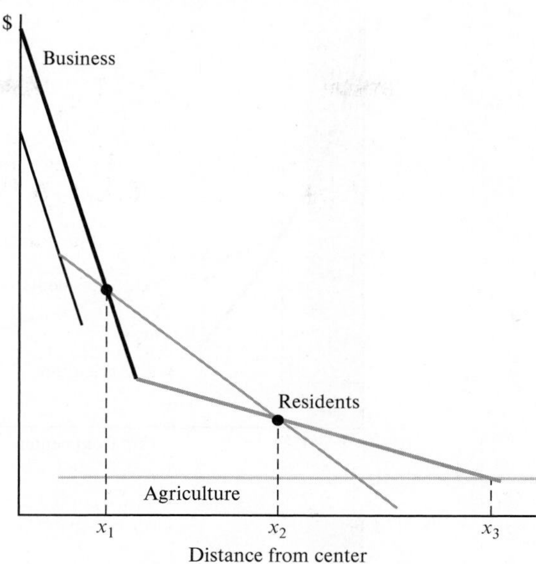

Changes in Employment and Residential Density

So far, we have assumed that both employment density and residential density are fixed. There is no input substitution by firms, and no consumer substitution by residents. As a result, all the changes in labor supply and labor demand are caused entirely by changes in the territories of business and residents. While the assumption of fixed density makes the numerical example simple and straightforward, the assumption is not realistic.

What are the implications of allowing consumer substitution and input substitution? For the business district, the streetcar generally increases land rent, causing input substitution that increases employment density. In other words, firms economize on land by operating in taller buildings on smaller production sites. For the residential district, residential density decreases wherever housing prices and land rent decrease, as households consume more housing and land. In contrast, residential density increases wherever land and housing prices increase, as households economize on housing and land by living in smaller houses on smaller lots.

The General Equilibrium Effects of Rising Sea Level

Consider the effects of climate change that triggers a rise in sea level that floods part of the production area of a city. In the upper panel of Figure 14-7, the initial (pre-flooding) equilibrium is shown by points *a* and *b*: the business area is x_1 km long and the residential area is $x_4 - x_1$ km long. The shaded rectangle out to km $\underline{x}$ shows the

FIGURE 14–7 General Equilibrium Effects of Rising Sea Level

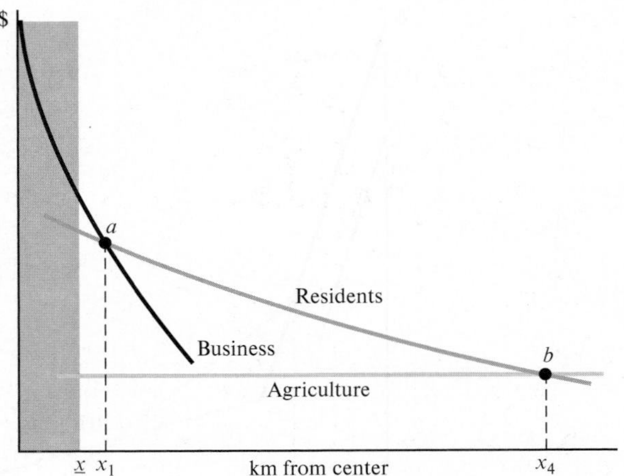

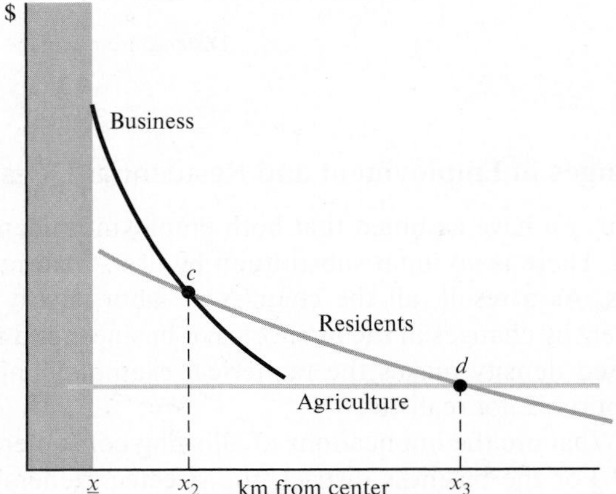

flooded area. The immediate effect of flooding is to decrease the demand for labor and generate excess supply of labor at the original wage.

The excess supply of labor decreases the wage. Applying the leftover principle, the business bid curve shifts upward and the resident bid curve shifts downward. In the lower panel of Figure 14–7, the new equilibrium is shown by points *c* and *d*: the business district is from $\underline{x}$ to x_2 and the residential district is from x_2 to x_3. The changes in the business and residential territories generate a net decrease in the equilibrium workforce.

How does flooding and the resulting changes in the labor market affect land rent? In the business area, land rent increases, as we would anticipate from simple supply-demand analysis: a decrease in the supply of production land will naturally increase its price. In the residential area, matters are more subtle, and not amenable to simple supply-demand analysis. But if we incorporate the labor market into the analysis, we see that the loss of production land decreases the city's wage and thus decreases residential land prices. The general-equilibrium approach provides some important insights into the effects of changes in one market (business land) on other markets (labor market and residential land market).

REVIEW THE CONCEPTS

1. The four key assumptions for a monocentric city are: (i) manufacturing output is exported through a [_____]; (ii) intra-city freight is on [_____]; (iii) workers commute on [_____]; (iv) office workers travel between firms for [_____].
2. Several innovations of the Industrial Revolution caused the development of large monocentric cities: (i) innovations in manufacturing increased [_____] in production; (ii) innovations in intercity transportation increased [_____]; (iii) innovations in intracity transportation increased the [_____] of cities; (iv) innovations in construction decreased the cost of [_____] buildings.
3. In a monocentric city, central land in the CBD is occupied by the land user with higher [_____] and thus a [_____] land bid curve. In the traditional monocentric city, central CBD land is occupied by [_____] firms.
4. The bid curve for office land is steeper than the bid curve for manufacturing land because the opportunity cost of [_____] is relatively high.
5. In a monocentric city, the rational location choice for a manufacturer is to locate close to the [_____] and far from its [_____] because the cost of transporting [_____] is high relative to the cost of transporting [_____].
6. A general-equilibrium model of an urban economy shows the interactions between the [_____] market and the [_____] market and thus the effects of changes in [_____] on business and residential [_____].
7. The introduction of a streetcar in a monocentric city causes excess labor [_____] and [_____] the wage. The change in wage shifts the bid curve for business land [_____] and shifts the bid curve for residential land [_____]. As a result, the business territory [_____].
8. The introduction of a streetcar in a monocentric city [_____] land rent near the city center and [_____] land rent near the city's original edge.
9. If firms engage in input substitution, an increase in land rent [_____] employment density.
10. If consumers engage in consumer substitution, an increase in the prices of housing and land [_____] residential density.
11. Suppose a rising sea level submerges some business land. There will be excess labor [_____], and the resulting [_____] in the wage shifts the bid for residential land [_____]. As a result, the residential territory [_____].
12. In a general-equilibrium model of an urban economy, an increase in the demand for labor [_____] the wage, which decreases the bid for [_____] land and increases the bid for [_____] land.

APPLY THE CONCEPTS

1. *Suburbanization of Manufacturing*
   Using Figure 14-2 as a starting point, suppose the freight cost per km decreases from \$6 per km to \$2 and the rate of change in labor cost increases from \$1 per km to \$3 per km. Illustrate the implications for the cost-minimizing location of a manufacturing firm.
2. *Centralized vs Dispersed Offices*
   Consider an office firm in a monocentric city. The labor-cost function is $w = 60 - 6x$, where x is the distance to the city center (from 0 km to 5 km). The interaction cost (for travel between office firms is $c = 12 + x^{\beta}$, where β is a parameter (a variable beyond the control of the firm).
   a. Based on the earlier discussion of the travel costs of office firms, a plausible value is $\beta =$ [______] (choose 0.50, 1.0, 2.0).
   b. Illustrate the cost-minimizing location for an office firm, including a value for x^*.
3. *Building Height Restrictions*
   Consider a monocentric city that establishes a maximum building height for business structures. The maximum height is the height of buildings one kilometer from the center.
   a. llustrate the effects of the restriction on the bid for business land.
   b. In the labor market, the restriction causes . . .
   c. In the residential land market, the changes in the labor market cause . . .
   d. Illustrate, using Figure 14-3 as a model.
4. *Improvement in Education System*
   Consider a monocentric city that improves its local schools, boosting student achievement in an efficient manner. To simplify matters, ignore any effects of increased achievement on worker productivity.
   a. In the residential land market, the improvement . . .
   b. In the labor market, the changes in the residential land market cause . . .
   c. In the business land market, the changes in the labor market cause . . .
   d. Illustrate, using Figure 14-3 as a model.
5. *Robotic Cars and Labor Market*
   Consider a monocentric city where everyone commutes to the city center by automobile. Suppose the introduction of a robot cars (self-driving cars) decreases the cost of commuting.
   a. In the residential land market, the introduction of robot cars . . .
   b. In the labor market, the changes in the residential land market cause . . .
   c. In the business land market, the changes in the labor market cause . . .
   d. Illustrate, using Figure 14-3 as a model.
6. *Business Tax*
   Suppose a monocentric city imposes a tax on manufacturing firms.
   a. In the business land market, the tax . . .
   b. In the labor market, the changes in the business land market cause . . .
   c. In the residential land market, the changes in the labor market cause . . .
   d. Illustrate, using Figure 14-3 as a model.

REFERENCES AND READING

1. Anas, Alex, Richard Arnott, and Kenneth A. Small, "Urban Spatial Structure." *Journal of Economic Literature* 36 (1998), pp. 1426–64.
2. Brueckner, Jan, J-F Thisse, and Yves Zenou, "Why Is Central Paris Rich and Downtown Detroit Poor? An Amenity-Based Theory." *European Economic Review* 43 (1999), pp. 91–107.
3. Brueckner, J., "The Structure of Urban Equilibria: A Unified Treatment of the Muth-Mills Model," in E. S. Mills, ed., *Handbook of Regional and Urban Economics, Volume 2,* 1987.
4. Fujita, Masahisa, *Urban Economic Theory*. Cambridge: Cambridge University Press, 1989.
5. Fujita, Masahisa and H. Ogawa, "Multiple Equilibria and Structural Transition of Non-Monocentric Urban Configurations." *Regional Science and Urban Economics* 18 (1982), pp. 161–196.
6. Gin, A., and J. Sonstelie, "The Streetcar and Residential Location in Nineteenth Century Philadelphia." *Journal of Urban Economics* (1992).
7. Glaeser, Edward, Matthew Kahn, and Chenghuan Chu, "Job Sprawl: Employment Location in US Metropolitan Areas." Brookings Institution Survey Series (2001, May): 1–8.
8. Glaeser, E., M. Kahn, and J. Rappaport, "Why Do the Poor Live in Cities? The Role of Public Transportation," *Journal of Urban Economics* (2008).
9. Kraus, Marvin, "Monocentric Cities," Chapter 6 in *A Companion to Urban Economics,* edited by Richard J. Arnott and Daniel P. McMillen. New York: Wiley-Blackwell, 2006.
10. LeRoy, S., and J. Sonstelie, "Paradise Lost and Regained: Transportation Innovation, Income, and Residential Location," *Journal of Urban Economics* (1983).
11. Mills, Edwin S, *Studies in the Structure of the Urban Economy*. Baltimore: Johns Hopkins, 1972.
12. Mills, Edwin S., "An Aggregative Model of Resource Allocation in a Metropolitan Area." *American Economic Review* 57 (1971), pp. 197–210.
13. McMillen, Daniel P., "Testing for Monocentricity," Chapter 8 in *A Companion to Urban Economics,* edited by Richard J. Arnott and Daniel P. McMillen. New York: Wiley-Blackwell, 2006.
14. Nechyba, Thomas, and Randall Walsh, "Urban Sprawl." *Journal of Economic Perspectives,* 18.4 (2004), pp. 177–200.
15. Plantinga, Andrew, and Stephanie Bernell, "The Association between Urban Sprawl and Obesity: Is It a Two-Way Street?" *Journal of Regional Science* 47.5 (2007), pp. 857–79.
16. Solow, Robert M., and William S. Vickrey, "Land Use in a Long, Narrow City." *Journal of Economic Theory* 3 (1971), pp. 430–47.
17. Wheaton, W., "Income and Urban Residence: An Analysis of Consumer Demand for Location." *American Economic Review* (1977).

CHAPTER 15

Neighborhoods

Love thy neighbor as yourself, but choose your neighborhood.
– LOUISE BEAL

When a household chooses a neighborhood, it chooses a set of neighbors for social interactions as well as a set of citizens who collectively determine the level of local public goods and local taxes. A key question is whether neighborhoods will be homogeneous or heterogeneous with respect to income, education, and race. As we will see, there are powerful forces that lead to relatively homogeneous neighborhoods, even in the absence of explicit preferences for like neighbors.

1. SEGREGATION: INCOME, EDUCATION, RACE

We start this chapter with the facts on residential segregation in U.S. cities with respect to income, educational attainment, and race. The most frequently used measure of segregation is the dissimilarity index, which runs from zero (neighborhoods are similar) to 100 (neighborhoods are perfectly dissimilar). At the low end, a dissimilarity value of zero indicates that neighborhoods in a particular city are identical with respect to the mixture of two groups (rich and poor or black and white). This is the case of perfect integration: each neighborhood's population mix matches the citywide mix. For example, if 10 percent of a city's households are black, then in each neighborhood, 10 percent of households are black. At the high end of the dissimilarity index, a value of 100 indicates perfect segregation: each neighborhood has a single household type, and there is no mixing of types at the neighborhood level. For example, there are exclusive white neighborhoods and exclusive black neighborhoods.

The calculation of a city's dissimilarity index for two population types is straightforward. The formula for the dissimilarity index is

$$D = 100 \cdot \frac{1}{2} \sum_{i=1}^{N} \left| \frac{a_i}{A} - \frac{b_i}{B} \right|$$

where there are N neighborhoods (indexed by i), a_i is the population of type a in neighborhood i, b_i is the population of type b in neighborhood i, A is the citywide population of type a, and B is the citywide population of type b.

TABLE 15-1 Dissimilarity Index for Low-Income Households in U.S. Metro Areas, 2010

	Large Metro Areas (population > 1 million)	All Metro Areas
Minimum	27	17
Maximum	47	49

Source: Florida, Richard, and Mellander, Charlotta, *Segregated City: The Geography of Economic Segregation in America's Metros.* Toronto: Martin Prosperity Institute, 2015.

Income Segregation

Table 15-1 shows the extent of segregation of low-income households in U.S. metropolitan areas in 2010. The results are derived from Census data, and a neighborhood is defined as a census tract. In the table, a low-income household is defined as a household whose income falls below the national poverty level (roughly $23,000 per year for a four-person household). For large metropolitan areas (population greater than 1 million), the least segregated area has a dissimilarity index of 27, compared to a value of 47 for the most segregated area. Among all metropolitan areas, the range is 17 for the least segregated area to 49 for the most segregated area.

The dissimilarity index shows the percentage of one group that must relocate to ensure that each neighborhood has the same residential mix. For the least segregated large metropolitan area, 27 percent of low-income households would have to relocate to equalize the residential mix across neighborhoods, that is, for each neighborhood (census tract), 15 percent of households are low-income households. For the most segregated large metropolitan area, the relocation share would be 47 percent. For all metro areas, 17 percent would have to relocate in the least segregated metropolitan area, compared to 49 percent in the most segregated metropolitan area.

Another measure of income segregation is the number of low-income households that live in predominately low-income neighborhoods. In Table 15-2, a low-income household is defined as a household with an income less than two-thirds of

TABLE 15-2 Income Segregation in U.S. Metropolitan Areas, 1980 and 2010

	Percent of Households in 2010	Percent of Households in 1980
Low-Income households in tracts with majority of		
Low-income households	28	23
Upper-income households	2	1
Middle-Income households in tracts with majority of		
Low-income households	11	8
Upper-income households	4	1
Upper-Income households in tracts with majority of		
Low-income households	4	3
Upper-income households	18	9

Source: Fry, Richard, and Taylor, Paul, *The Rise of Residential Segregation by Income.* Washington, DC: Pew Research Center, 2012.

TABLE 15-3 Dissimilarity Indexes, Educational Attainment in U.S. Metropolitan Areas, 2010

	Large Metro Areas (population > 1 million)	All Metro Areas
High School Dropouts		
Minimum	24	10
Maximum	45	50
College Graduates		
Minimum	28	14
Maximum	43	44

Source: Florida, Richard, and Mellander, Charlotta, *Segregated City: The Geography of Economic Segregation in America's Metros.* Toronto: Martin Prosperity Institute, 2015.

the national median income. In 2010, 28 percent of low-income households lived in neighborhoods (census tracts) where low-income households were in the majority. The corresponding figure for 1980 is 23 percent, indicating that the clustering of low-income households increased over this period. At the other end of the income distribution, the clustering of high-income households increased over this period. The last row of the table shows the percentage of high-income households living in neighborhoods where high-income households were in the majority. This measure of high-income clustering doubled from 9 percent in 1980 to 18 percent in 2010.

Education Segregation

Table 15-3 shows the extent of segregation with respect to educational attainment in U.S. metropolitan areas in 2010. As in the previous table, a neighborhood is defined as a census tract. Consider first the low end of the educational attainment ladder, people who did not complete high school (dropouts). For large metropolitan areas, the dissimilarity index for high-school dropouts is 24 for the least segregated area, compared to 45 for the most segregated area. Among all metropolitan areas, the range of the dissimilarity index is 10 for the least segregated area to 50 for the most segregated area.

Consider next the upper end of the educational attainment ladder, people with college degrees. For large metropolitan areas, the least segregated area has a dissimilarity index for college graduates of 28, compared to a value of 43 for the most segregated area. Among all metropolitan areas, the range of the dissimilarity index is 14 for the least segregated area to 44 for the most segregated area.

Racial Segregation

Figure 15-1 shows the racial mixing in U.S. metropolitan areas in 2010. For each group, the figure shows the racial composition of the neighborhood (census tract) of the typical metropolitan resident. For example, the typical Asian lived in a census tract with 49 percent White residents, 9 percent Black residents, 19 percent Hispanic residents, and 22 percent Asian residents. The typical White resident lived in a census tract with 75 percent White residents, 8 percent Black residents, 11 percent Hispanic residents, and 5 percent Asian residents.

FIGURE 15–1 Racial Mixing in U.S. Metropolitan Areas, 2010

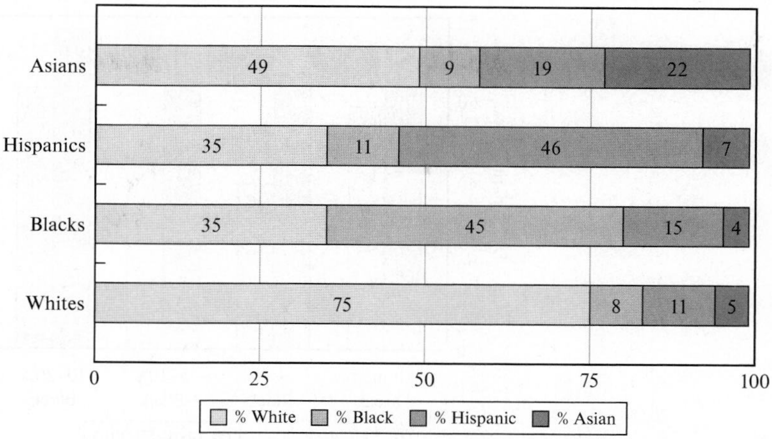

Source: Logan, John R., and Stults, Brian, "The Persistence of Segregation in the Metropolis: New Findings from the 2010 Census." Census Brief prepared for Project US2010, 2011.

To put these numbers in perspective, consider the racial composition of U.S. metropolitan areas in 2010. The racial breakdown was 58 percent White, 14 percent Black, 19 percent Hispanic, and 7 percent Asian. For each racial group, the typical metropolitan resident lived in a neighborhood with more than the national share of the same race (for Whites, 75% > 58%), and less than or equal to the national share of other races. For Asians and Hispanics, the share of the other race matches the national share: for Asians, 19 percent of neighbors are Hispanics; for Hispanics, 7 percent of neighbors are Asian.

Figure 15–2 shows Black-White dissimilarity values for U.S. metropolitan areas in 1980 and 2010. For metropolitan areas as a whole, the dissimilarity index decreased from 73 in 1980 to 59 in 2010. In the typical metropolitan area, to achieve the same Black-White mix in each census tracts, 59 percent of Blacks would be required to relocate. As shown in the Figure, the largest reductions in the dissimilarity index occurred in metropolitan areas with relatively small Black populations. For metro areas where Blacks are less than 5 percent of the population, the dissimilarity index decreased from 67 in 1980 to 40 in 2010. At the other extreme, for metro areas where Blacks are more than 20 percent of the population, the index decreased from 70 in 1980 to 59 in 2010. The decreases in segregation are largely a result of increased mixing in predominantly white neighborhoods.

To put these figures in perspective, consider the values of the dissimilarity index for other racial pairs. For U.S. metropolitan areas in 2010, the White-Hispanic dissimilarity value is 45, and the White-Asian dissimilarity value is 41. In other words, the residential mixing of Whites and Blacks is less than the residential mixing of Whites and other races.

Table 15–4 lists the values of the White-Black dissimilarity index for the 20 most segregated metropolitan areas. Between 1980 and 2010, the value of the index decreased in all metropolitan areas, with relatively small changes in the most segregated areas.

FIGURE 15-2 Black-White Dissimilarity Index, U.S. Metro Areas, 1980 and 2010

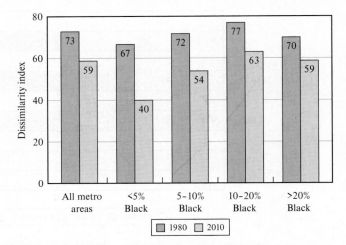

Source: Logan, John R., and Stults, Brian, "The Persistence of Segregation in the Metropolis: New Findings from the 2010 Census." Census Brief prepared for Project US2010, 2011.

TABLE 15-4 White-Black Dissimilarity Index for Most Segregated U.S. Metropolitan Areas

2010 Rank	Area Name	2010 Dissimilarity	2000 Dissimilarity	1990 Dissimilarity	1980 Dissimilarity
1	Detroit MI	79.6	85.9	85.6	83
2	Milwaukee WI	79.6	82.2	82.8	83.9
3	New York NY-NJ	79.1	81.3	82	81.7
4	Newark NJ-PA	78	80.4	82.7	82.8
5	Chicago IL	75.9	80.8	84.6	88.6
6	Philadelphia PA	73.7	76.5	81.4	82.6
7	Miami FL	73	72.4	71.8	79.3
8	Cleveland OH	72.6	77.2	82.8	85.8
9	St. Louis MO-IL	70.6	73.4	77.2	81.6
10	Nassau NY	69.2	73.6	76.4	76.9
11	Boston MA	67.8	71.5	73.7	79.8
12	Cincinnati OH	66.9	72.6	75.9	78.2
13	Birmingham AL	65.2	68.9	70.3	72.2
14	Los Angeles CA	65	67.4	73.1	81.1
15	Indianapolis IN	64.5	71	74.4	78.8
16	Baltimore MD	64.3	67.6	71.4	74.4
17	Washington DC	64.1	65.9	68.4	71.4
18	New Orleans LA	63.3	69	68.3	70
19	Pittsburgh PA	63.1	67.4	70.8	73.3
20	Memphis TN	62.2	65.7	65.5	68.8

Source: Logan, John R., and Stults, Brian, "The Persistence of Segregation in the Metropolis: New Findings from the 2010 Census." Census Brief prepared for Project US2010, 2011.

2. SORTING FOR LOCAL PUBLIC GOODS

The typical large metropolitan area has a number of municipalities, each providing a different mixture of local public goods such as public safety, libraries, and parks, along a system of taxes to finance the local public goods. In addition, households choose from a number of school districts, each with its own educational program. When a household chooses a house or apartment, it also chooses a bundle of local public goods and taxes. The bundle is determined by the political process, when citizens vote for their favored programs or elect representatives to make decisions. Neighbors are fellow citizens who collectively determine the level of local public goods and taxes. As we'll see, households favor neighbors who have (i) similar preferences for local public goods and (ii) similar demands for the private goods that are taxed to support local public goods.

Diversity in Demand for Local Public Goods

Citizens in a municipality or school district collectively determine the level of a public good and its budgetary cost. In a world (or metropolitan area) with differences in household income and preferences, households will differ in their desired level of local public goods. For example, households will differ on the size of library budgets and parks, the number of police officers and firefighters, and class sizes in local schools. Later in the book we will explore the political process that leads to collective decisions on local public goods. In this chapter, we focus on the implications of differences in desired levels of local public goods on location choices.

Consider a metropolitan area with a single school district and three hundred citizens. Suppose the citizens differ in income, with one hundred citizens of each type: low, medium, and high. The local public good is local schooling, with the quantity measured by the number of teachers. The larger the number of teachers for a given number of students, the smaller the class size and the higher the achievement of students. Because of the differences in income, citizens will disagree about the preferred level of the local public good (the number of teachers) and will use the political process–majority rule–to pick the number of teachers.

Figure 15-3 uses the consumer choice model to show the preferred number of teachers for each household type. The linear budget lines show the tradeoff between spending on local schools and all other goods, including private goods as well as other local public goods. We will assume for the moment that schools are financed by a head tax: if you have a head, you pay the same tax, regardless of income. As a result, each citizen faces the same tradeoff between education and other goods: each additional teacher has the same opportunity cost (in terms of foregone other goods) for each citizen. In graphical terms, the budget lines have a common slope. For the moment, we will assume that citizens have the same underlying preferences for education, so they have the same indifference curves.

As usual, the preferred bundle for each citizen is the affordable bundle at which the marginal rate of substitution (the slope of the indifference curve) equals the price ratio (the slope of the budget line). In graphical terms, the citizen's budget line is

FIGURE 15-3 Diversity in Demand for Local Public Goods

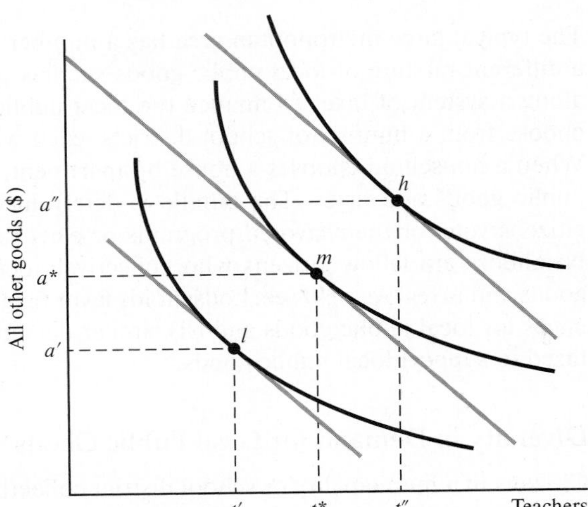

tangent to an indifference curve. In Figure 15-3, the preferred bundles are shown by points *l* (low income), *m* (medium income), and *h* (high income). In other words, a school teacher is a "normal" good as defined in economics: there is a positive relationship between income and the preferred number of teachers. In this case, the three types of citizens disagree about how many teachers to hire, with higher income citizens preferring more teachers (and higher taxes) and thus smaller class sizes.

How do the three citizen types reconcile their different preferred numbers of teachers? One option is to vote with ballots. As we'll see later in the book, the outcome of a direct vote will be the preferred option of the median voter, defined as the voter that splits the rest of voters into two equal halves, one that prefers fewer teachers and another that prefers more teachers. In this example, medium-income citizens determine the outcome of an election, so the political equilibrium will be t^* teachers. Two groups will be unhappy with outcome: low-income citizens would prefer fewer teachers ($t' < t^*$), and high-income citizens would prefer more teachers ($t'' > t^*$).

The alternative to voting with ballots is for citizens to vote with their feet. Each dissatisfied group could form a new homogeneous school district and hire its favored number of teachers. If there are no costs associated with forming smaller school districts, it's a no-brainer for low-income and high-income citizens. Each group would establish a 100-citizen school district and get its preferred number of teachers and other goods. The low-income citizens would achieve point *l*, with t' teachers and a' other goods, while the high-income citizens would achieve point *h*, with t'' teachers and a'' other goods. Of course, if a switch to a smaller school district increases average production cost, things are more complex.

Differences in the demand for local public goods cause households to sort with respect to income. Our hypothetical metropolitan area will have three school districts, each of which is homogeneous with respect to income. The same logic applies to differences in demand that arise from differences underlying preferences for local public goods rather than differences in income. For example, the demand for public education could depend on the educational attainment of the parents. In this case, diversity in demand for education could generate two school districts, one with parents who did not complete college and a second with college graduates.

Diversity in the Demand for the Taxed Good

Up to this point, we have assumed that a school budget is financed by a head tax, which is the same for each household within the school district. In the real world of local government, local public goods are financed by taxes on housing (property taxes), income, and consumer goods (sales tax). As we'll see, if citizens have varying demands for the goods taxed by local governments, this creates another incentive to form separate jurisdictions, to sort with respect to the demand for the taxed products.

Continuing our example, consider the middle-income school district. Suppose the cost of the preferred school program (t^* teachers) is $120 per capita, and a head tax of $120 per head will equalize taxes across citizens. Suppose the school district switches to a tax based on head weight. The average head weight in the district is 2 kilograms, so a tax of $60 per kilo will raise $120 on average, just enough to cover the cost of the school program. And if everyone has the same head weight (2 kilos), everyone will pay the same $120 tax.

Figure 15-4 shows the implications of diversity in the tax base (head weight). The gray rectangles on the left show the tax liabilities in the case of a uniform tax

FIGURE 15-4 Diversity in Demand for a Taxed Good

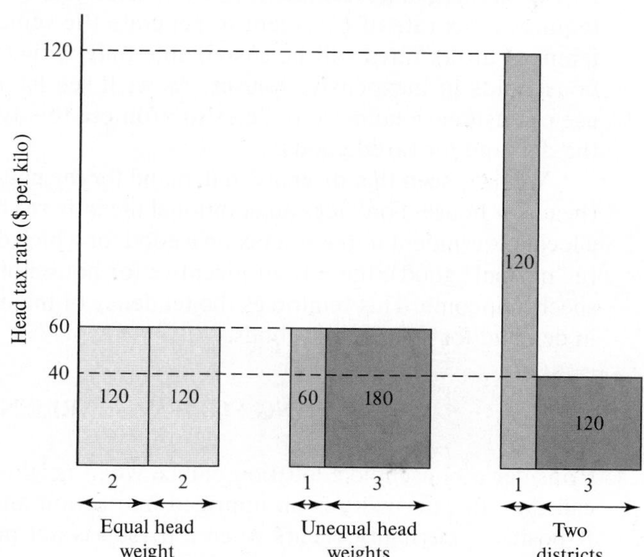

base (equal head weight). The height of the rectangle is the $60 tax, and the width is the 2 kilo weight, and the area of each rectangle is $120. The middle set of rectangles shows what happens in a single school district with two types of citizens, light heads (1 kilo) and heavy heads (3 kilos). With a tax rate of $60 per kilo, a light head pays only $60 while a heavy head pays $180. On average, citizens pay the $120 per-capita cost of the education program, but a heavy head pays more than a light head.

Differences in the tax base provide incentives for heavily taxed citizens to establish a new jurisdiction. In our example, heavy heads have an incentive to establish a new school district. As shown by the rightmost rectangle in Figure 15–4, heavy heads could form an exclusive school district and cut the tax rate to $40 per kilo. In that case, each citizen would pay $120 (equal to $40 times 3 kilos), the per-capita cost of the school program. If all heavy heads leave the original school district, the light heads left behind must increase the tax rate to $120 per kilo (the tall rectangle). It's important to note that this system requires some exclusion mechanism: if light heads were to move into the new heavy-head (low tax rate) district, the average tax liability in the heavy-head district would drop below $120, requiring an increase in the tax rate. Heavy heads would have an incentive to flee a municipality that experienced an influx of light heads.

What are the implications for household location decisions in real cities? Local governments tax housing rather than heads, but the same logic applies. Suppose a municipality has a per-household cost of $6,000 per year. A tax rate of 3 percent of value translates into a tax of $3,000 on a house with a market value of $100,000, compared to a tax of $9,000 on a $300,000. Under this tax system, households in large (high value) houses have an incentive to form exclusive jurisdictions with lower tax rates. For example, in a jurisdiction full of $300,000 houses, a tax rate of 2 percent will be sufficient to generate $6,000 to cover the cost of municipal government. In contrast, a jurisdiction full of $100,000 houses requires a tax rate of 6 percent to generate the same revenue per house. The differences in tax rates will be sustainable only if there is a mechanism to exclude households in inexpensive houses. As we'll see later in the book, municipalities use exclusionary land-use policies to promote this type of sorting with respect to the demand for taxed goods.

We have seen that diversity in demand for the goods taxed by local governments (heads or houses) provides an additional incentive to form local jurisdictions. When a local government imposes a tax on a good for which demand increases with income (a "normal" good), there is an incentive for households to sort themselves with respect to income. This reinforces the tendency of income sorting caused by diversity in demand for local public goods.

3. BIDDING FOR FAVORABLE NEIGHBORS

Consider a household's location choice when neighbors generate externalities. Recall that an externality is an unpriced interaction and can be positive or negative. A positive externality occurs when a person is not paid for an action that benefits someone else. A negative externality occurs when a person does not pay for an action that imposes a cost on someone else. Social interactions at the neighborhood level generate externalities for both children and adults.

1. Children imitate adults, and a neighborhood of educated and successful adults provides good role models. In school, kids learn more when they are surrounded by other kids who are motivated and focused.
2. For adults, information about employment opportunities often comes from informal sources such as neighbors and friends, and employed neighbors provide better job information. On the negative side, drug abuse among neighbors can generate an unpleasant living environment. These are externalities because neighbors don't charge each other for information that leads to job prospects, and drug abusers don't compensate their neighbors for the unpleasant environment.

These neighborhood externalities affect neighborhood choice. If households have the same preferences with respect to adult role models and school peers, all households will prefer the same sort of neighborhood. The positive externalities generated by a household generally increase with income and education level, so people generally prefer neighborhoods with large numbers of high-income, educated households. Of course, the number of such households is limited, so the question is, Who gets the favorable households as neighbors? In a market economy, favorable neighborhoods are allocated to the households who are willing to pay the most for them.

A Model of Bidding for Favorable Neighbors

Households compete for places in a desirable neighborhood by bidding for lots with houses. To illustrate a model developed by Becker and Murphy (2000), consider a city with two types of residents, blue and green. Suppose blue neighbors are more favorable than green neighbors, so everyone wants blue neighbors. Later in the chapter we'll consider a model in which residents have preferences for like and unlike neighbors, but for now we assume that blue is better for both blues and greens.

A neighborhood is defined as a 4×3 grid of 12 residential lots, with one house on each lot. Figure 15-5 shows a perfectly integrated neighborhood, with six residents

FIGURE 15-5 Perfectly Integrated Neighborhood

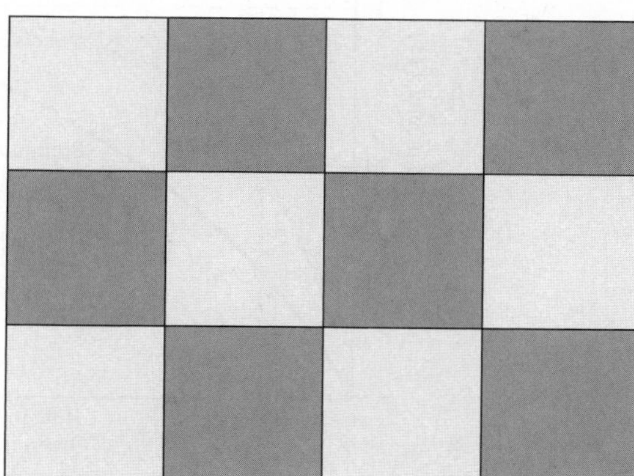

of each type. The checkerboard pattern is only one version of a perfectly integrated neighborhood. As long as there are six residents of each type, the neighborhood is perfectly integrated, regardless of the placement of the residents within the neighborhood. Consider a city with two distinct (not overlapping) neighborhoods (West and East) and 24 residents (12 of each type). For example, the two neighborhoods could be on the opposite sides of a highway or railroad tracks.

The allocation of residents across the two neighborhoods is determined by competitive bidding for land. An allocation is a locational equilibrium if three conditions are satisfied.

1. *Nash equilibrium.* No single resident has an incentive to relocate to the other neighborhood.
2. *Equal rent.* Every household in a particular neighborhood pays the same rent.
3. *Adding up.* All residents are accommodated, meaning that both neighborhoods are full.

Figure 15–6 provides a framework to determine the equilibrium allocation of the two types of households to the two neighborhoods. Moving from left to right along the horizontal axis, the number of blues in West increases and the number of greens decreases. A household's bid premium r (on the vertical axis) equals the bid for a West lot minus the bid for an East lot.

$$r = bid(west) - bid(east)$$

For both households, the premium curves are positively sloped. As the number of blues in West increases (and the number of greens decreases), both types are

FIGURE 15–6 Bid Premium Curves

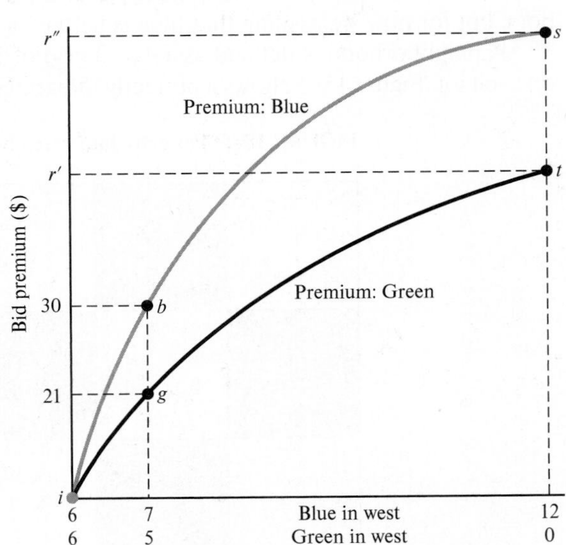

FIGURE 15–7 Segregation as a Stable Equilibrium

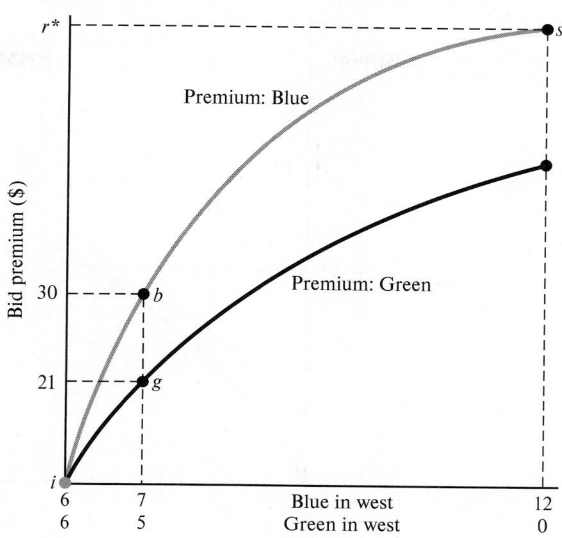

willing to pay more for a lot in West. At the same time in East, there are fewer blues and more greens, so both types are willing to pay less for a lot in East: the bid for East decreases. The combination of a higher bid for West and a lower bid for East means that the bid premium increases. For example, when the number of blues increases from 6 to 7, the premium of greens increases from zero to $21 (point *i* to point *g*) and the bid premium of blues increases from zero to $30 (point *i* to point *b*). When the number of blues increases to 12, the bid premium for blues increases to r'' and the bid premium for greens increases to r'.

In the case shown in Figure 15–7, perfect integration is a Nash equilibrium. At point *i*, the two neighborhoods are identical: each neighborhood has six residents of each type, so the bid premium is zero. This is an equilibrium because (i) there is no incentive for unilateral deviation; (ii) in each neighborhood, everyone pays the same rent; and (iii) all 24 households are accommodated.

Perfect integration is an unstable equilibrium. A small random deviation from integration will generate self-reinforcing changes in the same direction. Suppose a pair of residents swap neighborhoods: a blue moves from East to West, and a green moves from West to East. Given the new mix of 7 blues and 5 greens, each blue resident is now willing to pay a premium $30 (point *b*), and each green resident is willing to pay a smaller premium $21 (point *g*). Blue residents will outbid greens for lots in the bluer West, generating a still bluer neighborhood. As long as blues have a higher premium, they will continue to displace green residents. The relocation process ends at point *s*, the segregated outcome: West is all blue, and East is all green.

In this case, perfect segregation is the only stable equilibrium. The premium curve of the favorable type (blue) lies everywhere above the premium curve of

FIGURE 15-8 Mixing as Stable Equilibrium

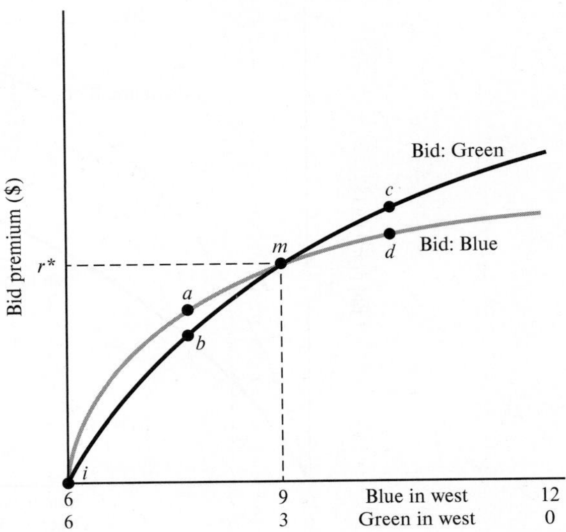

the unfavorable type (green). Although both blues and greens are willing to pay a premium for bluer neighborhoods, blues are willing to pay a larger premium over the full range of blueness, from just one blue beyond perfect integration to full segregation.

Mixing and Perfect Integration

The segregation outcome shown in Figure 15-7 results from the placement of the bid curves. In contrast, the placement of the bid curves in Figure 15-8 generates a stable equilibrium with a mix of blues and greens. Point *m* (9 blues and 3 greens) is a stable equilibrium because a random deviation will trigger changes that lead the market back to point *m*. An increase in the number of blues (points *c* and *d*) means that greens (point *c*) outbid the new blues (point *d*) for places in West, so the market moves back to point *m*. Similarly, a decrease in the number of blues (points *a* and *b*) means that blues outbid greens, so the market moves back to point *m*. Point *m* is the only stable equilibrium. Starting at point *i* (perfect integration), a random deviation to points *a* and *b* would cause blues to outbid the greens until we reach point *m*. Starting with perfect segregation (12 blue, 0 green), a random deviation to points *c* and *d* would cause greens to outbid blues until we reach point *m*.

Land Prices and Locational Equilibrium

One of the key concepts of urban economics is that prices adjust to generate locational equilibrium. To generate a Nash equilibrium in the market for neighborhoods, variation in the price of land offsets differences in the residential composition of the neighborhoods.

1. *Perfect segregation.* In Figure 15–7, point *s* shows the maximum premium from blue residents for a perfectly segregated neighborhood. Point *t* shows the premium from green residents for being the first green resident in an otherwise blue neighborhood. The equilibrium premium is somewhere between the two numbers associated with points *s* and *t*: savvy residents will recognize they must pay at least r', while savvy landowners will recognize that blue residents are willing to pay as much as r''.
2. *Mixed.* In Figure 15–8, each resident of West pays a premium of r^* for a favorable neighborhood. The 9 blue residents in West are just as happy as the 3 blue residents in East because West residents pay a premium for the more favorable neighborhood, while East residents get a discount for the inferior neighborhood. Similarly, the rent premium makes the green residents in the bluer West just as happy as green residents in the greener East.

Lot Size and Public Policy

Up to this point, we have assumed that each household occupies one unit of land. Of course, land is a normal good in the economic sense, and consumption increases with income. What are the implications of variable lot sizes for neighborhood choice and income segregation? As we'll see, when high-income residents consume more land, integration is more likely.

As a starting point, consider the situation shown in Figure 15–9. A blue resident is willing to pay a premium of \$30 to live in a neighborhood with 7 blue residents and 5 green residents (point *b*), while the premium for the green resident is only \$21

FIGURE 15–9 Lot Size and Integration

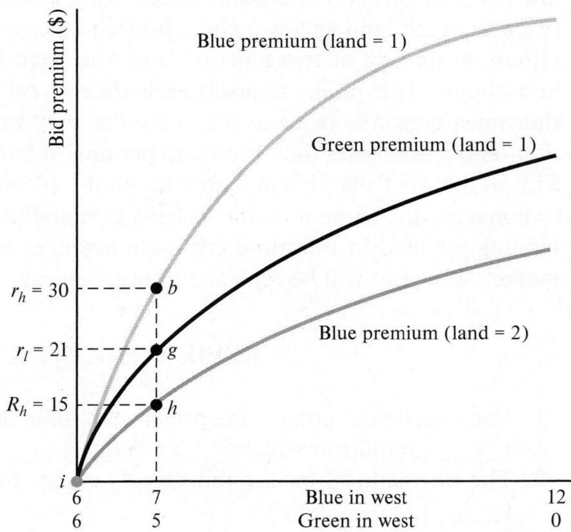

(point *g*). If both types of residents occupy one unit of land, blue households outbid green households, ultimately leading to segregation.

Things are different when blue residents consume more land. Suppose each blue resident occupies two units of land, compared to only one unit for a green resident. The $30 blue premium translates into a $15 premium per unit of land (point *h*). In this case, a blue resident has a lower premium per unit of land, so greens will outbid blues for land in the more desirable neighborhood. As a result, any deviation from the integrated equilibrium (e.g., 7 blues and 5 greens) will cause self-correcting rather than self-reinforcing changes. The result is integration, the symmetric equilibrium with six residents of each type in each neighborhood.

Another way to think about the effects of lot size is to take the perspective of landowners, who of course maximize their rental income. If you have two units of land to rent, you can either rent to a single blue resident for $30 or to a pair of green residents, each paying $21 for a total of $42. Obviously the pair of green residents is a more lucrative choice. A single blue resident loses the bidding battle because it competes against a pair of green residents.

This example illustrates the importance of land consumption in neighborhood choice and diversity. Suppose blues are high-income residents and greens are low-income residents. If the difference in land consumption between the two types of residents is large relative to the difference in the bid premium, a low-income resident (green) will have a larger premium per unit of land, integration is a stable equilibrium. On the other hand, if the difference in land consumption is relatively small, the neighborhoods will be segregated. For example, if the high-income household occupied only 1.25 units of land, its premium per unit of land would be $24 per unit of land ($30/1.25), and segregation would persist ($24 > $21).

Some local governments use minimum lot size zoning to control land use. Under this policy, the government specifies a minimum lot size for residential development and outlaws higher density. One possible consequence is income segregation. In Figure 15–9, integration is a stable equilibrium when high-income households occupy twice as much land as low-income households. Suppose the government specifies a minimum lot size of two units of land, the quantity chosen by high-income (blue) households. This policy imposes an extra cost on low-income (green) households—they must consume twice as much land as they would in the absence of the restriction—and it decreases their premium per unit of land to $10.50, which is less than the $15 premium of the high-income household. If low-income households are required to consume the same amount of land as high-income households, they lose in the bidding for land in the more desirable neighborhood. As a result, integration (the market outcome) will be replaced by segregation.

REVIEW THE CONCEPTS

1. For a particular citizen, the preferred bundle of education and other goods is the [_____] bundle at which [_____] equals [_____].
2. The provision of local public goods causes households to sort with respect to [_____].

3. The financing of local public goods causes households to sort with respect to [______].
4. If a taxed good is "normal" in an economic sense, diversity in demand for the taxed good causes households to sort with respect to [______].
5. As a variation on Figure 15-4, suppose the per-capita cost of local public services is $90. If the common head size is 2 kilos, the tax rate is $[______] per kilo. If head sizes are 1 kilo and 3 kilos, the tax rate in a light-head municipality is $[______] per kilo, compared to $[______] per kilo in a heavy-head municipality.
6. A positive externality occurs when someone is [______] for an action that [______]. In a neighborhood context, positive externalities tend to [______] with income.
7. For a Nash equilibrium in neighborhood choice, three conditions are satisfied: (i) no incentive for [______]; (ii) every household in a particular neighborhood pays [______]; (iii) all residents are [______].
8. Suppose all households prefer to live near blue households. Perfect integration is not a stable equilibrium if the [______] bid premium curve is steeper than the [______] bid premium curve. Perfect integration is a stable equilibrium if the [______] bid premium curve is steeper than the [______] bid premium curve.
9. Consider a mixed neighborhood equilibrium: Azul is 75 percent blue and 25 percent green; Verde is 75 percent green and 25 percent blue. A green household will be indifferent between Azul and Verde because [______] is lower in [______].
10. The [______] {↑, ↓, −} in segregation between 2000 and 2010 resulted largely from increased mixing in predominantly [______] neighborhoods.
11. For each pair of variables, indicate whether the relationship is positive, negative, neutral, or ambiguous.

Parameter	Choice Variable	Relationship
income diversity	number of school districts	[______]
head weight diversity with head tax	number of school districts	[______]
property value diversity with property tax	number of school districts	[______]

APPLY THE CONCEPTS

1. *House Size Tax and Number of Jurisdictions*
Consider a city where each household prefers the same spending on public education. Initially, schools are financed with the property tax based on market value. Suppose the city changes to a property tax based on house size (square meters of living space).
   a. The equilibrium number of school districts will decrease if [______] is large relative to [______].
   b. The equilibrium number of school districts will decrease to one if [______] is the same for all households.
2. *You Kids Get Off My Lawn!*
Suppose that people in your city generally prefer to live close to aged people. The bid premium for an aged household is $B(A) = A^{1/2}$, where A = number of aged

households. The bid premium for a young household is $b(A) = A/9$. There are two neighborhood (East and West), and each neighborhood accommodates 144 households.

a. Illustrate the Nash equilibrium in the West neighborhood, including the numbers of aged and young households.
b. The Nash equilibrium [______] (is, is not) a stable equilibrium because . . .
c. Suppose the city's objective is to generate perfect segregation as a Nash equilibrium. The appropriate tax on young households is $[______].

3. *Nerd Neighborhood*

People in your city generally prefer to live close to nerds. The bid premium for a nerd household is $B(N) = N^2$, where $N =$ number of nerd households. The bid premium for non-nerd households is $b(N) = 8 \cdot N$. Each neighborhood accommodates 12 households.

a. Perfect integration [______] (is, is not) an equilibrium, and it [______] (is, is not) stable because . . . Illustrate.
b. Perfect segregation [______] (is, is not) an equilibrium, and it [______] (is, is not) stable because . . . Illustrate.
c. Is there a mixed equilibrium, defined as an outcome between perfect integration and perfect segregation? If so, is it stable? Illustrate.

4. *Space on the Space Plane*

Consider a revenue-maximizing firm that provides rides on a space plane, an aircraft that takes off like an airplane, flies up and away from the earth until it is just about to go into orbit, and then returns to the earth. The total weight limit for passengers is 2,400 pounds. The willingness to pay for a ride is B for a high-income person, compared to b for a low-income person, where $B > b$. The body weight is W for a high-income person, compared to w for a low-income person, where $W > w$.

a. All the passengers will be low-income people if . . .
b. Suppose $\{B, W, b, w\} = \{1200, 200, 1080, w\}$. All the passengers will be low-income people if . . .

5. *Lots in Subdivision*

Consider a revenue-maximizing landowner that has 24 hectares of vacant land to sell in a new subdivision. The willingness to pay for a land is B for a high-income person, compared to b for a low-income person, where $B > b$. The demand for land (lot size) is S for a high-income person, compared to s for a low-income person, where $S > s$. The income of the high-income household is 40 percent higher than the income of the low-income household. The income elasticity of demand for land is 1.50.

a. All the land in the subdivision will be purchased by low-income households if . . .
b. Suppose $\{B, S, b, s\} = \{160, \text{S}, 120, 0.10\}$. All the land in the subdivision will be purchased by [______] households because . . .
c. Suppose the city's objective is to exclude low-income households from the subdivision. The city will succeed if the minimum lot size is at least [______].

REFERENCES AND READING

1. Baum-Snow, Nathaniel, and Byron Lutz, 2011, "School Desegregation, School Choice, and Changes in Residential Patterns by Race." *American Economic Review* 101, pp. 3019–46.
2. Becker, G., and K. Murphy, *Social Economics.* Cambridge: Harvard University Press, 2000.
3. Boustan, Leah Platt, "Racial Residential Segregation in American Cities," Chapter 14 in *The Oxford Handbook of Urban Economics and Planning,* edited by Nancy Brooks, Kieran Donaghy, and Gerrit-Jan Knaap. New York: Oxford University Press, 2011.
4. Collins, William, and Katherine Shester, "Slum Clearance and Urban Renewal in the United States." *American Economic Journal: Applied Economics* 5.1 (2013), pp. 239–73.
5. Cutler, David M., and Edward L. Glaeser, "Are Ghettos Good or Bad?" *Quarterly Journal of Economics* (1997), pp. 827–72.
6. Durlauf, Steven. "Neighborhood Effects," Chapter 50 in *Handbook of Regional and Urban Economics 4: Cities and Geography,* edited by Vernon Henderson and Jacques-Francois Thisse. Amsterdam: Elsevier, 2004.
7. Jargowsky, Paul A., "Urban Poverty, Economic Segregation, and Urban Policy," Chapter 13 in *The Oxford Handbook of Urban Economics and Planning,* edited by Nancy Brooks, Kieran Donaghy, and Gerrit-Jan Knaap. New York: Oxford University Press, 2011.
8. O'Sullivan, Arthur, "Schelling's Model Revisited: Residential Sorting with Competitive Bidding for Land." *Regional Science and Urban Economics* 39 (2009), pp. 397–408.
9. Pastor, Manuel, "Spatial Assimilation and Its Discontents: The Changing Geography of Immigrant Integration in Metropolitan America," Chapter 15 in *The Oxford Handbook of Urban Economics and Planning,* edited by Nancy Brooks, Kieran Donaghy, and Gerrit-Jan Knaap. New York: Oxford University Press, 2011.
10. Rosenthal, Stuart S., and Stephen Ross, "Change and Persistence in the Economic Status of Neighborhoods and Cities," Chapter 16 in *Handbook of Urban and Regional Economics Volume 5,* edited by Gilles Duranton, J. Vernon Henderson and William C. Strange. Amsterdam: Elsevier, 2015.
11. Ross, Stephen, "Social Interactions within Cities: Neighborhood Environments and Peer Relationships," Chapter 9 in *The Oxford Handbook of Urban Economics and Planning,* edited by Nancy Brooks, Kieran Donaghy, and Gerrit-Jan Knaap. New York: Oxford University Press, 2011.
12. Topa, Giorgio, and Yves Zenou, "Neighbourhood versus Network Effects," Chapter 9 in *Handbook of Urban and Regional Economics Volume 5,* edited by Gilles Duranton, J. Vernon Henderson and William C. Strange. Amsterdam: Elsevier, 2015.
13. Vigdor, Jacob, "Race: The Perplexing Persistence of Race," Chapter 7 in *Making Cities Work,* edited by Robert P. Inman. Princeton NJ: Princeton University Press, 2009.

CHAPTER 16

Land Use Policy

A tranquil city of good laws, fine architecture, and clean streets is like a classroom of obedient dullards, whereas a city of anarchy is a city of promise.

—Mark Helprin

So far our discussion of urban land use has focused on competitive bidding for land, with land allocated to the highest bidder. In this chapter we explore the effects of two types of local land-use policies.

1. *Zoning Plans.* A land-use zoning plan determines where different types of economic activity–industrial, commercial, residential–are located within the city
2. *Development Limits.* A city can limit residential development by (a) restricting the number of building permits, (b) imposing taxes on new housing, and (c) confining development to specific geographic areas.

As we will see, these land-use policies are motivated by environmental and fiscal concerns, and have important effects on the prices of land and housing.

1. ZONING: HISTORY & LEGAL BASIS

We will start our analysis of land-use policy with zoning, a policy under which a municipality divides land within its borders into separate zones for different types of economic activity. Local governments derive their power to control land use from the states. In most states, the enabling legislation for land-use policy is patterned after the Standard State Zoning Enabling Act, which was developed by the U.S. Department of Commerce in 1926 and includes the following language:

Grant of Power. For the purpose of promoting health, safety, morals, or the general welfare of the community, the legislative body of cities and incorporated villages is hereby empowered to regulate and restrict the height, number of stories, and size of buildings and other structures, the percentage of the lot that may be occupied, the size of yards, courts, and other open spaces, the density of population, and the location and use of buildings, structures, and land for trade, industry, residence, or other purposes.

TABLE 16–1 Zoning Classification, Portland, Oregon

	Residential: Single Dwelling	Residential: Multiple Dwelling	Commercial	Employment and Industrial
Classification Criterion	Minimum Lot Size (square feet)	Maximum Dwellings per Acre	Function	Function
Subclass	20,000	15	Neighborhood retail and services	General employment
Subclass	10,000	43	Regional retail and services: Pedestrians	Central industrial and service
Subclass	7,000	65	Regional retail and services: Automobiles	General industrial
Subclass	5,000	85+	Downtown	Heavy industrial
Subclass			Small and medium office clusters	
Subclass			Mixed commercial and residential	

Zoning is considered a legitimate exercise of the police power of local government if it promotes the public health, safety, and welfare.

In the typical city, land uses are classified into several general classes, and each class is divided into subclasses that vary in density and land-use intensity. Table 16–1 shows the zoning classification system of Portland, Oregon. There are two residential classes (for single and multiple dwellings), a commercial class (retail, services, offices), and an industrial class. The residential subclasses are based on lot size and density. The commercial subclasses are based on function, while the industrial subclasses are based on location and the level of objectionable impacts such as noise, air pollution, and traffic.

A Brief History of Zoning in the United States

Fischel (2004) summarizes the history of land-use zoning in the United States. Before comprehensive zoning, many cities used ordinances to control land use in specific areas. For example, to address concerns that skyscrapers would block views and light, cities regulated tall buildings. New York City implemented the first comprehensive zoning plan in 1916, and eight other cities adopted zoning plans in the same year. By 1936, zoning had spread to more than 1,300 cities.

Why didn't zoning develop earlier? Fischel argues that the urban transportation technology of the late 19th and early 20th centuries made zoning unnecessary, at least from the perspective of suburban homeowners. As we saw earlier in the book, manufacturers transported their output on horse carts, a slow and expensive mode that required firms to locate close to the city's central port or railroad terminal. The main form of public transit was the hub-spoke streetcar system. Low-income households lived in apartments close to the city center or along the spokes of the streetcar system. Commercial activities and apartments located along the streetcar lines, generating neighborhoods with mixed land use. Most homeowners lived a few blocks from the streetcar lines–inside the spokes–in neighborhoods separated from industry, commerce, and apartments. Homeowners placed a high value on their quiet, low-density neighborhoods and organized to prevent the extension of streetcar lines.

Innovations in transportation increased the location options for business, setting the stage for industrial zoning. Before the intracity truck, the externalities generated by industry and commerce (pollution, noise, congestion) were confined to the central areas of the city, far from the homes of suburban homeowners. The intracity truck (which dates to 1910) allowed firms to move away from the city's central export node and closer to their suburban workers. Once firms became more footloose, cities implemented zoning to separate industry from homes. A headline from the *New York Times* in 1916 read "Zoning Act Removes Fear of Business Invasion."

Innovations in mass transit increased the location options for workers, setting the stage for residential zoning. The motorized passenger bus, developed in 1920, allowed low-income workers to live between the spokes of the streetcar systems, where homeowners had been insulated from high-density housing. Cities developed residential zoning to keep apartments out of homeowner neighborhoods. In the leading case on the constitutionality of zoning (*Euclid v. Ambler* [1924]), U.S. Supreme Court Justice Sutherland wrote that apartments are "a mere parasite, constructed in order to take advantage of the open spaces and attractive surroundings created by the residential character of the district."

The Legal Basis for Zoning

Current zoning laws are the result of decades of legal decisions. Over the last eight decades, court decisions have established three criteria for the constitutionality of zoning: substantive due process, equal protection, and just compensation.

1. *Substantive Due Process.* Zoning must be executed for a legitimate public purpose using reasonable means. In *Euclid v. Ambler* (1924), the Supreme Court ruled that a zoning ordinance that excluded industrial activity from a residential zone satisfied the standards for substantive due process because it had some "reasonable relation" to the promotion of "health, safety, morals, and general welfare." The court did not say that the benefit of zoning must exceed its cost, only that the benefit must be positive. Fischel (1985) calls this benefit analysis, as opposed to benefit-cost analysis. The court defined the possible social benefits from zoning in broad terms, to include monetary, physical, spiritual, and aesthetic benefits.
2. *Equal Protection.* The equal-protection clause of the Fourteenth Amendment requires that all laws be applied in an impersonal (nondiscriminatory) fashion. Zoning is exclusionary in the sense that it excludes some types of people from a municipality, for example, people who live in apartments instead of single-family dwellings. Federal courts have upheld the constitutionality of exclusionary

zoning, finding in various cases that (a) the effects of zoning on people outside the municipality (outsiders) are unimportant (*Euclid v. Ambler,* 1924), (b) zoning did not cause specific personal damage (*Warth v. Selden,* 1975), (c) zoning did not arise from discriminatory intent on the part of zoning officials (*Village of Arlington Heights v. Metropolitan Housing Corporation,* 1977), and (d) zoning laws that discriminate on the basis of race are unconstitutional, but zoning laws that discriminate on the basis of income are legal (*Ybarra v. Town of Los Altos Hills*). In general, the federal courts have adopted a noninterventionist approach to exclusionary zoning. In contrast, some state courts have directed local zoning authorities to accommodate their "fair share" of low-income residents.

3. *Just Compensation.* The Fifth Amendment states "nor shall private property be taken for public use, without just compensation." This is the taking clause: If the government converts land from private to public use, the landlord must be compensated. Most zoning ordinances do not actually convert land to public use, but merely restrict private use and thus decrease its market value. According to Fischel (1985), the courts have provided mixed and confusing signals to local zoning authorities. The courts routinely uphold zoning laws that cause large losses in property values. Under the harm-prevention rule, compensation is not required if the zoning ordinance prevents a harmful use of the land. In other words, zoning is not a taking if it prevents the landowner from using land in ways that are detrimental to the general public.

2. THE ROLE OF ZONING

We turn next to three possible roles for zoning in an urban land market. First, zoning can serve as environmental policy, separating the generators of environmental externalities (commercial and industrial uses) from residents. Second, fiscal zoning can address a fiscal problem by excluding a household whose tax payment would be less than the cost of providing local services to the household. Third, zoning can mitigate the inefficiencies that result from the combination of density externalities and the free-rider problem.

Zoning to Mitigate Environmental Externalities

Zoning can be used to reduce the exposure to pollution. Industrial firms generate all sorts of externalities, including noise, glare, dust, odor, vibration, and smoke. Zoning is appealing as an environmental policy because it is simple: The easiest way to reduce the exposure to pollution is to put a buffer between a polluter and its potential victims. The problem with zoning as an environmental policy is that it doesn't reduce pollution to its socially efficient level, but simply moves it around.

The economic approach to pollution is to impose a tax equal to the marginal external cost of pollution. A firm subject to a pollution tax pays for pollution in the same way that it pays for raw materials, capital, and labor. The pollution tax gives the firm the incentive to economize on pollution in the same way that it economizes on other inputs to the production process. As a result, pollution is reduced in the most efficient manner. One approach to urban environmental policy is to combine pollution taxes with zoning. If a city places polluters in industrial zones and imposes a pollution tax, pollution would be reduced to the socially efficient level at the same time that exposure is controlled. In fact, a zoning plan that reduces the exposure would decrease the marginal external cost of pollution and thus decrease the pollution tax.

Retailers generate a number of externalities that affect nearby residents. Traffic generates congestion, pollution, noise, and parking conflicts. A traditional zoning plan deals with these externalities by confining retailers to special zones. A more flexible approach, "performance zoning," gives retailers more location options while enforcing performance standards for parking, traffic, and noise. For example, a city can require retailers to provide adequate off-street parking, pay for improvements in the transportation infrastructure to manage additional traffic, and design the retail site to control noise and other externalities.

Zoning to Prevent Fiscal Deficits

Another role for zoning is to exclude any land user that would not pay enough in taxes to cover the cost of providing local public goods. Local governments raise roughly three-fourths of their tax revenue from the property tax, so a household's local tax liability is determined largely by the value of its house or apartment. A household's use of local public services such as education, recreation, and public safety depends in part on the number of people in the household. A large household in a small dwelling is more likely to generate a fiscal deficit for the local government.

Consider a metropolitan area with a single municipality. The per-household cost of public services is $3,000 per year, and there are two types of households: half own $100,000 houses (type L for low value) and half own $200,000 houses (type H for high value). Local public goods are financed with a property tax. In Figure 16–1, house value is on the horizontal axis and the tax rate is on the vertical axis. The rectangles show the tax liabilities of the two types of houses. As shown by the left pair of rectangles, a tax rate of 2 percent generates an average of $3,000 per household, with $2,000 from type L (0.02 times $100,000) and $4,000 from type H (0.02 times $200,000). In this case, each L household generates a fiscal deficit of $1,000, which is offset by a $1,000 fiscal surplus from each H household.

The owners of the more expensive houses have an incentive to exclude the owners of less expensive houses. Suppose type H owners establish an exclusive municipality with a minimum house value of $200,000. In the right side of Figure 16–1, the new municipality has a tax rate of only 1.5 percent, which is just high enough to cover the cost of providing local public goods. In contrast, the type L owners are now forced to pay the full cost of local public goods, and the tax rate increases to 3 percent. The general lesson is that differences in house values generate incentive for citizens in expensive (high tax) houses to exclude citizens in inexpensive (low tax) houses.

One way to decrease the likelihood of fiscal deficits is to zone for minimum lot sizes. Housing and land are complementary goods, and in general the larger the lot,

FIGURE 16–1 Fiscal Deficits and Surpluses

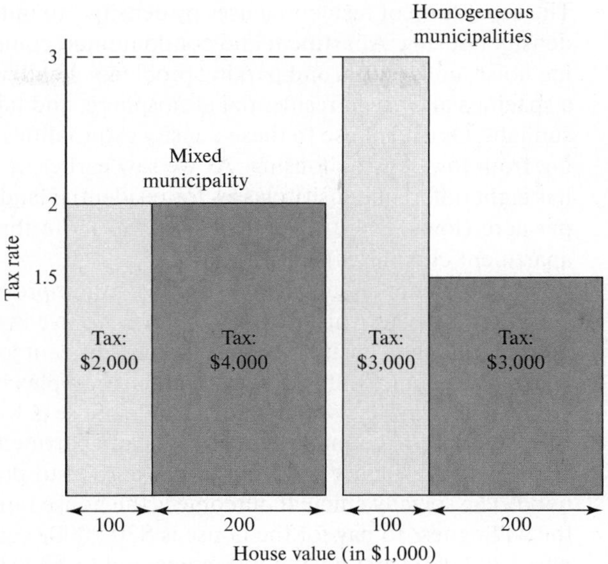

the higher the market value of the property (dwelling and land combined). A local government can use a minimum lot size to exclude households that would generate fiscal deficits. To compute the fiscally motivated minimum lot size, a local government computes the break-even value house value V': for a house with value V', the property tax paid equals the cost of providing public services to the household. The local government also computes the price of land R. Using the rough rule of thumb that the market value of a property (for land and dwelling) is about five times the value of land, the minimum lot size is

$$\text{lot size} = \frac{1}{5}\frac{V'}{R}$$

For example, if $V' = \$200{,}000$ and $R = \$240{,}000$ per acre, the target lot size is 1/6 acre:

$$\text{lot size} = \frac{1}{5}\frac{V'}{R} = \frac{1}{5}\frac{\$250{,}000}{\$240{,}000} = \frac{1}{6}$$

It is important to note that fiscally motivated zoning occurs at the level of the taxing jurisdiction. For example, a municipality with relatively high house values (a relatively low tax rate) has an incentive to outlaw low-value housing that would pay relatively low taxes. But within a taxing jurisdiction, zoning to exclude low-value or high-density housing is motivated by something other than fiscal reasons.

Zoning to Mitigate Density Externalities

The separation of residential uses by density can mitigate the externalities from high-density housing. Apartment and condominium complexes increase road traffic, causing noise, congestion, and parking problems. In addition, large buildings may disrupt a spacious and green residential atmosphere, and tall buildings may block views and sunlight. One response to these density externalities is to separate high-density housing from low-density housing. As we saw earlier in Table 16–1, the city of Portland has eight different density classes for residential land use, from roughly two dwellings per acre (low density single dwellings) to more than 100 dwellings per acre (large apartment complexes).

Under some circumstances, zoning can improve the efficiency of land markets. Consider a city in which everyone prefers to live in neighborhoods with low density rather than high density. Suppose there is a vacant lot in a low-density neighborhood. A firm that would build a large apartment complex is willing to pay $300,000 for the lot, while a firm that would build a single house is willing to pay $100,000 for the lot. In other words, the market outcome is an apartment complex. Suppose each of the 101 existing residents is willing to pay $2,000 to preserve the low-density neighborhood. The socially efficient outcome is the house rather than the apartment complex: the willingness to pay for the house is $302,000 (equal to $100,000 from the builder plus $202,000 from neighbors), compared to $300,000 from the apartment builder. In this example, the market outcome is inefficient.

Could a neighborhood association collect $202,000 from the affected neighbors and outbid the apartment builder? Such an outcome is unlikely because of the free-rider problem. The association does not have any taxing authority, so any contributions are voluntary. Each neighbor has an incentive to contribute less than his or her willingness to pay for preserving the moderate-density neighborhood, hoping that everyone else will contribute enough money to outbid the apartment builder. Given the incentive to get a free ride, the sum of the voluntary contributions is likely to be a small fraction of the $202,000 aggregate willingness to pay of the 101 neighbors, so the apartment builder is likely to outbid the neighbors, generating the inefficient result.

In this example, zoning for moderate density can promote efficient land use. Given the density externality (high density imposes costs on neighbors) and the free-rider problem, the banning of the apartment complex allocates the vacant lot to its highest and best use, broadly defined to include the implications of its use on neighboring properties. This is another example of a market failure caused by externalities that could be addressed with public policy.

Of course, zoning is a blunt policy instrument for dealing with the combination of density externalities and free riders, and it's easy to imagine circumstances in which residential zoning generates inefficient land use. For example, suppose the willingness to pay for preserving moderate density is only $500 per neighbor. In this case, the aggregate willingness to pay for the house is only $150,500 (equal to $100,000 from the builder plus $50,500 from neighbors), compared to $300,000 from the apartment builder. In this case, the market equilibrium–the apartment complex–is

FIGURE 16–2 The Market Effects of Low-Density Zoning

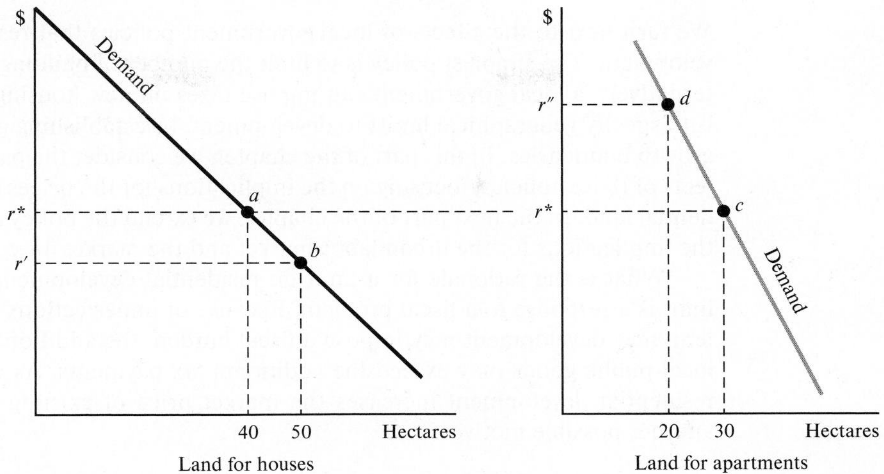

efficient. Nonetheless, each neighbor has an incentive to voice support for banning the apartment complex, and voice matters in zoning policy. If the collective voice in opposition to high density is loud enough, the city may make an inefficient choice, using residential zoning to ban the efficient apartment complex.

The Market Effects of Low-Density Zoning

Figure 16–2 illustrates the market effects of zoning in favor of low-density housing. In the market equilibrium shown by points *a* and *c*, land is allocated to the highest bidder, and the equilibrium price is the same (r^*) in both markets. At the equilibrium price, 40 hectares of land are allocated to houses and 30 hectares are allocated to apartments.

Suppose the city zones 50 hectares for low density (houses), leaving 20 hectares for high density (apartments). In Figure 16–2, the market goes to point *b* in the house market and to point *d* in the apartment market. The increase in the supply of land zoned for houses decreases the price from r^* to r', while the decrease in the supply of land zoned for apartments increases the price from r^* to r''. The price gap means that an apartment builder is willing to pay more for a vacant lot than a house builder: $r'' > r'$.

Does the gap in the willingness to pay between the two land users mean that the land market is inefficient? Recall that if there are density externalities, we must incorporate neighbors' willingness to pay for low density into the efficiency analysis. If the neighbors of a vacant lot are collectively willing to pay at least $(r'' - r')$ to prevent high-density housing, the zoning outcome is efficient in the sense that land is allocated to the highest and best use, broadly defined to include external effects. In contrast, if density externalities are small relative to the gap between the willingness to pay by apartment builders and house builders $(r'' - r')$, zoning generates an inefficient outcome.

3. LIMITS ON RESIDENTIAL DEVELOPMENT

We turn next to the effects of local-government policies that restrict residential development. The simplest policy is to limit the number of building permits issued. Alternatively, a local government can impose taxes on new housing. A third approach is to specify geographical limits to development, by establishing green belts or urban growth boundaries. In this part of the chapter, we consider the partial-equilibrium effects of these policies, focusing on the implications for the prices of housing and residential land. In the next part of the chapter, we extend the policy analysis to consider the implications for the urban labor market and the market for commercial land.

What is the rationale for a limit on residential development? In some cases, a limit is a response to a fiscal problem. Because of imperfections in the local tax system, new development may impose a fiscal burden: the additional cost of providing local public goods may exceed the additional tax payments. As we'll see, a limit on residential development increases the market price of existing housing, providing another possible motive.

Limits on Building Permits

Some cities limit residential development by restricting the number of building permits. A restriction could be direct, in the form of an explicit maximum number of permits per year, or could be indirect, in the form of a costly and time-consuming review process that discourages builders from applying for a permit.

Figure 16–3 shows the market effects of a direct policy under which a city issues a maximum of 100 permits per year.

- *Initial Equilibrium.* The demand curve intersects the supply curve (marginal-cost curve) at point *a*, generating an equilibrium price of $200,000 and an equilibrium quantity of 160.
- *Limit on Building Permits.* The supply curve is kinked, and goes vertical at the number of permits (100). The new supply curve intersects the market demand curve at point *b*, so the price of housing increases to $260,000. In other words, housing consumers bear part of the cost of the permit policy, paying an additional $30,000 for a house.

The permit policy also decreases the marginal cost of producing housing. As explained in a microeconomics course, a supply curve is also a marginal-cost curve. In the case of housing, the supply (marginal-cost) curve is positively sloped because an increase in the quantity of housing produced increases the demand for land, increasing its price. At the market-equilibrium quantity of 160 houses, the marginal cost of housing is $200,000 (point *a* on the supply and marginal-cost curve), which includes the price of the lot on which the house is built. The permit policy decreases the quantity of housing produced to 100 houses, decreasing the demand for land and its price. As shown by point *c*, the new marginal cost of housing is only $170,000, indicating that the lot price has decreased by $30,000 (equal to $200,000 – $170,000). In other words, landowners bear part of the cost of the building-permit policy.

FIGURE 16–3 The Market Effects of a Limit on Building Permits

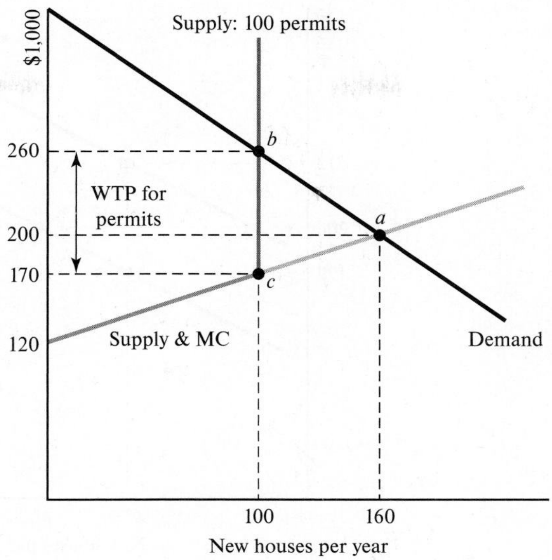

What is the monetary value of a building permit? A permit holder can build a new house at a cost of $170,000 (point *c*) and sell it at the new market price of $260,000 (point *b*), generating a surplus of $90,000. This is the maximum willingness to pay for a permit. A city that auctions 100 permits to the highest bidders could raise $9 million per year. Alternatively the city could accept proposals from developers and allocate the permits to the most appealing projects. In this case, a builder has an incentive to invest resources in plans and presentations to convince the city that his or her proposal merits approval. This is an example of rent seeking, defined as investing resources in the pursuit of favorable treatment by the public sector. Rent seeking is wasteful in the sense that the resources used for persuasion could instead be used in other ways.

Development Taxes

A residential development tax is imposed at the time a dwelling is built, and is paid in legal terms by the builder. In Figure 16–4, the initial (pre-tax) equilibrium is shown by point *b*, with price = $200,000 and a quantity = h^* new houses per year. A development tax shifts the supply curve for new housing upward by the amount of the tax ($20,000) and increases the equilibrium price to $212,000 (shown by point *d*). In other words, the builder shifts 3/5 of the tax ($12,000/$20,000) forward to housing consumers.

The builder shifts the remainder of the tax backward onto landowners. The development tax decreases the number of houses built, decreasing the demand for

FIGURE 16–4 Market Effects of a Development Tax

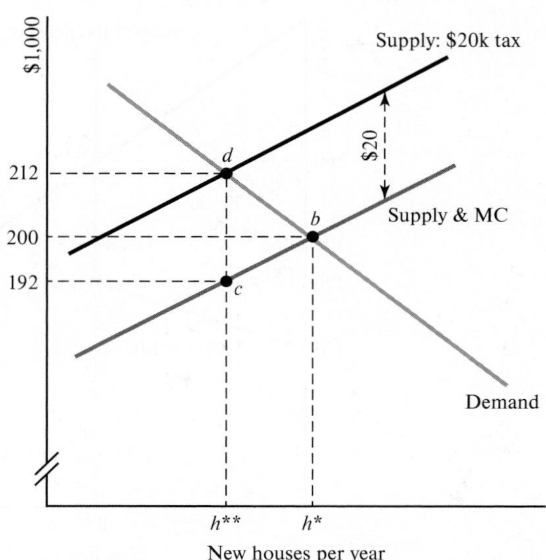

land and its price. In Figure 16–4, the marginal cost of housing decreases from $200,000 (point *b*) to $192,000 (point *c*), reflecting an $8,000 decrease in the cost of a plot of land for a new house. In other words, the builder shifts 2/5 of the tax ($8,000/$20,000) backward onto landowners.

Some cities impose development taxes to cover the additional cost of providing local public goods to new residential areas. For example, revenue from development taxes could be used to build infrastructure (roads, sewers, schools, and parks) to serve new residential areas. These sorts of development taxes are labeled "impact fees" or "system development charges."

Growth Boundary

Some cities limit residential development by confining development to specific geographical areas. The confinement policy could be an explicit ban on development outside a defined development area. Alternatively, a city could block the provision of vital public goods in certain areas. In both cases, residential development is confined within an urban growth boundary.

Figure 16–5 shows the effects of a growth boundary on the urban housing market. As usual, the initial market equilibrium is shown by point *b*. The growth boundary generates a kink in the supply curve at point *c*. For relatively small quantities of housing (less than h'), the growth boundary is irrelevant, so the supply curve is unaffected by the policy. The boundary becomes relevant at h' dwellings and its negative effect on housing supply increases as the potential market expands. The growth

FIGURE 16–5 Growth Boundary and the Housing Market

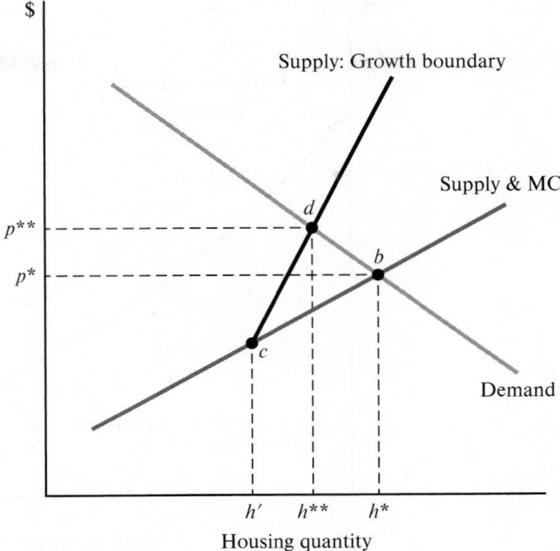

boundary increases the equilibrium price of housing from p^* to p^{**} and decreases the equilibrium quantity from h^* to h^{**}.

The increase in price from the growth boundary is beneficial for some people and costly for others. A person who owns housing at the time the growth boundary is announced gets a capital gain equal to $(p^{**} - p^*)$. In contrast, a newcomer to the housing market in the city pays a higher housing price.

Figure 16–6 shows the implications of a growth boundary for the urban land market. Consider a metropolitan area that is initially expected to expand to a circle with a radius of 12 miles. In other words, the initial urban land bid curve intersects the agricultural bid curve at a distance of 12 miles from the city center. Suppose a new growth boundary is 8 miles from the city center. For land between 8 and 12 miles from the center, the price drops to the agricultural bid, shown by the segment of the horizontal line between point *a* and point *b*. The households displaced by the growth boundary will bid up the price of land within the boundary. This is shown by the upward shift of the urban bid curve from the city center to a distance of 8 miles. In other words, landowners within the boundary gain at the expense of landowners outside the boundary.

How does the growth-boundary policy compare to the other policies that limit residential development–building permits and development taxes? All three policies increase the price and decrease the quantity of housing. The difference occurs in the land market. Building permits and development taxes decrease land prices. In contrast, a growth boundary produces winners and losers among landowners: there are benefits for landowners with favorable geography (inside the boundary) and costs for landowners with unfavorable geography (outside the boundary).

FIGURE 16-6 Growth Boundary and the Land Market

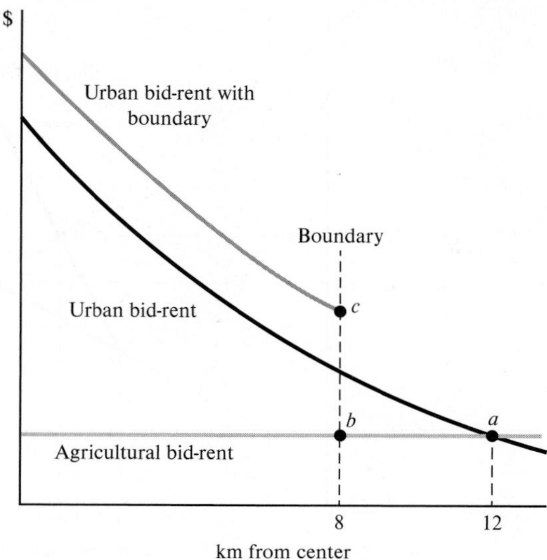

The Market Effects of Land-Use Regulations

The Wharton regulatory index measures the stringency of land-use regulations. The index has a value of zero for the average city, a positive value for cities with above-average stringency, and a negative value for cities with below-average stringency. Among the factors that increase the value of the index are (i) a lengthy review process for building projects, (ii) development taxes, (iii) requirements that builders provide open space, and (iv) large minimum lot sizes.

Table 16-2 shows the values of the Wharton index and the implications for housing prices in several municipalities. The regulatory price premium is computed as the

TABLE 16-2 The Regulatory Housing Price Premium

City (Municipality)	Regulation Index	Housing Price Premium ($)
Atlanta	0.70	89,606
Chicago	−1.15	−147,209
Dallas	−0.14	−17,921
San Francisco	1.96	250,896
Seattle	2.39	305,939

Sources: Gyourko, Joseph, Albert Saiz, Albert, and Anita Summers, "A New Measure of the Local Regulatory Environment for Housing Markets: The Wharton Residential Land Use Regulatory Index." *Urban Studies* 45, 2008, 693-729; Gyuorko, Joseph. "Housing: Urban Housing Markets," Chapter 5 in *Making Cities Work*, edited by Robert P. Inman. Princeton NJ; Princeton University Press, 2009.

FIGURE 16–7 Regulatory Housing Price Premium, Metropolitan

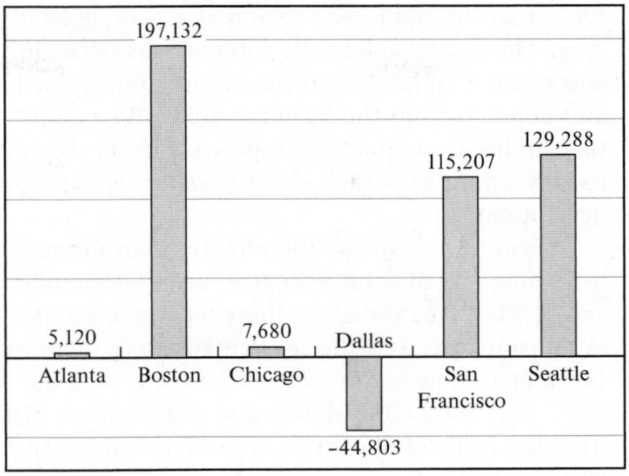

Sources: Gyourko, Joseph, Albert Saiz, Albert, and Anita Summers, "A New Measure of the Local Regulatory Environment for Housing Markets: The Wharton Residential Land Use Regulatory Index." *Urban Studies* 45, 2008, 693-729; Gyuorko, Joseph. "Housing: Urban Housing Markets," Chapter 5 in *Making Cities Work*, edited by Robert P. Inman. Princeton NJ; Princeton University Press, 2009.

difference in the price of housing, relative to the national average, that is attributable to the regulatory environment. In Chicago, a below-average stringency generates a price of housing that is $147,209 below the average. At the other extreme, Seattle's highly stringent environment generates a premium of $305,939. A household that moves from a house in Chicago to an otherwise identical house in Seattle would pay an additional $453,248.

Figure 16–7 shows the regulatory premia at the metropolitan level. The typical large metropolitan area has a large number of municipalities, each with its own set of residential land-use policies. In Figure 16–7, the premium for a particular metropolitan area is a weighted average of the premia of its individual municipalities. The regulation premium ranges from −$44,803 in Dallas to $197,132 in Boston.

4. GROWTH CONTROL AND LABOR MARKETS

So far we have explored the effects of growth-control policies on the markets for housing and residential land. In this part of the chapter we extend the analysis to explore the effects on the urban labor market and the market for commercial land. In addition, we look beyond the city to explore the effects of its policies on other cities in the regional economy.

Residential Limits and the Urban Economy

Earlier in the book we developed a general-equilibrium model of the urban economy. The model shows the interactions between urban land markets (for business and residential land) and the urban labor market (supply from the residential area and demand from the business area). We can use the model to show how a policy that limits residential development affects the rest of the urban economy. We will use an urban growth boundary as an example of a policy that limits residential development.

Figure 16-8 shows the effects of an urban growth boundary on the land and labor markets of a monocentric city. The initial equilibrium is shown by points *a* and *b*, where the initial business bid curve intersects the initial residential bid curve at a distance x_1 and the residential curve intersects the horizontal agricultural bid curve at x_2. The width of the CBD is x_1 and the width of the residential district is $(x_2 - x_1)$. Total labor demand in the business district equals the total labor supply from the residential district, so we have equilibrium in both the land market and the labor market.

A growth boundary at x_3 reduces the residential territory, decreasing labor supply. The resulting excess demand for labor increases the wage. The increase in the wage increases production cost and shifts the business bid curve downward, in accordance with the leftover principle. At the same time, the increase in the wage increases the price of housing, shifting the residential bid curve upward. Equilibrium is restored at points *c* and *d*, with a CBD width x_4 and a residential width $(x_3 - x_4)$.

FIGURE 16-8 General Equilibrium Effects of a Growth Boundary

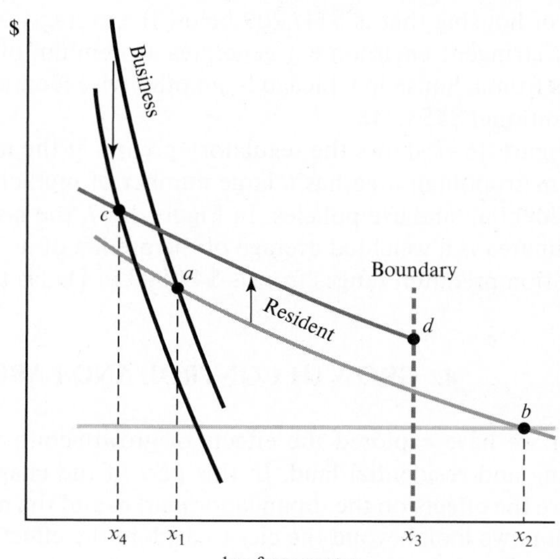

The key insight from this general-equilibrium analysis is that the effects of a policy spread beyond its original geography. The growth boundary directly affects the residential land market, but its effects are transmitted to the market for labor and the market for business land. The owners of business land lose because the increase in the wage increases production cost and decreases the bid for business land. In addition, the policy-directed shrinking of the residential district causes the business district to shrink.

In the previous section of the chapter, we explore two other residential policies: a limit on building permits and a tax on residential development. Both policies increase housing prices and decrease the number of residents in the city, so both policies decrease the supply of labor. The resulting changes in the urban labor market and the business land market are the same as triggered by an urban growth boundary: the excess demand for labor increases the equilibrium wage, which decreases the bid for business land. Equilibrium in the urban labor is restored with a higher wage and a smaller workforce. As in the case of an urban growth boundary, a residential policy affects other markets in the urban economy.

An Urban Growth Boundary and the Regional Economy

We turn next to the effects of one city's growth boundary on other cities in the regional economy. Recall the model of cities in a regional economy, which we developed in an earlier chapter. In our model of a two-city regional economy, the total workforce of the region is fixed, and workers are perfectly mobile between the cities. To simplify matters, we will assume that workers rent residential land from absentee landowners.

In Figure 16–9 the initial (pre-policy) equilibrium is shown by point *a*, with 5 million workers in each city, and a common utility level u^*. Suppose ControlCity

FIGURE 16–9 Intercity Effects of an Urban Growth Boundary

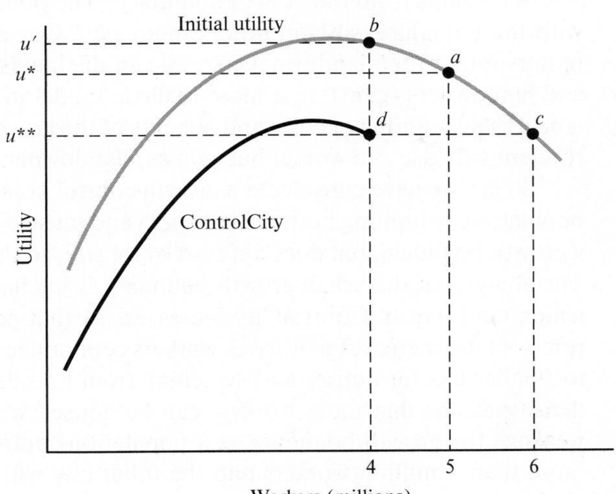

implements a precise growth-control policy: the city reduces its workforce from 5 million to 4 million by (a) specifying a minimum lot size per worker and (b) fixing the total land area of the city. The 1 million workers displaced by growth control in ControlCity move to the other city, increasing its workforce to 6 million. The immediate effect is to increase utility in ControlCity to u' (point *b*) and to decrease utility in the other city to u^{**} (point *c*). Workers are perfectly mobile between the two cities, so this utility gap will not persist.

The utility gap will be eliminated by changes in the land market. The region's workers compete for a fixed number of lots in ControlCity, and workers will bid up land rent in ControlCity. An increase in land rent decreases worker utility, and rent will continue to increase until the utility gap is eliminated. In Figure 16–9, the increase in land rent shifts the utility curve downward. Given the maximum of 4 million workers in ControlCity, the other city has a workforce of 6 million and a utility level of u^{**} (point *c*). In other words, the common (regionwide) utility level is anchored by point *c*. Therefore, land rent in ControlCity must rise to the point at which utility decreases to the utility anchor, u^{**}. This is shown by point *d* on the lower utility curve for ControlCity. In the new regional equilibrium, workers are indifferent between the two cities: the benefits of living in a smaller city (ControlCity) are fully offset by higher land rent and the resulting higher cost of living.

The growth-control policy decreases the utility of workers throughout the region. The workers in the uncontrolled city lose because their city grows, moving further downward along the negatively sloped utility curve. Both cities are initially too big, and the uncontrolled city moves even further from the utility-maximizing size. In ControlCity, locational equilibrium requires a sufficiently large increase in land rent to decrease utility to the level reached in the other city. The decrease in utility reflects the inefficiency of replacing two identical cities with a large city and a small city. The growth-control policy prevents the efficient movement of workers between cities, so the common utility is lower than it would be with two cities of equal size.

Who gains from the growth boundary? The policy increases land rent in the city with the boundary, so landowners there gain. Our model assumes that workers are renters rather than landowners, so we can distinguish between workers (utility loss) and landowners (gain). In a more realistic model in which workers own houses and land, the accounting of costs and benefits of the growth boundary is more complex. A resident will lose as a worker but gain as a landowner, and the net effect is ambiguous.

So far, we have considered a growth-control policy that precisely controls a city's population by limiting both the land area and lot size of the city. Suppose the city uses a growth boundary, but does not restrict lot size, so the density of the city can change. The analysis of the urban growth boundary is unchanged until we reach the stage at which land rent in ControlCity increases. At that point, the increase in the relative price of land increases density as workers economize on land, for example, by shifting to smaller lots for houses and switching from houses to apartments. The increase in density means that more workers can be housed within the growth boundary. This weakens the growth boundary as a population-control policy: ControlCity will have more than 4 million workers and the other city will have fewer than 6 million. The equilibrium utility level will be higher with flexible density because an increase in density weakens the distortionary effects of the urban growth boundary.

REVIEW THE CONCEPTS

1. According to the economist William Fischel, a key factor in the timing of industrial zoning was the development of the [_____] for the transport of [_____], and a key factor in the timing of residential zoning was the development of the [_____] for the transport of [_____].
2. In the classic Supreme Court case on zoning, the word "parasite" was used to describe [_____].
3. The three criteria for the constitutionality of land-use zoning are (i) [_____], (ii) [_____], and (iii) [_____].
4. Under the equal-protection criterion for zoning, discrimination based on [_____] is constitutional, but discrimination based on [_____] is unconstitutional.
5. In U.S. court cases concerning exclusionary zoning, the courts have found that the effects of zoning on [_____] (insiders, outsiders, extra-terrestrials) is unimportant.
6. The possible roles of land-use zoning are to (i) mitigate [_____], (ii) prevent [_____], and (iii) mitigate [_____].
7. Consider a variation on Figure 16–1. Suppose the per-household cost of public services is $6,000 and there are two house values: $100,000 and $300,000. In a mixed municipality, the tax rate is [_____] percent. In homogeneous municipalities, the tax rates are [_____] percent in the low-price municipality and [_____] percent in the high-price municipality.
8. Consider a municipality where the break-even house value is $250,000 and the price of land is $500,000 per acre. The fiscally motivated minimum lot size is [_____] acre.
9. The blocking of sunlight is an example of a density [_____]. Zoning to prevent blocking by an apartment building is efficient if neighbors' willingness to pay for [_____] is large relative to [_____] for apartment land.
10. A policy of zoning for low density residential development [_____] {↑, ↓, –} the price of land for apartments and [_____] {↑, ↓, –} the price of land for houses.
11. A limit on building-permits [_____] {↑, ↓, –} the price of housing, [_____] {↑, ↓, –} the marginal cost of housing, and [_____] {↑, ↓, –} the price of residential land. The willingness to pay for a building permit equals [_____] minus [_____].
12. The Wharton regulatory index has a [_____] value for a city with relatively high [_____] taxes and relatively large [_____].
13. Based on the Wharton regulatory index, a household that moves from Chicago to Seattle would pay an additional $[_____] (choose 153,000, 253,000, 453,000) for an identical house.
14. In a general-equilibrium context, an urban growth boundary generates excess labor [_____]. The equilibrium wage [_____] {↑, ↓, –} and the bid for business land [_____] {↑, ↓, –}.
15. In a regional economy, an urban growth boundary in one city [_____] {↑, ↓, –} utility in the control city because [_____] increases and [_____] {↑, ↓, –} utility in the uncontrolled city because [_____] increases.

16. For each pair of variables, indicate whether the relationship is positive, negative, neutral, or ambiguous.

Parameter	Choice Variable	Relationship
number of building permits	price of housing	[_____]
number of building permits	price of residential land	[_____]
residential development tax	price of housing	[_____]
residential development tax	price of residential land	[_____]
growth boundary in city A	1-city region: wage	[_____]
growth boundary in city A	1-city region: price of business land	[_____]
growth boundary in city A	2-city region: utility in city A	[_____]
growth boundary in city A	2-city region: utility in city B	[_____]
growth boundary in city A	2-city region: price of land in city A	[_____]
growth boundary in city A	2-city region: workforce in city B	[_____]

APPLY THE CONCEPTS

1. *Bidding for Development: Pareto and Nash*
Consider a 100-household neighborhood with a vacant lot that will be developed either as a house or an apartment complex. Each household is willing to pay $300 for a house rather than an apartment complex. The apartment builder has bid $100,000 for the lot, compared to a bid of $86,000 from the house builder.
   a. Zoning for low density [_____] (is, is not) efficient because . . .
   b. Suppose a neighborhood association stages a campaign of voluntary contributions in an attempt to outbid the apartment builder. An outcome under which each household contributes half of its benefit [_____] (is, is not) a Nash equilibrium because . . .
   c. Suppose half of the households contribute to the campaign, and each household contributes $$g$. The campaign will generate the Pareto-efficient outcome as a Nash equilibrium if $g =$ [_____] because . . .
2. *Permit Price*
Consider a city where the demand for new curve for new housing has a vertical intercept of $340,000 and a slope of −$1,000 per house. The marginal-cost curve (supply curve) has a vertical intercept of $100,000 and a slope of $2,000 per house. Suppose the city issues 40 building permits. Illustrate the effects of the permit policy on the housing market. Include numbers for the price of housing with and without the permit policy, and show the market value of a building permit.
3. *Who Pays a Development Tax?*
Consider a city where the initial equilibrium price of new housing is $200,000. The price elasticity of demand for housing is −1.0 and the long-run price elasticity of supply of housing is 4.0. Suppose the city imposes a development tax of $25,000 per dwelling. Illustrate the effects of development tax on the housing market. Include numbers for housing prices (with and without the tax) and the

marginal cost of production (with and without the tax). The portion of the tax not borne by consumers is borne by [______]

4. *Compensation for a Growth Boundary*
Consider a monocentric city with a CBD radius of 2 miles and a residential ring of 4 miles width. In the absence of a change in policy, the city's radius will increase from 6 miles to 9 miles. Suppose the city announces a new growth boundary at its current radius (6 miles). Your job is to design (i) a set of taxes on landowners who are winners from the policy and (ii) a set of subsidies for landowners who are losers from the policy.
   a. Taxes will be paid by landowners at $x =$ [______] (fill with 1, 5, 8) and subsidies will be paid to landowners at $x =$ [______] (fill with 1, 5, 8). Illustrate.
   b. Among residential landowners, the largest subsidies will be paid to landowners who are . . . Illustrate.

5. *Land-Use Policies and the Price of Land*
Consider the following: "Depending on the variable controlled by a land-use policy, the policy may either increase or decrease the equilibrium price of vacant land." The "variable" is the supply of or demand for vacant land.
   a. Illustrate the effect of a limit on building permits on the price of vacant land.
   b. Illustrate the effect of an urban growth boundary on the price of vacant land within the boundary.
   c. Illustrate the effect of an urban growth boundary on the price of vacant land outside the boundary.

6. *Development Tax and the Urban Labor Market*
Consider the general-equilibrium effects of a residential development tax.
   a. Illustrate the effects of the development tax on the urban labor market, including its effect on the equilibrium wage.
   b. Illustrate the effects of the labor-market effects of the development tax (from part (a)) on the bid for business land. Illustrate.

REFERENCES AND READING

1. Brueckner, J., "Urban Growth Boundaries: An Effective Second-Best Remedy for Unpriced Traffic Congestion?" *Journal of Housing Economics,* November 2007.
2. Dawkins, Casey J., "Exclusionary Land Use Policies: Economic Rationales and Legal Remedies," Chapter 20 in *The Oxford Handbook of Urban Economics and Planning,* edited by Nancy Brooks, Kieran Donaghy, and Gerrit-Jan Knaap. New York: Oxford University Press, 2011.
3. Fischel, William A., "A Theory of Municipal Corporate Governance with an Application to Land-Use Regulation," Chapter 22 in *A Companion to Urban Economics,* edited by Richard J. Arnott and Daniel P. McMillen. New York: Wiley-Blackwell, 2006.
4. Fischel, William. "An Economic History of Zoning and a Cure for Its Exclusionary Effects." *Urban Studies* 41 (2004), pp. 317–40.

5. Fischel, William, *The Economics of Zoning Laws.* Baltimore: Johns Hopkins, 1985.
6. Gyourko, Joseph, and Edward Glaeser, "Urban Growth and Housing Supply." *Journal of Economic Geography* 6 (2006), pp. 71–89.
7. Gyourko, Joseph, Albert Saiz, and Anita Summers, "A New Measure of the Local Regulatory Environment for Housing Markets: The Wharton Residential Land Use Regulatory Index." *Urban Studies* 45 (2008), pp. 693–729.
8. Gyuorko, Joseph, "Housing: Urban Housing Markets," Chapter 5 in *Making Cities Work,* edited by Robert P. Inman. Princeton, NJ: Princeton University Press, 2009.
9. Juntunen, Lorelei, Gerri-Jan Knaap, and Terry Moore, "Fiscal Impact Analysis and the Costs of Alternative Development Patterns," Chapter 31 in *The Oxford Handbook of Urban Economics and Planning,* edited by Nancy Brooks, Kieran Donaghy, and Gerrit-Jan Knaap. New York: Oxford University Press, 2011.
10. McDonald, John, and Daniel P. McMillen, "The Economics of Zoning," Chapter 19 in *The Oxford Handbook of Urban Economics and Planning,* edited by Nancy Brooks, Kieran Donaghy, and Gerrit-Jan Knaap. New York: Oxford University Press, 2011.
11. Rachelle Alterman, "Land Use Regulations and Property Values: The 'Windfalls Capture' Idea Revisited," Chapter 33 in *The Oxford Handbook of Urban Economics and Planning,* edited by Nancy Brooks, Kieran Donaghy, and Gerrit-Jan Knaap. New York: Oxford University Press, 2011.
12. Thomas Nechyba, "School Finance, Spatial Income Segregation and the Nature of Communities." *Journal of Urban Economics* 54.1 (2003, July), pp. 61–88.

CHAPTER 17

Urban Housing and Public Policy

Almost any man worthy of his salt would fight to defend his home, but no one ever heard of a man going to war for his boarding house.

—MARK TWAIN

Housing is different from other products in several respects. First, housing is durable: a carefully maintained dwelling can provide housing services for decades. Second, the housing stock is heterogeneous: dwellings differ in size, age, layout, design, and location. As a result, the urban housing market is a set of interdependent submarkets, with dwellings differing in quality and price. Third, housing is the most important means of wealth accumulation for many households, so changes in housing prices have relatively large effects on household wealth.

1. FILTERING: DURABILITY AND SUBMARKETS

We start with a model of the urban housing market as a set of interdependent submarkets. The submarkets are distinguished by the quality of housing services provided by the dwelling. The submarkets are interdependent because as prices change, dwellings move from one submarket to another, and so do consumers. The filtering model of housing shows that the movement of dwellings and consumers between markets is affected by changes in the relative prices of different quality levels.

The Filtering Model of Housing

Housing is durable in the sense that with proper maintenance, a dwelling can provide housing services for many decades. But in the absence of routine maintenance and repair, a dwelling will deteriorate, decreasing the quality of the dwelling over time. Imagine a quality ladder for housing, with the highest quality dwellings at the top of the ladder and progressively lower qualities as we move down the ladder. Each year, a property owner must decide where on the quality ladder to position a dwelling.

If the owner does nothing, the dwelling will drop one or more rungs on the ladder. With a moderate expenditure on maintenance and repair, the owner can keep the dwelling at the same level. To raise the quality of the dwelling, the owner must spend a substantial amount of money to renovate or remodel.

We will start with a simple model of two housing submarkets: high quality and low quality. We assume that all new housing is high-quality housing, and it is prohibitively expensive to upgrade a dwelling from low quality to high quality. The quantity of high-quality housing in year t equals the quantity of new housing in year t plus the quantity of high-quality housing left over from the previous year (year $t - 1$):

$$H_t = H_{t-1} \cdot (1 - f) + new$$

where f is the fraction of the high-quality dwellings that filter down to the low-quality submarket. For example, suppose $new = 18$, $H_{t-1} = 100$, and $f = 0.10$. In this case, $H_t = 108$:

$$H_t = 100 \cdot (1 - 0.10) + 18 = 108$$

In this case, the high-quality market has 18 new dwellings and 90 leftovers, for a total of 108. The quantity of low-quality housing in year t is the sum of low-quality housing that remains from the previous year plus any housing that filters down from the high-quality submarket:

$$L_t = L_{t-1} \cdot (1 - r) + f \cdot H_{t-1}$$

where r is the fraction of low-quality dwellings that are retired from the housing market. Continuing the numerical example, suppose $L_{t-1} = 200$ and $r = 0.06$. Given $H_{t-1} = 100, f = 0.10, L_t = 198$:

$$L_t = 200 \cdot (1 - 0.06) + 100 \cdot 0.10 = 188 + 10 = 198$$

Figure 17–1 illustrates the filtering process. Suppose a city starts with a fixed number of high-quality dwellings (65). Moving from left to right along the horizontal axis, the number of high-quality dwellings increases while the number of low-quality dwellings decreases. The positively sloped curve shows the maintenance cost required to keep a dwelling in the high-quality market. For example, the cost for dwelling #20 is \$115 (point a), compared to a cost of \$200 for dwelling #40 and \$250 for #50. The benefit of keeping a dwelling in the high-quality submarket is the difference between the price of high-quality and low-quality housing ($p_h - p_l$). The equilibrium is shown by point b: For the first 40 dwellings, the \$200 benefit of retaining high-quality status exceeds the cost, so 25 dwellings filter down to the low-quality market.

A change in the either price (p_h or p_l) will affect the equilibrium number of filtered dwellings. An increase in the price gap ($p_h - p_l$) increases the quantity of high-quality housing at the expense of low-quality housing. For example, if the price gap increases from \$200 to \$250, the number of leftover high-quality dwellings increases from 40 to 50 and the number of filtered dwellings decreases from 25 to 15. Similarly, a decrease in the price gap moves dwellings in the opposite direction.

FIGURE 17–1 The Filtering Process

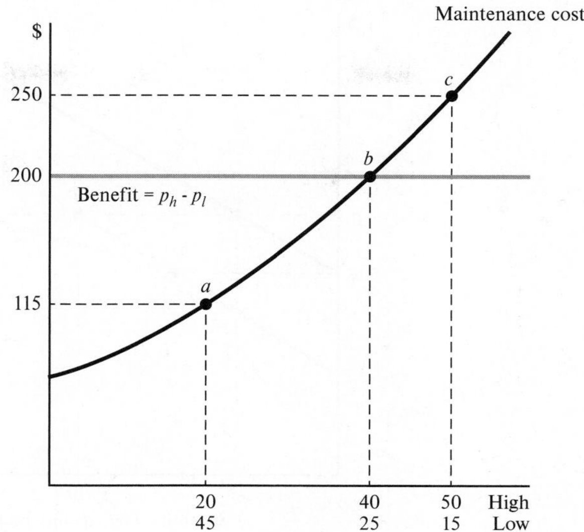

Supply of High-Quality Housing

The market supply of high-quality housing is the sum of new housing and leftover high-quality housing. In Figure 17–2, the higher curve is the supply of new housing. The minimum supply price of new housing is p_0: a builder requires a price of at least p_0 for a new dwelling. The quantity of new housing increases with the price. For example, at p' the quantity of new housing is 15 dwellings (point a). The middle curve is the supply curve for leftover high-quality housing. As we have seen, an increase in the price of high-quality housing increases the number of high-quality dwellings that remain in the high-quality market rather than filtering down to the low-quality market.

The market supply curve is the horizontal sum of the new supply curve and the leftover supply curve. For prices below the minimum supply price p_0, the market supply curve is the same as the leftover supply curve. The kink at point k shows the price at which new dwellings comes into play, and for $p > p_0$, the market supply curve is the horizontal sum of the supply curves for new housing and leftover housing. For example, at p^*, the market supply is 55, the sum of 15 new dwellings and 40 leftover dwellings.

Supply of Low-Quality Housing

The market supply of low-quality housing is the sum of filtered housing and leftover low-quality housing. In Figure 17–3, the higher curve is the supply of housing that filters downward from the high-quality submarket. As we have seen, the quantity of filtered housing increases with the price of low-quality housing. For example, at p'',

FIGURE 17-2 The Supply of High-Quality Housing

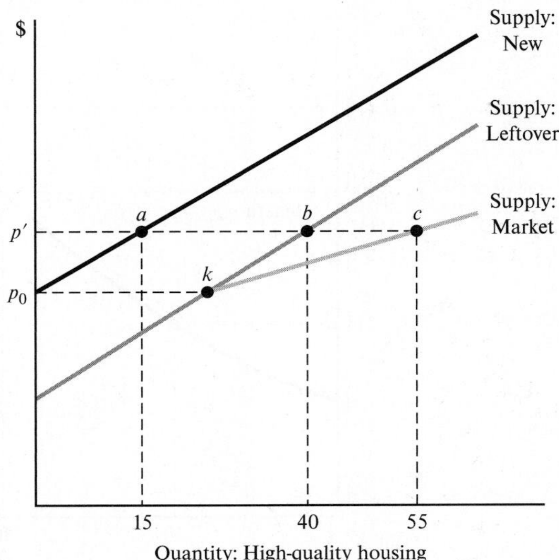

FIGURE 17-3 The Supply of Low-Quality Housing

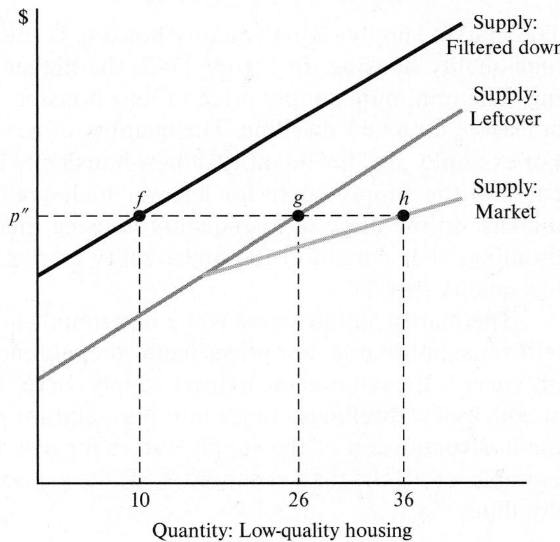

the quantity of filtered housing is 10 dwellings (point *f*). The middle curve is the supply curve for leftover low-quality housing. An increase in the price of low-quality housing increases the number of low-quality dwellings that remain in the low-quality market rather than being retired.

The market supply curve is the horizontal sum of the filtered supply curve and the leftover supply curve. For prices below the minimum supply price of filtered housing, the market supply curve is the same as the leftover supply curve. The kink at point *k* shows the price at which filtered dwellings come into play. For example, at p'', the market supply is 36 dwellings, the sum of 10 filtered dwellings and 26 leftover dwellings.

Applying the Filtering Model: Limit on Building Permits

We can use the filtering model to explore the effects of public policy on housing prices and quantities. Cities use a number of policies to limit the quantity of new housing, including explicit limits on building permits, development taxes, and growth boundaries. The filtering model shows how these policies affect the markets for high-quality and low-quality housing.

Figure 17–4 shows the effects of a limit on building permits on the high-quality submarket. The initial equilibrium is shown by point *c*, with an equilibrium price p^* and equilibrium quantity 55 dwellings, including 15 new dwellings and 40 used dwellings. If the city simply bans new housing (zero building permits), the supply curve for new housing disappears, so the new market supply curve is identical to the leftover supply curve. The ban increases the market price from p^* to p^{**} and decreases the equilibrium quantity to 48 dwellings.

Note that the effect of the new-housing ban is mitigated by a decrease in downward filtering. The increase in the price of high-quality housing increases the

FIGURE 17–4 A Building Ban and the High-Quality Submarket

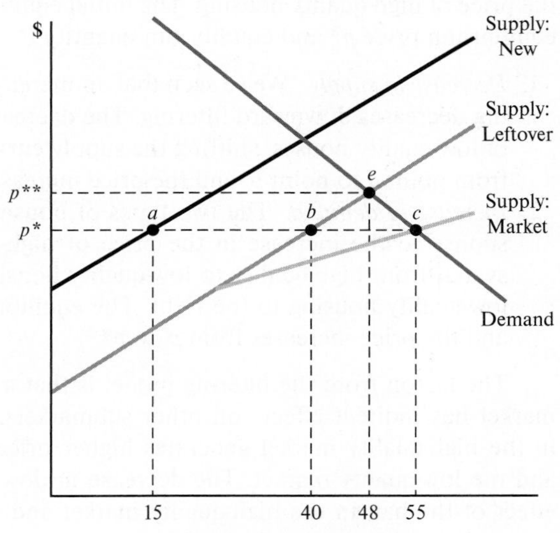

FIGURE 17–5 A Building Ban and the Low-Quality Submarket

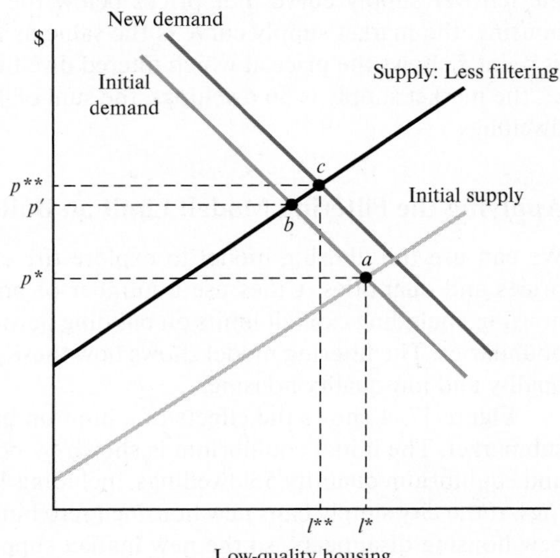

number of leftover dwellings—not filtered downward—from 40 to 48 dwellings. As a result, the quantity of high-quality dwellings decreases by only 7 dwellings, not 15 dwellings.

Figure 17–5 shows the effects of the new-housing ban on the low-quality submarket. There is a supply effect and a demand effect, both triggered by the increase in the price of high-quality housing. The initial equilibrium is shown by point *a*, with an equilibrium price p^* and equilibrium quantity l^*.

1. *Decrease in supply.* We've seen that an increase in the price of high-quality housing decreases downward filtering. The decrease in filtering decreases the supply of low-quality houses, shifting the supply curve to the left. The equilibrium goes from point *a* to point *b*, and the price increases from p^* to p'.
2. *Increase in demand.* The two types of housing are imperfect substitutes. In response to the increase in the price of high-quality housing, some consumers switch from high-quality to low-quality housing, shifting the demand curve for low-quality housing to the right. The equilibrium goes from point *b* to point *c*, and the price increases from p' to p^{**}.

The lesson from the filtering model is that a policy that is directed at one submarket has indirect effects on other submarkets. In this case, a supply restriction in the high-quality market generates higher prices in both the high-quality market and the low-quality market. The decrease in downward filtering mitigates the price effect of the ban in the high-quality market and causes an increase in the price of low-quality housing.

Filtering and Gentrification

We have seen that the filtering process links housing submarkets. As a result, a decrease in supply in one submarket increases prices in related submarkets. The same logic applies to a change in demand. For example, suppose that an influx of high-income households increases the demand for high-quality housing in a particular area of a city. The resulting increase in the price of high-quality housing affects the low-quality market in two ways.

1. *Less downward filtering.* The increase in the price of high-quality housing relative to the price of low-quality housing increases the payoff from keeping a dwelling in the high-quality market, so fewer dwellings filter down to the low-quality market.
2. *More upgrading.* For a sufficiently large increase in the relative price of high-quality housing, it will be economical to upgrade some low-quality dwellings to high-quality dwellings.

These two effects decrease the supply of low-quality housing and increase its price. In other words, an increase in the demand for high-quality housing increases the equilibrium prices of both high-quality and low-quality housing.

The gentrification process involves the displacement of low-income households by high-income households. In the typical gentrification scenario, there is an influx of high-income households into a low-income central-city neighborhood. The high-income households bid up the price of high-quality housing, triggering widespread upgrading of low-quality housing. The resulting decrease in the supply of low-quality housing increases its price. The increase in price causes some low-income households to relocate to areas with lower prices for low-quality housing.

2. SUPPLY-SIDE PUBLIC POLICY

In 2010, about 7 million low-income households in the United States had severe problems with housing affordability in the sense that they paid at least half their income on housing. In this part of the chapter, we explore housing assistance programs that operate on the supply side of the market. As we'll see, these supply-side policies are inefficient. For every dollar spent on public housing, a recipient receives a benefit of about $0.24. As we'll see in the next part of the chapter, there are more efficient ways of providing housing assistance to low-income households.

Public Housing

In 2012, about 1.1 million households lived in public housing, at a budgetary cost of $6.4 billion to the national government. Public housing is managed by local housing authorities, subject to rules set by the national government. From a tenant's perspective, the key rule is that housing rent is no more than 30 percent of household income. The national government pays the gap between the tenant contribution and the operating cost of public housing.

FIGURE 17–6 Public Housing

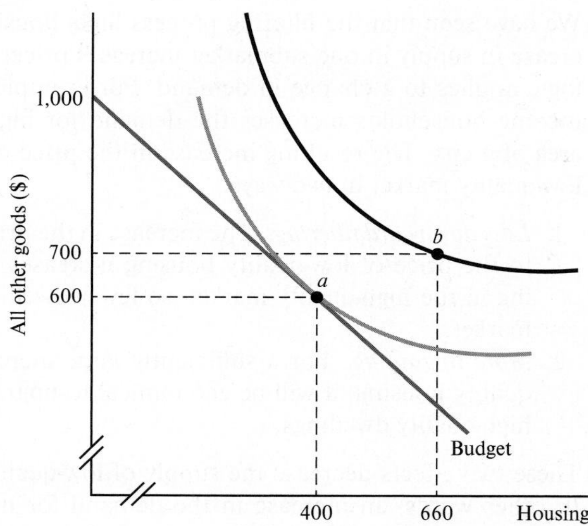

Figure 17–6 shows how public housing works. Consider a low-income household with an income of $1,000 per month. The market price of housing is $1 per unit of housing service. The typical low-income household starts at point *a*: in the absence of any assistance, the household maximizes utility by spending $400 of its $1,000 income on housing, leaving $600 to spend on all other goods.

Suppose an apartment in a public housing complex generates 660 units of housing service. For our hypothetical household, the monthly rent is $300 (equal to 30% of $1,000), leaving $700 to spend on other goods. Public housing adds point *b* to the consumer's budget set. In addition to all the points along the original budget line, the household has the option of point *b*, with 660 units of housing service and $700 on other goods. Utility is higher at point *b* than at point *a*, so the household will accept the offer of public housing.

What is the value of subsidized public housing to the recipient? An alternative to subsidized public housing is a cash payment that the household can spent any way it chooses. In Figure 17–7, we shift the consumer's initial budget line upward until it is tangent to the indifference curve that goes through the public-housing point (*b*). In this example, a cash payment of $240 makes the recipient indifferent: with a total income of $1,240 (equal to $1,000 of market income plus in $240 cash), the recipient chooses point *c* and reaches the same indifference curve as in the case of subsidized public housing. These numbers are consistent with studies that measure the value of public housing to recipients (Green and Malpezzi, 2003).

What is the bang per buck of public housing? The public housing unit generates 660 units of housing service, and if the market price of housing service is $1 per unit, the market value of public housing is $660. The production efficiency of

FIGURE 17-7 Value of Public Housing

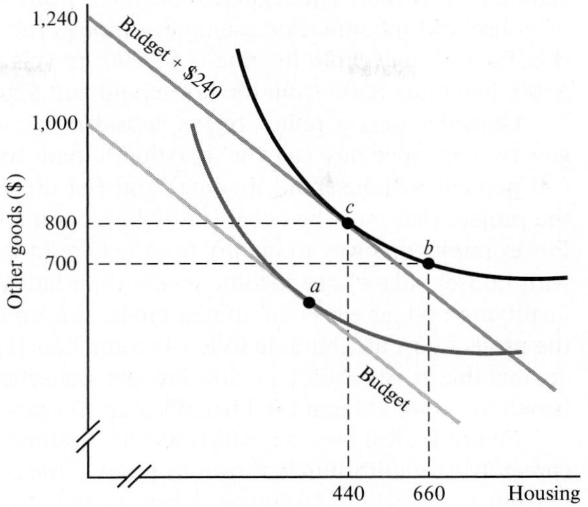

public housing is roughly 0.50, meaning that the cost of producing public housing is roughly twice the cost of housing produced by the private sector (Green and Malpezzi, 2003). In our example, the production cost of public housing unit is $1,320 (twice $660). The tenant pays $300 in rent, so the budgetary cost of the public housing is $1,020 (equal to $1,320 − $300 rent paid by the recipient). Therefore, it costs the government $1,020 to deliver a recipient benefit of $240, for benefit-cost ratio equal to 0.24. In other words, the bang per buck of public housing is $0.24.

Subsidies for Private Housing

The national government uses two types of programs to subsidize private housing for low-income households.

1. *Project-based rental assistance program.* The government specifies a maximum rent that a property owner can charge an eligible household, and covers the gap between the market rent and the tenant contribution. In 2012, about 1.2 million households received assistance under this program, at a budgetary cost of $9.4 billion.
2. *Tax credits for low-income housing.* The government provides tax subsidies to firms that build low-income housing. In 2012, the tax subsidies reduced federal tax revenue by about $6.5 billion.

Consider first the rent-assistance program. Under the Section 8–Project Based program, the government pays a property owner the difference between the "fair market rent" and the household's regulated payment to the owner. The fair market rent is determined by either the cost of building and managing the property, or the prevailing market rent. The regulated payment from a household is typically 30 percent of household income. For example, suppose the fair market rent of an apartment is $500 and household income is $1,000. In this case, the property owner receives $500, including $300 from the household and $200 from the government.

Consider next a policy of tax subsidies for low-income housing projects. The government specifies (a) the maximum rent to be charged eligible households (30 percent of household income) and (b) the minimum fraction of dwellings in the project that must be occupied by low-income households (known as set-asides). For example, one way to qualify for a tax credit is to fill at least 20 percent of units with households whose income is less than half the median income in the area. A qualifying builder earns an annual credit (for up to 10 years) equal to 9 percent of the project cost attributable to low-income housing. For example, if the project cost attributable to set-asides for low-income households is $5 million, the annual tax benefit is $450,000 and total benefit over 10 years is $4.5 million.

Figure 17–8 shows the market effects of supply-side housing subsidies. The initial (pre-policy) equilibrium is shown by point a: the equilibrium price is p^* and the equilibrium quantity is 70 dwellings. A subsidy paid to suppliers shifts the supply curve to the right: at a given market price (paid by tenants), firms provide a larger quantity of housing to the low-income market. In this case, the horizontal shift is 90 dwellings: at the original price p^*, a total of 160 dwellings are supplied, up from 70 dwellings. The new market equilibrium is shown by point c: the equilibrium price decreases from p^* to p^{**}, and the equilibrium quantity increases from 70 to 100 dwellings.

FIGURE 17–8 Market Effects of Supply-Side Policies

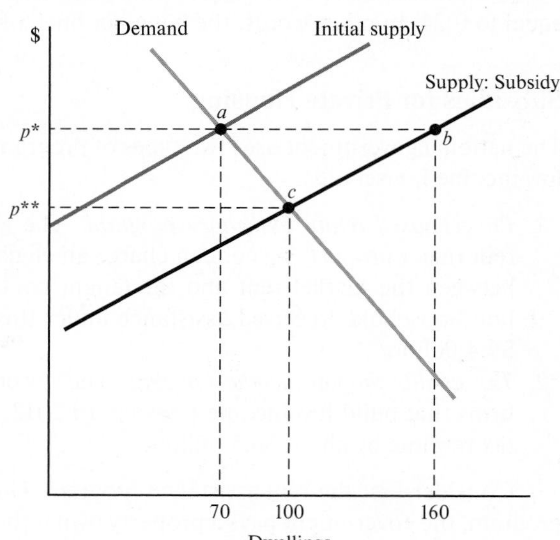

How efficient is the system of subsidizing the production of low-income housing? The cost of low-income housing generated by the tax-credit program exceeds the cost of unsubsidized housing by a large margin. Quigley (2000) estimates that the production efficiency of the program is about 0.62, meaning that each dollar of tax revenue lost generated only $0.62 worth of housing.

Filtering and Crowding Out

In Figure 17–8, a supply-side policy shifts the supply curve to the right by 90 dwellings and increases the equilibrium number of dwellings by only 30 dwellings. Why is the increase in the equilibrium quantity less than the horizontal supply shift? The policy-induced increase in supply decreases the equilibrium price of housing, which decreases the quantity of unsubsidized dwellings supplied. In other words, housing policies cause "crowding out": public and subsidized private housing displaces unsubsidized housing, so the net increase in the total quantity of housing is less than the quantity of public and subsidized private housing. In Figure 17–8, the 90-dwelling increase in supply displaces 60 unsubsidized dwellings, so the net increase is only 30 dwellings.

The filtering model explains the decrease in the quantity of unsubsidized housing. As the price of low-income housing decreases, the quantity decreases for two reasons.

1. *More retirement.* The decrease in price makes low-quality housing less profitable, and the response for some property owners is to retire the dwellings, either through abandonment or conversion to another use.
2. *Slower downward filtering.* The price of low-quality housing decreases relative to the price of medium-quality housing, causing the owners of medium-quality dwellings to slow the movement of dwellings downward along the quality ladder.

Gyourko (2009) reports that estimates of the crowding-out fraction range from one-half to two-thirds, meaning that for every 90 additional low-income dwellings from public housing or subsidized private housing, between 45 and 60 unsubsidized dwellings are retired from the market, leaving a net addition of 30 to 45 dwellings.

3. DEMAND-SIDE PUBLIC POLICY

An alternative to boosting the supply of low-income housing is to provide housing coupons or vouchers to low-income households, allowing the recipients to make their own choices in private housing markets. In 2012, about 2.2 million households received vouchers under the program known as "Section 8 Tenant Based Rental Assistance," at a budgetary cost of $19.2 billion.

The face value of a voucher is determined by a household's income and the fair market rent in the area. A voucher can be used only for housing that meets a minimum quality standard. The value of a voucher is

$$\text{Face value} = \text{Fair market rent} - 0.30 \cdot \text{Income}$$

The fair market rent is computed as the 45th percentile of rent, meaning that 45 percent of dwellings rent for less. To illustrate, suppose the fair market rent in a metropolitan area is $540. If an eligible household's income is $1,000, the household receives a voucher with a face value of $240. The voucher can be used on any dwelling that meets the minimum quality standard. The recipient has an incentive to find the most economical dwelling because the voucher doesn't vary with the actual rent paid.

Housing Vouchers and Efficiency

Figure 17–9 shows the effect of a $240 voucher on a low-income household. The light line is the initial budget line, and the household maximizes utility at point *a*. The dark line is the budget line with a $240 voucher. The endpoint of the new budget line *m* indicates the minimum quality standard: vouchers must be used on dwellings that generate at least 350 units of housing services. Under the voucher program, the household maximizes utility at point *c*, choosing a dwelling with 440 units of housing service and thus a market value of $440. The household receives a voucher of $240, so the net cost of housing is only $200, leaving $800 of the household's own income for all other goods.

How does the efficiency of a voucher compare to the efficiency of public housing? In Figure 17–9, point *b* shows the public-housing outcome from Figures 17–6 and 17–7. The voucher point and the public-housing point are on the same indifference curve, meaning that the recipient is just as well off under both programs. The two programs differ in their budgetary costs. The voucher policy has a budgetary cost of $240 per recipient, compared to $1,020 for public housing. Based on these

FIGURE 17–9 Recipient Response to a Housing Voucher

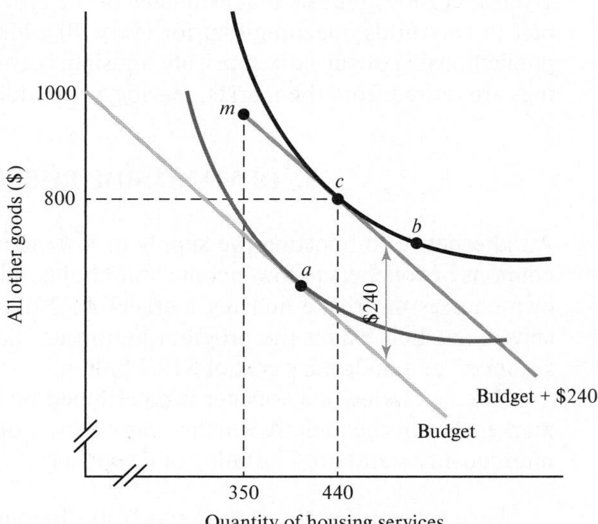

calculations, a reallocation of the low-income housing budget from public housing to vouchers would (a) cut the budgetary cost to roughly a quarter of its original level or (b) roughly quadruple the number of households receiving assistance.

The Market Effects of Vouchers

We can use the filtering model to explore the market effects of housing vouchers for low-income households. Figure 17-10 shows the effects of vouchers on the market for low-quality housing. The vouchers increase the demand for housing, shifting the demand curve to the right and increasing the equilibrium price from p^* to p^{**}. The quantity of low-quality housing supplied increases from L^* to L^{**} as the market moves upward along the supply curve. This supply response results from changes in retirement and filtering.

1. *Lower retirement rate.* The increase in the price of low-quality housing increases the payoff from keeping dwellings in the market rather than retiring them.
2. *Higher filtering rate.* The increase in the price of low-quality housing relative to the price of medium-quality housing increases the payoff from downward filtering to the low-quality market, so the quantity of low-quality dwellings increases at the expense of medium-quality dwellings.

Figure 17-11 shows the implications of vouchers for the medium-quality submarket. The more rapid downward filtering decreases the supply of medium-quality dwellings, shifting the supply curve to the left and increasing the equilibrium price

FIGURE 17-10 Market Effects of Vouchers: Low-Quality Housing

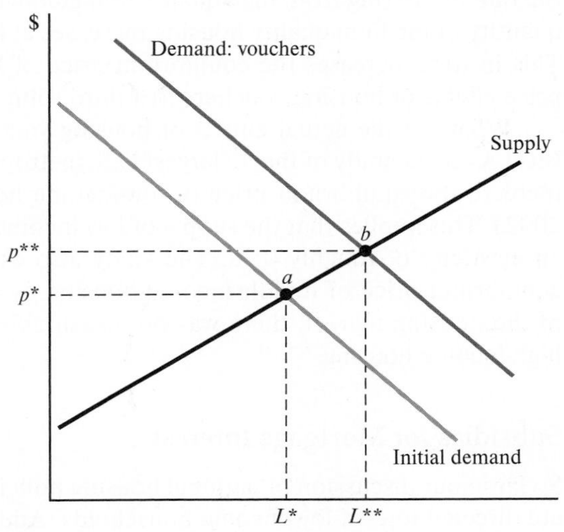

FIGURE 17-11 Market Effects of Vouchers: Medium-Quality Housing

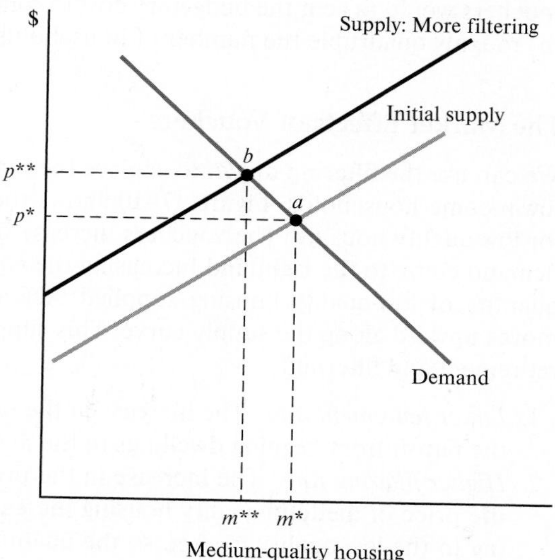

from p^* to p^{**} and decreasing the equilibrium quantity from m^* to m^{**}. Therefore, a voucher program for low-income households increases the price of housing for middle-income households.

Continuing up the quality ladder, consider the implications of vouchers for the high-quality submarket. The increase in the price of medium-quality housing increases the rate of filtering from high-quality to medium-quality housing. In other words, the quantity of medium-quality housing increases at the expense of high-quality housing. This in turn increases the equilibrium price of high-quality housing, spreading the price effects of housing vouchers to a third submarket.

What are the actual effects of housing vouchers on prices in housing submarkets? A recent study of the 90 largest U.S. metropolitan areas estimates that vouchers increase the equilibrium price of low-income housing by about 16 percent (Susin, 2002). This implies that the supply of low-income housing is relatively inelastic, with an elasticity of roughly 0.38. The study also estimates that vouchers increase the equilibrium price of middle-income housing by about 3 percent. At the upper end of the housing market, there was no measurable effect of vouchers on the price of high-income housing.

Subsidies for Mortgage Interest

So far in our discussion of national housing policies, we have considered policies that are directed toward low-income households. Adding up the supply-side and demand side policies, the annual spending on housing assistance is roughly $42 billion ($6b for public housing, $9b for project-based rental assistance, $7b for tax credits, $19b for vouchers) or about $133 per capita per year. The national government also has policies that benefit middle-income and high-income households. In 2010, tax breaks for homeowners reduced federal tax revenue by $87 billion per year ($279 per capita per year). This is an example of a tax expenditure: instead of giving money directly to homeowners (an expenditure), the government cuts their taxes.

The mortgage tax expenditure comes from the deductibility of mortgage interest in the computation of the federal income tax. A household can deduct mortgage interest from its gross income as one step in computing taxable income. The size of the deduction is determined by the homeowner's marginal tax rate (the increase in tax per dollar increase in taxable income). For a homeowner with a marginal tax rate of 15 percent, every dollar of mortgage interest decreases the tax liability by $0.15. The higher the marginal tax rate, the greater the subsidy of mortgage interest: for a homeowner with a marginal tax rate of 28 percent, the subsidy is $0.28 per dollar of mortgage interest.

Figure 17–12 shows the tax benefits from the mortgage subsidy for different income groups. The annual benefits are measured in billions of dollars. Households with income between $100,000 and $200,000 receive roughly 42 percent of the total tax benefits, and households with income exceeding $200,000 receive roughly 35 percent of the benefits. That leaves roughly 23 percent for all the other income groups combined. Households with income less than $50,000 receive only 3 percent of the tax benefits. The tax benefit increases with income for three reasons.

1. *Increasing marginal tax rate.* Under a tax system with progressive tax rates, the marginal tax rate increases with income, so the subsidy per dollar of mortgage interest increases with income.

FIGURE 17–12 Tax Benefits from the Mortgage Subsidy

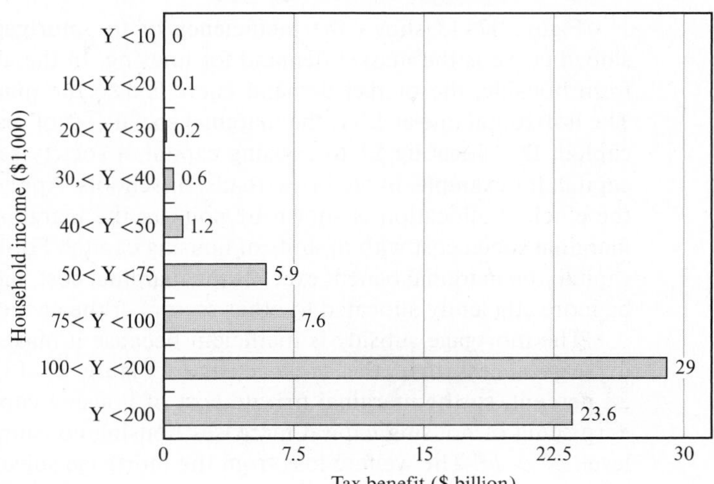

Source: Fischer, William, and Huang, Chye-Ching, "Mortgage Interest Deduction Is Ripe for Reform," Center for Budget and Policy Priorities, June 25, 2013.

FIGURE 17-13 Inefficiency of the Mortgage Subsidy

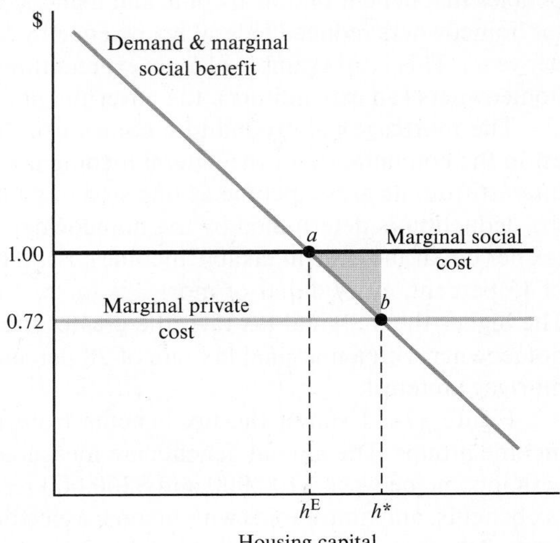

2. *Itemizing deduction.* The subsidy is paid only to households who itemize their deductions on their tax forms, and low-income households are less likely to itemize; instead they take the standard deduction.
3. *Housing is a normal good.* Housing consumption increases with household income, and so does the amount of mortgage interest that can be deducted from gross income.

Figure 17-13 shows the inefficiency of the mortgage subsidy. The negatively sloped curve is the market demand for housing. In the absence of external benefits from housing, the market demand curve is also the marginal social benefit curve. The horizontal line at 1.0 is the marginal social cost of resources invested in housing capital. By allocating \$1 to housing capital, a society sacrifices \$1 worth of other capital, for example, in factories, roads, or schools. Applying the marginal principle, the efficient allocation is shown by point *a*: the marginal social benefit equals the marginal social cost with h^E units of housing capital. For larger quantities of housing capital, the marginal benefit exceeds the marginal cost, meaning the resources would be more efficiently allocated to other sectors of the economy.

The mortgage subsidy is inefficient because it makes the private cost of housing capital less than the social cost. In Figure 17-13, the marginal tax rate is 28 percent, so the marginal private cost of housing capital is only \$0.72. The underpricing of housing capital increases housing consumption beyond the efficient level: $h^* > h^E$. The welfare loss from the mortgage subsidy is shown by the shaded triangle, the area between the marginal social cost of housing capital (\$1) and the marginal social benefit (shown by the demand curve). The amount of resources invested in housing capital is excessive: some of the resources invested in housing would be more productive if they were invested in other capital such as factories, roads, or schools.

4. HOMELESSNESS AND PUBLIC POLICY

The U.S. Department of Housing and Urban Development (HUD) reports that on a single night in January 2009, there were more than 640,000 sheltered and unsheltered homeless people nationwide (HUD, 2010). The HUD definition of a homeless individual is a person who lacks a fixed nighttime residence and whose primary nighttime residence is (a) a supervised public or private shelter designed to provide temporary living accommodations, (b) an institution that provides a temporary residence for individuals intended to be institutionalized, or (c) a place not intended to be used as a regular sleeping place.

Figure 17-14 shows the composition of the homeless population. Over three-fourths of the homeless are single, and just over half are single men. Children under 18 account for almost two-fifths of the homeless. The share of homeless that are veterans (13 percent) is just above the veteran share of the general population (11 percent). In contrast, the share of the homeless that suffer from mental disorders (30 percent) is five times the share of the population with mental disorders (6 percent). About a third of the homeless suffer from addiction disorders, including alcohol and other drugs.

FIGURE 17-14 The Homeless Population

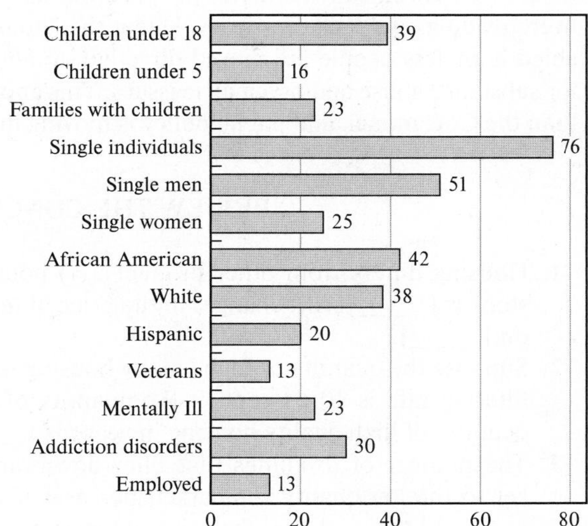

Source: National Coalition for the Homeless, "Who Is Homeless?" 2009.

Several federal agencies provide serves to homeless persons. Many of the federal programs were authorized by the McKinney-Vento Homeless Assistance Act of 1987. The agencies include the Department of Education (education for homeless children), the Federal Emergency Management Agency (emergency food and shelter program), and the Department of Health and Human Services (health care), and the Veterans Administration (health care, homeless providers grants). The Department of Housing and Urban Development provides housing and services for homeless individuals, including support for shelters and subsidies for housing designed to serve the homeless population (single residence occupancy [SRO] units and emergency housing).

What causes homelessness? A person will be not have a fixed residence if his or her income is sufficiently low relative to the price of housing. Studies of homelessness suggest that homeless rates are higher in areas with the following characteristics.

1. Relatively high prices for low-quality housing. Honig and Flier (1993) estimate that the elasticity of homelessness with respect to rent on low-quality housing is 1.25, meaning that a 10 percent increase in rent increases homelessness by 12.5 percent.
2. Weak labor markets: slow employment growth.
3. Low institutionalization rates for the mentally ill.

Although homelessness is a complex problem with many causes, there is evidence that the problem could be mitigated by policies that improve the functioning of the low end of the housing market (O'Flaherty, 1996; Green and Malpezzi, 2003).

A key policy question is, What comes first for a chronically homeless person, housing or the resolution of any substance abuse or psychiatric issues? Under the continuum of care model (CoC), substance-abuse and psychiatric issues are resolved first, with the person remaining homeless (in a shelter or on the street) in the meantime. Many chronically homeless people avoid the shelter system because of its rules, overcrowding, and lack of privacy. Under the "housing-first" approach, the most disabled homeless people are moved directly into affordable housing before treatment for substance abuse and psychiatric issues. This approach has proven more successful than the CoC model, and public policy is moving in that direction (Meschede, 2011).

REVIEW THE CONCEPTS

1. Housing differs from other products: (i) housing is [_____]; (ii) the housing stock is [_____]; (iii) changes in the price of housing have relatively large effects on [_____].

2. Suppose the quantity of high-quality housing is 50 in year *t*-1, and the downward filtering rate is 10 percent. If the quantity of new housing is 12 per year, the quantity of high-quality housing in year *t* is [_____] dwellings.

3. The number of dwellings that filter downward from the high-quality submarket to the low-quality submarket increases if the price of high-quality housing [_____] {↑, ↓, –} or if the price of low-quality housing [_____] {↑, ↓, –}.

4. The market supply curve for high-quality housing is the [_____] sum of the supply curves for [_____] housing and [_____] housing.

5. The market supply of low-quality housing equals [_____] housing plus [_____] housing.
6. A ban on new housing [_____] {↑, ↓, –} the price of high-quality housing, so it decreases [_____]. As a result, the net change in the quantity of high-quality housing is [_____] (<, >, =) the loss of new housing.
7. A ban on new housing [_____] {↑, ↓, –} the price of low-quality housing because the ban (i) decreases [downward_filtering] and (ii) increases [_____].
8. Gentrification [_____] {↑, ↓, –} the price of low-quality housing because it decreases [_____] and increases [_____]. Both effects result from an [_____] {↑, ↓, –} in the price of high-quality housing.
9. The bang per buck of public housing is roughly $[_____] (choose 0.10, 0.24, 0.90, 1.5).
10. Under a system of tax subsidies for low-income housing projects, the government specifies (i) [_____] and (ii) [_____] of dwellings for low-income households.
11. Consider a voucher policy that makes recipients just as well off as they would be with public housing. A reallocation of the housing budget from public housing to vouchers would [_____] {↑, ↓, –} the number of households receiving assistance by a factor of roughly [_____] (choose 2, 4, 10).
12. A program of housing vouchers [_____] {↑, ↓, –} the price of medium-quality housing because the program [_____] {↑, ↓, –} the price of low-quality housing and increases [_____].
13. The annual budgetary cost of housing programs for low-income households is [_____] (<, >, =) the annual tax revenue lost from subsidies for mortgage interest. The household benefit from the mortgage subsidy [_____] {↑, ↓, –} with income at a relatively [_____] (choose slow, fast) rate.
14. The welfare loss from the mortgage subsidy is shown by the area between the [_____] curve and the [_____] curve, from the [_____] quantity to the [_____] quantity.
15. Homelessness rates are relatively high in areas with (i) high [_____]; (ii) weak [_____] markets; (iii) low institutional rates for the [_____].
16. Compared to the veteran share of the general population (11 percent), the veteran share of the homeless population is [_____] (lower, roughly the same, a bit higher, much higher).
17. For each pair of variables, indicate whether the relationship is positive, negative, neutral, or ambiguous.

Parameter	Choice Variable	Relationship
price (high quality)	f: filter rate	[_____]
price (low quality)	f: filter rate	[_____]
wage of repair workers	f: filter rate	[_____]
number of public housing units	price (low quality)	[_____]
number of public housing units	number of private housing units	[_____]
number of public housing units	r: retirement rate	[_____]
number of housing vouchers	price (low quality)	[_____]
number of housing vouchers	price (medium quality)	[_____]

APPLY THE CONCEPTS

1. *Choose a Quality Level*
Suppose dwelling quality is measured on a scale of 1 to 20, and the monthly cost of producing a particular quality equals the square of the quality level: For quality level 1, the cost is $1; for quality level 2, the cost is $4, and so on. In other words, $C(q) = q^2$ and marginal cost is $mc(q) = 2q$. The daily rent on a dwelling equals the price per unit of quality times the quality level. At a price of $20, the profit-maximizing quality level is $q^* =$ [______]. Illustrate.
2. *Hurricane Katrina*
Hurricane Katrina destroyed a large fraction of the housing stock of New Orleans, with relatively large losses in the low-quality submarket. To simplify, suppose that the hurricane destroyed only low-quality houses, and assume that there are only two quality levels, low and high. Predict the effect of the hurricane on the equilibrium price of high-quality housing. Illustrate.
3. *Bang per Buck of Low-Income Housing Tax Credits?*
Suppose you incur a cost of $200,000 to build a low-income house that qualifies for the low-income housing tax credit.
   a. Over the period that generates an annual tax credit, your total tax credit is $[______].
   b. Based on Quigley's results, the market value of the house is $[______].
4. *Tiny Effects of Public Housing?*
According to Mr. Wizard, "The long-run market effects of public housing are tiny. Starting with an equilibrium with a private supply of 120 dwellings, the building of 60 public housing dwellings will increase the equilibrium quantity of housing by only 10 dwellings." Use a supply-demand graph to illustrate Mr. Wizard's economic logic.
5. *Price Effects of Vouchers*
Consider the Susin (2003) study of the price effects of vouchers. Suppose the initial price of low-income housing is $p^* = \$500$ and the price elasticity of demand for low-income housing is -0.82. Suppose a program of housing vouchers increases the demand for low-income housing by 24 percent. Illustrate the market effects of the voucher program, and include the new equilibrium price p^{**}.
6. *Ask Dr. Elastic*
Your objective is to maximize the welfare of low-income households, and you must choose between housing vouchers and subsidies for the production of low-income housing. You can ask Dr. Elastic, who knows every economic elasticity ever measured, a single question.
   a. Your question is . . . ?
   b. Under what circumstances (what values of the relevant elasticities) will vouchers be better than subsidies? Illustrate.
   c. Under what circumstances (what values of the relevant elasticities) will subsidies be better than vouchers? Illustrate.
7. *Deadweight Loss from the Mortgage Subsidy*
Suppose the marginal value of a square foot of factory space is constant at $1.00. The marginal benefit of a square foot of housing space is $1.00 for 1,000 square

feet and $0.80 for 1,200 square feet. Suppose the government provides a 20 percent mortgage subsidy, cutting the net price of housing to consumers from $1.00 to $0.80 per square foot. Illustrate the market effects of the subsidy, including the value of the deadweight loss from the subsidy.

REFERENCES AND READING

1. Brueckner, Jan, and Stuart Rosenthal, "Gentrification and Neighborhood Cycles: Will America's Future Downtowns Be Rich?" *Review of Economics and Statistics,* 91.4 (2009), pp. 725–43.
2. Case, Bradford, "Housing Price Indexes," Chapter 14 in *A Companion to Urban Economics,* edited by Richard J. Arnott and Daniel P. McMillen. New York: Wiley-Blackwell, 2006.
3. Diehang Zheng, Yongheng Deng, Peter Gordon, and David Dale-Johnson, "An Examination of the Impact of Rent Control on Mobile Home Prices in California," *Journal of Housing Economics* 16 (2007), pp. 209–42.
4. DiPasquale, Denise, Dennis Fricke, and Daniel Garcia-Diaz, "Comparing the Costs of Federal Housing Assistance Programs." *Federal Reserve Bank of New York Policy Review* (June 2003), pp. 147–66.
5. Ellen, Ingrid Gould, and Katherine O'Regan, "Gentrification: The Perspectives of Economists and Planners," Chapter 16 in *The Oxford Handbook of Urban Economics and Planning,* edited by Nancy Brooks, Kieran Donaghy, and Gerrit-Jan Knaap. New York: Oxford University Press, 2011.
6. Glaeser, Edward, and Charles Nathanson, "Housing Bubbles," Chapter 11 in *Handbook of Urban and Regional Economics Volume 5,* edited by Gilles Duranton, J. Vernon Henderson, and William C. Strange. Amsterdam: Elsevier, 2015.
7. Goering, John. "The Impacts of New Neighborhoods on Poor Families: Evaluating the Policy Implications of the Moving to Opportunity Demonstration." *Federal Reserve Bank of New York Policy Review* (June 2003), pp. 113–40.
8. Green, Richard, "Housing Markets, Prices, and Policies," Chapter 18 in *The Oxford Handbook of Urban Economics and Planning,* edited by Nancy Brooks, Kieran Donaghy, and Gerrit-Jan Knaap. New York: Oxford University Press, 2011.
9. Gyourko, Joseph, and Raven Molloy, "Regulation and Housing Supply," Chapter 19 in *Handbook of Urban and Regional Economics Volume 5,* edited by Gilles Duranton, J. Vernon Henderson, and William C. Strange (2015).
10. Han, Lu, and William Strange, "Microstructure of Housing Markets: Search, Bargaining, and Brokerage," Chapter 13 in *Handbook of Urban and Regional Economics Volume 5,* edited by Gilles Duranton, J. Vernon Henderson and William C. Strange (2015).
11. Malpezzi, Stephen, and Kerry Vandell, "Does the Low-Income Housing Tax Credit Increase the Supply of Housing?" *Journal of Housing Economics* 11 (2002), pp. 360–80.
12. Malpezzi, Stephen. "Welfare Analysis of Rent Control with Side Payments: A Natural Experiment in Cairo, Egypt." *Regional Science and Urban Economics* 28 (1998), pp. 773–95.

13. O'Flaherty, Brendan, "Homelessness in the United States," Chapter 12 in *The Oxford Handbook of Urban Economics and Planning,* edited by Nancy Brooks, Kieran Donaghy, and Gerrit-Jan Knaap. New York: Oxford University Press, 2011.
14. Office of Management and Budget. Budget of the United States Government Fiscal Year 2002, Table 8-1. Washington, DC: 2002.
15. Olsen, Edgar, and Jeffrey Zabel, "United States Housing Policies," Chapter 14 in *Handbook of Urban and Regional Economics Volume 5,* edited by Gilles Duranton, J. Vernon Henderson, and William C. Strange (2015).
16. Rosenthal, Stuart, "Are Private Markets and Filtering a Viable Source of Low-Income Housing? Estimates from a 'Repeat Income' Model," *American Economic Review,* 104.2 (2014), pp. 687–706.
17. Saiz, Albert. "The Geographic Determinants of Housing Supply." *Quarterly Journal of Economics* 125.3 (2010), pp. 1253–96.
18. Seko, Miki, "Housing Demand: An International Perspective," Chapter 11 in *A Companion to Urban Economics,* edited by Richard J. Arnott and Daniel P. McMillen. New York: Wiley-Blackwell, 2006.
19. Smeeding, Timothy M. "Alternative Methods for Evaluating Selected In-Kind Transfer Benefits and Measuring Their Effect on Poverty." Technical Paper no. 50. Washington, DC: U.S. Bureau of the Census, 1982.
20. Susin, Scott, "Rent Vouchers and the Price of Low-Income Housing." *Journal of Public Economics* 83 (2002), pp. 109–52.
21. U.S. Department of Housing and Urban Development, Fiscal Year 2012 Program and Budget Initiatives–Affordable Housing Rental Assistance.
22. U.S. Government, www.whitehouse.gov/sites/default/files/omb/budget/... /teb2013.xls

PART FOUR

Urban Transportation

Part Four of the book explores the two components of the urban transportation system. Chapter 18 looks at cars and roads, focusing on three externalities that cause inefficiency: congestion, environmental degradation, and traffic accidents. Naturally, we discuss various policy responses to the externalities. Chapter 19 explores the economics of urban public transit, focusing on an individual traveler's choice of travel mode (car versus bus versus rail) and a city's choice of a public transit system (buses vs. light rail vs. heavy rail). The chapter explains why so few commuters in the United States choose public transit, and why in most U.S. cities, a bus system is more efficient than light rail or heavy rail.

CHAPTER 18

Cars and Roads

I started to slow down but the traffic was more stationary than I thought.

—FROM AN AUTOMOBILE INSURANCE CLAIM FORM

This first of two chapters on urban transportation explores the economics of cars and roads. The car is the principal means of travel in U.S. cities, comprising 88 percent of commuting trips (travel to work) and 90 percent of all trips. This policy-oriented chapter focuses on three external costs generated by cars: congestion, pollution, and traffic accidents. An external cost is a cost experienced by someone other than the person deciding how much of an activity to undertake. The economic approach to an external cost is to use a tax to internalize the externality and thus ensure that the decision-maker incurs the full cost of his or her choices. This simple approach lets markets work: once the external cost is internalized, individual decision-makers will make efficient choices.

1. CONGESTION EXTERNALITIES

Consider first the external cost generated by using crowded roads and highways. An additional driver slows traffic and thus imposes an external cost on other drivers. The economic approach to congestion is straightforward. There is an external cost associated with using a highway—an additional vehicle slows down other vehicles—and a congestion tax equal to the marginal external cost will internalize the externality and generate an efficient outcome. The efficient level of congestion is not zero, just as the efficient level of pollution is not zero.

The Cost of Travel: External, Private, and Social

We will start with the calculation of the marginal external cost of travel. An additional vehicle on the road decreases the space between vehicles, and drivers naturally slow down to maintain safe distances between vehicles. The slowing of traffic forces each other road user to spend an additional m minutes traveling on the road. If there are v other road users and the opportunity cost of travel time is c per minute, the marginal external cost of an additional vehicle is

$$\text{Marginal external cost} = m \cdot v \cdot c$$

For example, suppose $m = 0.01$ (an additional vehicle increases the travel time of each other user by 0.01 minutes), $v = 1200$ (there are 1200 other users), and $c = \$0.20$ (the opportunity cost of travel time is \$0.20 per minute). In this case, the marginal external cost of an additional vehicle is

$$\text{Marginal external cost} = m \cdot v \cdot c = 0.01 \cdot 1200 \cdot \$0.20 = \$2.40$$

An additional vehicle imposes a cost of \$2.40 on other highway users.

The marginal external cost depends on traffic volume. When the volume is relatively low, the marginal external cost will be relatively low for two reasons. First, the value of m (the additional time per vehicle) will be relatively low, and will actually be zero when the volume is low enough that all vehicles can travel at the legal speed limit. Second, the value of v (the number of affected users) will be relatively low. In contrast, when traffic volume is relatively high, an additional vehicle will increase travel time by a relatively large amount (large m) and a relatively large number of vehicles will be slowed (large v).

The private cost of travel is the cost experienced by an individual driver. In Figure 18-1, the private trip cost is the lower of the two curves. This curve shows the sum of the monetary and time cost of travel along a stretch of highway. The monetary cost is constant at \$2.00 per trip, and the time cost for uncongested travel is \$1.00. The

FIGURE 18-1 Travel Cost: Private, External, Social

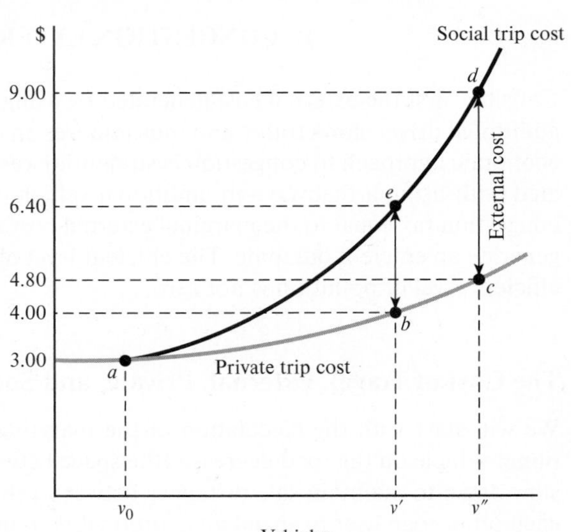

private cost curve is horizontal at \$3.00 (\$2.00 + \$1.00) as long as everyone travels at the legal speed limit, which happens up to a volume of v_0. For higher volumes, the spacing between vehicles decreases, causing drivers to slow down to maintain safe distances between vehicles. A slower speed means more travel time and thus a higher time cost. For example, at a volume of v', the time cost doubles to \$2.00, so the private cost of the trip is \$4.00, with \$2.00 in monetary cost and \$2.00 in time cost.

The upper curve in Figure 18-1 shows the social cost of travel, equal to the sum of private cost and external cost. The gap between the two curves is the marginal external cost travel. At volume v', the private cost is \$4.00 and the external cost is \$2.40, so the social cost is \$6.40. As the volume of travel increases, the external cost increases, widening the gap between the two curves. At volume v'', the private cost is \$4.80 and the external cost is \$4.20, so the social cost is \$9.00.

Market Equilibrium vs. Efficient Outcome

Figure 18-2 shows the market equilibrium and the efficient outcome. The demand curve, which shows travelers' willingness to pay to use the highway, is negatively sloped: an increase in the cost of using the road decreases the number of people for whom the cost exceeds the willingness to pay, so fewer people will use the road. The equilibrium is shown by point *c*, where the market demand curve intersects the private-cost curve. We use an * (asterisk) to identify the equilibrium, so the equilibrium volume is v^*. For a total of v^* travelers, the benefit of using the highway (the willingness to pay, shown by the demand curve) is greater than or equal to the private cost of the trip (shown by the private-cost curve).

FIGURE 18-2 Equilibrium versus Efficient Outcome

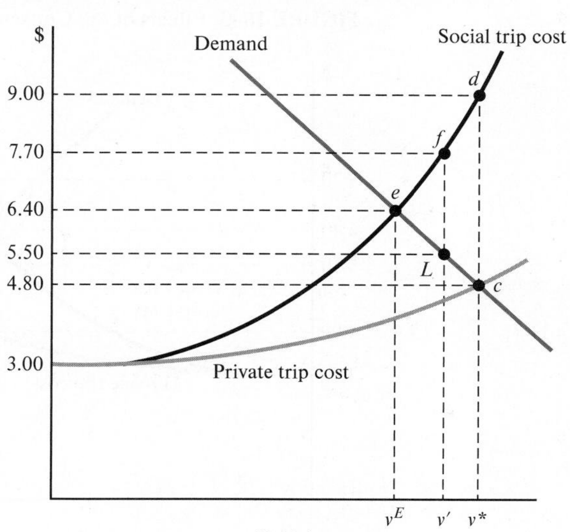

We can use the marginal principle to find the efficient number of vehicles. The efficient level of an activity is the level at which the marginal social benefit equals the marginal social cost. There are no positive externalities associated with travel, so the demand curve shows the marginal social benefit of travel. The marginal social cost is shown by the social-cost curve, which includes both the private and external cost of travel. We use E to indicate the efficient outcome. The demand curve intersects the social-cost curve at point e, so the efficient volume is v^E vehicles. For the first v^E vehicles, the social benefit of travel (the willingness to pay) is greater than or equal to the social cost, so their use of the highway is socially efficient.

The equilibrium volume v^* exceeds the efficient volume v^E because each user ignores the external cost imposed on other users. In Figure 18–2, Lois is willing to pay \$5.50 for a trip (shown by point L on the demand curve) and her use of the road has a social cost of \$7.70 (shown by point f). As one of v^* users, her private cost is the equilibrium private cost \$4.80. Lois will use the road because her willingness to pay exceeds the private cost (\$5.50 > \$4.80). But her use of the road is inefficient because her willingness to pay is less than the social cost (\$5.50 < \$7.70). Lois ignores the external cost of her decision, so she uses the highway even though her travel is inefficient.

The Congestion Tax

The economic approach to congestion is to internalize the congestion externality with a congestion tax. In Figure 18–3, a congestion tax of \$2.40 per trip shifts the private-cost curve upward by \$2.40.

1. *Decrease volume.* The tax decreases the number of vehicles from v^* to v^E. At point L on the demand curve, Lois's willingness to pay (\$5.50) is now less than

FIGURE 18–3 Effects of the Congestion Tax

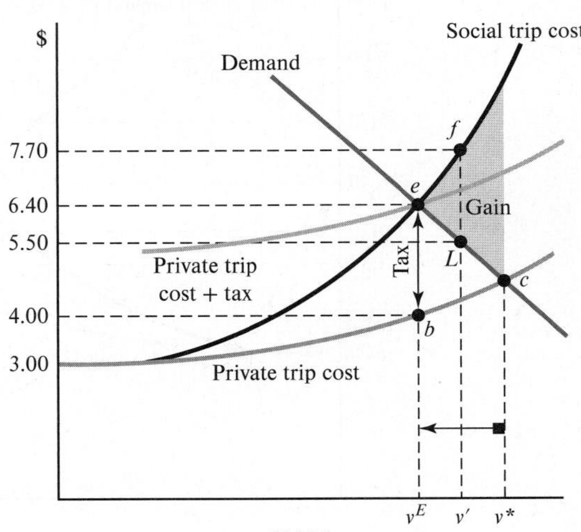

her \$6.40 cost (the private trip cost plus the \$2.40 tax), so she will not use the highway. Similarly, for travelers v^* through v^E, the willingness to pay is now less than the cost, so they no longer use the highway.

2. *Efficiency gain.* The gain from keeping Lois (in vehicle v') off the road equals the social cost avoided minus her benefit foregone. The cost avoided is the \$7.70 social cost (point *f*), and the benefit foregone is her \$5.50 willingness to pay for the trip (point *L*). So the gain from keeping Lois off the highway is \$2.20. For the market as a whole, the efficiency gain from keeping vehicles v^* through v^E off the road is shown by the shaded area, the area between the social cost curve and the demand curve from v^* to v^E.

In considering the individual benefits and costs of a congestion tax, it's important to note that a congestion tax generates revenue that can be used to cut other taxes. In our example, the congestion tax is \$2.40 per traveler, which translates into a tax cut less than \$2.40 because the congestion tax causes some travelers to stop using the road. To simplify, suppose v^E is five-sixths of v^*: the congestion tax cuts traffic volume by a sixth. In this case, the tax cut associated with a \$2.40 congestion tax is \$2.00 per consumer. For example, if $v^* = 600$ and $v^E = 500$, total tax revenue is \$1,200, or \$2.00 per consumer.

Figure 18–4 shows the consequences of a congestion tax for a consumer who pays the tax and continues to use the highway. A consumer at point *H* on the demand curve has a relatively high willingness to pay for highway travel (\$9.00). After the tax, the price of travel is \$6.40, so the consumer will continue to use the highway. The tax decreases traffic volume and decreases the private cost from \$4.80 (point *c*) to \$4.00 (point *b*), a savings in time cost of \$0.80. The net gain is \$0.40 = \$0.80 time savings + \$2.00 tax refund − \$2.40 tax.

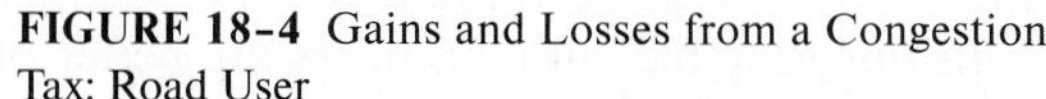

FIGURE 18–4 Gains and Losses from a Congestion Tax: Road User

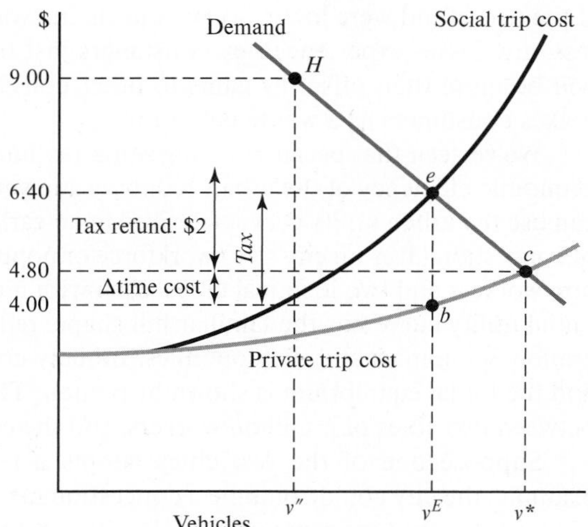

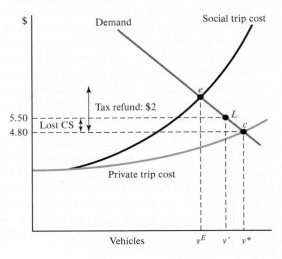

FIGURE 18–5 Gains and Losses from a Congestion Tax: Diverted Driver

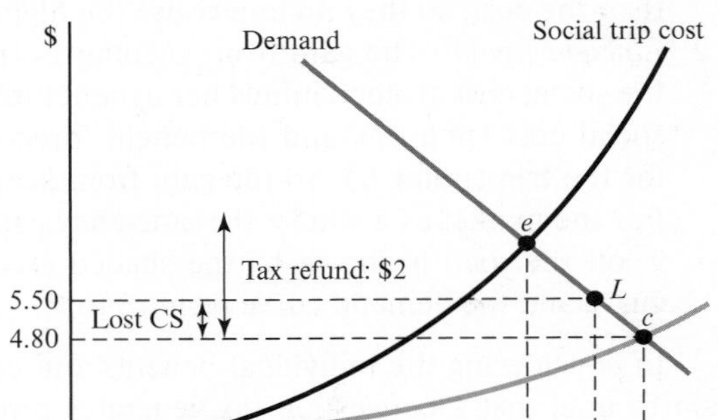

Figure 18–5 shows the consequence of a congestion tax for a consumer who stops using the highway. For a consumer at point L on the demand curve, the \$5.50 willingness to pay exceeds the \$4.80 pre-tax price, but is less than the \$6.40 post-tax price. The consumers experience a loss of a consumer surplus of \$0.70, equal to the \$5.50 willingness to pay minus the \$4.80 private trip cost. The net gain for the consumer is \$1.30 = \$2.00 tax refund − \$0.70 loss in consumer surplus.

In this example, all consumers are better off as a result of the congestion-tax policy because the tax refund is large enough to cover any loss of consumer surplus. If the tax refund were lower, some consumers would experience net losses. Nonetheless, any losses experienced by consumers just below point e on the demand curve will be more than offset by gains to other consumers, so the congestion-tax policy makes consumers as a whole better off.

We've seen that because a congestion tax internalizes an externality, it increases economic efficiency of the urban economy and generates a welfare gain to society. We can use the urban utility curves (derived in an earlier chapter) to show the implication of congestion taxes on city size (workforce or population). Consider a region of 12 million workers and two identical cities, each with 6 million workers. In Figure 18–6, the initial utility curve has the familiar hill shape, reflecting the tension between agglomeration economies and diseconomies. Initially congestion is unpriced in both cities, and the initial equilibrium is shown by point a. The region's workforce is split equally between two cities of 6 million workers, and the common utility level is u^*.

Suppose one of the two cities adopts a revenue-neutral congestion tax. For example, the city could combine a congestion tax with a decrease in its income tax. In Figure 18–6, the tax program shifts the city's utility curve upward. The internalization

FIGURE 18–6 A Congestion-Tax City Grows

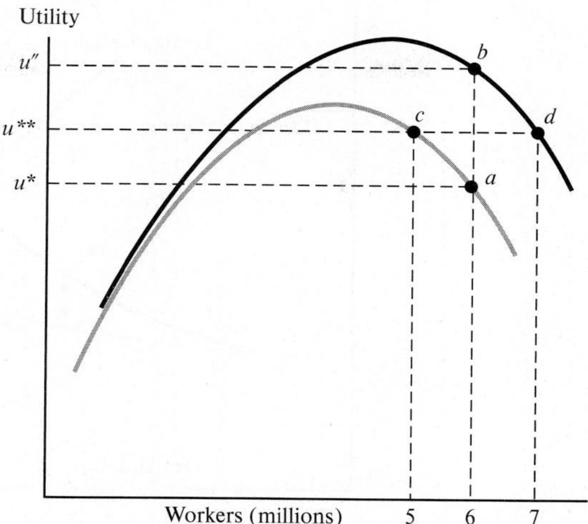

of congestion externalities decreases the magnitude of diseconomies of agglomeration, so it reduces the downward drag on utility as city size increases. The vertical shift is relatively small for a small workforce, where congestion is light, and relatively large for a large workforce, where congestion is heavy. In the congestion-tax city, the utility level increases from u^* (point *a*) to u'' (point *b*). In the absence of migration, utility in the congestion-tax city would exceed the utility in the other city by $u'' - u^*$. This is not a Nash equilibrium because there is an incentive for unilateral deviation. In response to the utility gap, workers will migrate to the congestion-tax city, and migration will continue until utility is equalized across the two cities.

The new regional equilibrium is shown by points *c* and *d*. This is a Nash equilibrium because both cities have the same utility level u^{**}, and the workforces in the two cities add up to the fixed regional workforce. The congestion-tax city (shown by point *d*) gains 1 million workers, while the other city (shown by point *c*) loses 1 million workers. Utility increases from u^* to u^{**} in both cities, meaning that workers in both cities benefit from an efficiency-enhancing congestion tax in one city. Workers in the other city benefit because the decrease in its workforce causes the city to move upward along its negatively sloped utility curve from point *a* to point *c*, where $u^{**} > u^*$. The benefits of a congestion tax in a one city spread to other cities in the region.

2. IMPLEMENTING A CONGESTION TAX

In this part of the chapter, we look at the practicalities of implementing a congestion tax. In addition, we explore an alternative approach known as value pricing, a system under which travelers pay a toll to use special congestion-free lanes.

FIGURE 18–7 Peak vs. Off-Peak Congestion Tax

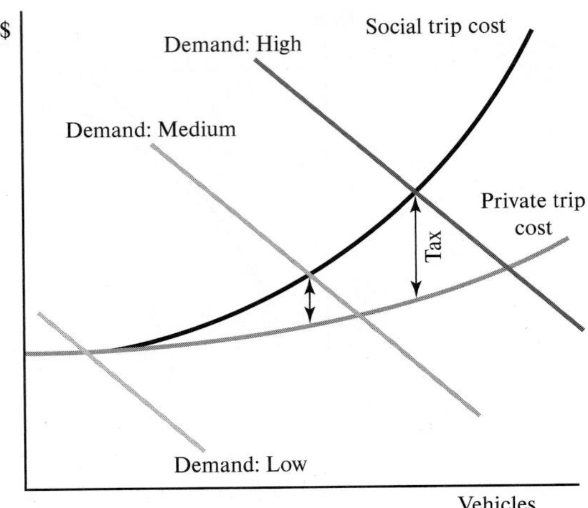

Implementing a Congestion Tax

The efficient congestion tax on a roadway varies with the volume of traffic. Figure 18–7 has three demand curves, representing high, medium, and low demand for travel along a roadway. The efficient congestion tax is shown by the vertical gap between the two cost curves (private and social cost), computed at the efficient volume. When travel demand is relatively high, there is a relatively large gap between private and social cost, and thus a relatively large congestion tax. In the case of low demand, the market demand curve intersects the private cost curve along its horizontal segment. In this case, traffic flows at the speed limit, and there is no congestion externality and thus no congestion tax.

Figure 18–8 shows estimates of the efficient congestion taxes per mile for three metropolitan areas. For the two U.S. cities, the peak-demand tax is roughly ten times the off-peak tax. For London, the peak-demand tax is five to six times the peak tax for the U.S. cities, and the differences in the off-peak taxes are even larger. On average, the efficient peak-demand congestion tax for U.S. cities is $0.085 per mile.

Modern technology allows the efficient implementation of roadway use taxes. Under a vehicle identification system (VIS), each car is equipped with a transponder—an electronic device that allows sensors along the road to identify a car as it passes. The system records the number of times a vehicle uses a congested roadway, and sends a bill to the driver at the end of the month. For example, if the congestion tax is $0.24 per mile, a driver who travels 10 miles along a roadway 20 times per month would have a monthly tax bill of $48.00 (20 times $2.40). An alternative approach, which avoids issues of privacy, is to use anonymous debit cards to charge for using congested roads.

FIGURE 18-8 Congestion Taxes in Selected Cities

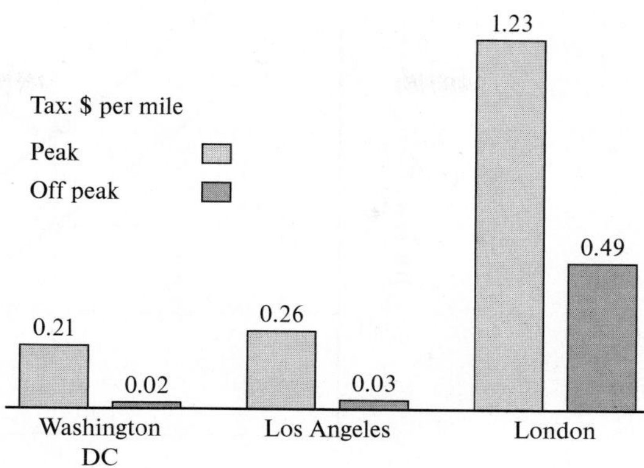

Source: Parry, Ian and Small, Kenneth, "Should Urban Transit Subsidies Be Reduced?" *American Economic Review* 99, 2009, 700–724.

Singapore was the first city to use prices to charge for using roadways. The city started with the Area Licensing System (ALS) in 1975, a cordon pricing system under which drivers were charged about $2 per day to travel in a special toll zone in the central area of the city. In 1998, the city switched to Electronic Road Pricing (ERP), a smart-card system with user charges that increase with the level of congestion. The system has 28 gantries that charge users for entering the central area during the daytime. In addition, 14 of the city's highways are subject to tolls during the morning peak period on weekdays.

Several cities have adopted cordon systems under which drivers are charged for entering a central area. Drivers in central London pay to use the streets on weekdays between 7:00 a.m. and 6:30 p.m. The cordon fee, implemented in 2003, reduced congestion and increased travel speeds. Stockholm introduced a variable-rate cordon system in 2006: the charge for entering the central core area varies by time of day. The Stockholm pricing scheme increased transit ridership and increased travel speeds. In the United States, a proposal for a similar cordon system for New York City precipitated a spirited political debate, and was eventually blocked by the state legislature.

Value Pricing and HOT Lanes

A recent development in road pricing is labeled value pricing, a system under which drivers pay to use special high-speed "express" or toll lanes. Some express lanes are converted carpool lanes, labeled HOT lanes (for high occupancy or toll) because users must either have a minimum number of occupants (2 or 3) or pay a toll. In some cases, the toll varies with travel demand, rising during peak demand to limit

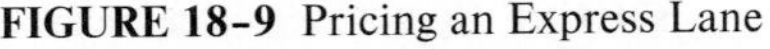
FIGURE 18–9 Pricing an Express Lane

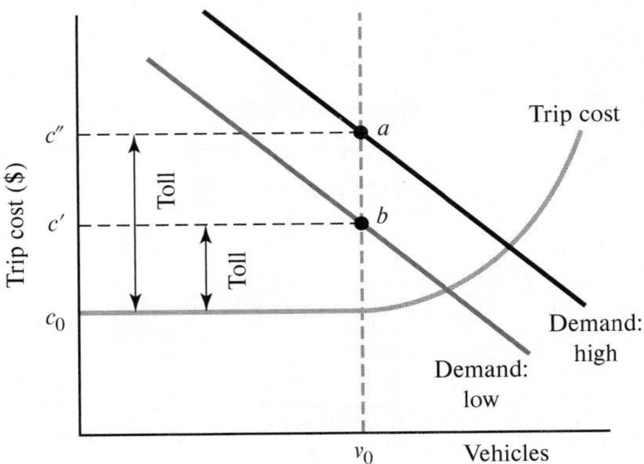

traffic volume and keep speeds at a target level. This system makes the lanes of a roadway differentiated products, with higher prices for high-quality (faster) express lanes. This is similar to consumers paying a higher price for better seats in a theater or athletic event: the best seats are allocated to consumers who are willing to pay the most for them.

Figure 18–9 shows the mechanics of value pricing for an express lane. Suppose a firm builds a new express lane and commits to congestion-free travel: traffic volume will not exceed v_0. When the demand for the express lane is relatively high, the full cost (including the toll) required to generate a volume v_0 is c''. The toll is shown by the gap between c'' and c_0, the private trip cost at the free-flow volume. When demand is relatively low, the toll is smaller, equal to $(c' - c_0)$. The express lane will be a rational choice if the savings in time costs exceed the toll, a likely case for travelers with relatively high opportunity cost of travel.

The switching of travelers to an express lane benefits the travelers who remain on the regular roadway. In Figure 18–10, the demand curve for the regular roadway shifts to the left by the number of diverted drivers $(v' - v''')$. The equilibrium volume decreases from v' to v'' and the equilibrium trip cost decreases from c' to c''. Notice that the equilibrium volume decreases by $(v' - v'')$, which is less than the horizontal shift of the demand curve. The decrease in travel time increases the number of travelers as the market moves downward along the demand curve. In the transportation world, the increase in volume from v''' to v' is an example of latent demand: a decrease in travel cost increases the number of travelers. In economics this is an example of the law of demand: a decrease in price increases the quantity demanded.

The use of value pricing and HOT lanes has increased in recent years. Several metropolitan areas in North America have converted carpool lanes or built new lanes for premium pricing, including Orange County (CA), San Diego, Toronto, Minneapolis, and Denver. In other cities, private firms have taken the initiative, proposing

FIGURE 18–10 Effects of an Express Lane on the Regular Roadway

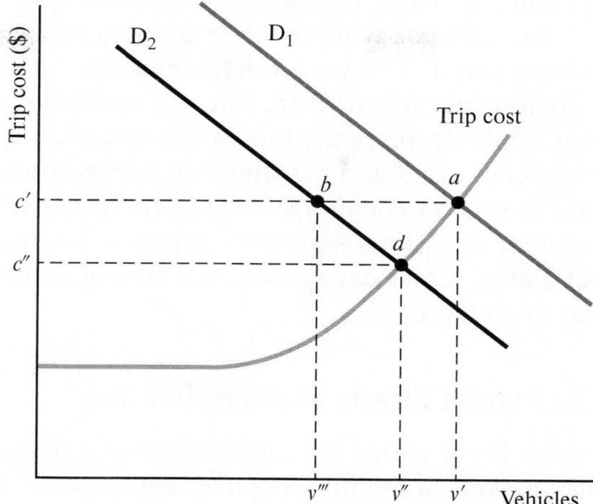

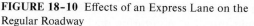

new highways with the expectation of using value pricing to make a profit. For example, a consortium submitted a proposal for new HOT lanes on the Washington Beltway and Interstate 395 in Virginia.

3. ENVIRONMENTAL EXTERNALITIES

Motor vehicles generate two types of environmental externalities: air pollution and greenhouse gases. The air pollutants include particulate matter, nitrogen oxides, volatile organic compounds, sulfur oxides, carbon monoxide, and ozone (a result of atmospheric reactions of other pollutants). These pollutants cause health problems related to respiratory systems and cause premature deaths. The estimated air-pollution cost per mile driven is $0.013, over 99 percent of which comes from particulate matter (Small and Verhoef, 2007). Roughly three-fourths of the pollution cost from motor vehicles comes from premature deaths. Motor vehicles also emit carbon dioxide, and the estimated carbon-related external cost of gasoline is $0.061 per gallon, or $0.003 per mile driven in the United States. Adding the two environmental costs together, the external environmental cost per mile driven is $0.016.

Externality Tax versus Gasoline Tax

As for other external costs, the economic approach to air pollution is to use a pollution tax to internalize the externality. A tax equal to the marginal external cost of pollution would cause drivers to incorporate the full costs of driving into their decisions, leading to the efficient level of driving and air pollution. A pollution tax would (i) encourage people to buy cars with lower pollution and carbon emissions per mile driven and (ii) drive fewer miles. To implement this pure pollution tax, we would install a monitoring device in each car to measure its emissions and then periodically charge the owner for the emissions.

An alternative approach is to use a gasoline tax to increase the private cost of auto travel. The tax would encourage fuel efficiency and thus reduce carbon emissions per mile driven. The tax would also increase the cost per mile driven, so it would decrease the total miles driven and decrease air pollution. But because a gasoline tax doesn't distinguish between low-emission cars and high-emission cars, it doesn't encourage consumers to buy low-emission cars. Of course, if government emissions standards generate relatively small differences in emissions per gallon across car models, the lack of incentives to buy cleaner cars would be less of an issue.

The Market Effects of a Gasoline Tax

Figure 18–11 shows the implications of a unit gasoline tax in a perfectly competitive market. In the initial market equilibrium shown by point *a*, the price of gasoline is $4.00 per gallon and the equilibrium quantity is g^*. The tax is assumed to be $0.32 per gallon, including $0.26 for air pollutants ($0.013 per mile times 20 miles per gallon) and $0.06 for carbon emissions. The tax shifts the market supply curve upward by $0.32, and the new market equilibrium is shown by point *c*, with a price of $4.16 and a quantity g^{**}. The increase in the equilibrium price is half the tax (the vertical shift of the supply curve), meaning that consumers and producers split the tax equally. This is consistent with studies of the effect of gasoline taxes on equilibrium prices.

As explained in a typical course in intermediate microeconomics, the fraction of a tax shifted forward to consumers is determined by the price elasticities of demand

FIGURE 18–11 Market Effects of a Gas Tax

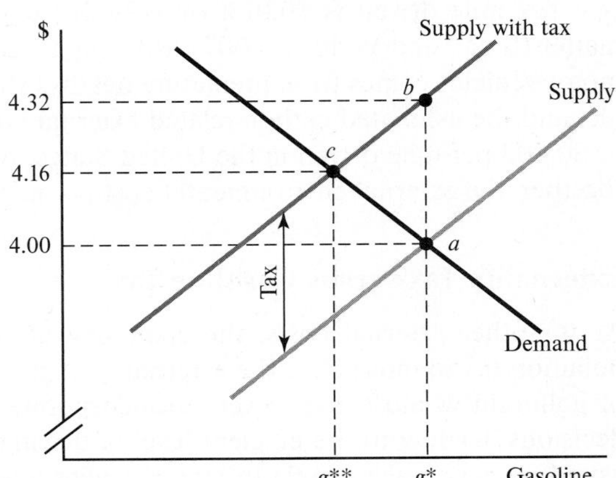

and supply for the taxed good. If we define s as the fraction of the tax shifted forward to consumers,

$$s = \frac{\Delta p^*}{Tax} = \frac{e_S}{e_S - e_D}$$

The fraction of the tax shifted backward onto input suppliers is $(1 - s)$. For example, suppose the price elasticity of demand for gasoline is -1.0 and the price elasticity of supply is 1.0. In this case, half the gasoline tax will be shifted forward to consumers:

$$s = \frac{e_S}{e_S - e_D} = \frac{1}{1 - (-1)} = \frac{1}{2}$$

In our numerical example, a unit tax of \$0.32 increases the gasoline price by \$0.16, leaving half the tax to be borne by producers. Studies of the market effects of the gasoline tax indicate a roughly equal sharing of the tax, suggesting that the price elasticity of demand is roughly equal to the price elasticity of supply.

Who bears the producer burden of the tax? Recall that the long-run market supply curve of a product is positively sloped if input prices increase as the total output of the industry increases. This is the case of an increasing-cost industry. In the gasoline market, the input whose price increases with the total output of the industry is the price of crude oil: the larger the quantity of gasoline produced, the larger the demand for crude oil and the higher its price. Moving in the other direction, a tax that decreases the quantity of gasoline produced decreases the demand for crude oil, decreasing its price. Therefore, a gasoline tax will be borne by consumers and the suppliers of crude oil.

4. EXTERNALITIES FROM TRAFFIC ACCIDENTS

Consider next the external costs generated by traffic accidents. In addition to the costs of bodily harm and property damage, traffic accidents also use resources to handle insurance claims and legal issues. Adding all the costs associated with traffic accidents, the average accident cost per mile driven is \$0.14 (Small and Verhoef, 2007). This figure includes both the private and external cost of accidents. On average, the marginal external cost of traffic accidents is \$0.061 per mile driven.

Social Cost of Traffic Accidents

The largest cost of traffic accidents is the cost associated with traffic deaths. The value of a statistical life (VSL) is computed by examining people's willingness to pay to avoid the risk of death. For example, suppose the typical person is willing to pay \$5,500 to reduce the probability of dying in an accident from 0.001 (one chance in one thousand) to zero. If every person in a group of 1,000 experiences the same 0.001 reduction in the probability of death, they would collectively be willing to pay \$5.5 million for one statistical life saved. In this example, the implied value of a statistical life (VSL) is \$5.5 million.

TABLE 18-1 Social Cost of Traffic Accidents

Type	Cost ($ per vehicle mile)
Death or injury	0.103
Productivity loss	0.013
Medical expenses	0.008
Property damage	0.007
Legal, police, fire	0.004
Insurance administration	0.003
Traffic delay	0.002
Total	0.140

Source: Small, Kenneth and Verhoef, Erik, *The Economics of Urban Transportation.* New York: Routledge, 2007; Parry, Ian W.H. "Comparing Alternative Policies to Reduce Traffic Accidents." *Journal of Urban Economics* 56, 2004, 346-368.

Table 18-1 shows the components of the social cost of traffic accidents. The numbers are the accident cost per mile driven. The largest cost is for death and injury, and the numbers are based on VSL = $5.5 million. The second largest component incorporates the productivity lost during the recovery time of accident victims. The costs associated with medical expenses and property damage are not far apart. The cost of traffic delay incorporates the cost of congestion when an accident reduces the carrying capacity of roadways.

Inefficiency from Underpricing Accident Costs

Small and Verhoef (2007) estimate that on average, the marginal external accident cost is $0.061 per mile driven. Figure 18-12 shows the inefficiency generated by this external cost. The marginal private cost of driving includes the private cost of

FIGURE 18-12 Traffic Accidents and Efficiency

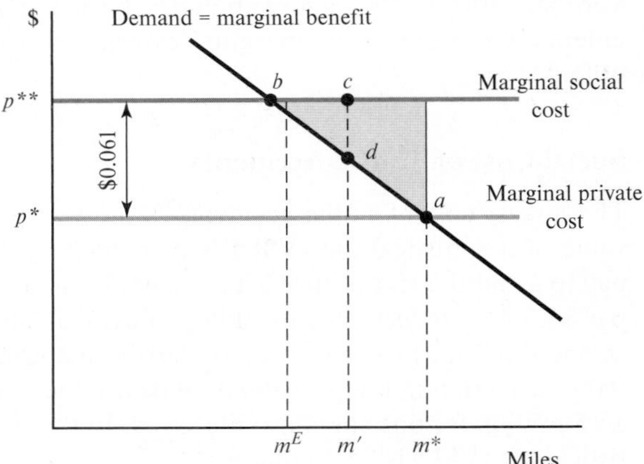

accidents (the driver's own risk of death and injury, medical expenses, property damage). The rational individual choice is shown by the intersection of the demand curve and the private-cost curve at point a. The marginal social cost of driving exceeds the private cost by the \$0.061 marginal external cost. The efficient outcome is shown by point b, with $m^E < m^*$.

The shaded area shows the efficiency loss resulting from the underpricing of traffic accidents. This is the familiar deadweight loss, computed as the area between the marginal social cost curve and the demand curve, from the market equilibrium (m^*) to the efficient outcome (m^E). To illustrate, consider the efficiency loss from driving mile m'. The cost is shown by point c and the benefit is shown by point d, and the efficiency loss is shown by the gap between the two points. Adding up the gaps between marginal social cost and the demand curve from the equilibrium m^* to the efficient m^E, we get the shaded area as the efficiency loss from underpricing traffic accidents.

The marginal external accident cost varies across drivers and vehicles. For drivers who consume alcohol before driving, the external cost is roughly seven times the average external cost, or \$0.427 per mile. For young drivers (age $<$ 25 years), the external cost is roughly \$0.109 cents per mile, compared to \$0.034 for drivers ages 25 to 70. For accidents involving at least one vehicle designated as a "light truck" (a van, pickup truck, or sport utility vehicle), the probability of being killed is much higher. In an accident involving a light truck and a car, the probability that a car occupant is killed is 61 percent higher than in an accident involving two cars (White, 2004). For a pedestrian, the difference in the probability of being killed is 82 percent higher when being struck by a light truck rather than a car.

One possible response to external accident cost is pay-as-you-drive pricing. The external accident cost depends on miles driven, and a VMT (vehicle mile traveled) tax increases the marginal cost of driving. For a VMT tax designed to internalize external accident cost, the tax would be \$0.061 per mile. The VMT tax could vary with the type of vehicle, with a higher tax on light trucks. In Figure 18–12, a VMT tax would decrease miles driven from the inefficient m^* miles to the socially efficient m^E miles. As shown by Parry (2004), the possible efficiency gains from a VMT tax are substantial.

Safety Equipment and Risk Compensation

So far in our discussion we have implicitly assumed that accident costs depend only on the miles driven. In fact, the probability of an accident also depends on driver behavior. Compared to middle-aged drivers, the external accident cost of young drivers is over three times larger. And drivers of all ages make decisions that affect the probability of an accident: how fast to drive, how much attention to devote to driving, and how much space to allow other cars.

An important policy issue concerns the effect of vehicle-safety policies on driver behavior. Starting in 1966, the U.S. government established standards for new cars. Among the mandated features are head restraints, seat belts, dual braking systems, and airbags. The widespread implementation of laws requiring vehicle occupants to wear seat belts saved lives overall, but death rates for pedestrians and bicyclists

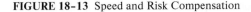

FIGURE 18–13 Speed and Risk Compensation

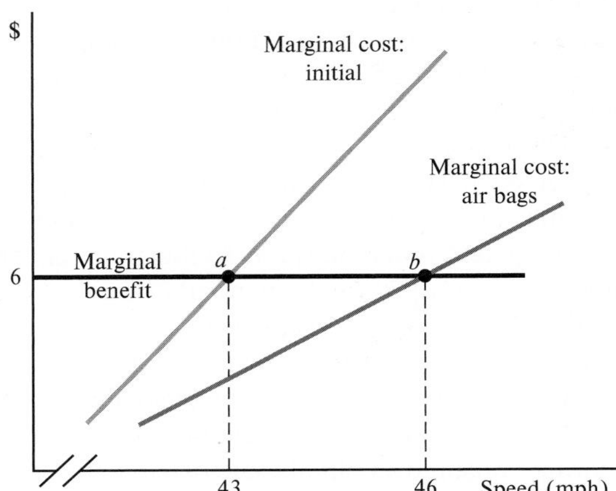

increased. This puzzling effect is explained by the theory of risk compensation (Peltzman, 1975). Seat belts and other safety features make drivers feel safer because the consequences of an accident are less severe if the driver is buckled in. People who feel safer drive faster and less cautiously, so there are more accidents and thus more pedestrian and bicyclist deaths.

Figure 18–13 illustrates a driver's decision about how fast to drive. The benefit of driving faster is a shorter trip and thus more time for other activities. In this example, the marginal benefit of speed is constant at $6: each additional unit of speed (mile per hour) generates a $6 benefit in extra time. Speed is costly because it increases the probability of being in a traffic accident and increases the cost of an accident (property damage, injuries, death). In Figure 18–13, the marginal cost of speed increases with speed: the expected accident cost increases at an increasing rate with speed. Applying the marginal principle, a driver will choose the speed at which the marginal benefit of speed equals the marginal cost. The initial rational choice is 43 mph. Going faster is irrational because the marginal cost associated with going 44 mph instead of 43 mph exceeds the $6 marginal benefit.

Consider the effects of installing airbags. A car with airbags has a lower accident cost (lower injury cost) and has a lower marginal-cost curve. In Figure 18–13, the installation of air bags tilts the marginal-cost curve downward. The rational choice shifts from point *a* to point *b*, meaning that the rational speed increases from 43 to 46 mph. In general, features like airbags decrease the consequences of accidents for drivers and their passengers, causing faster and less cautious driving.

How does mandated safety equipment affect the total number of traffic deaths? For drivers and their passengers, faster driving increases the number of accidents, but the safety equipment decreases the probability of dying in an accident. The net effect of these two conflicting effects is a decrease in highway deaths for people in cars: the increase in the number of accidents is dominated by a lower probability of dying in an accident. In contrast, the increase in speed and reckless driving and the resulting increase in the number of accidents increases death rates for pedestrians and bicyclists.

REVIEW THE CONCEPTS

1. Suppose (i) an additional vehicle increases the travel time per user by 0.02 minutes, (ii) there are 1,100 other road users, and (iii) the opportunity cost of travel time is $0.15 per minute. The marginal external cost of an additional vehicle is $[_____].
2. The social trip cost equals [_____] plus [_____].
3. The equilibrium traffic volume is shown by the intersection of the [_____] curve and the [_____] curve.
4. The equilibrium traffic volume is [_____] (<, >, =) the efficient volume because [_____] exceeds [_____].
5. The congestion tax is computed as [_____] at the [_____] traffic volume.
6. The efficiency gain from a congestion tax is shown by the area between the [_____] curve and the [_____] curve from [_____] to [_____].
7. A person who continues to use a roadway after the imposition of a congestion tax will be better off if (i) the decrease in [_____] is relatively large and (ii) reduction of [_____] is relatively large.
8. A person who stops using a roadway because of a congestion tax will be better off if the loss of [_____] is small relative to the reduction of [_____].
9. Under value pricing for roads, road lanes are [_____] products like [_____], and fast lanes are allocated to travelers with the highest [_____].
10. Using an express lane subject to value pricing will be a rational choice if a traveler's savings in [_____] exceeds the toll, a likely case for travelers with relatively [_____].
11. Suppose the travel cost for a roadway decreases. The resulting increase in the number of travelers is an example of [_____] in the transportation world and an example of the [_____] in economics.
12. In the United States, the environmental cost per mile driven is roughly $[_____] (choose 0.001, 0.016, 0.600, or 0.900).
13. Roughly one [_____] (choose half, third, quarter, tenth) of a gasoline tax will be shifted forward to [_____] in the form of a [_____]. The remainder of the tax is borne by [_____].
14. The largest component of the cost of traffic accidents is the cost associated with [_____]. The value of a statistical life is roughly $[_____].
15. On average, the marginal external accident cost of driving is roughly $[_____] per mile driven. For drivers under the influence of alcohol, the marginal external cost is roughly [_____] times higher.

16. The efficiency loss from accident externalities is shown by the area between the [_____] curve and the [_____] curve from the [_____] number of miles to the [_____] number of miles.

17. One approach to accident externalities is a tax per [_____], also known as a VMT.

18. Mandated safety equipment such as seat belts and air bags [_____] {↑, ↓, −} the marginal cost of [_____] and increases the equilibrium [_____]. As a result, the roads are more dangerous for [_____] and [_____].

19. For each pair of variables, indicate whether the relationship is positive, negative, neutral, or ambiguous.

Parameter	Choice Variable	Relationship
c: opportunity cost of travel time	marginal external cost	[_____]
v: traffic volume	marginal external cost of travel	[_____]
gasoline tax	price of gasoline	[_____]
gasoline tax	price of crude oil	[_____]
mandated safety features	travel speed	[_____]
mandated safety features	pedestrian deaths	[_____]

APPLY THE CONCEPTS

1. *Thump-Thump Data*

Your task is to compute the peak-period congestion tax for the 8-mile trip along I-5 from Vancouver to Portland. At the equilibrium volume $V = 1100$, the trip takes 30 minutes, compared to 29.98 minutes with $V = 1099$. The opportunity cost of travel is $0.30 per minute. Illustrate the equilibrium and the efficient outcome. The marginal external cost at the initial equilibrium is [_____], which [_____] {>, <, =} the efficient congestion tax.

2. *Who Is Better Off?*

Your city imposed a congestion tax of $3 per trip, and traffic volume decreased from 120 to 80 and travel time decreased by 4 minutes. The city will reduce its head tax to ensure revenue neutrality.

a. The congestion tax will make a traveler better off if . . .

b. The congestion tax will make a diverted driver (a person who stops using the highway) better off if . . .

3. *Congestion Tax and the Chamber of Commerce*

The citizens of Snarlsville will vote on a revenue-neutral congestion tax. Your task is to develop a position of the Chamber of Commerce on the proposed tax, that is, whether citizens of Snarlsville should vote yes or no. The key question is whether the tax will be good or bad for business in the city.

a. Briefly state the position of Snarlsville's Chamber of Commerce (vote yes or no). Explain the economic logic of the position.

b. Consider Smileville, the other city in the regional economy. The city's Chamber of Commerce is concerned about business activity in Smileville. Briefly state the position of Smileville's Chamber of Commerce on Snarlsville's congestion tax (vote yes or no). Explain the economic logic of the position.

4. *Pricing Environmental Externalities*
Suppose the initial marginal cost per mile traveled by car is \$0.32, and the initial mileage for the typical driver is 1,000 per month. Assume the elasticity of miles driven with respect to the price is −1.0. Suppose the government uses a per-mile tax to internalize the environmental externalities associated with car travel (for air pollution and CO_2). Illustrate the effects of the tax on equilibrium miles driven, including a new value for miles driven.
5. *Gasoline Tax in Small City*
Consider the effects of a gasoline tax of \$0.32 per gallon. Figure 18–11 shows the effects of a national tax. For a tax imposed by one of a dozen small municipalities in a large metropolitan area, the consumer's share of the tax will be [______] (choose >, <, =) one half because . . .
6. *Speeding Penalty*
The marginal benefit of speed is constant at \$3 per mph. The marginal cost of speed is $mc(s) = 0.04 \cdot s$, where s is speed in miles per hour. The legal speed limit is 50 mph. The fine for speeding is f times the speed gap (speed −50 mph), for example, f for 51 mph and $2f$ 120 for 52 mph. The probability of being caught and fined for speeding is 0.01.
   a. Illustrate the equilibrium speed for $f =$ \$0 and $f =$ \$60, including values for the equilibrium speeds s^* (for $f =$ \$0) and s^{**} (for $f =$ \$60).
   b. Suppose the city's objective is to decrease the equilibrium speed to the legal limit (50 mph). In this case, $f =$ [______]. Illustrate.
7. *Bikers Against Seat Belts*
In a column of *The State Paper* (Columbia, South Carolina) on April 5, 2004, columnist John Monk describes the efforts of motorcycle riders to defeat a proposed law that would allow police to issue \$25 tickets to automobile drivers and passengers who are not wearing seat belts. The law would not apply to motorcycles, yet the bikers showed up in groups of a dozen or more, some dressed in full biker regalia, to urge legislators to reject the law. It is sensible for bikers to oppose the proposed law because . . . Illustrate.
8. *Ma'am, Step Away from the Car*
In Vaporville, a tow truck takes 30 minutes to clear a highway accident, and the opportunity cost of highway travel time is \$0.20 per minute. To simplify, assume that an accident simply stops traffic until any disabled vehicles are removed. Suppose a helicopter can deliver a laser beam to instantly vaporize any vehicle involved in an accident. Vilfredo Pareto the vapogunner is a former used-car seller and an expert in car repair, and provides vaporizing services at the same price as tow-truck services.
   a. Suppose 1,200 people would be delayed by an accident. Vilfredo's efficiency rule is to vaporize a disabled car if . . .
   b. At what time of day is Vilfredo most likely to vaporize a vehicle?
   c. To get drivers to voluntarily make an efficient choice–either a tow-truck or a vaporizer–the city could impose an accident tax equal to [______].
9. *Youngsters Pay to Drive*
The demand curve for car travel by the typical young driver (age < 25 years) has a vertical intercept of \$1.00 and a horizontal intercept of 200 miles per week.

Initially, the cost of insurance is a fixed amount per week, and the marginal private cost of driving is constant at $0.20 per mile. Suppose insurance companies switch to a VMT equal to the marginal accident cost of young drivers (rounded to the nearest cent). Illustrate the effects of the switch in pricing. Include on your graph the values for (i) the initial and the new price and (ii) the initial and the new miles driven.

REFERENCES AND READING

1. Chouinard, Hayley, and Jeffrey M. Perloff, "Incidence of Federal and State Gasoline Taxes." *Economics Letters* 83 (2004), pp. 55–60.
2. Crandall, Robert W., Howard K. Gruenspecht, Theodore E. Keeler, and Lester B. Lave, *Regulating the Automobile*. Washington DC: Brookings Institution, 1986.
3. de Palma, Andre, Robin Lindsey, and Nathalie Picard, "Urban Passenger Travel Demand," Chapter 16 in *A Companion to Urban Economics,* edited by Richard J. Arnott and Daniel P. McMillen. New York: Wiley-Blackwell, 2006.
4. Duranton, Gilles, and Turner, Matthew, "The Fundamental Law of Road Congestion." *American Economic Review* (2011).
5. Kahn, Matthew E., "Air Pollution in Cities," Chapter 29 in *A Companion to Urban Economics,* edited by Richard J. Arnott and Daniel P. McMillen. New York: Wiley-Blackwell, 2006.
6. Kanemoto, Yoshitsugu, "Urban Transport Economic Theory," Chapter 15 in *A Companion to Urban Economics,* edited by Richard J. Arnott and Daniel P. McMillen. New York: Wiley-Blackwell, 2006.
7. Parry, Ian W. H., "Comparing Alternative Policies to Reduce Traffic Accidents." *Journal of Urban Economics* 56 (2004), pp. 346–68.
8. Parry, Ian, and Antonio Bento, "Estimating the Welfare Effect of Congestion Taxes: The Critical Importance of Other Distortions within the Transport System." *Journal of Urban Economics* 51 (2002), pp. 339–65.
9. Parry, Ian, and Kenneth Small, "Should Urban Transit Subsidies Be Reduced?" *American Economic Review* 99 (2009), pp. 700–24.
10. Peltzman, Sam, *Regulation of Automobile Safety.* Washington DC: American Enterprise Institute, 1975.
11. Rietveld, Piet, "Urban Transport Policies: The Dutch Struggle with Market Failures and Policy Failures," Chapter 18 in *A Companion to Urban Economics,* edited by Richard J. Arnott and Daniel P. McMillen. New York: Wiley-Blackwell, 2006.
12. Small, Kenneth A., "Transportation: Urban Transportation Policy," Chapter 3 in *Making Cities Work: Prospects and Policies for Urban America,* edited by Robert P. Inman. Princeton, NJ: Princeton University Press, 2009.
13. Small, Kenneth, and Erik Verhoef, *The Economics of Urban Transportation.* New York: Routledge, 2007.
14. Small, Kenneth, Clifford Winston, and Jua Yan, "Differentiated Road Pricing, Express Lanes, and Carpools: Exploiting Heterogeneous Preferences in Policy Design," Brookings-Wharton Papers on Urban Affairs, 2006, pp. 53–86.

CHAPTER 19

Urban Public Transit

> *While real trolleys in Newark, Philadelphia, Pittsburgh, and Boston languish for lack of patronage and government support, millions of people flock to Disneyland to ride fake trains that don't go anywhere.*
>
> —KENNETH T. JACKSON

This second chapter on urban transportation explores the economics of urban public transit. In the United States, the market share of public transit is less than 5 percent, but the market share is much higher in many U.S. cities and in many other nations. We will explore transportation modal choice from two perspectives. First, an individual traveler decides whether to drive, ride the bus, or take a train. Second, a local government designs a transportation system, including roads and possibly a transit system. The key question for local transit planners is, What is the appropriate mix of cars, buses, light rail, and heavy rail? We will also explore the economic rationale for the large subsidies for public transit systems.

1. MODAL CHOICE: INDIVIDUAL TRAVELER

For the United States as a whole, 4.7 percent of commuters use public transit. The transit share is 11 percent for central city residents, compared to 2 percent for suburban residents. In the New York metropolitan area, about a quarter of workers use public transit. The transit share is between 10 and 14 percent in three metropolitan areas: Chicago, Philadelphia, and Washington, DC. There are eight metropolitan areas in the trillion-mile club (annual passenger miles of at least a trillion miles): New York (18.4 trillion), Chicago (7.3), Los Angeles (2.8), Washington, DC (2.2), San Francisco (2.1), Boston (1.9), Philadelphia (1.5), and Seattle (1.0). Together these metropolitan areas are responsible for roughly four-fifths of the public transit passenger miles of the 38 largest metropolitan areas.

Figure 19-1 shows the distribution of public transit ridership across modes of travel. The numbers are daily commuters, in thousands. For example, daily bus ridership is 3,207,000 and streetcar ridership is 73,000. The bus is responsible for over

FIGURE 19–1 Public Transit Ridership

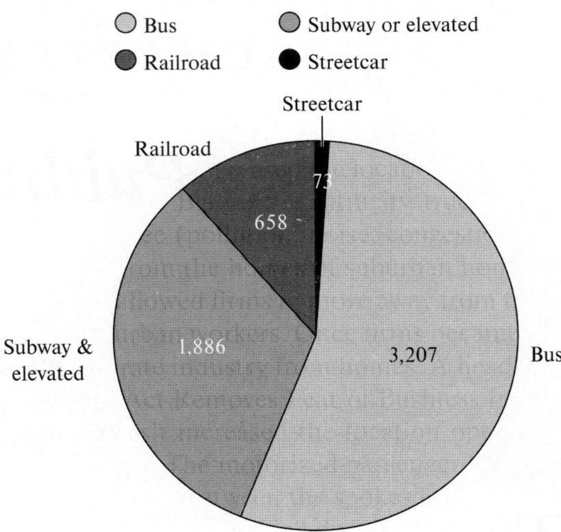

Source: US Census Bureau, "Numbers in 1,000 Commuters per Day," *Journey to Work,* 2004.

half of commuter transit trips, followed by heavy rail (subway or elevated trains) and commuter rail. The streetcar (aka light rail) is responsible for a relatively small share of commuter transit.

Trip Cost for Alternative Modes

Consider a city where commuters have three travel options: car, bus, or rail. The rail mode is either heavy rail such as subways or elevated trains, or light rail such as streetcars. The commuter's objective is to choose the travel mode that minimizes the cost of travel, which includes both monetary and time costs.

We can divide the cost of a commuter trip into three components: monetary costs, the opportunity cost of walking and waiting time, and the opportunity cost of time spent in a vehicle.

$$\text{Trip cost} = \text{monetary cost} + \text{walk and wait time cost} + \text{in-vehicle time cost}$$

For bus or rail, the monetary cost is simply the fare charged by the transit authority. For commuting by car, the monetary cost is the sum of (i) fuel cost, (ii) maintenance cost and depreciation attributable to a commute trip, and (iii) parking cost.

The cost associated with walking and waiting is applicable to transit trips. A transit rider spends time walking between (i) a residence and a transit stop and (ii) a transit stop and a workplace. In addition, a rider spends time waiting for the transit vehicle to arrive at the stop. The cost of walking and waiting equals the actual time in hours T_W times the marginal disutility of walk and wait time d_W:

$$\text{Walk and wait time cost} = T_W \cdot d_W$$

The marginal disutility of walk and wait time is the dollar amount a commuter is willing to pay to avoid one hour of access time. On average, the marginal disutility of walk and wait time is 80 to 100 percent of a commuter's wage.

The cost associated with in-vehicle time is applicable to both car and transit trips. This is the opportunity cost of time spent in a vehicle, either a car or a transit vehicle such as a bus, streetcar, or subway train. The in-vehicle time cost equals the actual vehicle time in hours T_V times the marginal disutility of in-vehicle time d_V:

$$\text{In-vehicle time cost} = T_V \cdot d_V$$

The marginal disutility of in-vehicle time is the dollar amount a commuter is willing to pay to avoid one hour of time in a vehicle. On average, the marginal disutility of in-vehicle time is 50 percent of a commuter's wage. Notice that the disutility of in-vehicle time is much less than the marginal disutility of walking and waiting.

A Numerical Example of Modal Choice

We will use a simple numerical example to illustrate a worker's choice of a commuting mode. Consider a worker whose hourly wage is \$24 (\$0.40 per minute). The marginal disutility of walk and wait time equals the wage, while the marginal disutility of in-vehicle time is half the wage. Table 19-1 tallies the daily commuting costs for the three modes.

1. *Car.* The in-vehicle time is 80 minutes (40 minutes each way), so the time cost is \$16 = 80 minutes × \$0.20 per minute. Adding the \$6 monetary cost, the total cost is \$22.
2. *Bus.* The cost of walk and wait time is \$8 = 20 minutes × \$0.40 per minute and the cost of in-vehicle time is \$18 = 90 minutes × \$0.20 per minute. The in-vehicle time is longer than for the car mode because buses and cars use the same roads, but buses stop to pick up passengers. Adding the \$3 monetary cost to the time cost, the total cost is \$29.
3. *Rail.* The cost of walk and wait time is \$18 = 45 minutes × \$0.40 per minute and the cost of in-vehicle time is \$12 = 60 minutes × \$0.20 per minute. The in-vehicle time is shorter than for the car mode because rail transit is not subject to road congestion. The walk and wait time is longer than for the bus mode because rail stations are more widely spaced than bus stops. Adding the \$3 monetary cost to the time cost, the total cost is \$33.

TABLE 19-1 Numerical Example of Modal Choice

	Car	Bus	Rail
Monetary cost (\$)	6	3	3
Walk and wait time (minutes)	0	20	45
Walk and wait cost (\$)	0	8	18
In-vehicle time (minutes)	80	90	60
In-vehicle cost (\$)	16	18	12
Total cost	22	29	33

FIGURE 19–2 Commuting Cost: Car vs. Bus vs. Rail

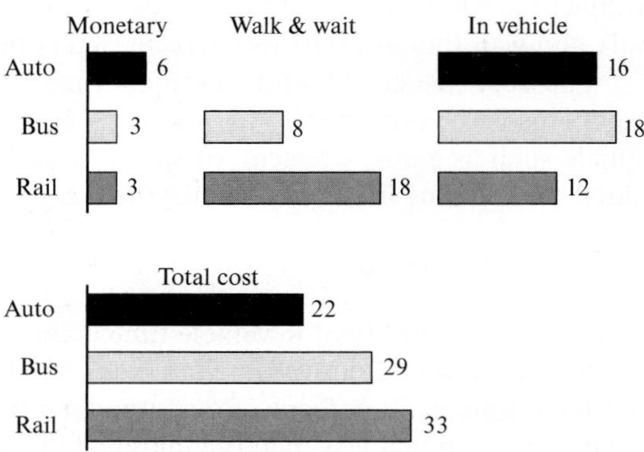

Figure 19–2 provides a graph of the numerical example shown in Table 19–1 The car is the least costly mode because of its large cost advantage in walk and wait time. The walk and wait cost for the car is zero, compared to $8 for the bus and $18 for rail commuting. The differences are relatively large because the disutility of waiting and walking is relatively high. Compared to car commuting, rail commuting has a lower in-vehicle cost ($12 versus $16) and a lower monetary cost ($3 versus $6), but these advantage are not large enough to offset its higher walk and wait cost. For the bus, its $3 monetary advantage over the car is overwhelmed by its $8 disadvantage in walk and wait cost and its $2 disadvantage in in-vehicle cost.

Figure 19–3 shows the effects of two changes in our numerical example that tip the balance from car commuting to riding transit.

1. *Increase population density.* In a high-density city, more commuters will live close to bus stops. As a result, bus ridership will be higher, so (i) buses can run more frequently (lower wait and walk time cost) and (ii) express buses are feasible (lower in-vehicle time cost). If we reduce the time cost for the bus by half, the total cost drops to $16, which is below the car commuting cost of $22. If we reduce the time cost of rail by half, the total cost decreases to $18. In this example of a high-density city with better transit service, both transit modes are less costly than car commuting.
2. *Decrease income.* A decrease in the wage decreases the marginal disutility of both walk and wait time and in-vehicle time. If we cut the wage to $0.10 per minute, the bus is less costly than auto commuting.

Elasticities of Demand for Public Transit

Small and Verhoef (2007) summarize what we know about the responsiveness of transit riders to changes in price and service. The overall price elasticity of demand for urban transit is −0.40: a 10 percent increase in fares decreases ridership by

FIGURE 19-3 Tip the Balance in Favor of Transit

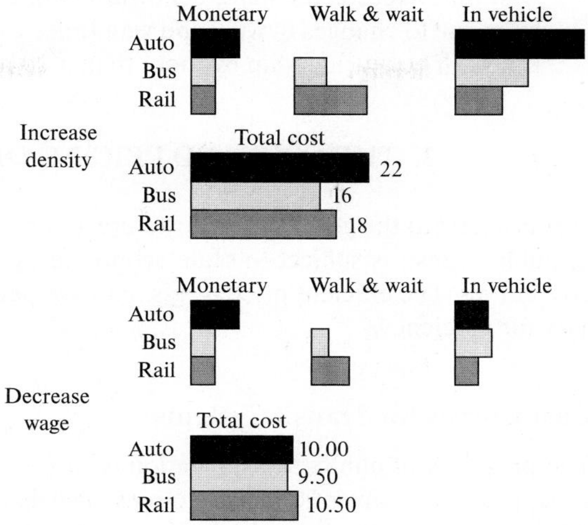

4 percent. As shown in Table 19-2, the demand for bus transit is more price-elastic than the demand for rail transit, and the demand for off-peak travel is more elastic than the demand for peak-period travel. Because transit demand is price-inelastic, an increase in fares will increase total fare revenue.

Consider next the responsiveness of travelers to changes in transit service. There are two key observations from empirical studies of transit ridership.

1. *Relatively responsive to changes in service.* Transit ridership is more responsive to changes in service than to changes in price. For example, a study of Boston commuters concluded that the elasticity of ridership with respect to travel time is −0.80, compared to a price elasticity of −0.50. Therefore, if a 10 percent increase in service is combined with a 10 percent increase in fares, ridership will increase: the negative effect from higher fares will be more than offset by a positive effect from better service.
2. *Relatively responsive to changes in walk and wait time.* Transit ridership is more responsive to changes in walk and wait time than to changes in in-vehicle time.

TABLE 19-2 Price Elasticities of Transit Demand

Time of Day	Bus	Rail
Peak demand	−0.40	−0.24
Off-peak	−0.80	−0.48
Overall	−0.50	−0.30

Source: Parry, Ian, and Small, Kenneth, "Should Urban Transit Subsidies Be Reduced?" *American Economic Review* 99, 2009, 700–724.

This is consistent with the observation that the marginal disutility of walk and wait time exceeds the marginal disutility of in-vehicle time. Given relatively large response to changes in walk and wait time, a 10 percent decrease in walk and wait time will boost ridership by more than a 10 percent decrease in in-vehicle time.

2. THE COST AND PRICING OF PUBLIC TRANSIT

We turn next to the general cost structure and pricing of public transit. The provision of public transit is subject to scale economies, generating negatively sloped average-cost curves. The efficient price is less than average cost, so transit subsidies are necessary for efficiency.

Cost Curves for Transit Systems

The provision of public transportation is subject to two types of economies of scale. First, there are conventional economies of scale in production resulting from indivisible inputs. Some inputs such as tracks, trains (heavy and light rail vehicles), and trolley power systems cannot be efficiently scaled down. For example, it is impractical to build quarter-width or eighth-width rail tracks and run skinny trains on them. Once these indivisible inputs are in place, an increase in ridership spreads their substantial fixed cost over more riders, and the average cost per rider decreases. Of course, the size of these indivisible inputs and their fixed cost varies for different systems (Small and Verhoef, 2007): the construction cost per route mile is $202 million for heavy rail, compared to $63 million for light rail. For bus systems that run on regular roadways, economies of scale are limited by the size of the indivisible input, the bus.

The second source of economies of scale is related to the interactions between transit service and ridership. An increase in ridership improves transit service and decreases the average time cost of riders. To illustrate the notion of economies of scale in ridership, imagine a bus operator that provides just-in-time service. The operator sends a bus to a bus stop as soon as the number of people waiting for the bus reaches some target quantity, say 24 riders. If commuters appear at the rate of one per minute, the bus headway (the time between buses) is 24 minutes and the average wait time is 12 minutes. If the arrival rate of riders triples to 3 per minute, the headway decreases to 8 minutes and the average wait time decreases to 4 minutes. In general, an increase in bus ridership decreases waiting time and the average time cost of commuters.

The cost curves for a transit system incorporate the monetary costs of the transit provider and the time costs of riders. The cost of the provider include capital and operating costs. As shown in Figure 19–4, the average-cost curve for a transit is negatively sloped: As ridership increases, the average capital cost decreases because of conventional economies of scale in production and the average time cost of riders decreases because of ridership economies. The marginal cost is less than the average cost, a result of simple arithmetic: if the average cost is decreasing, the marginal cost must be below the average cost.

FIGURE 19–4 Economies of Scale in Transit: Indivisible Inputs and Ridership Economies

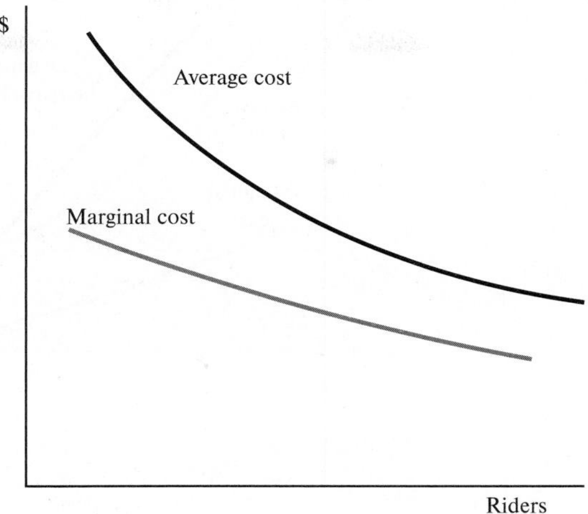

Ridership economies in transit provide an interesting counterpoint to congestion externalities in driving. An additional transit rider increases the frequency of service and thus generates an external benefit for other riders. As a result, the marginal rider cost is less than the average rider cost. In contrast, an additional driver slows down traffic and imposes an external cost on other drivers. As a result, the marginal driver cost (the social trip cost) exceeds the average driver cost (private trip cost).

Efficient Ridership and Pricing

We can use Figure 19–5 to show the socially efficient transit ridership. The market demand curve shows the marginal benefit of ridership. In this figure, the cost curves include the production costs of transit, but not the time costs of travelers. A change in time costs shifts the market demand curve for transit. The efficient outcome is shown by point a, where the market demand curve (marginal social benefit curve) intersects the marginal cost curve. The efficient price of transit service is p^E. This is another example of the marginal principle: for efficiency, choose the level of an activity at which marginal cost equals marginal benefit. Starting from any ridership less than R^E, the marginal benefit of an additional rider exceeds the marginal cost, so adding riders promotes efficiency. Starting from any ridership exceeding R^E, the marginal cost of the last rider exceeds the marginal benefit, so subtracting riders promotes efficiency.

The policy challenge associated with the efficient outcome is that the transit authority runs a deficit. At ridership R^E, the average cost is ac^E and the price is $p^E < ac^E$, and the shaded rectangle shows the transit deficit. In the interests of

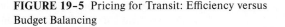

FIGURE 19-5 Pricing for Transit: Efficiency versus Budget Balancing

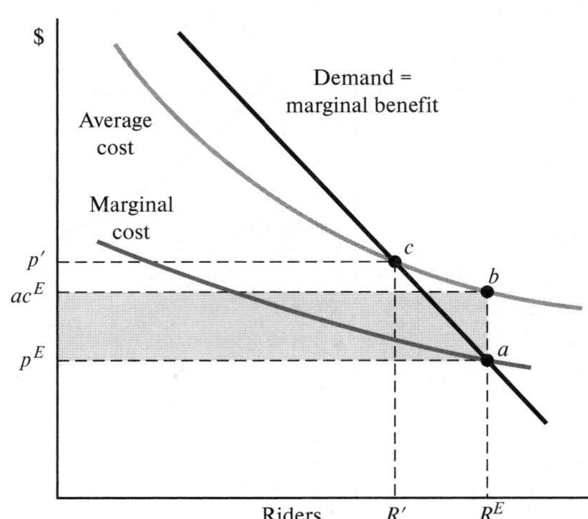

efficiency, the total revenue from riders will fall short of the cost of providing transit service. The transit deficit could be eliminated by increasing the price to p', which as shown by point c, decreases ridership to R' and increases the average cost to p'. This budget-balancing allocation is inefficient because for riders R' through R^E, the marginal benefit exceeds the marginal cost.

Transit Subsidies

Transit subsidies are substantial and vary across metropolitan areas. For the 20 largest metropolitan areas, the average subsidy is 44 percent of operating cost for rail systems, 69 percent for bus systems, and 54 percent for transit systems as a whole. The lowest subsidy rates are in New York (around 40 percent for MTA New York City and Metro-North Commuter Railroad) and San Francisco (42 percent for BART), while the highest subsidy rates are in Texas cities (82 percent in Houston and 88 percent in Dallas).

Are these substantial subsidies justified on efficiency grounds? Parry and Small (2009) estimate the efficient subsidies in Los Angeles, Washington, DC, and London. For Los Angeles bus service, economies of scale in production and ridership are large enough to justify an operating subsidy of about 47 percent for peak travel and 81 percent for off-peak travel. For Washington, DC, rail service, the efficient subsidies are 48 percent for peak travel and 84 percent for off-peak travel. In London, the efficient subsidies for rail service are 28 percent during the peak period and 60 percent during the off-peak period.

Although transit subsidies are justified on efficiency grounds, the current system of transit subsidies does not provide incentives for cost minimization by the monopoly providers of public transit. There is evidence that the subsidies increase operating costs because of excessive labor compensation, misallocation of workers (high-skill workers performing low-skill tasks), and inefficient mixes of capital and labor. As explained by Parry and Small (2009), the solution is to switch from operator-based subsidies to user-side subsidies. Under a user-based plan, the government would pay a transit operator a fixed subsidy per passenger trip or per passenger mile. For example, if the subsidy is $0.10 per passenger mile, a transit operator that provides 200 million passenger miles would receive a payment of $20 million.

3. CHOOSING A TRANSIT SYSTEM

In this part of the chapter we take the perspective of a transportation planner who must choose a public transit system. The options are bus, light rail (streetcars and trolleys), and heavy rail (subways and elevated trains). The planner also must choose a price for the transit system. As we'll see, the key factor in system choice is the total demand for transit, which is determined largely by the density of population and employment.

In evaluating the merits of alternative transit systems, a planner considers the average cost of serving travelers. We've seen that transit systems are subject to large economies of scale, so the average cost of transit service–including capital cost, operating costs, and riders' time costs–decrease as ridership increases. The key question for the planner is, How many riders will a transit system serve?

1. *Large ridership.* The efficient choice is a heavy-rail system, with relatively high capital cost but relatively low operating cost and time cost.
2. *Small ridership.* The efficient choice is not to provide public transportation, but instead to rely on private transportation in cars. If there is public concern about the mobility of low-income people, the subsidization of taxi service in a low-density environment is more efficient than a subsidized bus system.
3. *Medium ridership.* Most U.S. cities lie between the two extremes, with potential ridership that is large enough to support an efficient bus system.

Ridership and Average Cost

Figure 19-6 shows the average-cost curves for three alternative transportation systems. The cost curves come from Small and Verhoef (2007), who updated a pioneering study of transportation costs. The cost curves are for a 10-mile trip from a residential area to a high-density employment area. The curves incorporate capital costs, operating costs, and the time costs of travelers.

1. *Car and road system.* The horizontal cost curve incorporates the costs of (i) acquiring and operating a car, (ii) travel time, (iii) building and maintaining roads, and (iv) congestion and environmental externalities. The average-cost curve is horizontal because the authors assume that as traffic volume increases, the roadway is widened to keep travel time constant.

FIGURE 19–6 Long-Run Average Costs for Alternative Transportation Systems

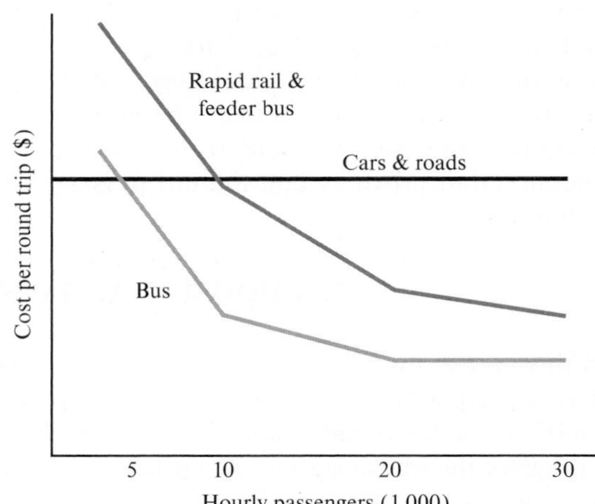

2. *Bus system.* The negatively sloped curve incorporates the costs of (i) acquiring and operating buses, (ii) travel time, (iii) building and maintaining roads for buses, and (iv) environmental externalities. The curve is negatively sloped because of economies of scale in production and ridership.
3. *Heavy-rail system.* The heavy-rail system includes a rail network and rail vehicles, along with a fleet of feeder buses that transports riders (i) between homes and train stations, and (ii) between train stations and workplaces. The negatively sloped curve incorporates the costs of (i) building and maintaining the rails and the exclusive right-of-way, (ii) acquiring and operating rail vehicles and feeder buses, (iii) travel time, and (iv) environmental externalities. The curve is negatively sloped because of economies of scale in production and ridership.

The cost curves in Figure 19–6 represent transportation costs in a U.S. city with typical residential density. For relatively low volumes of traffic, the car and road system is the most efficient. The bus becomes competitive with the car at a volume of about 6,000 passengers per hour. For larger volumes of traffic, the bus system is more efficient than both the car and heavy rail. For the typical city in the United States, ridership is not large enough to justify the large capital costs of a heavy-rail system.

In cities with relatively high density, transit ridership is large enough to justify heavy-rail systems. Specifically, in high-density cities, the average-cost curve for rail intersects the cost curve for buses at a ridership of 30,000 passengers. In New York and Chicago, ridership reaches this level in some corridors, so heavy rail is the efficient choice. In contrast, new heavy-rail systems (in Washington, DC, Atlanta, Miami, and Baltimore) have not generated enough riders to drop the average cost of the heavy-rail system below the average cost of a bus system.

Light Rail versus Buses

In the last several decades, many medium-sized cities have built light-rail systems, which are modern versions of the trolley and streetcar systems built in the late 1800s and early 1900s. How does the cost of light rail compare to the cost of a bus system?

1. *Higher construction cost.* The construction cost of light rail per daily trip is \$35,000 (Small and Verhoef, 2007). In contrast, a normal bus system that uses regular roads doesn't have any construction cost, and the construction cost of an exclusive busway is \$3,000 per daily trip.
2. *Higher operating cost.* The operating cost of light rail exceeds the operating cost of buses. A study of transit options in Rotterdam (the Netherlands) estimated an operating cost of \$3.12 per vehicle mile for light rail, compared to \$1.39 for buses. A study of transit in Cairo, Egypt, estimated an operating cost of \$0.047 per passenger mile for light rail, compared to \$0.0146 for a regular bus and \$0.0142 for a minibus.

The lesson is that compared to a bus system, light rail may have higher capital and operating costs. In Figure 19–6, the average-cost curve for light-rail would lie above the average-cost curve for buses. The widespread appeal of costly light-rail systems is caused in part by the financial support from federal grants.

Figure 19–7 shows how the population densities in four metropolitan areas compare to the threshold density required for viable mass transit. Each census tract is

FIGURE 19–7 Population Density and the Viability of Light Rail

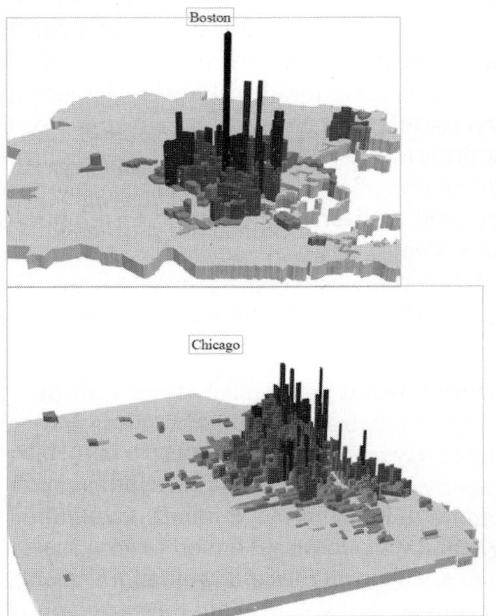

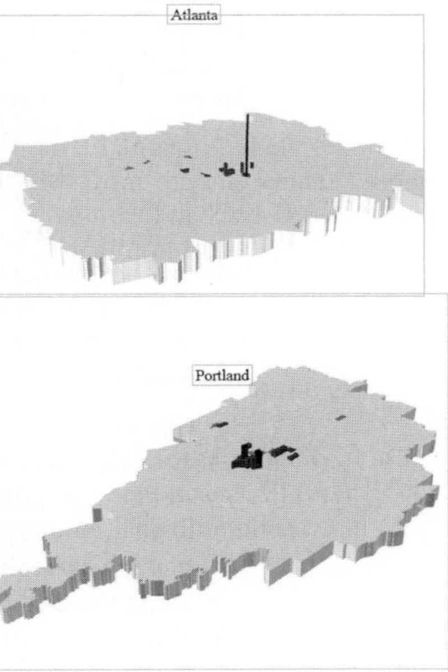

extruded to the density required to support light rail (37 per hectare or 9,472 per square mile), generating a plateau at a height of 37. Each tract is then extruded again to show the actual population density. If the actual density exceeds the threshold density, the tract is extruded above the transit plateau. In Boston and Chicago, the actual population exceeds the light-rail threshold for light rail for a large part of the city. In contrast, Atlanta and Portland have much lower population densities, and a small fraction of their residents live in tracts that rise above the transit plateau.

In recent years innovations in bus service have focused on incorporating some of the desirable features of rail transit into the bus experience (Small, 2009). The set of innovations known as *bus rapid transit* include boarding stations, real-time information at stations, off-vehicle fare payment, and faster travel because of restricted rights-of-way and preferential traffic-signal timing. In Curitiba, Brazil, the prototype bus rapid transit system carries almost 2 million passengers per day. In North America, when Los Angeles upgraded regular bus routes to bus rapid transit, the average travel speed increased by 25 percent to 14 miles per hour. In Vancouver, similar upgrades led to similar increases in travel speed.

Privatization

Most cities in the United States restrict entry into the market for transit service, resulting in transit monopolies. Firms are prohibited from providing services that compete with the local transit operator. For example, a taxi cannot serve as a common carrier, meaning that a taxi cannot pick up additional passengers, either along the route chosen by a passenger or along a route chosen by the driver.

Under privatization, private firms are allowed to provide some types of urban transportation services. Some cities specify transit service characteristics (for example, fares and bus stops) and contract with private firms to provide the service. This approach is sometimes used to serve low-density areas, for example with dial-a-ride taxi service. A more aggressive approach is for the public sector to exit a particular transit market and allow firms to enter. In some cases, entering firms are regulated like public utilities, and in other cases, firms are subject to the usual regulations for safety.

Privatization can be used to diversify the set of transit options available in U.S. cities. The conventional system has two extremes–solo rider taxis and large transit vehicles–leaving room between the extremes for private firms. The term *paratransit* describes a wide variety of services that fall between the extremes of the taxi and the conventional bus.

1. *Shared-ride taxis.* During World War II, shared-ride taxis thrived in Washington, DC. Cab drivers displayed their destinations, allowing travelers along the route to hail cabs going their way.
2. *Jitneys (6–15 passengers).* Compared to a conventional bus, a jitney or minibus has lower capital and operating costs and can provide more frequent service along low-density routes.
3. *Subscription vans and buses (10–60 passengers).* Riders pay in advance for commuter service. Compared to public buses, operating costs are lower, in part because private firms pay lower wages.

Transit Systems and Land-Use Patterns

There is no doubt that urban transportation systems affect land use patterns. As we saw in earlier chapters, the large monocentric city of the early 20th century resulted from the combination of (i) streetcars for commuters, (ii) horse carts for manufacturing inputs and outputs, and (iii) sidewalks for face time among information (office) workers in the city center. The development of the truck and the interstate highway system contributed to the suburbanization of manufacturing employment, and the development of information technology contributed to the suburbanization of information employment. The development of the automobile freed workers from their reliance on walking and streetcars, contributing to suburbanization. These fundamental changes in transportation technology changed land-use patterns.

How does a city's public transit system affect land-use patterns? Specifically, does building a rail transit system increase density around transit stations and thus increase the demand for rail transit? The experience in Atlanta suggests that transit supply does not create transit demand. The MARTA system is a heavy-rail system with 74 miles of track. Between 1990 and 1999, the population of Atlanta grew by 700,000, but only 2 percent of the additional residents chose residential locations that were accessible to MARTA (within 800 meters of a station), and only 1 percent of the additional jobs were accessible to MARTA (Bertaud, 2003). This suggests a weak connection between transit design and urban form, at least in Atlanta.

The experience of BART in San Francisco also suggests a weak connection between transit design and land-use patterns. Studies of the system suggest that it had a moderately positive effect on employment near the stations in downtown San Francisco, but not much of an effect elsewhere (Cervero and Landis, 1995). This is consistent with studies of other rail systems. The general conclusion is that if land-use policies such as zoning and property taxation generate a high-density area, rail transit provides an efficient system to transport a large number of workers to the dense employment area.

REVIEW THE CONCEPTS

1. For the United States as a whole, roughly one in [_____] commuters use public transit, compared to roughly one in [_____] central-city commuters and one in [_____] commuters in the New York metropolitan area.
2. The cost of a commuter trip equals [_____] + [_____] + [_____].
3. On average, the marginal disutility of walk-wait time is [_____] percent of the wage, compared to [_____] percent for in-vehicle time.
4. The relative cost of bus transit is lower in high-density environments because of shorter [_____] and the feasibility of [_____].
5. The overall price elasticity of demand for public transit is −[_____]. The demand for peak period travel is [_____] elastic than the demand for off-peak travel. An increase in transit fares [_____] {↑, ↓, −} total fare revenue.
6. Transit ridership is more responsive to change in [_____] than to changes in [_____], and more responsive to changes in [_____] time than to changes in [_____] time.

7. The provision of public transportation is subject to economies of scale in [______] and economies of scale in [______].
8. An increase in transit ridership [______] the average time per rider because an increase in ridership [______] the bus headway, defined as the time [______].
9. Scale economies in ridership mean that an additional rider generates an [______] for other riders. In contrast, traffic congestion means that an additional driver imposes an [______] on other travelers.
10. A transit subsidy is justified on efficiency grounds because for the efficient number of transit riders, [______] < [______].
11. Transit subsidies [______] {↑, ↓, –} transit operating cost, and solution to this problem is to switch from [______] subsidies to a subsidy per [______].
12. The long-run average cost curve for an automobile-based system is [______] because as traffic volume increases, the roadway is [______].
13. The long-run average cost curve for a bus system is [______] sloped because of economies of scale in [______] and economies of scale in [______].
14. Compared to an equivalent bus line, a light-rail line typically has a [______] (choose higher, lower) capital cost per passenger and a [______] (choose higher, lower) operating cost per passenger.
15. The experience of Atlanta suggests that transit [______] does not create transit [______]: a [______] fraction of new residents and new jobs located close to the transit network.
16. For each pair of variables, indicate whether the relationship is positive, negative, neutral, or ambiguous.

Parameter	Choice Variable	Relationship
disutility of walk and wait	bus cost relative to car cost	[______]
disutility of in-vehicle time	rail cost relative to car cost	[______]
traveler income	bus cost relative to car cost	[______]
price of bus	bus ridership	[______]
price of bus	bus total fare revenue	[______]

APPLY THE CONCEPTS

1. *Changes in Transit Service*
   Consider a city that decreases the distances between bus stops, which decreases the walking time of bus riders by 20 percent, increases the in-vehicle (line-haul) time by 10 percent, and increases operating cost by 5 percent. On the typical bus line, the initial ridership is 1,000 riders per hour. Suppose the elasticity of transit ridership with respect to (i) line-haul time = −0.40, (ii) access time = −0.70, and (iii) fare = −0.40.
   a. Suppose the fare is fixed. Predict the change in ridership.
   b. Suppose the transit operator passes on the higher operating cost in the form of an increased fare. Predict the change in ridership.

2. *Pricing Bus Service*
Suppose the demand curve for bus service is linear, with a vertical intercept of \$5.00. If the objective of the city is to maximize bus fare revenue, the appropriate price is \$[_____] because . . .
3. *Auto Pricing and Transit Deficit*
Consider a city where the fixed cost of a transit system is \$140 per hour. The long-run marginal cost is constant at \$1 per rider. The demand curve is linear, with a vertical intercept of \$11 and a slope of \$0.10 per rider.
   a. Illustrate the equilibrium under marginal-cost pricing, including values for price, ridership, and the transit deficit per rider.
   b. Suppose the city internalizes the externalities from automobiles, and the willingness to pay for transit increases by \$4 at each ridership level. Illustrate the new equilibrium, including values for price, ridership, and the transit deficit per rider.
4. *Ridership Economies*
You dispatch city buses to pick up riders at point A and transport them to point B. The capacity of the bus is 60 riders, and your objective is to fill each bus. Riders arrive at point A at a rate of r riders per minute. The opportunity cost of waiting for a bus is $t =$ \$0.20 per minute. Suppose new apartment complex increases the number of riders and increases the arrival rate from $r = 4$ to $r = 5$. The ridership economies generated by the apartment complex decrease the average cost of bus travel by \$[_____], computed as . . .
5. *Sidewalk Drones*
Suppose a city with a bus system gives each of its citizens a personal sidewalk drone. A sidewalk drone transports one dangling commuter at an altitude of 3 meters above sidewalks for a maximum distance of 1 kilometer. The drones are small enough to be carried in a large purse or a briefcase and are equipped with a force-field accessory that makes travel comfortable even in nasty weather. Use a graph like Figure 19–5 to illustrate the effects of sidewalk drones on the (i) the efficient ridership, (ii) the deficit per rider under efficient pricing, and (iii) the budget-balancing ridership. Recall that the cost curves include transit production costs, but not rider time costs.
6. *Disutility of Vehicle Time: Bus vs. Car*
In drawing the cost curves in Figure 19–6, the authors assumed that the disutility of time spent riding a bus is the same as the disutility of time driving a car. Consider two possible factors that affect the disutility of travel time: (i) the armpit factor and (ii) the media-access effect (read a book or check social media).
   a. How do these two factors affect the disutility of travel?
   b. Draw a new set of cost curves consistent with your personal preferences and travel disutilities. Explain the placement of your cost curves relative to the curves in Figure 19–6.
7. *Average Cost for Light Rail*
Use a graph like Figure 19–6 to show the long-run average cost of a light-rail system. Draw the light-rail curve along with the curves for BART and a bus system. Explain your placement of the light-rail curve in terms of capital cost and operating cost.

REFERENCES AND READING

1. American Public Transit Association, *Transit Fact Book 2010.* Washington, DC, 2010.
2. Bertaud, Alain. "Clearing the Air in Atlanta: Transit and Smart Growth or Conventional Economics?" *Journal of Urban Economics* 54 (2003), pp. 379–400.
3. de Palma, Andre, Robin Lindsey, and Nathalie Picard, "Urban Passenger Travel Demand," Chapter 16 in *A Companion to Urban Economics,* edited by Richard J. Arnott and Daniel P. McMillen. New York: Wiley-Blackwell, 2006.
4. Duranton, Gilles, and Matthew Turner, "Urban Growth and Transportation." *Review of Economic Studies* 79 (2012), pp. 1407–40.
5. Giuliano, Genevieve, "Transportation Policy: Public Transit, Settlement Patterns, and Equity in the U.S.," Chapter 25 in *The Oxford Handbook of Urban Economics and Planning,* edited by Nancy Brooks, Kieran Donaghy, and Gerrit-Jan Knaap. New York: Oxford University Press, 2011.
6. Gomez-Ibanez, Jose A. "A Dark Side to Light Rail?" *Journal of the American Planning Association* 51 (Summer 1985), pp. 337–51.
7. Kahn, Matthew. "Gentrification Trends in New Transit-Oriented Communities: Evidence from 14 Cities That Expanded and Build Rail Transit Systems." *Real Estate Economics* 35 (2007).
8. Nelwon, Peter, et al., "Transit in Washington, DC: Current Benefits and Optimal Level of Provision." *Journal of Urban Economics* 62 (2007), pp. 231–51.
9. Parry, Ian, and Kenneth Small, "Should Urban Transit Subsidies Be Reduced?" *American Economic Review* 99 (2009), pp. 700–24.
10. Reynolds-Feighan, Aisling, and Roger Vickerman, "Transportation Economics for Planners in the 21st Century," Chapter 24 in *The Oxford Handbook of Urban Economics and Planning,* edited by Nancy Brooks, Kieran Donaghy, and Gerrit-Jan Knaap. New York: Oxford University Press, 2011.
11. Rietveld, Piet, "Urban Transport Policies: The Dutch Struggle with Market Failures and Policy Failures," Chapter 18 in *A Companion to Urban Economics,* edited by Richard J. Arnott and Daniel P. McMillen. New York: Wiley-Blackwell, 2006.
12. Small, Kenneth A., "Transportation: Urban Transportation Policy," Chapter 3 in *Making Cities Work: Prospects and Policies for Urban America,* edited by Robert P. Inman. Princeton NJ: Princeton University Press, 2009.
13. Small, Kenneth, and Erik Verhoef, *The Economics of Urban Transportation.* New York: Routledge, 2007.

PART FIVE

Local Government, Education, and Crime

Part Five of the book explores the various roles of local government in a federal system of government. Chapter 20 provides an overview of the role of local government and explores several mechanisms for making decisions, including voting with ballots and voting with feet. As we'll see, majority rule is generally not efficient rule. Chapter 21 looks at the two largest revenue sources for local government: intergovernmental grants and the property tax. We explore the issue of who actually pays property taxes and how local governments respond to grants from states and the national government. Chapter 22 focuses on K–12 education and uses the production-function approach to assess the contributions of various inputs (teachers, parents, peers) to student achievement, measured in the short run by test scores and in the long run by adult income. Chapter 23 uses the model of a rational criminal as a framework to evaluate the merits of various policies developed in response to crime, including investment in human capital.

CHAPTER 20

The Role of Local Government

Pedro: Do you think people will vote for me?
Napoleon Dynamite: Heck yes! I'd vote for you.
Pedro: Like what are my skills?
Napoleon Dynamite: Well, you have a sweet bike. And you're really good at hooking up with chicks. Plus you're like the only guy at school who has a mustache.

—FROM THE MOVIE *NAPOLEON DYNAMITE* (2004)

Democracy is the worst form of government except all the others that have been tried.

—WINSTON CHURCHILL

Local governments provide a wide variety of goods and services, including schooling, public safety, parks, and transit systems. In this chapter we provide an overview of local public goods and discuss the role of local government in a federal system of government. We explore alternative mechanisms to choose the level of local public goods, including majority rule, benefit taxation, and sorting households with respect to demand for local public goods, also known as "voting with your feet." As we'll see, majority rule is unlikely to generate the efficient level of a local public good.

In 2012, more than 90,000 local governments provided goods and services in the United States, including more than 38,000 general-purpose governments and more than 51,000 special-purpose governments.

1. General purpose governments perform a number of functions, including financial administration, police protection, highway administration, hospitals, and utilities. The tally of general-purpose governments include counties (3,031), municipalities (19,519), and townships (16,360).
2. Special-purpose governments perform a single function or a few functions. The tally includes 12,880 independent school districts and 38,266 special districts. A special district may serve a single function in a large municipality or may serve as a regional entity in a rural setting. Among the special districts are mosquito-abatement districts, utility districts, water and sewer districts, and transit authorities.

TABLE 20–1 Per-Capita Spending by Local Governments, 2012

Total	Education	Police	Public Assistance	Highways	Public Transit	Fire Protection	Other
4,919	1,711	300	262	190	171	134	2,151

Source: 2012 Census of Governments, Washington, DC: US Census Bureau.

1. ROLE OF LOCAL GOVERNMENT

Table 20–1 shows per-capita spending by local governments in 2012. Roughly one-third of local spending went to education, and the other large spending programs include police, public assistance (including transfer payments and housing assistance), highways, public transit, and fire protection.

Three Roles for Government

What is the role of local government in the market economy? Musgrave and Musgrave (1980) distinguish between three roles for government.

1. *Stabilization.* The government uses monetary and fiscal policy to control unemployment and inflation.
2. *Income redistribution.* The government uses taxes and transfers to alter the distributions of income and wealth.
3. *Resource allocation.* The government makes decisions about what to produce and how to produce it. When the government actually produces a particular good or service, it makes these resource allocation decisions directly. When the government subsidizes or taxes private activities, it influences the resource allocation decisions of the private sector.

The national government has assumed the responsibility for stabilization policy for two reasons. First, although each local government could print its own money and execute its own monetary policy, such a system would be chaotic. Instead, the national government prints the money and manages a national monetary policy. Second, because a large fraction of local income is spent on goods produced outside the local area, local monetary and fiscal policies would be relatively weak and ineffective. Fiscal policy is more effective at the national level because a relatively small fraction of national income is spent on imports.

Consider next the distribution role of government. Local attempts to redistribute income will be frustrated by the mobility of taxpayers and transfer recipients. Suppose that a city imposes a tax on its wealthy citizens and provides transfer payments to the poor. To escape the tax, some wealthy households will leave the city, causing a decrease in total tax revenue. At the same time, some poor households will migrate to the relatively generous city, causing a decrease in the transfer payment per recipient. In combination, the flight of the wealthy and the migration of the poor will weaken the city's redistribution program. A national redistribution program is more effective because there is less mobility between nations than between cities.

The third role of government is resource allocation, which involves decisions that determine how an economy's resources are allocated to different goods and services. As shown in Table 20-1, local governments provide education, police services, public transit, highways, and fire protection. Among the "other" goods and services are parks and water systems.

Local Government in a Federal System

Under the federal system of government, the responsibility for providing public goods is divided between the national, state, and local governments. Some goods, such as defense and space exploration, are provided at the national level. Others, such as education and police protection, are provided at the local level. Oates (1972) discusses the advantages and disadvantages of the local provision of public goods.

1. *Diversity in demand.* As we will see later in the chapter, households differ in their demands for local public goods, and this diversity can be accommodated by a system of small municipalities and school districts, each providing a different mix of local public goods and taxes.
2. *Externalities.* For some locally provided products, benefits spill over to people outside the municipality or school district. In this case, local voters will ignore the benefits of outsiders, generating inefficient choices.
3. *Scale economies.* If there are scale economies in the provision of public goods, a system of small local governments has a relatively high production cost.

The local provision of a public good is efficient if the advantages outweigh the disadvantages. In other words, local provision is efficient if (1) diversity in demand is relatively large, (2) externalities are relatively small in a geographic sense, and (3) scale economies are relatively small.

What are the facts on scale economies in the provision of local public goods? There have been dozens of studies of the relationship between production costs and jurisdiction sizes. The evidence suggests that there are moderate scale economies in the provision of water and sewage services. Because these services are capital intensive, average cost decreases as population increases. In contrast, studies of other local public goods (police protection, fire protection, schools) suggest that scale economies are exhausted with a relatively small population–about 100,000. Many small cities use intergovernmental contracts and joint service contracts to join forces and exploit scale economies in the provision of public services.

The most important trade-off associated with local service provision is between diversity of demand and externalities. Metropolitan government will be more efficient than municipal government if interjurisdictional spillovers are large relative to diversity in demand. In this case, the advantages of a small local government (the ability to accommodate diverse demands for local public goods) are relatively small, and the disadvantages (the inefficiencies associated with externalities that cross municipal boundaries) are relatively large. Therefore, a metropolitan system of government will be more efficient.

One solution to the spillover problem is a system of subsidies from a higher level of government. If the municipality receives a subsidy equal to the marginal external benefit of the public good, it bases its spending decisions on the marginal social benefit of the good. In the next chapter, we'll explore the effects of intergovernmental grants on local spending.

Another response to spillovers is to grant governmental bodies the power to deal with specific urban problems that cross municipal boundaries. Many economists and geographers believe that metropolitan areas–not municipalities or states–are the most important spatial units in today's economy. As discussed by Anthony Downs (1998), it would be sensible to establish policy-making organizations for the entire metropolitan area because the various spatial sections of each metropolitan area are linked together in a series of densely interlocking networks. These networks transcend the boundaries of most individual communities.

Among these networks are streets and highways, water systems, sewage-disposal systems, school systems, airsheds, and watersheds. Some of the problems that cross jurisdictional boundaries are highway congestion, air pollution, crime, and low educational achievement. In the current political system, the power to deal with these problems is divided among many small jurisdictions, most of which contain only a small fraction of the people affected by the problems. Two metropolitan areas–Portland, Oregon, and the Twin Cities in Minnesota–have governmental bodies with the power to deal with problems that cross municipal boundaries.

2. LOCAL PUBLIC GOODS: EFFICIENCY AND MECHANISMS

A local public good has three characteristics, two of which it shares with a conventional public good. A public good is defined as a good that is available for everyone to consume, regardless of who pays and who doesn't. More precisely, a pure public good has two features.

1. *Nonrival.* One person's benefit from a public good does not reduce another person's benefit from the public good. For example, farmer A's benefit from a flood-control dam doesn't reduce farmer B's benefit from the dam.
2. *Nonexcludable.* It is impractical to exclude people who don't pay for the good. If one farmer refuses to participate in a voluntary arrangement to pay for a dam, the farmer would still benefit from flood protection.

Some examples of public goods are national defense, space exploration, the protection of the earth's ozone layer, and fireworks shows. Many of the goods provided by local governments are impure or contestable in the sense that if enough people use the good, each person reduces the benefit to others. For example, if enough people use a city park, they get in others' way, and frisbees fly into birthday cakes. As we saw earlier in the book, streets and highways are subject to congestion during peak travel periods.

For a local public good, we add a third characteristic. The benefits of a local public good are confined to a relatively small geographical area—a municipality or a metropolitan area. Unlike national defense, which generates benefits for the entire nation, most of the benefits of the local police force and local fire department go to local citizens. Similarly, local citizens get most of the benefits from local streets and highways. The appropriate size of the jurisdiction is determined by the "localness" of the public good— the geographical extent of the benefits from the good. The more widespread the benefits, the larger the jurisdiction required to contain all the beneficiaries.

The Efficient Level of a Local Public Good

Consider a three-person city that provides public parks. Citizens in the city vary in their demand for park land and will collectively decide how many acres to provide. Specifically, the number of park acres will be determined by majority rule.

Figure 20-1 shows three individual demand curves for park land, one for each citizen. An individual demand curve shows a consumer's willingness to pay for a product, so it is a marginal-benefit curve. Lois has the relatively low marginal-benefit curve mb_1 and is willing to pay \$20 for the 6th acre of park land (point *a*). In contrast, Marian has a medium demand and marginal benefit curve mb_2, and is willing to pay \$28 for the 6th acre (point *b*). Hiram, with the high marginal-benefit curve mb_3, is willing to pay \$40 for the 6th acre (point *c*).

What is the social benefit of park land? Because land in an uncrowded park is a non-rival good, the social benefit is the sum of the private benefits. To compute the marginal social benefit of a public good, we add the individual marginal benefits. In Figure 20-1, the marginal social benefit of the 6th acre is \$88 (point *d*), equal to the

FIGURE 20-1 The Efficient Level of a Public Good

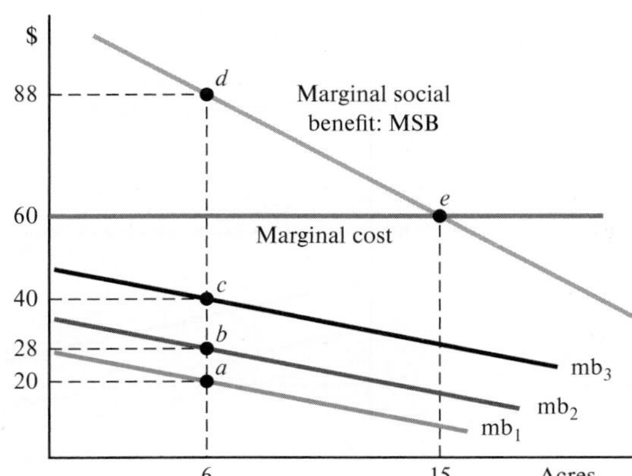

sum of the marginal private benefits of $20 for Lois, $28 for Marian, and $40 for Hiram. Similarly, for other park sizes, we add the individual marginal benefits to get the marginal social benefit. For example, as shown by point *e*, the marginal social benefit of the 15th acre is $60. The marginal social benefit curve is the vertical sum of the individual demand (marginal benefit) curves.

What is the efficient size of the public park? At the efficient level, the marginal social benefit of park land equals the marginal cost. In Figure 20–1, the marginal cost is $60 per acre, so the efficient land area is 15 acres. For any quantity less than 15 acres, citizens in the city would collectively be willing to pay more than $60 for an additional acre, so an additional acre would increase social welfare. For example, suppose the city starts at 6 acres. As shown by point *d* on the marginal social benefit curve, citizens are willing to pay a total of $88 for one more acre. If the marginal cost is only $60, another acre would generate a net gain of $28 for citizens in the city. In contrast, for any amount exceeding 15 acres, the total willingness to pay for the last acre is less than the marginal cost, so a program with fewer acres would more efficient.

Majority Rule and the Decisive Median Voter

Figure 20–2 shows that voters in the 3-person city will disagree about the size of the park. If the cost per acre is $60, a voter's tax bill equals $20 times the number of acres. For each voter, the marginal cost of an acre of park land is $20. Applying the marginal principle, each voter will prefer the number of acres at which the voter's marginal benefit equals the $20 marginal cost. For Lois, the marginal benefit equals the marginal cost at point *a*, so she favors 6 acres. Similarly, Marian favors 12 acres (point *m*), and Hiram favors 22 acres (point *h*). The diversity in demand for the public good means that citizens disagree about how much of the local public good to provide.

Under majority rule, voters will choose Marian's preferred program of 12 acres. Suppose the city holds a series of pairwise elections between the favored programs.

FIGURE 20–2 Voter Disagreement

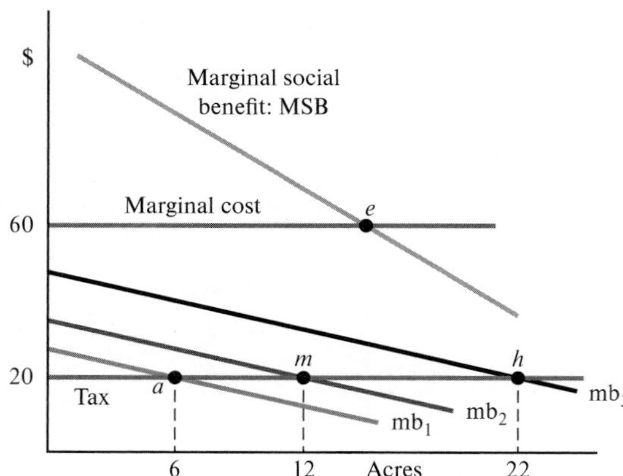

TABLE 20-2 The Median Voter Is Decisive

Election	Vote for 6 Acres	Vote for 12 Acres	Vote for 22 Acres
6 vs. 12	Lois	Marian & Hiram	–
12 vs. 22	–	Marian & Lois	Hiram

As shown in Table 20-2, in an election between 6 acres (Lois's favorite) and 12 acres (Marian's favorite), Hiram joins Marian to approve Marian's favorite. In an election between Marian's favorite and Hiram's favorite (22 acres), Lois joins Marian to approve Marian's favorite. Marian's preferred size wins both elections because she is the median voter, defined as the voter who splits other voters into two equal halves. Marian wins because she can always get one voter to join her to defeat any alternative to her favored program. This is the median-voter result: the outcome of majority rule is the preference of the median voter.

Majority voting is unlikely to generate the efficient level of a public good. In our example, Marian the median voter favors a quantity (12 acres) that is less than the efficient quantity (15 acres), so the city chooses an inefficiently small park. If the city had a direct election between the efficient program (15) and the program favored by the median voter (12), the median program would win: Lois would join Marian to defeat the efficient program. Because there is no reason to expect the median voter to favor the efficient quantity, majority voting is likely to generate an inefficient outcome.

To illustrate the power and inefficiency of the median-voter result, consider a simple thought experiment. Suppose the marginal private benefit of the high-demand consumer increases. Figure 20-3 shows the implications for the level of the public good chosen by majority rule and the efficient level. The increase in the marginal private benefit shifts the marginal social benefit curve upward, and the efficient

FIGURE 20-3 Majority Rule Is Not Efficient Rule

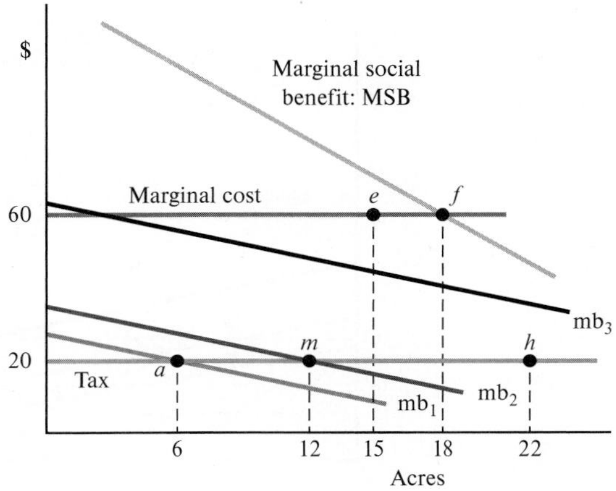

number of acres increases from 15 (point *e*) to 18 (point *f*). But since the preferences of the median voter haven't changed, the voting outcome doesn't change (point *m*, with 12 acres). The median voter is decisive, so the preferences of other voters are irrelevant.

Benefit Taxation

As we've seen, the equilibrium under majority rule is unlikely to be efficient. One way to promote the efficient choice under majority rule is to vary the tax liabilities of individual citizens: a citizen who receives a relatively large benefit pays a relatively high tax.

Under a Lindahl tax (named after economist Erik Lindahl), a citizen's tax liability is proportional to the citizen's willingness to pay for the public good. Figure 20–4 continues our example of a city's park program. The first step for the government is to determine the efficient level of the public good, which in our example is 15 acres (point *e*). The second step is to allocate the cost of the public good according to citizens' willingness to pay (marginal benefit). At the efficient quantity, Hiram's marginal benefit is $30, so that's his tax liability per acre. Similarly, Marian pays a tax of $18 per acre, and Lois pays $12 per acre.

The benefit-tax plan covers the cost of the efficient park program and generates unanimous support for the program. The taxes paid by the three citizens add up to $60 per acre, the price of an acre. For each citizen, the marginal cost (the tax per acre) equals the marginal private benefit at 15 acres, so each voter favors a program with 15 acres. The benefit tax generates the efficient outcome because it matches diversity in demand for the public goods with diversity in tax liabilities. The citizens with the greatest benefits pay the highest acre tax. The citizens with relatively low benefits pay relatively low taxes, so they vote in favor of a relatively large program.

FIGURE 20–4 Benefit Taxation

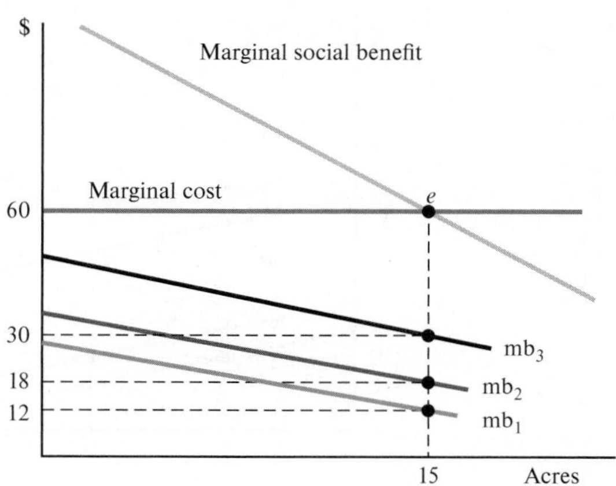

Is benefit taxation practical? One problem is that we cannot observe citizens' marginal-benefit curves, so we cannot precisely determine the appropriate taxes. We can't simply ask citizens to reveal their willingness to pay because each citizen has an incentive to understate their willingness to pay if that means a lower tax. But for some public goods such as parks or public safety, the benefit from local public goods may be roughly proportional to property value, so a property tax serves roughly as a benefit tax. Similarly, if the benefits from local public goods increase with income, an income tax serves roughly as a benefit tax.

The Tiebout Model: Voting with Feet

As we've seen, majority rule generates an equilibrium quantity equal to the preferred choice of the median voter. For other voters, the equilibrium quantity is either too large or too small. One option for dissatisfied citizens is to vote with their feet. A citizen could move to a jurisdiction that provides a level of public goods closer to the citizen's preferred level. In our example, suppose the citizens live in a metropolitan area with many municipalities, each of which has its own park program. Lois could move to a municipality with a relatively small park (6 acres), and Hiram could move to a municipality with a relatively large park (22 acres). By voting with their feet, citizens sort themselves into communities of like-minded citizens, and each citizen gets its favored program.

The Tiebout model is a formal model of interjurisdictional mobility. The simple version of the Tiebout model is based on five assumptions.

1. *Municipal choice.* A household chooses the municipality (or school district or other local jurisdiction) that provides the household's favored level of local public goods. There are enough municipalities to ensure that every household finds the perfect jurisdiction.
2. *Perfect information and mobility.* All citizens have access to all relevant information about the alternative municipalities, and moving is costless.
3. *No interjurisdictional spillovers.* There are no spillovers (externalities) associated with local public goods: All the benefits from local public goods accrue to citizens within the municipality.
4. *No scale economies.* The average cost of production is independent of output.
5. *Head tax.* A municipality pays for its public goods with a head tax: If you have a head, you pay the head tax.

Under the Tiebout process, households will sort themselves into municipalities according to their demand for parks. Suppose three low-demand citizens form a municipality called Loisville. The marginal social benefit of six acres is three times $20, or $60, the same as the marginal social cost of park acreage. When each voter pays a tax of $20 per acre, they will all prefer six acres, so they will vote unanimously for the efficient park. Similarly, if three Marians form a municipality, they will choose the efficient park for medium demanders—12 acres. The sorting of citizens into homogeneous municipalities eliminates the inefficiencies of majority rule because everyone in a homogeneous municipality has the same preferred level of the local public good.

3. A CLOSER LOOK AT THE MEDIAN-VOTER RESULT

We have explained the median-voter result in the context of a direct election with three citizens. In this part of the chapter, we'll take a closer look at voting, showing the general applicability of the median-voter result and its limitations. Many local jurisdictions, including most central, large, and heterogeneous populations, and decisions about local public goods are determined by voting with ballots rather than feet.

The Median Voter in a Representative Democracy

In a representative democracy, elected officials make budgetary decisions. A citizen votes for the candidate whose expressed budget position is closest to the citizen's preferred budget. Suppose there are two candidates for a seat in a legislative body, and the key issue is spending on public education. There is a uniform distribution of voter preferences, and there are 10 voters in each \$1 interval from \$1 to \$11. We can use Figure 20–5 to show the Nash equilibrium.

- *Panel 1: Small and big budgets.* Penny initially proposes a \$3 budget and Buck proposes a \$9 budget. Penny gets voters with preferred budgets through \$5, while Buck gets voters with preferred budgets of \$7 and higher. The two candidates split the voters with a preferred budget of \$6. The result is a tie vote, 55 to 55.

FIGURE 20–5 The Median Voter in a Representative Democracy

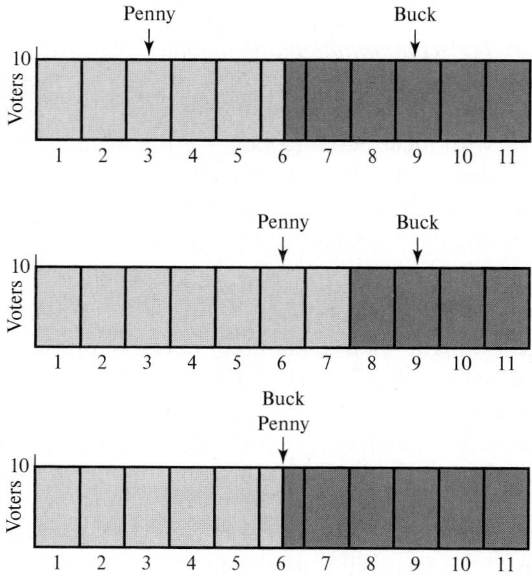

- *Panel 2: Unilateral deviation by Penny to the median budget ($6).* Suppose Penny increases her proposed budget to the median budget: half the voters prefer a budget less than $6, and half prefer a larger budget. Penny's unilateral deviation tilts the election in her favor. She gets voters with preferred budgets $1 through $7, while Buck gets voters with higher preferred budgets. Penny wins, 70–40.
- *Panel 3: Unilateral deviation by Buck to the median budget.* If buck proposes the median budget, his unilateral deviation causes 15 voters to switch in his favor. Penny gets voters with preferred budgets $1 through $5, while Buck gets voters with preferred budgets $7 through $10. The candidates split the voters with a $6 preferred budget, generating a tie vote, 55–55.

When both candidates reach the median budget, there is no incentive for unilateral deviation. Any move away from the median would move a candidate away from a majority of voters and toward a minority of voters, so the candidate will lose the election. In the Nash equilibrium, both candidates propose the budget of the median voter.

The key to the median-voter result is the competition for voters in the middle. As long as Penny proposes a smaller budget than Buck, citizens with relatively small preferred budgets will continue to vote for her. The benefit of moving toward the median is that Penny takes some votes in the middle from Buck. Similarly, Buck doesn't have to worry about people with relatively large preferred budgets but can concentrate instead on the battle for voters in the middle. The result is that the two candidates adopt virtually the same position, the position of the median voter. The median-voter result suggests the choices made by elected officials will match the preferences of the median voter.

Implications of the Median-Voter Result

The median-voter result provides a strategy to predict the outcome of an election. We identify the median voter, and then estimate his or her preferred budget. As a practical matter, it may be difficult to identify the median voter. One approach is to assume that the desired spending depends on income, so the person with the median income is the median voter. Of course, if the desired spending depends on other variables (for example, household size, age, or political philosophy), a prediction based on the preferences of the median-income voter will be a rough estimate.

We can also use the median-voter result to estimate the elasticities of demand for local public goods. Consider two cities, one with a small police budget ($100 per capita) and a low median income ($1,000), and a second with a large police budget ($125 per capita) and high median income ($1,200). Assume that the "price" of police services (the opportunity cost of money spent on police) is the same in the two cities. The income elasticity of demand for police services is defined as the percentage change in the police budget divided by the percentage change in income. City L, with 20 percent higher income, has a 25 percent larger police budget, so the income elasticity of demand is 1.25 (25 percent divided by 20 percent).

TABLE 20–3 Income and Price Elasticities of Demand for Local Public Goods

Public Good or Service	Income Elasticity	Price Elasticity
Total expenditures	0.34 to 0.89	−0.23 to −0.56
Education	0.24 to 0.85	−0.07 to −0.51
Parks and recreation	0.99 to 1.32	−0.19 to −0.92
Public safety (police and fire)	0.52 to 0.71	−0.19 to −1.0
Public works	0.79	−0.92 to −1.0

Source: Inman, Robert, "The Fiscal Performance of Local Governments." In *Current Issues in Urban Economics,* eds. Peter Mieszkowski and Mahlon Straszheim. Baltimore: Johns Hopkins University Press, 1979.

Table 20–3 summarizes the results of empirical studies based on the median-voter model. For total expenditures, the estimated income elasticity is between 0.34 and 0.89. The largest income elasticity is for parks and recreation.

We can also use the median-voter result to estimate the price elasticities of demand for local public goods. If the price of local public goods varies across municipalities, we can use the median-voter model to draw the demand curve for local public goods and compute the price elasticity of demand. To plot the demand curve for local spending, we need information on price (the opportunity cost of local spending) and quantity (the local spending level). As shown in Table 20–3, the demands for local public goods are price-inelastic; the price elasticities are all less than or equal to 1.0 in absolute value.

Limitations of the Median-Voter Result

The median-voter model has a number of unrealistic assumptions. Although the model provides a useful framework for thinking about voting outcomes, three assumptions limit the model's applicability.

1. *Ideology.* The model assumes that politicians care only about winning elections, meaning that they slavishly adhere to voter preferences. Alternatively, a candidate could base his or her position on basic principles and ideology, and use election campaigns to persuade voters that the candidate's position is the best position. In other words, a candidate could be a leader rather than a follower.
2. *Single issue.* If there are several issues (e.g., police budget, park budget, policies for the homeless) in an election campaign, each candidate will offer a bundle of proposed policies to voters, and the median voter is elusive.
3. *All citizens vote.* In real elections, only a fraction of eligible voters cast ballots. From the perspective of an individual citizen, the benefit of voting will be relatively small if (i) the candidates are so close to each other that it makes little difference who wins (voter indifference) or (ii) the best candidate is so far from a citizen's position that the citizen is alienated from the election process (voter alienation). If some citizens abstain from voting, the median-voter result will not necessarily occur because changes in the candidates' positions affects voter participation.

REVIEW THE CONCEPTS

1. A pure public good is [______] in consumption and [______].
2. The marginal social benefit curve for a public good is the [______] sum of [______] curves.
3. In Figure 20–1, suppose that for 15 acres, $mb_1 = \$12$ and $mb_2 = \$18$. Then $mb_3 = \$$[______].
4. Under majority rule, voters will choose the level of the public good preferred by the [______].
5. In Figure 20–2, suppose Marian's marginal-benefit curve shifts to a position above Hiram's curve. Under majority rule, the equilibrium number of acres is [______] acres.
6. Under Lindahl (benefit) taxation, a voter's tax bill for a public good is proportional to the voter's [______].
7. Lindahl (benefit) taxation promotes efficient choice of public goods because each citizen pays a tax equal to the [______] of the [______] quantity of the public good.
8. For each pair of variables, indicate whether the relationship is positive, negative, neutral, or ambiguous. For a local public good, G^* is the equilibrium level under majority rule and a head tax, and G^E is the efficient level. The marginal private benefit of an individual citizen is *mpb*.

Parameter	Choice Variable	Relationship
number of citizens	G^E	[______]
marginal cost of public good	G^E	[______]
mpb	G^E	[______]
mpb: median voter	G^*	[______]
mpb: non-median voter	G^*	[______]

APPLY THE CONCEPTS

1. *Fire Protection*
   The marginal private benefit of a county's flood-protection program is $mb(G) = V/100 - G/2$ where V is the market value of the property and G is the height of a flood-protection dam. For example, the marginal private benefit for a citizen with a market value of \$200,000 is $mb(G) = 200 - G/2$. There are three citizens, with $V = \$60{,}000$, \$80,000, and \$160,000. The marginal cost of flood protection is \$150. Illustrate the efficient outcome (G^E) and the outcome under majority rule (G^*), including values for G^E and G^*.
2. *Negative Benefit*
   Consider the example shown in Figure 20–1. Suppose Lois leaves town and is replaced by Sneezy, whose allergies are triggered by plants in public parks. Sneezy's marginal private benefit of park land is –\$8 per acre. Illustrate the efficient outcome, including a value for A^E.

3. *Efficient Park*
Suppose the marginal private benefit of park acreage is $mb = 12 - A/10$, where A is the number of acres. The marginal cost of park acreage is \$400. Consider a city of 100 citizens.
   d. The efficient park acreage is A^E = [______]. Illustrate.
   e. Suppose the city tentatively decides on $A = 20$. Describe a Pareto improvement in which each citizen gets the same benefit from an additional acre of park.
4. *Efficient vs. Equilibrium Fireworks.*
The city of Rocketville has 9 citizens with incomes ranging from \$1 to \$9, with one citizen at each integer value. The marginal private benefit of rockets in a fireworks display is $mb(R) = w - R/9$, where w is income and R is the number of rockets. The marginal cost of a rocket is \$18, and rockets are financed with a head tax (the same tax per citizen).
   a. Illustrate the efficient outcome, including a value for R^E.
   b. Illustrate the outcome under majority rule, including a value for R^*.
   c. Suppose the income of the citizen with the lowest income ($w = \$1$) increases to \$4. Consider the qualitative implications for R^E and R^*. Will the values increase, decrease, or not change?
5. *Fire Protection Upgrade*
An upgrade of a city's fire-protection system has an annual cost of \$300 and will decrease the probability that any particular house is destroyed by fire by 0.001 (one in a thousand). For simplicity, assume that fire insurance is not available, and any house fire reduces the market value of a house to zero. There are 3 houses, with property values \$100,000 for Wanda's house, \$200,000 for Tupak's house, and \$300,000 for Trey's house.
   a. Is the upgrade efficient? Explain.
   b. Under a tax system that generate unanimous support for an efficient upgrade, the tax liabilities are [______] for Wanda, [______] for Tupak, and [______] for Trey.
6. *Surplus from Lindahl Tax*
Under the Lindahl benefit tax shown in Figure 20–3, each citizen pays a per-rocket tax equal to the citizen's marginal benefit at the efficient level (\$12, \$18, \$30). Consider the net benefit or surplus experienced by Lois, whose marginal-benefit curve has a vertical intercept of \$28. For Lois, the net benefit or surplus is \$[______]. Illustrate.
7. *Benefit Tax Numbers*
Consider a four-citizen community where the marginal private benefits of a public good G are:

$$mpb_1 = \frac{1}{G}; \qquad mpb_2 = \frac{2}{G}; \qquad mpb_3 = \frac{3}{G}; \qquad mpb_4 = \frac{4}{G}$$

The marginal cost of the public good is \$2.
   a. The efficient level is G^E = [______] Illustrate.
   b. Compute the benefit-tax liabilities per unit of G for the four citizens. Illustrate.

8. *Predict the Election Outcome*
The citizens of a city have the following preferred park budgets per capita: {$1, $1, $2, $3, $4, $8, $9}.
  a. Suppose Penny proposes a budget of $2 and Buck proposes a budget of $8. Predict the outcome of the election: Who wins, and what is the park budget? Illustrate.
  b. Predict the Nash equilibrium. Who wins, and what is the park budget?

9. *Torn by Indifference?*
Consider the example shown in Figure 20–5. Some of the residents of MehVille abstain from voting if the difference between the two candidates is relatively small. Specifically, half of voters abstain if the difference between the two candidates is less than $2. If the difference is at least $2, everyone votes. Is the median-voter outcome a Nash equilibrium? Illustrate by considering a unilateral deviation by Buck from $6 to $8.

10. *Alienation?*
Consider the example shown in Figure 20–5. A resident of GapVille abstains from voting if the gap between the citizen's preferred budget and the best candidate's expressed budget is greater than $3. Is the median-voter outcome a Nash equilibrium? Illustrate by considering a unilateral deviation by Buck from $6 to $7.

REFERENCES AND READING

1. Ding, Weili, and Steven Lehrer, "Do Peers Affect Student Achievement in China's Secondary Schools?" *Review of Economics and Statistics* 89 (2007), pp. 300–12.
2. Hanushek, Eric, *The Economic Value of Higher Teacher Quality*. Washington, DC: The Urban Institute, 2010.
3. Krueger, Alan, "Experimental Estimates of Educational Production Functions." *Quarterly Journal of Economics* (1999), pp. 497–32.
4. Oates, Wallace E., *Fiscal Federalism*. New York: Harcourt Brace Jovanovich, 1972.
5. Sund, Krister, "Estimating Peer Effects in Swedish High School Using School, Teacher and Student Fixed Effects." *Economics of Education Review* 28 (2009), pp. 329–36.
6. Tiebout, C., "A Pure Theory of Local Expenditures." *Journal of Political Economy* 64 (1956), pp. 416–24.
7. U.S. Bureau of the Census. Census of Governments. 2012.

CHAPTER 21

Local Government Revenue

Sonja: What are you suggesting, passive resistance?
Boris: No, I'm suggesting active fleeing (as he leaps out a window).

—*From the movie* Love and Death (*1975*)

As we saw in the previous chapter, local governments provide a wide variety of goods and services, including schooling, public safety, parks, and transit systems. In this chapter we discuss two of the largest revenue sources of local government: the residential property tax and intergovernmental grants. We address two key questions.

1. Who actually pays the property tax? The person who pays the property tax in a legal sense may change his or her behavior to avoid paying the tax, and this "active fleeing" triggers changes in markets that shift the tax to someone else.
2. What fraction of an intergovernmental grant is spent on the targeted local public good? Local governments respond to intergovernmental grants by cutting taxes, so part of a grant is spent on private goods.

Figure 21-1 shows the distribution of local government revenue from various sources. Roughly one-third of revenue comes from grants from higher levels of government (states and the federal government). School districts are heavily dependent on intergovernmental grants. The property tax generates 27 percent of local revenue, compared to 6 percent from sales taxes and 2 percent from income taxes. Revenue from charges and utilities is responsible for 29 percent of local government revenue. Special districts are heavily dependent on charges and utility revenue.

1. THE PROPERTY TAX

The property tax is an annual tax on residential, commercial, and industrial properties. The total value of a particular property is the value of the structure plus the value of land. For example, suppose a property has a market value of $300,000, with $240,000 for the structure and $60,000 for the land. With a 1 percent property tax, the annual tax liability will be $3,000, equal to $2,400 for the structure plus $600 for the land.

FIGURE 21–1 Revenue Sources for Local Governments

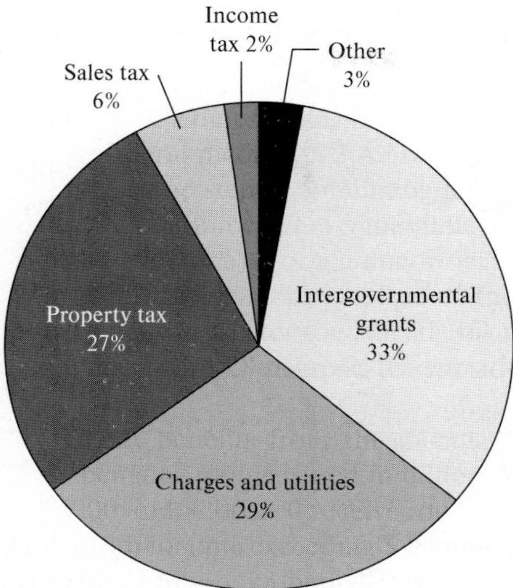

Source: 2012 Census of Governments, Washington, DC: U.S. Census Bureau.

The property tax has a long history, dating back to the ancient worlds of Egypt, Babylon, Persia, and China. As explained by Youngman (2016), the property tax has two key attributes in its favor.

1. *Visibility.* The property tax is highly visible to taxpayers, in contrast to enormously complex income taxes and sales taxes that are applied to thousands of purchases every year. The annual property tax bill provides a clear signal about the cost of local public goods. Taxpayers can compare the tax cost to the benefits of local public goods (schools, fire protection, libraries, and roads), and vote accordingly. In other words, the visibility of the property tax allows citizens to make informed electoral choices.
2. *Resource Immobility.* Part of the property tax is levied on land, a resource that is perfectly immobile even in the long run. Land owners cannot "actively flee" the tax, so the land portion of the tax does not distort behavior and cause inefficiency. In contrast, a local sales tax or a local income tax causes consumers and workers to flee to nearby jurisdictions with lower taxes.

A recent report explores differences in property-tax rates across U.S. cities (Lincoln Institute of Land Policy, 2016). Table 21–1 shows tax rates for some of the cities with the highest and lowest effective tax rates on homestead property (owner-occupied dwellings). The effective tax rate equals the tax liability as a percentage of market value for the median-value home in the city. The table shows the reasons for a relatively high or relative low effective tax rate. The tax rate will be relatively high in cities that have (i) a high reliance on the residential property tax compared to other taxes, (ii) relatively low home values, and (iii) high spending by local governments.

TABLE 21-1 Highest and Lowest Effective Property Tax Rates, 2015

City	Tax Rate (%)	Reliance on Property Tax	Home Values	Local Spending
Bridgeport, CT	3.88	High		
Detroit, MI	3.81		Low	
Aurora, IL	3.72	High		
Newark, NJ	3.05	High		
Milwaukee, WI	2.68	High	Low	
Boston, MA	0.67	Low	High	
Birmingham, AL	0.66	Low		
Denver, CO	0.66	Low	High	
Cheyenne, WY	0.65	Low		
Honolulu, HI	0.30	Low	High	Low

Source: Lincoln Institute, *50-State Property Tax Comparison StudyrFor Taxes Paid in 2015,* June 2016.

For example, Detroit has a relatively high effective tax rate because home values are relatively low. The high rate in Milwaukee results from a high reliance on the residential property tax and low home values. In contrast, the low effective tax rates in Boston and Denver result from a low reliance on the property tax and high home values.

A Simple Model of the Residential Property

We can use a simple model to illustrate the incidence of a residential property tax. Consider a residential city where all land is used for rental housing in the form of mobile homes. The rental housing industry is perfectly competitive, and, in equilibrium, each firm makes zero economic profit. Housing firms produce rental housing with two inputs.

1. *Structures.* A mobile home is a form of physical capital that housing firms rent from capital owners who live elsewhere. A mobile home can be moved costlessly from one city to another.
2. *Land.* Housing firms rent the land under the mobile homes from absentee landowners. The lot size is fixed.

The housing firm rents housing (mobile home and land) to consumers. The initial (pretax) housing rent is \$5,000 per year, equal to \$4,000 for structure rent and \$1,000 for land rent.

We assume that the property tax is paid in a legal sense by housing firms. To simplify matters, suppose the property tax is \$800 per mobile home and \$200 per standard lot. In other words, the property tax is a unit tax rather than a tax based on value. We are interested in the effect of the property tax on housing firms, housing consumers, landowners, and capital owners.

The Land Portion of the Property Tax

Figure 21-2 shows the market effects of the land portion of the property tax. The supply of land is perfectly inelastic, with a fixed supply of 600 lots. The demand for

FIGURE 21-2 The Land Portion of Property Tax

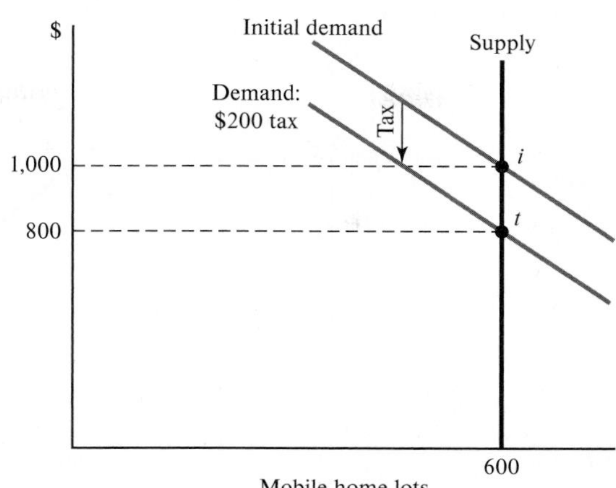

land comes from housing firms, who use it as an input to rental housing. The demand curve intersects the supply curve at point *i*, generating an initial land rent of $1,000 per lot.

The demand curve shows housing firms' willingness to pay for land. If a housing firm pays a tax of $200 per lot, the firm is willing to pay $200 less to the landowner. In Figure 21-1, the $200 land tax shifts the demand curve downward by $200. As shown by point *t*, the new equilibrium rent is $800. The tax decreases land rent paid to landowners by the full amount of the tax because the supply of land is perfectly inelastic. For any land rent above $800, the net price of land to housing firms (rent plus the tax) would exceed $1,000, and the quantity demanded would be less than the fixed supply of 600 lots. Excess supply would cause rent to decrease until it reaches $800.

Structure Portion: Partial-Equilibrium

We start our analysis of the structure portion of the property tax with partial-equilibrium analysis. We explore the effect of the tax on one market (structures) in the taxing city. The analysis is partial because it ignores the effects of the tax on other markets and other cities.

In Figure 21-3, point *a* shows the initial equilibrium in the structure market. The initial supply curve for mobile homes is horizontal at $4,000 per structure. A housing firm rents mobile homes from capital owners, and the annual payment for the structure–the return to capital–is the firm's only production cost. As usual, the supply curve is a marginal-cost curve and shows the housing firm's cost per mobile home. The supply curve is horizontal because the supply of capital (mobile homes) to a single city is perfectly elastic. The initial supply curve intersects the demand curve at point *a*, with a quantity of 600 structures and a structure rent of $4,000.

FIGURE 21–3 Partial Equilibrium Effects of Structure Tax

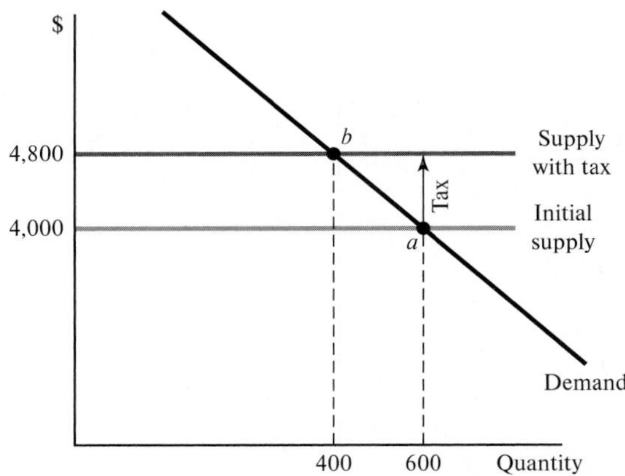

A structure tax of $800 increases the marginal cost of housing to $4,800. A housing firm pays $4,000 to a capital owner and $800 to the government, so the supply curve is horizontal at $4,800. The new equilibrium is shown by point *b*, with a price of $4,800 and a quantity of 400 dwellings. In other words, the entire structure tax is passed forward onto consumers, who pay $800 more for housing.

Because we assume that the housing industry is perfectly competitive, firms don't pay any of the property tax. They shift the land portion backward onto landowners and shift the structure portion forward to consumers. They get the money to pay the $1,000 tax by paying $200 less for land and charging $800 more to consumers. This is not unique to the housing market but is the normal consequence of a tax on a competitive industry. A tax is shifted backward onto input suppliers and forward onto consumers, leaving producers with zero economic profit, just as they had before the tax.

Structure Portion: A General-Equilibrium Approach

A general-equilibrium approach explores the implications of a property tax in one city on economic activity in other cities. In Figure 21–4 the equilibrium in the housing markets in a two-city regional economy is shown by points *a* and *b*. The negatively sloped curves show housing rent (the return to structural capital) in the two cities. As the quantity of housing increases, the housing rent and thus the rate of return to the owners of structural capital decreases.

For a Nash equilibrium in the capital market, the two cities have the same rate of return. If the returns were different a capital supplier would move a mobile home to the city with a higher rent (rate of return). In Figure 21–4, the initial equilibrium is shown by points *a* and *b*: the common rate of return to structural capital is $4,000, and the fixed amount of capital (1,200 mobile homes) is divided equally between the two cities.

FIGURE 21-4 General Equilibrium in a Two-City Region

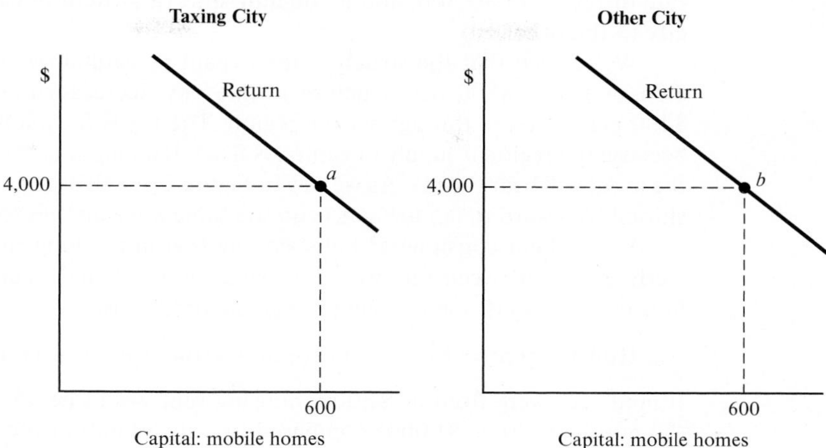

Figure 21-5 shows the effects of a \$800 tax on structural capital. The tax shifts the return curve in the taxing city downward, so that at the initial quantity (600 units), the rate of return is only \$3,200 (point *c*). The tax generates a gap between the rates of return in the two cities and thus gives capital suppliers an incentive to shift their capital from the taxing city to the other city. As capital leaves the taxing city, the market moves upward along the return curve to higher rates of return. As capital enters the other city, the market moves downward along the return curve to lower rates of return. The combination of these changes narrows and ultimately eliminates the tax-generated gap in the returns to capital between

FIGURE 21-5 General Equilibrium Effects of the Structure Tax

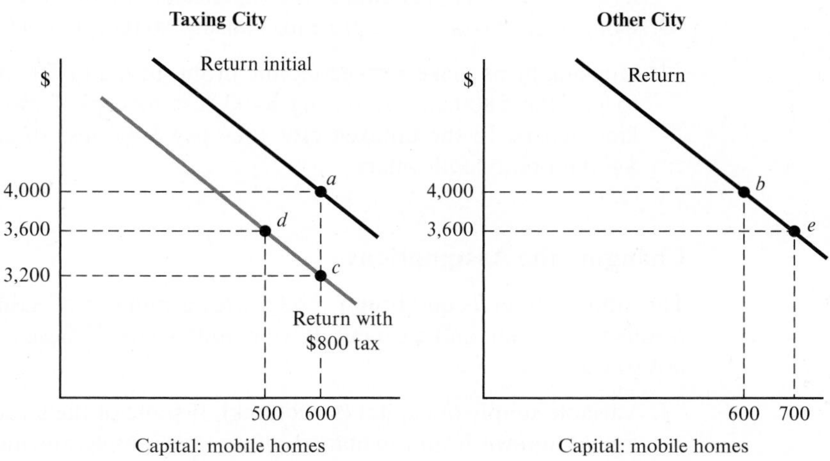

the two cities. As shown by points *d* and *e*, equilibrium is restored with a common rate of return of $3,600, and a 100-unit shift of structural capital from the taxing city to the other city.

We've seen that the structure tax is paid by capital owners throughout the region. A tax of $800 per structure in one city decreases the return on capital by $400 per structure throughout the region. The tax is fully shifted to capital owners because the regional supply of capital is fixed. If an input is fixed in supply, owners of the input will bear the tax. As we saw in Figure 21–4, this is true for the land tax (fully shifted backward to landowners) and the same logic applies to the structure tax.

What about consumers? Let's assume that in the long run, consumers are perfectly mobile between the two cities. Housing firms make zero economic profit, so housing rent is just high enough to pay the firm's cost:

Housing rent = Return to capital + structure tax + land rent.

If land rent were fixed at $1,000, housing rent would be $5,400 in the taxing city ($3,600 + $800 + $1,000) compared to only $4,600 in the other city ($3,600 + $1,000). To reach locational equilibrium, the price of land will adjust to equalize housing rent and thus make consumers indifferent between the two cities. To close the gap in housing rent, land rent decreases to $600 in the taxing city and increases to $1,400 in the other city. As a result, housing rent is $5,000 in each city, so consumers will be indifferent between the two cities. The structure tax causes landowners in the taxing city to lose $400 per lot, while landowners in the other city gain $400 per lot.

We can summarize our discussion of the incidence of the structure portion of the property tax. Recall that we are assuming for now that the supply of capital (structures) in the region is fixed.

1. Capital owners bear the tax. The return to capital falls by $400 per structure in both cities.
2. Landowners in the region experience zero-sum changes in rent, with landowners in the untaxed city gaining at the expense of landowners in the taxed city.
3. Consumers pay the same price for housing, so they do not bear any part of the tax.
4. Housing firms make zero economic profit. In the taxed city, they get the money to pay the $800 tax by paying $400 less to capital owners and $400 less to landowners. In the untaxed city, they pay $400 less to capital owners but pay $400 more to landowners.

Changing the Assumptions

The simple general-equilibrium model uses a number of assumptions to make the results transparent and clear-cut. If we modify some of these assumptions, things are not so tidy.

1. Variable supply of capital (structures). If some of the structures that flee the tax are withdrawn from the market rather than simply moving to the other city, the

initial excess supply of structures in the other city won't be as large, so the return on capital won't drop as far. The equilibrium housing rent will exceed $5,000, meaning that part of the structure tax will be shifted to consumers, leaving a smaller burden on capital owners.

2. More than two cities in the region. If there were 10 cities in the region, the effects of the structure tax would be spread over five times as much capital. As a result, the decrease in the return to capital would be one-fifth as large: The return to capital would drop by $80 instead of $400. To equalize housing rent between the cities, the price of land would increase by $80 in the untaxed cities and decrease by $720 in the taxing city. Notice that the changes in land rent in the region sum to zero: Nine cities experience an $80 rise and one experiences a $720 decline.

2. FROM MODELS TO REALITY

To explain the effects of the property tax on different sorts of people, we have used a number of modeling artifices that may seem to limit the applicability of the results. But in fact we can apply the lessons from the artificial model to real markets.

Rental Property Owners and Homeowners

What about rental property owners and homeowners? Our model of the housing market has four economic actors: consumers, owners of housing firms, landowners, and capital owners. In the rental housing market, these roles are merged into two: Housing firms own property (land and structures) and consumers rent housing from firms. In the homeowner market, the roles are merged into one, with consumers as property owners. We can distinguish between insiders (property owners in the taxing city) and outsiders (property owners outside the taxing city).

1. *Insiders.* Property owners in the taxing city lose as both owners of land and owners of capital. They lose as landowners because (1) the land portion of the tax decreases land rent and (2) part of the structure portion is shifted onto land. In addition, like other capital owners in the region, they lose because the return to capital decreases. In general, the property tax decreases the market value of property. This is sensible because the property now carries a tax liability, so potential buyers are willing to pay less for the property.
2. *Outsiders.* Although property owners in other cities don't pay the tax in a legal sense, they are affected by the tax. Outsiders gain as landowners because land rent in their city rises to equalize housing rents. Like other capital owners, they lose as the regionwide return on capital decreases. So the net effect on their income and the market value of their properties is ambiguous.

Practical Guide for Policy Makers

Consider next the lessons for policy makers. We've explored the effects of the residential property tax with different models and assumptions. Suppose an elected official asks, Who actually pays the property tax? The appropriate response depends on the official's perspective. We can distinguish between a city perspective and a national perspective.

1. *Mayor.* Consider a mayor who wants to predict the effect of a structure tax on citizens in the city, one of 50 cities in a regional economy. Given the large number of cities, the region-wide return to capital will decrease by a relatively small amount (1/50 of the tax), leaving a large fraction to be borne by land (49/50) in the taxing city. So the mayor can assume that most of the tax will be borne by local landowners.
2. *President.* Consider next a president who wants to predict the effect of a uniform property tax across cities in the nation. With the same tax rate in all cities, structures have nowhere to flee from one city's property tax. If the national supply of capital is fixed, the entire tax will be borne by the owners of capital. In this case, capital owners cannot shift the tax to anyone else because they do not respond to the tax: They don't move their capital between cities, and they don't decrease the total amount of capital in the nation. Of course, if the supply of capital is variable rather than fixed, capital owners can shift the tax to households in the form of higher housing rent throughout the nation.

The Tiebout Model and the Property Tax

As explained in this and earlier chapters, the provision and financing of local public goods causes household sorting of two sorts.

1. Diversity in the demand for local public goods causes sorting with respect to the demand for local public goods.
2. Diversity in demand for the goods taxed to finance local public goods causes sorting with respect to the demand for the taxed good.

When local public goods are financed by taxes on housing, households sort with respect to house value. This Tiebout sorting prevents a household with an expensive house (and a large property tax bill) from giving a "free ride" to households with relatively cheap houses (small property tax bills). The sorting process has important implications for the incidence of the property tax.

Consider a metropolitan area where the per-household cost of public goods is \$3,000 per year. There are two types of households: half own \$100,000 houses and half own \$200,000 houses. Local public goods are financed with a property tax. In Figure 21–6, house value is on the horizontal axis and the tax rate is on the vertical axis. The rectangles show the tax liabilities of the two types of houses: light gray for \$100,000 houses and dark gray for \$200,000 houses. As shown by the left pair of rectangles, if there is a single mixed municipality, a tax rate of 2% generates an average of \$3,000 per household, with \$2,000 from light gray (0.02 times \$100,000) and \$4,000 from dark gray (0.02 times \$200,000). In this case, a dark-gray household pays more than its share of the cost of local public services.

FIGURE 21–6 Fiscal Deficits and Surpluses

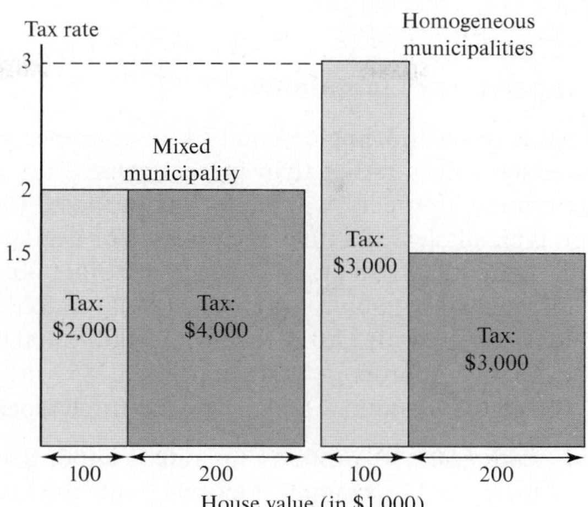

The owners of the more expensive houses have an incentive to exclude the owners of less expensive houses. Suppose dark-gray owners establish an exclusive municipality with a minimum house value of $200,000. In the far right of Figure 21–6, the new municipality has a tax rate of only 1.5 percent, which is just high enough to cover the cost of providing local public goods ($200,000 times 0.015 = $3,000). In contrast, the light-gray owners are now forced to pay the full cost of local public goods, and the tax rate increases to 3 percent to cover the cost of providing local public goods ($100,000 times 0.03 = $3,000). The general lesson is that differences in house values generate incentive for citizens in expensive (high tax) houses to exclude citizens in inexpensive (low tax) houses. In the two-municipality outcome, each household pays its share of the cost of local public goods. Differences in house values cause offsetting differences in tax rates to ensure that each household pays the same amount in property taxes.

Because households sort themselves into homogeneous communities, the property tax is a user fee, not a conventional tax. A household's property tax liability is determined by its consumption of the local public good, not by its property value. In the Tiebout world, households get what they pay for, and the question of who pays the property tax is simple: Just as a consumer pays $10 to get a book, a household pays a property tax of $3,000 to get $3,000 worth of local public goods. There is no tax shifting because the tax is a user fee.

How realistic is the Tiebout model and the user-fee view of the property tax? Given the large number of municipalities in the typical metropolitan area, households can choose from a wide variety of municipalities and local governments. But the sorting with respect to the demand for local public goods and property value is imperfect, even in suburban areas. And the Tiebout model is clearly inapplicable to central cities, where a single municipality serves a large and diverse population. In large central cities, the property tax is not a user fee, but a conventional tax.

Property Tax Limitations

In the real-world implementation of a property taxes, tax liabilities are based on assessed values rather than market values. Tax authorities use various methods to determine a property's value for tax purposes (assessed value), and assessed values are typically less than market values. For example, if a property has a market value of \$300,000 and an assessed value of \$200,000, a tax rate of 15 mills (1.5 percent) generates a tax liability of \$3,000 (equal to \$200,000 times 0.015) and an effective tax rate of 10 mills (1.0 percent = \$3,000/\$300,000).

Limits on property taxes started in 1852 in Delaware, and are currently in force in 46 states (Paquin, 2015). There are three types of limits.

1. *Rate Limit.* A property tax rate is either fixed or subject to a maximum rate of increase. For example, Georgia limits the tax rate for school districts to 20 mills (2.0 percent). In 2013, a total of 38 states enforced rate limits.
2. *Assessment Limit.* The annual percentage increase in assessed value is either fixed or limited by an index or formula. For example, in California the maximum annual increase in assessed value is 2 percent. In 2013, a total of 11 states enforced broad assessment limits. Eight other states implemented narrowly defined limits that apply to select local governments or geographical areas, or are limited in other ways.
3. *Levy Limit.* The growth rate total property-tax revenue is limited. For example, Indiana restricts the annual growth rate for non-school local property tax revenue to either 6 percent or the statewide average annual growth rate in nonfarm personal income, whichever is lower. In 2013, a total of 36 states enforced levy limits.

The first property tax revolt came during the Great Depression, a result of a mismatch between property tax liabilities and citizens' willingness to pay for local public services. Between 1929 and 1933, the share of income absorbed by the property tax doubled, reaching 11.3 percent in 1932. Over this period, personal income was cut in half while property tax revenue decreased by only 9 percent. The decrease in citizens' ability to pay property taxes nearly tripled the delinquency rate. Fearing massive defaults on municipal bonds, the business community supported protax campaigns by paying for lapel buttons, mass mailings, and parades. The parades featured the descendants of canine war heroes, who barked and carried signboards urging people to pay their taxes. In 1933, more than 3,000 local tax leagues were agitating for tax reform. The clear message was that local government should scale back its operations to reflect lower income during the Great Depression. In the words of one agitator, "I buy less food, less tobacco, less recreation, and I'd like to buy less government" (Beito, 1989, p. 18). In mass meetings organized by the tax leagues, citizens demanded the elimination of local services, including weed inspectors and county nurses.

The tax revolt of the 1930s resulted in the passage of tax limits that reduced the tax burden. Between 1929 and 1939, a total of 11 states passed tax limits, with nine states passing rate limits and two states passing levy limits. Between 1932 and 1940, the share of income absorbed by property taxes decreased from 11.3 percent to 5.8 percent. The decrease in the tax share resulted from a combination of income growth and the tax limits. By 1940, personal income had almost reached the level observed in 1930, while the share of income absorbed by the property tax was 5.8 percent, compared to 6.3 percent in 1930.

The modern tax revolt started in 1978 with the passage of Proposition 13 in California. During the period 1960 to 1975, the share of national income absorbed by the property tax was high by recent historical standards–about 4.2 percent, compared to 3.4 percent during the late 1940s and 1950s. By 1995, dozens of states had enacted new tax limits, and the share of income absorbed by property taxes dropped to 3.3 percent. In contrast with the earlier tax revolt, the supporters of modern tax limits expected local governments to provide the same level of service with less money. In California, 38 percent of the citizens believed that state and local governments could absorb a 40 percent cut in tax revenue without cutting services. In Massachusetts, 82 percent of the supporters of Proposition 2 1/2 believed that the proposition would cut taxes without reducing the quality of local public services. In Michigan, three-fourths of the supporters of the Headlee Amendment expected the government to absorb the revenue cut by simply becoming more efficient.

Assessment limits can generate horizontal inequities among homeowners. The limits typically restrict the growth rate of assessed value but reset the assessed value when a property is sold. In some states, the assessed value is reset to the current market value. As a result, long-time owners pay lower property taxes than new owners. The tax gap between long-time and new owners depends on (i) the maximum growth rate of assessed value, (ii) the growth rate of market value, and (iii) the length of ownership. In Los Angeles, the average gap is roughly 35 percent: the property tax of a new homeowner is roughly 35 percent higher than the property tax of an existing homeowner who (i) has owned a home for the average number of years in the city and (ii) lives in a house with the same market value. The tax gap is roughly 37 percent in New York City, 30 percent in San Francisco, 29 percent in Miami, 18 percent in Detroit, 16 percent in Portland, Oregon, 5 percent in Chicago, 2 percent in Oklahoma City, and 1 percent in Austin. The tax gaps are relatively low in cities where the growth rate in market value is close to or less than the allowable growth rate in assessed value.

In 1992, the U.S. Supreme Court refused to overturn California's Proposition 13 on federal constitutional grounds. In a dissenting opinion, Justice John Paul Stevens noted the windfall benefits for "the Squires," his label for people who invested in California real estate in the 1970s (Youngman, 2016).

> As a direct result of this windfall for the Squires, later purchasers must pay far more than their fair share of property taxes. The specific disparity that prompted petitioner to challenge the constitutionality of Proposition 13 is the fact that her annual property tax bill is almost five times as large as that of her neighbors who own comparable homes. . . . Indeed, some homeowners pay 17 times as much in taxes as their neighbors with comparable property. For vacant land, the disparities may be as great as 500 to 1. . . .

> These disparities are aggravated by section 2 of Proposition 13, which exempts from reappraisal a property owner's home and up to $1 million of other real property when that property is transferred to a child of the owner. This exemption can be invoked repeatedly and indefinitely, allowing the Proposition 13 windfall to be passed from generation to generation. . . . Such a law establishes a privilege of a medieval character: Two families with equal needs and equal resources are treated differently solely because of their different heritage.

Sources: Nordlinger v. Hahn, 505 U.S. 1, 29–30, 112 U.S. 2326, 2341–2342, 120 L. Ed. 2d 1, 24–25 (1992) (Stevens, J. dissenting).

3. INTERGOVERNMENTAL GRANTS

This part of the chapter explores the economics of intergovernmental grants, examining how local governments respond to transfers of funds from higher levels of government. Intergovernmental grants provide about two-fifths of the revenue of local government and about one-fourth of the revenue of municipalities. Roughly half of this grant money goes to education, and the rest supports other local programs such as public welfare, housing and community development, highways, health programs, and hospitals. At the municipal level, about one-fifth of grant money supports the general operations of local government, and another fifth supports education. Two redistributional programs–public welfare and housing programs–together get about a quarter of the grant money received by municipalities.

Why don't local governments pay their own way, supporting their spending programs with local taxes? First, intergovernmental grants can be used to internalize inter-jurisdictional spillovers. Second, if the desired spending on local public goods rises faster than the local tax base, there will be a mismatch between desired spending and local revenue. At the national level, tax revenue increases more rapidly with income, providing an opportunity to transfer surplus funds to local governments. Of course, a more straightforward response to the mismatch problem would be to increase local tax rates.

We will explore the responses of local government to two types of grants. A lump-sum grant is a fixed grant, independent of a local government's spending on a local public good. In contrast, under a matching grant, a higher level of government matches local spending, for example, $1 of grant money for every $1 spent locally.

Lump-Sum Categorical Grants

Most lump-sum intergovernmental grants come with strings attached. The money from a conditional or categorical grant must be spent on a specific program. Conditional grants are provided for education, public welfare, health and hospitals, highways, housing, and community development. Within each expenditure group are program-specific grants. For example, education grants to local governments include specific grants for remedial reading, school libraries, special education, and other programs. We will use a grant for special education as an example.

FIGURE 21–7 Response to Lump-Sum Categorical Grant

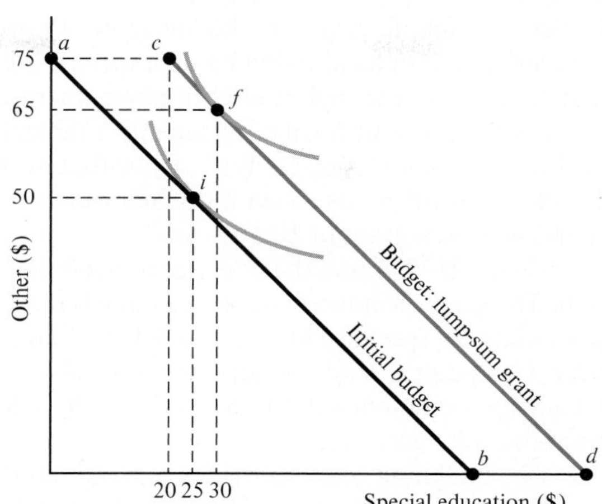

We can use the consumer-choice model, applied to the median voter, to explore the effects of grants. In Figure 21–7, Marian the median voter initially maximizes utility at point *i*, where the indifference curve is tangent to the budget line, meaning that the marginal rate of substitution equals the price ratio. The best affordable bundle has $25 on special education and $50 on other goods, including other public goods and private goods. Under majority rule, the city will choose the preferred budget of the median voter. In this case, the city spends $25 per household on special education, leaving Marian $50 for other goods.

Suppose the state gives the city a lump-sum grant of $20 per capita for special-education programs. The grant shifts the budget line from *ab* to *acd*. Point *c* is in the new budget set because Marian could spend all her own money ($75) on other goods and use the $20 grant to support special education. For spending on special education above $20, there is a dollar-for-dollar trade-off between special education and other goods. The new utility-maximizing point is point *f*, meaning that the grant increases Marian's desired spending on special education to $30 (up by $5) and her desired spending on other goods to $60 (up by $15). In other words, one-fourth of the grant is spent on special education, and the rest is spent on other goods.

Why does a categorical grant of $20 increase spending on the target program by less than $20? The city can spend part of the grant on other goods because it decreases its own contribution to special education. Before the grant, $25 of local tax money was spent on special education. After the grant, total spending on special education is $30, and the city can combine the $20 grant with just $10 of local tax money. The grant frees up $15 worth of local tax money, which can be spent on other local public goods and private goods.

Matching Grants

Under a matching grant, the higher level of government contributes some amount for every dollar of local spending on a specific local public good. Under a one-for-one matching grant, the higher level of government gives one dollar in grant money for every dollar spent by local government. A matching grant decreases the opportunity cost of local public goods: With a one-for-one match, local citizens sacrifice only \$0.50 in private goods to get a dollar's worth of local public goods (\$0.50 of local spending plus a grant of \$0.50).

Figure 21–8 shows the effect of a one-for-one matching grant for special education. The grant decreases the slope of the budget line, from \$1 worth of other goods per dollar on special education to \$0.50. Marian's utility-maximizing point moves from *i* to point *g*, and spending on special education increases from \$25 to \$40. Under the one-for-one grant, \$20 of the city's \$40 special-education budget comes from the state government.

The matching grant provides a larger stimulus to special education than an equivalent lump-sum grant. Although the state transfers the same amount for each type of grant (\$20), the matching grant increases spending on special education to \$40, while the lump-sum grant increases spending to only \$30. Both grants increase Marian's real income by \$20, increasing her demand for special education and other goods. The matching grant also has a substitution effect because it cuts the opportunity cost (price) of special education in half. The decrease in the relative price of special education causes consumer substitution of special education for other goods.

What about spending on other goods? Under a one-for-one matching grant, the local contribution to a \$40 special-education budget is \$20. This leaves \$55 to spend on other goods, including other public goods and private goods, up from \$50 before the grant. In other words, the city spends one-fourth of the \$20 matching grant on other goods. Like a lump-sum grant, a matching grant increases spending on other

FIGURE 21–8 Response to a Matching Grant

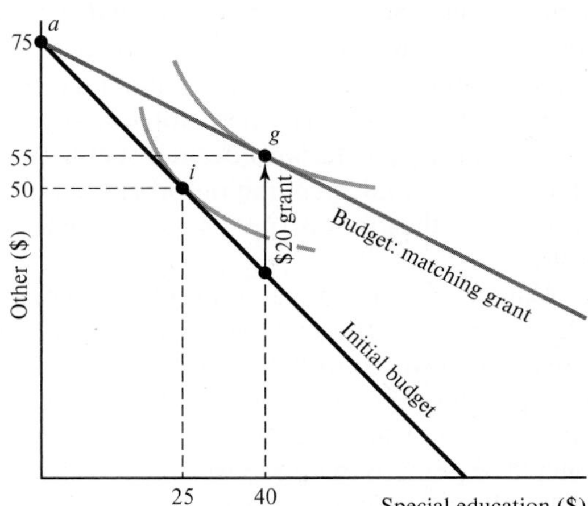

goods as the local government cuts its own contribution to the program covered by the grant.

Up to this point, we have assumed that there is no upper limit on the matching grant. In many cases, the government specifies a maximum grant amount, and this type of grant is called a closed-ended matching grant. If the desired spending after the grant is less than the limit, the limit is irrelevant and the closed grant is equivalent to the open grant. If however, the desired spending exceeds the limit, the constraint is binding, and a closed grant generates a lower level of spending than an open grant.

The Flypaper Effect

We have applied the model of consumer choice to the median voter to show that an intergovernmental grant will increase spending on local public goods and private goods. Empirical studies of the local response to grants conclude that each dollar from a lump-sum grant increases local government spending by about $0.25 to $0.50 (Oates, 1999; Ryu, 2017). In contrast, an additional dollar of household income increases local spending by about $0.05 to $0.10. In other words, a lump-sum grant has a larger stimulative effect than an equal increase in income. The relatively large stimulative effect of intergovernmental grants is known as the flypaper effect: The grant money sticks where it first hits (the local government) rather than being passed on to households in the form of lower taxes.

What explains the flypaper effect? Economists have grappled with this question and have developed several possible explanations (Inman, 2008).

1. *Fiscal illusion.* Voters suffer from fiscal illusion in the sense that they treat a lump-sum grant as if it were a matching grant. As we've seen, a matching grant has both an income effect and a substitution effect, and thus generates a larger increase in local government spending.
2. *Mental accounting.* To economize on cognitive effort, humans have "bins" for different types of spending—one for private spending and another for public spending. A lump-sum grant goes into the public bin, so public spending increases by a relatively large amount.
3. *Budget-maximizing bureaucrats.* An intergovernmental grant provides an infusion of funds into an inherently inefficient budgeting process, one that is biased toward excessive government spending. If the objective of public officials (bureaucrats) is to maximize the government budget, they will increase the budget beyond the efficient level, and stop just short of eliminating the surplus from the local public good. A lump-sum grant increases the potential surplus from local public goods, and bureaucrats boost the budget by a relatively large amount.
4. *Concealment.* Public officials conceal information about lump-sum grants from voters, who then don't recognize that a lump-sum grant is available for tax relief.

Welfare Reform: Matching Grants to Lump-Sum Grants

A key component of the welfare-reform plan adopted in 1996 is the replacement of federal matching grants with lump-sum grants (also known as block grants). Under

FIGURE 21–9 Switch to Lump-Sum Grants Decreases Welfare Spending

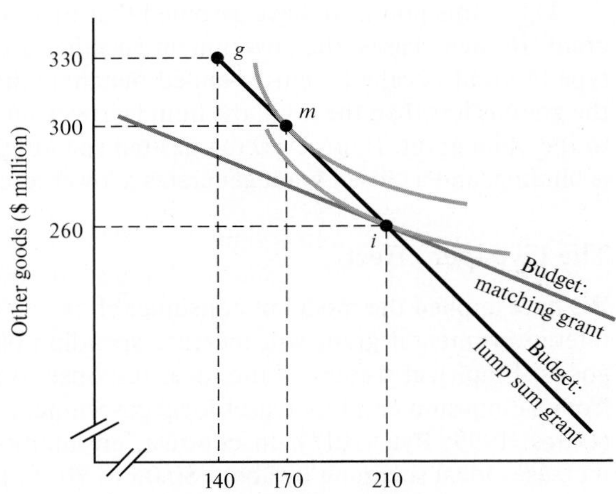

the old system, each state picked a level of welfare spending, and the federal government used matching grants to support local efforts. For low-income states, the federal rebate per dollar spent on welfare was $0.78, so from a state's perspective, each dollar spent on welfare cost the state only $0.22. The rebate was lower for high-income states, with a one-for-one match for the highest income states. Under the new grant system, the federal grant no longer depends on how much the state spends on welfare. There are no matching funds, so the state's price of a dollar spent on welfare is $1.00.

Figure 21–9 uses the consumer choice model to show the effects of welfare reform on the budget choices of a low-income state. The budget line for the median voter under the matching grant is relatively flat, reflecting the low local price of welfare spending. The voter's initial preference (and thus the state's initial choice) is shown as point *i*, with $210 million on welfare and $260 million on other goods. The new lump-sum grant is $140 million, so the new budget line is shown by the line connecting points *g*, *m*, and *i*. The lump-sum grant is large enough that the median voter has the option of picking the initial matching-grant point *i*.

Although the initial allocation is feasible, it is not the rational choice. Under the lump-sum grant, the state will actually spend less on welfare programs. To maximize the utility of the median voter, the state picks the point where the slope of the indifference curve (the marginal rate of substitution) equals the slope of the budget line (the price ratio):

Utility-maximizing rule: Marginal rate of substitution = Price ratio

For the initial choice (point *i*), the marginal rate of substitution equals the price ratio, $0.22. The switch to the lump-sum grant increases the price of welfare spending to $1, so to maximize utility, the median voter moves to point *m*, where the marginal rate of substitution is 1.0. In other words, the median voter chooses to spend less on welfare programs and more on other goods. Comparing point *m* to point *i*, the state will spend $40 million less on welfare programs and $40 million more on other goods (other public goods and private goods). The switch to a lump-sum grant increases the price of welfare spending, causing a substitution effect that decreases welfare spending.

The predicted changes in welfare spending are large. For a low-income state, the price hike from $0.22 to $1.00 is projected to decrease welfare spending by 40 to 66 percent (Inman and Rubinfeld, 1997). For a high-income state, the price hike is smaller (from $0.50 to $1.00), and the switch to lump-sum grants is projected to decrease welfare spending by 1 to 18 percent. Congress was apparently aware that welfare reform would cause states to cut their welfare spending. The law requires states to continue to spend at least 80 percent of the amount spent under the old matching-grant policy.

REVIEW THE CONCEPTS

1. Housing firms shift the land portion of the property tax onto [______] because the supply of land is [______].
2. In the partial-equilibrium analysis, housing firms shift the structure portion of the property tax onto [______] because the supply of capital is assumed to be [______].
3. In the general-equilibrium model of a two-city region, housing firms shift the structure portion of the property tax onto [______] because the region-wide supply of capital is assumed to be [______].
4. In the general-equilibrium analysis, the structure portion of the property tax generates zero-sum changes in [______] across cities. These changes generate locational indifference for [______].
5. A mayor of a small city can assume that the bulk of a local property tax will be borne by [______].
6. In general, housing consumers will not bear the burden of a property tax because the tax is borne by [______] and [______].
7. To predict the response of a local government to an intergovernmental grant, we examine the rational choice of the [______] voter.
8. A categorical grant [______] {↑, ↓, –} spending on the target public good by an amount [______] (<, >, =) the grant and [______] {↑, ↓, –} spending on other goods.
9. A lump-sum grant [______] the budget line of the decisive voter, while a matching grant [______] the budget line of the decisive voter.
10. Compared to a lump-sum grant, a matching grant has a [______] stimulative effect because it decreases the [______] of a local public good and has a [______] effect.

11. For each pair of variables, indicate whether the relationship is positive, negative, neutral, or ambiguous.

Parameter	Choice Variable	Relationship
land tax	price of housing	[_____]
land tax	price of land	[_____]
structure tax: General equilibrium	price of housing	[_____]
structure tax: General equilibrium	price of land in taxing city	[_____]
structure tax: General equilibrium	price of land in other city	[_____]

APPLY THE CONCEPTS

1. *A Tax on Mobile Home Pads.*
The residents of mobile home parks own their dwellings and rent pads (the land under the mobile home) from landowners. In Padville, all land is initially occupied by mobile homes, and each resident rents one padacre (a standard pad). Each landowner owns one padacre. Initially, there are 100 residents, and the price of land is $200 per padacre. Suppose the city imposes a tax of $40 per padacre, regardless of how the land is used. The tax is paid in legal terms by the land user (the resident). Illustrate the effects of the land tax on the equilibrium price of pads (the price paid by the resident to the landowner).
2. *Tax Revenue versus Total Burden.*
Consider the land tax in Figure 21-2 and the partial-equilibrium analysis of the structure tax in Figure 21-3.
   a. For the land tax, the deadweight loss (also known as excess burden) is $ [_____].
   b. For the structure tax, the deadweight loss (also known as excess burden) is $ [_____].
3. *Effects the Property Tax.*
Consider the general-equilibrium view of the structure portion of the property tax. Based on the example in the chapter (fixed supply of capital and perfectly mobile consumers), identify the monetary effects for each of the following individuals. The dollar values can be positive, negative, or zero.
   a. For Rene, a renter in the taxing city, the monetary effect is [_____].
   b. For Landry, who owns three lots in the taxing city, the monetary effect is [_____].
   c. For Loren, who owns two lots in the other city, the monetary effect is [_____].
   d. For Cap, who owns five structures in the taxing city, the monetary effect is [_____].
   e. For Talulah, who owns four structures in the other city, the monetary effect is [_____].
4. *Education Lottery.*
Consider a city that initially spends $20 million of its $100 million budget on public schools, a choice consistent with the preferences of the median voter.

The income elasticity of demand for public schools is 1.5. Suppose the city gets $10 million from a new state lottery, and by law must spend all $10 million on public schools. Illustrate the effects of the lottery on the city's spending choices, including new values for spending on public schools (S**) and other goods (A**).

5. *Library Grant.*

Consider the hiring of city librarians. The daily wage of a librarian is $100, and the city initially hires $L^* = 10$ librarians. Suppose the state offers a 25 percent matching grant for librarians: $m = 0.25$. The wage elasticity of demand for city librarians is -0.50.

a. Use a graph like Figure 21-8 to illustrate the effects of the matching grant on librarians and other goods. Include the new number of librarians L^{**}.

b. The city's own spending on librarians changes from $1,000 to $ [_____]. The grant is [______] and spending on other goods changes by $ [_____].

REFERENCES AND READING

1. Beito, David T., *Taxpayers in Revolt.* Chapel Hill, NC: University of North Carolina Press, 1989.
2. Courant, Paul, Edward Gramlich, and Daniel Rubinfeld, "The Stimulative Effects of Intergovernmental Grants: Or Why Money Sticks Where It Hits," in Peter Mieszkowski and William Oakland (eds.), *Fiscal Federalism and Grants-in-Aid*, Washington, D.C.: Urban Institute Press, 5-21.
3. Filimon, Radu, Thomas Romer, and Howard Rosenthal, "Asymmetric Information and Agenda Control." *Journal of Public Economics* 17 (1982, February), pp. 51-70.
4. Hines, James, and Richard Thaler, "Anomalies: The Flypaper Effect." *Journal of Economic Perspectives* 9 (1995, Fall), pp. 217-26.
5. Inman, Robert P., "The Flypaper Effect," NBER Working Paper, 2008.
6. Inman, Robert P., "Finances: Financing City Services." Chapter 11 in *Making Cities Work: Prospects and Policies for Urban America*, edited by Robert P. Inman. New York: Princeton University Press, 2009.
7. Lincoln Institute of Land Policy, 50 State Property Tax Comparison Study for Taxes Paid in 2015 (June 2016).
8. Lincoln Institute of Land Policy, Significant Features of the Property Tax, http://datatoolkits.lincolninst.edu/subcenters/significant-features-property-tax/Report_Tax_Limits.aspx.
9. Oates, Wallace E., *Fiscal Federalism.* New York: Harcourt Brace Jovanovich, 1972.
10. Oates, Wallace, "Lump-sum Intergovernmental Grants Have Price Effects," in Peter Mieszkowski and William Oakland (eds.), *Fiscal Federalism and Grants-in-Aid*, Washington, D.C.: Urban Institute Press, 1979, pp. 23-30.
11. Paquin, Bethany P., "Chronicle of the 161-Year History of State-Imposed Property Tax Limitations," Working Paper WP15BP1 Lincoln Institute of Land Policy (2015).

12. Tiebout, C., "A Pure Theory of Local Expenditures." *Journal of Political Economy* 64 (1956), pp. 416–24.
13. Ryu, Jay E., "Measuring the Flypaper Effect: The Interaction Between Lump-Sum Aid and the Substitution Effect of Matching Aid," *Public Finance and Management* 17 (2017), pp. 48–70.
14. U.S. Bureau of the Census. Census of Governments, 2012.
15. Youngman, Joan, *A Good Tax: Legal and Policy Issues for the Property Tax in the United States.* Lincoln Institute of Land Policy, Cambridge, MA, 2016.
16. Zodrow, George R. "The Property Tax as a Capital Tax: A Room with Three Views." *National Tax Journal* 54 (2001), pp. 139–56.

CHAPTER 22

Education

Human history becomes more and more a race between education and catastrophe.

—H. G. WELLS

This chapter explores the economics of education. Roughly half of local-government expenditures in the United States go to local schools, and spending on K–12 education (kindergarten through high school) is roughly seven times the spending on police, the second largest spending category. As we've seen in earlier chapters, educational achievement varies significantly across space, both within and across metropolitan areas. As a result, the quality of local schools is an important factor in the location decisions of households and firms. And since an educated workforce is more productive and innovative, local education affects urban economic growth.

The economic analysis of education is based on the education production function, which represents the relationship between the inputs and outputs of the education process. The inputs include variables controlled by schools (teachers, class size, curriculum) as well as variables beyond the control of schools, including the home environment. Until recently, education output has been defined in terms of scores on cognitive tests. Recent advances in economic theory and empirical technique allow us to take a longer-term view, measuring output as the change in lifetime earnings attributable to education. This approach provides a framework for benefit-cost analysis of changes in educational inputs. For example, a decrease in class size (more teacher time per student) increases student achievement lifetime earnings, but does the additional benefit exceed the additional cost?

1. SPENDING AND ACHIEVEMENT

In the United States in 2014, the average expenditure per K–12 student was $11,009. Table 22–1 shows per-pupil spending in the five states with the highest spending and the five states with the lowest spending. Spending per pupil varies significantly across the nation, from a low of $6,500 in Utah to a high of $20,600 in New York. Between 1960 and 2014, real spending per pupil more than quadrupled.

TABLE 22–1 Per Pupil Spending in Selected States, 2014

State	Spending per Pupil ($)
New York	20,600
District of Columbia	18,500
Alaska	18,400
New Jersey	17,900
Connecticut	17,800
Mississippi	8,300
Oklahoma	7,800
Arizona	7,500
Idaho	6,600
Utah	6,500

Source: U.S. Census Bureau, *U.S. Annual Survey of School System Finances*, 2014.

Table 22–2 provides an international perspective on educational achievement. The table shows the average test scores for the mathematics portion of the Programme for International Student Assessment examination (PISA). The United States is ranked 27th among the 34 OECD countries. The performance gap between U.S. students and students in Shanghai-China is equivalent to two years of schooling. Although the United States spends more per student than most countries, the additional spending does not translate into higher performance. The Slovak Republic spends roughly half as much as the United States, but the test scores are similar. For the reading and science portions of the PISA exams, the scores for U.S. students were close to the OECD averages.

Table 22–3 shows student achievement data for the United States as a whole, for large cities as a group, and for selected cities. The National Assessment of

TABLE 22–2 International Student Test Scores

Country	Mathematics PISA Score
OECD Average	494
Shanghai-China	613
Singapore	573
Korea	554
Japan	536
Switzerland	531
Netherlands	523
Finland	519
Canada	518
Ireland	501
Russian Federation	482
Slovak Republic	482
United States	481
Greece	485
Kazakhstan	432
Mexico	413

Source: OECD Programme for International Student Assessment (PISA), *Results from PISA 2012.*

TABLE 22-3 Student Achievement in Selected Cities, 2009

Jurisdiction	Percent Below Basic Level
United States	29
Large Cities	40
San Diego	32
Boston	33
New York City	40
Chicago	49
Atlanta	54
Los Angeles	54
Baltimore	57
Cleveland	58
Detroit	77

Source: Digest of Education Statistics 2010. Washington, DC: National Center for Education Statistics, Table 145.

Educational Progress (NAEP) measures achievement levels in reading and mathematics. The table shows the percentage of eighth graders who scored below the basic level on the NAEP mathematics exam. Nationwide, 29 percent of students scored below the basic level, compared to 40 percent for all large cities. Among the large cities listed in the table, student performance was above average in San Diego, Boston, and New York, and below average in Detroit, Cleveland, and Baltimore.

Figure 22-1 illustrates differences in educational achievement within a metropolitan area. The figure provides data on student performance and socioeconomic

FIGURE 22-1 Mathematics Scores and Economically Disadvantaged Students

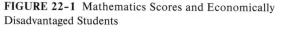

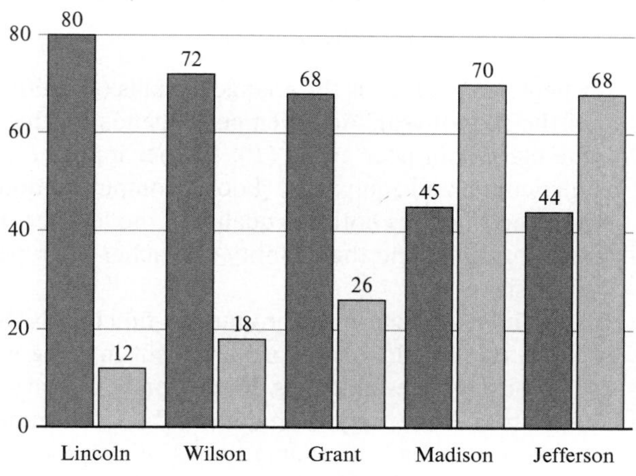

Source: Oregon Department of Education. *Report Cards, 2009-2010.*

characteristics for several high schools in the Portland, Oregon, school district. There is substantial variation in student achievement across the high schools: the percentage of students who meet state standards for mathematics ranges from 44 percent to 80 percent. The percentage of students who are economically disadvantaged ranges from 12 percent to 70 percent.

As documented by Dobbie and Fryer (2009), the United States has a persistent and widespread racial achievement gap, a fact demonstrated by student performance on grade-four NAEP tests. In reading, 43 percent of white students are proficient, compared to 12 percent of black students. In math, 51 percent of white students are proficient, compared to 14 percent of black students. On every subject at every grade level, there are large achievement gaps between white and black students, and the gaps widen as children move through the school system. Although part of the achievement gap can be explained by differences in socioeconomic background (including the income and education level of parents), two-thirds of the gap remains after controlling for differences in background.

2. THE EDUCATION PRODUCTION FUNCTION

The purpose of education is to develop cognitive, social, and physical skills. The basic cognitive skills (reading, writing, mathematics, logic) are necessary for employment and participation in a democracy. These skills also increase the enjoyment of leisure activities: they allow people to read books, understand jokes, and compute bowling scores. Schools also develop social skills: they teach children how to exchange ideas and make group decisions. Finally, schools develop physical skills: they teach children how to exercise and play.

The education production function shows the relationship between the inputs and outputs of the educational process. For a school year, the production function is

$$Achievement = f(H, P, T, Z)$$

where *Achievement* is the change in skills (cognitive, social, physical) over the course of the school year. Achievement depends on the student's home environment (H), the classroom peer group (P), teacher input (T), and other inputs (Z) such as the curriculum and equipment (books, computers, and lab equipment). The teacher variable incorporates both the quality of the teacher (productivity in terms of improving student skills) and the quantity of teacher input per student, which is determined by class size.

The first input in the production function is the home environment (H). Parents play a role in educational achievement in three ways. First, parents set the rules of the household, establishing an environment that is either favorable or unfavorable to education. For example, an unfavorable environment is one in which children watch television instead of reading books or doing their homework. Second, parents can motivate their children by encouraging reading and studying, helping with homework, and rewarding success. Third, parents can provide instructional materials such as books and home computers, encouraging independent learning. Based on dozens of empirical studies, it is clear that the home environment has a large effect on educational achievement, with achievement generally increasing with the income and educational attainment of parents.

Peer Effects

The second input in the production function is the student's classroom peer group (*P*). A child learns more if he or she is surrounded by smart and motivated children. Smart peers promote achievement because of cooperation (children learn from one another) and competition (children compete with one another). Motivated peers promote achievement because the teacher can spend less time disciplining and motivating students and more time teaching. In addition, an unmotivated student provides an undesirable role model for other students.

Recent studies estimated the magnitude of peer effects in secondary schools (high schools). Chinese students take two admissions tests, one to get into high school and a second to get into college. To measure the quality of a student's peers, we can use the average score on the high-school exam for the student's classmates. To measure achievement of the high-school experience, we can use the student's score on the college exam. Ding and Lehrer (2007) estimate that a 1 percent increase in peer quality increases achievement by 0.088 percent. Sund (2009) measures peer effects in Swedish high schools: if the quality of a student's classmates increases from the median quality (50th percentile) to a quality level at the 84th percentile, the student's achievement increases from the median achievement level to the 54th percentile.

There are important tradeoffs associated with peer effects. A key policy issue concerns mixing students of different abilities in a single class. The alternative is to sort students into classes of differing abilities, a practice known as ability grouping or tracking. A high achiever who is switched from a class with other high achievers to a mixed class will bear a cost in terms of lower educational achievement, but will generate benefits for his or her classmates in higher achievement. An unsettled question is whether the loss of the high achiever is larger or smaller than the gain of the lower achievers. In other words, we don't know whether a switch from tracking to mixing increases educational achievement as a whole. Another unsettled question is who gains the most from the presence of a high achiever—low achievers or middle achievers.

School Inputs: The Value-Added of Teachers

There is substantial variation across schools in student achievement, measured in the short run by scores on cognitive tests, and in the long run by adult earnings. The most important factor behind differences in achievement is teacher productivity. In other words, the most productive schools are the schools with the most effective teachers.

To measure the productivity differences across teachers, we can compare an above-average teacher to an average teacher. Let's define a "superior" teacher as one whose average student test score places the teacher in the 84th percentile among teachers: in terms of student test scores, the superior teacher does better than 84 percent of teachers. Consider the following thought experiment developed by Chetty (2014) and implemented by Hanushek (2010). Suppose we replace an average teacher (at the 50th percentile) with a superior teacher (84th percentile), and then measure the resulting change in student test scores. The test score of the typical student will increase, moving the student from the 50th percentile of students to the 58th percentile.

We can translate changes in student test scores into changes in lifetime earnings. The lifetime earnings of a student at the 58th percentile is roughly $21,311 greater than the earnings of the student at the 50th percentile. For the typical student in a class of 20 students, the benefit of this teacher substitution is $21,311, so for a class of 20 students, the economic value of a superior teacher relative to an average teacher is $426,220. It is important to note that this is the annual value of a superior teacher: a superior teacher generates these future earnings gains each year.

The same logic applies to other sorts of teacher substitutions. For example, suppose we replace an average teacher (50th percentile) with a teacher at the 69th percentile. In this case, the typical student will move from the 50th percentile to the 54th percentile. This change in educational achievement will increase the lifetime earnings per student by $10,607, meaning that the lifetime earnings of a 20-student class increases by $212,140. On the opposite side of the distribution of teacher productivity, suppose we replace an average teacher with a below-average teacher, for example, a teacher at the 31st percentile. The typical student will move from the 50th percentile to the 46th percentile, and the lifetime earnings of students in a 20-student class will decrease by more than $200,000.

The evidence on the effects of teacher quality on lifetime earnings has important implications for teacher personnel decisions. There would be a large payoff from taking low-productivity teachers out of the classroom, a process known as "deselecting" teachers. Hanushek (2010) estimate that if the United States were to replace the bottom 8 percent of teachers with average teachers, student test scores would increase by roughly 45 percent. This achievement gain is large enough to eliminate the performance gap between students in the United States and most other countries.

Although it is clear that teachers differ in productivity, a list of characteristics that identify a productive teacher has proven elusive. Teaching requires subtle skills that cannot be easily measured, so it is difficult to predict in advance which teachers will be the most productive. In looking for teacher characteristics that explain productivity differences, researchers focus on education level (years of graduate coursework), experience (years of teaching), and communication skills (verbal ability).

1. *Education level.* There is no evidence that teachers who complete graduate courses in education are more productive than teachers with only a bachelor's degree. In other words, graduate coursework in education does not increase teacher productivity.
2. *Experience.* The consensus among researchers is that teaching experience increases productivity for the first few years (roughly 3 years) of teaching.

3. *Verbal skills.* The most effective teachers have superior communication skills. Students learn more from teachers with high scores on standard tests of verbal ability.

School Inputs: Teachers and Class Size

There is evidence that class size affects student achievement. This is sensible because a decrease in class size increases the teacher time per student. There is evidence that the achievement gains from small classes are relatively large for low-income and low-achieving students. The fact that students learn more in smaller classes doesn't necessarily mean that small classes are more efficient. Reducing class size requires an increase in the number of teachers, and the efficiency question is whether the benefit exceeds the cost.

A recent study estimates the effects of class size on short-term and long-term outcomes in Sweden (Fredricksson, Okeert, and Ossterbeek, 2013). Using data on class sizes for grades 4–6 (ages 10–13), the authors measure the effects of decreasing class size by one student. In the short run, student performance on standardized tests increases. In the long run, the average adult (age 27–42) who spent grades 4–6 in smaller classes (one student less than the average) experiences the following effects.

1. The probability of getting a college degree is 0.80 percentage points higher.
2. Income (earnings) is 1.2 percent higher, a result of higher wages and more work hours.

The long-term effects are large enough that a decrease in class size passes a benefit-cost test: the benefits (increase in earnings) exceed the cost (additional teacher cost) by a large margin.

Figure 22–2 shows the implications of the Swedish study. The horizontal axis measures (i) the number of teachers for a set of 100 students (moving from left to right) and

FIGURE 22–2 Efficient Class Size

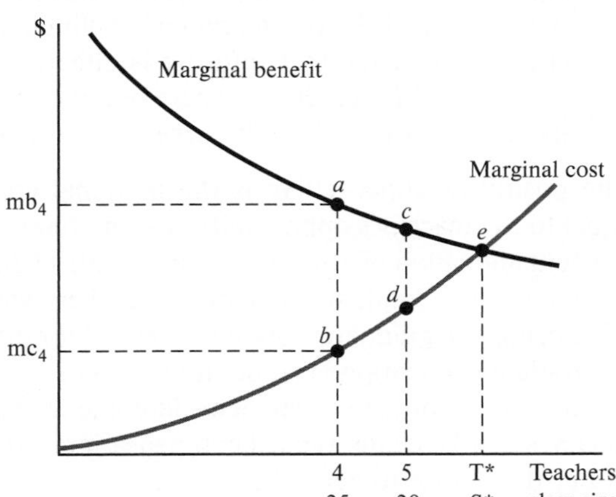

(ii) class size (students per teacher, moving right to left). Starting from a class size of 25 (four teachers), the marginal benefit of a teacher (point *a*) exceeds the marginal cost (point *b*), so hiring the fifth teacher to reduce class size to 20 is efficient. As shown by point *e*, the efficient number of teachers is T* and the efficient class size is S*.

Teacher Compensation and Productivity

As we've seen, teachers are the key input to the education production process, and teachers vary in their productivity. It would be reasonable to expect that differences in teacher wages would match the differences in productivity, with superior teachers getting higher wages than mediocre teachers. The market for teachers doesn't work that way. Instead, the wage of the typical teacher is largely determined by two factors: teaching experience (years teaching) and the teacher's own educational attainment.

1. *Experience.* In 2008, a teacher with 20 years of experience earned 1.44 times as much as a 3-year teacher. This is puzzling because empirical work suggests that teacher productivity increases for only the first few years of experience.
2. *Graduate Education.* In the United States, the wage premium for a master's degree in education is roughly 26 percent: On average, a teacher with a master's degree earns roughly 26 percent more than a teacher without one. This is puzzling because empirical work suggests that graduate education doesn't increase teacher productivity.

The puzzle about teacher compensation is that schools pay for two characteristics—experience beyond the third year and graduate course work—that do not increase student achievement.

Figure 22-3 illustrates the puzzle of graduate education. The horizontal axis measures the hours allocated by a teacher to two types of after-school activities: graduate education or tutoring. Tutoring is defined as instructional time with a single student or perhaps a few students.

1. The marginal benefit (mb) of graduate education is close to zero, as represented by the lower of the two marginal-benefit curves.
2. There is evidence that tutoring is effective in increasing student achievement (Dobbie and Fryer, 2013). Therefore, the marginal-benefit curve for tutoring lies above the marginal-benefit curve for graduate education.

The positively sloped curve is the marginal cost of time allocated to either task, equal to the teacher's opportunity cost of after-school hours. Points t and g show the efficient allocation of after-school time, with T* hours allocated to tutoring and $G^* < T^*$ allocated to graduate education. Teachers will choose the efficient combination of tutoring and graduate work if the reward for tutoring is w_T per hour and the reward for graduate education is w_G per hour, where $w_G < w_T$.

We can contrast the efficient outcome in Figure 22-3 with the actual outcome in U.S. schools. Under typical compensation system, $w_T = 0$ and w_G is relatively large rather than close to zero. As a result, teachers do not allocate after-school time in an efficient manner, but spend too much after-school time in graduate coursework

FIGURE 22–3 Graduate Education vs. Tutoring Time

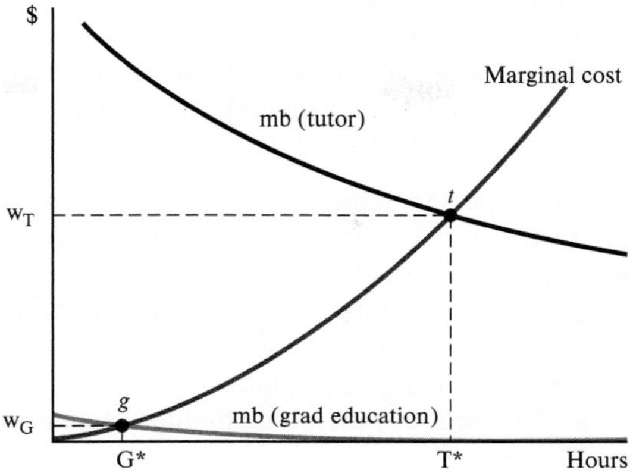

rather than in tutoring. From the school-district perspective, a reallocation of funds from graduate-school rewards to tutoring rewards would increase achievement without an increase in budgetary cost.

Innovations in Charter Schools

Some recent innovations in K–12 education provide important insights into the education production process. A charter school is more flexible than a traditional school in terms of its curriculum and management. Several cities have experimented with "no-excuse" charter schools, which have an extended school day, emphasize discipline, establish high expectations for student achievement, and monitor student progress with frequent testing. Recent studies suggest that no-excuse schools produce significant achievement gains for students.

A good example of a no-excuse charter school system is Promise Academy in Harlem, New York City. The schools have an extended school day and year, and also provide after-school tutoring for children in need of remedial work in reading and mathematics. On average, an academy student spends about twice as much time on school work as a student in a traditional school. The schools emphasize the culture of achievement and hard work. A key objective of the Promise Academy is to recruit and retain high-productivity teachers, and the schools use student scores on standardized tests to measure teacher performance and reward superior teachers. In the early years of Promise Academy, the turnover rate of teachers was relatively high (almost 50 percent in the first year) as the schools searched for the most effective teachers.

A recent study shows that Promise Academy schools generate large achievement gains (Dobbie and Fryer, 2009).

1. The typical student entering an academy school in sixth grade scored in the 39th percentile among New York students in both mathematics and reading. By the

eighth grade, the percentile ranking of the typical academy student rose to 74th in mathematics and 53rd in reading.

2. For middle schoolers, the typical black student entered the charter school at the 20th percentile of white achievement in mathematics (80 percent of white students had higher scores). After three years, the typical black academy student reached the 55th percentile (45 percent of white students had higher scores).

The reported achievement gains are remarkably large, and the authors suggest that further study is necessary to confirm the magnitude of the gains and determine their causes. The authors provide two tentative conclusions. First, it is plausible that the primary source of the achievement gains is high teacher productivity, a result of deselecting mediocre teachers and hiring superior teachers. Second, it is possible that the large gains resulted from the combined effects of several features of the schools, including higher teacher productivity and the focused learning environment.

A recent study of students in boarding schools provides some insights into the effect of the home environment (Curto and Fryer, 2011) on educational achievement. The idea behind a boarding school is to take a student out of an unfavorable home environment. Like other no-excuse charter schools, SEED schools in the District of Columbia and Baltimore have an extended school day, provide extensive after-school tutoring, monitor progress with frequent testing, and have high expectations for student achievement.

The reported achievement effects of SEED schools are large. To measure the effect of a SEED boarding school, suppose we move a student who attends a traditional public school and lives at home into a SEED boarding school. The authors report that each year spent at the new school generates a gain of 9 percentile points in mathematics and 8 percentile points in reading. For example, a student who enters at the 20th percentile in math will move to the 29th percentile after year one, to the 37th percentile after year two, and so on to the 56th percentile after year four. The achievement gains are a bit larger than the gains generated in regular no-excuse charter schools, indicating that there are benefits associated with boarding schools. A careful accounting of all the costs of boarding suggests that the achievement gains are not large enough to offset the substantial cost associated with housing students five days a week.

Overall Effects of Educational Spending

Recent empirical work on the education production function looks beyond test scores to estimate the effects of educational spending on long-term outcomes such as adult earnings. Jackson, Johnson, and Persico (2016) explore the connection between educational spending and adult outcomes (ages 40–50). Consider the effects of a 10 percent increase in per-pupil spending, in force for all 12 years that a student attends public school. The boost in spending generates (i) a 0.31 year increase in school attainment (0.31 more years of education), (ii) a 7 percent increase in adult wages, and (iii) a 3.2 percentage point decrease in the incidence of adult poverty.

The positive effects of increased spending are stronger for children from low-income families. For a 10 percent boost in spending, the effects are stronger in several ways.

1. Larger increase in the probability of high school graduation: 9.8 percentage point increase for low-income students, compared to 2.4 percentage points for nonpoor students.
2. Larger increases in adult wages: 9.6 percent for low-income students, compared to 5.5 percent for nonpoor students.
3. Larger decreases in poverty rates: 6.1 percentage point decrease for low-income students, compared to no effect for nonpoor students.

The estimated effects on earnings suggest that education spending passes the benefit-cost test: the benefit-cost ratio is roughly 3.0.

The authors explore the mechanisms behind the positive effects of spending on adult outcomes. A 10 percent increase in spending per pupil (i) decreases the student-teacher ratio by 5.7 percent (a change in class size of roughly one student), (ii) increases the length of the school year by 1.36 days, and (iii) increases teacher salaries by 4 percent. A higher teacher salary helps attract and retain high-productivity teachers. To summarize, an increase in spending buys better teachers who spend more time per day with each student over a longer school year.

3. SPENDING INEQUALITIES AND PUBLIC POLICY

The traditional funding source for K–12 education is the local property tax. Starting in the 1970s, citizens in many states challenged the constitutionality of property-tax funding, citing the substantial inequalities across school districts in spending per pupil and student achievement. In most state constitutions, education is identified as a fundamental right for all citizens. In contrast, education is not mentioned in the U.S. Constitution, so inequalities in spending are not proscribed by the U.S. Constitution.

As a result of state court cases challenging the constitutionality of education finances, states have developed several alternative notions of equity in K–12 education (Yinger, 2004).

1. *Adequacy.* Each local school district provides an education that meets or exceeds some minimum statewide standard.
2. *Access equality.* Voters in each school district have access to the same effective tax base. This means that a given property tax rate will generate the same revenue per pupil in every school district.
3. *Educational Equality.* Each school district provides the same level of education. Although several court cases have adopted a standard of educational equality, no court has indicated how a state is to measure equality.

Given these alternative notions of equity, there is substantial variation across states in systems of education finance. Most states that confront the issue of equity focus on reducing spending inequalities.

Intergovernmental Grants: Foundation Plans

The states use several types of intergovernmental grants to address spending inequalities across school districts. Under a system of foundation grants, a state provides larger grants to school districts with relatively low property tax bases. The foundation grant per pupil is

$$Grant = Foundation\ level - Foundation\ tax\ rate \cdot L$$

where L is the local property value per pupil (local tax base per pupil). The foundation grant equals the difference between the foundation level and the local revenue that could be generated if the district were to impose the foundation tax rate. To illustrate, consider a state with a foundation level of \$5,000 and a foundation tax rate of 2 percent (0.02). For a school district with $L = \$200{,}000$, the foundation grant is \$1,000:

$$Foundation\ grant = \$5{,}000 - 0.02 \cdot 200{,}000 = \$1{,}000$$

Note that the foundation grant is independent of the actual local tax rate. Continuing our example, Table 22–4 shows spending options with different local tax rates. Given the local tax base of \$200,000 per pupil, for every percentage point of the tax, local tax revenue and spending increases by \$2,000. If the school district chooses a tax rate of 1.7 percent, it generates \$3,400 of local revenue per pupil. Adding the local tax revenue to a \$1,000 foundation grant, the district has \$4,400 per pupil to spend. A higher tax rate of 1.8 percent generates \$3,600 in local property taxes but does not change the grant, so education spending increases by \$200. Moving in the opposite direction, a decrease in the local tax rate to 1.5 percent decreases the local contribution by \$400 and decreases education spending by the same amount.

The idea behind a foundation grant is to provide more money to school districts with lower tax bases. The foundation tax rate determines the rate at which the grant varies with the local property tax base. Continuing our example, a foundation tax rate of 0.02 means that each additional dollar of property value decreases the grant by \$0.02. For a district with $L = \$220{,}000$ the foundation grant is \$600 instead of \$1,000:

$$Foundation\ grant = \$5{,}000 - 0.02 \cdot 220{,}000 = \$600$$

This district gets \$400 less in a foundation grant because its tax base is \$20,000 higher: $\$400 = 0.02 \cdot \$20{,}000$.

TABLE 22–4 Tax and Spending Options with a Foundation Grant

Local Tax Rate	Local Tax Revenue	Foundation Grant	Education Spending
1.7 percent	\$3,400	\$1,000	\$4,400
1.8 percent	\$3,600	\$1,000	\$6,000
1.5 percent	\$3,000	\$1,000	\$4,000

Response to a Foundation Grant

As we saw in an earlier chapter, we can combine the consumer-choice model with the median-voter result to predict the response of local government to an intergovernmental grant. In Figure 22–4, point *a* shows the initial (pre-grant) utility-maximizing choice of the median voter, with spending per pupil equal to \$3,400. The median property value is \$200,000, and to generate \$3,400 for education, the local tax rate is 1.7 percent. A foundation grant of \$1,000 shifts the budget line to the right by \$1,000, and point *b* shows the new utility-maximizing bundle of education and other goods, where the marginal rate of substitution equals the price ratio. The \$1,000 grant increases spending on education by \$600 and increases spending on other goods by \$400.

The rational response by the median voter is to spend part of the grant on other goods, including other local public goods and private goods. To allow citizens to spend part of the grant on private goods, the school district cuts the property tax rate. Given the \$4,000 target education spending and a \$1,000 foundation grant, the local contribution is only \$3,000. Therefore, the district cuts the tax rate from 1.7 percent to 1.5 percent:

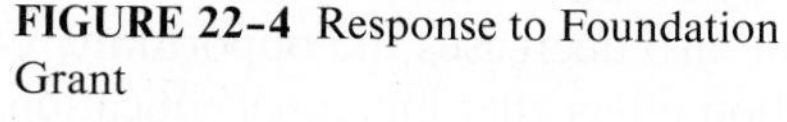

$$\$3{,}000 = 0.015 \cdot \$200{,}000$$

The tax cut from 1.7 percent to 1.5 percent frees up \$400 to spend on other goods. To summarize, a foundation grant increases education spending and also provides tax relief that increases spending on other goods.

The numerical example in Figure 22–4 is consistent with empirical studies of responses to foundation grants (Evans, Murray, and Schwab, 2001; Card and Payne, 2002). On average in low-spending school districts, 60 percent of a foundation grant

FIGURE 22–4 Response to Foundation Grant

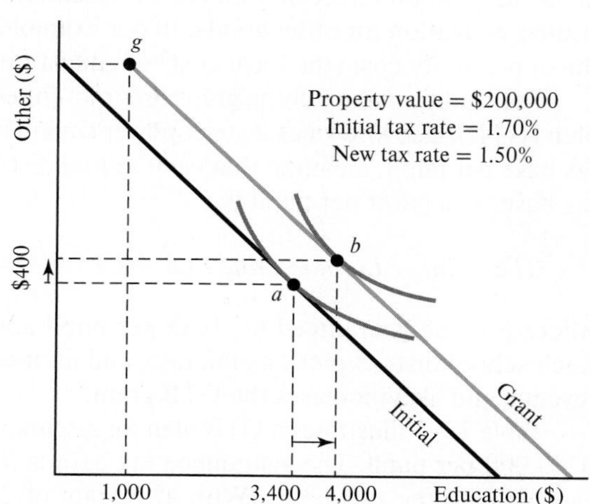

is allocated to education, leaving 40 percent for other goods. This is another example of the flypaper effect: A relatively large fraction of grant money sticks where it first hits (the school district).

The purpose of a system of foundation grants is to decrease inequality in education spending across school districts. The largest grants are given to the school districts with the lowest property values, so the greatest stimulus for education occurs in low-wealth districts. As we'll see later in the chapter, empirical studies suggest that foundation grants do in fact reduce education spending gaps.

Matching Grants: Guaranteed Tax Base

We turn next to a system of matching grants for education spending. Under a matching grant, every dollar generated from local taxes is matched by m dollars of additional revenue from the state. For example, if $m = \$0.25$, each dollar of local tax revenue increases the state grant by \$0.25, so the school district gets \$1.25 worth of education for a local cost of only \$1. In general, the local cost per dollar of education spending is

$$\textit{local cost per dollar} = \frac{1}{1+m}$$

where m is the match rate. In our example, the local cost per dollar of education is

$$\textit{local cost per dollar} = \frac{1}{1.25} = \$0.80$$

Compared to a foundation grant, a matching grant has a larger stimulative effect because it has both an income effect and a substitution effect. Like the foundation grant, the matching grant increases the median voter's real income, increasing the desired spending on all "normal" goods, including education (the income effect). A matching grant also decreases the opportunity cost of education spending, generating a substitution effect that increases education spending as the median voter substitutes education for other goods. In our example, a matching rate of 0.25 decreases the opportunity cost (the local cost) of education spending from \$1.00 to \$0.80.

The traditional matching-grant program for education is the guaranteed tax base plan (GTB), also known as district power equalizing. The state specifies a guaranteed tax base per pupil, meaning that each school district has access to the same effective tax base. The grant per pupil is

$$\textit{GTB grant} = \textit{Local tax rate} \cdot (B - L)$$

where B is the guaranteed tax base per pupil and L is the local tax base per pupil. Each school district picks its tax rate, and an increase in the tax rate increases local revenue and also increases the GTB grant.

Table 22–5 illustrates a GTB plan for a school district with a local tax base of $L =$ \$200,000 per pupil. The guaranteed tax base is $B =$ \$250,000, so there is a \$50,000 gap between the two bases. With a tax rate of 2 percent, the district raises \$4,000

TABLE 22-5 Tax and Spending Options with a Guaranteed Tax Base

Local Tax Rate	Local Tax Revenue	Grant	Education Spending
2 percent	$4,000	$1,000	$5,000
3 percent	$6,000	$1,500	$7,500

locally and gets a grant of $1,000, for a total of $5,000. An increase in the tax rate to 3 percent increases local tax revenue by $2,000 (to $6,000) and increases the grant by $500, for a total increase of $2,500. The local cost per dollar of education is $0.80:

$$\text{Local cost per dollar} = \frac{\Delta \text{Local taxes}}{\Delta \text{Education Spending}} = \frac{2000}{2500} = \$0.80$$

In general, the local cost per dollar of education under a GTB plan equals the ratio of the local tax base to the guaranteed tax base. In our example, the local cost per dollar is

$$\text{Local cost per dollar} = \frac{L}{B} = \frac{\$200{,}000}{\$250{,}000} = \$0.80$$

Effects of Equalization Plans on Spending and Achievement Inequalities

In the 1970s and 1980s, a series of state court cases mandated reforms of education finance systems. The resulting wave of education-finance reform was based on the notion of equity in education spending, defined generally as equal spending per pupil across school districts. Evans, Murray, and Schwab (2001) summarize studies of this wave of reform. States had the option to either "level up" (increase spending in low-spending districts) or "level down" (decrease spending in high-spending districts). Most states used foundation plans to "level-up" spending, but there were exceptions. On average, the equalization programs decreased spending disparities across school districts within a state by 16 percent to 38 percent. Overall, low-spending school districts used roughly 40 percent of additional grant money to reduce local taxes and used 60 percent to increase spending per pupil.

The next wave of education-finance reform started in the 1990s. This wave of reform is based on the notions of both equity and *adequacy*, where adequacy is defined by the level of spending per pupil. The inclusion of adequacy as a criterion for finance systems means leveling-down is no longer a practical option for states.

In a study of the most recent wave of reform, the empirical analysis focuses on low-income versus high-income districts (LaFortune, Rothstein, and Schanzenbach, 2015). The key question is how equalization programs affect spending disparities across school districts with varying average household income. There are three key results.

1. Larger grants to low-income school districts. In the state of Ohio in 1991 (before reform), the typical low-income school district (lowest quintile) received $1,102 more per pupil than a high-income district (top quintile). In 2011, the

gap between the grant to a low-income district and the grant to a high-income district was $3,387 per pupil.

2. Larger increase in spending per pupil in low-income school districts. On average across states, the implementation of reforms increased per-pupil spending in low-income districts by $1,023, compared to $510 in high-income districts. The $1,023 increase in spending is roughly 10 percent of spending in low-income school districts.
3. Decrease in achievement gaps. The changes in relative spending decreased achievement gaps: the test scores of low-income districts increased relative to the scores of high-income districts.

In 1994, the state of Michigan adopted Proposal A, comprehensive overhaul of the state's school finance system. The state eliminated the local property tax as a source of education funding and increased the state sales tax to make up for lost revenue. Proposal A largely eliminated local discretion over school spending and increased the state share of K–12 spending. The state share of school expenditures increased from 32 percent in 1994 to 79 percent in 1995. The state provides larger grants to low-spending districts and allows low-spending districts to increase spending more rapidly than other districts. The finance system relies largely on a system of foundation grants, with additional funding through categorical grants for special education, "at-risk" students and other programs.

The Michigan reforms decreased spending disparities across school districts. In 1991, spending per pupil at the 95th percentile was $8,620, compared to $4,680 at the 5th percentile. In 2000, the values were $9,285 for the 95th percentile and $6,385 for the 5th percentile. In other words, the 95/5 ratio decreased from 1.84 to 1.46. Between 1991 and 2000, average spending per pupil increased by 26 percent for the state as a whole, compared to 3.1 percent for the school districts in the top spending decile and 42.8 percent for school districts in the lowest decile. Overall, urban school districts experienced smaller spending gains than other districts (20 percent versus 27 percent). Many of the districts experiencing the smallest gains are in the Detroit area, but most large inner-city districts experienced large gains (Detroit, 32 percent; Flint, 38 percent; Lansing, 32 percent).

There is some evidence that the Michigan reform package increased student achievement. Roy (2011) estimates that a $1,000 increase in per-pupil spending in lower grades increases test performance (passing rates) by 0.20 to 0.40 standard deviations for reading and 0.40 to 0.55 standard deviations for mathematics. Papke (2005) estimates that a 10 percent increase in per-pupil spending increases test performance (passing rates) by about 2.2 percentage points.

As we saw earlier in the chapter, the study by Jackson, Johnson, and Persico (2016) shows that increases in educational spending increase adult earnings. The data for the study come from Michigan's Proposal A. The study showed that the positive effects of increased spending are larger for low-income students: there is a larger bang per education buck (dollar) for low-income students. The Michigan reform program increased spending in low-income school districts by relatively large amounts, so the program sent more bucks to districts where the bang per buck is larger.

How do central-city schools fare under equalization programs? Central-city schools have relatively high costs because a large fraction of their students come from low-income families. Central-city schools devote more time and resources to security measures, dealing with family and health crises, and teaching children with weak educational preparation and English skills. Central-city schools have relatively high costs and had above-average spending levels before reforms were implemented. As a result, they often receive relatively small benefits from equalization programs, and in some cases actually get less money (Courant and Loeb, 1997; Duncombe and Yinger, 1997). If the funding formulas were modified to incorporate cost differences, some central-city school districts would receive substantially larger intergovernmental grants as part of an equalization program.

REVIEW THE CONCEPTS

1. The replacement of an average teacher (50th percentile) by a teacher at the 84th percentile [______] {↑, ↓ –} the test score of the typical student, moving the student from the 50th percentile to the [______] (45th, 58th, 99th) percentile.
2. For a class of 20 students, the economic value of a superior teacher (84th percentile) relative to an average teacher is over [______] ($10,000, $50,000, $426,000).
3. The wage of the typical teacher is largely determined by [______] and [______].
4. An increase in graduate education [______] {↑, ↓ –} teacher productivity.
5. Teaching experience increases teacher productivity for the first [______] (1, 3, 9, 20) years.
6. To promote efficiency in allocating teacher time, the monetary reward for an hour of tutoring [______] (<, =, >) the monetary reward for an hour of graduate study.
7. The study of the long-term effects of school spending suggests that a 10 percent increase in spending increased [______] and [______] and decreased [______].
8. An increase in the local tax rate [______] {↑, ↓ –} the value of a foundation grant and [______] {↑, ↓, –} the value of a matching grant.
9. Consider a state with a foundation level of $6,000 and a foundation tax rate of 3 percent. For a school district with a property value per pupil of $180,000, the foundation grant is $[______].
10. For an equalization program, roughly [______] (1, 10, 60, 90) percent of a grant is spent on education.
11. Suppose the matching rate for a GTB grant is one-third. The local cost per dollar of education is $[______].
12. The stimulative effect of a grant is larger for a [______] (foundation, GTB) grant because it has a [______] effect.

13. The positive effects of increased school spending are [______] for low-income students than for high-income students.
14. For each pair of variables, indicate whether the relationship is positive, negative, neutral, or ambiguous.

Parameter	Choice Variable	Relationship
Local tax base per pupil	Foundation grant	[______]
Local tax rate	Foundation grant	[______]
GTB match rate	Local cost per dollar of education	[______]
Local tax rate	GTB grant	[______]

APPLY THE CONCEPTS

1. *Verbal Ability vs. Experience*
   Consider two inputs to teacher productivity, verbal ability (measured by SAT score) and teaching experience (in years).
   a. Based on the empirical results concerning teacher productivity presented in this chapter, draw an education isoquant, with experience on the horizontal axis (0 to 20 years) and verbal ability on the vertical axis (200 to 800).
   b. Suppose the price of experience is $1,000 per year and the price of verbal ability is $10 per point on the SAT exam. Use the input choice model to show the cost-minimizing input mix.
2. *Efficient Number of Teachers*
   Consider a school with 720 students. Class size is determined by the number of teachers hired (t). Total achievement is computed as $A = 360 \cdot ln(t)$, where ln is the natural logarithm. Using the rules of differentiation, the marginal benefit of a teacher is $mb(A) = 360/t$. The monetary value of achievement is $1 per unit, and the marginal cost of a teacher is $w = \$10$. Illustrate the efficient outcome, including a value for the efficient number of teachers (t^E) and the efficient class size (S^E).
3. *Tutoring Time*
   Suppose the marginal benefit of after-school tutoring time (h) is $mb(h) = 200/h$ and the marginal cost is $mc(h) = 2 \cdot \text{h}$. Illustrate the efficient outcome, including values for the efficient number of hours (h^E) and the wage per hour of tutoring.
4. *Foundation Grant*
   Consider a school district with $\text{L} = \$200{,}000$. The initial education spending is $E^* = \$3{,}000$. The foundation level is $6,000 and the foundation tax rate is 2 percent. Assume that 60 percent of a grant is spent on education.
   a. Illustrate the effects of the foundation grant on education spending, including values for the grant (G), the new education spending (E^{**}), and the change in spending on other goods (ΔA).
   b. The initial (pre-grant) local tax rate is $t^* =$ [______] and the new tax rate is $t^{**} =$ [______].

5. *Response to GTB Grant*
Consider a school district with an initial (pre-grant) education spending $E^* =$ \$6,000. The matching rate for a GTB grant is $m = 0.25$. The price elasticity of demand for school spending is -1.50. Illustrate the effects of the GTB program on education spending, including values for the new price of education ($p^{**} =$ local cost per dollar) and the new spending on education (E^{**}).

REFERENCES AND READING

1. Card, David, and Abigail Payne, "School Finance Reform, the Distribution of Test School Spending, and the Distribution of Student Test Scores." *Journal of Public Economics* 83 (2002), pp. 49–82.
2. Chaudhary, Latika, "Education Inputs, Student Performance, and School Finance Reform in Michigan." *Economics of Education Review* 28 (2009), pp. 90–98.
3. Chetty, Raj, John Friedmand, Nathaniel Hilger, Emmanueal Saez, Diane Witmore Schanzenbach, and Danny Yagan, "How Does Your Kindergarten Classroom Affect Your Earnings? Evidence from Project STAR," NBER Working Paper (2010).
4. Chetty, Raj, John Friedman, and Jonah Rockoff, "Measuring the Impacts of Teachers II: Teacher Value-Added and Student Outcomes in Adulthood." *American Economic Review* 104 (2014), pp. 2633–79.
5. Courant, Paul N., and Susanna Loeb, "Centralization of School Finance in Michigan." *Journal of Policy Analysis and Management* 16. 1 (1997), pp. 114–36.
6. Cullen, J.B., and S. Loeb, "K-12 education in Michigan." In C. Ballard, P. N. Courant, D. C. Drake, R. Fischer, and E. R. Gerber (Eds.), *Michigan at the Millennium: A Benchmark and Analysis of its Fiscal and Economic Structure.* Ann Arbor, Michigan: Center for Local, State, and Urban Policy, 2003.
7. Ding, Weili, and Steven Lehrer, "Do Peers Affect Student Achievement in China's Secondary Schools?" *Review of Economics and Statistics* 89 (2007), pp. 300–312.
8. Dobbie, Will, and Roland Fryer, "Are High-Quality Schools Enough to Close the Achievement Gap? Evidence from a Bold Social Experiment in Harlem," Working Paper, Harvard University 2009.
9. Dobbie, Will, and Roland Fryer, "Getting beneath the Veil of Effective Schools: Evidence from New York City," *American Economic Journal: Applied Economics* 5 (2013): 28–60.
10. Duncombe, William, and John Yinger, "Why Is It So Hard to Help Central- City Schools?" *Journal of Policy Analysis and Management* 16. 1 (1997), pp. 85–113.
11. Evans, William N., Sheila E. Murray, and Robert M. Schwab, "Schoolhouses, Courthouses, and Statehouses after Serrano." *Journal of Policy Analysis and Management* 16. 1 (1997), pp. 10–31.
12. Evans, William N., Sheila E. Murray, and Robert M. Schwab. "The Property Tax and Education Finance, Uneasy Compromises." In *Property Taxation and Local*

Government Finance, edited by Wallace E. Oates. Cambridge, Mass.: Lincoln Institute of Land Policy, 2001.

13. Fredriksson, Peter, Bjorn Ockert, and Hessel Oosterbeek, "Long-Term Effects of Class Size." *Quarterly Journal of Economics*, 128 (2013), pp. 249–285.
14. Hanushek, Eric, *The Economic Value of Higher Teacher Quality*. Washington, DC: The Urban Institute, 2010.
15. Hanushek, Eric A., and Steven G. Rivkin. "Generalizations about Using Value-Added Measures of Teacher Quality." *American Economic Review: Papers and Proceedings* 100 (2010), pp. 267–71.
16. Jackson, C. Kirabo, Rucher C. Johnson, and Claudia Persico, "The Effects of School Spending on Educational and Economic Outcomes: Evidence from School Finance Reforms." *Quarterly Journal of Economics* (2016), pp. 157–218.
17. Kreuger, Alan, "Experimental Estimates of Education Production Functions," *Quarterly Journal of Economics* (1999), pp. 497–532.
18. LaFortune, Julien, Jesse Rothstein, and Diane Whitmore Schanzenbach, "School Finance Reform and the Distribution of Student Achievement," *National Bureau of Economic Research*, November 2015.
19. Papke, Leslie, "The Effects of Changes in Michigan's School Finance System." *Public Finance Review* 36. 4 (2008), pp. 456–74.
20. Sund, Krister, "Estimating peer effects in Swedish High School Using School, Teacher and Student Fixed Effects." *Economics of Education Review* 28 (2009), pp. 329–36.
21. Roy, Joydeep, "Impact of School Finance Reform on Resource Equalization and Academic Performance: Evidence from Michigan," *Education Finance and Policy*, 6. 2 (Spring 2011), pp. 137–67.
22. Tiebout, C, "A Pure Theory of Local Expenditures." *Journal of Political Economy* 64 (1956), pp. 416–24.
23. Yinger, John (ed.), *Helping Children Left Behind: State Aid and the Pursuit of Educational Equity*. Cambridge: MIT Press, 2004.
24. U.S. Bureau of the Census. Census of Governments, 2012.

CHAPTER 23

Crime and Public Policy

Erle Gardner, the writer of detective stories, was paid by the word, and his villains were always killed by the last bullet in the gun. When asked why his heroes were so careless with their first five shots, he responded, "Every time I say bang in the story, I get three cents. If you think I'm going to finish the gun battle while my hero has fifteen cents worth of unexploded ammunition in his gun, you're nuts."

—BARTLETT'S BOOK OF ANECDOTES (2000)

This chapter explores the economics of crimes that involve the transfer of property. We develop a model of a rational, utility-maximizing criminal, who commits a property crime if the expected benefit exceeds the expected cost. The traditional approach to controlling crime is to allocate resources to police, criminal courts, and prisons to increase the certainty and severity of punishment for crime. As we will see in the chapter, there is another approach that rests on a solid theoretical and empirical foundation: invest in education to decrease dropout rates and increase the returns to lawful employment.

1. CRIME FACTS

Although crime that is motivated by the acquisition of property can be modeled with conventional models of rational choice, the motives for violent crime are more complex. Nonetheless, violent crime is relevant to urban economics because it affects location choices and the markets for housing and land. In 2010, the victimization rate for violent crime (assault, robbery, rape/sexual assault, and homicide) was 19.3 per 1,000 persons. Roughly half of violent crimes are assaults that do not cause injuries. The homicide rate was 6 per 100,000 persons.

Table 23-1 shows the victimization rates for property crime, reported as the number of victims per 1,000 persons or households. Robbery is a crime of force, defined as a property transfer that involves direct interaction between a criminal and a victim. In contrast, other property crimes (burglary, motor-vehicle theft, general theft) are crimes of stealth and do not involve contact between the criminal and the victim.

Figure 23-1 shows victimization rates by income and geography. In the upper panel, victimization rates generally decrease as income increases. A household in the lowest income group is victimized at a rate that is 40 to 50 percent higher than

TABLE 23-1 Victimization Rates for Property Crime

	Rate per 1,000 Persons or Households
Robbery	2.2
Household burglary	26.3
Motor vehicle theft	6.6
Theft: Less than $250	94.8
Theft: $250 or more	27.0

Source: U.S. Bureau of Justice, *Criminal Victimization in the United States,* 2011.

FIGURE 23-1 Crime Victimization: Income and Geography

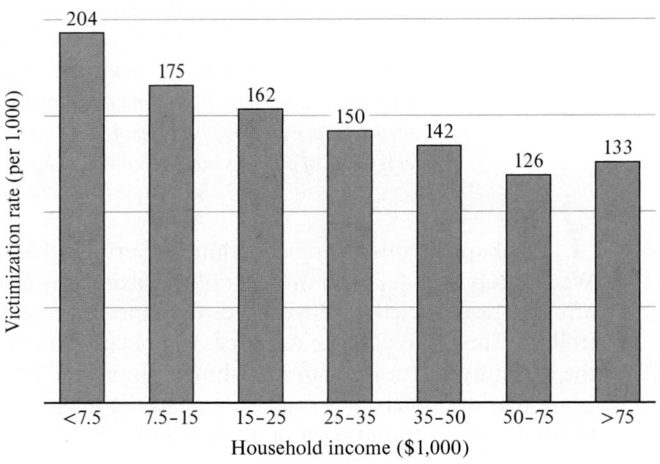

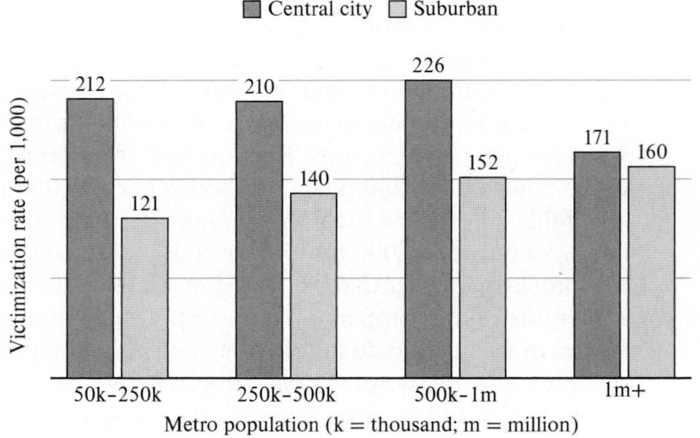

Source: U.S. Bureau of Justice, *Criminal Victimization in the United States,* 2011.

the typical middle-income or high-income household. In the lower panel, victimization rates in central cities exceed victimization rates in suburbs, but the difference is relatively small in the largest metropolitan areas. For central cities, the largest metropolitan areas have the lowest victimization rates. This is a dramatic reversal from 10 to 15 years ago, when the central cities of the largest metropolitan areas had the highest victimization rates.

Figure 23–2 shows the time trends in the victimization rates of property and violent crime. As shown in the upper panel, the victimization rate for property crime in 2010 was just over one-fourth the victimization rate experienced in 1975. For violent crime, between 1973 and 1993 the victimization rate was relatively stable. As

FIGURE 23–2 Time Trends in Crime Victimization

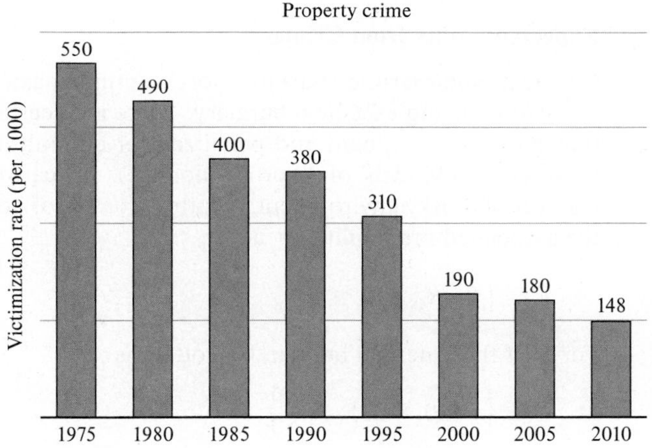

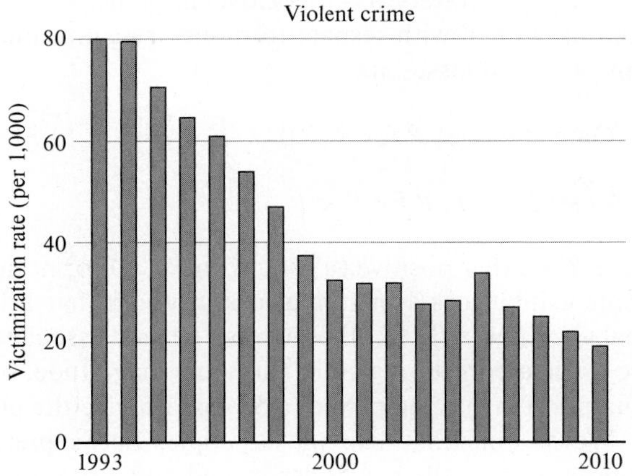

Source: U.S. Bureau of Justice, NCVS Victimization Analysis Tool, 2017.

shown in the lower panel of the figure, the victimization rate for violent crime in 2010 was roughly one-fourth the peak rate experienced in 1993.

2. A MODEL OF THE RATIONAL CRIMINAL

In this part of the chapter we explore the decision of whether to commit a property crime. We develop a model of a rational criminal, who commits a crime if the expected benefit exceeds the expected cost. We use the model to show the effects of public policy on the benefits and costs of crime, and thus crime rates. The policy responses include changes in the certainty and severity of punishment for crime. The model explains why the incidence of criminal behavior is relatively high among high-school dropouts and other low-income individuals.

Expected Utility from Crime

Consider Notarbartolo (Bart for short), a utility maximizer who is considering taking a day to plan and execute a burglary. There is uncertainty because there is a chance that Bart will be caught and penalized for committing the crime. As explained in Chapter 24 (Models of Microeconomics), we can use a lottery to represent the features of a risky environment. A lottery is a list of possible outcomes R_1 and R_2 and the associated probabilities r_1 and r_2.

$$L = \{R_1, R_2; r_1, r_2\}$$

For Bart the potential burglar, the lottery is

$$L = \left\{\$120, -\$25; \frac{3}{5}, \frac{2}{5}\right\}$$

$R_1 = \$120$ is the loot from the crime, and $R_2 = -\$25$ represents the penalty resulting from being caught committing the crime. The probability of success is $r_1 = 3/5$ and the probability of failure (being caught and penalized) is $r_2 = 2/5$.

The crime lottery has a positive and a negative payoff, and we can use a utility function defined with respect to monetary gains and losses. The changes in utility from gains and losses are

Gain: $\Delta u = g \,.\, R$ for $R > 0$

Loss: $\Delta u = l \,.\, R$ for $R < 0$

where R is either positive (a gain, with $R_1 > 0$) or negative (a loss, with $R_2 < 0$). Most people exhibit loss aversion: a loss in wealth has a larger effect on utility than an equal gain in wealth. In other words, the pain associated with a loss exceeds the pleasure associated with a gain of the same magnitude, so $l > g$. A common numerical assumption is that the pain of a \$1 loss is twice the pleasure of a \$1 gain: $l = 2 \cdot g$.

We assume that like most people, Bart's preferences exhibit loss aversion. Suppose $g = 3$ utils per dollar gained and $l = 6$ utils per dollar lost. In this case, a loss is twice as painful as a gain is pleasurable. In Figure 23-3, the horizontal axis

FIGURE 23–3 Expected Utility From Crime

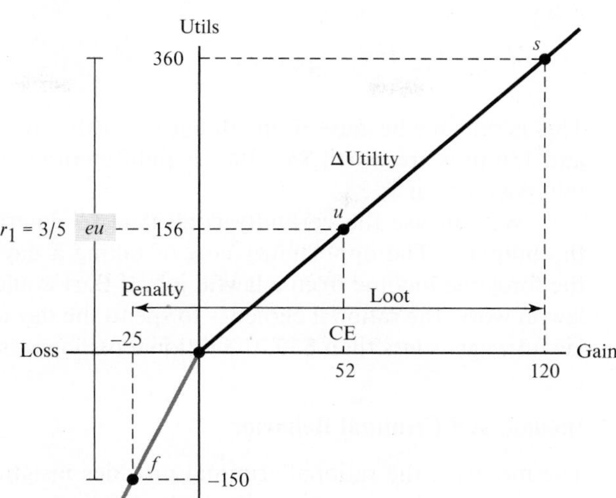

shows the gain (on the right) and the loss (on the left), and the vertical axis shows the change in utility in utils. For a gain, the slope of the utility curve is $g = 3$ utils per dollar. For a loss, the slope of the utility curve is $l = 6$ utils per dollar.

Figure 23–3 shows how to compute the expected utility of the crime lottery. Point *s* shows the outcome with a successful burglary (change in wealth = \$120 and change in utility = 360 utils) and point *f* shows the outcome with a failed crime (change in wealth = −\$25 and change in utility = −150 utils). The expected utility from crime is the weighted average of the two outcomes, with weights equal to the respective probabilities of success and failure.

$$eu = \frac{3}{5}\, 360\ utils - \frac{2}{5}\, 150\ utils = 156\ utils$$

In Figure 23–3, the slider is three-fifths of the distance from the utility of the failed outcome and the utility of the successful outcome, so the expected utility of the crime lottery is $eu = 156$ utils.

Certainty Equivalent and the Crime Decision

As explained in Chapter 24 (Models of Microeconomics), the certainty equivalent of a lottery translates expected utility into a certain dollar amount. Using *CE* as the symbol for certainty equivalent,

$$u(CE) = eu(Lottery)$$

In words, the utility of the certainty equivalent equals the expected utility of the lottery. In the case of gain-loss lottery with a positive expected utility, the certainty equivalent is the expected utility divided by *g*, the change in utility per dollar gained.

$$CE = \frac{eu}{g}$$

In our example, $g = 3$ and the expected utility is 156 utils, so the certainty equivalent is \$52:

$$CE = \frac{eu}{g} = \frac{156}{3} = \$52$$

This is sensible because if one dollar is worth 3 utils, then 1 util is worth 1/3 dollar and 156 utils are worth \$52. Bart is indifferent between the crime lottery and a certain payment of \$52.

We can use the certainty equivalent to determine whether Bart will commit the burglary. The opportunity cost of taking a day to plan and execute a crime is the foregone income from a lawful job. If Bart could earn at least \$52 for certain in lawful work, the rational choice is to spend the day on a lawful job. In contrast, if his lawful wage is less than \$52, the rational response is to commit the burglary.

Income and Criminal Behavior

The model of the rational criminal provides insights into the greater prevalence of crime among low-income individuals. Crime is a rational choice if the benefit of crime (measured as its certainty equivalent) exceeds the opportunity cost (the lawful wage). As a worker's wage increases, the opportunity cost of criminal activity increases, so the likelihood of committing crime decreases. In our original example, the certainty equivalent of crime is \$52, so crime is the rational choice for a worker whose lawful wage is less than \$52.

Figure 23–4 illustrates the relationship between lawful wages and crime rates. Suppose workers earn wages that range from \$1 to \$100. There are two workers at each integer wage, so there is a total of 200 workers. The positively sloped curve shows for each wage, the number of workers whose wage is no higher than the wage.

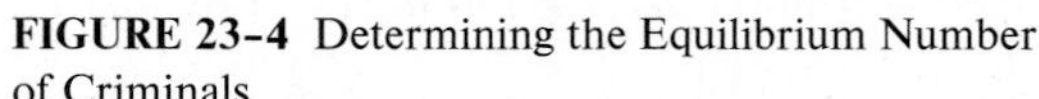

FIGURE 23–4 Determining the Equilibrium Number of Criminals

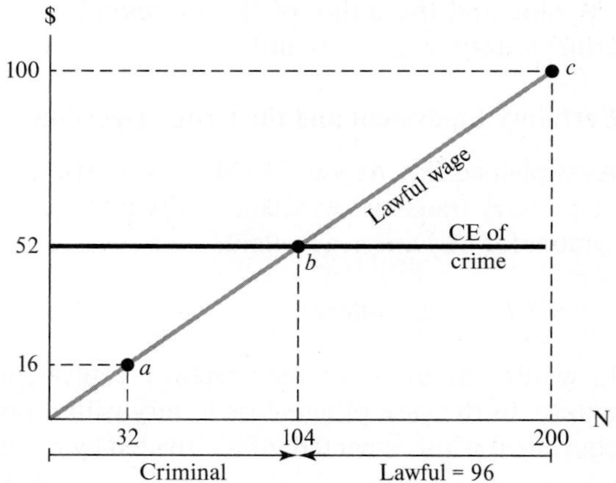

Point *a* shows that there are 32 workers with wages less than or equal to \$16, while point *b* shows that there are 104 workers with wages less than or equal to \$52. The horizontal curve shows the certainty equivalent of crime. For CE = \$52, crime is rational choice for the 104 workers whose lawful wages are less than or equal to \$52. That leaves 96 workers with wages exceeding the certainty equivalent of crime, so there are 96 lawful workers.

Anguish Costs and Internal Penalties

Up to this point, our model of the rational criminal has considered readily measurable costs and benefits. One implication of the analysis is that two people who face the same benefit (loot), cost (penalty), and probability of being penalized for crime will make the same choice. Both workers will commit the crime if the certainty equivalent of crime exceeds the lawful wage. This is not consistent with reality: people make different choices even if they face the same crime benefits and costs. Most people have an aversion to committing anti-social acts and won't commit crime even if the payoff is very large. In other words, most people incorporate the moral consequences of crime into their decisions, and that's enough to prevent criminal behavior.

We can incorporate morality and aversion to committing crime by adding an internal penalty from a crime. An internal penalty quantifies the anguish a person feels when he or she commits a crime. The internal penalty is self-imposed and certain. In our graphical model, an internal penalty representing anguish cost shifts the expected utility point downward along the utility axis. For example, suppose Bart's internal penalty is 36 utils. Starting from the situation shown in Figure 23-3, the expected utility from crime decreases from 156 utils to 120 utils:

$$eu = \frac{3}{5}\, 360\ utils - \frac{2}{5}\, 150\ utils - 36\ utils = 120\ utils$$

The certainty equivalent of the crime decreases from \$52 to \$40 (equal to 120/3). As a result, crime is rational for lawful wages up to \$40, compared to \$52 without the internal penalty.

People vary in their anguish costs and internal penalties for committing crime. For most people, the internal penalty from committing crime is large enough to drop the certainty equivalent of crime below the lawful wage. For people with a relatively large internal penalty, crime is not a rational choice.

Insights from Neuroscience

Recent developments in neuroscience provide insights into the decision-making process behind criminal choices. In the last few decades, neuroscientists have explored the brain activity associated with making decisions, and can now map and measure the neural activity involved in all sorts of choices. Specifically, neuroscientists observe neural activity representing both the benefit and the cost of a particular action. To decide whether to take an action like committing a crime, a person compares the anticipated benefit of the action to its anticipated cost. The principal decision-making region of the brain is the prefrontal cortex (PFC). The PFC observes the benefit and valuation activity in various regions of the brain, and uses these activity levels as inputs into the decision-making process. The valuation of benefits and costs are essentially gut feelings in the sense that they are instantaneous valuations of the perceived benefit or cost of an action. In other words, the PFC uses gut feelings as inputs into the decision-making process.

The PFC is not a simple calculator of gut-feeling benefits and costs, but incorporates other factors into the decision-making process. The PFC uses cognition (conscious thought) to consider a broad set of possible consequences of an action. The dorsal-lateral portion of the PFC (the DLPFC) is responsible for introducing other factors into the decision-making process. In particular, the DLPFC incorporates the possible future consequence of an action, causing a person to make a thoughtful rather than an impulsive choice. There are two implications for the analysis of criminal behavior.

1. *Present bias.* Humans are subject to present bias: we accurately incorporate the present consequences of an action into our decision making, but either ignore or underestimate the future consequences. This present bias can lead to misguided decisions, but the bias can be counteracted by cognitive processing utilizing the DLPFC.
2. *Differing ability to overcome present bias.* People vary in the strength of activity from the DLPFC. A person whose DLPFC is less active in relative terms is more likely to make impulsive choices. In other words, people differ in their ability to overcome present bias.

The notion of present bias provides one possible explanation of why two people who face the same crime opportunity make different choices: an impulsive person commits the crime, while a more thoughtful person does not.

3. PUBLIC POLICY AND CRIME

So far we have explored the choices of an individual who deploys the logic of expected utility to decide whether to commit a crime. The key insight is that crime is a rational choice if the certainty equivalent of crime exceeds the lawful wage. In this part of the chapter we widen our perspective to explore how public policy can affect crime rates by (i) changing the certainty equivalent of crime and (ii) changing the lawful wage.

Investment in Human Capital

Consider the effects of investment in human capital. Suppose a public investment in education or job training increases human capital and worker productivity. For example, a local government could provide funds to schools to hire more teachers or to hire more productive teachers. The resulting increase in human capital increases worker productivity, so it increases the lawful wages of some workers.

FIGURE 23–5 Reduce Crime with an Increase in Human Capital

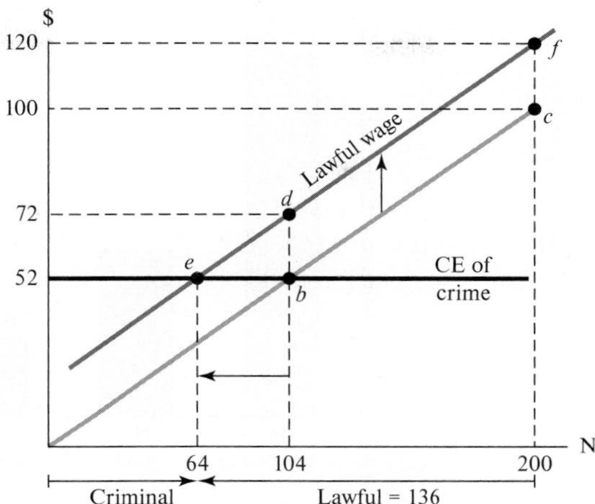

Figure 23–5 shows the effects of a change in the distribution of wages across workers. For each worker, the lawful wage increases by \$20, so the lowest wage is \$21 rather than \$1, and the highest wage is \$120 rather than \$100. The lawful-wage curve upward by \$20 and to the left by 40 workers: for worker #104, the lawful wage is now \$72 rather than \$52; for worker #64, the lawful wage is now \$52 rather than \$32. The new equilibrium is shown by point *e*: if the certainty equivalent of crime is \$52, the number of criminals is 64 rather than 104. In this case, 40 workers switch from crime to lawful work. The lesson is that one way to reduce crime is to invest in education to increase human capital and lawful wages.

Empirical studies have measured the sensitivity of crime to changes in the wages of low-skill workers. Grogger (1991, 2000) shows that low-skill wages and crime rates move in opposite directions. The estimated elasticity of crime with respect to wages is between −1.0 and −2.0 (Gould, Weinberg, and Mustard, 2002). In other words, a 10 percent increase in the wages of low-skill workers decreases crime by between 10 and 20 percent.

Consider next the effects of policies that increase high-school graduation rates. Figure 23–6 shows the relationship between a white male's level of education and the likelihood of being in jail, prison, or another institution related to the criminal-justice system. The numbers show that high-school dropouts are 13 times more likely to be institutionalized than college graduates. Between the two extremes, there is a negative relationship between education and institutionalization rates.

There is evidence that investment in high-school education is an efficient way to reduce crime (Lochner and Moretti, 2004). Each additional year of high school decreases the crime participation rate and generates large reductions in crime. For example, the estimated elasticity of arrest rates with respect to high-school graduation rates is −2.0 for violent crime and −1.3 for motor-vehicle theft. We can compute the benefits and costs of promoting graduation.

FIGURE 23–6 Institutionalization Rates and Education, U.S. White Males

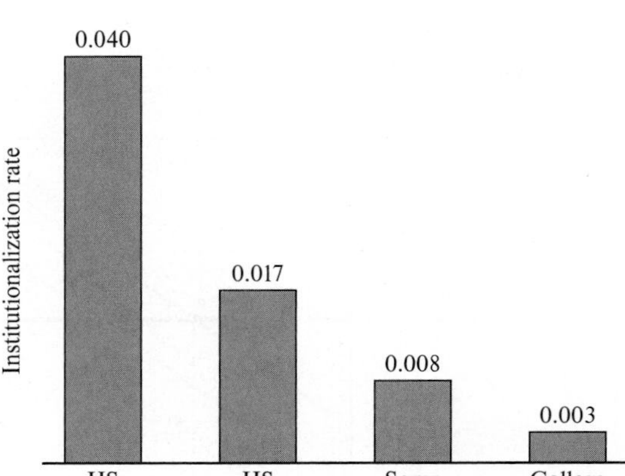

Source: Rafael, Steven, and Michael Stoll, *Do Prisons Make Us Safer? The Benefits and Costs of the Prison Boom*, New York: Russell Sage, 2008.

1. *Cost.* The annual cost per pupil is \$6,000, so if getting a student from dropout to graduate status requires one additional year of schooling, the cost is \$6,000.
2. *Benefit.* The wage premium for high-school graduation is about 50 percent, so a high-school graduate earns roughly \$8,400 in additional income per year for the rest of his or her working life. The resulting decrease in crime generates a benefit to society of roughly \$1,600 per year for the rest of the person's potential crime career.

To summarize, a one-time investment of \$6,000 yields a return of \$1,600 per year for 30 or 40 years.

The Certainty of Punishment

In 2004, nationwide spending on the criminal-justice system was \$640 per capita. An increase in spending on police and the courts provides more resources for patrol, investigation, and prosecution. If an increase in spending increases the probability that a criminal will be caught and penalized, the certainty equivalent of crime decreases, decreasing the number of workers for whom crime is the rational choice.

Figure 23–7 shows that an increase in the probability of being caught and penalized decreases the certainty equivalent of crime. Starting from the situation shown in Figure 23–3, suppose the probability of success decreases from 3/5 to 1/2, so the probability of being penalized increases from 2/5 to 1/2. The utilities associated with success (360 utils) and failure (−150 utils) don't change, but now there is only a 50-50 chance of success. As a result, the expected utility from crime decreases from 156 utils to 105 utils:

$$eu = \frac{1}{2}\,360\ utils - \frac{1}{2}\,150\ utils = 105\ utils$$

FIGURE 23–7 Probability of Success and Certainty Equivalent

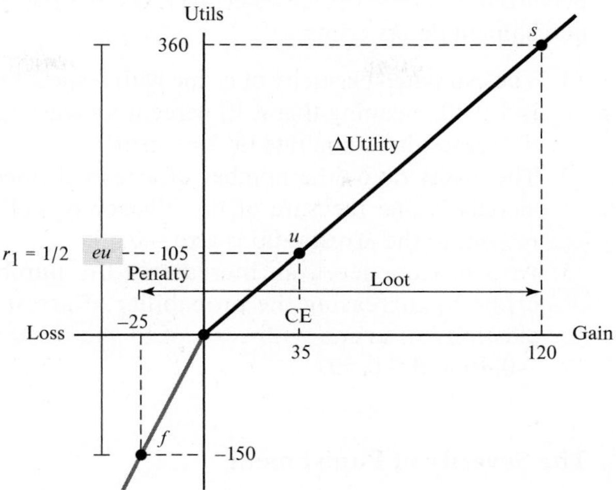

The certainty equivalent of the crime decreases from \$52 to \$35. Crime is now the rational choice if Bart's lawful wage is less than \$35, compared to a threshold wage of \$52 before the increase in the probability of being caught and penalized.

Figure 23–8 shows that an increase in the probability of being penalized for crime decreases the number of criminals. The increase in the probability decreases the certainty equivalent of crime, so fewer workers have wages below the certainty equivalent. In this case, the certainty equivalent decreases from \$52 to \$35, so the number of criminals decreases from 104 (point *a*) to 70 (point *b*). The number of lawful workers increases from 96 to 130.

FIGURE 23–8 Probability of Success and Crime

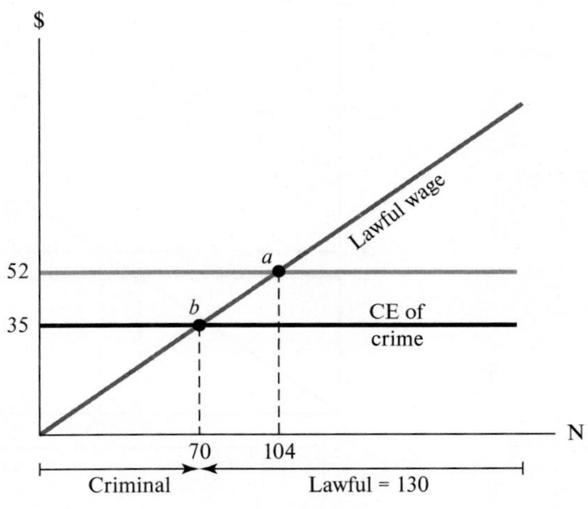

Empirical studies provide evidence that an increase in the probability of being penalized for crime decreases crime rates. In other words, increasing the certainty of punishment deters crime.

1. The estimated elasticity of crime with respect to the probability of imprisonment is −0.30, meaning that a 10 percent increase in the likelihood of imprisonment decreases the crime rate by 3 percent.
2. The arrest ratio (the number of arrests divided by the number of crimes convicted) is one measure of the efficacy of police. The elasticity of crime with respect to the arrest ratio is also −0.30.
3. At a broader level, an increase in the number of police officers decreases crime by increasing the probability of arrest and conviction. The estimated elasticity of crime with respect to the number of police officers is between −0.40 and −0.50.

The Severity of Punishment

Another option for public policy is to increase the severity of punishment. Suppose an increase in spending on prisons increases the length of prison sentences. Part of a penalty for crime is the opportunity cost of time spent in prison, so a longer prison sentence means a larger crime penalty. An increase in the penalty decreases the certainty equivalent of crime, so fewer workers have wages below the certainty equivalent. As a result, the number of criminals decreases.

Figure 23-9 shows that an increase in the crime penalty decreases the number of criminals. Starting from the situation shown in Figure 23-3, suppose the crime penalty increases from $25 to $35. In this case, the crime-failure outcome is a loss

FIGURE 23-9 The Crime Penalty and Crime

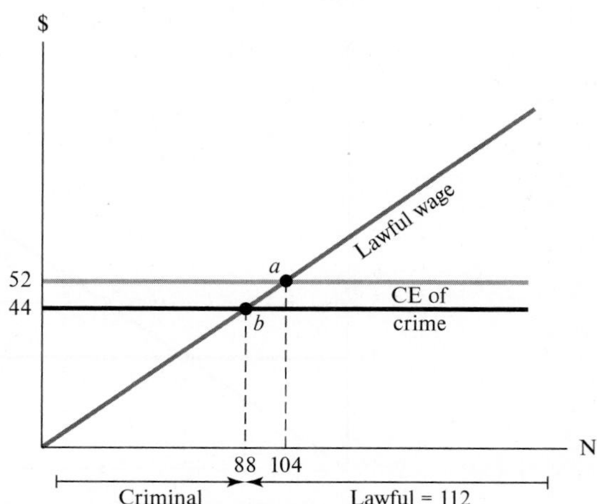

of \$35 and a utility loss of 210 utils (equal to \$35 times $l = 6$ utils per dollar). The expected utility from crime decreases from 156 utils to 132 utils:

$$eu = \frac{3}{5}\,360\ utils - \frac{2}{5}\,210\ utils = 132\ utils$$

The certainty equivalent of the crime decreases from \$52 to \$44 (equal to *132/3*). The decrease in the certainty equivalent means that crime is the rational choice for fewer workers. In this case, the number of criminals decreases from 104 (point *a*) to 88 (point *b*).

There is a general consensus that increasing the size of crime penalties has a relatively small effect on crime. For example, increasing the length of a prison term for a particular crime from 2 years to 3 years causes a relatively small decrease in crime. There are diminishing returns to prison time: the second year has a smaller deterrent effect than the first year, the third year has a smaller deterrent effect than the second, and so on.

Although the reasons for diminishing returns to the length of prison terms are not fully understood, several factors appear to be in play.

1. *Present bias.* For a criminal who underestimates future costs, a distant additional year of prison will have a relatively small weight for decisions in the present.
2. *Aging criminals.* A criminal in prison cannot commit crime on the streets, and an additional year in prison prevents some crime. But as a criminal ages, the frequency of criminal activity decreases. So adding a year to the prison term of a relatively old inmate prevents a relatively small number of crimes.
3. *Hardening the criminal.* Prisons are unpleasant places, and a longer prison term may further decrease a person's aversion to committing anti-social acts. In other words, prison time could decrease a convict's internal penalty from committing crime. As a result, the certainty equivalent of crime increases, at least partly offsetting the decrease in the certainty equivalent from a longer prison term.
4. *Prison schooling.* If inmates learn from each other by talking about their successes and failures, a longer prison term means more learning and more skillful criminals. This decreases the probability of being penalized, which increases the certainty equivalent of crime. The schooling effect at least partly offsets the decrease in certainty equivalent from a longer prison term.

The Role of Prisons

Over the last few decades, the number of people incarcerated (in prisons and jails) in the United States has increased seven-fold, to 2.3 million in 2008 (Cook and Ludwig, 2010). Figure 23–10 shows the incarceration rates for OECD countries. The tallest bar is for the United States (760), and the next tallest bars are for Russia (624), South Africa (329), and Israel (325). The U.S. incarceration rate is seven times the median rate of OECD countries. The incarceration rate is 116 in Canada, 85 in Ireland, and

FIGURE 23–10 Incarceration Rates of OECD Countries

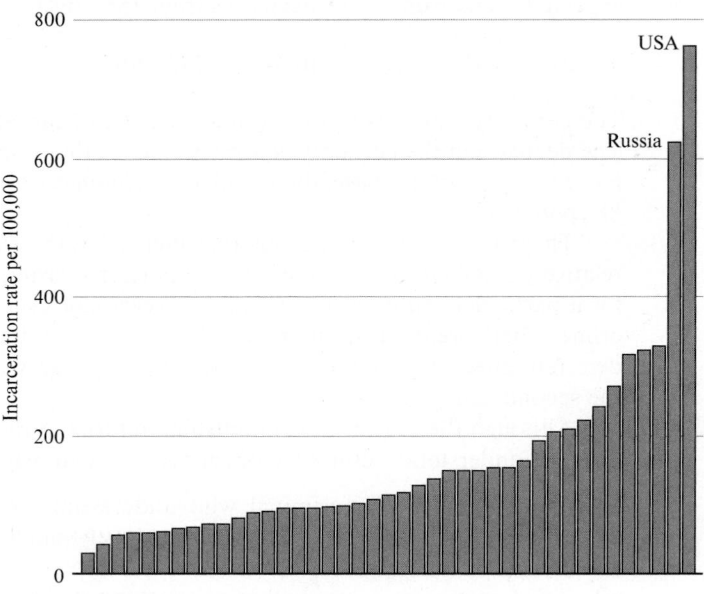

Source: OECD. *Factbook 2010. Economic, Environmental and Social Statistics,* 2010.

67 in Finland. In the United States in 2008, the per-capita cost of incarceration and supervised release was $70 billion, or about $230 per capita.

The estimated elasticity of crime with respect to the prison population is −0.25 for property crime and −0.40 for violent crime. The prison system decreases crime rates in three ways. We've already discussed the deterrent effect of prisons: the threat of prison time decreases the certainty equivalent of crime, decreasing the number of criminals. The second function of prisons is incapacitation–taking criminals out of circulation. The annual incapacitation benefit equals the number of crimes a criminal would have committed outside prison (the number of crimes prevented) times the victim cost per crime. The question is whether the incapacitation benefit exceeds the cost of holding the criminal in prison. For example, a study of the Texas prison system computed an annual cost of $36,000 and annual incapacitation benefit of $15,000 (Spelman, 2005).

The third function of prisons is rehabilitation. The idea is to provide criminals with the skills and attitudes necessary for success in the lawful world after release. The evidence for the effects of rehabilitation programs is not encouraging. Roughly two-thirds of inmates are rearrested within three years of release, and roughly half return to prison within three years. Dozens of studies have estimated the effects of adult rehabilitation programs, and the consensus is that the programs are ineffective. In contrast, rehabilitation programs for juvenile delinquents generate modest reductions in crime.

4. THE EFFICIENT LEVEL AND MIX OF CRIME

Policies designed to reduce crime use resources—labor, capital, land, and materials—that could be used to produce other goods and services. For example, police officers and prison guards could be teachers or carpenters, and the concrete used in prisons could be used for factories or apartment buildings. In this part of the chapter, we explore the benefits and costs of crime control. As we'll see, the socially efficient level of crime is not zero because some crimes are more costly to prevent than to experience. We'll also see the economic logic behind the adage *the punishment should fit the crime.*

The Efficient Amount of Crime

We can use the marginal principle to determine the efficient level of crime control. The benefit of crime control is a reduction in victim cost. Miller, Cohen, and Wiersema (1996) estimate the victim cost per crime is $370 for larceny, $1,500 for burglary, $4,000 for auto theft, and $13,000 for armed robbery. In Figure 23–11, the marginal benefit of crime prevention is constant at $1,500 per crime prevented. The marginal-cost curve for crime control is positively sloped: the first crime is easier to prevent than the second, which is easier to prevent than the third, and so on. This is sensible because some crime can be prevented with inexpensive measures such as patrol and vigilance, but preventing crime by the most skillful and determined criminals is costly.

For the efficient level of crime control, the marginal benefit (lower victim cost) equals the marginal prevention cost. In Figure 23–11, the efficient choice is shown by point *c*, with 60 crimes prevented and 40 crimes experienced. For the first 60 crimes prevented, the $1,500 benefit exceeds the marginal cost, but beyond that point, it is less costly to experience crime than to prevent it.

FIGURE 23–11 The Efficient Level of Crime

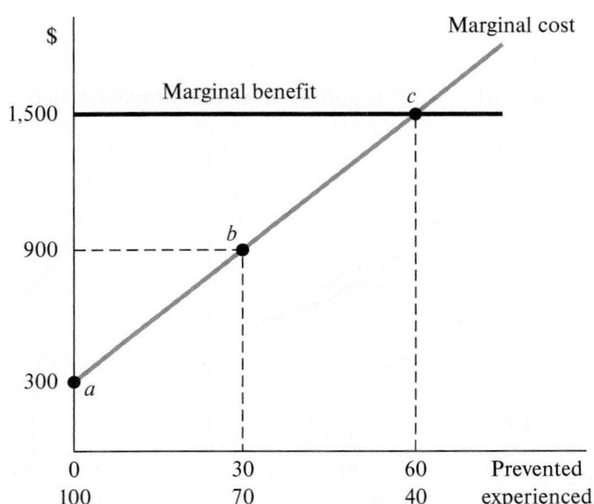

Occupational Choice and Marginal Deterrence

A person who commits property crime makes an occupational choice, choosing crime over lawful work. In addition, a criminal chooses what type of crime to commit, for example, burglary instead of robbery. Public policy determines the penalties for different crimes, presenting criminals with a menu of expected payoffs (certainty equivalents) for different crimes. A rational criminal can use the crime menu to decide how to allocate time between lawful work and various types of crime. As we'll see, a change in public policy that affects the payoff of one type of crime changes the mix of crime, affecting the social cost of crime.

Figure 23-12 illustrates occupational choice that includes crime as an option. Consider a city with 30 workers, two types of property crime (burglary and robbery), and lawful work (carpentry). For each occupation, the payoff curve is negatively sloped, reflecting decreasing marginal productivity. The carpenter payoff curve is a labor demand curve, and is negatively sloped because an increase in the number of carpenters decreases the market-clearing carpenter wage. For the crime payoff curves, an increase in the number of criminals decreases the payoff because the most lucrative targets are tapped first, so the larger the number of criminals, the lower the loot of the marginal target. In the terms we used earlier in the chapter, the payoff from a crime is its certainty equivalent.

In our analysis of occupational choice, we take a long-run perspective, and assume that workers are perfectly mobile between the three occupations. There are two conditions for occupational equilibrium.

1. *Nash equilibrium:* No incentive for unilateral deviation. The three occupations have the same payoff, so no single worker has an incentive to change occupations.
2. *Adding up constraint.* All 30 workers are employed in some occupation.

The initial equilibrium is shown by points *a, b,* and *c*. All three occupations have a payoff π^*, with 10 workers in each occupation.

FIGURE 23-12 Equilibrium Occupational Choice

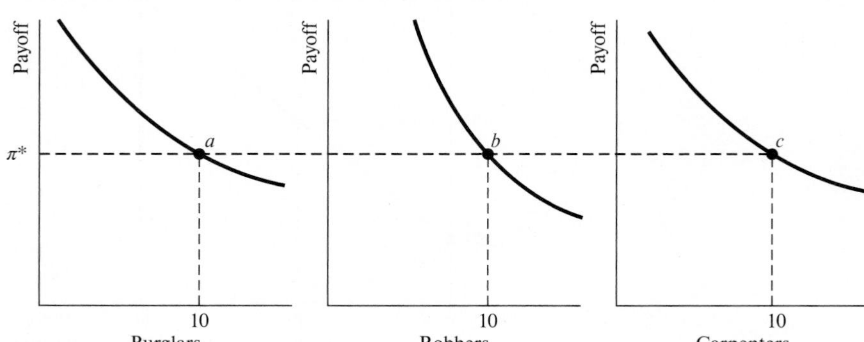

FIGURE 23–13 The Burglary Penalty and Occupational Mix

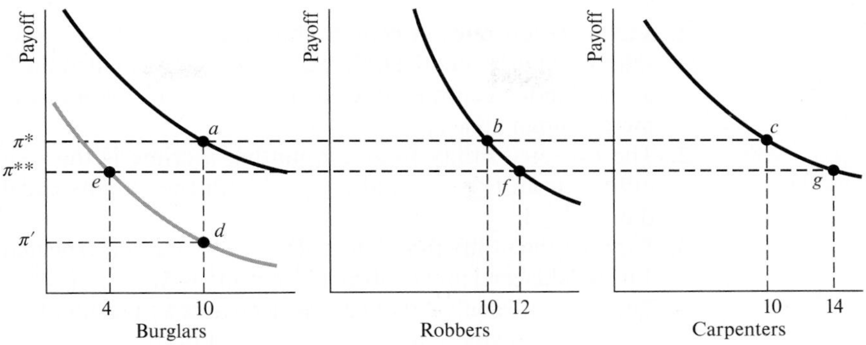

Figure 23–13 shows the occupational implications of an increase in the penalty for burglary. For the initial equilibrium shown by points *a, b,* and *c*, the workforce is divided equally between the three occupations. An increase in the penalty shifts the burglary payoff curve downward. At the initial number of burglars (10), the payoff per burglar decreases from π^* to π'. The burglary payoff is now less than payoffs to robbery and carpentry, so the labor market is no longer in equilibrium.

The lower payoff to burglary causes some burglars to switch to robbery, and others to switch to carpentry. The increase in the number of robbers decreases the payoff in robbery, and the increase in the number of carpenters decreases the payoff in carpentry. Conversely, the decrease in burglars increases the payoff in burglary above π'. The movement out of burglary will continue until occupational equilibrium–with equal payoffs for the three occupations–is restored at points *e, f,* and *g*. The new equilibrium payoff is $\pi^{**} < \pi^*$: the policy-induced decrease in the burglary payoff spreads to other occupations. In the new equilibrium, a total of 6 criminals switch occupations: 2 switch to robbery, and 4 switch to carpentry. In other words, one-third of the displaced burglars switch to another crime.

What are the implications of the increase in the burglary penalty for the total cost of crime? In our example, the number of burglaries decreases by 6, for a savings in victim costs of $9,000 (equal to 6 times $1,500) and the number of robberies increases by 2, for an additional victim cost of $26,000 (equal to 2 times $13,000). In this case, the change in policy increases crime victim cost by $17,000. In general, since the victim cost of a robbery is roughly nine times the victim cost of a burglary, the total victim cost will increase if fewer than nine burglaries are prevented for every additional robbery.

The principle of marginal deterrence is that the expected penalty for committing a crime should be larger for crimes with higher victim costs. For example, burglary generates a relatively small victim cost, so it should carry a relatively small expected penalty. Although "getting tough" on burglary decreases the number of burglaries, it causes criminal substitution in favor of other crimes, some of which have higher victim cost. The challenge for policy makers is to develop a menu of expected penalties to provide criminals the incentive to choose the efficient mix of crimes.

REVIEW THE CONCEPTS

1. Victimization rates in central cities are [_____] (<, >, =) than victimization rates in suburbs, but the difference is relatively small in the [_____] metropolitan areas. Among central cities, the lowest victimization rates occur in the [_____] metropolitan areas.
2. The expected utility from committing a crime is the weighted average of the utilities from [_____] and [_____] with the weights equal to the [_____] and the [_____].
3. Suppose the utility function is $u(w) = w^{1/2}$ and the expected utility from crime is 7 utils. The certainty equivalent of crime is $[_____].
4. The certainty equivalent of crime decreases as a result of an [_____] {↑, ↓, –} in the crime penalty or a [_____] {↑, ↓, –} in the probability of successful crime.
5. Crime is a rational choice if the [_____] of crime exceeds the [_____].
6. Compared to a college graduate, a high-school graduate is roughly [_____] (choose 2, 5, 6, 13) times more likely to be incarcerated.
7. Recent advances in neuroscience suggest that humans are subject to varying degrees of [_____] bias, and the bias tends to [_____] {↑, ↓, –} criminal activity.
8. Investment in human capital [_____] {↑, ↓, –} crime rates by increasing [_____].
9. The elasticity of crime with respect to the probability of imprisonment is –[_____] (choose 0.05, 0.10, 0.3, or 3.0).
10. The U.S. incarceration rate is roughly [_____] (choose 0.50, 2, 3, or 7) times the median incarceration rate of OECD countries.
11. The prison system decreases crime rates through (i) [_____], (ii) [_____], and (iii) [_____].
12. Increasing the prison time for crime has a relatively [_____] effect on crime, and the deterrent effect is subject to [_____].
13. Several factors play a role in the diminishing returns to the length of prison sentences: (i) [_____], (ii) [_____], (iii) [_____], and (iv) [_____].
14. The elasticity of crime with respect to wages is between –[_____] 8 and –[_____].
15. For motor-vehicle theft, the elasticity of arrest rates with respect to high-school graduation rates is –[_____] (choose 0, 0.10, 1.3, 3.0).
16. Getting a student from dropout status to graduation status has a one-time cost of roughly $[_____] and an annual benefit to society of roughly $[_____] in lower crime cost.
17. For the efficient amount of crime control, [_____] equals [_____].
18. For a Nash equilibrium in the model of occupational choice, the payoffs of the alternative occupations are [_____].
19. An increase in the burglary penalty [_____] {↑, ↓, –} the number of burglars, [_____] {↑, ↓, –} the number of robbers, and [_____] {↑, ↓, –} the number of lawfully employed workers.
20. It is possible that an increase in the burglary penalty will increase the social cost of crime because the social cost of [_____] exceeds the social cost of [_____].
21. For each pair of variables, indicate whether the relationship is positive, negative, neutral, or ambiguous.

Parameter	Choice Variable	Relationship
probability of crime success	certainty equivalent of crime	[_____]
crime penalty	certainty equivalent of crime	[_____]
certainty equivalent of crime	number of criminals	[_____]
lawful income	likelihood of committing crime	[_____]
victim cost per crime	efficient crime level	[_____]
police wage	efficient crime level	[_____]

APPLY THE CONCEPTS

1. *Crime Lottery and Criminals*
Suppose as in Figure 23-3, $g = 3$ and $l = 6$. Consider a crime lottery $L = \{\$60, -\$20; \frac{1}{2}, \frac{1}{2}\}$. Lawful wages go from \$1 to \$50, with two workers at each integer wage. In the case of an equal payoff between criminal and lawful work, the worker chooses crime.
a. Illustrate this crime lottery, including values for expected utility and the certainty equivalent.
b. The equilibrium number of criminals is [_____].

2. *Loss Aversion and Lottery Probabilities*
Consider a worker who experiences loss aversion, and $l = 2 \cdot g$. In other words, the pain from a \$1 loss is two times the pleasure from a \$1 gain. The crime lottery is $L = \{\$30, -\$30; r_1, r_2\}$. The expected utility of the lottery will be zero if r_1 = [_____] and r_2 = [_____]. Illustrate.

3. Using the example shown in Figure 23-3 as a starting point, suppose that potential victims take measures to protect their property, and the loot decreases from \$120 to \$50. Illustrate the values associated with the new lottery, including the new value of the certainty equivalent.

4. *Women and Crime*
During the 1970s, the crime rate for women increased five times faster than the crime rate for men. Suppose that for Betty, $g = 3$ and $l = 6$. In 1970, Betty's crime lottery is $L = \{\$120, -\$15; \frac{1}{3}, \frac{2}{3}\}$.
a. In 1970, Betty's rational choice is commit crime if her lawful wage is less than \$[_____]. Illustrate.
b. Suppose the physical fitness of women improves between 1970 and 1980. A plausible new value for r_1 is [_____] (choose *1/4 or 1/2*). Betty's rational choice is commit crime if her lawful wage is less than \$ [_____]. Illustrate.
c. The fertility of women decreased between 1970 and 1980 (fewer children). Use the value for r_1 from (b). A plausible new value for R_2 is [_____] (choose −\$10 or −\$30). Betty's rational choice is commit crime if her lawful wage is less than \$ [_____]. Illustrate.

5. *Budget-Balancing Prison Change*
Consider a state with a fixed prison capacity. The state (i) increased the average prison term from 5 years to 6 years and (ii) decreased the probability of being penalized for crime from 1/5 to 1/6. Predict the qualitative effect of the change

in policy on the equilibrium level of crime and explain the economic logic of your prediction.

6. *Crime in Low-Income Neighborhood*
   Consider a city where the burglary rate in a low-income neighborhood is 60, compared to 20 in a high-income neighborhood. The two neighborhoods have the same victim cost per burglary ($1,500). The higher crime rate in the low-income neighborhood is efficient if . . . Illustrate.
7. *Education and Crime*
   Consider a city with 20 workers and two occupations: robber and electrician. For each occupation, the payoff curve (the payoff as a function of the number of workers) has a slope of -2 utils per worker. In the initial equilibrium, there are 10 robbers and 10 electricians, and a payoff of 20 utils. Suppose the government subsidizes community-college programs and thus increases the productivity of electricians, shifting the payoff curve upward by 12 utils. Illustrate the new equilibrium, including values for the number of electricians, the number of robbers, and the equilibrium payoff.
8. *Marginal Deterrence and Crime Cost*
   Consider a city with 36 workers and three occupations: burglary (b), robbery (r), and plumbing (p). For each occupation, the payoff curve is negatively sloped, and the slopes of the three curves are equal. In the initial equilibrium, $b = r = p$. Suppose the city increases the penalty for burglary. The new equilibrium number of burglars = 8.
   a. Illustrate the equilibrium including values for the number of robbers and plumbers.
   b. Predict the effect of the increase in the burglary penalty on the social cost of crime and explain the economic logic of your prediction.

REFERENCES AND READING

1. Bartel, Ann P., "Women and Crime: An Economic Analysis." *Economic Inquiry* 42 (1979), pp. 29–51.
2. Cohen, M., R. Rust, S. Steen, and S. Tidd, "Willingness-to-Pay for Crime Control Programs." *Criminology* 42 (2004), pp. 89–109.
3. Cook, Philip J., "Crime: Crime in the City," Chapter 10 in *Making Cities Work: Prospects and Policies for Urban America*, edited by Robert P. Inman. Princeton, NJ: Princeton University Press, 2009.
4. Cullen, J. B., and S. D. Levitt, "Crime, Urban Flight, and the Consequences for Cities." *Review of Economics and Statistics* 81 (1999), pp. 159–69.
5. Goldsmith, William W., "The Drug War and Inner-City Neighborhoods," Chapter 11 in *The Oxford Handbook of Urban Economics and Planning*, edited by Nancy Brooks, Kieran Donaghy, and Gerrit-Jan Knaap. New York: Oxford University Press, 2011.
6. Gould, Eric D., Bruce A. Weinberg, and David B. Mustard, "Crime Rates and Local Labor Market Opportunities in the United States: 1979–1997." *Review of Economics and Statistics* 84 (2002), pp. 45–61.

7. Grogger, Jeffrey. "An Economic Model of Recent Trends in Violence." Chapter 8 in *The Crime Drop in America*, edited by Alfred Blumstein and Joel Wallman. New York: Cambridge University Press, 2000.
8. Levitt, Steven D. "Understanding Why Crime Fell in the 1990s: Four Factors That Explain the Decline, and Six That Do Not." *Journal of Economic Perspectives* 18 (2004), pp. 163–90.
9. Lochner, Lance, and Enrico Moretti, "The Effect of Education on Crime: Evidence from Prison Inmates, Arrests, and Self Reports." *American Economic Review* 94 (2004), pp. 155–89.
10. Miller, T., M. A. Cohen, and B. Wiersema, *Victim Costs and Consequence: A New Look*. Washington, DC: National Institute of Justice, 1996.
11. O'Flaherty, Brendan, and Rajiv Sethi, "Urban Crime," Chapter 23 in *Handbook of Urban and Regional Economics Volume 5*, edited by Gilles Duranton, J. Vernon Henderson, and William C. Strange. Amsterdam: Elsevier, 2015.
12. Raphael, Stephen, and Melissa Sills, "Urban Crime, Race, and the Criminal Justice System in the United States," Chapter 30 in *A Companion to Urban Economics*, edited by Richard J. Arnott and Daniel P. McMillen. New York: Wiley-Blackwell, 2006.
13. Raphael, Steven, and Michael Stoll. "The Effects of Prison Releases on Regional Crime Rate." *Brookings-Wharton Papers on Urban Affairs* (2004), pp. 207–43.
14. Sen, Anindya, "Does Abortion Lead to Lower Crime? Evaluating the Relationship between Crime, Abortion, and Fertility." *The B.E. Journal of Economic Analysis and Policy* 7.1, Article 48 (2007).
15. Spellman, William, "Jobs or Jails? The Crime Drop in Texas." *Journal of Policy Analysis and Management* 24 (2005), pp. 133–65.

CHAPTER 24

Models of Microeconomics

It can scarcely be denied that the supreme goal of all theory is to make the irreducible basic elements as simple and as few as possible without having to surrender the adequate representation of a single datum of experience.

—ALBERT EINSTEIN, FROM "ON THE METHOD OF THEORETICAL PHYSICS," JUNE 10, 1933

Albert Einstein said, in effect, that everything should be as simple as it can be but not simpler!

—ROGER SESSIONS, "HOW A 'DIFFICULT' COMPOSER GETS THAT WAY," JANUARY 8, 1950

Urban economics is applied microeconomics, and this book applies a variety of microeconomics concepts to explore urban economic phenomena. This chapter reviews four key models that are developed in the typical course in intermediate microeconomics.

1. *Model of Producer Choice:* Cost minimization, input choice, and input substitution.
2. *Model of Consumer Choice:* Utility maximization, product choice, and market demand.
3. *Model of Perfect Competition:* Long-run supply and market equilibrium.
4. *Model of Expected Utility:* Expected monetary value, expected utility, and certainty equivalent.

1. INPUT CHOICE: COST MINIMIZATION

This part of the chapter reviews the model of producer choice. A producer chooses the bundle of inputs that minimizes the cost of producing a target quantity of output. In casual terms, the producer choose the cheapest satisfactory bundle of inputs where "satisfactory" indicates that the inputs produce the target output quantity and "cheapest" indicates that the chosen input bundle produces the target quantity of output at the lowest possible cost.

Production Function and Isoquants

A production function represents the relationship between inputs and output. For a firm that uses two inputs, the production function is $q = f(z_1, z_2)$, where q is the quantity of output produced with input quantities z_1 z_2. In the upper panel of Figure 24-1, the latitude of the box (running left to right) shows the quantity of

FIGURE 24-1 Production Surface and Isoquants

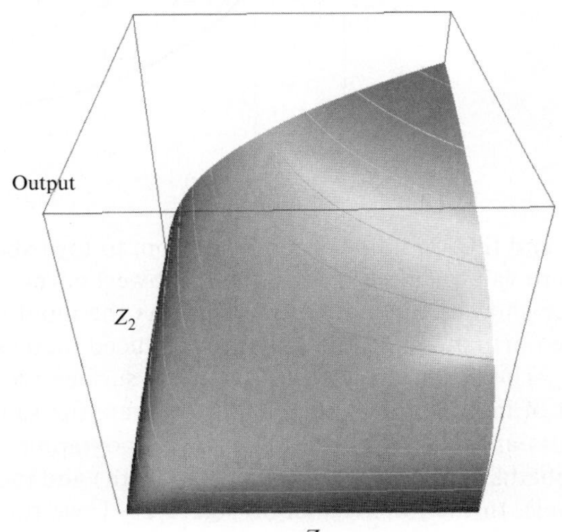

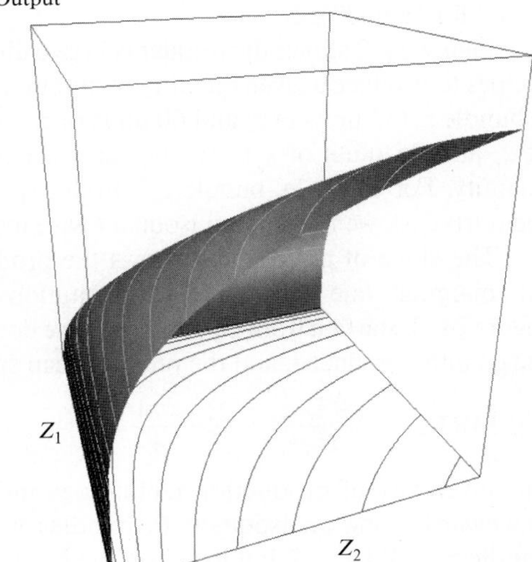

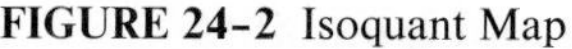

FIGURE 24–2 Isoquant Map

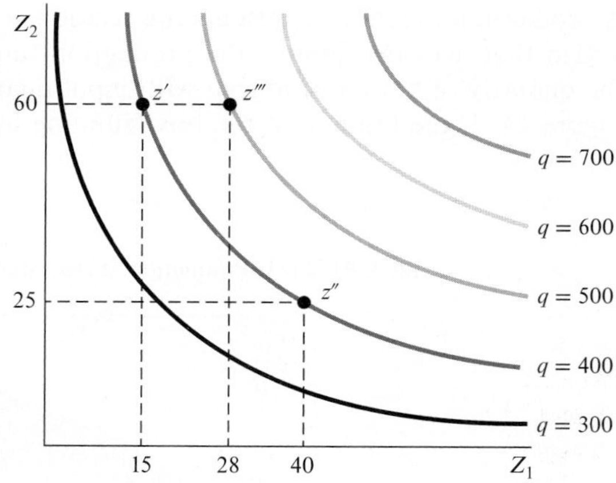

z_1, and the longitude (running bottom to top) shows the quantity of z_2. The origin (zero values for each) is in the southwest corner of the box. The height of the surface shows the quantity produced. As the input quantities increase with moves to the north and east, the quantity produced increases.

The lightly shaded curves on the surface are contours, each of which shows a set of input bundles (z_1, z_2) that generate the same quantity of output. These contours are analogous to isolines on topographical maps (common elevation) and isobaths on ocean maps (common depth) and indifference curves (common utility level). In the lower panel of Figure 24–1, we rotate the graph to show the projections of the contours onto the floor of the box. Each projection is an isoquant, which shows a set of input bundles that generate a particular quantity of output ("iso" for "equal").

Figure 24–2 shows the isoquants in two dimensions. Each isoquant provides a set of recipes to produce a given quantity of output. For example, one way to produce $q = 400$ is bundle z' (15 units of z_1 and 60 units of z_2), and another option is bundle z'' (40 units of z_1 and 25 units of z_2). An increase in either input quantity increases the output quantity. For example, bundle z''' produces more output than bundle z''. Moving to the northeast, we move to an isoquant with more of both inputs and thus more output.

The slope of an isoquant shows the production tradeoff between the two inputs, the marginal rate of technical substitution (MRTS) between the two inputs. In Figure 24–3, starting from bundle z', a move downward along the isoquant doesn't change the quantity produced, and the producer can substitute 3 units of z_2 for one unit of z_1:

$$\text{MRTS} = -\frac{\Delta z_2}{\Delta z_1} = -\frac{21 - 24}{5 - 4} = \frac{3}{1}$$

The convexity of production technology means that MRTS decreases as we move downward along an isoquant to bundles with more z_1 and less z_2. Starting from bundle z', MRTS = 3, but lower on the isoquant at bundle z'', MRTS = 1. In general,

FIGURE 24–3 Convex Isoquant

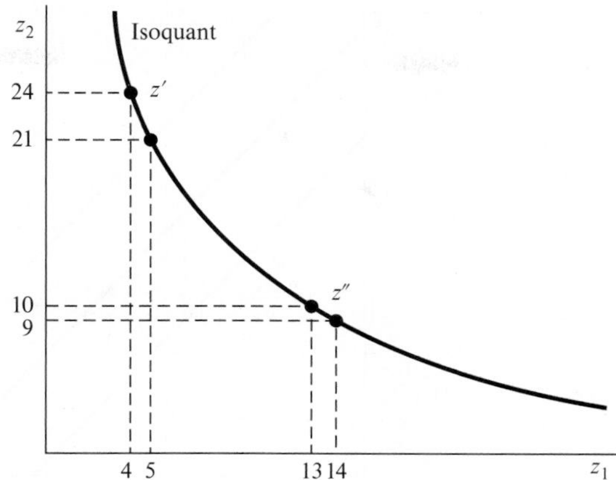

as the quantity of the first input increases, the isoquant becomes flatter, indicating a smaller MRTS.

The MRTS is determined by the relative productivity of the two inputs. The marginal product of z_1 is defined as the increase in the quantity produced from a one-unit increase in z_1. The MRTS equals the ratio of the marginal products of the two inputs (mp_1 and mp_2):

$$\text{MRTS} = \frac{mp_1}{mp_2}$$

For example, if $mp_1 = 6$ and $mp_2 = 2$, the first input is three times as productive, on the margin. In this case, MRTS = 3, meaning that the firm can substitute 3 units of z_2 for one unit of z_1:

$$\text{MRTS} = \frac{mp_1}{mp_2} = \frac{6}{2} = 3$$

Production Cost and Cost Minimization

Figure 24–4 introduces the cost side of input choice. An isocost is the production analog of a consumer budget line, and shows the set of input bundles that can be purchased at a given total cost ("iso" for equal). For a firm that uses two inputs, the cost equation is

$$c = w_1 z_1 + w_2 z_2$$

The slope of an isocost is the market tradeoff between the two inputs, the change in z_2 per unit change in z_1 required to keep total cost at some fixed level. We can rearrange the cost equation into slope-intercept form:

$$z_2 = \frac{c}{w_2} - \frac{w_1}{w_2} z_1$$

FIGURE 24–4 Production Isocosts

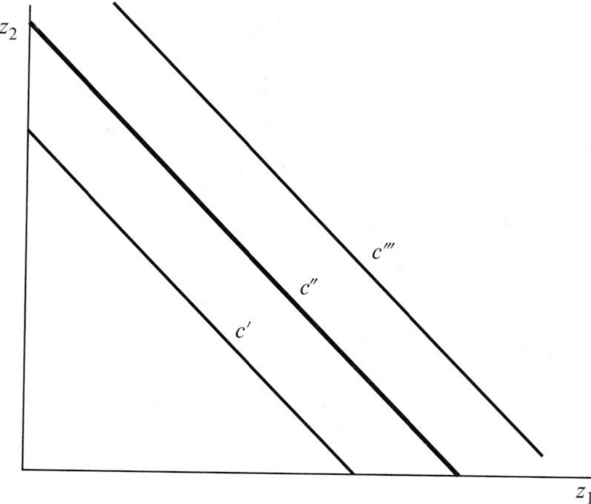

The vertical intercept of the isocost is (c/w_2) and the slope is the input price ratio (w_1/w_2). For example, if $w_1 = 8$ and $w_2 = 4$, the input price ratio is 2. As we move from one isocost to a higher isocost, total cost increases, from c' to c'' to c'''.

The objective of a cost-minimizing firm is to minimize the cost of producing a target quantity of output. In Figure 24–5, total cost is minimized at bundle z^*, the bundle on the target isoquant that lies on the lowest (most southwesterly) isocost. The cost of producing the target quantity is minimized at the input bundle where the isoquant is tangent to an isocost. In other words, the two curves have the same slope, and the cost-minimizing rule is

$$\text{MRTS} = \frac{w_1}{w_2}$$

FIGURE 24–5 Cost Minimization

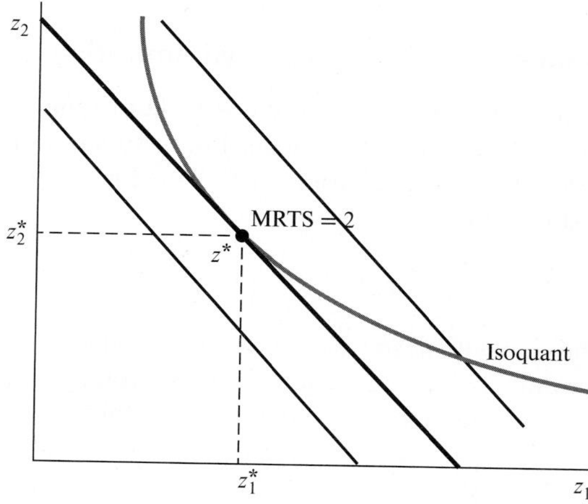

The MRTS is the ratio of marginal products of the two inputs, so we can also write the cost-minimizing condition as

$$\frac{mp_1}{mp_2} = \frac{w_1}{w_2}$$

For example, suppose the input price ratio is 2. To minimize the cost of producing the target quantity, the firm finds the point on the target isoquant at which MRTS = 2. If z_1 is twice as costly as z_2, the firm will minimize production cost at the input bundle such that z_1 is twice as productive as z_2, on the margin.

Input Substitution

We've seen that a cost-minimizing firm chooses the input bundle at which MRTS equals the input price ratio. A change in an input price will cause a firm to choose a different input bundle, a process known as input substitution.

Figure 24-6 shows input substitution in response to an increase in an input price. The initial cost-minimizing input bundle z^* is produced at a cost c^*. An increase in w_1 increases the slope of the isocost (dashed line labeled c′) and the cost of the initial input bundle increases: $c' > c^*$. At the initial input bundle, MRTS < input price ratio, so the long-run cost of producing the target output quantity is no longer minimized at z^*. At the higher w_1, MRTS = input price ratio at bundle z^{**}, where the firm produces the target output quantity with less of the first input ($z_1^{**} < z_1^*$) and more of the second input ($z_2^* > z_2^{**}$). The input substitution decreases the cost of producing the target quantity of output: $c^{**} < c'$.

FIGURE 24-6 Input Substitution

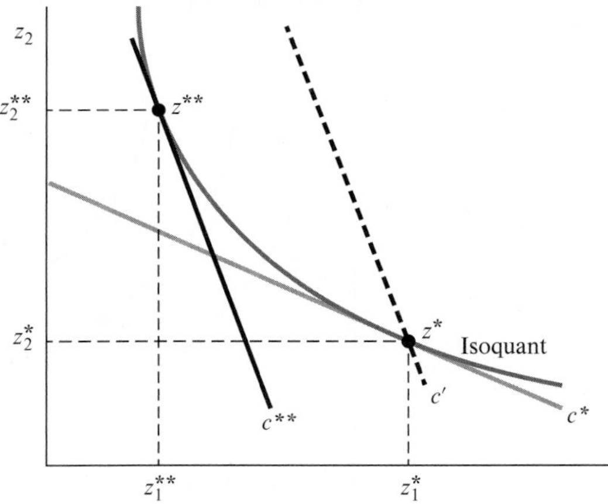

2. CONSUMER CHOICE

This part of the chapter reviews the model of consumer choice and uses the model to explain the logic behind individual demand curve and the market demand curve. A consumer allocates a fixed income among consumer products, with the objective of maximizing utility. In casual terms, the consumer chooses the best affordable bundle of consumer goods, where "best" indicates utility maximization and "affordable" indicates that the consumer has a fixed income to spend on the goods.

Utility Maximization

In Figure 24-7, consumer preferences are represented by indifference curves, the consumer analog of production isoquants. An indifference curve shows bundles of goods x_1 and x_2 that generate a given level of utility. For example, all the bundles shown by indifference curve u' generate the same level of utility. The slope of an indifference curve is the consumer's marginal rate of substitution (MRS) between the two goods, defined as the change in the quantity of the good on the vertical axis (x_2) required to offset a one-unit increase in the good on the horizontal axis (x_1).

$$\frac{\Delta x_2}{\Delta x_1} = MRS$$

This is the consumer's subjective tradeoff between the two goods. Under the assumption of non-satiation (more is better), utility increases as a consumer moves to a higher (more northeasterly) indifference curve, from u' to u'' to u'''.

In the consumer choice model, the consumer has a fixed income or budget to spend on two goods. The consumer budget constraint is

$$w = p_1 x_1 + p_2 x_2$$

FIGURE 24-7 Indifference Curve Map

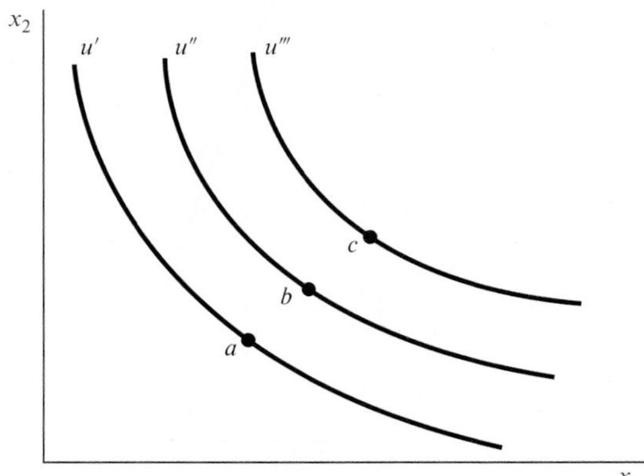

FIGURE 24-8 Budget Line and Budget Set

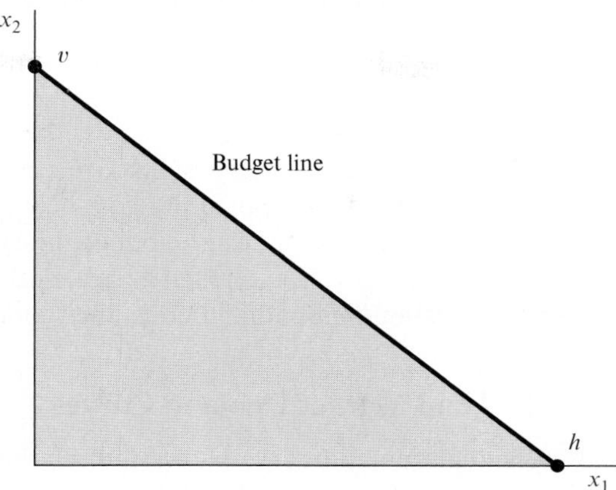

where w is the fixed income and p_1 and p_2 are the prices of the two goods. In Figure 24-8, the budget set (the shaded area) shows all the affordable bundles and the budget line (the border of the budget set) shows the set of bundles that exhaust the budget. The slope of the budget line is the price ratio of the two goods:

$$\frac{\Delta x_2}{\Delta x_1} = -\frac{p_1}{p_2}$$

The slope shows the market tradeoff between the goods, that is, the opportunity cost of x_1 in terms of x_2. For example, if $p_1 = 6$ and $p_2 = 2$, the consumer sacrifices 3 units x_2 for each unit of x_1.

Figure 24-9 shows the outcome of utility maximization. The consumer's objective is to reach the highest affordable indifference curve, resulting in bundle x^*,

FIGURE 24-9 Utility Maximization

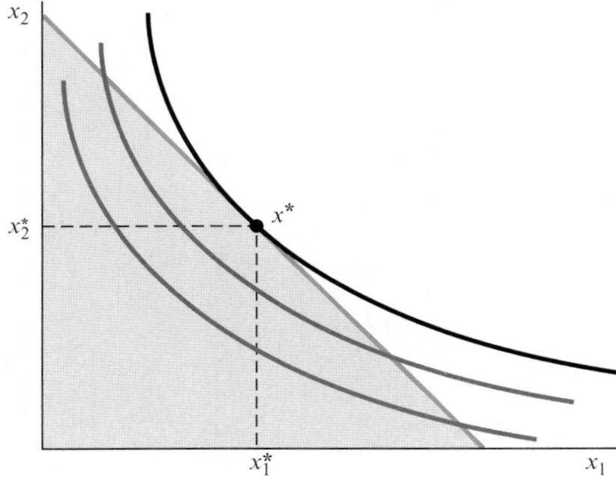

with x_1^* units of good 1 and x_2^* units of good 2. At the utility-maximizing bundle, the indifference curve is tangent to the budget line, meaning that the MRS equals the price ratio:

$$MRS = \frac{p_1}{p_2}$$

In other words, the consumer's subjective tradeoff between the two goods equals the market tradeoff (the opportunity cost of x_1 in terms of x_2). At any other affordable bundle (any other point on the budget line), MRS will not be equal to the price ratio, and the consumer could reach a higher utility level (reach a higher indifference curve) by changing the bundle of consumer goods.

Individual and Market Demand Curves

The individual demand curve shows the relationship between a consumer's utility-maximizing quantity of a good and its price, ceteris paribus. To draw a demand curve for x_1, we vary p_1 and hold fixed the values of p_2 and w.

Figure 24–10 shows a consumer's response to an increase in p_1, given fixed values for p_2 and w.

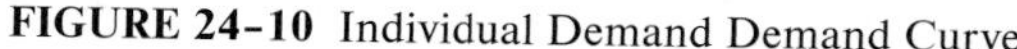

FIGURE 24–10 Individual Demand Demand Curve

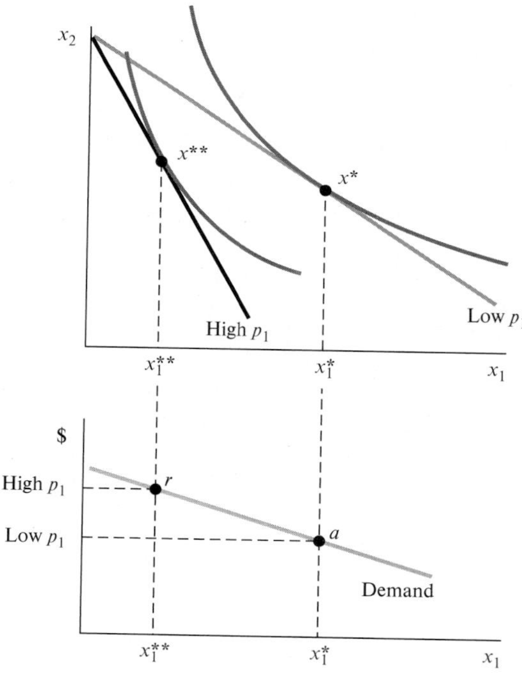

FIGURE 24–11 Individual to Market Demand

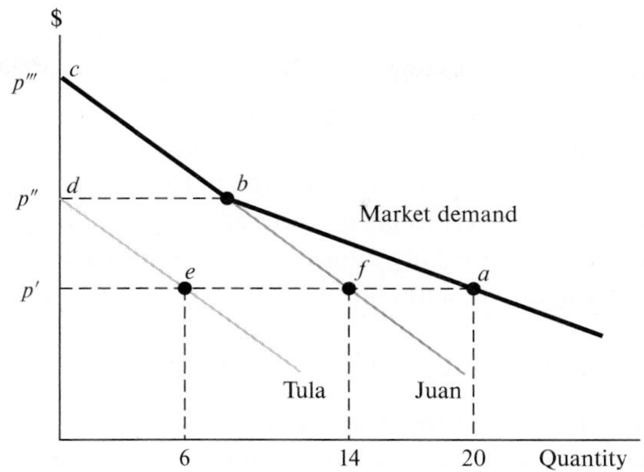

1. *Upper panel: Consumer choice model.* At a low price (low p_1), utility is maximized at bundle x^*, with x_1^* units of x_1. An increase in price to high p_1 tilts the budget line inward, increasing its slope. At the higher price, utility is maximized at bundle x^{**}, with $x_1^{**} < x_1^*$.
2. *Lower panel: Demand curve.* Point *a* on the demand curve is associated with the low-price bundle x^* and the quantity x_1^*. Point *r* on the demand curve is associated with the high-price bundle x^{**} and quantity x_1^{**}.

An increase in price decreases the utility-maximizing quantity, causing the consumer to move upward along the demand curve.

The market demand for a product is the sum of the individual demands. The market demand curve is the horizontal sum of the individual demand curves. Figure 24–11 shows a market demand curve in the case of two consumers, Juan and Tula. It is negatively sloped because (i) each individual demand curve is negatively sloped and (ii) the number of active consumers (people who buy a positive quantity) increases as the price decreases. In Figure 24–11, the first consumer (Juan) becomes active when the price drops below p''' (point *c*) and the second consumer (Tula) becomes active once the price drops below p'' (point *d*). The addition of the second consumer generates a kink in the market demand curve at point *b*. At the price p', both consumers are active, and the market demand is the sum of the quantities demanded: $20 = 6 + 14$.

The same logic applies to markets with many consumers. At a given price, the market quantity demanded is the sum of the individual quantities demanded at that price. For example, if there are *n* consumers with identical demand curves, the market quantity demanded at some price equals *n* times the individual quantity demanded at that price.

3. PERFECT COMPETITION: SUPPLY AND DEMAND

In this part of the chapter we explore the long-run equilibrium in a perfectly competitive market. The model of perfect competition, also known as the model of demand and supply, is based on the assumption of perfect competition. Each firm recognizes that it cannot control the market price of the good it produces, but instead takes the market price as given. Although perfectly competitive markets are rare, the notion of perfect competition is a useful approximation in many markets and provides a benchmark for comparing alternative market structures. In the long run, firms are perfectly flexible in choosing inputs and can enter or exit the market.

Long-Run Supply Curve for Constant-Cost Industry

The long-run supply curve incorporates the entry and exit of firms in response to changes in price. The model of perfect competition employs three assumptions.

1. *Constant returns to scale in production.* In the long run, firms are perfectly flexible in their choice of inputs, and as they scale their production operations up or down, input quantities change proportionately. For example, to double the quantity produced, a firm doubles all its inputs.
2. *Constant input prices.* The prices of inputs such as labor, capital, and materials do not vary with the total quantity of output produced in the market.
3. *Equal access and identical firms.* Firms have equal access to production technology and inputs to the production process. All firms are identical, so we can focus on a representative firm.

The first two assumptions mean that the firm's total-cost curve is linear:

$$C(q) = cq$$

Marginal cost is constant and is equal to average cost:

$$mc(q) = ac(q) = c$$

The assumption of identical firms means that the market quantity $Q(p)$ equals the quantity per firm $q(p)$ times the number of firms n:

$$Q(p) = q(p)n$$

Figure 24–12 shows long-run supply curves for the representative firm and the market.

1. *Firm.* The long-run supply curve $q(p)$ is horizontal at the long-run marginal cost c. The quantity supplied is zero for any price less than the long-run marginal cost. For price = marginal cost, the quantity is indeterminate: at a price equal to marginal cost, any quantity of output is consistent with profit maximization.
2. *Market.* The market quantity equals the firm quantity times the number of firms. The market supply curve is horizontal at the long-run marginal cost of production.

FIGURE 24–12 Individual and Market Supply: Constant-Cost Industry

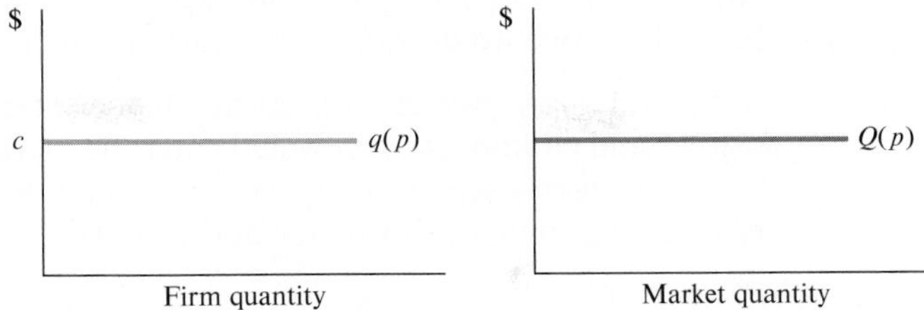

This is the case of a constant-cost industry. Input prices do not vary with the market quantity produced, so long-run marginal cost is constant and the long-run supply curve is horizontal. For any price less than the long-run marginal cost, the quantity supplied is zero.

Long-Run Equilibrium for a Constant-Cost Industry

A market has reached a long-run equilibrium at price p^* if four conditions are satisfied.

1. *Profit maximization.* The market supply curve incorporates profit maximization, so if the market is on the supply curve, firms are maximizing profit.
2. *Utility maximization.* The market demand curve incorporates utility maximization, so if the market is on the demand curve, consumers are maximizing utility.
3. *Market clearing.* At p^*, the quantity supplied equals the quantity demanded.
4. *Zero economic profit.* There is no incentive for additional firms to enter the market, and no incentive for active firms to exit the market.

Figure 24–13 shows the long-run market equilibrium. The horizontal market supply curve intersects the demand curve at the equilibrium price p^* and equilibrium

FIGURE 24–13 Long Run Equilibrium: Constant-Cost Industry

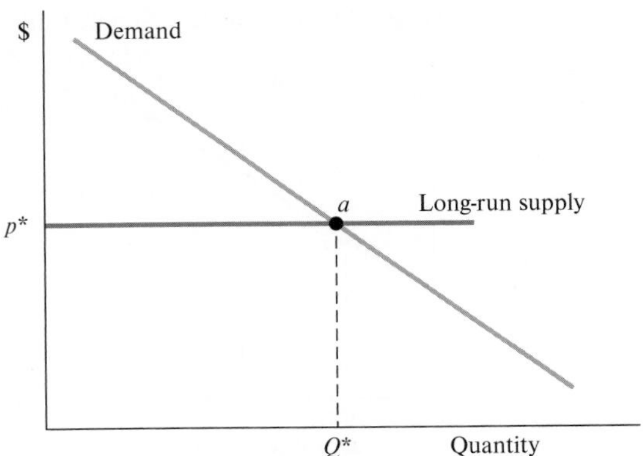

quantity Q^*. For a constant-cost industry, the long-run equilibrium price equals the constant long-run marginal cost of production, which equals the long-run average cost. Any other price would violate the fourth equilibrium condition.

1. *Price > Long-run average cost.* At any higher price, economic profit would be positive, and additional firms would enter the market.
2. *Price < Long-run average cost.* At any lower price, economic profit would be negative, and some firms would exit the market.

The Long-Run Equilibrium for an Increasing-Cost Industry

Up to this point, we have assumed that the prices of inputs used in production are unaffected by changes in the total quantity produced. Combined with the assumption of constant returns to scale, this means that the long-run marginal cost curve is horizontal: the marginal cost is unaffected by changes in the total quantity produced. In other words, the assumption of constant input prices generates a horizontal long-run market curve.

An alternative scenario is that the price of a key input changes with the total quantity produced. For example, consider the market for new housing in a metropolitan area. The supply of land is fixed: in the words of Will Rogers, "The problem with land is that they're not making it anymore." An increase in the quantity of new housing produced increases the demand for all inputs to the production process, including land. As more housing producers compete for scarce land, the price of land increases, increasing the marginal cost of producing housing. The increase in an input price increases the long-run marginal cost of production, generating a positively sloped long-run supply curve. This is the case of an increasing-cost industry.

Figure 24–14 illustrates the connection between input prices and the long-run supply curve. On the left side, the initial quantity of housing supplied is h' and the initial price is p'. On the right side, supply curve for land is vertical at the fixed quantity $\bar{z}$, and the demand curve associated with housing quantity h' is D'. The land

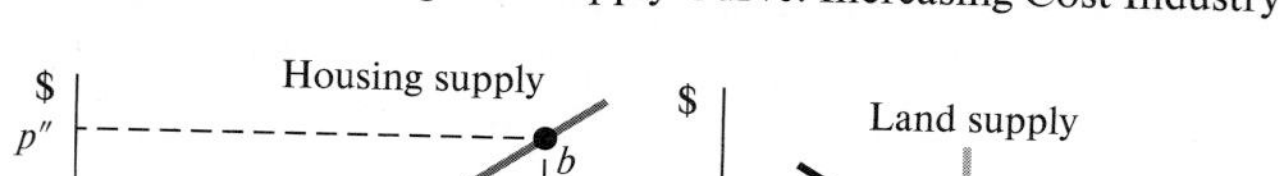

FIGURE 24–14 Long-Run Supply Curve: Increasing-Cost Industry

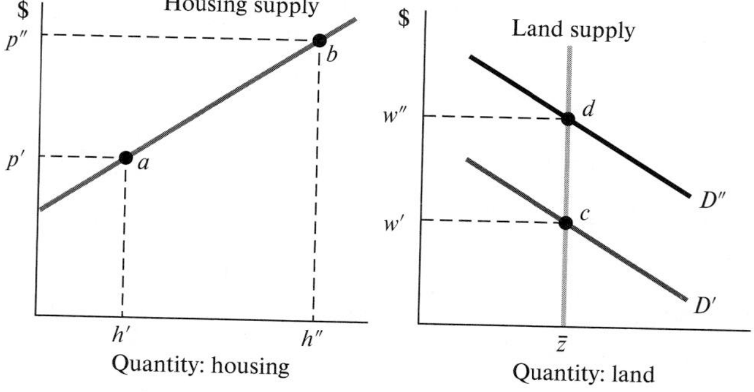

demand curve intersects the land supply curve at point *c*, generating an initial land price w'.

Consider the effects of an increase in housing production on the land market. Suppose the quantity of housing produced increases from h' to h''. The increase in housing production increases the demand for land, shifting the land demand curve from D' to D''. The increase in demand increases the equilibrium price of land from w' to w'' (point *c* to point *d*).

An increase in the price of land increases the marginal cost of producing housing, so the price of housing must be higher to ensure zero economic profit. On the left side of Figure 24–14, this is shown by the move from point *a* to point *b* along the housing supply curve. To summarize, an increase in the quantity of housing from h' to h'' increases the price of land and thus increases the zero-profit price of housing from p' to p''. Therefore, the long-run supply curve for housing is positively sloped.

Figure 24–15 shows the long-run equilibrium in a perfectly competitive market. As we've seen, a market has reached a long-run equilibrium at price p^* if (i) firms are maximizing profit (the market is on the supply curve), (ii) consumers are maximizing utility (the market is on the demand curve), (iii) the market clears (the market is at the intersection of the demand curve and the supply curve), and (iv) each firm makes zero economic profit. At any price other than the equilibrium price p^*, the quantity demanded will differ from the quantity supplied. In this case, there will be pressure to change the price.

1. *Excess Demand.* At $p' < p^*$, the quantity demanded exceeds the quantity supplied ($Q_d' > Q_s'$), so there will be pressure to increase the price. An excluded consumer has an incentive to bid up the price to get the good at the expense of another consumer.
2. *Excess Supply.* At $p'' > p^*$, the quantity supplied exceeds the quantity demanded ($Q_s'' > Q_d''$), so there will be pressure to decrease the price. A firm with leftover output has an incentive to cut its price to sell more.

FIGURE 24–15 Long Run Equilibrium: Increasing Cost Industry

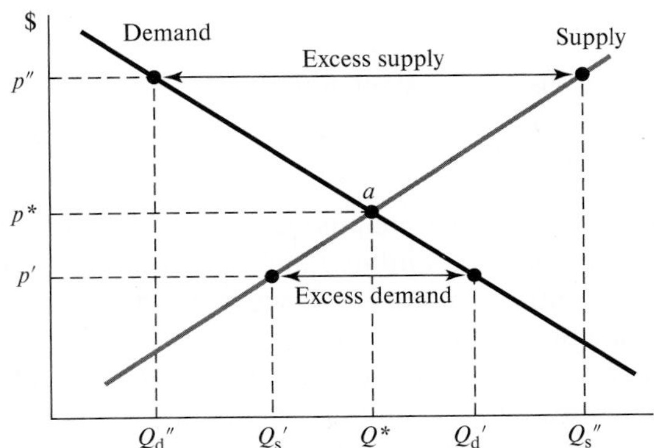

4. UNCERTAINTY

This part of the chapter explores decision-making in an uncertain environment, where the benefits or costs of an action are uncertain. The model of expected utility generates several useful concepts, including expected monetary value, expected utility, and certainty equivalent. We apply these concepts in the chapter on Agglomeration Economies and the chapter on Crime and Public Policy.

We can use the notion of a lottery to represent the features of a risky environment. A lottery is a list of possible outcomes R_1 and R_2 and the associated probabilities (r_1 and r_2):

$$L = \{R_1, R_2; r_1, r_2\}$$

For example, suppose you own a stock that could have a value of \$100 or \$4. If both values are equally likely, the stock-price lottery is

$$L = \left\{\$100, \$4; \frac{1}{2}, \frac{1}{2}\right\}$$

In words, the stock lottery is a 50 percent probability of getting \$100 and a 50 percent probability of getting \$4. If for another stock there is a 75 percent chance of the high value and a 25 percent chance of the low value, the lottery is

$$L = \left\{\$100, \$4; \frac{3}{4}, \frac{1}{4}\right\}$$

The lottery framework provides a convenient and flexible way to represent risky environments.

Expected Monetary Value and Expected Utility

We can use lottery information to compute the expected monetary value of an event such as selling a stock. The expected monetary value of a lottery (EV) equals the weighted average of lottery values, with weights equal to the probabilities of the values. In the case of two possible values,

$$\text{EV}\{R_1, R_2; r_1, r_2\} = r_1R_1 + r_2R_2$$

In the case of the stock lottery,

$$\text{EV}\left\{\$100, \$4; \frac{1}{2}, \frac{1}{2}\right\} = \frac{1}{2}\$100 + \frac{1}{2}\$4 = \$52$$

In words, the expected monetary value of equal chances of either \$100 or \$4 is \$52.

We can use a utility function to translate monetary values into levels of satisfaction or utility. Figure 24–16 shows a conventional utility curve, with utility (in utils) as a function of wealth w (in dollars). The utility curve is concave, indicating that utility increases as wealth increases, but at a decreasing rate. In other words, the economic agent experiences diminishing marginal utility of wealth. As wealth increases, each additional dollar of wealth increases utility by a progressively smaller amount.

FIGURE 24-16 Diminishing Marginal Utility

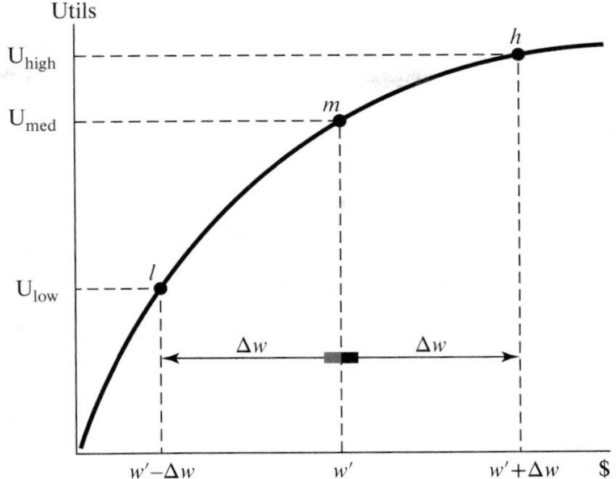

One implication of diminishing marginal utility is that a loss of wealth has a larger effect on utility than a gain in wealth. In Figure 24-16, suppose we start at point m, with wealth w' and a medium utility U_{med}. An increase in wealth to $w' + \Delta w$ increases utility to U_{high}, while a decrease in wealth to $w' - \Delta w$ decreases utility to U_{low}. Although the change in wealth is Δw in both cases (increase or decrease), the utility loss exceeds the utility gain. As wealth decreases, the utility lost per dollar lost increases, so wealth losses have relatively large negative effects on utility. In the opposite direction, as wealth increases, the utility gained per dollar decreases, so wealth gains have relatively small positive effects on utility. In general, diminishing marginal utility means that the displeasure associated with losing wealth exceeds the pleasure of gaining wealth.

We can use a utility function to measure the consequences of a lottery in utility terms. The expected utility of a lottery is the weighted average of the utilities generated by different outcomes, with the weights equal to the probabilities of two outcomes.

$$EU\{R_1, R_2; r_1, r_2\} = r_1 \cdot u(R_1) + r_2 \cdot u(R_2)$$

For the stock lottery, the expected utility of the lottery is

$$EU\left\{\$100, \$4; \frac{1}{2}, \frac{1}{2}\right\} = \frac{1}{2}u(\$100) + \frac{1}{2}u(\$4)$$

In our examples of lotteries, we often use the utility function $u(w) = w^{1/2}$. For this utility function, utility is the square root of wealth. Using this utility function, the expected utility of the stock lottery is

$$EU\left\{\$100, \$4; \frac{1}{2}, \frac{1}{2}\right\} = \frac{1}{2}10\ utils + \frac{1}{2}2\ utils = 6\ utils$$

The utility function $u(w) = w^{1/2}$ is consistent with diminishing marginal utility, but it is just an example. This particular utility function makes it easy to construct examples of lotteries that are numerically manageable.

FIGURE 24–17 Expected Utility

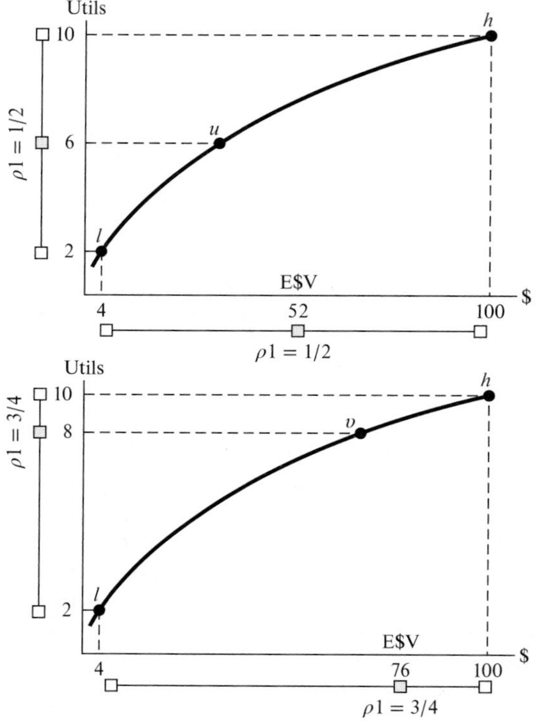

Figure 24–17 shows the computation of the expected utility of a lottery. Continuing the stock example, as shown by point h, the utility value of the high price is $u(\$100) =$ 10 utils. As shown by point l, the utility value of the low price is $u(\$4) = 2$ utils. The expected utility is the weighted average of the two utility numbers, with probability weights r_1 and r_2, given $r_1 + r_2 = 1$.

1. *Upper panel:* $r_1 = 0.50$. The probability slider along the vertical axis is at the midpoint between the high utility (10 utils) and the low utility (2 utils), equal to 6 utils. On the horizontal axis, the expected monetary value of the lottery is \$52.
2. *Lower panel:* $r_1 = 0.75$. The probability slider is three-fourths of the distance between the low utility and the high utility, so the expected utility is 8 utils:

$$EU\left\{\$100, \$4; \frac{3}{4}, \frac{1}{4}\right\} = \frac{3}{4}10\ utils + \frac{1}{4}2\ utils = 8\ utils$$

As expected, an increase in the probability of the favorable outcome (high utility) moves the expected utility closer to the utility of the favorable outcome. On the horizontal axis, the expected monetary value of the lottery is \$76:

$$\text{EV}\left\{\$100, \$4; \frac{3}{4}, \frac{1}{4}\right\} = \frac{3}{4}\$100 + \frac{1}{4}\$4 = \$76$$

Certainty Equivalent

Up to this point, we have computed the benefit of a lottery as its expected utility, measured in utils. In contrast, the certainty equivalent measures the benefit of a lottery in dollars. Specifically, the certainty equivalent of a lottery is the certain wealth (in dollars) that generates the same utility as a lottery. Using CE as the symbol for certainty equivalent,

$$u(CE) = EU(Lottery)$$

In words, the utility of the certainty equivalent equals the expected utility of the lottery.

Figure 24–18 shows how to compute the certainty equivalent of a lottery. The expected utility of the stock lottery is 6 utils (the average of 10 utils with the favorable outcome and 2 utils with the unfavorable outcome). We use the utility curve to determine the certain wealth that generates the same 6 utils of utility. Point u provides a pivot to translate utility of 6 utils into wealth of \$36. A certain wealth of \$36 generates 6 utils, the same as the expected utility from the lottery.

$$u(\$36) = 6\ utils$$

The certainty equivalent of \$36 makes the agent indifferent between a certain payment of \$36 and taking a chance by playing the lottery, with equal chances of getting either \$100 or \$4.

In this book we often use a specific utility function in our numerical examples: $u(w) = w^{1/2}$. We can invert this utility function to get an expression for the certainty equivalent $w(u)$. Solving for w in terms of utility, the certainty equivalent is

$$CE = w(u) = u^2$$

In the stock-price lottery, the expected utility of the lottery is 6 utils:

$$CE = w(6\ utils) = 6^2 = \$36$$

FIGURE 24–18 Certainty Equivalent

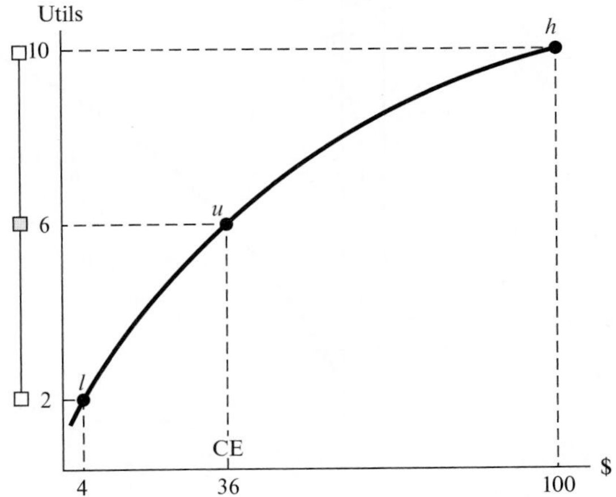

The certainty equivalent is an agent's willingness to pay for a lottery. In the stock lottery, our agent would be willing to pay up to $36 to buy the stock today, knowing that the price tomorrow could be $100 or $4. A certain payment of $36 today (6 utils sacrificed today) is exactly offset by an expected utility payoff of 6 utils tomorrow, when the stock will be sold at either $100 or $4. An agent who pays the certainty equivalent $36 for the stock will be indifferent about playing the stock lottery. Naturally, the agent would prefer to pay a smaller amount for the stock. For any price less than the $36 certainty equivalent, the agent will be better off. For example, if the agent paid a price of only $25 today, the utility lost today (5 utils) would be more than offset by an expected utility payoff of 6 utils tomorrow.

The risk premium of a lottery is defined as the gap between the certainty equivalent and expected monetary value of a lottery.

Risk Premium = *Expected monetary value* − *Certainty equivalent*

In the stock lottery example, the risk premium is $16:

Risk Premium = $52 − $36 = $16

The word *premium* indicates that an agent demands a premium—an extra amount of money—to take a risky action. In this case, the agent is willing to pay only $36 for an asset with an expected monetary value of $52. The $16 gap between the willingness to pay and the expected monetary value is the premium the agent requires to take the risk.

Figure 24-19 shows all four measures of the stock-price lottery. The expected utility is 6 utils (the midpoint of the vertical slider), and the certainty equivalent is $36 (below point *u*). The expected monetary value is $52 (the midpoint of the horizontal slider), and the risk premium is the $16 gap between the certainty equivalent and the expected monetary value.

FIGURE 24-19 Certainty Equivalent and Risk Premium

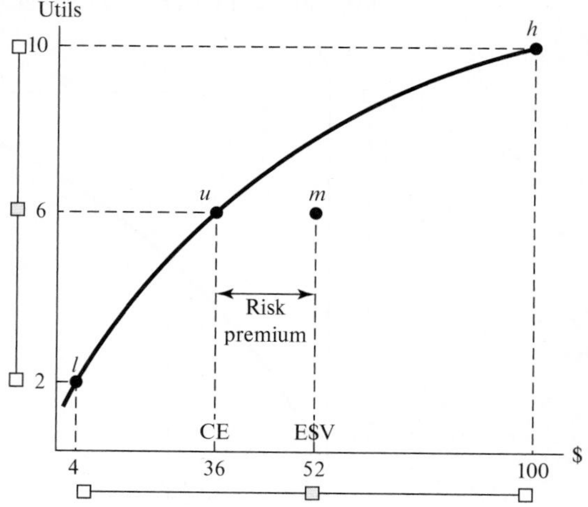

Loss Aversion and Certainty Equivalent

So far we have considered lotteries with non-negative monetary outcomes. An alternative is a lottery that has a potential gain $R_1 > 0$ and a potential loss $R_2 < 0$. In this case of a gain-loss lottery, we can use a utility function defined with respect to monetary gains and losses. The changes in utility for gains and losses are computed as

$$\Delta u = g \cdot R \text{ for } R > 0$$

$$\Delta u = l \cdot R \text{ for } R < 0$$

where R is either positive (a gain, with $R_1 > 0$) or negative (a loss, with $R_2 < 0$). Most people exhibit loss aversion: a loss in wealth has a larger effect on utility than an equal gain in wealth. In other words, the pain associated with a loss exceeds the pleasure associated with a gain of the same magnitude, so $l > g$. A common assumption is that the pain of a \$1 loss is twice the pleasure of a \$1 gain: $l = 2 \cdot g$.

Figure 24–20 shows how to compute the values of a gain-loss lottery. Suppose there are equal chances of either gaining \$30 or losing \$7. The lottery is

$$L = \left\{ \$30, -\$7; \frac{1}{2}, \frac{1}{2} \right\}$$

Suppose $g = 3$ and $l = 6$: a \$1 loss is twice as painful as a \$1 gain is pleasurable. The horizontal axis shows the gain (on the right) and the loss (on the left), and the vertical axis shows the change in utility in utils. For a gain, the slope of the utility curve is $g = 3$ utils per dollar. For a loss, the slope of the utility curve is $l = 6$ utils per dollar. The expected utility of the lottery is

$$eu = \frac{1}{2} 90 \textit{ utils} - \frac{1}{2} 42 \textit{ utils} = 24 \textit{ utils}$$

FIGURE 24–20 Loss Aversion and Gain-Loss Lottery

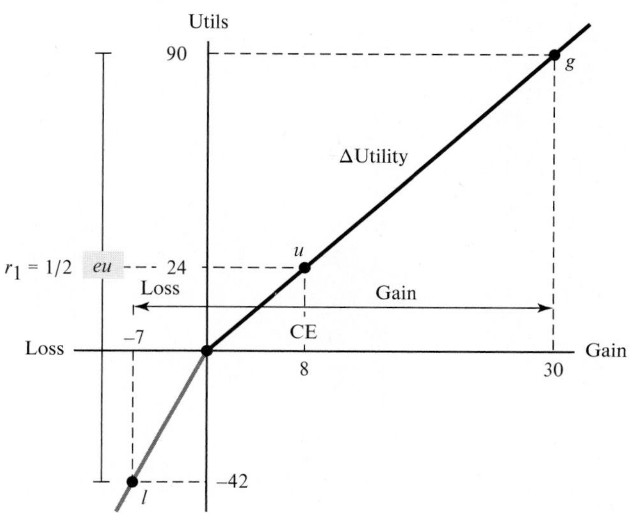

As we've seen, the certainty equivalent translates the expected utility of lottery into a dollar value. In the case of a gain-loss lottery with a positive expected utility, we compute the certainty equivalent by dividing the expected utility by g, the change in utility per dollar gained.

$$CE = \frac{eu}{g}$$

In our example, $g = 3$ and the expected utility is 24 utils, so the certainty equivalent is \$8:

$$CE = \frac{eu}{g} = \frac{24}{3} = \$8$$

This is sensible because if one dollar is worth 3 utils, then 1 util is worth *1/3* dollar and 24 utils is worth \$8. In this example, an agent will be indifferent between (i) a lottery with an expected utility of 24 utils and (ii) a certain payment of \$8.

Index

C

D

F

G

H

L

M